HOT
WACKS
BOOK
Supplement 4

THE HOT WACKS PRESS

PO Box 544, Owen Sound, ON, N4K 5R1, CANADA
Fax 519 376 9449 - E-Mail hotwacks@log.on.ca
Web-Page http://log.on.ca/hotwacks

Dedicated to Jerry Garcia... keep on truckin'.

Also dedicated to producers of fine recordings the world over and collectors who take the time to write and share information on these recordings.

With thanks to:
Beanie for patience. Mom for encouragement. Kurt for feeding the monster. Elvis for the attitude. And Ed Sullivan for February 9 1964.

© 1996

HOT WACKS BOOK
Supplement 4

is a copyright protected publication of

ROBERT WALKER AND THE HOT WACKS PRESS

PO Box 544, Owen Sound, ON, N4K 5R1, CANADA
Fax 519 376 9449 - E-Mail hotwacks@log.on.ca
Web-Page http://log.on.ca/hotwacks

Hot Wacks books have been

PRINTED IN CANADA

for 10 years by the experts at
WEBCOM
3480 Pharmacy Avenue
Scarborough, Ontario M1W 3G3

ISBN 0-9698080-5-4

Intro: Future Wacks

Hot Wacks Book XV (1992 - see page 227) was the last complete bootleg discography. Up until Book XV, each edition contained the information from the previous book plus any new releases. However, the book was becoming too big. Book XIV was 496 pages and, with the explosion of new releases on both vinyl and CD, Book XV was more than 800 pages. This was not only a monster to produce but expensive to ship. On top of that, it became a bit redundant and expensive for those of you who bought every edition of the book to have to buy the old information with the new.

Hot Wacks Book Supplements (see page 227) are designed to keep you up-to-date with the ever-expanding world of bootlegs. They contain new releases along with old listings not found in Hot Wacks Book XV.

Plans call for THE ULTIMATE WACKS to be published in 1997. This will be a hard-cover, large-format book jam-packed with: interviews with bootleggers, photo discographies, bootleg memorabilia as well as the most complete bootleg listings ever. A CD-ROM is also in the works. This is being put together by Collector's Guide Publishing who's recent CD-ROM 'The Illustrated Collector's Guide To Led Zeppelin On CD-Rom' (see page 228) is a big hit with Zep collectors. The Hot Wacks CD-ROM should be out for the fall of '96. Hot Wacks also has a Web-Page (http://log.on.ca/hotwacks) listing books and new releases.

As many of you well know, Hot Wacks does not include every bootleg that has ever been released. Not everything that comes out is available here in Canada because of the limited runs of some items and because contacts with some producers or distributors have not been established. While we have access to a great number of items through various collections, there are still some things that get by.

With this in mind, The Hot Wacks Press asks for your help to keep future books up to date. If you have some things in your collection that do not appear in Book XV, Supplements 1, 2, 3 or 4 please write with the information about these items. Please send a picture or photocopy of the cover(s) along with song listings, the source and sound quality of the recording. Feel free to include any comments you want about the recording, performance, or cover.

If you have a collection that you feel is unique and would care to share it with the rest of the world please write, FAX (519-376-9449) or E-mail (hotwacks@log.on.ca) with information about your collection.

If you are a producer of bootlegs, vinyl or CD, please send sample copies or information about your product. We don't need your address or number, just the tracks facts.

A History Of Bootlegs

In 1969 bootleg Rock records made their appearance in the United States and Europe. Previously bootlegs consisted mainly of Jazz and Blues artists. These, however, did not receive the attention that Rock bootlegs did as the artists were not big money-makers. Dean Meador, writing in "Hot Wacks Quarterly" (A History Of Bootleg Recordings, Issue #4), traced bootlegs back to the turn of the century.

"Mapleson, the librarian of the Metropolitan Opera at that time, received a cylinder recorder from Thomas Edison. He took his gift up into the fly-loft on several occasions during the Met's 1901-03 seasons and recorded bits and pieces of performances. Even though Mapleson had his machine a long way from the stage area and his medium had limitations (his cylinders ran for only a few minutes at a time, making it impossible to capture all of a long aria or duet), he produced an astonishing number of unique recording documents".

"Mapleson and his cylinders provided a taste of actual performances during that period. Mapleson gave collectors a chance to obtain and hear performers, singers, artists and speakers of that era who never appeared on commercial recordings, others in roles they didn't duplicate on authorized discs".

The record that started it all for Rock boots was Bob Dylan's "Great White Wonder". This double album originally came in a plain white jacket without any printed label or title. Since sound recordings did not receive copyright protection in the USA until February 15, 1972, GWW received wider distribution than the bootlegs of today. However, claims that it sold some 350,000 copies are extremely unlikely. It is further interesting to note that when Columbia Records released the same material in authorized form years later as "The Basement Tapes" the official version sold quite well.

A distinction had best be made at this point between bootleg, pirate and counterfeit records. A bootleg consists of unreleased material recorded at concerts, studio outtakes, and radio or TV broadcasts. A pirate album consists of released material without attempting to make the LP look like an original. A counterfeit album is an exact copy of an officially released album.

Record industry spokespeople often include bootlegs with counterfeit and pirate recordings when making statements about the loss of revenue from record piracy. Bootlegs, with their small pressings, should not be included in this figure as the record labels do not lose revenue from a recording which is not in their catalog.

These same spokespeople completely overlook the historical significance of bootlegs as well. While this is obvious when speaking in terms of Opera, Jazz and Blues boots, Rock has not been around for the same amount of time. With Rock's seemingly unending loss of performers due to untimely deaths, this will soon become evident. Albert Goldman, in his bestseller "Elvis", is one of the first biographers to appreciate the historical significance bootlegs have.

"Not just the man but the performer continued to emerge after his death. Though RCA had nothing better to offer than gleanings from its soon-exhausted archives, the record bootleggers, those great friends of the fans, cut the legal knots that had long restrained the release of Elvis's most significant live sessions. The legendary Elvis of the Louisiana Hayride, the Dorsey Brothers shows and the Hawaiian benefits appeared. All the jams from the Singer Special were offered in two beautifully-packaged albums from California that far surpassed both in interest and in appearance any legitimate offerings of RCA Victor. In yet another illicit release came at last the most sought-after tape in the history of rock 'n' roll: the fabled 'Million Dollar Quartet', an impromptu sing in the Sun Studio around Christmas 1956, by the three greatest heroes of rockabilly: Elvis, Jerry Lee Lewis and Carl Perkins (minus the anticipated fourth voice, Johnny Cash). Though in this instance the reality of the recording hardly matched the glamour of its legend, the value of the disc as a document was enormous. At last you were inside the Sun Studio listening attentively as Sam Phillips' greatest singers did what they most enjoyed doing: pickin' and singin' their favorite rock songs and hymns".

Currently the average pressing in the USA of a bootleg is 1,000 copies; in Europe 500 to 1,000 copies; and a few hundred copies in Japan. Australia, which just recently became a steady source of supply, quite likely has runs as small as Japan. Canada deserves mention if only for the fact that an entire run of Bruce Springsteen boxed sets was seized before they could be distributed. With that exception, Canada is not a bootleg-producing country.

All of the early American bootleg labels have ceased operating. This is the case with RUBBER DUBBER, IMMACULATE CONCEPTION RECORDS (ICR), CONTRABAND MUSIC (CBM), DITTOLINO DISCS, KUSTOM RECORDS, TRADE MARK OF QUALITY (TMOQ), PIG'S EYE, HIGHWAY HI FI (HHCER), PHONYGRAF and one outfit that used a different name for each release (Hen, Steel Led, etc.). Their product was a thick, black record in a white jacket. To simplify matters they are referred to in this text as White Cover Folks (WCF).

The second generation of bootleggers, which includes WIZARDO RECORDS (WRMB), IDLE MIND PRODUCTIONS (IMP), HOFFMAN AVENUE RECORDS (HAR), K&S RECORDS and THE AMAZING KORNYFONE RECORD LABEL (TAKRL), is also out of business.

At the present time the vast majority of releases is coming out of Europe. If anything, the Europeans have improved on their sound quality and packaging, both of which they have been leaders in for years. Most of their product matches, and in some cases surpasses, legitimate record releases.

(December 22 1985 Kurt Glemser - Editor of HOT WACKS - Books I thru XI)

The Last 10 Years

1986 saw the rise and fall of BOX TOP RECORDS. This label re-released many old classics, most on colored vinyl, from original plates. These came in a thin cover with a color snap-shot of the artist on the front and a sticker with the song listings on the back. Titles were rubber-stamped on the front. In the spring of 1987, after two years of production, ROCK SOLID RECORDS/INTERNATIONAL RECORDS (RSR/International) went out of business.

1988 witnessed the short-lived return of the TRADE MARK OF QUALITY (TMOQ or TMQ) and THE AMAZING KORNYPHONE RECORD LABEL (TAKRL) labels working together to provide 'A High Standard Of Standardness'. Records came in one-color covers with the artists' name and the album title on the front and a jacket-sized label logo on the back. There were two separate batches of releases and each had the song listings for all albums in that batch on sheets enclosed in the record jackets. Each release was limited to 500 copies.

1989 brought the introduction of the bootleg CD and the demise of vinyl. In some cases bootleg CDs are a waste of technology since these are taken from the original boots of the same name, not new or better sources. After all, who wants a bad recording containing pops and crackles that'll last forever. In other instances when a good source is available, such as with "Ultra Rare Trax" (The Beatles) or "Dallas '75" volumes 1 and 2 (Led Zeppelin), the results are incredible.

1990 through 1995 can only be described as the time of the bootleg CD. Using loopholes in the copyright laws of some European and Far East countries, bootleggers flooded the market with CD re-issues of old boots as well as a wealth of new, often soundboard, recordings.

Many of the items coming out of Europe were available in North America through mail-order and, because of various copyright laws, in stores in Europe and Japan. However, recent changes in European, US and Canadian laws (see page 13) are hindering production and distribution. There is some speculation that bootlegging may come to an end as a result of these changes but I suggest that the action will just relocate. As long as fans crave the live and unusual, bootlegs will exist.

Please note, THE HOT WACKS PRESS does not sell the records or CDs listed in this book, this is a discography not a catalog. Most of these items are long out of circulation and not available.

(March 1996 Bob Walker - Editor/Publisher of HOT WACKS Books XII to SUPPLEMENT 4).

STOP AND READ THIS

Abbreviations have been used in order to save space, making Hot Wacks more compact and easier to use. These are:
R = Recording: Ex = excellent, Vg = very good, G = good, s = stereo, m = mono.
S = Source (recording location and/or date of recording).
C = Comments: Eb = European bootleg*, ECD = European CD*, ACD = Asian CD*,
Dcc = deluxe color cover/insert, Dbw = deluxe black & white cover/insert, GF = gatefold,
DL = deluxe label, CV = colored vinyl, MCV = multi-colored vinyl, SS = song separation.
*(source of development, manufacture or distribution)

Sound Quality

The HOT WACKS rating system is based on the sound quality of bootleg releases, not legitimate albums and CDs. Sound quality has come a long way since the old days of boots in the early 70s. We were very forgiving in those days, simply amazed that we could hear our faves live and ignoring some of the less than perfect recordings. So what if it was an audience recording from the back of a stadium with some drunken lout yelling for "Hard Rain", "Heart Breaker" or "Whipping Post". It was our band LIVE.

The introduction of high quality bootleg CDs has spoiled some of us. No longer will some collectors accept less than perfect recordings. I've talked to some collectors who will not even consider listening to an audience recording. How soon we forget.

Sure, excellent sound quality is desirable but sometimes it's just not available. Do we ignore the Australian Zep shows or Quarrymen rehearsals because of the less than perfect quality? I think not. I hope not. When we start putting the sound quality of recordings ahead of historic importance we are buying bootlegs for the wrong reasons.

Enough soapboxing, let's look at how recordings are graded for this 4th edition of The Hot Hot Wacks Book Supplement. The big thing to keep in mind is the state of live recording at the time of the performance. Remember, DAT portables did not always exist.

Excellent (Ex): Everything is nice and clear - instruments and voice(s) are well defined.
Very Good (Vg): Lacks the edge of an Ex recording. Good (G): Still quite listenable but not for everyone. Poor: For the hard-core collector.

Soundboard Recording (Soundboard): Professional recording from the mixing board at a concert, a recording studio source or from a radio or television broadcast. Audience Recording (Audience): Amateur recording on portable audio or video equipment.

An Ex Soundboard recording more often than not differs from an Ex Audience recording and this should be kept in mind when looking at the gradings. Soundboard recordings tend to provide an even balanced recording while Audience recordings rely on the quality of the sound system, the recording equipment and the position of the recorder.

Soundboard VS Audience:

What's the Difference, and Which is Better?

By Hugh Jones - Assisted by Bruce Deerhake - © 1995 HJR/Proximity Productions
(Hugh Jones is the editor and publisher of Proximity, The Led Zeppelin Collector's Journal, and Bruce Deerhake runs the pre-eminent Zeppelin homepage on the Internet. Thus, all recording examples used in the following piece refer to Led Zeppelin recordings)

When tape or bootleg collectors get together, a lot of catch phrases get bandied about, and healthy debate often ensues as folks compare the relative merits of DAT vs. analog, Maxell vs. TDK, KTS vs. Silver Rarities, or audience vs. soundboard.

Today's technical lecture concerns the two ways in which live concerts are most often recorded: either with microphones from the audience, or via patch cords carrying a signal from the PA system's soundboard directly to the tape recorder.

Professionally recorded concerts are generally captured on tape using a combination of these two methods, however the majority of bootleg recordings are one or the other. The debate has to do with which of these two methods produces a more accurate representation of the sound that was heard at the concert - and the reason it's such an unending controversy is because there really is no definitive 'better' or 'worse' in this situation. Ultimately, it's a matter of personal taste, colored by many factors involved in how the recording was made.

ROOM SOUND and REVERB

Generally speaking, soundboard recordings which are made unprofessionally are 'unbalanced,' and have a 'dry' sound that is very different than what you hear at a show. There are several reasons for this, the most significant one being that there is no 'room' sound in the recording. When you're standing in a room listening to music - or any kind of sound - what you hear is affected dramatically by the shape of the space, the type of floor, wall and ceiling surfaces in it, and the other objects (and even people) in the room. If you have ever had the opportunity to hear a band play a soundcheck in an empty club or hall, and then hear the same band at the show later when the place is packed with people, you've no doubt noticed a big difference in the sound.

This is because of reverberation. After sound waves are emitted, they physically collide with anything in their path. If they hit a hard surface, they bounce back, and will continue bouncing against each obstacle they encounter, diminishing in strength with each surface they hit. Envision a superball bounced hard in a small, empty room - it keeps bouncing off any surface it hits until it runs out of energy. As the sound waves bounce around like this, they hit your ears at different times and from different directions, creating what is known as reverb, or 'room ambience'.

If sound waves hit a soft, absorbent surface, they don't bounce as much, and the effect of reverberation is not created. Consequently, your ears don't catch the sound coming from all those different angles, they just hear the waves originally emitted from the sound source. A room with hard surfaces that produces lots of reverb is known as a 'live' room, and one with absorbent surfaces which eliminate reverb is known as a 'dead' room.

Recording studios go to great lengths to control room ambience, and to completely eliminate it in their control rooms, where playbacks are usually listened to and evaluated. This is so that the engineers can get a completely unbiased impression of what has been committed to tape. On most recordings, however, a certain amount of reverb is desirable in the finished product, and in a studio setting this is usually added electronically during the final mixing process.

This ambience is something that needs to be present in just the right amount to sound good. Too little, and music sounds flat; too much, and you get the 'echo chamber' effect where everything runs together and sounds distorted (which is often what happens at Rock shows in cavernous arenas or stadiums, the ultimate in 'live' rooms, and a recording engineer's worst nightmare).

Generally speaking, a soundboard recording from a concert will have little or no true room ambience. Usually there will be some reverberation on individual components (most often the vocals) which is introduced electronically, by a reverb or echo unit, as the signal runs through the soundboard on its way from the microphone to the speakers. On most bootleg soundboards, however, this is not enough to keep the recording from having that flat, 'lifeless' feel.

'FOH' and MONITOR MIXES

Another problem with soundboard tapes is that their mix is entirely dependent upon where in the sound system's chain they are taken from.

Almost all PA systems consist of two soundboards; one for the 'front of house' (known as 'FOH') mix that the audience hears, and another for the 'monitor' mix, which is what the band hears on stage. Often each member of the band receives an individual monitor mix emphasizing what he/she most needs to hear while playing.

If you listen to the beginning of the well-known Zeppelin soundboard tape from Dallas '75 (which incidentally is one of the best-mixed board tapes out there), you can hear Bonzo soundchecking his monitor, in his inimitable fashion. He taps the snare a few times and yells "louder!" Taps it a few more times and again, "louder!" A few more, harder hits on the drum, and still not enough - a more insistent "louder!" and finally he's happy, uttering a gutteral "yeeaah" and launching immediately into the intro of "Rock & Roll". You can bet that if the recording had been made using Bonham's monitor mix, the drums would have overpowered the rest of the band. Thankfully, this tape seems to have come from the FOH board, and though it is a bit dry, all the elements are well-balanced with each other.

If a recording is made from the monitor mixing board instead of the FOH board, it usually will be mostly vocals, since they are the one component which can't be heard on stage over the drums and electric instruments without being pumped loudly through the monitors. The Vancouver '71 tape used to make the famous "Mudslide" boot comes to mind as an example of this particular problem.

Even with a board tape made at the FOH mixer, sometimes one or two elements of the band will dominate the mix. This usually occurs at smaller venues, because the guitar and bass amplifiers (especially when you're talking about Page and Jones) are producing much more sound in the hall than the drums and vocals, and thus don't need as much of the PA system's reinforcement to be heard by the audience.

Some classic examples of this syndrome are the soundboard tapes of the "Whole Lotta Love" Rock & Roll medleys recorded in relatively small halls on Zeppelin's UK tour of 1973. These potentially great recordings give us Plant and Bonham loud and clear, while Jimmy's guitar is frustratingly quiet and Jones' bass almost non-existent.

RECORDINGS FROM THE CROWD

Getting back to audience tapes, excellent recordings should result when well-placed, high quality equipment is set up in a room where music is being played - at least theoretically. While terrific recordings can indeed be made this way, most bootleg audience recordings are a hit-and-miss proposition. If the sound is good coming from the PA and the taper is standing in just the right spot in the room, you end up with a recording that sounds like the "Seattle Supersonic" CD or the LA '77 recording that yielded "Listen To This, Eddie". Though neither one is technically perfect, these recordings provide a very good mix of music and room ambience, and many people prefer this rougher sound to the clean quality of even a well-balanced soundboard tape like Dallas '75, because in capturing more crowd noise it approximates more closely the feeling of actually being at the show.

On the other hand, too many audience tapes sound like the Bath Festival recording from 1970 - a great performance that is virtually unlistenable due to the poor quality of the recording - or the notorious Madison Square Garden show from September 1971, where the audience members close to the microphone (and even the tapers) chatter and shout so much that you wind up hearing more of them than the band!

When a live recording is made professionally, it is almost always recorded off the soundboard, but there are at least two additional microphones placed somewhere out in the hall and more on the stage. These are to pick up audience noise and room ambience. When the recording is mixed for final release, the 'ambient' room mics are blended in with the 'dry' soundboard source to give an overall sound as close as possible to what was heard in the hall by people attending the show. Of course, this method can go awry sometimes too - witness the recent nationwide broadcast of Page And Plant's San Jose concert, which had way too much audience noise mixed in. The excellent DAT audience tape made at the Tacoma Dome a few nights later is in many ways a superior recording to the professional one sent out over the airwaves.

DISTINGUISHING THE TWO TYPES OF RECORDINGS

With really good audience recordings, or really bad soundboard tapes, it is sometimes difficult to tell which is which. Because of this, discrepancies in 'source' descriptions occasionally show up on tape trading lists.

One way to identify a soundboard tape is to listen to the audience noise. If the level of the crowd is very low between songs, and non-existent during them, it's most likely a soundboard even if the sound quality of the music is poor. The little bit of crowd noise that does come through on a soundboard would be only what was picked up by microphones on stage used to amplify the vocals and instruments. These mics are fairly directional, and they're pointed away from the crowd so they only pick up the sound source directly in front of them.

Conversely, if a recording sounds superb but audience whoops and whistles are audible during the performance and the crowd response between songs is at least as loud as the music, then you're listening to a top-notch audience tape.

THE BOTTOM LINE. . .

. . . is that with either type of source, presuming it's a decent recording to begin with, you're gaining some qualities and sacrificing others. For example, on a tape like the Cleveland '77 soundboard, Bonzo's drums sound phenomenal - clear and powerful. On the other hand, Jimmy's guitar doesn't fare nearly as well - the room sound that's missing would really add some dimension to the 100+ decibels of sound cranking out of his Marshall stacks.

The opposite example would be the Seattle '75 audience recording, which interestingly enough was actually recorded with mics placed in the concourse immediately outside the arena! No one element of the band sounds as clean as it does on the previous tape, but the crowd noise is fairly low and the balance of instruments and voice is excellent, giving an overall effect much closer to what was actually heard in the hall.

As recording technology moves forward and high quality equipment continues to come down in price, more people have DATs and good stereo condenser microphones to bring to concerts so audience recordings are getting better. While audience tapes from large arenas will almost always have that big-room ambience that immediately brands them as 'bootleg sound', some of the recordings I've heard from small clubs recently have been every bit as good as a well-balanced soundboard, to the point of being nearly indistinguishable. And, of course, the room sound in the smaller halls works in favor of the overall mix.

Ultimately, it's all a matter of taste, and, of course, sound quality ratings will always be subjective. Regardless, I hope the information provided here will help people to judge quality, to create accurate descriptions of recordings they have, and to make decisions about recordings they want to get. In the final analysis, if it's your favorite band or the best show you ever saw, who cares what it sounds like - you know you've gotta have it!

Bootlegs: A Beginner's Guide

By Dave Thompson from the October '95 issue of 'Discoveries' (see page 238)

Half a block off Carnaby Street, the soul of swinging London, a dusty record store was nestled between a souvenir shop and a shoemaker's shop. It was nothing special from the outside, and not that much better within; just an owner who looked like Neil from "The Young Ones", and a shifting stock of Japanese imports, and French 'Stooges' records.

But root through the racks often enough, and sooner or later you'd make a rare find, or overhear a conversation which would lead you to an even rarer one, like this: Customer: "Anything interesting come in lately?" Neil: "Yeah, a couple of Bowie things, and - oh, are you interested in this?" And he'd reach for a shelf high over the cash register and pull down ... well, that's the point. You never knew what he'd pull down, but they certainly weren't records that you'd seen before. Pink Floyd, "The Coming of Kahoutek"; David Bowie, "His Master's Voice"; Roxy Music, "When We Were Young"; and within weeks, it seemed, of the first time you heard of her, Patti Smith, "Teenage Perversity And Ships In The Night" - with a guest appearance from Iggy Pop.

You'd turn and look, and Neil would smile, and in that magic moment you were hooked. Welcome to the world of bootlegs. Some background: the first bootleg, a collection of Dylan's so-called Basement Tapes, appeared in America in 1969. Inspired on the one hand, by the rash of unreleased Zimmersongs being covered by sundry British bands ("This Wheel's On Fire", "Mighty Quinn"); on the other, by tapes of a 14-song acetate of publishers' demos which were then in circulation. It involved combining seven of these songs with a mishmash of other unreleased Dylan material, finding a "no questions asked" pressing plant willing to produce 2,000 copies of the ensuing double album, and slipping the two discs into a plain white sleeve. Dylan's own official new album, "Nashville Skyline", had just been released to poor sales and poorer reviews, but among Dylan's most fanatical acolytes, that didn't matter a lot. "Great White Wonder" more than made up for the disappointment.

"Official" response to this first bootleg was muted. Radio and press alike picked up on GWW but while Dylan's label, Columbia, did make litigious noises, the only positive response was another new Dylan album, "Self Portrait". Drawn from a variety of live and abandoned studio sources, "Self Portrait" was presumably Dylan's own idea of what a bootleg should be.

But if that was the case, it just proved how out of touch Dylan had suddenly become. His fans wanted outtakes, but they wanted outtakes from his good albums. Not from "Nashville Skyline". And especially not when the underground floodgates had only just started to open. "Flower", "Troubled Troubadour", "A Thousand Miles Behind", "Stealin", live and studio, basement and gaslight .... In 1974, on his first tour since the mid-1960s, Dylan would try and pre-empt the inevitable flood of in concert bootlegs by rush-releasing a double album called, prosaically, "Before the Flood". He should have thought of that title five years before.

The second band to come under the bootleggers' scrutiny was the Rolling Stones, and they, too, immediately acted to counteract the ensuing rash of bootleg live '69 albums. Unfortunately, "Get Yer Ya-Yas Out", also completely missed the point of what was fast shaping up to be an industry in its own right. Bootleg buyers rarely, maybe never, buy boots instead of authorized product. They buy them in addition to ... then they sit around comparing the untouched, un-overdubbed, unofficial release with the wartless wonder handed down from on high, and thank the Lord that someone out there is willing to make the music available.

When DJM released Elton John's "11-17-70" live album, they did so fully aware that a bootleg version of the same radio broadcast was already in circulation, but they still cropped 20 minutes off the show, 20 minutes which the bootleggers, of course, had left intact. Bootleg labels sprang up as fast as bootleggable bands came to the fore, each one establishing its own coterie of supporters. For some, like Trade Mark of Quality and Smokin' Pig, it was the established old guard of Dylan, the Stones and the Beatles who paid the bills. For others, spearheaded by the Amazing Kornyfone Record Label and its subsidiary Ze Anonym Plattenspieler, any artist was fair game. And for others still, like the loathsome Contraband, it was simply enough to watch for whatever the other labels produced, then "reissue" it with a new name, new artwork, and a new low in sound reproduction.

Sparks' "One And A Halfnelson", David Bowie's "In America", Deep Purple's "On The Wings of a Russian Foxbat", Led Zeppelin's "Mudslide", the Who's "Decidedly Belated Response", Genesis' "Swelled And Spent" ... you didn't even need to smuggle your recorder into gigs! If a show was broadcast over FM radio, or if a band played a set on Don Kirschner's "Rock Concert," they became fair game to the bootleggers.

But while live performances were the easiest to source, "Great White Wonder" alone proved the viability both of acquiring, and marketing studio material. And again, there were ways and means ...

The apocryphal "Unscrupulous Record Company Staffers" walking out after-hours with a box of tapes beneath one arm; the studio spring cleanings which dumped tons of unwanted (and presumably, unchecked) master tapes into nearby garbage bins; the friend of a friend who knew a disgruntled roadie (the infamous tape of Linda McCartney's backing vocal rendition of "Hey Jude" was sourced in this fashion); and last but not least, the artists themselves, bucking their own record company's contractual policy by producing, or at least getting involved in, their own bootlegs! (Lowell George once acknowledged that he had even remixed two Little Feat bootlegs prior to release.)

There were also a number of highly-regarded bootlegs which rounded out their in-concert contents with various legitimately-released, but now unavailable, rarities. The Who's "Who's Zoo" collection of B-sides and alternate mixes has still to be satisfactorily replicated by the legitimate copyright owners, and that despite the wealth of official compilations (beginning with the two volume "Rarities") which culminated in last year's "Maximum R & B" box.

The 1975 Genesis souvenir, "As Though Emerald City", featured two U.K. B-sides "Happy the Man" and "Twilight Alehouse," which have yet to receive a full American release (or a British rerelease, at that); 10CC's "Going Pink On Purpose" appended a five track US radio broadcast with seven non-album tracks, a full 15 years before those same songs were officially compiled (on Castle's "The Early Years").

Of course, releases such as these only further complicated the divide between simple bootlegging and outright piracy. But who got hurt? Not the record companies, for whom deleted material is essentially lost revenue anyway; not the fans, who were still being presented with material which the bands in question had deemed fit to release; and certainly not the bands themselves.

Neither has the traffic been all one way, flowing from the artist's (or label's) vaults to the bootlegger's pressing plant. The music industry has also learned much from the bootleg sector. In 1971, The Who's seminal "Live At Leeds" was released in a sleeve designed to duplicate the spartan artwork which then accompanied most bootlegs. At the other end of the decade, a bootleg collection of previously released Beatles rarities, "Collectors Item", became the ipso facto role model for Capitol's own "Rarities" compilation.

The very terminology of unauthorized recordings has also been hijacked by the majors. The word "bootleg" itself has attained a romantic quality in the overground Rock lexicon which is completely at odds with the actual commodity's outlaw standing in that community. As early as 1975, A&M Records was pressing a Nils Lofgren live promo album, "Back It Up", under the subtitle of "An Authorized Bootleg" (as though that were not a contradiction in terms!). The following year, Shelter produced a similar, and similarly misnomic, "Official Live Bootleg", documenting an early Tom Petty show. And 1994 saw Ice Cube cobble together a collection of B-sides and live tracks under the title "Bootlegs and B-Sides".

Then there are the two veritable grand-daddies of the official boot, Dylan's "Bootleg Series" (a three-disc set which, somewhat contrarily, was largely comprised of material which never had been bootlegged!), and Frank Zappa's "Beat the Boots", a remarkable offering which not only legitimized a total of 16 existing bootlegs (spread over two BTB volumes), but also offered them up with their original underground artwork.

Zappa's own motives in this enterprise were cynical at best. A fierce opponent of bootlegging, he saw the sets' purpose as twofold: one, to reroute some of the bootleggers' money into his own pocket; and two, to highlight the often poor quality of the "real" bootlegs by mastering his copies from original vinyl editions.

The countering argument is, if the bootleggers had not preserved this music in the first place, Zappa would have been unable to capitalize upon it later for whatever reason. The same can be said for the contents, in part if not entirely, of a great many of today's most cherished "archive" releases. It is horrifying to note how many priceless master tapes have been wiped out by uncaring label and studio staff, to the point where a legitimate release for a legendary session can often only be put together from bootleg recordings! Swathes of the Beatles' "Live At The BBC" collection bear witness to that!

Much of "Great White Wonder" (and its myriad of successors) long ago gained a legal release, as Bob Dylan's mid-70s "Basement Tapes" album. Later this year, another legendary Dylan boot, the live "Royal Albert Hall 1966", will become volume two of the "Bootleg Series". The list goes on. Bowie's "In Person" became Griffin Records' "Live At Santa Monica"; Prince's pirate "Black Album" became Prince's official "Black Album"; and Virgin tacked a Pistols boot onto copies of the "Kiss This" compilation. In every case, sales far outstripped the original pirate production.

Yet still the Bootleggers bootleg. Why? For some, obviously, the motivation is money. But for others, producing, even compiling, bootlegs is a labor of love, a fan's chance to share his interest with others - one recent Genesis bootleg box was even titled "From One Fan To Another".

With this in mind, it should be noted that many bootleggers make no secret about their desire to go "overground", at least to the point where they are not infringing sundry copyright laws. It is this desire which has led to the amazing proliferation of European-manufactured CDs, many of which consign (under new titles) existing vinyl boots to digital immortality, and almost all of which exist in nose-thumbing defiance of the individual artist and/or his/her label.

Even within such a tightly constrained community as the European Economic Community, national copyright laws are wildly out of sync with one another. In Italy, for example, any live recording made before 1965 is considered Public Domain, and the only constraints on releasing this material revolve around the payment of royalties! Other countries have equally contradictory laws, to the point where albums which would be regarded as unquestionably piratical in one land, are perfectly legitimate in another.

Luxembourg, Germany, the former Eastern Block, Australia and Japan are among the other countries in which the thin line between out-and-out bootlegs and unauthorized-but-loophole-legal albums is distorted enough to give manufacturers and collectors alike a field day. And the major labels, a major headache.

'The Ethics (or Lack Thereof) in Bootleg Collecting'

By Rush Evans from the July '95 issue of 'Discoveries' (see page 238)

At a recent Austin Record Convention, I bought a bootleg of a Springsteen show from 1975 that had been performed in the very room in which the convention was being held. The dealer's table was just about twenty feet in front of the stage at Austin's Palmer Auditorium. My friend also bought one; he'd actually attended that 1975 show, and he'd even sat at the same spot on which he was now standing to buy the CD of the same performance. (The show, by the way, had cost him eight bucks in 1975, the bootleg cost him twenty in 1995, a bargain by bootleg standards.)

I was only 13 when Bruce came to Austin in 1975, I barely knew who he was and I was not yet a concertgoer. Being able to hear the show now is great. I mean, I'm as worthy to hear it as any of those attending that night, aren't I? I'm a loyal Springsteen fan, I've bought all his released material and attended every concert appearance anywhere near me since 1978, certainly I'm entitled to hear the other shows he's performed, I'm not taking any money out of his pockets, right? Such is the rationalization process of a bootleg collector.

Most artists have a strong personal anger towards the bootleg industry, and I can't say I blame them. Not only is their creative output an incredibly personal expression of themselves, it's also their product with their name on it. If they can't control their own output, then their artistic statement has been altered and their privacy has been violated. I can certainly understand that the creative process is reliant on a great degree of privacy. I'd be livid if anyone were to even see an early unpolished version of this very article (not that there's any demand).

But this brings up a moral dilemma for the collector: since a live performance is public in nature, should it not be considered an invasion? Are studio bootlegs, therefore, a more offensive intrusion? Am I more guilty for listening to Springsteen working in the studio on a never-released song called "Chevrolet Deluxe" than for listening to that live '75 show? An artist might very well argue that both are equal; studio recordings are not intended for public consumption, and live performances are only intended for the members of the public who have elected to attend, with the purchase of a ticket.

Which brings up the financial issue: are fans taking money straight out of an artists pockets by supporting an industry made up of thieves, who've literally stolen the music for resale? The fan's most common rationale is, "Hey, I buy all his legit stuff, too, he gets plenty of my money already!". But an artist would be quick to point out that any public performance of his or her product should be compensated. In fact, with regard to the composer or publisher, ASCAP and BMI exist solely for this reason, even tracking radio air play.

Artists have battled the bootleg industry in various ways, some of which have inadvertently validated the industry. Paul McCartney released his MTV Unplugged performance in order to prevent its being bootlegged. From a fan's perspective, we might never have gotten this excellent album out of Mr. McCartney had he not felt the need to defy the bootleggers. (His plan sort of backfired, by the way. An alternate version of the performance with extra songs came out as a bootleg video.) Bob Dylan released a boxed set actually called "The Bootleg Series" which included many songs that had been bootlegged for years. The greater irony is that the set is excellent; these songs that he'd chosen not to release over the years were often far superior to those that had been released, which is I guess the real reason studio bootlegs exist. Sometimes, the artist just can't objectively see the quality or lack thereof in his or her own music.

One must also wonder if the forthcoming rare Beatles recordings would have ever seen the light of day had it not been for the interest that has been generated for their material through the years by bootleg releases. John Lennon himself has been rumored to have been the original source for many bootlegged Beatles recordings; supposedly he traded tapes to bootleggers for Beatles recordings that he'd been looking for! Yoko Ono shared Lennon's rare solo recordings with fans by playing many hours of his home experimentations on the syndicated radio series, "The Lost Lennon Tapes". The bootleg-gers wasted no time "releasing" them in a series of LPs and CDs under the same name. Beatles rari-ties have surfaced for some thirty years, with the some of the best material, like the excellent "Ultra Rare Trax" series showing up in the bootleg market as recently as the early 1990s.

Frank Zappa was a very outspoken opponent of bootlegs, which never seemed to faze his fans: the demand for bootlegs of his shows kept the product flowing for years from the bootleggers. Considering his hatred for the industry, it was particularly surprising to see the way he chose to battle them. When he took ten of the most popular Zappa bootlegs and issued them legitimately, he was, in essence, acknowledging that they were worthy of release. Again, had it not been for the bootleggers, many fans never would have heard these shows, the legal or the illegal versions. The legitimate releases of these albums even maintained the "integrity" of the original bootleg album covers, thus raising the question of whether he might have been vulnerable to a lawsuit from the bootleggers for a type of "copyright" infringement. This might sound like a ludicrous suggestion, but don't laugh: remember we live in a country in which burglars have successfully sued their victims and songwriter John Fogerty has been sued for plagiarizing himself.

The Grateful Dead's major quarrel with bootleggers has had more to do with the often inferior quality of the releases than with financial or artistic control. Nils Lofgren actually learned his guitar parts for Springsteen songs from bootleg recordings when he was invited to join the E Street Band, despite his boss' (pardon the pun) very public aversion to them. It's the casual endorsements like these that help to ease the inherent guilt of a collector of such nefarious recordings.

Speaking of relieving guilt, one method many collectors have found of bypassing the evil, opportunistic bootlegger is through tape trading. Fans have managed to hook up with one another and trade dubs of live performances that have been made by members of the audience on portable tape recorders. I've met people of similar musical interests through tape trading and no money has ever traded hands. I've managed to find recordings of performers who mean a lot to me, but are not quite in the commercial bracket that would merit a bootleg release (let's not forget, this is a business like any other, dictated by supply and demand, if not taxes). I count among the most valued items in my collection, tapes of little known acts like the long-defunct Texas trio, Uncle Walt's Band (one of whom, David Ball, is now finally enjoying tremendous commercial success in country music). I'm also afraid I could never part with the outstanding live recordings of Loudon Wainwright III, which capture his personality and spirit far better than any studio recording (though I know for a fact that he strongly disapproves of unauthorized recordings).

The only people involved in a tape trade are the fans and admirers of the music; the profit motive has been removed, creating a type of "honor among thieves" scenario. Even the legality of tape trading is somewhat vague, much like that of dubbing audio or videotapes at home for personal use. To some degree, there has even been unspoken endorsement from performers on the subject of tape trading. On the recent Jimmy Page/Robert Plant tour, certain sections of the arenas in which they've played have been set aside just for those who wish to bring recording devices to the show. Clearly, Page and Plant are not concerned with any possible financial loss, as they've already done quite well in the profit department.

But some artists might argue, quite understandably, that the money is the least of it, even when discussing tape trading. The simple fact that their creative control has been removed from something that has their name on it (even if it's just handwritten by someone who paid the full ticket price for the concert) is enough. This, quite simply, is what they do for a living. They come up with thoughts, feelings, ideas, arrangements, melodies, and emotions, put them together in some configuration that expresses them best, then sell them to you and me. It's certainly one of the most honorable professions in the world, one which affects each of us in such a personal way that we have great reverence and admiration for those in the art creation business. When the ability to express themselves their own way has been removed by some tape or bootleg CD, have their artistic expressions on their legitimate releases been somehow undermined as well?

As for the recording quality issue, artists often spend a great deal of their own time and money to ensure that the finest, cleanest, most properly balanced version of a song reaches the consumer. The individual instruments and effects are placed at particular points with great care and precision, usually by producers and engineers who are also a great expense in the album-making process. None of this is particularly important to a bootlegger. The most basic rules of the free marketplace take precedence over such tedious matters: fans want the studio alternates and live performances and they're willing to pay for them, no matter what they sound like. Again, there are exceptions, especially in recent years. The quality of many bootleg recordings is occasionally superior to legitimate releases. One of the reasons for this is the bootleggers' growing access to soundboards at concerts, where the best possible mix has already been designed for the show, and the ambient audience noise has been averted. Also, modern studio technology has helped in the remixing of old recordings. The "Ultra Rare Trax" version of the Beatles' "There's A Place" sounds as though it were recorded today, making the legitimate version almost unlistenable.

Have I managed to come down firmly on both sides of this very moral issue? Probably. I only know that Bruce Springsteen is entitled to whatever reasons he may have for choosing not to release the 20 minute, slow version of 'The E Street Shuffle' with the monologue intro from that Austin 1975 show. I just hope that if he knew how much hearing it has meant to me, he'd forgive me for listening to it.

Legal Issues

The following has been reprinted with permission from the September 1995 issue of
ICE - THE MONTHLY CD NEWSLETTER (PO Box 3043, Santa Monica, CA 90408 USA)

For the first time in nearly five years, the RIAA and U.S. Customs officials have taken significant action against the importing of bootleg CDs into the U.S.. According to an RIAA press release, on July 21, customs officials in New York City intercepted a parcel of "2,900 alleged bootleg CDs" shipped from Luxembourg. "A controlled delivery, under the auspices of customs, was then made to Zapp Records, Inc. in Greenwich Village. At that location, an additional 5,500 alleged unauthorized CDs, primarily in the bootleg form, were confiscated". The press release goes on to commend officials and describe the action as the "first seizure under the new federal anti-bootlegging statute".

That statute added special language to existing United States Code to specifically address "sound recordings and music videos of live musical performances". It comes as a direct result of the U.S. signing the GATT treaty. Prior to that, according to the RIAA press release, "generally only state statutes had been available to law enforcement and the RIAA's anti-piracy unit to protect artists' recording rights against bootleggers.

The new laws are unique in that they shift the focus of illegality from copyright infringement to "the unauthorized fixation of a live performance", according to an RIAA internal memorandum. To simplify, CDs of live performances made without the consent of the artist are now illegal for that act alone. With the question of copyright secondary, customs officials can seize live CDs purely on the basis of being "unauthorized fixation(s)". Curiously, the new law does not apply to studio outtakes, as under its definition, such recordings are already "fixed", though they remain protected under existing copyright laws.

Perhaps most important, the new code applies regardless of whether the recording or manufacturing occurred outside of the United States. "Such copies", the memorandum states, "are subject to seizures and forfeiture in the United States in the same manner as property inspected in violation of customs laws. These 'live' bootlegs can now be seized by U.S. Customs at the Point of Importation". Also altered by the legislation are penalties for bootlegging. A single violation can now bring up to five years imprisonment and fines of up to $250,000.

The updated federal statute has given Customs plenty of incentive to inspect CD shipments. An unconfirmed source tells ICE that customs began this new wave of enforcement by holding and inspecting more than 50 CD shipments at Newark (New Jersey) Airport, including the Zapp container, as well as packages of legally imported CDs destined for stores in New York City. Reports of other shipments and parcels seized have followed in the weeks since the Zapp bust. On August 4 (1995), customs officials, aided by the FBI and state and local police, struck hard again. According to a report in the New Haven Register, some 50,000 bootleg CDs were confiscated from a Connecticut-based distributor/importer. He is rumored to have operated the Kiwi label, among others.

The busts sent a chill through stores around the country specializing in live CDs, closing a few temporarily. The prevailing opinion in the bootleg community is that the actions are limited to those importing CDs directly from foreign countries, and not average retailers. "It's back to business as usual", reports a frequent bootleg shopper in New York City, but others aren't quite as confident. There's already word of domestic bootleg labels losing shipments, delaying production and generally laying low to see how the current situation plays out. Meanwhile, customs inspections are forcing foreign labels to reassess American shipments, sure to cause delays or threaten availability stateside in the short run. And who's to say if stores are really safe? The bottom line is, if customs continues this level of inspection and seizure, bootleg CDs will become much scarcer in this country, regardless of the continuing legal issues in Italy and elsewhere.

Customs is not the only source of new problems for bootleggers. The updated federal law also opens the door to new civil actions against bootlegging. Nine Inch Nails is reportedly the first band to do so, taking action against a store in Los Angeles and a Long Island wholesaler selling bootleg videos of the band. Over 1,000 NIN boot CDs were also said to be taken from the Long Island dealer, and a lawsuit may be pending. As charges of copyright infringement are difficult to prosecute criminally, Nine Inch Nails stands more likely to receive retribution through civil suits and collected damages. In doing so, the act may start a trend for bands seeking to fight bootlegging.... Legal changes aside, there are other signs that the recent (albeit limited) tolerance of bootlegs by some in the music industry may be eroding. Even boot collector Eddie Vedder indicted bootleggers with ticket scalpers and other undesirables when he spoke to the crowd at a recent Pearl Jam concert in Milwaukee.... And the situation isn't any better Down Under. The days of legalized bootlegging in Australia are now over. Under the headline of "Bootleg Loophole Closed," the Melbourne Herald-Sun reported that as of July 1, labels "selling bootleg live recordings of artists will face fines of $250,000, when amendments tightening copyright laws come into effect. Individuals will face up to six months in jail or fines up to $50,000".

The following has been reprinted with permission from the March 1996 issue of
ICE - THE MONTHLY CD NEWSLETTER (PO Box 3043, Santa Monica, CA 90408 USA)

It's been over six months since U.S. Customs officials and the RIAA stepped up their enforcement against the importation of bootleg CDs into America. Has the situation changed? Says one European label, "It's now almost impossible getting goods into the United States. Airport customs have been alerted to stop commodities bearing the CD description. It's just a no-go situation for importers. We've now temporarily closed our European production house". Of course, some CDs are getting through, but confiscations remain common, and recent busts at a midwest record convention are keeping dealers on edge.

And the problems are not exclusively Stateside. In early February, officials in Luxembourg took action against bootleg labels operating in that country, confiscating a number of new titles and taking a few well-known imprints out of commission. Until now, the tiny nation had remained bootleg-friendly, despite the changes across Europe and the U.S.. One informed dealer suggests the Luxembourg action will only add greater delays to an industry where production now takes months instead of weeks - when it happens at all.

As if that were not enough, U.S. officials are urging Japan to change its copyright protection window from 25 to 50 years, in accordance with the GATT treaty. The major target of the campaign to change the law is counterfeit compilation CDs sold on street corners, but the law could also make trouble for Japanese bootleg labels, especially those in the Beatle trade.

Meanwhile, back in Canada...

Press release dated January 8 1996.
ANTI-BOOTLEG LAW ADDED TO COPYRIGHT ACT

Recent amendments to the Copyright Act will for the first time protect Canadian performers and recording artists exploited by the sale of bootleg recordings. "Bootleg" is a term used to describe a type of record piracy that involves unlawfully recording a performer's performance at a concert or in a live broadcast without the authorization or consent of the performer. These amendments to the Copyright Act will bring Canadian copyright law into conformity with the laws of one hundred and twenty other countries that are members of the World Trade Organization. The new copyright in a performer's performance has a life of fifty years and will retroactively apply to any performances that have been recorded and copied without authorization of the performer.

On January 1, 1996, the "Anti-Bootleg" amendments to the Copyright Act became law. It is now an infringement of copyright and unlawful for any person to make an unauthorized recording of a performer's performance and to distribute or sell copies of bootleg recordings, imported into or manufactured in Canada after January 1, 1996, can be sued by the owner of copyright in the performance and/or criminally prosecuted for the offence of copyright infringement. Maximum penalties for a conviction of the offence of copyright infringement are $1,000,000 or imprisonment for up to 5 years, or both.

Brian Robertson, president of the Canadian Recording Industry Association, said that "the anti-bootleg amendments that now bring recording artists within the protection of copyright law are another positive step that will assist the music industry's efforts to battle piracy of sound recordings. Manufacturers and importers of bootleg recordings do not pay royalties to the recording artist and do not invest in the development their careers". In 1994, the sales of pirated sound recordings in Canada were $30 million dollars and world-wide were estimated at $2.9 billion dollars.

For further information: Ken Thompson, Canadian Recording Industry Association, (416) 967-7272

From The Trenches

The following articles have been written by people in the trenches... collectors. Some say that we at HOT WACKS are (or who should be) the experts. The way I see it, it's you the collectors compiling that seemingly never-ending collection who are the real experts. Sure, we listen and document a lot of the material that goes into HOT WACKS but it's the collectors who write with new information and facts missing from past editions that make the book as complete as it is. Please feel free to send in any data you may have or to contribute an article about your favourite group.

The Beatles: History of "Get Back" Bootlegs

The following has been reprinted from the book that comes with the "Get Back Journals 2" boxed set (see page 45). Please keep this in mind when you see phrases such as "...this set...". While no credit is given in the book, there's no doubt this excellent article was written by a very knowledgeable fan.

For over 20 years, the collecting public has been fed a continuing stream of bootlegs drawn from the Twickenham sessions. These have usually been chopped up, placed out of sequence, and presented in inferior sound quality.

Of course, bootleggers can only work from material at their disposal, and in the beginning the only material available was the film "Let It Be". The first Twickenham material to appear, then, came from the soundtrack of the film on a double album called "Cinelogue: Let It Be", which was released in February, 1974 by Contra Band Music (CBM). Of course, this was back in the days before home video, so fans were more delighted to be able to enjoy the "Let It Be" soundtrack on record!

The release of the "Let It Be" videotape in 1982 provided a new audio source, and bootlegs produced after that date were mastered from the video soundtrack, rather than film. The first of these was "In a Play Anyway", a 2 LP set on Circuit Records (matrix number TWK 2262). A further reissue by Beeb Transcription Records (on a new plate TR-2170) was titled "The Last Blast". It was released in 1988 and its sound quality is slightly inferior. Of course, most of the film soundtrack from Twickenham is completely useless because longer source tapes have surfaced (and the few bits that you would still need can be found on this set and on the "Get Back Journals").

In late 1974 the first completely unreleased Twickenham outtakes surfaced on the legendary "Sweet Apple Trax" LPs. These were originally released as two two-LP sets by CBM using the Instant Analysis label (matrix numbers 4185 - REV-2000 and 4181 - STD-2002). This phenomenal series was among the most enjoyable vinyl bootlegs of its era, and many of us listened to it for hours on end, leading to a lifelong addiction to this stuff! By the way, these LPs were originally announced under the title "The Apple Treasure Chest Masters, Vol. 1 & 2". When they finally appeared, they had "deluxe" printed sepia-toned jackets. A late ´70´s repress from the original plates came with blank white labels and black and white covers which were copies of the originals.

The "Sweet Apple Trax" LPs were copied almost immediately by Kornyphone, which combined the material onto a single double set called "Hahst Az Sun" (TAKRL-2950). This prompted CBM to remaster its own release as a double album in order to compete. It was distributed under the title "Hot As Sun" (matrix number 4216 REV 2000 / 4217 BLD 2002) on the Instant Analysis label. In 1980 single LP repressings of "Hot As Sun" were distributed as "Sweet Apple Tracks Crate 1" and "Sweet Apple Tracks Crate 2". It might be noted that the Kornyphone issue "Hahst Az Sun" rearranged the songs and omitted a few seconds here and there. This set was copied many times and reissued as a variety of single LP bootlegs, and with a full color cover as "Sweet Apple Trax" on the Newsound Records label (matrix NR 909-1). The Newsound plates were also used for a picture disc which came out under the titles "Sweet Apple Trax Vol. 1" and "Sweet Apple Trax Vol. 2". The original source tapes were remastered by Audifon records for the first 2 records of the 3 LP set "The Beatles" (commonly known as "The Black Album" released in May, 1981). These plates were subsequently used for the first three albums of the original "Get Back Journals" vinyl boxed set. More recently, an hour of the original tapes were released on CD in "Songs From The Past Vol. 3". All of the material was included on the first "Get Back Journals" CD set.

The next batch of Twickenham outtakes to appear was on the EPs "Twickenham Jams", which popped up in February 1977 (matrix VC-4591), and "Watching Rainbows" which appeared in May 1977. This material soon appeared on bootleg albums of the same names. "Watching Rainbows" (which had more material than the EP of the same name) came from Audifon in March of 1978. "Twickenham Jams" was a straight knock-off on the label Smilin' Ears (filling out the LP with non-"Get Back" sessions material). Most of the "Watching Rainbows" performances showed up on "The Black Album" in better quality, and the few moments that didn't are included here on "Get Back Journals 2". It might be noted that a second edition of "Watching Rainbows" came out in July of 1978. This upgraded the sound quality of the "Watching Rainbows" / "Madman" / "Mean Mr. Mustard" tape, cutting off some of the "Watching Rainbows" jam in the process (but don't worry, it was restored back on "Get Back Journals"). Copies of the "Watching Rainbows" LP appeared on the 2 LP set "Behind Closed Doors" and the boxed set "So Much Younger Then".

Collectors had to wait a couple of years for the next batch of Twickenham outtakes to surface. Oddly enough, the first taste of a new tape came in the form of a sampler tape, reproduced at the end of a one-sided record from Tobe Milo called "Man of The Decade" which came out in early 1980. This rather useless bootleg reproduced bits and pieces of various January 3rd performances which were unbootlegged up to that time. Later in the year the entire tape appeared on an album called "Vegemite". This record was quite difficult for American collectors to find, and was the first product from a bootlegger who later went on to fame for his CD product under the "Goblin" label. The 2 LPs of "Vegemite" (BT-6896) gave us our first exposure to the January 2nd / 3rd material, albeit in lousy sound quality. The set was copied in 1981 by JPM Records as 2 single LPs and retitled "The Dream is Over Vol. 1" (JPM1081) and "The Dream is Over Vol. 2" (JPM 280102) in slightly lesser sound quality. These, in turn, were quickly copied by Sweet Sound Records as "Sweet Apple Trax Vol. III" (W-909) in even worse sound quality, and the Sweet Sound masters (which was not even complete) was copied I onto picture disc by another bootlegger (matrix SA-3909). Great Live Concerts copied it as a double album called "Apple Trax Vol.2" (15802), and Strawberry Records later copied this issue as part of its 6 LP compilation "Apple Trax", and single LP series "Applemania". Knock-offs aside, all of the material here appears on the "Get Back Journals" CDs, as well as "Songs From The Past Vol. 4" and "Songs From The Past Vol. 5" CDs - usually in much improved sound quality.

In May 1981 one of the classic bootlegs appeared on the Ruthless Rhymes label - "The Beatles Black Album", (a parody of the legitimate "White Album"), which could only have appeared during the late, lamented vinyl age. This bootleg included a wonderful "alternate" poster which neatly complemented the original. The first two LPs here were simply repressings of the TAKRL "Hahzt As Sun" plates, but the third album offered a significant upgrade in quality to the "Watching Rainbows" material, as well as adding 5 numbers which hadn't appeared up to that point. This set was subsequently repressed by Box Top, and the stampers were used for the first 3 LPs of the vinyl "Get Back Journals" set. A copy of the "Black Album" (from a different bootlegger) was issued on the EVA label on plate LP A/B/C/D/E/F. This omitted one of the versions of "One After 909".

At the end of '81 a new "Get Back" session bootleg began to filter out of Europe (with both a black-and-white and full-color cover). This was called "Her Majesty" and featured a few new songs from Twickenham, plus a whole bunch of Apple stuff which hadn't been heard before. It was almost as awful in sound quality as "Vegemite", and is completely useless at this point, since all of its material has appeared in better quality on CD. An American bootleg called "Wonderful Picture of You" copied the "Get Back" material on it from "Her Majesty". This title has also been copied as part of the boxed set called "Apple Trax", and by Great Live Concerts as "Sweet Apple Trax Vol.3" (15803). Finally, someone had the bright idea of copying the entire LP onto CD - direct from vinyl.

In September 1983, King Records put out "I Had a Dream", a new bootleg of "Get Back" sessions which was entirely Apple. This was followed the next month by "Almost Grown" (MLK-002), an enjoyable hodge-podge of material from both Twickenham and Apple. Many of the performances there were later included in the original "Get Back Journals" and "Songs From The Past Vol. 5" (CD). By that time the entire LP was quite useless.

Almost a year later, in September 1984, King Records issued the last in its series of "Get Back" bootlegs called "Singing The Blues" (MLK-003). Only a couple of songs came from Twickenham and these, too, are now found elsewhere in better sound quality.

In September of 1986 the most ambitious "Get Back" bootleg to date surfaced, called "The Get Back Journals". This came two ways, in a deluxe film box, and in regular small boxes held together by a simple color wrap-around. While the set had eleven discs, it was flawed by poor sound quality and even worse pressing quality. It was reissued in 1993 on CD with a couple of hours of new material added, and a significant upgrade in the sound quality. Needless to say, it contained much material unavailable to collectors up to that time (much of it from Apple). The entire vinyl set was copied by SUMA records under a variety of names and having even worse sound quality.

In January 1988 Core Ltd. released "Code Name Russia" (BL 888-2), an excellent quality bootleg comprised entirely of Twickenham outtakes. Most of the performances here were entirely new, and quite enjoyable - and most of them were copied onto CD in September 1988 from the tape source as part of the "Songs From The Past" series (Volume 2 and a small part of Volume 1, to be precise). "Songs From The Past" Vol. 1 and 2 have, in turn, been rendered obsolete by the two "Get Back Journals" CD sets (at least as far as Twickenham material is concerned).

At the end of '88 another "Get Back" session bootleg appeared on the Tiger Beat label (a subsidiary of the legendary Starlight Records company). The LP, "Bye Bye Love", was a knock-off of (most of) the soundtrack from a videotape of "Let It Be" outtakes which was in common circulation among collectors (more of the video soundtrack appears on Tiger Beat's "Classified Documents Vol. 3" LP). It's extraordinarily difficult to listen to, both because the performances are poor and choppy and the sound quality sucks. Needless to say, the "Get Back Journals" set will try to see to it that you never need go out of your way to find this hunk of vinyl.

In 1989 "Songs From The Past" Vol. 3-5 appeared. While Vol. 3 offered us an hour of the "Sweet Apple Trax" master tape, Vol. 4 and 5 gave us a significant upgrade of much of the material which had previously appeared on "Vegemite" (with some bits omitted here and there, and some bits added). It's all academic at this point, since if you have both "Journals" CD boxes you don't need the "Songs From The Past Vol. 3-5" CDs at all.

1990 saw the rise of Yellow Dog Records. Throughout this decade they have issued a number of important releases featuring "Get Back" material. The first two of these ("Unsurpassed Masters Vol. 5" and "Celluloid Rock") featured only material from Apple. The next two ("Get Back and 22 Other Songs" and "Complete Rooftop Concert") both centered on Apple also, but featured some new and/or upgraded Twickenham performances as part of their "bonus" tracks. These were followed by the outstanding release "All Things Must Pass, Part I", which contained "Get Back" session performances featuring George on lead vocal. This disc was split almost evenly between Apple and Twickenham, with many of the performances being previously unheard. Needless to say, all the Twickenham material contained on the discs mentioned about can be found on the two "Get Back Journals" boxes.

Yellow Dog's next "Get Back" release was "WBCN Get Back Reference Acetate" which contained Apple material coupled with a 33+ minute "bonus" track of January 14th material (primarily dialogue, and painfully boring dialogue at that). This material, drawn from the identical source tape, later appeared (along with more dull January 14th dialogue), on "Rockin' Movie Stars, Volume 3". This was the last Yellow Dog "Get Back" release for some time, and the void was filled by a company calling itself "Blue Kangaroo", which released three discs full of (mostly) new material. The first of the volumes of "'69 Rehearsals" contained only Apple material. The latter two featured much new Twickenham material (which is gathered on this set and returned to its original context). Also released during this period was "Hail Hail Rock'n'Roll", which featured a number of new Apple performances, but only four Twickenham performances, and "Core of the Apple", which is equally short on Twickenham.

Yellow Dog returned to the "Get Back" sessions with the 1994 release of "All Things Must Pass, Part 2", another excellent quality set of performances featuring George on vocal. This was followed immediately by "The Auction Tapes, Volume 1" which was a hodgepodge of Twickenham and Apple material, some of it previously unheard and all of it in great quality. The Twickenham material from these two discs is, of course, found on the "Journals" boxes, and expect the Apple material to be found on a future release. Yellow Dog followed these with "Rock and Roll", an exceptional disc which featured more than 50 oldies performances from the sessions, a virtual encyclopedia of the group's roots. This disc is a necessary complement to the "Journal" boxes because it upgrades the sound quality on some material on "The Get Back Journals". Because you'll need it anyway for the "Journals 1" upgrade, we elected not to include the new Twickenham material on it here on "Journals 2".

1994 also saw the advent of Orange Records, a subsidiary of Yellow Dog, which released an eight-volume set of "Get Back" material entitled "Rockin' Movie Stars". While much of this material was previously unheard, the discs were haphazardly arranged, often duplicating each other and sometimes containing incomplete or inferior versions of things already issued. With the exception of the third volume (which contains a chronologically-correct presentation of much of the horrid January 14th session), none of these discs feature Twickenham material not found on the "Journals" boxes.

Late in 1994, Yellow Dog issued the first of three boxed sets entitled "The Ultimate Collection". Each of these four-CD sets features one full disc of Twickenham material (the rest being non-"Get Back" session material). Taken together, the three discs present ALL extant January 2nd tapes, as well as the first half hour of January 3rd. Since these releases cover this portion of the "Get Back" sessions so comprehensively, we have ignored that area completely on this boxed set.

So, you're probably saying "thanks for the history lesson, guys, but what releases do I need to have all of Twickenham?". Well, thanks to this release, very few. To be precise, "Get Back Journals" (Vigotone VIGO101-108), "Get Back Journals 2" (this set), "Rock and Roll" (Yellow Dog YD054), "Rockin' Movie Stars Volume 3" (Orange 7) and the three "Ultimate Collection" boxes (Yellow Dog) will give you all of the Twickenham material currently available. So, until "Journals 3..."

Essential Nirvana: Obscure And Oblique

By Lori Weiner

Kurt Cobain was a gifted and prolific musician who left behind a great many unreleased songs. David Grohl, Nirvana's drummer, is a talented singer/songwriter who was stymied by Cobain's total artistic domination of the band; the songs he wrote and recorded under the monicker "Late!", immediately before joining Nirvana, have never been widely released. Thus is the Nirvana collector led through the gates of heaven - or into the bowels of hell, depending on one's point of view - as (s)he begins to explore unreleased Nirvana.

As of this writing, there is a significant amount of notable material unavailable on CD. This article will concentrate solely on what is available as product - either compact disc or vinyl. With luck - and time - the many treasures currently enjoyed only by Nirvana tape traders will come into the marketplace as CDs/records.

Kurt Cobain, for all his punk sensibilities, was a consummate professional when it came to creating music. He meticulously worked and reworked songs, changing timing, lyrics, and solos until he was completely satisfied with the outcome. Especially in the Sub Pop years, Cobain made a practice of previewing his new material live. The three-CD boxed set, "A Season In Hell Part One", contains "preview" versions of "In Bloom" and "Lithium." A Compendium of historical live performances (a Seattle show shortly after Grohl's joining, and the final performance of his predecessor, Chad Channing) and demos/B-side, "A Season In Hell" also includes the only live versions currently available of "Swap Meet", "D-7", and "Here She Comes Now". Both live performances are Northwest USA club dates, and the air is electric with excitement, joy, and anticipation. The band has never sounded stronger, and most importantly, Cobain is still innocent, untainted by fame and its trappings. He is as excited and invigorated as the crowd, a feeling which unfortunately would leave him very soon after these performances.

Also included on the live portion of "A Season In Hell" is a song identified as "Token Eastern Song," long rumored but never making an appearance on CD. The track in question, from a different venue, appeared on the second volume of the "Outsesticide" series credited as "In His Hands". While it is pos- sible that the song is indeed the vaunted "Token Eastern Song", most collectors do not believe this to be the case. "In His Hands" is a punk-informed ballad with lyrics foreshadowing the themes of "Pennyroyal Tea": there is a line about "taking medications til the stomach's full". It is one of the most moving songs Cobain wrote, and it dates from a period of tremendous growth in his songwriting (1989- 90).

From the same period as "In His Hands" comes "Sappy", a song with which Cobain and Nirvana wrestled for four years. The first known recording of "Sappy" was made in Madison, WI with producer Butch Vig, slated for inclusion on what was to be the second Sub Pop LP. Instead, Nirvana signed to Geffen Records and recorded the album that made and broke them, "Nevermind". The demo version of "Sappy' is well represented on bootleg CD, available from multiple sources. The entire demo tape, which also includes early versions of "Lithium", "In Bloom", and "Stay Away" (then titled "Pay To Play"), is available in outstanding quality on the 6-CD "Into The Black" boxed set. Two live versions of "Sappy" are included on "A Season In Hell", and a somewhat different live version appears in outstanding soundboard quality on "Out Of The Blue".

"Sappy" was renamed "Verse Chorus Verse" and recorded during the sessions for Nirvana's final LP, "In Utero". Cobain wanted the song to be the title track. In the end, it was cut from the album, ending up as an uncredited track on the "No Alternative" AIDS benefit CD.

Another outstanding song dating from Cobain's prolific 1989 period is "Junkyard", available on the "Wired" and "Outcesticide Vol. I" CDs. It seems to have been performed only during the 1989 European tour, as no versions of "Junkyard" appear on any of the 1989 US dates documented on CD. "Junkyard" is not as melodic as "Sappy", retaining the grit and bombast of "Bleach"-era material, but its structure shows tremendous development over the near-metronomic pace of much of "Bleach". The careful lis- tener will note that, in this song, Cobain is experimenting with texture and beginning to master the hybrid of punk and pop that made Nirvana so remarkable.

A song titled "Help Me" appears on the "Out Of The Blue" CD from 1989. While promising, the song is not well developed, and appears to have been abandoned by Cobain before it was completed.

As Nirvana became more popular, they lost much of their spontaneity and variations in sets became less common. During the "Nevermind" tour of Europe, the band often closed the show with "Endless, Nameless", a ten-minute-plus jam with minimal riffing and vocals. "Endless, Nameless" appears on most copies of the "Nevermind" CD as a hidden track.

Cobain's chronic stomach ailment was aggravated by stress of touring, and after his marriage to Courtney Love in February 1992 he returned to Los Angeles. There was no "Nevermind" US tour, though the band played several isolated shows, most notably England's Reading Festival and Portland, Oregon's "No On 9" benefit. At these shows, the band previewed "Pennyroyal Tea", "Dumb" and "All Apologies". "Into The Black" contains the Reading show, with all three "previews" in digital quality. "Live Tits", a show from Hamburg in 1991, includes very early versions of "Dumb" and "Pennyroyal Tea", the latter with different lyrics.

Nirvana performed in Rio De Janiero in early 1993. They were not happy to be there and let the crowd know by mangling "Smells Like Teen Spirit" with a trumpet solo (courtesy of Flea, Red Hot Chili Peppers) and playing obscurities from their Sub Pop days, such as "Dive", totally unrecognisable to the football field full of trendies. Then in rehearsal for "In Utero", Kurt led the band through radically different versions of "Heart Shaped Box" and "Scentless Apprentice". The concert is documented on the "Hollywood Rock Festival' 2-CD set.

After "In Utero" was completed, but several months prior to its release, Nirvana played the 1993 New Music Seminar in Roseland, NY. The show was energetic and the new material polished. For the first time, fans witnessed an acoustic set complete with cello. The sound was augmented by the second guitar of Big John, formerly of British punk band The Exploited. Cobain mentioned in an interview with England's The Face that he was "disgusted by the male meathead quotient" in the crowd. He didn't mention that earlier in the day he had nearly died from a heroin overdose.

By the time "In Utero" was released, Kurt Cobain was exhausted emotionally and physically. He and his wife narrowly averted losing custody of their child, and the many problems surrounding the recording of "In Utero" had been making headlines for months. His stomach ailment was no better and there was a great deal more pressure on him than ever before. He was not looking forward to the tour for the new record, and the "In Utero" performances were largely lethargic and predictable, not matching the energy of tours gone by. Each show featured an acoustic set and the song lists were adhered to with military-like precision. Now with guitarist Pat Smear, they added a cover of David Bowie's "The Man Who Sold The World" to their later sets, as well as Leadbelly's "Where did You Sleep Last Night?". These songs were performed essentially identically at each show. Nirvana had become a business and operated like one. There are many CDs documenting "In Utero" shows. The best is "Roma" (KTS), boasting unparalleled sound quality and a very energetic performance. Several days later, Kurt Cobain OD'd and the remainder of the tour was cancelled. Two months later, he committed suicide.

The Nirvana collector can look forward to many more minutes of listening pleasure as the vaults continue to open. Eagerly awaited are the demos Kurt and Pat Smear were working on at the time of Cobain's death, a studio session with Screaming Trees' Mark Lanegan (with Cobain providing the vocals to "Ain't That A Shame") and Nirvana's final studio session in January 1994. One of the songs rumored to have been recorded is "On The Mountain", which has been performed by Hole on MTV Unplugged. We can only wait - and enjoy what is already here.

Pink Floyd Verses The Beatles?

Still More Floyd Musings By Keith From Toronto

In one corner we have the group that began it all. They set off the 60s rock music invasion and merely changed the face of popular music for all time. If that wasn't enough, they also were a major influence for the group in the other corner. So chalk up an early point for Pink Floyd.

Just kidding folks. Of course it's the Beatles who came first. But let me clarify what this article is about. It has nothing to do with an actual competition between Pink Floyd and the Beatles. Instead, I want you to think of all the similarities, oddities and parallels between the two bands. There are quite a few.

You can probably come up with some quick and easy ones. Both groups come from England. Both had members that knew each other from their school days. Both had more than one songwriter and one vocalist. Both were five piece bands at one stage. Both groups came out of the 1960s. And both experienced creative differences causing very public and not too pleasant splits involving their bass players. But get past these and you get down to the real comparison. Pink Floyd and the Beatles have many more things in common.

WHAT'S THIS GOT TO DO WITH BOOTLEGS?

What's all this got to do with bootlegs you may ask? Well, it's through listenings to the bands' unofficial material that helps complete our analysis. So, once again, dig out all your HOT WACKS books. Refer to all of the Beatles, solo Beatles, Floyd and solo Floyd sections in The Last Wacks Book XV and Supplements 1 through 4 for additional reference. And don't forget to include Syd Barrett just before the Beatles section.

While I usually confine myself to listens to CD boots only, this time out I previewed material released on vinyl going as far back as to what was circulating in 1976. In spite of the scads of CD material around, not everything has made it to the new format. All references in this article are for CD unless otherwise noted, however. OK? With the housekeeping out of the way, we can begin.

WHAT'S IN A NAME?

Both the Beatles and Floyd had different names in their earliest incarnations. Pre-Beatles were the Quarry Men, Johnny and The Moondogs, the Beatals, Long John and The Silver Beatals, the Silver Beetles, the Beetles and, finally, the more familiar Beatles.

Pre-Pink Floyd were called the T-Set, Sigma Six, Megadeaths, the Screaming Abdabs, the Architectural Abdabs, the Abdabs, Leonard's Lodgers, the Pink Floyd Sound and finally, Pink Floyd. See a pattern here?

Both groups had their eventual and final lead guitarists play in other bands. George Harrison played for the Les Stuart Quartet. Syd Barrett with Geoff Mott and the Mottoes and Those Without. David Gilmour with Jokers Wild.

Both groups also had members juggling instruments before settling on a final arrangement. Roger Waters says he ended up on bass by default, it was all that was left to try! While this is a bit different from Paul McCartney taking over from Stuart Sutcliffe, the bass does end up as the final instrument for both songwriters. (More on the two bass players later.)

But back to the name thing. The Beatles were named by Stuart Sutcliffe, not John Lennon as myth has it (though everyone agrees it was John who came up with the b.e.a.t. spelling in the name). Depending on who you believe, Stuart either took the name from (1) the movie "The Wild Ones", starring a young Marlon Brando (the name of the bike gang in the film was the Beetles) or (2) as a play on Buddy Holly's band - the Crickets. The Crickets variation is the most popular choice as truth but, note, the "Beatles Anthology" video makes a reference to "The Wild Ones" version.

It was Syd Barrett who coined Pink Floyd, definitely based on early musical influences - blues players Pink Anderson and Floyd "Dipper Boy" Council (some say the odd combination happened on the spur of the moment as Barrett spied the names on records in his collection).

Ironically, both Stuart Sutcliffe and Syd Barrett would depart their respective groups before seeing widespread success. Unfortunately, Sutcliffe did not live to see his band mates make good, dying on April 10, 1962, just the day before the band returned to Germany for a seven-week engagement at the newly-opened Star Club in Hamburg.

It was also a day in April but six years later (April 6) when Pink Floyd officially announced the departure of Syd Barrett. The reason? Not from Barrett's literal death but rather his slowly dying mental capacity. Sadly, it was too much drugs and not enough rock and roll that ruined another good one in Syd Barrett.

Fans of both bands will surely agree that the loss of these two individuals represents a loss of true genius. While Sutcliffe was not respected for his musical abilities, he was for his art and his influence on John Lennon's persona. Just as Barrett was respected for his music (less so for his art abilities) and the effect he had on all four remaining Floyds. Why, there is a little bit of Syd Barrett that continues to haunt Floyd and Roger Waters even to this day.

Syd and Stu are an odd parallel to be sure. We can take it even further by noting that both individuals answered to a three letter name beginning with an "s".

As for the band make-up itself, the Beatles were active as a five piece for a couple of years while all five official Floyds only worked together for a few months (January to April 1968).

It's worth pointing out though, that Ringo Starr's appearance on the scene, replacing Pete Best (and well after Sutcliffe had departed to study art in Germany), was as natural a fit as David Gilmour's. In both situations, the groups had played or socialised with their new members before. In Gilmour's case, he and Syd were old friends from high school and shared many a guitar lick together. It is also rumored that Gilmour's band, Jokers Wild, often played on the same bill as Floyd. Once, at a party for the girlfriend of Storm Thorgerson (Floyd album designer), the group even played together as a "super group". Or so say some Floyd history books. They also say Paul Simon played at this party. Hmmmm?

Ringo would occasionally sit in on drums with the Beatles in their Hamburg, Germany days. Ringo was playing with Rory Storm and the Hurricanes at the time. This group also shared the stage with the Beatles for a time at the Kaiserkeller club and played with the Beatles as a "super group" on occasion.

The Beatles first producer, George Martin, felt Pete Best was the weak link in the Beatles sound. His view helped prompt Best's outing by the others to bring in Ringo (they got their manager, Brian Epstein, to do the "deed").

In Syd's case, it was his inability to perform that was the problem. He'd become too unreliable at live gigs to play on stage. After an attempt at him being, more or less, just the songwriter for the group, he was asked to go. As for Floyd's first managers, they decided to stick with Barrett. Both Peter Jenner and Andrew King felt Syd was the key player in the group and the others would amount to very little. Wrong! Is this decision as foolish as Decca records not signing up the Beatles? (See below for more on Decca records and signing up the bands.)

By the way, departed Beatles drummer Pete Best can be heard playing on the Tony Sheridan "My Bonnie" sessions, with the Beatles credited as the Beat Brothers. These sessions have long been available beyond bootlegs and also feature John Lennon singing "Ain't She Sweet" as well as a fine instrumental by Harrison and Lennon called "Cry For A Shadow" (this song is on the "Beatles Anthology 1").

But let's back up a few years before those recordings. The earliest recorded material featuring the Quarry Men is found on several boots. Titles include "The Quarry Men At Home" (Chapter One CO 25190, 1992), "Liverpool May 1960" (FU 207, 1994) and segments found on the Box Set "Artifacts" (BIG MUSIC, KTS, set one, BIGBX 4018, 1993).

There are many other titles featuring the material as well. What you should look for is the period 1958 to 1960. Also note, most of the boots list the material as coming from Liverpool, England and state "recorded at Paul McCartney's house". In the book "Black Market Beatles", this is refuted information (the authors say the material comes instead from the rehearsals in the Fall of 1960 in Hamburg). The "Beatles Anthology 1" features three examples of songs from this period and states they were recorded in Liverpool at Paul's house.

Hunter Davies (official Beatles biographer) in his book, "The Beatles" (second revised edition), says that Astrid Kircherr (Hamburg friend, lover to Stu and first photographer of the group) owns a copy of a tape Stuart gave her featuring John, Paul, George and Stuart rehearsing at the Liverpool Art College. Could this be the source for this early material? Perhaps. According to Kircherr, John talked the college into buying a tape recorder for the band to use.

Whatever the truth about the source, there is one significant song worth pointing out. Check out the release on bootleg of the first (for certain) Liverpool material recorded by John, Paul and George (also with Stu) in 1958, "That'll Be The Day". (There are Buddy Holly and the Crickets again.)

The version on the "Artifacts" Box Set comes from two separate radio broadcasts of the song with the excerpts edited together. It is known that the group recorded an acetate at Liverpool's Kensington Recording Studio in 1958, also taping a Harrison/McCartney tune called "In Spite Of All The Danger". It's presumed that Paul McCartney himself owns the original copy of this material. (The "Beatles Anthology 1" features full versions of both songs in a scope on all the Bootleggers - thanks Paul.)

As for Pink Floyd, we have to advance eight years to October 1966. The group went to the Thompson Private Recording Company, in London, to record their earliest material. What survives is often referred to as coming from the "original EMI acetate". But this has nothing to do with the record company, just the manufacturer of the acetate itself. The Thompson tapes feature a Syd Barrett original, "Lucy Leave" and also "King Bee", by blues man Slim Harpo.

This material is available on several boots. Check out "Magnesium Proverbs" (The Gold Standard NIGHT TRIPPER GD - 10, 1994), "A Saucerful Of Outtakes" (Chapter One CO 25195, 1994) or "Pink Floyd Jewel Box 4" (Home Records HR - 5947 - 3, 1994).

Compare the two groups and you can hear few common denominators at this point. The quality of the Floyd material is superior so let's go to the Beatles Decca audition for a fairer comparison. Both have short songs (the norm for the day).

The Decca audition tapes were made in Decca's North London recording studios (Pete Best plays on these and not Ringo). As is notorious in bootlegdom, the early underground releases were not actually the true Decca auditions at all, so be careful. What you want to hear are the 15 songs captured on January 1, 1962 including "The Sheik Of Araby", "Money" and "Besame Mucho".

Yellow Dog's, "The Silver Beatles The Original Decca Audition Tapes 1962 And The Cavern Club Rehearsals" (Yellow Dog, YD 011, 1991) is a great release to use for this particular Beatles/Floyd taste test.

Most notable is the better recording quality. But there is a decidedly different sound to the group itself here. Beatleologists often comment that George Martin added something to the Beatles sound. You can quickly hear how Martin's efforts paid off.

The Beatles' later releases of the same songs have a far less derivative "late 50s sound" than what is recorded at Decca. Listen to "Money" for the best example. There is more going on than just the switch of drummers between Decca and EMI just over a year later. While the Beatles' early EMI material sounds dated too, it at least sounds like the 60s (in fact creating the mould for the others to follow, including Pink Floyd).

But back to Decca. To be fair, time was tight for the group at this audition and they may have been less inclined to approach the session as if it were just like a stage performance. (Apparently Manager Brian Epstein chose all the material to be recorded and in what order; thinking to feature each members' talents - but note, there were no vocals for Pete Best) Maybe it was just nerves. Whatever, the songs aren't really up to speed. (Note, the "Beatles Anthology 1" features only five songs from this session but adds rare versions of "Besame Mucho" and "Love Me Do", recorded at EMI with Pete Best on drums.)

Now, all you Beatle fans may strike me down for saying it, but they really don't sound like they are the next big thing here. Do they? Please, don't let hindsight interfere with your analysis either. Indeed, by putting the groups together, I think there's an edge to Pink Floyd. "Lucy Leave" is infectious. Ask your-self which group you would sign? Who sounds most original?

You do have to factor in the fact that the Beatles had hit big by the time Syd Barrett and the rest of Floyd recorded their material. But could four years of Beatles recordings on the scene have made such a difference in approach for Floyd? You be the judge.

A second Floyd example of early material is also found on "A Saucerful Of Outtakes". Here we get a much longer version of "Interstellar Overdrive" (an early Floyd signature tune) than released on their first official album, "Piper At The Gates Of Dawn". The band recorded the material in February 1967 at the Sound Techniques Studio, Chelsea, England. This is still before they signed a record deal. The demo material helped seal their contract with EMI however. Polydor records was interested in the group but, after hearing the results of the Sound Techniques sessions, EMI outbid everyone else and signed Floyd.

Ironically, one of the executives making the decision for EMI was Beecher Stevens, who allegedly had worked for Decca and was a part of the crowd of decision-makers who turned down the Beatles. Does signing Floyd make up for this earlier mistake?

While crediting George Martin for being able to capture the sound of the Beatles on records, we have to credit Joe Boyd for Floyd. Their first studio releases reflected the sound he generated at Sound Techniques Studios, something Norman Smith was not able to duplicate as well at Abbey Road Studios when he took over as Floyd's "in house" producer at the insistence of EMI (note, Smith was the engineer who was also working with George Martin and the Beatles).

Smith did provide all of the same recording techniques the Beatles were using. And much of Floyd's early studio work reflects Beatle shades, with double tracked vocals and such. But I would say that the Norman Smith sound is not derivative of Pink Floyd's true sound. That comes later and post-Syd Barrett.

Another studio personnel connection is Alan Parsons. Coincidentally, Parsons began working at Abbey Road studios as a tape operator/second engineer while the Beatles were working on the "Abbey Road" album. He had graduated to first engineer by the time of "Dark Side Of The Moon", contributing many of the connections and segue bits found on the Floyd's most successful album - sound connections not altogether dissimilar to side 2 (or songs 7-17 on the CD) of the Beatles "Abbey Road" album. Parsons also worked for a time as Floyd's live concert mixer. What great sound those gigs must have had!

But back again to our direct comparison. We later have both bands working in the same Abbey Road studios (actually next door to each other). Floyd is allowed to observe the Beatles in action too, a privilege not everyone got in 1967.

On one occasion at least, Paul, George and Ringo dropped in on Syd, Roger, Rick and Nick. The three Beatles offered some moral support to the four Floyds while they were recording the "Piper At The Gates Of Dawn" album.

As for the music itself, take the songs listed as "Screaming Guitar Blues" and "Shuffle Boogie Blues" on the "Liverpool May 1960" Beatles CD mentioned earlier. Compare these to Floyd's "Interstellar Overdrive" from the Sound Techniques sessions. These three pieces are long and show the two acts in improv mode.

While the "Screaming Guitar Blues and Shuffle Boogie Blues" are just jams and on acoustic guitar, they do feature competent playing and have an honest, early rock n' roll "feel". No one should ever say the Beatles were bad musicians, even at this early point with mistakes intact. I like the sparks we get here far better than what we get with Decca.

Certainly the greatest difference between the Beatles and Floyd is the actual length of songs. While the early Floyd (on record) went after shorter pieces and even the singles market, the later version, minus Syd, is best known for album-length cuts. The Beatles, of course, will forever claim the greatest ability to pen spectacular pop tunes - considerably shorter but no less complete.

While this may be a telling difference between the bands in the long run, all of the material noted so far lets you judge ability and potential. Can you imagine the Beatles having even greater success with longer, improvised pieces? Interesting thought but maybe an impossibility in 1962. Even in 1967, it is pressure from EMI that forces Floyd to record far shorter versions of their on-stage material. Ironically, it's the Beatles who help break the radio barrier over long cuts with the release of "Hey Jude" in 1968. You can hear a semi-live performance of this song, as played on the David Frost show, on "Strawberry Fields Forever" (Fab 4 Records FAB 5555, 1989) - great live vocal by Paul.

LIVE ON STAGE

This leads us to live performances. Here, the similarity between the bands is weakest. For the Beatles, concerts were almost as short as their songs. Again, we have to consider that the Beatles really began it all. There were no huge stadium tours before the Beatles. No huge amps. No fancy lights (though Floyd was working on it). We really have to go back to Hamburg and the Star Club material (recorded by fellow rocker, Kingsize Taylor on a cheap tape recorder - was it the same one used to capture the 1960 rehearsals from two years earlier?) to get a feel for what the Beatles were capable of doing in an extended set.

The Star Club performances in late 1962 have been widely bootlegged but are also available on commercial release, most commonly on vinyl as "Live At The Star Club".

To compare the bands, we go "pre-stadium" for Floyd as well. A good example is material featured on "A Saucerful Of Outtakes". Listen especially to "Astronomy Domine" taken from a May 12 concert (Games For May event) in London.

This features Floyd's first use of quad sound and is something Norman Smith turned the band onto by accident in the studio. Apparently he played back some of their material through four speakers in the control room and forever changed the way the group wanted to present their material to an audience. So Smith deserves some credit at least for providing such divine inspiration for Floyd.

What I find interesting here though, is that the Beatles stopped touring mostly because they became fed up with their inability to play live what they were doing in the studio. Ironically, Floyd took up the challenge and pushed the envelope to recreate all their studio sounds live.

It may look and sound easy now but go back to 1967 and consider how radical and revolutionary surround sound would have come across. While the conditions for both bands were very different, let's give credit to Floyd in wanting to bring absolute control over the sound to the live-playing environment.

I'm sure if the Beatles had begun to tour again, as discussed during the "Let It Be" sessions, they would have found a less frenzied audience and experienced far more satisfaction in actually playing live again. They could have done what Floyd did. Too bad they didn't. All we have after their last live gig at Candlestick Park in San Francisco 1966 (see CANDLESTICK PARK Masterdisc MDCD - 007, 1993) is the great rooftop concert recorded atop the Apple building in 1969.

This event, of course, is seen and heard in the "Let It Be" film. On bootleg, we get the full rooftop audio portion on several titles including "Get Back" (GHOST Records CD 53-43, 1991). Some absolutely great playing, especially by John and George.

By the way, I use the Harrison rooftop version of the solo on "One After Nine O Nine" to prove how good a lead player George Harrison really is. The material is vintage early 1960. See "Liverpool May 1960", mentioned earlier, for the first version of this song, Yellow Dog's, "The Silver Beatles The Original Decca Audition Tapes 1962 And The Cavern Club Rehearsals" (Yellow Dog, YD 011, 1991) for further evolution and, finally, "The Beatles Sessions" (Masterdisc MDCD 002, 1994) for the full blown studio version also released on "Anthology 1". Although the song is over 25 years old, Harrison's lead playing is contemporary to this day. For my mind, George does the concise, tightly worked lead guitar solo better than almost anyone.

True, Harrison might not wail like a Clapton or a Gilmour but what style would you want on songs like "One After Nine O Nine" anyway? And, to his credit, Harrison called in his buddy Clapton to play on "While My Guitar Gently Weeps" and he provided just what was needed. (A solo Paul McCartney would use David Gilmour as session lead guitarist on more than one occasion years later.) You can hear an entirely different version of "Gently Weeps", minus Clapton, on "The Beatles Sessions" mentioned above and yet another version (only Harrison on acoustic) on "Artifacts" set one, disc 4 (4201). Expect this to be on "Anthology 3".

Calling on others is something Gilmour and Waters never hesitated to do, even when both were in Floyd, something less likely for McCartney or Lennon to do, especially while in the Beatles.

EGOS

Which brings us to egos. The most obvious comparison between bands is the break-up of partnerships between Lennon and McCartney, and Waters and Gilmour. The fact that both McCartney and Waters played bass may be just a coincidence (but is it really?).

In a recent interview in "Bass Player" magazine (August 1995), McCartney talks about the power that the bass player has over a band. He says in effect, the band can't go anywhere without the bass leading them there. Is this a metaphor for his asserting leadership? I think it might be.

Of course, Roger Waters is no spring chicken in this regard either. As bass players go, both McCartney and Waters provided significant control of the band over and above the actual result of playing the bass in a foursome. As an aside though, listen to Floyd without Roger Waters and you do miss his driving bass. Guy Pratt (Floyd touring band) is obviously highly competent but I'd say he has yet to exert the kind of presence McCartney is talking about. This may be the only other weak link left in the new Floyd's sound (along with less spectacular lyrics). Just gear it up a notch Guy and David.

With the break-up of the respective creative partnerships in the Beatles and Floyd, we do lose that magical thing (whatever it is) that really made the groups tick. Ignoring the valuable contributions of a George Harrison or a Rick Wright, this argument centers on the most prolific forces in the group only. When these players could no longer cooperate that was that.

They may not have had to continue to like each other but they did have to like working together. What we hear and see in the "Let It Be" film is tension as much as anything else. But the outcome is still remarkable. This echoes the experiences for Floyd in making the "Wall". But any, what I call, "good" tension was falling apart.

Speaking of tension and falling apart, Richard Wright actually got booted out of Pink Floyd during the "Wall" period. Not unlike Ringo's sudden departure during the making of the "White Album". Both events arose from the bass players' badgering on and on about Ringo and Richard's poor playing. Of course, Ringo came back. Richard didn't (at least until Roger departed). Say, there's another fluke connection. Ringo is actually a Richard too.

To grasp what gives (or gave) here, just take in the "Let It Be" movie and compare to "The Wall Rehearsals" (ROTATION ROTA 04, 1994) or "Behind The Wall" (STONEHENGE STBX 022/23/24, 1994) or "Brick By Brick" (Great Dane GDR CD 9313, 1994). You'll hear Roger Waters sound very similar, as leader, to Paul McCartney in "Let It Be".

Now, there may be nothing wrong with asserting control but if you can't motivate your colleagues, you've got problems. The above examples demonstrate the beginning of the end for both bands.

While we're talking about "Let It Be", refer to the Floyd CD, "Just Warmin' Up" (Octopus OCTO 055, 1995). This demonstrates David Gilmour in charge and he is a tad more playful in his methods. Like Lennon, McCartney and Harrison on "Let It Be", there is also some monkeying around with words - "Shine on you crazy bastard" is an example.

RESPECT

In spite of it all, most times in Floyd, respect for individual musicianship stayed constant. Even during the breakup between Waters and Floyd, and through Gilmour's and Nick Mason's resurrection in 1987, Waters and Gilmour never put each others' abilities down.

This can't be said for Lennon and McCartney. Lennon's "How Do You Sleep" is cutting via wicked lyrics such as "the sound you make is musak to my ears" or "the only thing you done was yesterday". These are not great testimonials to McCartney. Check out "Imagine -The Alternate Album" (Sidewalk Music SM 89009), "Imagine The Sessions" (VIGOTONE VT-CD 08) or "Jealous Guy - The Imagine Sessions" (LUNA Records LU 9308, 1993) for rehearsals and alternate takes of this song.

While you're at it, listen closely to Gilmour's singing on "Lost For Words" on the "Just Warmin' Up" CD. You get a real intense "they tell me to go fuck myself" at the end of this song. We all assume, of course, Gilmour is referring to Roger Waters referring to Gilmour. But, again, nowhere in any lyrics does Gilmour ever slag Water's ability as a writer.

There is one other comparison worth noting here. In both groups, the other band mates seemingly let the bass players lead them or, as Hunter Davies says, "steer them into new projects". When the rest of the members finally refused to be steered, and steered so absolutely, a split was inevitable.

Some critics trash Floyd for continuing without Waters. The loudest of these is Roger Waters himself. He even uses an analogy between the Beatles and Floyd, saying continuing would be like three of the Beatles going on. It would not be Beatles nor is it Floyd.

But let's look at this in light of John Lennon's murder.

Is it The Beatles? Certainly they try to be, using Lennon demo tapes and adding their own voices to the mix. But they even went further than this to capture the "Beatles sound". Added material was recorded in the Abbey Road studios of old, going so far as to rebuild the studio and return the glazed sewage pipes that acted as acoustic reflectors, giving the room its specific ambient sound.

The new songs are "Free As A Bird", "Real Love" and "Grow Old With Me" (yet to be worked on). Some bootlegs feature these in Lennon demo form. The "Free As A Bird" demo showed up on the internet - Scott Chatfield posted the song @ http://www.moosenet.com/beatles.html (Obvious Moose Beatles Page) as did Sam Choukri, on his John Lennon page, http://www.missouri.edu/~c588349/johnpage.html.

Where did they get the song? Well, "Free As A Bird" shows up on the yet-to-make-it-onto CD, "Lost Lennon Tapes, Vol 19" (BAG Records 5091). Anyone who followed the radio series in detail will have heard it and had an opportunity to tape the song off-air too.

"Christmas Present" (White Fly WF 001/3), a three-disc set, lists the song "Real Life" (sic?) piano demo". (The set also features "How Do You Feel" mentioned above.) "Pill" (Missing In Action MIA ACT.12) lists "Real Love". This CD also features "Girls And Boys", supposedly the first version of the song. The commercially-released "Imagine" soundtrack album also features a Lennon only version of the song.

"Grow Old With Me" is found on the official "Milk And Honey" album but another version is on the bootleg, "John's Lost Home Demos, Vol 1" (John Records John 001). The Beatles new recording (if they finish it off) could be yet a third version of this song, as there were many. Yoko states on the liner notes to "Milk And Honey" that only a few different demos of "Grow Old" survived a robbery. The one used on the "Milk And Honey" album is the one that "was meant to be".

The three surviving Beatles are using material originated by Lennon. But what if the reconstituted Floyd decided to record material from any of Roger's solo albums? Would this lessen Roger's criticism? Just a thought.

Actually, I concede that groups who carry on after an integral member leaves are definitely not the same. (So long Grateful Dead, we'll miss you) Indeed, they can never be the same. As to whether they should try to continue or not, well, Gilmour's version of Floyd is doing quite well, to quote John Lennon, "thank you very much, you've got a lucky face". (For a take on who's really Pink, read Keith's article in Supplement 3, More Floyd Musings - Editor)

And the surviving Beatles? Well, while critics and purists may have a hard time with it, I think I can speak for most everyone else when I say go for it, PLEASE!!!

But let's end on a less speculative note.

It's no secret that the Beatles were a great influence on Syd Barrett and Roger Waters. Both mention John Lennon in particular as a force in their musical upbringing. Did you know Syd Barrett had to miss a Beatles performance because of an interview for art college? As a career choice, before music takes over, this really echoes John Lennon's background. But, if the situations had been reversed, I have no doubt Lennon would have taken in the show rather than the interview.

There is one other thing in common between the two groups I should mention. Both groups developed their particular style through extended stays as housebands in clubs. We had the Beatles at the Cavern Club in Liverpool and their stints at the Top Ten and Star Clubs (among others) in Hamburg, Germany. Floyd, following the pattern, became the house staple at the UFO club in London. Of note, this is the club frequented by none other than the Beatles themselves.

The Beatles' response to Pink Floyd was enthusiastic too. On the "Magnesium Proverbs" CD mentioned earlier, we hear McCartney defend the band in a brief clip into track 8: "What they're saying and what they're doing is sort of nothing strange about it, it's just dead straight. But it's that they're talking about things that are a bit new, you know. And they're talking about things which people don't know too much about yet".

"And so, they tend to get, you know, people sort of put them down a bit and say, 'wah', 'weirdo', 'psychedelic' and things. But it's really just what's going on around and they're just trying to look into it a bit".

"So next time you see the word, you know, like sort of any word, any new, strange word; like, 'psychedelic', you know, 'drugs'. The whole bit, you know, 'freak out music' and all of that. Don't immediately take it as that, you know. Because your first reaction is gotta be one of fear, you know?"

Scary stuff this Floyd. Reactions much like that of some parents to the scruffy Silver Beatles, "Teddy Boys", the lot of them.

Going further, Nicholas Schaffner in his book, "Saucerful Of Secrets The Pink Floyd Odyssey" (Dell Publishing, 1991), quotes International Times publisher Barry Miles (known simply as Miles) as saying McCartney went so far as to figuratively pass the mantle over to Floyd in 1967. Supposedly McCartney acknowledged that the Beatles were a little more restricted in their ability to marry rock and roll with electronics. Psychedelic music indeed!

Let's advance that train of thought even further. There are two Beatle songs that reflect a Floydian ambience. Clearly "What's The New Mary Jane" and "Revolution Number Nine" are unlike any other Beatles songs. You may want to add "You Know My Name, Look Up The Number" here too.

Of course, you can hear "Revolution Number Nine" on the "White Album" with its collection of sounds and repeating words but there is an alternate version to this. "Off White Vol 3" (Red Phantom RPCD 1138, 1993) has a second mix. Both versions go well with Roger Water's "Several Species Of Small Furry Animals Gathered Together In A Cave And Grooving With A Pict" found on the legitimate

"Ummagumma" Pink Floyd release.

You'll need to find one of the many bootlegs to feature it before you can hear "Mary Jane" however. A few titles include "Off White Vol. 3" as well as the "Artifacts" box set noted earlier (CD4 #4021). There are several different mixes of the song too.

It's rumored Syd Barrett appears on the original recording but this is not the case. The song does resemble a bit of Syd's style however. "Mary Jane" is slang for Marijuana (echoes of Syd's "Let's Roll Another One" having to be changed to "Candy And A Currant Bun" for commercial release) and the whole song could easily fit with the likes of Syd's "Apples And Oranges" which has an "I thought you might like to know" nod to the Beatles' "Sgt. Pepper" in its lyrics. There's also "Jugband Blues", "Vegtable Man" or even Water's "Corporal Clegg" for comparison.

Let's use "Vegetable Man" here. You can find this on the "Total Eclipse" box set (Great Dane Records GDR CD 9320A) as well as on other collections featuring Floyd BBC material circa 1967 and '68, including, again, "Magnesium Proverbs".

Syd's use of the "Vegetable man where are you?" refrain is truly the forerunner for John's "What a shame Mary Jane had a pain at the party". Just nonsense for both, and note the sustained echo endings in each song. The time period for these two recordings is exactly a year apart (August 1967 for Syd and August 1968 for John). Who's copying who now?

And there are a few more comparisons left. The Beatles began using sound effects around the time of "Revolver" and throughout "Sgt. Pepper". Floyd came to the fore during the same period and (as noted before, via producer Norm Smith) began using sound effects regularly in what would become a Floyd signature pattern. The Beatles mostly left this approach after "Pepper".

Certainly, the most common cross-over period between bands is through the Beatles "Pepper" and "Mystery Tour" albums. Consider the songs "Flying", the end bit of "Lovely Rita", or even George's "Blue Jay Way" - all have a resemblance to Floyd.

One of the Beatles' strengths was their ability to assimilate trends and make them uniquely Beatle trends. In the above examples I think we see the Beatles lending their stamp of approval on the direction Floyd wanted to go. And go Floyd did.

AND IN THE END?

Well, in the end you can love both bands equally. There doesn't have to be a winner or loser here. Bootleggers may love the Beatles just a bit more though. Consider the higher volume of Beatles bootleg material available. In "The Last Wacks" alone, Beatles' listings number 62 pages compared to Floyd's 19.

Obviously, the "inner circle" of the Floyd camp is far tighter in loyalty and in preventing leaks compared to the Beatles camp. Unfortunately, the one thing we don't have for our comparison, is an abundance of Floyd alternate and rehearsal takes.

We do have loads of material being developed by Floyd in live performance however. While the Beatles did their work in the studio and brought it to the live arena, Floyd worked their material extensively before live audiences (while simultaneously exploring in the studio).

Listen to the early versions of "Dark Side Of The Moon" for proof. See "Speak To Me" (Silver Shadow CD 9314, 1993) for a great sounding, early live and pre-"Dark Side Of The Moon" show in Japan. There is also the more famous Rainbow Theatre show where "Dark Side" premiered as "Eclipse". See "Pink Floyd Live" (The Swinging Pig TSP-CD-049, 1994) for one of the best sounding versions of this February 1972 performance.

Finally, we have both groups using backward tape loops. Remember the "Paul is dead. Miss him. Miss him" clue found on the "White Album"? Play "I'm So Tired" backwards and you'll hear it.

Compare this to what you hear when you play "Empty Spaces" from the "Wall" album backwards, just before the song "Young Lust". You'll hear: "Congratulations. You have just discovered the secret message. Please send your answers to Old Pink, care of the funny farm, Chalfont." Coincidence that both of these albums were double albums with mostly white covers? Of course it is.

And let's not forget the connecting of songs. The whole concept of the "concept album" takes off with "Sgt. Pepper" but Floyd caps the process off with "Dark Side Of The Moon". By the way, Paul McCartney was interviewed for the talking odds-and-end bits for "Dark Side" but his material didn't make it onto the final record.

Had enough? You know, there are probably more things in common between the bands but I think that's it for one day.

End words to Paul McCartney: "The love you take is equal to the love you make" and to Roger Waters: "It's tough banging your head on some mad bugger's Wall". Agreed! Until next time, I'll see you in the trenches.

Please address any responses c/o The Hot Wacks Press.

Punk Legs:
THE HISTORICAL IMPORTANCE OF BOOTLEGS TO THE PUNK / ALTERNATIVE MUSIC SCENE
By Lori Weiner

In his book about the bootleg business ("Great White Wonders" in the UK, "Bootleg" in USA), Clinton Heylin identifies the "Big 5" as the artists most often bootlegged: Beatles, Dylan, Stones, Zeppelin, and Springsteen. While these artists may account quantity, a large number of punk, post-punk and, in the age of CD, "alternative" recording artists have enjoyed the careful ministrations of bootleggers for over fifteen years. While they can never compete with the "Big 5" in terms of sheer number of titles, fans of these artists hotly pursue and, once captured, enjoy the rare live performances and studio outtakes of their favorite bands equally.

During the vinyl heyday, there were two definitive camps of "punk" musicians who charmed the boot-leggers. Patti Smith and the Sex Pistols received the initial attention. Smith in particular was the underground darling of the NYC art/punk intelligentsia, and her 1976 "Radio Ethiopia" tour saw no fewer than five illicit titles, including one double, issued in the States and UK. The Sex Pistols were bootlegged even before their debut LP was released. "Spunk" and its many recyclings are rough, radically different versions of legendary tracks in sparkling clear studio quality. In addition to Smith and the Pistols, significant bootleg recordings were issued documenting the wider picture of the scene: the Clash, Devo, Siouxsie and the Banshees, the Buzzcocks, New York Dolls, and the Runaways (not quite a punk band but whose salability coincided with the punk movement) all saw seminal released courtesy of their friends at TAKRL, ZAP and Flat, among other labels (Smilin' Ears and Excitable Recordworks also paid close attention to the "newer" acts).

After the "first wave" of punk music came the New Wave. Beginning in early 1979 and continuing throughout the 1980s, British artists who blended the aggressive rock and flippant attitude of the punks with pop sensibilities garnered much media attention and fan popularity. Bootleggers responded enthusiastically, issuing a number of titles by the original incarnations of The Pretenders and B-52's; Joy Division (whose product was generally European) and its spinoff, New Order; the early U2; Talking Heads; The Cure; Public Image Limited (Johnny Rotten's post Pistols project); and Elvis Costello, along with quite a few titles by the now-mainstream Clash. Centrifugal Records appeared as a label devoting itself entirely to the "Class of '79", releasing extremely rare performances by the Pretenders, B-52s, Buzzcocks, and Clash (this particular label had a baffling habit of issuing their product as two 12" 45 rpm discs instead of a single 33 1/3 rpm record). Excitable Recordworks and its cousin Impossible Recordworks also documented 1979-80, as did numerous one-off labels.

The music originally called "punk," then "new wave," was mutating again, this time into two distinct camps. The first was "speed metal" which was largely ignored by bootleggers until 1986, when Elektra Records released the ground-breaking "Master Of Puppets" LP by San Francisco speedsters Metallica. Suddenly Metallica bootlegs were springing like snakes from Medusa's forehead.

This particular period of time coincided with the beginning of the end of vinyl; the traditional American bootleg labels which had nurtured the punk/new wave artists were long gone, replaced by Europeans who were just beginning to exert a firm grip on the bootleg trade. They quickly took to the task and flooded consumers with their glossy covers (occasionally even gatefold) and superb sound quality. Guns N'Roses was heavily bootlegged during this period, as were Kiss and Led Zeppelin (what else is new?). There were also quite a few Jimi Hendrix titles on such labels as Toasted Records.

The 1990s saw wonderful, terrible changes in bootleg technology and marketing. The CD was embraced as the medium of choice and sizable loopholes in copyright law were discovered in Germany, Italy, and Luxembourg. About the same time, Nirvana was setting pop music on fire. After years of pallid disco and lite-rock kibble, exciting, dangerous rock music was back on radio. As one might imagine, Nirvana ushered in a brand new, highly lucrative market to the bootlegger. Times and people, however, were different than they had been ten years before. Rock music had been sliced, diced, and peeled in too many directions. There were too many divergent tastes within the community of "rock" fans to reach real consensus.

Add to this confusion the fact that, for the first time, it was possible for the bootlegger to earn an "honest" living at her/his work, actually operating a legal business and able to be self-supporting, and we arrive at a relationship that appears to be a one-sided issue of dollars (or Marks, Lira, or ¥en).

"Alternative" bootlegs, particularly Nirvana bootlegs appearing after the suicide of leader Kurt Cobain, mercilessly duplicate one another and offer very little in the way of "new" material. While this had been a consistent annoyance even during the age of vinyl, the financial possibilities of the CD bootleg have served to intensify the problem exponentially. It is also common to find studio tracks with crowd noise overdubbed, a problem reported with live CDs of many different artists, not just alternative acts. (German Records is one CD label notorious for these studio recordings.)

Vinyl bootlegs, with their minuscule pressings and strict illegal status, were by necessity "labors of love" which were barely expected to pay for themselves. This would seem to ensure that whoever took the time, trouble, and expense to produce bootleg vinyl was an astute fan who wanted to release only the most delectable and collectible of recordings by their personal favorite(s). In the case of CDs, while it is clearly impossible and unwise to generalise, it appears as though many of the perpetrators are shrewd business people who know what sells. The legal status afforded these CDs in their countries of origin make it advantageous to follow the market instead of one's passions. With the ever-changing status of live CDs overseas, it will be interesting to read the next chapter.

The Rolling Stones

STICKY FINGERS' ESSENTIAL BOOTLEGS
By John Carr
(John Carr is the Editor of Sticky Fingers a publication dedicated to the Rolling Stones and their music. Sticky Fingers is published 6 times a year. John Carr can be contacted at 12190 1/2 Ventura Blvd., #411, Studio City, CA 91604. Send $4 for a sample issue or $20 for a 1 - year subscription.)

The Rolling Stones did not start out to become The Greatest Rock & Roll Band in the World. They were primarily a group of art students and knockabouts who loved American Blues music and wanted to bring it into England. Even in the early years, the group centered around the duo of Mick Jagger and Keith Richards; however, the band didn't really take root until Brain Jones, a blues disciple who called himself Elmo Lewis, joined the band as leader. Brian, with his Edwardian look and astute knowledge of the Blues masters, played a large part in the Rolling Stones' early success. However, by 1966 his star was already dimming as the songwriting duo of Jagger and Richards gained ascendancy over the band. Most of the Stones' early releases were interpretations of Blues and Rock & Roll standards. In England, during the early Sixties, Chuck Berry and Bo Diddley were lumped together with the other Blues artists by most musicians, except the Traditionalists. In the US they were usually considered Rockers with the other early pioneers of Rock & Roll, such as Elvis, Carl Perkins, Little Richard and Jerry Lee Lewis.

When the Rolling Stones burst onto the London scene, they were viewed as iconoclasts and outlaws. They broke all the traditional rules for British pop stars; they wore street clothes on stage; had a hip, 19 year-old manager; a blatantly defiant attitude; unconventional lifestyles and didn't give a shit about success or being proper - at a time when everyone in the British music business had his place and position. Their music, in contrast to the harmonies and group sing-alongs of the Mersey Groups, was down right dangerous - straight from the dark heart of the American South.

1. BRIGHT LIGHTS BIG CITY: Twentieth Anniversary Edition (Swingin' Pig TSP-CD-010)
The earliest surviving Rolling Stones recordings are the IBC demos, which feature 5 songs (although 6 were originally recorded) from their stage show, including "Bright Lights, Big City" and "Road Runner". The IBC demo are available from The Swingin' Pig label (insofar as the Stones have a bootleg label, the Pig would have to be it. They inherited most of the old masters from the Trade Mark of Quality and Smokin' Pig labels, and were the first to bring Stones bootlegs into the CD era with their "Ultra Rare

Trax Vol. I & II"). In addition to the IBC demos, "Bright Lights Big City" includes 4 studio outtakes from Chess Studios 1964 (including the classic "High Heel Sneakers"), 4 rehearsal songs from the 1972 tour, and one outtake from RCA studios, "Looking Tired", and an excellent Blues rocker that was originally on the song list for the album "Could You Walk On Water?", which Decca refused to release.

Most Rolling Stones fans and collectors divide their large body of work into three eras - the Brian Jones era, the Mick Taylor era and the Ronnie Wood Era. Each period has its own distinctive sound and rich body of work.

THE BRIAN JONES ERA

The Brian Jones Era began when Brian joined together with Keith Richards and Mick Jagger to form a Blues tribute band. During the early years, Rolling Stones were on a crusade to bring the Blues to Britain. When it ended, the Rolling Stones were the second-Greatest Rock Group in the World.

2. BEAT-BEAT-BEAT-AT THE BBC (Invasion Unlimited IU 9428-2 2-CDs)
Here in one convenient 2-CD slimline package are the best surviving recordings of the Rolling Stones 1963 to 1965 British Broadcasting Corporation (BBC) radio performances. Despite a lack of decent liner notes, this is an essential collection. It is the bootleg equivalent of the Beatles "Live at the BBC", both in sound quality and number of songs. In terms of quality, the Stones collection is definitely superior to the Beatles; for example, both collections contain versions of some of the same cover songs, such as Chuck Berry's "Carol". The Stones version is the winner by a knockout. About a third of the recordings have a substantial amount of noise, but the fervor of these early performances shines through. Other shows, like the Camden Theatre show, sound as if they were taped only yesterday, Beat-Beat-Beat-At The BBC Is an essential document of the Brian Jones Era; it is debatable whether ABKCO has access to better masters than these, since in recent years the BBC has played the best of the surviving tapes on the air. I keep this one with my studio albums for quick reference and enjoyable play.

3. THE FIRST DECADE (Big Music - BIG BX 003 4-CDs)
Surprisingly, there are not a large number of studio outtakes from the Brian Jones Era: Decca's vaults have never been as thoroughly looted as EMI's for Beatles outtakes. There are some outtakes from Chess Studios, RCA and Olympia, but not in the numbers you might expect, considering the Rolling Stones stature and the many documented sessions they've done. The best of this material can be found in mostly excellent sound on the box set "The First Decade". As a bonus, "The First Decade" also contains 5 of the IBC demos, the best of the BBC releases, 10 of the best studio outtakes of that period and that's all on the first CD! The second CD concludes the studio half of the collection, containing most of the best studio outtakes from 1968 to 1972. Of course, by then Brian was out of the picture for most of these sessions and we see the band metamorphose from the Second-Greatest Rock Group in the World to the Greatest Rock & Roll Band in the World. The third and fourth CDs are live concerts, starting with the best surviving live show of the Brian Jones Era, "Honolulu Stadium", Honolulu. From this July 28th, 1966 radio soundboard we find 2 songs, "Mother's Little Helper" and "Satisfaction"; the rest of the historical show can be found on Insect Record's (Scorpio's) "In Action". After an early version of "You Can't Always Get What You Want" from the unreleased "Rock & Roll Circus", the rest of the live performances consist of classic live audience and soundboard performances from Hyde Park and later featuring Mick Taylor.

THE MICK TAYLOR ERA

4. TIME TRIP-Vols. I, II & IV (Scorpio RS 100- 1, RS 100-2, RS 23-94-07)
These three collections contain the essential studio outtakes of the Mick Taylor Era. Mick Taylor was the legendary Peter Green's replacement with John Mayall's Blues Breakers in 1967. His virtuoso guitar work on "Blues Crusade" displays some of the finest playing of that time; he combined the finesse of Peter Green's melodic guitar leads with the powerhouse playing of the young Eric Clapton. He was an inspired pick to replace the dispirited Brian Jones and gave the Rolling Stones a world class contender during the age of the Guitar Hero. His soaring tone, and smooth as glass leads have been highly imitated, but rarely matched since the early seventies. It was during this time that the Stones penned many of their most enduring classics, "Gimme Shelter", "Brown Sugar", "Honky Tonk Woman", "Bitch", "Midnight Rambler", "All Down The Line", "Tumbling Dice", and so many others. "Time Trips Vol. I & II" contain a number of studio outtakes from "Sticky Fingers" and "Exile On Main Street" albums in excellent fidelity. (Time Trip Vol. III is mostly a collection of familiar Trident mixes in so-so quality). "Time Trip IV" is the best of the lot; it has some "Beggars Banquet" and "Let It Bleed" outtakes (with Ry Cooder on slide guitar on most of the "Beggars" outtakes)

including a few takes that in some cases are superior to the album versions! These 3 volumes are must-haves for every Stones fan.

5. LIVER THAN YOU'LL EVER BE (Swingin' Pig TSP-CD-043)
The majority of the essential bootlegs from here onward are live studio albums, since most of the Rolling Stones best work has been on the concert stage. As Bill Graham said in his autobiography, "On any given night, they (Rolling Stones) were the very best Rock & Roll band in the world.... Truthfully, they got to me every night. They were that strong. Fucking monsters." The 1969 tour was the first with Mick Taylor and the first of the big Stones tours. When this audience tape of the 1969 Oakland concert was released in 1970, it brought bootleg albums into the mainstream - it was even reviewed by Rolling Stone magazine. The resulting sales forced Decca to release an official album of the "Let It Bleed Tour", "Get Yer Ya-Yas Out!". "Liver Than You'll Ever Be" was the best bootleg audience tape of its time, comparable to many studio live albums. This was the first tour with Mick Taylor and a groundbreaking tour on many levels. This show has been booted and re-booted under so many names it would take a page to list them all; the best of the lot are The Swingin' Pig's "Liver Than You'll Ever Be", which includes some alternate songs from the San Diego 1969 concert, and Great Dane's "Revolution Sixtinine". Many consider the San Diego concert, "Stoneage" on the World Productions label, the best sounding of the 1969 tour, but it hasn't been available since 1989. The Los Angeles shows were also quite good; the best bootleg of the Los Angeles concerts is "Born In A Crossfire Hurricane".

6. GET YOUR LEEDS LUNGS OUT (Swinging' Pig TSP-CD-030)
There are no high-quality audience tapes from the 1970 European Tour, but we do have this excellent 1971 radio broadcast from Leeds University, during the Stones' Farewell Tour of England, as they prepared to go into tax exile in the south of France. The sound on this bootleg is excellent, and while the performance isn't as polished as those of the 1972 and '73 tours that followed, it is just as heartfelt. They do a standout take of Chuck Berry's "Let It Rock" and the best live version I've heard yet of "Stray Cat Blues".

7. PHILADELPHIA SPECIAL I & II (Swingin' Pig TSP-CD-050-2/CD 2-CDs each)
These two CD sets contain most of the soundboard tracks from Philadelphia and Fort Worth shows that were considered for a live 1972 album. Most of these songs are from the mixing board and are not finished mixes; therefore, they are much closer to the actual performances than the studio-mixed soundtrack for "Ladies & Gentlemen: The Rolling Stones". This tour was a big media event and it was the first time the Stones used elaborate staging and walls of speakers; the sound and musical performance suffered as a result. Still, they produced some excellent music, including Chuck Berry's "Bye Bye Johnny", and the version of "Love In Vain" on Philly II is the best ever.

8. WELCOME TO NEW YORK (Swingin' Pig TSP-CD-038)
This is the soundboard from the Madison Square Garden Show of September, 26, 1972. This is an exceptional soundboard of a very good show; unfortunately, it's been sonically "enhanced" giving it a ghost-like whisper between songs. As with most stage soundboards, there is very little audience noise between tracks which some people find distracting. The best of the "Exile On Main Street" tour audience recordings is Gold Standard's "Tropical Windsongs", which features the second show from Honolulu, Hawaii. There are some sound level problems with the opening number, "Brown Sugar", but after that the sound is great. Surprisingly, the audience feedback and reaction enhance the listening experience of this show, almost giving it that you-are-there feeling which makes it such a rare and special recording.

9. THE BRUSSELS AFFAIR (Chameleon CHAM 8812)
This 1973 concert originally aired on Radio Luxembourg on October 17 and is considered by most Rolling Stones fans to be their finest live album - official or bootleg! The band is tight - the result of a heavy schedule in the USA the year before, and Mick Taylor's soaring, singing leads touch the stratosphere. During this concert they played the best live versions yet recorded of many of the band's classic songs, such as "You Can't Always Get What You Want", "Gimme Shelter", "Brown Sugar", "All Down The Line", and many others. It's now several years out of print, but many of the songs from Brussels, along with some from a Wembley, September, 1973 soundboard, were used on two 1975 King Biscuit Flower Hour shows; both of these shows in their entirety are on a recent 2CD compilation "Headin' For An Overload". There is some song duplication, but all the Brussels songlist is repeated here. These are from a pristine master tape and sound as good as the day they aired. In short, an excellent substitute for a show every Stones fan should own. It doesn't get any better than this! And a fitting end to the Mick Taylor Era.

THE RON WOOD ERA

10. EXILE AUX ABATTOIRS (Great Dane CD 9106)
A number of well-known guitarists were considered as Mick Taylor's replacement; twenty years later it is quite obvious why most of them were passed over for Ron Wood, former lead guitarist for the Small Faces. Most lead guitars love the spotlight, but Woody was used to sharing it with Rod Stewart and Jeff Beck. He was also a long-time fan of the group and fit in immediately as One Of The Boys. It's hard to imagine anyone else surviving twixt Keith and Mick for over 20 years! Plus, Woody is a great foil for the Riffmeister, Keith Richards; they swap fills and chords much like Brian and Keith did in the early days. And, now with Bill Wyman gone, he has become the group historian and archivist. Unfortunately, there are no high-quality known soundboards of the 1975 Tour of America. The best of the audience tapes is "Whores In The Night" taped by the Whistler - the version of "Wild Horses" with chimes is my all-time favorite. Unfortunately, this show has only appeared on a rare Japanese CD and the LP is long out of print. There are some very good audience recordings of the New York and LA Forum shows. However, the Stones did almost the identical song list (with the exception of "Wild Horses!") on the 1976 Tour of Europe. Vigotone's "Live in Frankfurt 1976" is a decent soundboard recording, although it only runs about 45 minutes. There's almost too much of Knebworth on "Hot August Night" and half a dozen other titles of varying lengths that this particular concert appears under. "Exile Aux Abattoirs" is an excellent soundboard of a French TV show and a good representation of the 1976 concert.

11. BACK IN THE USA (Beautiful Buzz-002)
With the "Some Girls" album, the Rolling Stones reclaimed the No. 1 spot on the charts and left enough outtakes to do a couple more albums. The recent "Back in the USA" offers major upgrades on many of the "Some Girls" outtakes, plus offers a few songs from the RCA, Hollywood 1978 sessions. Most of the 17 tracks on this album are familiar to fans, but here they sound better than ever before. Highlights are a killer version of the Willie Dixon classic, "I Ain't Superstitious", and "One Night With You". Frankly, I've been disappointed with most of the "Some Girls" outtake discs. They were all pretty good, but frequently they had that out-of-kilter sound that comes from having the radio dial just a little shy of the station. "Back In The USA" is not easy to find, but if you see it - grab it!

12. SOME GIRLS ARE BIGGER THAN OTHERS (Home Records HR5985-1)
There were several radio shows during the 1978 "Some Girls Tour", including Lexington, Kentucky and Passaic, New Jersey, best known as "Garden State 78" and "Memphis Tennessee". This radio soundboard from the neglected 1978 tour is one of the great shows of the Ron Wood Era; the sound is excellent and the 'boys' are on the money. The show opens with a rousing version of Chuck Berry's "Let It Rock" and then continues with blistering takes on "Some Girls" favorites, such as "Miss You", "Shattered", "The Whip Comes Down" and "Beast of Burden". The standout track, besides the rare version of Presley's "Hound Dog" (a tip-of-the-hat to Memphis' favorite son) is Woody's bluesy take on "Love In Vain", where he puts his own imprint on a song forever associated with Mick Taylor. This punchy 1-CD set has more highpoints than "Love You Live" and "Still Life" combined.

13. HAMPTON '81 (The Swingin' Pig TSP-CD- 100- 1/2 2-CDs)
The Stones best shows follow strong albums; the 1981 "Tattoo You Tour", was no exception. Few realized at the time that it would be the last tour for almost a decade. The Stones did a number of radio shows, including the King Biscuit Flower Hour (Michigan), and Washington DC, which appears on the American Concert Series as "Time Is On Our Side". There was also a Pay-Per-View on Cable TV from Hampton, Virginia recorded live at the Hampton Coliseum on December 18, 1981. Swingin' Pig has given the Hampton concert an attractive 2 CD box set, which contains the entire performance of 25 songs. The stand out cuts are "Time Is On My Side" and the rarely performed "Let It Bleed". One interesting collection, on the Golden Stars label, "Fever In The Funkhouse Part One and Part Two", contains some of best cuts of both the Hampton, Virginia show and the Pontiac, Michigan show.

14. CRUSHED PEARL (A Vinyl Gang 041)
There was no follow-up tour for the "Dirty Work" album although Keith certainly did his damned best to get Mick to go on the road again. There have been a few "Dirty Work" outtakes albums, but nothing to write home about until this Japanese CD recently appeared. Most of the songs here are different from the old vinyl bootleg, "Dirtiest Work". The sound quality is very good with an occasional dip here and there. There is an outtake of "Dirty Work" that should have been on the original album and a version of "Fight" that sounds like an exorcism! This is the type of bootleg that forces you to re-examine the old myths about this album, like the one that Jagger was aloof and distant - if he was, it wasn't on these songs. This is the kind of album that leaves you wondering just how much of this good stuff is still sitting in the vault!

15. ATLANTIC CITY '89 (The Swingin' Pig TSP-CD 075-3)
There were a number of radio shows and one Network TV show from Atlantic City. For these shows the Rolling Stones added a full horn section and backup singers to their already-elaborate stage show. Yet, the Stones still managed to remain at the center of the show, Jagger and Keith playing off each other and Woody as well. Lisa Fischer's dynamite vocals added a new dimension to classics such as "Gimme Shelter" and "Miss You". What makes Atlantic City special are the additional guests such as Eric Clapton playing on "Little Red Rooster", and John Lee Hooker's "Boogie Children". There are some very good audience recordings of the "Steel Wheels Tour" (such as Big Music's "Back In Business") but with great soundboards from Atlantic City, Dallas and Toronto to choose from, they're only for hometown fans. The tour ended in Tokyo at the beginning of 1990 and Templar's "Tokyo Dome" is an excellent soundboard of one of the Tokyo shows.

16. SEVENTH OF JULY (Chameleon CHAM 2-9000 2-CDs)
The "Steel Wheels" tour turned into the "Urban Jungle" European tour in the Summer of 1990; the best of these shows is a BBC broadcast called "Seventh Of July". This is a great performance in excellent sound quality; in fact, the last 6 songs are among the Stones' finest performances anywhere, anytime - the mix is that good! Highlights of this fine album include a pounding version of "Paint It Black" and a rousing "Gimme Shelter". If you just want one concert from the 1989-1990 tours, this is the one to get.

17. VOODOO AT HALLOWEEN (Moonlight Records ML9512/13 2-CDs)
This collection from a digital stage-mix recorded in Oakland, California on Halloween Night is the best performance yet released of the 1994 North American "Voodoo Lounge" tour. Forget the Miami Pay-Per-View (where Chuck Leavell's piano drowns out the guitars) and the New Orleans muddy radio show - the one to get is "Voodoo At Halloween". The up-front live sound on these discs brings Charlie Watts and his famous cowbell on the intro to "Honky Tonk Women" right into your living room! The audience is barely audible on this recording; it's just you, Mick, Keith, Charlie, Ronnie, and the rest of the band. Until the release of this fine performance, the cry from die-hard Stones fans was "Where are the guitars?" Now we know. If you just want a "Voodoo Lounge" CD sampler, "Sparks Will Fly" from Kiss The Stone will do. "Sparks Will Fly" is the Giants Stadium, New Jersey show mastered from the official tour video.

18. LIVE IN JAPAN (Octopus 105/106 2-CDs)
This is an excellent show mastered from a 1975 Japanese "Voodoo Lounge" TV broadcast at the Tokyo Dome; the mix is better than any of the official US shows. Some critics have complained about Jagger wearing out in the second half but I've got the video and I don't see it. I like this show better than the discs from Rio, Buenos Aires, and South Africa. Plus, there's a great version of "Love Is Strong" (which was not played much in Europe for some reason) and a superlative version of "Sweet Virginia". Kiss The Stone has the same concert out under the title "Eastern Promise", but there's a glitch in "Sparks Will Fly" and the cover sucks.

19. HAVING A LAUGH AT BRIXTON (BAL 1979A/B 2-CDs)
This great performance is from an excellent audience tape at the Brixton Academy. This is from a show that was legendary even before it happened. Has the hype dwarfed reality once again? No, this is a wonderful club show (the Stones cut their teeth on live shows at the Crawdaddy and Marquee clubs in London in the early Sixties), where the Stones expanded on their US "Voodoo Lounge" repertoire with an expanded acoustical segment and songs like "Down In The Bottom", "Black Limousine" and "Connection", that they hadn't played live in decades. "Beggars Banquet" (Stones fanzine) called this concert "the most potent repertoire the Stones have delivered in the 13 months since they started this tour." It's truly amazing that in their third decade as a band the Rolling Stones could deliver what may be their finest single performance. On top of this, there were reports of other great club gigs in Amsterdam and Paris, but none of these have shown up yet in high-quality record-ings. I can't wait until the soundboards from these shows turn up!

This list is by no means to be considered definitive; there are too many other great shows that had to be overlooked due to space considerations. Due to the success of the "Voodoo Lounge" tour, which grossed over a 100 million dollars, there's been an avalanche of new and re-issued Rolling Stones releases. And not just "Voodoo Lounge" shows either - we've seen a new version of the 1965 radio show at the L'Olympia Theatre in Paris ("Raw Power"), the first Oakland November 9, 1969 show ("Bring It Back Aliver"), and many others. While I consider "Voodoo Lounge" to be the best Stones album since "Some Girls", I don't think the band, after hearing "Having A Laugh At Brixton" and "Stripped", has yet reached its peak. Where do they go from here? Well, hopefully onto a new and better album in '97 and to a small amphitheater near you!

A

AC/DC

LP - MADE IN GERMANY
RULPS RECORDS
S1: Are You Ready/ Back In Black/ Fire Your
Guns/ Sin City/ The Jack
S2: Razor's Edge/ That's The Way I Wanna R
And R/ Money Talks/ High Voltage
R: Exs.   S: Cologne '91 (first part of show).
C: Eb. Dcc. 500 Copies. 50 copies on CV - red,
yellow or blue. 'Are You Ready' on S1 should
read 'Shoot To Thrill'.

LP - MADE IN
GERMANY 2
CAT NO. 7
S1: Dirty
Deeds Done...
(5:00)/ Whole
Lotta Rosie
(4:25)/ Let
There Be
Rock (13:07)
S2:
Heatseeker
(3:55)/ Who
Made Who
(4:30)/
Highway To
Hell (4:35)/
TNT (3:35)/
For Those
About To
Rock... (6:45)
R: Exs.
S: Cologne
'91 (second
part of show).
C: Eb. Dcc.
500 Copies.
50 copies on
CV - red, yellow or blue.

LP - FIRE ENGINE
S1: Shoot To Thrill (5:07)/ Back In Black (4:08)/
Hell Ain't A Bad... (4:08)/ Fire Your Guns (3:10)/
The Jack (6:35)
S2: Dirty Deeds... (4:40)/ High Voltage (9:35)/
TNT (3:40)/ Highway To Hell (4:37)
S: Nepstadion, Budapest.   C: Eb. Dcc. 500
Copies. 50 copies on CV - red, yellow or blue.

AEROSMITH

CD - ANGELS FALLIN' INTO ARENA
AE-001/002
CD1: Eat The Rich/ Toys In The Attic/ Rag Doll/
Fever/ Monkey On My Back/ Amazing/ Mama Kin/
Angel/ Cryin'/ Rats In The Cellar
CD2: Stop Messin' Around/ Walk On Down/
Janie's Got A Gun/ Love In A Elevator/ Dude
(Looks Like A Lady)/ Sweet Emotion/ Dream On/
Livin' On The Edge/ Walk This Way/ Livin' On The
Edge
R: Vg. Soundboard.   S: Yokohama Arena Apr.
27 '94.   C: Japanese CD.

CD - CLASSICS LIVE OUTTAKES
BONDAGE MUSIC BON 026
Back In The Saddle/ Same Old Song And Dance/
My Fist, Your Face/ Last Child/ No Surprise/
Sheila/ She's On Fire/ The Hop/ Walk This Way/
Let The Music Do The Talking/ Dream On/ Toys In
The Attic/ Bolivian Ragamuffin/ (demo)/ Bitch's
Brew (demo)/ Jailbait (demo)
R: Ex. Soundboard.   S: Centrum, Worcester,
MA Mar. 12
'86. Tracks
13-15 demos.
C: Japanese
CD. Pic CD.
Time 72:43.

CD - COVER-
ING' EM
OCTOPUS
OCTO 103
Come
Together
(4:36)/
Walking The
Dog (4:11)/
Rattlesnake
Shake (9:32)/
Milk Cow
Blues (4:37)/
I'm Not
Talking
(2:39)/ Red
House
(8: 05)/ Perry
Mason
Theme
(1:56)/ Train
Kept A Rollin' (4:12)/ Smokestack Lightning
(4:24)/ Helter Skelter (3:18)/ Love Me Two Times
(3:16)/ Mama Kin (4:08)/ Train Kept A Rollin'
(4:07)/ Stop Messin' Around (4:49)/ Bonus Tracks:
Scream In Pain (4:38)/ Lookin' Like A Lady (5:24)
R: Ex.   S: Tracks 1-8 and 14 live various loca-
tions '90-'91. Tracks 9-11 rehearsal studio demos
'90. Tracks 12-13 jamming with Guns 'N' Roses
live in Europe '92. Tracks 15-16 'Permanent
Vacation' '87.   C: ECD. Dcc. Pic CD.

CD - FEVER LIVE
RSM 049
Love In An Elevator/ Back In The Saddle/ Fever/
What It Takes/ Rag Doll/ Last Child/ Cryin'/ Shut
Up And Dance/ The Other Side/ Janie's Got A
Gun/ Dude (Looks Like A Lady)/ Dream On/ Walk
This Way/ Livin' On The Edge
R: Vg-Ex. Audience.   S: Great Woods,
Mansfield, Mass. '93.   C: ECD. Dcc. 74:28.

CD - GET AMAZED!
POLYPHONIA DISCS 095432
Living On The Edge (acoustic version)/ Don't Stop/ Can't Stop Messin'/ Head First/ Amazing (orchestral version)/ Line Up (smoky bar-mix)/ Crazy (acoustic version)/ Blind Man (harder-mix)/ Livin' On The Edge (demo)/ Amazing (acoustic version)/ Line Up (Butcher Bros. mix)/ Crazy (orchestral version)/ Blind Man/ Deuces Are Wild/ Shut Up And Dance (live version)
R: Exs. Soundboard.   S: B-sides and different versions of the 'Get A Grip' album.   C: ECD. Dcc. Time 72:26.

CD - HARD NOX AND DIRTY SOX
TUFF BITES TB 94.1005
Love In An Elevator (5:58)/ Eternal Fever (4:37)/ Crying (5:22)/ Shut Up And Dance (6:54)/ Stop Messin' Around (4:05)/ Rag Doll (4:27)/ Janie's Got A Gun (5:35)/ Dude Looks Like A Lady (4:42)/ Dream On (5:02)/ Walk This Way (4:43)/ Living On The Edge (5:27)
R: Exs. Soundboard.   S: Brussels, Belgium Oct. 31 '93.   C: ECD. Dcc. Digi-pack.

CD - HOUSE ON FIRE
OCTOPUS OCTO 071
Train Kept A Rollin' (4:10)/ Same Old Song And Dance (5:14)/ Big Ten Inch Record (4:35)/ Walk On Water (4:47)/ Walking The Dog (4:31)/ Chip Away The Stone (5:21)/ Last Child (4:14)/ Rattlesnake Shake (9:53)/ One Way Street (7:33)/ Stop Messin' Around (4:09)/ Let The Music Do The Talking (5:23)/ Mama Kin (4:06)/ Milk Cow Blues (4:37)/ I'm Not Talking (4:22)/ Toys In The Attic (4:06)
R: Ex. Audience.   S: Live in USA '94. C: ECD. Dcc. Pic CD.

CD - LOVE ME LIKE A BIRD DOG
HAIGHT STREET RECORDS HS010
Love Me Like A Bird Dog/ Take It Easy/ One Time/ Joe's Funky/ Love Me Like A Bird Dog/ Once Is Enough/ Girl Keeps Coming Apart/ Hollywood/ Danger Street/ Sleeping Sickness/ St. John/ Joe's Funky/ Got To Find A Way/ Simorah/ Dude Looks Like A Lady/ Permanent Vacation
R: Ex. Soundboard.   S: Tracks 1-5 Rick Robin Sessions NYC Feb. '87. Tracks 6-17 studio rehearsals spring '86.   C: Japanese CD. Dcc. Time 75:08.

CD - MAMA KIN'S
KTS OF AUSTRALIA 001 A
Train Kept A Rollin' (3:59)/ Same Old Song & Dance (5:20)/ Big Ten Inch Record (4:16)/ Rock'n My World (5:11)/ Walking The Dog (4:05)/ Chip Away The Stone (4:53)/ Last Child (4:32)/ Rattlesnake Shake (10:18)/ One Way Street (6:55)/ Xmas Lies (5:05)/ Let The Music Do The Talking (5:15)/ Walk This Way (5:59)/ Mama Kin (4:06)/ Milk Cow Blues (4:53)/ I'm Not Talking (2:40)
S: Boston Dec.19 '94.   C: Australian CD.

CD - PLUGGELECTRIC
SWINDLE RECORDS SWN 032
ACOUSTIC SET: Big Ten Inch Record (4:03)/ Hangman Jury (6:15)/ Dream On (4:52)/ Train Kept A Rollin' (3:20)/ Walking The Dog (3:50)/ Toys In The Attic (3:56)/ ELECTRIC SET: Cryin' (4:44)/ Janie's Got A Gun (5:38)/ Livin' On The Edge (6:05)/ Walk This Way (4:03)/ Dude (Looks Like A Lady) (4:51)/ Love In An Elevator (4:55)/ Red House (5:24)/ Mama Kin (3:55)/ Dream On (4:57)/ Amazing (5:28)
R: Exs. Soundboard.   S: Live during '90/'93 US tours.   C: ECD. Dcc. Pic CD. Some songs fade-in.

CD - TAKE ONE BITE
AIR VOX RECORDS AC-40001-2
CD1: Eat The Rich/ Toys In The Attic/ Rag Doll/ Fever/ Monkey On My Back/ Amazing/ Mama Kin/ Angel/ Cryin'/ Rats In The Cellar
CD2: Stop Messin' Around/ Walk On Down/ Janie's Got A Gun/ Love In An Elevator/ Dude (Looks Like A Lady)/ Sweet Emotion/ Peter Gunn Theme/ Dream On/ Living On The Edge/ Walk This Way
R: G. Audience.   S: Yokohama Arena Apr. 27 '94.   C: Japanese CD. Dcc. Time CD1 54:01. CD2 50:45.

CD - UNWIRED
OCTOPUS OCTO 090
Smokestack Lightning (4:37)/ Monkey On My Back (4:22)/ Season Of Wither (4:54)/ Love Me Two Times (3:11)/ Dream On (4:18)/ Is Anybody Out There? (2:27)/ Hangman Jury (5:51)/ End Of The Line (3:15)/ No More, No More (2:56)/ Hangman Jury (6:14)/ Big Ten Inch Record (4:09)/ Dream On (5:05)/ Train Kept A Rollin' (3:07)/ Walking The Dog (3:51)/ Toys In The Attic (4:05)
R: Ex.   S: Tracks 1-9 acoustic session, Kansas City '90. Tracks 10-15 acoustic set NYC '91. C: ECD. Dcc. Pic CD.

<h1 style="text-align:center">ALCATRAZZ</h1>

CD - BACK AGAIN
CRYSTAL SOUND CS-18
Opening (Incubus)/ Too Young To Die, Too Drunk To Live/ Hiroshima Mon Amour/ Night Games/ Big Foot/ Island In The Sun/ Kree Nakoorie/ Since You've Been Gone/ Suffer Me/ Desert Song/ Jet To Jet/ Evil Eyes/ Lost In Hollywood/ All Night Long/ Something Else
R: Exs. Audience recording.   S: Nagoya, Jan. 26 '84.

CD - MAKE NO PRISONERS
PROJECT K PKCD-94003/004
CD1: Too Young To Die/ Hiroshima Mon Amour/ Night Games/ Big Foot/ Island In The Sun/ Kree Naccrie (Yngwie Guitar Solo)/ Since You've Been Gone/ Suffer Me/ Desert Song
CD2: Jet To Jet/ Evil Eye/ All Night Long/ Lost In Hollywood/ Kojyo No Tsuki/ Something Else/ Suite

Opus 3/ Merlin's Castle/ Electric Dust/ Suite Opus 3
R: Good-Vg audience recording and studio tracks.
S: Nakano-Sunplaza, Tokyo Jan. 29 '84. CD2 tracks 7-10 'Rising Force' demo tapes.

CD - PRISONER IS BACK
CRYSTAL SOUND CS-009
Opening (Incubus)/ Too Young To Die, Too Drunk To Live/ Hiroshima Mon Amour/ Desert Song/ Night Games/ Big Foot/ Island In The Sun/ Kree Nakoorie/ Since You Been Gone/ Suffer Me/ Jet To Jet/ Evil Eyes (Rising Force)/ Lost In Hollywood/ All Night Long
R: Vg audience recording.　S: Festival Hall, Osaka, Japan Jan. 24 '84.

ALICE COOPER

LP - YOU'RE ALL CRAZIER THAN I AM
BLACK DEATH 9401201
S1: Under My Wheels/ Billion Dollar Babies/ I'm Eighteen/ It Is My Body/ I Love The Dead/ Go To Hell/ It's Hot Tonight
S2: Welcome To My Nightmare*/ Steven*/ No More Mr. Nice Guy*/ Devils Food/ Black Widow/ Unfinished Sweet/ Escape/ 3-M-Microscreen
R: Exs.　S: Halloween's Day, Wendler Arena, Saginaw, Michigan '78 except *LA Forum.
C: Eb. Dbw. Red Vinyl. Fred says 'Among the best recordings I've ever heard... better than official live albums'.

LP - NOBODY LIKES ME
BEELZEBUB 1991001
S1: House On Fire/ No More Mr. Nice Guy/ This Maniac's In Love.../ Screaming/ Welcome To My Nightmare/ Ballad Of Dwight Fry
S2: Hello Hooray/ Trash/ Billion Dollar Babies/ I'm Eighteen/ I'm Your Gun/ Unknown
S3: Road Rats/ I Love The Dead/ Poison
S4: Spark In The Dark/ Only My Heart Talking/ Bed Of Nails/ Schools Out
R: Exs.　S: Complete show. Ellenfeldstadion, Neukirchen A.D. Saar July 14 '90.　C: Eb. Dbw. MCV.

ALICE IN CHAINS

CD - RIFUGIUM PECCATORUM
LAST BOOTLEG RECORDS LBR 020
Junkhead (5:32)/ Would? (3:37)/ Man In The Box (4:41)/ Real Thing (4:49)/ Love, Hate, Love (6:43)/ Sea Of Sorrow (5:32)/ Bleed The Freek (4:34)/ Dam The River (5:28)/ We Die Young (2:53)/ Them Bones (3:48)/ Rooster (5:17)/ Godsmack (4:01)/ It Ain't Like That (4:14)/ Dirt (5:24)/ Hate To Feel (5:46)/ Angry Chair (4:15)
R: Exs. Soundboard. Tracks 8-16 Ex. Audience.
S: Tracks 1-7 NYC during '93 US tour. Tracks 8-16 Europe '93.　C: ECD. Dcc. Pic CD.

ALLMAN BROTHERS BAND, THE

CD - A HOT STEAMY SUMMER NIGHT
RSM 044
Blue Sky (8:58)/ All Night Train (4:39)/ Same Thing (7:51)/ Seven Turns (4:25)/ Jessica (17:33)/ No One To Run With (6:20)/ Back Where It All Begins (13:25)/ Whipping Post (11:48)
R: Ex. Soundboard.　S: The Walnut Creek Amphitheatre, Raleigh, North Carolina July 1 '94.
C: ECD. Dcc. Time 74:59.

CD - MY BROTHERS KEEPER
CAPRICORN RECORDS CR 2037/38
CD1: Statesboro Blues (5:57)/ Done Somebody Wrong (4:07)/ Ain't Wasting Time No More (5:45)/ One Way Out (6:35)/ Stormy Monday (8:32)/ You Don't Love Me (17:23)/ In Memory Of Elizabeth Reed (16:04)/ Midnight Rider (3:07)
CD2: Whipping Post (21:16)/ Jam (10:36)/ Mountain Jam (35:47)*
R: G-Vg. Soundboard.　S: Syracuse, New York Mar. 27 '72. *Stoneybrook, New York '71.
C: Dcc.

CD - NEW ORLEANS TAPE
MAIN STREET MST 106/2
CD1: Statesboro Blues/ Trouble No More/ Don't Keep Me Wondering/ Done Somebody Wrong/ One Way Out/ In Memory Of Elizabeth Reed
CD2: Midnight Rider/ Hoochie Coochie Man/ Hot' Lanta/ You Don't Love Me/ Mountain Jam
R: G-Vg. Soundboard.　S: The Warehouse, New Orleans Dec. 31 '70.　C: ECD. Dbw. Red type. Time CD1 39:22. CD2 48:35.

CD - OF THE ROAD
HQ 07
Can't Take It With You (3:53)/ Crazy Love (3:30)/ In Memory Of Elizabeth Reed (8:33)/ The Judgment (16:07)/ Jessica (5:56)/ You Don't Love Me (4:47)/ Blue Sky (3:50)/ Never Knew How Much, I Needed You (4:55)/ Statesboro Blues (5:57)/ Whippin' Post (10:18)/ Let Me Ride (1:50)/ Danny Boy Boy (2:58)/ The Preacher (1:58)
R: Exs. Soundboard.　C: ECD. Dcc. Digi-pack. Gold disc.

CD - ONE MORE RIDE
IT'S ITS-1005
One More Ride/ Home Jam/ Little Martha/ Statesboro Blues/ In Memory Of Elizabeth Reed/ Midnight Rider/ Hootchie Koochie Man/ One More Ride/ Allman Jam/ Instrumental Jam
S: 'Idle Wild South' outtakes, Georgia Feb. '70 and Florida July '70.

CD - ONE WAY OUT
MAIN STREET MST 112/2
CD1: Statesboro Blues/ Done Somebody Wrong/ Ain't Wasting Time No More/ One Way Out/ Stormy Memory/ You Don't Love Me
CD2: In Memory Of Elizabeth Reed/ Midnight Rider/ Whipping Post

R: Vg.   S: Syracuse University Apr. 4 '72.

CD - SOMEBODY'S CALLING
IT'S ITS-1006/7
CD1: Come On In My Kitchen #1/ Come On In
My Kitchen #2/ Seven Turns #1/ Seven Turns #2/
Low Down Dirty Mean #1/ Low Down Dirty Mean
#2
CD2: Midnight Rider/ Low Down Dirty Mean/
Melissa/ Seven Turns/ Come On In My Kitchen
R: Ex. Soundboard.   S: CD1 Aug. '90 rehearsal.
CD2 studio recordings.

CD - SONGS FROM THE ROAD
KISS THE STONE KTS 441
Statesboro Blues (5:35)/ Blue Sky (9:09)/ Same
Thing (8:02)/ Soulshine (6:32)/ Seven Turns
(4:23)/ Midnight Rider (3:08)/ Southbound (7:13)/
No One To Run With (5:52)/ Back Where It All
Begins (12:07)/ One Way Out (12:09)
R: Exs. Soundboard.   S: The Garden State Arts
Center, Homedale New Jersey Aug. 16 '94.
C: ECD. Dcc. Pic CD.

CD - SOUTH MEETS EAST
VINTAGE RARE MASTERS VRM-008-9
CD1: Statesboro Blues/ Don't Keep Me
Wondering/ Done Somebody Wrong/ One Way
Out/ In Memory Of Elizabeth Reed/ Midnight
Rider/ Hot Lanta
CD2: Whipping Post/ You Don't Love Me, Soul
Serenade
R: Ex. Soundboard. Some hiss.   S: Fillmore
East, NYC June 26 '71.   C: Japanese CD. Dbw.
Orange type. Time CD1 42:40. CD2 43:21.

CD - SOUTHROAD CONNECTION
MAN 001/2
CD1: Statesboro Blues (6:12)/ Blue Sky (8:27)/ All
Night Train (4:38)/ Same Thing (7:50)/ Seven
Turns (4:27)/ Jessica (17:40)/ Soulshine (6:38)/
Midnight Rider (3:21)/ In Memory Of Elizabeth
Reed (19:10)
CD2: No One Left To Run With (6:36)/ Back
Where It All Begins (13:26)/ Dicky Betts Guitar
Solo (2:33)/ One Way Out (9:32)/ Southbound
(7:00)/ Whippin' Post (11:54)/ Trouble No More
(3:49)/ Hot 'Lanta (5:01)/ Done Somebody Wrong
(4:11)/ Southbound (acoustic) (4:39)/ Sweet
Melissa (acoustic) (4:40)/ Midnight Rider
(acoustic) (2:55)
R: Exs. Soundboard.   S: Walnutcreek
Amphitheatre, Raleigh, North Carolina July 1 '94.
C: ECD. Pic CD.

CD - SOUTHERN HARMONY
OCTOPUS OCTO 037
Statesboro Blues (5:59)/ Blue Sky (8:27)/ All Night
Train (4:40)/ The Same Thing (7:50)/ Seven Turn
(4:25)/ No One To Run With (6:19)/ Back Where It
All Begins (13:24)/ One Way Out (12:02)/
Whipping Post (11:53)
R: Exs. Soundboard.   S: Italy '94.   C: ECD.
Dcc. Pic CD.

CD - SYRIA MOSQUE
CAPRICORN CR-2027
Statesboro Blues/ Trouble No More/ Don't Keep
Me Wondering/ In Memory Of Elizabeth Reed/
Midnight Rider/ You Don't Love Me/ Whipping
Post/ Terraplane Blues, Come In My Kitchen,
Jesus Make Up My Dying Bed
R: Poor soundboard recording.   S: The Syria
Mosque, Pittsburgh Jan. 17 '71. Track 8 Duane
home jam.

CD - TONI BROTHERS BAND - WE'RE A FAM-A-LEE
TEDDY BEAR TB 78
Come Into My Kitchen (5:27)/ Seven Turns (4:18)/
Goin' Down The Road, And Feelin' Bad (5:22)/
Midnight Rider (3:02)/ Southbound (5:34)/ In
Memory Of Elizabeth Reed (9:36)/ Melissa (4:54)/
Never Knew How Much, I Needed You (4:31)/ Let
Me Ride (0:58)/ Danny Blue Boy (3:05)/ The
Preacher (2:02)/ Come And Go Blues (5:00)
R: Ex.   S: Acoustic - various locations '81-'92.
C: ECD. Pic CD.

CD - WELCOME TO HOLLYWOOD
ARCHIVO ARC 025
Statesboro Blues/ Done Somebody Wrong/ One
Way Out/ Stormy Monday/ You Don't Love Me/
Trouble No More/ In Memory Of Elizabeth Reed/
Whipping Post/ Johnny B. Goode/ Dust My
Broom
R: Vgs. Audience recording.   S: Hollywood Bowl
Aug. 6 '72.

CD - WILD BLUESY ROAD
KOBRA RECORDS KRCR 02/2
CD1: Statesboro Blues/ End Of Line/ Blue Sky/
Nobody Knows/ Low Down Dirty Mean/ Melissa
(acoustic)/ Come On My Kitchen (acoustic)/
Midnight Rider (acoustic)/ Goin' Down This Road
Feelin' Bad (acoustic)/ Hoochie Coochie Man
CD2: Kind Of Bird/ Get On With Your Life/ In
Memory Of Elizabeth Reed/ Revival/ Jessica/
Whipping Post
R: Exs. Soundboard.   S: Pacific Amphitheatre,
CA 11-10-'91.   C: ECD.

AMOS, TORI

CD - AMERICAN HEARTBREAKER
ALL OF US AS 22
Crucify (13:28)/ Icicle (4:50)/ Precious Things
(5:55)/ Leather (4:23)/ God (8:25)/ Silent All
These Years (5:33)/ The Waitress (4:27)/ Here In
My Head (5:09)/ Baker Baker (5:04)/ Cornflake
Girl (6:15)/ American Pie (2:25)/ Smells Like Teen
Spirit (4:05)/ Past The Mission (4:26)/ Winter
(7:18)
R: Ex. Audience.   S: Milan Apr. 18 '94.
C: ECD. Dcc. Pic CD.

CD - CORNFLAKE GIRL
GRAPEFRUIT GRA-009-A
Crucify (6:08)/ Silent All These Years (5:16)/

Happy Phantom (3:43)/ Girl (4:25)/ Whole Lotta Love (4:12)/ Leather (3:36)/ Smells Like A Teen Spirit (3:44)/ China (5:44)/ Cornflake Girl (3:16)/ Pretty Good Year (2:36)/ Baker Baker (3:16)/ God (3:37)/ Sugar (3:27)/ Precious Things (5:45)/ Tear In Your Hand (5:19)/ Winter (7:02)
R: Ex.   S: San Juan USA '92. New York '94. Toronto, Canada '92.   C: Australian CD.

CD - COVERING' EM
OCTOPUS OCTO 104
Whole Lotta Love (1:55)/ Thank You (2:23)/ Love Song (3:35)/ Little Drummer Boy (4:32)/ Angie (5:23)/ Wrapped Around Your Finger (6:25)/ Famous Blue Raincoat (5:49)/ A Case Of You (5:21)/ Ain't No Sunshine (5:00)/ Imagine (3:29)/ Home On The Range (4:52)/ American Pie (2:34)/ Smells Like Teen Spirit (3:58)
R: Ex.   S: Various locations in the USA.
C: ECD. Dcc. Pic CD.

CD - FORGOTTEN EARTHQUAKES
AMOS 951
Upside Down/ Thoughts/ Sugar/ Flying Dutchman/ Humpty Dumpty/ The Pool/ Take To The Sky/ Sweet Dreams/ Crucify/ Angie/ Smells Like Teen Spirit/ Thank You/ Here In My Head/ Mary/ Song For Eric/ Ode To The Banana King/ The Happy Worker/ Leather (solo piano version)/ Sarah Sylvia Cynthia Stout/ China (solo piano version)
S: B-Sides and rarities.   C: ECD. Dcc. Pic CD. Time 77:34.

CD - LITTLE RARITIES II: EVEN MORE RARITIES
PIANO CLASSICS PIC 04
A Case Of You/ Honey/ Black Swan/ Home On The Range With Cherokee Addition/ Sister Janet/ Daisy Dead Petals/ Strange Fruit/ All The Girls Hate Her/ Over It/ If 6 Was 9/ Little Drummer Boy/ Sarah Cynthia Sylvia Stout/ Ring My Bell/ WHFS Interview (Tea With The Waitress)
R: Exs. Soundboard.   C: ECD. Dcc. Time 75:12.

CD - PIANO GIRL UP NORTH
HOME RECORDS HR6049-2
Leather/ Crucify/ Icicle/ Whole Lotta Love/ God/ Past The Mission/ Me And A Gun/ China/ Cornflake Girl/ Cloud On My Tongue/ Bells For Her/ Winter
R: Ex. Audience.   S: Live In Montreal, Canada, Nov. 8 '94.   C: ECD. Picture CD. Time 64:47.

CD - SPACE DOGGIN' BRUINS
STRANGLED RECORDS STR 006/7
CD1: Sugar/ Crucify/ Icicle/ Precious Things/ Happy Phantom/ Pretty Good Year/ God/ Silent All These Years/ Past The Mission/ Leather/ The Waitress/ Teen Spirit/ Me And A Gun/ Baker Baker
CD2: Cornflake Girl/ Winter/ China/ All The Girls Hate Her/ Cloud On My Tongue/ Take To The Sky (NJ Oct. 11 '92)/ Little Earthquakes (Seattle Aug. 29 '92)/ Girl (CA Sept. 5 '92)/ Mary (Detroit Oct. 30 '92)/ Imagine (UK Dec. 12 '92)/ Angie

(Germany June 8 '92).
R: Vg-Ex. Audience.   S: UCLA Campus Mar. 22 '94.   C: ECD. Dcc. Pic CD. Time CD1 67:20. CD2 53:07.

CD - WHITE HORSES
REAL LIVE RL CD 34
Crucify/ Silent All These Years/ Precious Things/ Happy Phantom/ Leather/ Upside Down/ Little Earth Quakes/ Whole Lotta Love/ Me And A Gun/ Winter/ Smells Like Teen Spirit/ Mother/ China/ Song For Eric
R: Exs. Soundboard.   S: Boulder, Colorado Sept. 29 '92.   C: Time 74:10.

CD - ULTRA RARE TORI
AR4/ BM2
The Big Picture/ Cool On Your Island/ Fayth/ Fire On The Side/ Pirates/ Floating City/ Heart Attack At 23/ On The Boundary/ You Go To My Head/ Etienne Trilogy: The Highlands: Etienne: Sky Boat Song/ Ain't No Sunshine (a)/ A Case Of You (a)/ Imagine (a)/ Sentimental Journey (b)/ Little Drummer Boy (c)/ Sarah Cynthia Sylvia Stout Would Not Take The Garbage Out/ Ring My Bell (e)
R: Exs. Soundboard except - (a) and (b) Audience. (c), (d) and (e) Vg. Soundboard.
S: Official 'Y Kant Tori Read' LP '88 except (a) live '91 (b) live '92 (c) from 'We've Got Your Yule Logs Hangin' '92 (d) from 'Speaking Of Christmas & Other Things' (e) '92 from NME 'Ruby Trax' compilation.   C: Time 74:23.

AYERS, KEVIN

CD - RAPT IN THOUGHT
CANTERBURY DREAM CTD-017/018
CD1: Lady Rachel/ Stop This Train (Again Doing It)/ There Is Loving/ Margaret/ Whatevershebringswesing/ Shouting In Bucket Blues/ Didn't Feel Lonely Till I Thought Of You/ Observations/ Stranger In Blue Suede Shoes/ Interview/ Farewell Again (Another Dawn)
CD2: Shouting In A Bucket Blues/ Star/ Love's Gonna Turn You Round/ Mr. Cool/ Ballad Of Mr. Snake/ Blue
R: Poor.   S: CD1 tracks 1-6 BBC '72. Tracks 7-11 London Apr. '75. CD2 London Oct. 27 '76.
C: Japanese CD.

CD - SPANISH TROUBADOUR
CANTERBURY DREAM CTD-023/024
CD1: May I/ Shouting In A Bucket Blues/ Steppin Out/ Everybody's Something And Some People's All the Time Blues/ Champagne And Valium/ Super Salesman/ Decadence/ Animals/ It Begins With Blessing, Once I Awakened, But It Ends With A Curse/ Stranger In Blue Suede Shoes
CD2: Am I Really Marcel?/ Don't Fall In Love With Me/ Stop This Train (Again Doing It)/ Stepping Out/ Fool After Midnight/ Wish I Could Fall/ Only Heaven Knows/ Too Old To Die Young/ The

Howlin' Man/ Never My Baby/ Budget Tours Part
1/ Budget Tours Part 2
R: Poor.   C: Japanese CD.

B

BAD COMPANY

CD - CRIME STORY
BABY CAPONE 027/2
CD1: How About That (6:00)/ Holy Water (4:15)/
Rock 'N' Roll Fantasy (3:17)/ Ready For Love
(5:29)/ If You Needed Somebody (5:48)/ Here
Comes Trouble (4:20)/ Shooting Star (6:29)/ Bad
Company (8:34)/ This Could Be The One (5:40)/
Good Lovin' Gone Bad (4:45)/ Can't Get Enough
(4:39)/ Take This Town (5:39)/ Movin' On (3:21)/
Feel Like Makin' Love (5:42)
CD2: Bad Company (4:24)/ Rock Steady (3:45)/
Ready For Love (4:46)/ Can't Get Enough (3:25)/
Movin" On (3:22)/ One Night (6:41)/ Shake It Up
(4:41)/ No Smoke (5:32)/ Boys Cry Tough (5:18)/
Tell It Like It Is (4:15)/ Drums Solo, Can't Get
Enough (8:14)/ Holy Water (6:25)/ Bad Company
(7:13)/ Ready For Love (7:12)
R: Exs. Soundboard.   S: CD1 Electric Ladyland
Studios, New York Dec. 13 '92. CD2 tracks 1-5
BBC Studios '74 Session. Rest Universal
Amphitheatre, Los Angeles Dec. 24 '90.
C: ECD. Dcc. Pic CDs.

CD - LITTLE MISS FORTUNE
ZA 41/42
CD1: Deal With The Preacher/ Rock Steady/ Little
Miss Fortune/ Ready For Love/ Whisky Bottle/
Feel Like Makin' Love/ Shooting Star/ Seagull
CD2: Bad Company/ Easy On My Soul/ Movin'
On/ Can't Get Enough/ The Stealer/ Good Lovin'
Gone Bad/ I Just Want Make Love To You*
R: G-Vg. Audience.   S: Budokan, Tokyo Mar. 3
'75. *New York '74 with Jimmy Page and Robert
Plant.   C: Japanese CD.

BAD RELIGION

7" - BAD RELIGION
S1: Rock 'N' Roll*/ Riding The Storm**
S2: Johnny B. Good*/ Louie Louie*
R: G. Audience.   S: Skylight Club Mar. 31 '83.
**Olympic Auditorium '84.   C: USA.
Orange/black sleeve. Clear vinyl. 45 RPM.

7" - GENERATOR DEMOS
S1: Generator   S2: Atomic Garden
R: Exs. Soundboard.   C: USA. White sleeve
with yellow/back. 45 RPM.

CD - KROQ CHRISTMAS PARTY
KROQ2
Christmas Medley/ American Jesus/ Recipe For
Hate/ Stranger Than Fiction/ Struck A Nerve/ The
Handshake/ 21st Century Digital Boy/ Fuck

Christmas/ Individual/ Modern Man/ Modern Day
Catastrophists/ Sanity/ Leave Mine To Me/
Generator/ Do You Want/ Yesterday/ Anaesthesia/
Lookin' In/ 21st Century Digital Boy/ Recipe For
Hate/ Kerosene/ What Can You Do?/ American
Jesus/ 21st Century Digital Boy/ The Handshake/
Incomplete/ Infected/ Silent Knight
R: Exs. Soundboard.   S: Tracks 1-8 KROQ
Christmas Party Dec. 10 '94. Tracks 9-19
Goteborg Oct. '94. Tracks 20-27 demos and
rehearsals '94. Track 28 from KROQ charity cas-
sette 'No Toys For O.J.' released Dec. '94.
C: ECD. Dcc. Pic CD.

CD - RADIATION HAZARD
KISS THE STONE KTS 442
The Hand Shake/ Too Much To Ask/ Stranger
Than Fiction/ American Jesus/ Infected/ Change
Of Ideas/ Atomic Garden/ The Answer/ Flat Earth
Society/ Individual/ Modern Man/ Modern Day
Catastrophe/ Sanity/ Leave Mine To Me/ Do What
You Want/ Yesterday/ Anaesthesia/ Looking In/
21st Century Digital Boy/ Recipe For Hate/
Generator/ American Jesus/ Portrait Of Authority/
Get Off/ Pessimistic Lines/ Kerosene/ 1,000 More
Fools/ Men With A Mission/ Fuck Armageddon ...
This Is Hell/ Atomic Garden
R: Vg-Ex. Audience.   S: Tracks 1-19 Goteberg,
Sweden 8/10/94. Tracks 20-30 Amsterdam,
Holland 4/7/93.   C: ECD. Pic CD. Time 76:36.

CD - STRANGER THAN PULP FICTION ...
PITCHFORK RECORDS PF-1100
Noel, Joy To The World/ American Jesus/ Recipe
For Hate/ Stranger Than Fiction/ Struck A Nerve/
Modern World/ 20th Century Digital Boy/ Fuck
Christmas/ Silent Night/ Fuck Christmas/ Struck A
Nerve/ I Saw The Light/ American Jesus/
Operation Rescue/ Along The Way/ Do What You
Want/ Too Much To Ask/ Struck A Nerve/ Suffer/
What Can You Do?/ Generator/ No Control/
Anathesia/ Get Off/ 20th Century Digital Boy/
We're Only Gonna Die/ Fuck Armageddon This Is
Hell/ Atomic Garden
R: Vg-Exs.   S: Tracks 1-7 Los Angeles Dec. 10
'94. Tracks 8-13 Los Angeles Dec. 15 '93. Tracks
14-28 Los Angeles May '94.   C: Time 72:00.

BAD RELIGION / NOFX

CD - EAT OR DIE
BAD RELIGION Goteborg Nov. '94: The Hand
Shake/ Too Much To Ask/ Stranger Than Fiction/
American Jesus/ Infected/ Change Of Ideas/
Atomic Garden/ The Answer/ Flat Earth Society/
Individual/ Modern Man/ Modern Day
Catastrophists/ Sanity/ Leave Mine To Me/
Generator/ Do What You Want/ Yesterday/
Anaesthesia/ Lookin' In/ 21st Century Digital Boy/
NO FX Europe 93: Together On The Sand/
Nowhere/ Stickin' In My Eye/ Bob/ You Are
Bleeding/ Straight Edge/ Lisa And Louise/ Shower
Days/ Kill All The White Men
R: Exs. Soundboard.   C: ECD. Time 78:56.

BAND, THE

CD - LIVE AT THE HOLLYWOOD BOWL
GOLD STANDARD 195-TB-16-07
The Shape I'm In/ Look Out Cleveland/ The Weight/ King Harvest/ Unfaithful Servant/ Jemima Surrender/ Rocking Chair/ Time To Kill/ Organ Improvisation, Chest Fever/ The Night They Drove Old Dixie Down, Across The Great Divide/ Up On Cripple Creek/ Strawberry Wine/ I Shall Be Released/ This Wheel's On Fire/ Baby Don't Do It
R: Vg audience recording. Some static.
S: Hollywood Bowl Oct. 7 '70.

BAND OF GYPSYS, THE

CD - RESURRECTION (A REUNION CONCERT)
JMH 004
Killing Floor (5:05)/ Manic Depression (6:03)/ Spanish Castle Magic (5:18)/ Message To Love (6:22)/ Little Wing (5:06)/ Castle Made Of Sand (3:20)/ Hey Joe (5:57)/ Who Knows (13:19)/ Machine Gun (9:22)/ Telephone Interview With Al Hendrix (4:25)/ Fire (3:36)/ Red House (7:51)/ All Along The Watchtower (6:14)
R: Ex.   S: Kabuky Theatre, San Francisco Dec. 27 '84.   C: ECD. Dcc.

BAUHAUS

CD - IN THE FLAT FIELD
HAND MADE HAM 016
Bela Lugosi's Dead (10:07)/ In The Flat Field (4:46)/ Boys (3:45)/ Telegram Sam (4:01)/ Poem (2:59)/ God In The Alcove (4:09)/ Spy In The Cab (5:05)/ Scopes (2:34)/ Terror Couple Kill Colonel (3:53)/ Dancing Stigmata (4:26)/ Martyr (0:56)/ My Kind Of Town Chicago Is Double Dare (7:30)
R: Vg-Ex. Soundboard.   S: Chicago, Space Palace Aug. 5 '80.   C: ECD. Dcc.

BEACH BOYS, THE

CD - LEI'D IN HAWAII REHEARSAL
VIGOTONE VIGO-133
God Only Knows/ California Girls/ Surfer Girl/ You're So Good To Me/ The Letter/ Help Me Rhonda/ Heroes And Villains/ Their Hearts Were Full Of Spring/ Sherry, She Needs Me (backing track recorded '65, vocals added '76)/ We're Together Again (alternate mix)/ We're Together Again (backing track)/ We're Together Again (instrumental)/ We're Together Again (alternate mix 2) (recorded Sept. 11 '68)/ Introduction By Art Linkletter/ Little Deuce Coupe/ In My Room/ Be True To Your School/ Surfer Girl/ KFWB Theme/ Closing Credits/ God Only Knows*/ Good Vibrations*
R: Ex. Soundboard. *G. S: Tracks 1-8 Lei'd in Hawaii Rehearsal Aug. 25 '67. Tracks 9-13 studio outtakes. Tracks 14-20 Hollywood Bowl Nov. 1 '63. Tracks 21-22 live in Sydney Feb. 13 '78.
C: Dcc. Time 55:33.

CD - LIVE AT THE FILLMORE EAST
MOONLIGHT.ML 9507
Heroes And Villains/ Do It Again/ Cottonfields/ Help Me Rhonda/ Wouldn't It Be Nice/ Your Song/ Student Demonstration Time/ Good Vibrations/ California Girls/ I Get Around/ It's About Time/ Do It Again*/ Wild Honey*/ Help Me Rhonda*(Elton John on piano)
R: Vgs/m.   S: The Fillmore East, New York June 27 '71. *London '72.

CD - LONG LOST SURF SONGS VOL. 1
SILVER RARITIES SIRA 149
Surfin' Safari ('62 Ariola single version, similar to stereo overdub on 'Lost And Found')/ Mr. Moto / Interview (Beach Boys Oxnard, CA July 14 '62 plus interview with Brian)/ Gonna Hustle You (late '62 - Brian Wilson demo later recorded by Jan and Dean as 'The New Girl In School')/ Farmers Daughter ('63 - alternate take and different mix)/ Lana ('63 - alternate take and different mix)/ Rocking Surfer ('63 alternate take and different mix)/ Chopsticks Boogie ('63 - alternate take and different mix)/ Papa Oom Mow Mow (Sydney Stadium, Australia Jan. '64)/ Little Deuce Coupe (Sydney Stadium, Australia Jan. '64)/ What I'd Say (Sydney Stadium, Australia Jan. '64)/ I Get Around ('64 session and track - stereo)/ Honda 55 ('64 unfinished track - Japanese TV commercial)/ In My Room (Red Skeleton TV Show 12/5/64)/ Little Honda (Sept. '64 outtake from Beach Boys concert LP)/ Karen (TV show theme '64)/ I Get Around ('Ready Steady Go' TV show 6/11/64)/ When I Grow Up ('Ready Steady Go' TV show 6/11/64)/ The Monkey's Uncle (Annette & The Beach Boys - stereo - Mar. '65)/ Good To My Baby/ In The Back Of My Mind/ Please Let Me Wonder (sessions)/ Do You Wanna Dance (sessions)
R: Vg-Ex. Some G.   C: ECD. Dbw. Time 62:18.

CD - LONG LOST SURF SONGS VOL. 2
SILVER RARITIES SIRA 150
Help Me Rhonda (Andy Williams Show 2/5/65)/ Their Hearts Were Full Of Spring (Andy Williams Show 2/5/65)/ Little Honda (Andy Williams Show 2/5/65 - with Andy Williams - performed as 'Little Cycle' because of advertising restrictions)/ California Girls (Jack Benny TV Show 3/11/65 with Brian Wilson)/ Sketch (Jack Benny TV Show 3/11/65 with Jack Benny and Bob Hope)/ Intro (introduction to 'Pet Sounds' sessions Jan - Apr. '66)/ Wouldn't It Be Nice (Brian Wilson guide vocal)/ That's Not Me (unfinished and remixed from 'American Band' video)/ I Just Wasn't Made For These Times (unfinished and remixed from 'American Band' video)/ Wouldn't It Be Nice (unfinished and remixed from 'American Band' video)/ Studio Chat/ Don't Talk (track session)/ Here Today (unfinished and remixed from 'American Band' video)/ Hang Onto Your Ego (additional vocals)/ Interview (WDRC, Hartford - '66 - interview with Love and Jardine by Dicky Robinson about 'Pet Sounds')/ Good Vibrations

(selections from 'The Best Summers Of Our Lives' radio biography '76)/ Heroes And Villains (different mix)/ Barnyard (extra vocals)/ Blind Mice (mono version from 'Smile' period)/ Interview (Brian Wilson with Jack Wagner talking about 'Smiley Smile' '67)
R: Vg-Ex. Some G.   C: ECD. Dbw. Time 59:23.

CD - LONG LOST SURF SONGS VOL. 3
SILVER RARITIES SIRA 151
Here Comes The Night #1/ Here Comes The Night #2/ Here Comes The Night #3/ Here Comes The Night #4/ Here Comes The Night #5/ Here Comes The Night #6/ Here Comes The Night #7/ Here Comes The Night #8 (tracks and vocal over-dubs from 'Wild Honey ' LP sessions)/ With A Little Help From My Friends (slow version released on 'Rarities' Lp)/ The Letter ('Rarities' Lp)/ I Was Made To Love Him (longer ending from 'Rarities' LP)/ With A Little Help From My Friends (speed-corrected version)/ Do It Again (from The Ed Sullivan Show '68)/ Good Vibrations (from The Ed Sullivan Show '68)/ Cease To Exist (Charles Manson)/ Never Learn Not To Love (Beach Boys single version)/ Bluebirds Over The Mountain (Dutch 7" version with overdub)/ Time To Get Alone (rough mix)/ Rock And Roll Woman (Brighton Dome May 30 '69)/ Breakaway (Czechoslovakia)/ It's About Time (drum track)/ Tears In The Morning (different vocal, lyric and mix)/ My Solution (outtake Oct. 31 '70)/ Musical Parts (Dennis Wilson - introduced by Steve Aspin)/ Barbara (Dennis Wilson)/ Sounds Of Free (Dennis And Rumbo - released in '70 as a single only in Europe and UK)
R: Vg-Ex. Some G.   C: ECD. Dcc. Time 59:56.

CD - LONG LOST SURF SONGS VOL. 4
SILVER RARITIES SIRA 152
Forever (David Frost Show '71)/ Vegetables (David Frost Show '71)/ Falling In Love (David Frost Show '71)/ Walls, Awake (Brian Wilson and David Sandler demo Oct. 71)/ Long Promised Road (St. John University, New York 8/3/72)/ Disney Girls (St. John University, New York 8/3/72)/ Wonderball (St. John University, New York 8/3/72 - combination of 'Wonderbill' and 'Don't Worry Bill')/ Surfs Up (Grand Cala Du Disque, Dutch TV show Feb. 24 '72)/ I've Got A Friend (Radio Luxembourg concert 10/5/72 - important live performance by Dennis)/ Jam (Radio Luxembourg concert 10/5/72)
R: Vg. Some G.   C: ECD. Dcc. Time 58:48.

CD - LONG LOST SURF SONGS VOL. 5
SILVER RARITIES SIRA 152
Vote '72 (summer '72 - Beach Boys promote vot-ing)/ Marcella ('72 - slightly different mix)/ Melody ('70 - Melody Alan Jardine and Johnny Rivers)/ California Saga (Hartford, Conn.)/ River Song (only live recording)/ Jumpin' Jack Flash (Colby College, Maine '73)/ God Only Knows (acoustic version Miami, Florida Apr. '73)/ Caroline No (acoustic version Miami, Florida Apr. '73)/ Ding

Dang (outtake fall '73)/ Good Timin' (summer '74)/ River Song (summer '74 - incomplete studio ver-sion)/ Don't Talk (Tampa, Florida 12/4/74)/ Dragin' (Michigan State University, East Lansing May 18 '74 with Roger McGuinn)/ The Trader (Nassau Coliseum, Long Island, New York June 6 '74)/ All This Is That (Nassau Coliseum, Long Island, New York June 6 '74)/ Help Me Rhonda (Nassau Coliseum, Long Island, New York June 6 '74 with Dennis Wilson lead vocal)
R: Vg. Some G.   C: ECD. Dcc. Time 58:15.

CD - LONG LOST SURF SONGS VOL. 6
SILVER RARITIES SIRA 154
California Girls (June 27 '74 - Mike Love (vocals), Charles Lloyd (flute) and John McLaughlin (acoustic guitar))/ I'm Waiting For The Day (Greensboro, North Carolina 5/4/75 with Billy Hinsche on lead vocal)/ You're So Good To Me (Greensboro, North Carolina 5/4/75)/ In the Back Of My Mind (St. Louis May '75)/ Surf's Up (May '75 - vocals by Bobby Lamm of 'Chicago')/ Wishing You Were Here (Madison Square Gardens 12/6/75)/ I Wanna Pick You Up (outtake from '15 Big Ones' sessions Jan. - May '76)/ Rock And Roll Music (outtake from '15 Big Ones' ses-sions Jan. - May '76 different mix)/ We Gotta Groove (outtake from '15 Big Ones' sessions Jan. '76)/ Honkin' Down The Highway (outtake from '15 Big Ones' sessions Jan. '76 with Billy Hinsche on lead vocal)/ That Same Song (rehearsals ses-sion, NBC special 'It's OK' 5/8/76)/ Interview (BBC - Brian Wilson interview with Bob Harris Nov. 16 '76)/ Back Home (Madison Square Gardens Nov. 25 '75 - Brian lead vocals)/ Wild Honey (Madison Square Gardens Nov. 25 '75)
R: Vg. Some G.   C: ECD. Dbw. Time 58:44.

CD - MEET THE GRATEFUL DEAD
CAPRICORN RECORDS CR-2046
Deal (5:44)/ Me And My Uncle (3:07)/ Birdsong (6:06)/ Playin' In The Band (6:04)/ Dire Wolf (7:25)/ Searchin' (5:08)/ Riot In Cell Block #9 (6:02)/ Good Vibrations (5:33)/ I Get Around (2:24)/ Okie From Muskogee (3:37)/ Johnny B. Good (3:21)/ Sing Me Back Home (9:39)/ Uncle John's Band (6:09)
R: Ex. Soundboard.   S: Fillmore East Apr. 27 '71.   C: Time 70:18.

CD - MERRY CHRISTMAS FROM THE BEACH BOYS
FRONTLINE FLCD-14
Christmas Time Is Here Again/ Child Of Winter/ Winter Symphony/ Michael Row The Boat Ashore/ Seasons In The Sun/ Holy Evening/ Christmas Day/ So Get That Girl/ Santa's Got An Airplane/ I Saw Mommy Kissing Santa Claus/ Christmas Carol Medley/ Kona Christmas Aka Mele Kaliki Mako/ Bells Of Christmas/ Jingle Bell Rock/ Have Yourself A Merry Christmas/ Do You Hear What I Hear?/ Mystery/ two other tracks
C: Vg sound.   S: Studio sessions.

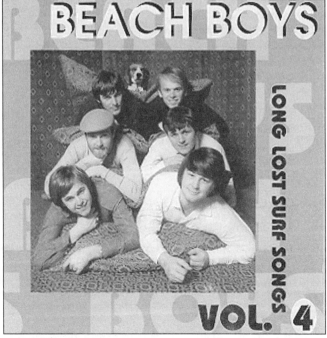

CD - MIKE LOVE, NOT WAR
SPANK PRODUCTIONS SP-108
Help Me Rhonda/ I Get Around/ Medley: Fun Fun
Fun, Shut Down, Little Deuce Coupe, Surfin'
U.S.A./ Surfer Girl/ Papa-Oom-Mow-Mow/ You're
So Good To Me/ You've Got To Hide Your Love
Away/ California Girls/ Sloop John B/ Wouldn't It
Be Nice/ God Only Knows/ Papa-Oom-Mow-Mow/
Little Deuce Coupe/ Surfer Girl/ Monster Mash/
Louie Louie/ Surfin' USA/ Don't Worry Baby/ I Get
Around/ Johnny B. Goode/ What I'd Say
C: Vgm.   S: Tracks 1-11 Michigan State
University Oct. '66. Tracks 12-20 Sweden Nov.
'64. Track 21 Sydney Jan. '64.
C: Japanese CD.

CD - ON THE BEACH
DYNAMITE STUDIO DS94J094
California Girls/ Darlin'/ Little Deuce Coupe/ In My
Room/ Good Timin'/ Sumahama/ Help Me
Rhonda/ I Get Around/ Surfin' U.S.A./ Good
Vibrations/ Fun Fun Fun
R: Vg sound. Hiss.   S: Enoshima Beach,
Kanagawa Aug. 4 '79.   C: Japanese CD.

CD - ROCKIN' RARITIES
HB 002
More Smile Session/ Special Feeling/ It's Over
Now (2 takes)/ Marching Along/ Please/ Still
Dream Of It/ My Diane/ Baby Blue/ Honkin' Down
The Highway/ You've Lost That Lovin' Feelin'/ We
Gotta Groove/ California Dreaming/ California
Feeling/ Santa Ana Winds/ Monterey Saga/
Brian's Back/ Tears In The Morning (2 versions)/
Do You Wanna Dance?/ Calendar Girl/ Good
Vibrations*/ Bermuda Shorts
R: Ex. Soundboard. *Vg. Soundboard.
S: Studio outtakes.   C: Time 75:57.

BEATLES, THE
(also see page 230)

CD - THE ACOUSTIC SUBMARINE
TEDDY BEAR TB 66/2
CD1: Do You Want To Know A Secret (2:26)/ And
I Love Her (2:24)/ I'm A Loser (2:36)/ Help (2:23)/
Yesterday (2:07)/ Yes It Is (2:55)/ Norwegian
Wood, The Bird Has Flown (2:25)/ I'm Looking
Through You (2:28)/ We Can Work It Out (4:30)/
I'm Only Sleeping (2:56)/ Yellow Submarine
(2:40)/ A Day In The Life (4:20)/ The Fool On The
Hill (2:42)/ Christmas Time Is Here Again (5:43)/
The Happy Rishikesh Song (1:53)/ Jubilee (2:34)/
Child Of Nature (2:33)/ Goodbye (2:23)/ Everyone
Had A Hard Year (1:50)/ What's The New Mary
Jane (6:31)
CD2: Heather (2:12)/ Back In The USSR (3:00)/
Dear Prudence (4:34)/ Ob-La-Di Ob-La-Da (2:46)/
While My Guitar Gently Weeps (3:14)/ Blackbird
(2:20)/ Rocky Raccoon (3:33)/ Julia (2:50)/
Mother's Nature Son (2:45)/ Hey Jude (5:00)/
Because (2:19)/ I Lost My Little Girl (4:03) Teddy
Boy (5:54)/ Mama You've Been On My Mind
(2:00)/ For You Blue (2:22)/ Two Of Us (3:20)/

Across The Universe (3:44)/ I Me Mine (1:47)/
Maggie Mae (1:48)
R: Vg-Ex. Some G.   S: Acoustic outtakes.
C: ECD.

CD - ALTERNATE MASTERS
FAB GEAR CPCS 9402
Twist And Shout (stereo remix version)/ Please
Please Me (true stereo version)/ Thank You Girl
(true stereo version)/ I'll Get You (Capitol stereo
version)/ Money (stereo remix version)/ This Boy
(Capitol simulated version)/ Komm, Gib Mie Deine
Hand (stereo German version)/ Sie Liebt Dich
(stereo German version)/ I Call Your Name
(Capitol stereo version)/ I'll Cry Instead (Capitol
mono long version)/ If I Fell (original soundtrack
mono version)/ And I Love Her (original soundtrack mono version)/ Anytime At All (Capitol mono
version)/ When I Get Home (Capitol mono version)/ She's A Woman (Capitol stereo version)/ I
Feel Fine (alternate stereo mix)/ Kansas City, Hey
Hey Hey Hey (stereo remix version)/ Bad Boy
(original mono version)/ Yes It Is (simulated
stereo version)/ Dizzy Miss Lizzy (original stereo
mix)/ I'm Looking Through You (Capitol stereo
version)/ Think For Yourself (alternate stereo mix)/
The Word (Capitol alternate stereo mix)/ Drive My
Car (alternate stereo mix)/ And Your Bird Can
Sing (Capitol simulated stereo version)/ Dr.
Robert (Capitol mono version)/ Paperback Writer
(simulated stereo version)/ Taxman (edited mono
version)/ I'm Only Sleeping (alternate stereo version)/ Got To Get You Into My Life (stereo remix
version)
R: Ex.   C: Japanese CD. Dcc. Pic CD. 73:10.

CD - THE ALTERNATE VERSIONS VOL. 1 -
THE BEAT YEARS 1963-65
INVASION UNLIMITED IU 9539-1
CD1: I Saw Her Standing There/ There's A Place/
Misery/ Do You Want To Know A Secret/ From Me
To You/ Thank You Girl/ One And One Is Two/ I'm
In Love/ Please Mister Postman/ It Won't Be
Long/ Hold Me Tight/ Don't Bother Me/ Can't Buy
Me Love/ A Hard Day's Night
CD2: Leave My Kitten Alone/ I'm A Loser/ She's A
Woman/ I Feel Fine/ Honey Don't/ If You've Got
Trouble/ That Means A Lot/ Ticket To Ride/ Yes It
Is/ Help!/ Run For Your Life/ Norwegian Wood/
Day Tripper/ We Can Work It Out/ I'm Looking
Through You/ 12-Bar-Original
R: Vg-Ex.   S: Alternate and unreleased out-
takes.   C: ECD.

CD - THE ALTERNATE VERSIONS VOL.2 -
THE PSYCHEDELIC YEARS 1966-68
INVASION UNLIMITED IU 9540-1
CD1: Tomorrow Never Knows/ Rain/ Paper Writer/
For No One/ Here, There And Everywhere/
Strawberry Fields Forever/ A Day In The Life/
Lucy In The Sky With Diamonds/ It's All Too Much/
The Fool On The Hill
CD2: Ariel Instrumental/ Your Mother Should
Know/ Lady Madonna/ Across The Universe/ Not

Guilty/ Ob-La-Di, Ob-La-Da/ While My Guitar Gently Weeps/ Happiness Is A Warm Gun/ I'm So Tired/ What's The New, Mary Jane?/ Hey Jude/ Revolution No.9/ Goodbye
S: Alternate and unreleased studio outtakes.
C: ECD.

CD - ATLANTA / MUNICH / SEATTLE
SPANK RECORDS SP 145 CD
Intro By Paul Drew/ Twist And Shout/ She's A Woman/ I Feel Fine/ Ticket To Ride/ Everybody's Trying To Be My Baby/ Can't Buy Me Love/ Baby's In Black/ I Wanna Be Your Man/ Help?/ I'm Down/ Rock And Roll Music/ Baby's In Black/ I Feel Fine/ Yesterday/ Nowhere Man/ I'm Down/ Twist And Shout/ You Can't Do That/ All My Loving/ She Loves You/ Things We Said Today/ Roll Over Beethoven/ Can't Buy Me Love/ If I Fell/ I Want To Hold Your Hand
R: Poor-G.   S: Tracks 1-11 Atlanta Stadium, Atlanta, Georgia Aug. 18 '65. Tracks 12-17 Circus Krone, Munich, Germany June 24 '66. Tracks 18-26 Seattle Center Coliseum, Seattle, Washington Aug. 21 '64.   C: Japanese CD. Dcc. Time 69:10.

CD - ATLANTA '65
MASTERDISC MDCD 006
MC/ Twist And Shout/ She's A Woman/ I Feel Fine/ Ticket To Ride/ Everybody's Trying To Be My Baby/ Can't Buy Me Love/ Baby's In Black/ I Wanna Be Your Man/ Help/ I'm Down
R: Vg.   S: Fulton County Stadium, Atlanta Aug. 18 '65.   C: Japanese CD.

CD - THE BEATLES IN ITALY: 1965
BULLDOG RECORDS BG CD 006
Twist And Shout/ She's A Woman/ I'm A Loser/ Interview/ Twist And Shout/ She's A Woman/ I'm A Loser/ Can't Buy Me Love/ Baby's In Black/ I Wanna Be Your Man/ A Hard Days Night/ Everybody's Trying To Be My Baby/ Rock And Roll Music/ I Feel Fine/ Ticket To Ride/ Long Tall Sally
R: Poor-G.   S: Tracks 1-4 Milan, June 24 '65. Tracks 5-16 Rome June 27 '65.   C: ECD. Box set with t-shirt, two 2 foot by 3 foot posters and a 16 page color book. Time 36:20.

CD - THE ED SULLIVAN SHOW
MELVIN RECORDS MMCD 05A/05B
CD1: All My Loving/ Till There Was You/ She Loves You/ I Saw Her Standing There/ I Want To Hold Your Hand/ She Loves You/ This Boy/ All My Loving/ I Saw Her Standing There/ From Me To You/ I Want To Hold Your Hand/ Twist And Shout/ Please Please Me/ I Want To Hold Your Hand/ The Radio Show/ I Saw Her Standing There, I Want To Hold Your Hand, All My Loving, She Loves You
CD2: Intro/ Twist And Shout/ She's A Woman/ I Feel Fine/ Dizzy Miss Lizzy/ Ticket To Ride/ Everybody's Trying To Be My Baby/ Can't Buy Me Love/ Baby's In Black/ I Wanna Be Your Man/ A Hard Day's Night/ Help!/ I'm Down/ Intro/ Twist

And Shout/ She's A Woman/ I Feel Fine/ Dizzy Miss Lizzie/ Ticket To Ride/ Everybody's Trying To Be My Baby/ Can't Buy Me Love/ Baby's In Black/ I Wanna Be Your Man/ A Hard Day's Night/ Help!/ I'm Down
R: G. Some G-Vg.   S: CD1 The Ed Sullivan Show. Tracks 1-5 Feb. 9 '64. Tracks 6-11 Feb. 16 '64. Tracks 12-14 Feb. 16 '64. Track 15 Zaal Treslong Studio, Hillgom Dutch TV show 'Beatles In Netherlands'. Track 16 John, Paul, George and sit-in drummer Jimmy Nicol singing along with records on Dutch TV show. CD2 Sam Houston Coliseum, Houston Aug. 19 '65. Tracks 1-13 afternoon show. Tracks 14-25 evening show.
C: Japanese CD. This is one of those releases that makes me ask 'why?' This material has been out before in better quality. The cover is a copy of the Melvin Records vinyl release and the type is so small you can't read it. The songs are misnamed on the discs. Thanks to Belmo for pinning this one down. Time CD1 76:28. CD2 75:46.

CD - THE GET BACK JOURNALS II
VIGOTONE VIGO138-145
CD1: Sun King/ Improvisation/ All Things Must Pass/ All Things Must Pass/ All Things Must Pass/ All Things Must Pass/ All Things Must Pass/ All Things Must Pass/ Improvisation/ All Things Must Pass/ All Things Must Pass/ All Things Must Pass/ All Things Must Pass/ All Things Must Pass/ Unknown/ Back In The USSR/ Every Little Thing/ Piece Of My Heart/ Sabre Dance/ Piece Of My Heart/ Over And Over Again/ I've Been Good To You/ Maxwell's Silver Hammer/ I Want You/ I'm Gonna Pay For His Ride/ Don't Let Me Down/ Oh! Darling/ C'mon Marianne/ I've Got A Feeling/ I've Got A Feeling/ High School Confidential/ I've Got A Feeling/ Hear Me Lord/ Hear Me Lord/ Improvisation/ Tracks Of My Tears/ Dizzy Miss Lizzy/ Money (That's What I Want)/ Fools Like Me/ Sure To Fall/ Right String, Wrong Yo-Yo/ I'm Talking About You
C: Features a great deal of previously unheard 'All Things Must Pass' rehearsals, which includes George's 'you're so full of shit' comment to Paul (which is clearly not the 'punky put on' that Beatles' history has painted it to be). Certainly the highlight of this disc is a lengthy oldies jam session from January 6th, featuring never-before-heard performances of 'Sure To Fall' and 'Right String, Wrong Yo-Yo'. Time 73:38.
CD2: Live Show Dialogue/ Don't Let Me Down/ Don't Let Me Down/ Don't Let Me Down/ Don't Let Me Down/ Don't Let Me Down/ Don't Let Me Down/ Don't Let Me Down/ Don't Let Me Down/ Don't Let Me Down/ Don't Let Me Down/ Don't Let Me Down/ Don't Let Me Down/ Don't Let Me Down/ Don't Let Me Down/ Don't Let Me Down / Send Me Some Lovin'/ Don't Let Me Down/ Don't Let Me Down/ Two Of Us/ Two Of Us/ Two Of Us/ Two of Us/ Two of Us/ Two of Us
C: Fragments of a lengthy conversation about the planned live performance which clearly illustrate how Yoko had usurped John's role in the decision

making process of the group. This is followed by an incredibly extensive look at the evolution of 'Don't Let Me Down', with over forty minutes of rehearsal presented in their original context for the first time. Capping off the disc is an unedited presentation of the 'fight' between Paul and George, which was presented in a distorted manner in the film 'Let It Be'. Time 70:74.

CD3: Frere Jaques/ It Ain't Me Babe/ Hear Me Lord/ Hear Me Lord/ Hear Me Lord/ Let's Dance/ All Things Must Pass/ She Came In Through The Bathroom Window/ Carry That Weight/ The Long And Winding Road/ Golden Slumbers/ Carry That Weight/ The Long And Winding Road/ Instrumental/ Instrumental/ Lady Madonna/ Instrumental)/ She Came In Through The Bathroom Window/ Improvisation/ Instrumental/ Mr. Epstein Said It Was White Gold/ Lowdown Blues Machine/ What'd I Say/ Carry That Weight / Shout!/ Get Back/ I've Got Rings On My Fingers/ For You Blue/ For You Blue/ My Back Pages/ I've Got A Feeling/ She Came In Through The Bathroom Window/ Stuck Inside Of Mobile With The Memphis Blues Again/ Improvisation

C: Contains a number of interesting items, including a lengthy McCartney piano session. The unquestionable highlight, though, is the earliest known performance of 'Get Back', presented here for the very first time. Much of the explosive dialog from January 7th is also here. Time 73:05.

CD4: I Shall Be Released/ To Kingdom Come/ For You Blue/ For You Blue/ Improvisation/ Bo Diddley/ What the World Needs Now Is Love/ Instrumental/ First Call/ She Came In Through The Bathroom Window/ I've Got A Feeling/ Oh! Darling/ The Long And Winding Road/ Maxwell's Silver Hammer/ Maxwell's Silver Hammer/ Maxwell's Silver Hammer/ Maxwell's Silver Hammer/ Maxwell's Silver Hammer/ Maxwell's Silver Hammer/ Rule Britannia/ Improvisation/ Improvisation/ Speak To Me/ Oh! Darling/ Maxwell's Silver Hammer/ Maxwell's Silver Hammer

C: Completion of the January 7th debate over the fate of the live performance and, in fact, The Beatles as a group, George suggests that perhaps 'a divorce' is in order. The mood lightens as the group spends a great deal of time rehearsing 'Maxwell's Silver Hammer'. Time 70:58.

CD5: Improvisation/ A Shot of Rhythm And Blues/ (You're So Square) Baby I Don't Care/ Across The Universe/ Across The Universe/ Across The Universe/ Give Me Some Truth/ improvisation/ Across The Universe/ Across The Universe/ Improvisation/ Across The Universe/ A Case Of The Blues/ Cuddle Up/ Give Me Some Truth/ Across The Universe/ Give Me Some Truth/ From Me To You/ Across The Universe/ Across The Universe/ Rock and Roll Music/ Lucille/ Lotta Lovin'/ Across The Universe/ Gone Gone Gone/ Dig A Pony/ One After 909/ One After 909/ One After 909/ One After 909/ What'd I Say/ One After 909/ Improvisation/ Don't Let Me Down/ Don't Let Me Down/ Don't Let Me Down/ Don't Let Me

Down/ Don't Let Me Down/ Devil In Her Heart/ Devil In Her Heart/ Don't Let Me Down/ School Day/ F.B.I./ She Came In Through The Bathroom Window/ Improvisations/ Honey Hush/ Honey Hush/ Stand By Me/ Hare Krishna Mantra/ 'Well, If You're Ready'/ Hare Krishna Mantra

C: Concludes a very extensive overview of the January 7th session contained on this set (nearly three hours worth). John's attempts to lead the band through rehearsals of 'Across The Universe' prove disastrous, and the group only comes to life when they perform oldies such as 'Rock And Roll Music'. Time 70:36.

CD6: Two Of Us/ You Got Me Going/ Twist And Shout/ Don't Let Me Down/ I've Got A Feeling/ St. Louis Blues/ One After 909/ Too Bad About Sorrows/ Just Fun/ She Said, She Said/ All Things Must Pass/ Improvisation/ All Things Must Pass/ All Things Must Pass/ All Things Must Pass/ All Things Must Pass/ All Things Must Pass/ All Things Must Pass/ All Things Must Pass/ All Things Must Pass/ All Along The Watchtower/ Mean Mr. Mustard/ Don't Let Me Down/ All Things Must Pass/ Fools Like Me/ You Win Again/ Improvisation/ She Came In Through The Bathroom Window/ I Me Mine/ I Me Mine/ How Do You Think I Feel/ The Ballad Of Bonnie And Clyde/ Hello Muddah, Hello Fadduh!/ I Me Mine/ I Me Mine/ I Me Mine/ I Me Mine/ Almost Grown/ What Am I Livin' For?/ Rock And Roll Music/ I Me Mine/ I Me Mine/ I Me Mine/ I Me Mine/ Another Day/ For You Blue/ For You Blue

C: Focuses primarily on the January 8th sessions, featuring the best group performance of 'All Things Must Pass'. The two group performances of 'I Me Mine' which were edited together in 'Let It Be' are heard in their original form here. Also of note is the earliest known performance of Paul's 'Another Day'. Time 71:22.

CD7: For You Blue/ Improvisation/ Two Of Us/ Two Of Us/ Two Of Us/ Two Of Us/ Two Of Us/ Unknown)/ Two Of Us/ I've Got A Feeling/ One After 909/ One After 909/ She Came In Through The Bathroom Window/ She Came In Through The Bathroom Window/ She Came In Through The Bathroom Window/ She Came In Through The Bathroom Window/ Right String, Wrong Yo-Yo/ Boogie Woogie/ Baa, Baa, Blacksheep/ Mr. Bassman/ Get Back/ Instrumental/ La Penina/ Instrumental/ Across The Universe/ Across The Universe/ Across The Universe/ Across The Universe/ Across The Universe/ Across The Universe/ Teddy Boy/ Junk/ Across The Universe/ Across The Universe/ Shakin' In The Sixties/ Move It/ Good Rockin' Tonight/ Let It Be/ Let It Be/ Let It Be/ That'll Be The Day/ I've Got A Feeling/ Jenny Jenny/ Slippin' And Slidin'/ Let It Be/ Let It Be/ Let It Be

C: Chronicles the January 9th session, including rehearsals of 'Two Of Us', 'She Came In Through the Bathroom Window', 'Across The Universe' and 'Let It Be'. Note Paul's sly comment on 'oriental influence' that which he wishes wasn't present. Time 72:25.

CD8: I'm Talking About You/ A Quick One While

He's Away/ A Quick One While He's Away/ Improvisation/ improvisation/ Till There Was You/ Maxwell's Silver Hammer/ Mack The Knife/ Maxwell's Silver Hammer/ Maxwell's Silver Hammer/ Don't Be Cruel/ On a Sunny Island, Brazil, Groovin', I Got Stung/ Brazil/ It's Only Make Believe/ Through A London Window/ The Long And Winding Road/ Instrumental/ Martha My Dear/ Get Back/ Instrumental/ The Back Seat of My Car/ Improvisation/ It's Just For You/ It's Just For You/ As Clear As A Bell Says La Scala, Milan/ Hello Dolly/ Madman/ Mean Mr. Mustard, Madman/ Watching Rainbows/ Improvisation/ Improvisation/ Oh! Darling/ Ob-La-Di, Ob-La-Da
C: Begins with George's dramatic post-lunch departure from the group, on Jan. 10 and the other Beatles surprising reaction (or virtual non-reaction) to it. The remainder of the disc contains a number of George-less performances of varying degrees of interest (if not musical quality). Time 72:10.
R: Ex. Soundboard.   C: Four double CDs in a white cardboard box inside a full color cardboard slipcase. Comes with a 28 page 10" x 10" book with colour and B&w pictures. Includes a history of 'Get Back' bootlegs article which can be found reprinted on pages 15-18 of this Supplement. This set is an excellent example of what can be done by people who care as opposed to some of the boring 'product' released by an 'industry' interested in the bottom line. When will they realise that this is what collector's want and that they don't mind paying for quality.

CD - IN CASE YOU DON'T KNOW
SPANK SP 110
Kansas City, Hey-Hey-Hey! (undubbed)/ She Loves You/ Twist And Shout/ I Saw Her Standing There/ Long Tall Sally/ Introduction/ Roll Over Beethoven/ From Me To You/ I Saw Her Standing There/ This Boy/ All My Loving/ I Wanna Be Your Man/ Please Please Me/ Till There Was You/ She Loves You/ I Want To Hold Your Hand/ Twist And Shout (incomplete)/ Kansas City, Hey-Hey-Hey!/ I'm A Loser/ Boys/ Closing Theme
R: Tracks 1-5 Ex. Soundboard. Tracks 6-21 G-Vg. Soundboard. Lots of screaming.   S: Track 1 'Shindig' Oct. 3 '64. Tracks 2-5 'Drop In' Oct. 30 '63. Tracks 6-17 Washington Coliseum Feb. 11 '64. Tracks 18-21 'Shindig' Oct. 3 '64.
C: Japanese CD. Dcc. Time 52:19.

CD - JAMMING WITH HEATHER
BECAUSE BECD 001
Two Of Us (4:33)/ I've Told You Before, Get Out Of My Door (8:15)/ I've Got A Feeling (4:04)/ Don't Let Me Down (4:09)/ All Things Must Pass (3:33)/ Bathroom Window (with false start) (4:01)/ Take This Hammer, Long Lost John, Daddy Where You Been So Long, Run For Your Life (8:48)/ I've Got A Feeling, Hear Me Lord, Carry That Weight, Long Instrumental, Louie Louie, My Imagination (15:51)
R: Ex. Soundboard.   S: Tracks 1-7 Apple

Studios Jan. '69. Tracks 8 Twickenham Studios Jan. '69.   C: Japanese CD. Dcc.

CD - JIMMY NICOL AND THE BEATLES
DESPERADO RECORDS DP1
Abbey Road Rehearsal/ Pathe News (Arrival In Amsterdam)/ She Loves You/ All My Loving/ Twist And Shout/ Roll Over Beethoven/ Long Tall Sally/ Can't Buy Me Love/ I Want To Hold Your Hand/ All My Loving/ She Loves You/ Till There Was You/ Roll Over Beethoven/ Can't Buy Me Love/ This Boy/ Thanks To Jimmy/ Twist And Shout/ Extract From Interview 5/6/64/ I Saw Her Standing There/ I Saw Here Standing There/ I Want To Hold Your Hand/ All My Loving/ She Loves You/ I Saw Her Standing There/ 5 other tracks
S: Tracks 1-2 from a news film. Tracks 3-8, 18 Ropack TV, Holland. Tracks 9-17 Copenhagen. All other tracks from TV & radio.

CD - JOHN, PAUL, GEORGE AND STU - LIVERPOOL 1960
FU 207
I'll Follow The Sun (first version) (1:47)/ Long Rambling Blues (7:30)/ Blues & Roll Expectations (instrumental jam) (11:47)/ Hallelujah, I Love Her So (2:32)/ That's Not A Banjo, It's Blues Guitar (instrumental jam) (4:49)/ Dreaming Old Mississippi Blues (instrumental jam, some vocal) (7:39)/ Cold As Ice/ Elvis' Nightmare (unreleased) (5:45)/ Oh Pretty Darling (unreleased) (5:42)/ One After 909 (first version) (2:21)/ Brown-Eyed Handsome Man (instrumental jam) (3:43)/ Screaming Guitar Blues (instrumental jam) (11:28)/ Shuffle Boogie Blues (instrumental jam) (17:11)/ Won't You Try (unreleased) (1:46)
R: G.   S: Paul's house, Liverpool '60.
C: ECD. Dcc.

CD - THE LONG AND WINDING ROAD
BOYS 001/7
CD1: I Want To Hold Your Hand (2:56)/ I Saw Her Standing There (2:58)/ Anna (3:02)/ Don't Bother Me (2:18)/ It Won't Be Long (2:32)/ Please Please Me (2:07)/ Ask Me Why (2:19)/ A Taste Of Honey (2:04)/ There's A Place (2:12)/ Love Me Do (2:21)/ P.S. I Love You (2:07)/ Please Mr. Postman (2:42)/ 'Till There Was You (2:17)/ Boys (2:38)/ Twist And Shout (2:41)/ Baby It's You (2:52)/ Chains (2:11)/ From Me To You (1:53)/ She Loves You (2:32)/ Hold Me Tight (2:44)/ Not A Second Time (2:22)/ Devil In Her Heart (2:32)/ Money (That's What I Want) (2:38)/ Can't Buy Me Love (2:09)/ You Can't Do That (2:42)/ Do You Want To Know A Secret (2:05)/ Thank You Girl (2:25)/ Komm Gib Mir Deine Hand (2:40)/ My Bonnie (2:22)/ Ain't She Sweet (2:09)/ Hello, Little Girl (1:57)/ Three Cool Cats (2:26)
CD2: All My Loving (2:05)/ Little Child (1:55)/ Misery (2:06)/ Any Time At All (2:48)/ A Hard Day's Night (3:23)/ Roll Over Beethoven (2:43)/ When I Get Home (2:31)/ And I Love Her (2:34)/ The Night Before (2:28)/ I Should Have Known Better (2:42)/ This Boy (1:58)/ I'll Get You (2:16)/

Sie Liebt Dich (1:51)/ I'm Happy Just To Dance With You (4:02)/ I'll Cry Instead (2:01)/ If I Feel (2:26)/ Matchbox (1:59)/ Tell Me Why (2:39)/ I Call Your Name (2:25)/ Kansas City - Hey, Hey, Hey, Hey (2:13)/ Mr. Moonlight (2:13)/ Rock & Roll Music (2:48)/ Eight Days A Week (3:10)/ I Don't Want To Spoil The Party (2:47)/ Every Little Thing (2:09)/ Honey Don't (2:59)/ I'm A Loser (2:34)/ I Feel Fine (2:07)/ She's A Woman (3:07)/ Baby's In Black (1:59)/ I'll Follow The Sun (1:52)/ I'm Looking Through You (2:12)
CD3: What You're Doing (2:37)/ Wait (2:11)/ Everybody's Trying To Be My Baby (2:46)/ Dizzy Miss Lizzy (2:30)/ Help! (2:15)/ Another Girl (2:13)/ Tell Me What You See (2:43)/ I'm Down (2:22)/ Ticket To Ride (2:56)/ I Need You (2:35)/ Yes It Is (2:53)/ The Word (2:34)/ Norwegian Wood (This Bird Has Flown) (1:53)/ Drive My Car (2:22)/ No Reply (2:21)/ Think For Yourself (2:25)/ You've Got To Hide Your Love Away (2:13)/ Got To Get You Into My Life (2:18)/ Dr. Robert (2:04)/ And Your Bird Can Sing (2:03)/ You Like Me Too Much (2:38)/ Yesterday (2:07)/ Act Naturally (2:28)/ Girl (2:24)/ You're Gonna Lose That Girl (2:15)/ All My Loving (3:00)/ She Loves You (2:19)/ I Saw Her Standing There (2:38)/ I Want To Hold Your Hand (2:38)/ Please Please Me (1:57)/ Twist And Shout (2:13)/ Long Tall Sally (2:06)/ Things We Said Today (2:15)
CD4: Can't Buy Me Love (2:39)/ Boys (2:02)/ A Hard Day's Night (5:52)/ And I Love Her (2:42)/ I Should Have Known Better (2:38)/ If I Feel (2:08)/ You Can't Do That (2:27)/ Run For Your Life (2:22)/ You Won't See Me (3:33)/ Michelle (2:29)/ Taxman (2:56)/ Paperback Writer (3:22)/ Rain (3:11)/ I'm Only Sleeping (3:21)/ If I Needed Someone (2:33)/ Good Day Sunshine (2:06)/ I've Just Seen A Face (1:50)/ She Said She Said (2:23)/ Things We Said Today (3:06)/ We Can Work It Out (3:06)/ Day Tripper (2:43)/ I Want To Tell You (2:06)/ Tomorrow Never Knows (3:11)/ Eleanor Rigby (2:04)/ In My Life (2:30)/ Here There And Everywhere (2:20)/ Nowhere Man (2:39)/ Sgt. Pepper's Lonely Hearts Club Band (2:18)/ With A Little Help From My Friends (2:50)
CD5: Getting Better (2:53)/ Lucy In The Sky With Diamonds (3:46)/ Fixing A Hole (2:41)/ She's Leaving Home (3:50)/ Being For The Benefit Of Mr. Kite (3:00)/ When I'm Sixty-Four (3:16)/ Lovely Rita (2:54)/ Good Morning, Good Morning (2:47)/ Sgt. Pepper's Lonely Hearts Club Band (Reprise) (1:50)/ A Day In The Life (5:08)/ Magical Mystery Tour (2:44)/ The Fool On The Hill (3:01)/ Your Mother Should Know (2:24)/ I Am The Walrus (4:30)/ Hello Goodbye (3:34)/ All You Need Is Love (3:29)/ Baby You're A Rich Man (2:43)/ Strawberry Fields Forever (4:03)/ Penny Lane (3:17)/ The Inner Light (2:17)/ Lady Madonna (2:34)/ Back In The U.S.S.R. (2:54)/ Dear Prudence (3:49)/ The Continuing Story Of Bungalow Bill (3:02)
CD6: Ob-La-Di Ob-La Da (3:24)/ While My Guitar Gently Weeps (4:26)/ Martha My Dear (2:23)/ Rocky Raccoon (3:30)/ I'm So Tired (2:03)/

Birthday (2:40)/ I Will (1:57)/ Sexy Sadie (2:54)/ Blackbird (2:27)/ Revolution (3:40)/ Julia (2:51)/ Cry Baby Cry (2:54)/ Long, Long, Long (3:06)/ Hey Jude (7:17)/ Yellow Submarine (3:46)/ All Together Now (2:06)/ Come Together (4:06)/ Something (3:09)/ Oh Darling (3:22)/ Octopus's Garden (3:16)/ Here Comes The Sun (3:33)/ Medley Til' The End (9:49)
CD7: Give Piece A Chance (4:44)/ My Sweet Lord (4:13)/ It Don't Come Easy (3:02)/ Maybe I'm Amazed (3:36)/ Instant Karma (We All Shine On) (3:14)/ What Is Life (3:55)/ Photograph (3:46)/ Another Day (4:02)/ Power To The People (2:45)/ Hi, Hi, Hi (2:49)/ You're Sixteen (2:26)/ Let It Be (3:39)/ Across The Universe (3:30)/ For You Blue (2:25)/ Ballad Of John & Yoko (3:13)/ Imagine (2:57)/ Live And Let Die (3:05)/ Don't Let Me Down (3:37)/ Get Back (3:05)/ Whatever Gets You Through The Night (3:07)/ Band On The Run (4:45)/ The Long And Winding Road (3:35)
S: The only source information is: 'Unreleased Tracks, Alternate Mixes, And A Number Of Incredible Rare Recordings Never Published Before, In Various Location '64/'70'. That pins it down. While it may indeed contain all of this, some material appears to be from official releases and takes this set from being a boot to being a pirate. One interesting thing about this set is that a lot of the songs have an intro clip from interviews with The Beatles, Pete Best, Brian Epstein, George Martin and others.   C: ECD. Box set. Photo book. Pic CDs.

CD - THE LOST PEPPERLAND REEL
VIGOTONE VIGO 132
THE LOST REEL: All Versions In Mono From Master Tape: All You Need Is Love (early mix with extended fade) (4:31)/ Lucy In The Sky With Diamonds (version with Boob singing opening line) (3:36)/ Good Morning Animal Noises (1:39)/ Intro Sgt. Pepper (crowd noise only) (0:55)/ Billy Shears Applause (0:36)/ Yellow Submarine (2:44)/ Its All too Much (complete long version) (8:16)/ All Together Now (2:15)/ Only A Northern Song (3:27)/ RARITIES: Hey Bulldog (mono version) (3:04)/ Mellotron Music No. 4 (Lennon sound experiment July '68) (1:47)/ Penny Lane Overdub Session (EMI Studio 2 Nov. 9 '67) (6:32)/ Good Morning, Good Morning (Lennon home demo late Jan. '67) (1:04)/ Breakdown (John and Ringo from Pepper Session) (1:46)/ She Can Talk To Me 1 (Lennon Home Demo Mar. '68) (1:22)/ She Can Talk To Me 2 (Lennon Home Demo Mar. '68) (1:54)/ Across The Universe (Lennon Home Demo Mar. '68) (1:30)/ You Know My Name (Lennon Home Demo Mar. '68) (2:46)/ Chi Chi S (John and Ringo '68?) (3:09)/ Mellotron Music No. 5 (Lennon sound experiment July '68) (1:44)
R: Tracks 1-11 Ex. Soundboard. Tracks 11-20 G-Vg. Some G.   C: Dcc. Pic CD.

CD - POLLWINNERS GO TO BLACKPOOL
M-BEAT MUSIC MBCD 001
Introduction By Jimmy Saville And Murray The K/

She Loves You/ You Can't Do That/ Twist And Shout/ Long Tall Sally/ Can't Buy Me Love/ I Feel Fine/ She's A Woman/ Baby's In Black/ Ticket To Ride/ Long Tall Sally/ Oh I Do Like To Be Beside The Seaside/ I Feel Fine/ I'm Down/ Act Naturally/ Ticket To Ride/ Yesterday/ Help/ She Loves You/ Moonlight Bay/ Twist And Shout/ Roll Over Beethoven/ I Wanna Be Your Man/ Long Tall Sally/ Medley: Love Me Do, Please Please Me, From Me To You, She Loves You, I Want To Hold Your Hand/ Can't Buy Me Love/ Shout
R: Tracks 1-6 G-Vg. Soundboard. Tracks 7-11 Poor. Audience. A bit fast. Tracks 12-18 G. Soundboard. Track 19 G. Soundboard. Track 20 G-Vg. Soundboard. Tracks 21-27 Vg. Soundboard.   S: Tracks 1-6 NME Pollwinners Concert, Empire Pool, Wembley Apr. 26 '64. Tracks 7-11 NME Pollwinners Concert, Empire Pool, Wembley Apr. 11 '65. Tracks 12-18 Blackpool Night Out, Arc Theatre, Blackpool Aug. 1 '65. Track 19 Little Theatre, Southport Aug. 27 '63. Track 20 Morecombe And Wise Show Dec. 2 '63. Tracks 21-27 Around The Beatles recording session Apr. 19 '64 before the audience was added.   C: ECD. Dcc. Time 68:51.

CD - ROCKIN' MOVIE STARS VOL. 1
ORANGE 003
Discussion/ I've Got A Feeling/ Maxwell's Silver Hammer/ Maxwell's Silver Hammer 2/ A Shot Of Rhythm And Blues Baby, I Don't Care, Across The Universe Rehearsal/ Don't Let Me Down, Devil In Her Heart, Don't Let Me Down/ Thirty Days, Be Bop A Lula, Whole Lotta Lovin'/ Jam/ Money/ Talkin' Bout You
R: Ex. Soundboard.   S: 'Let It Be' sessions.
C: ECD. Dcc. Time 72:49.

CD - ROCKIN' MOVIE STARS VOL. 2
ORANGE 004
Dialogue/ Don't Let Me Down/ Gimme Some Truth, God/ Maxwell's Silver Hammer, I Want You, Jam/ Don't Bring Me Down, Hear Me Lord, Don't Let Me Down/ Frere Jacque, It Ain't Me Babe, Hear Me Lord/ Let's Dance/ All Things Must Pass/ She Came Through The Bathroom Window/ Long And Winding Road, Golden, Slumbers/ Carry That Weight, The Castle Of The King Of The Birds/ Lady Madonna/ Child Of Nature, I Shall Be Released, Speak To Me/ Well Alright, Two Of Us/ Piano Solo/ I'm So Tired, Obla Di Obla Da
R: Ex. Soundboard.   S: 'Let It Be' sessions.
C: ECD. Dcc. Time 70:30.

CD - ROCKIN' MOVIE STARS VOL. 3
ORANGE 007
Paul On Piano: Death Cab For Cutie, Martha My Dear, San Francisco Blues, Oh Baby, I Need You/ More Early Morning Piano: The Day I Went Back To School, Woman/ Dialogue: About Making A Film With A Script/ Peter Sellers Arrives, Conversation/ More Peter Sellers/ More Dialogue
R: Ex. Soundboard.   S: 'Let It Be' sessions.
C: ECD. Dcc. Time 72:15.

CD - ROCKIN' MOVIE STARS VOL. 4
ORANGE 008
Two Of Us (Various Versions)/ I've Got A Felling (Various Versions)/ Madman/ Mean Mr. Mustard, Madman/ Watching Rainbows/ Jam #1/ Jam #2/ Oh Darling, Obla Di Obla Da/ Maxwell's Silver Hammer/ Don't Be Cruel, Costa Del Sol, Groovin', My One And Only Prayer, Through A London Window
R: Ex. Soundboard.   S: 'Let It Be' sessions.
C: ECD. Dcc. Time 60:46.

CD - ROCKIN' MOVIE STARS VOL. 5
ORANGE 009
Let It Down, Browneyed Handsome Man, I've Got A Feeling, Jam Plus Tuning Guitars, Child Of Nature/ I Shall Be Released, Don't Let Me Down/ Don't Let Me Down, Go Johnny Go, I've Got A Feeling/ Speak To Me, I've Got A Feeling/ Long And Winding Road, Golden Slumbers, Carry That Weight, Long And Winding Road, The Castle Of The King Of The Birds, Lady Madonna/ Across The Universe, Rock And Roll Music
R: Ex. Soundboard.   S: 'Let It Be' sessions.
C: ECD. Dcc. Time 62:08.

CD - ROCKIN' MOVIE STARS VOL. 6
ORANGE 010
Don't Let Me Down/ Two Of Us (Paul and George Conflict)/ Two Of Us/ Hear Me Lord, Carry That Weight/ She Came In Through The Bathroom Window/ White Gold/ Dialogue: Communications And Discipline/ For You Blue, Dialogue, What The World Needs Now/ I've Got A Feeling/ Oh Darling, Maxwell's Silver Hammer, Rule Britannia, Maxwell's Silver Hammer
R: Ex. Soundboard.   S: 'Let It Be' sessions.
C: ECD. Dcc. Time 71.57.

CD - ROCKIN' MOVIE STARS VOL. 7
ORANGE 011
Warming Up Jam/ Two Of Us/ Let It Be/ That'll Be The Day/ Jenny Jenny Jenny, Slippin' And Slidin'/ Let It Be ('God Bless You' version)/ Long And Winding Road/ Piano Theme/ Martha My Dear, John John/ Another Day, Two Of Us
R: Ex. Soundboard.   S: 'Let It Be' sessions.
C: ECD. Dcc. Time 57:08.

CD - ROCKIN' MOVIE STARS VOL. 8
ORANGE 012
All Along The Watchtower, Domino/ I Me Mine/ Almost Grown, Nobody Else Will Do, Rock And Roll Music/ I Me Mine/ Two Of Us, Ba Ba Black Sheep/ Don't Let Me Down/ Suzy's Parlour/ I've Got A Feeling/ Bathroom Window, Be Bop A Lula/ Get Back (No Pakistani's)/ La Penina/ Across The Universe/ Shakin' In The Sixties, Come On Everybody, Good Rockin' Tonight/ Tennessee
R: Ex. Soundboard.   S: 'Let It Be' sessions.
C: ECD. Dcc. Time 64:23.

CD - SHEA! / CANDLESTICK PARK
SPANK SP-109
Introduction/ Twist And Shout/ I Feel Fine/ Dizzy
Miss Lizzy/ Ticket To Ride/ Can't Buy Me Love/
Baby's In Black/ A Hard Day's Night/ Help!/ I'm
Down/ Rock And Roll Music/ She's A Woman/ If I
Needed Someone/ Day Tripper/ Baby's In Black/ I
Feel Fine/ Yesterday/ I Wanna Be Your Man/
Nowhere Man/ Paperback Writer/ Long Tall Sally
(incomplete)
R: G-Vg. Soundboard.   S: Tracks 1-10 Shea
Stadium, NYC Aug. 15 '65. Tracks 11-21
Candlestick Park, San Francisco Aug. 29 '66.
C: Japanese CD. Dcc. Pic CD. Time 53:24.

CD - STRAWBERRY FIELDS FOREVER
FAB 4 RECORDS FAB 5555
Strawberry Fields Forever #1/ Strawberry Fields
Forever #2/ Strawberry Fields Forever #3/
Strawberry Fields Forever #4/ Strawberry Fields
Forever #5/ Strawberry Fields Forever #6/
Strawberry Fields Forever #7/ Strawberry Fields
Forever #8/ Strawberry Fields Forever #9/ The
Bus (unreleased instrumental from 'Magical
Mystery Tour')/ The Fool On The Hill (original
demo)/ All You Need Is Love ('Our World' TV spe-
cial)/ Tea Room Music (impromptu jam from
'David Frost Show')/ Hey Jude (live from 'David
Frost Show')/ I Am The Walrus (basic track and
vocals only)/ Spiritual Regeneration (India '67)/
Yer Blues (acappela Lennon and Jagger)/ What's
The New Mary Jane? (original mix)/ It's All Too
Much (not 'Piece Of Mind' as listed on cover)/ The
Barber Of Seville (vocals by John, Paul, George
and Ringo)
R: Vg-Ex. Some G.   C: Japanese CD. Dcc.
Time 66:02.

CD - SWEETEST APPLES 1966-69
MAMBO SUN MS-39436-ABP
Helter Skelter (mono mix Sept. 9 '68) (3:37)/
Magical Mystery Tour (film version) (1:36)/
Strawberry Fields Forever (EMI mix Dec. 12 '66)
(3:26)/ Glass Onion (early mix with different
instrumental sections) (2:52)/ Aerial Tour (instru-
mental - mono mix Sept. 8 '67) (2:07)/ Blue Jay
Way (overdub session Oct. 6 '67) (3:43)/ A Day In
The Life (EMI take 5 Jan. 20 '67) (4:22)/ Across
The Universe (mono mix Aug. 2 '68) (3:46)/ Dear
Prudence (alternate take Aug. 28 '68) (3:45)/
While My Guitar Gently Weeps (EMI take 1 July
25 '68) (3:18)/ Child Of Nature (Esher Demo May
'68) (2:34)/ While My Guitar Weeps (Esher Demo
May '68) (2:34)/ Something (Apple Studios July
11 '69 - different vocals, extended jam) (5:28)/ Let
It Be (early rehearsal, Twickenham Studios Jan
'69) (2:51)/ The Long And Winding Road (take 2
Feb. 8 '68) (3:38)/ Child Of Nature ('Let It Be' out-
take, Twickenham Studios Jan. '69) (1:50)/ Old
Brown Shoe (rehearsal, Twickenham Studios Jan.
'69) (2:59)/ Get Back (up tempo version,
Twickenham Studios Jan. '69) (2:11)/
Commonwealth (Twickenham Studios rehearsal
Jan. '69) (3:58)/ No Pakistanis (Apple Studios

Jan. 23 '69) (3:53)/ I've Got A Feeling (heavy ver-
sion Jan. 22 '69) (2:48)/ I Lost My Little Girl
(Twickenham Studios Jan. '69) (4:07)/ Watching
Rainbows (Twickenham Studios Jan. '69) (4:08)/
All Things Must Pass (Twickenham Studios Jan.
'69) (3:08)
R: Vg-Ex. Some G-Vg.   C: Japanese CD. Dcc.
Pic CD.

CD - UNPLUGGED
INVASION UNLIMITED IU 9541-1
CD1: Cry Baby Cry/ Child Of Nature/ The
Continuing Story Of Bungalow Bill/ I'm So Tired/
Yer Blues/ Everybody's Got Something To Hide
Except Me/ And My Monkey/ What's The New
Mary Jane/ Revolution/ While My Guitar Gently
Weeps/ Circles/ Sour Milk Sea/ Not Guilty/
Piggies
CD2: Julia/ Blackbird/ Rocky Raccoon/ Back In
The USSR/ Honey Pie/ Mother Nature's Son/ Ob-
La-Di, Ob-La-Da/ Junk/ Dear Prudence/ Sexy
Sadie/ Helter Skelter/ Spiritual Regeneration/
Rishikesh No.9
S: Acoustic outtakes.   C: ECD.

CD - THE WORLD'S BEST - NEW REMASTER
EDITION
FAB GEAR CPSC 9401
I Want To Hold Your Hand (alternate stereo ver-
sion)/ She Loves You (simulated stereo version)/
From Me To You (original stereo mix)/ All My
Loving (five counts hi-hat opening stereo version)/
A Hard Days Night (US single mono mix)/ I
Should Have Known Better (alternate stereo
remix)/ And I Love Her (unedited stereo long ver-
sion, guitar riff repeated six times at the end)/ I
Feel Fine (alternate stereo mix, whispering before
intro)/ Ticket To Ride (short edit stereo version)/
Help! (US Capitol stereo version, 'James Bond'
intro)/ Yesterday (US Capitol mono mix)/ We Can
Work It Out (alternate stereo mix, different mix of
organ)/ Day Tripper (alternate stereo mix)/
Norwegian Wood (alternate stereo remix)/ Girl
(alternate stereo remix, vocal track moved center)/ Here There And Everywhere (alternate
stereo remix)/ Strawberry Fields Forever (alternate stereo version, sound effects and ending
remixed)/ Penny Lane (trumpet ending stereo version, Capitol promo single)/ I Am The Walrus
(alternate stereo mix, six beats intro and extra
beats after third verse)/ Hey Jude (short edit version)/ Revolution (original stereo mix)/ Across The
Universe (original mono mix from Brazilian single)/ Ballad Of John And Yoko (single mono mix,
Australian single)/ Let It Be (mono version,
Japanese single)/ Beatles Movie Medley (single
stereo version, promo remix)
R: Ex.   S: Collection of Beatles rarities.
C: Japanese CD. Dcc. Pic CD. Time 74:32.

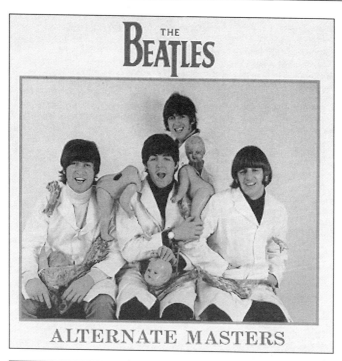

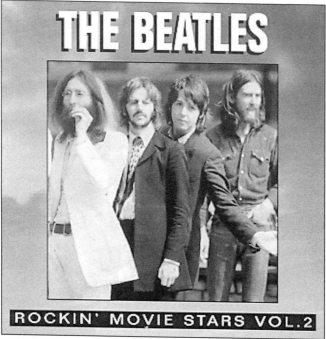

BECK

CD - SUICIDAL JERK
KTS OF AUSTRALIA 004 A
Suicidal Jerk/ Phew/ Fuckin' With My Head/
Disappear/ Stop Joking Around/ Corvette
Bummer/ Whiskey Clone, Hotel City 1997/
Asshole/ I Get Lonesome/ 1 Foot In The Grave/
Loser/ Glove/ Maximum Possession/ Wake Up/ All
The Way/ Homophobic/ Mother Fucker/ Power Of
Value
S: Oct. 28 '94.   C: Australian CD.

CD - TOTAL PARANOIA
CRACKER CR-15
Corvette/ Colour/ F...kin With My Head (Mountain
Dew Rock)/ Mutherf..er/ Few/ Pay No Mind
(Snoozer)/ Burnt Orange Peel/ Unknown/ It's Not
Easy/ Monkey See/ Go For Land/ One Foot In
The Grave/ Now I'm Breakin' Die/ Blues By
Myself/ Looser/ From My Brain/ Blackhole/
Beercan
R: Vg. Audience.   S: First Avenue Club,
Minneapolis June 26 '94.   C: Japanese CD.
Time 72:26.

BECK, JEFF

CD - ACADEMY OF MUSIC 1971
M-9503
Max's Piano, Going Down/ Ice Cream Cakes/
Tonight I'll Be Staying Here With You/ Jeff's
Boogie/ Jody/ Morning Dew/ I Ain't Superstitious/
New Ways Train Train/ Got The Feeling/ Situation
R: Poor-G. Audience.   S: Academy Of Music,
NY Nov. 6 '71.   C: Japanese CD. Dcc. 72:34.

CD - BLUE WIND
OFF BEAT RECORDS XXCD 22
Star Cycle/ El Becko/ Too Much To Lose/ The
Pump/ Cause We're Ended As Lovers/ Space
Boogie/ Led Boots/ Diamond Dust/ Air Blower,
Drum Solo, Scatterbrain/ Blue Wind
R: Vg.   S: Green Dome, Sapporo, Japan Dec.
14 '80.   C: Japanese CD.

CD - DEFINITELY MAYBE
IMPROVISATION LABEL IL-366811
Constipated Duck/ She's A Woman/ Freeway
Jam/ Definitely Maybe/ Superstition/ Air Blower/
Cause We've Ended As Lovers/ Jeff's Boogie/
Jeff's Jam 1/ Got The Feeling/ You Know What I
Mean/ Diamond Dust/ Jeff's Jam 2
R: Audience recording.   S: First show, O'Keefe
Center, Toronto, Canada July 23 '75.

CD - LED BOOTS
FILL IN FI-941001
Blue Wind/ Goodbye Pork Pie Hat/ Going Down/
Star Cycle/ El Becko/ Too Much To Lose/ The
Pump/ Cause We've Ended as Lovers/ Space
Boogie/ Led Boots
R: Poor sound.   S: Hammersmith Odeon,
London Mar. 10 '81.

CD - LED BOOTSLEG
TARANTURA TJB-001
Come Dancing/ Goodbye Pork Hat/ Sophia/ Play
With Me/ Led Boots/ Head For Backstage Pass/
Love Is Green/ Blue Wind
S: 'Wired' outtakes.   C: Japanese CD.

CD - SCATTERBRAIN
IMPROVISATION LABEL IL-366816
Constipated Duck/ She's A Woman/ Freeway
Jam/ Definitely Jam/ Superstition/ Air Blower/
Cause We've Ended As Lovers/ Freezer/ Got The
Feeling/ Thelonius, You Know What I Mean
R: G-Vg analogue recording.   S: Ken Taikukan,
Nagoya, Japan Aug. 5 '75.

CD - SHE'S A WOMAN
FILL IN FI-941003
Constipated Duck/ She's A Woman/ Freeway
Jam/ Definitely Maybe/ Superstition/ Cause We've
Ended As Lovers/ You Know What I Mean
R: G-Vg audience recording.   S: Aug. 7 '75.

CD - STAR CYCLE 1980
MY PHENIX CO ZA 44
Star Cycle/ El Becko/ Too Much To Lose/ The
Pump/ Cause We've Ended As Lovers/ Led
Boots/ Scatterbrain/ Blue Wind
R: G-Vg. Audience.   S: Yokohama Bunka-
Kaikan, Yokohama, Japan Dec. 16 '80.
C: Japanese CD. Dcc. Time 58:28.

CD - SUPERSTITION
ZA49
Going Down/ Superstition/ Tonight I'll Be Staying
Here With You, People Get Ready/ New Ways,
Train Train/ Definitely Maybe/ Plynth, Shotgun
(includes bass solo)/ Got The Feeling/ Let Me
Love You/ Jeff's Boogie/ Wake Up This Morning
R: G-Vgm. Audience.   S: Civic Center, San
Jones, CA 11/8/72.   C: Japanese CD. 65:04.

CD - WORLD ROCK FESTIVAL 1975
JB-001
She's A Woman/ Free Way Jam/ Definitely
Maybe/ Air Blower/ Superstition/ Cause We've
Ended As Lovers/ You Know What I Mean/
Constipated Duck/ She's A Woman/ Air Blower
R: G-Vg sound.   S: Tracks 1-7, World Rock
Festival, Sapporo, Japan Aug. 3 '75. Tracks 8-10
Nagoya, Japan Aug. 5 '75.

BECK, BOGART AND APPICE

CD - BECK, BOGART, APPICE
TOP/BB-74005D
CD1: Gonna Be Satisfied/ Livin' Alone/ Song For
Lovely Ladies/ Lady/ Jizz Whizz-Morning Dew
CD2: Prayin'/ Superstition/ Your Lovemaker's
Coming Home/ You Shook Me-Rainbow Boogie
R: Poor stereo. Audience recording, hiss.
S: Rainbow Theatre, London Jan. 26 '74.

CD - MAPLE LEAF GARDEN 1973
M 9504
Superstition/ Livin' Alone/ I'm So Proud/ Lady/
Morning Dew (Drum Solo)/ Sweet Sweet
Surrender/ Lose Myself With You (includes Bass
Solo)
R: Poor. Audience.   S: Maple Leaf Garden,
Toronto Apr. 13 '73.   C: Japanese CD.
Time 52:56.

BECK, JEFF WITH JAN HAMMER

CD - FREEWAY JAMMIN' WITH JAN
JB 002/3
CD1: Jammin' With Jan/ You Know What I Mean/
Freeway Jam/ Sophie/ Earth (Still Our Only
Home)/ Diamond Dust/ Full Moon Boogie/ Led
Boots
CD2: Oh, Yeah!*/ The People*/ Darkness, Earth
In Search Of A Sun/ You Know What I Mean/
Scatterbrain/ Freeway Jam/ Earth (Still Our Only
Home)/ Diamond Dust/ Full Moon Boogie/ Blue
Wind
R: CD1 G-Vg. Audience. CD2 Ex. Audience.
S: CD1 Oakland June 5 '76. CD2 Minneapolis
June 26 '76.   C: Japanese CD. Dcc. *Jan
Hammer Group Only. CD1 42:32. CD2 66:18.

BELLY

CD - LIVE AND HUNGRY
KISS THE STONE KTS 459
Full Moon-Empty Heart/ Dusted/ Feed The Tree/
Slow Dog/ Red/ Seal My Fate/ Gepetto/ Now
They'll Sleep/ Superconnected/ Now They'll
Sleep/ Untitled And Unsung/ Seal My Fate/ Feed
The Tree/ Gepetto/ White Belly/ Slow Dog/ Are
You Experienced?/ Acoustic: Untitled And
Unsung/ Judas My Heart/ Red
R: Ex.   S: Tracks 1-9 Glastonbury Festival June
23 '95. Tracks 10-17 London, Mar. 18 '95. Tracks
18-20 Dec. 2 '94.   C: ECD. Dcc. Pic CD.
Time 75:34.

BENATAR, PAT

CD - WE BELONG TO PAT BENATAR
RSM 023
Instrumental/ Heartbreaker/ Live For Love/ One
Love/ Invincible/ Somebody's Baby/ Hit Me With
Your Best Shot/ Everybody Lay Down/ True Love/
Disconnected/ We Belong/ Promises In The Dark/
Hell Is For Children
R: Exs. Soundboard.   S: Electric Ladyland, New
York '93.   C: ECD. Dcc. Time 58:35.

BIG BROTHER AND THE HOLDING COMPANY

SHE'S THE BOSS
DYNAMITE STUDIO DS94J103/104
CD1: Call On Me/ Combination Of The Two/ Blow
My Mind/ Down On Me/ All Is Loneliness/ Road
Block
CD2: Light Is Faster Than Sound/ Bye, Bye Baby/
Comin' Home/ Ball And Chain/ I Know You Rider/

Farewell Song
R: G-Vg audience recording.   S: California Hall,
San Francisco Feb. 16 '67.   C: Japanese CD.

BJORK

CD - BIG TIME HAPPINESS
RISE TWO CD 8736-1J
Human Behavior/ Untitled/ One Day/ Venus As A
Boy/ Come To Me/ The Anchor Song/ Big Time
Sensuality/ Aeroplane/ Big Time Sensuality/
Come To Me/ Benus As A Boy/ Big Time
Sensuality/ Satisfaction/ Big Time Sensuality/
Violently Happy
R: Ex.   S: Tracks 1-6 Manchester Academy
Sept. 14 '93. Track 7 'Smash Hits Party'. Track 8
'Late Night with Jools Holland'. Tracks 9-10 'The
Beat'. Tracks 11,15 'Top Of The Pops'. Track 12
'Dance Energy'. Track 13 'The Brit Awards' with
PJ Harvey. Track 14 Nice, France.

CD - CIRKUS
MOONRAKER 022
Headphones (Dat-Intro)/ Army Of Me/ The
Modern Things/ Human Behavior/ Isobel/ Venus
As A Boy/ Possibly Maybe/ Before You Come
Back/ The Anchor Song/ Hyper Ballad/ Enjoy/ I
Miss You/ Crying/ Violently Happy/ I Dare You/ It's
Oh So Quiet/ Big Time Sensuality
R: Ex. Audience.   S: Circus Tent, Gothenburg,
Sweden Oct. 7 '95.   C: ECD. Dcc. Time 76:32.

CD - UNPLUGGED
SWINDLE SWN 016
Human Behavior (4:18)/ One Day (6:24)/ Come
To Me (3:51)/ Big Time Sensuality (5:09)/
Aeroplane (4:11)/ Like Someone In Love (4:08)/
Crying (4:11)/ The Anchor Song (3:27)/ Violently
Happy (6:22)
R: Exs. Soundboard.   S: MTV Unplugged, New
York Nov. 7 '94.   C: ECD. Dcc. Pic CD.

BLACK CROWES, THE

CD - BLESSED CHLOROFORM
EPL-CD 1000-0055/6
CD1: Hotel Illness (4:33)/ Tied Up And Swallowed
(5:07)/ Could I've Been So Blind (6:35)/ My
Morning Song (13:04)/ Ballard In Urgency (5:18)/
P-25 London/ No Speak No Slave (6:15)/ Wiser
Time (7:28)/ The High Head Blue (4:28)/ A
Conspiracy (5:05)/ Sting Me (5:29)/ Feelin' Alright
(5:17)/ Remedy (6:33)
CD2: Hard To Handle (5:03)/ Bad Luck, Blue
Eyes Goodbye (7:51)/ Non Fiction (4:30)/ Long
Time Gone (10:01)/ Jealous Again (6:49)/ She
Talks To Angels (9:05)/ A Thorn In My Pride
(10:40)/ Black Moon Creeping (7:56)/ Twice As
Hard (4:51)/ Stare It Cold (5:23)
R: Vg. Audience.   S: CD1 The Meanfiddler,
London, England Oct. 31 '94. CD2 Meanfiddler,
London, England Nov. 1 '94.   C: Secret show.
C: ECD. Dcc. Pic CDs. Group advertised as 'A
Blessed Chloroform'.

CD - BLESSED IN CHLOROFORM
RED PHANTOM RPCD 1191
Gone (5:22)/ Hotel Illness (4:19)/ Tied Up And
Swallowed (5:53)/ Could I've Been So Blind
(6:39)/ My Morning Song (13:07)/ Ballad In
Urgency (5:20)/ P25-London (3:46)/ No Speak No
Slave (6:10)/ Wiser Time (7:13)/ High Head Blues
(4:11)/ A Conspiracy (4:54)/ Sting Me (4:55)/
Remedy (6:27)
R: Vg. Audience.   S: Europe '94.   C: ECD.
Dcc. Pic CD.

CD - FROSTBITE JUBILEE
BLY006/7
CD1: Gone/ Twice As Hard/ Hotel Illness/ High
Head Blues/ Morning Song/ Descending/ Non-
Fiction/ Sting Me
CD2: Black Moon/ P-25 London/ Hard To Handle/
Jealous Again/ Seein' Things/ Wiser Time/ Mellow
Down/ Remedy
R: Ex audience recording.   S: '1st Avenue',
Minneapolis '94.

CD - THE HALLOWEEN SECRET
TEDDY BEAR TB 81
Gone (5:35)/ Hotel Illness (4:13)/ Tied Up And
Swallowed (5:33)/ Been So Blind (5:50)/ Ballad In
Urgency (5:48)/ P.25 London (4:14)/ No Speak No
Slave (5:28)/ Wiser Time (8:00)/ The High Head
Blues (4:30)/ Conspiracy (5:20)/ Sting Me (4:38)/
Feeling Allright (5:00)/ Remedy (7:14)
R: Exs. Audience.   S: London 'Secret Gig' Oct.
31 '94.   C: ECD. Dcc. Pic CD.

CD - HIGH HEAD BLUES
KISS THE STONE KTS 414
Conspiracy (7:00)/ High Head Blues (7:19)/ Sister
Luck (5:46)/ Hard To Handle (4:10)/ Cursed
Diamond (5:59)/ Jealous Again (5:25)/ Remedy
(6:43)
R: Ex. Audience.   S: Live Jan. '95.   C: ECD.
Dbw. Pic CD.

CD - NEWPORT 1992
THE SWINGIN' PIG TSP 206-2
CD1: No Speak No Slave/ My Morning Song/
Sting Me/ Hard To Handle/ Jam/ Thorn In My
Pride
CD2: Bad Luck Blue Eyes Goodbye/ Black Moon
Creeping/ Sometimes Salvation/ Thick N'Thin/
Stare It Cold/ Three Little Birds/ You're Wrong/
Jealous Again
R: Exs. Soundboard.   S: Newport, Rhode Island
Nov. 19 '92.   C: ECD.

CD - OUT OF THE NEST (EARLY DEMOS)
BLUE MOON RECORDS BMCD 5
Mercenary Man/ Karel The Psychic/ If/ Medicine/
Redneck Blues/ It's Not Fair/ Your Definition/ The
Long Day/ Serving Time/ Redneck Blues/ It's Not
Fair/ Jealous Again/ She Talks To Angels/ You're
Wrong/ She Talks To Angels/ Jealous Again/ She
Talks To Angels/ You're Wrong
R: Poor-G. Hiss.   S: Tracks 1-4 garage demos

'86. Tracks 5-7 A&M demos, NYC Oct. '87. Tracks
8-11 studio demos '88. Tracks 12-14 National
Studios, NYC '90. Tracks 15-17 acoustic '90.
Tracks 18-19 acoustic rehearsal '90.

CD - SONGS OF THE FLESH
KISS THE STONE KTS 444
Black Moon Creeping/ Thick 'N Thin/ A
Conspiracy/ High Head Blues/ Hard To Handle/
Waitin' Guilty/ Cursed Diamond/ Jealous Again/
No Speak No Slave/ She Talks To Angels/ Wiser
Time/ Shake Your Money Maker/ Remedy
R: Exs. Soundboard.   S: Live Jan. '95.
C: ECD. Dcc. Pic CD. Time 71:04.

CD - SOUL SOAKED
TEDDY BEAR TB 53
You're Wrong (5:54)/ Boomer's Story (5:24)/ Live
Too Fast Blues (3:20)/ Having A Good Time
(8:29)/ Hard To Handle (3:50)/ Jam (7:40)/ Three
Little Birds (6:04)/ Get Back (5:12)/ Dreams
(9:06)/ Jealous Guy (4:34)/ Soul - Soaked (5:46)
R: Exs. Soundboard.   S: Various locations
'90/'93. Tracks 1, 6 and 11 previously unreleased.
C: ECD. Dcc. Pic CD.

CD - STONE THE CROWES
BABY CAPONE BC 009/2
CD1: Intro (1:57)/ No Speak No Slave (3:13)/
Sting Me (7:00)/ Hard To Handle (4:40)/ My
Morning Song (9:34)/ Thorn's Progress (7:46)/
Thorn In My Pride (11:30)/ Bad Luck Blue Eyes
Goodbye (7:00)/ Twice As Hard (4:30)/ Black
Moon Creeping (6:30)/ Thick 'N' Thin (3:30)/ Hotel
Illness (4:00)
CD2: Stare It Cold (4:00)/ Three Little Birds
(5:42)/ Sometimes Salvation (5:30)/ Jealous
Again (5:50)/ Remedy (11:36)/ Seeing Things
(7:02)/ Sister Luck (5:47)/ Shake 'Em (14:41)/
She Talks To Angles (6:46)/ Dreams (8:42)
R: Exs. Soundboard.   S: Houston, Texas Feb. 6
'93.   C: ECD. Dcc. Pic CD.

CD - UNWIRED
OCTOPUS OCTO 100
Jealous Again (6:01)/ Your Wrong (6:12)/ Seeing
Things (6:49)/ Boomer's Story (5:21)/ Live Too
Fast Blues (3:31)/ She Talks To Angels (9:05)/
Thorn In My Pride (7:24)/ Darling Of The
Underground Press (4:25)/ Jealous Again (5:09)/
She Talks To Angels (6:15)/ Non Fiction (4:35)/
Long Time Gone (7:01)
R: Ex. Soundboard.   S: Tracks 1-8 Ronnie
Scott's, London June 20 '91. Tracks 9-10 MTV
Unplugged '92. Tracks 11-12 Mean Fiddler,
London Nov. 1 '94.   C: ECD. Dcc.

BLACK FLAG

CD - LAST SHOW
HAWK 065
Retired At 21/ Annihilate This Week/ Bastard In
Love/ Drinking And Driving/ Paralyzed/ In My
Head/ White Hot/ Black Love/ Kickin' And Stickin'/

Society's Tease/ This Is Good/ I Can See You/
Nothing Left Inside/ Gimme Gimme Gimme/ Louie
Louie
R: Vg.   S: Detroit. June 28 '86.   C: ECD. Dcc.
Time 69:22.

7" - THE UNHEARD '83 DEMOS
S1: What Can You Believe
S2: Modern Man/ Slip It In
R: Ex. Soundboard.   C: USA. B&w sleeve
unfolds to poster. 45 RPM.

BLACK SABBATH

LP - BLACK HAVEN SABBATH
S1: Snowblind/ Black Sabbath/ Iron Man
S2: Paranoid/ Killing Yourself To Live/ Hole In The
Sky/ War Pigs
S3: Dirty Woman/ Drum Solo/ Rock And Roll
Doctor/ Guitar Solo
S4: Improvisation/ Electric Funeral/ Guitar Solo/
NIB / Gypsy
R: Exs. Exm.   C: Dcc. Matrix number scratched
out.

CD - BOSTON 1992
LIVE STORM LSCD 52575
CD1: Mob Rules/ Computer God/ Children Of The
Sea/ Time Machine/ War Pigs/ I/ Die Young/
Guitar Solo
CD2: Black Sabbath/ Master Of Insanity/ After All
(The Dead)/ Iron Man/ Heaven And Hell/ Neon
Knights/ Paranoid
R: Vgs.   S: Orpheum Theater, Boston Aug. 9
'92.   C: ECD.

CD - GILLAN THE HERO
NIGHTLIFE N 014
Children Of The Grave/ Hot Line/ War Pigs/ Iron
Man/ Zero The Hero/ Heaven And Hell/ Guitar
Solo, Digital Bitch/ Black Sabbath/ Smoke On The
Water/ Paranoid
R: Vg-Ex. Soundboard.   S: Worchester, Mass.
'83.   C: Japanese CD. Dcc. Limited numbered
edition of 1,000. Time 74:50.

CD - KILLING YOURSELF TO DIE
BONDAGE MUSIC BON 041
Supertzar, Sympton Of The Universe/ Snowblind/
War Pigs/ Black Sabbath/ Dirty Women, Drums
Solo/ Rock 'N' Roll Doctor/ Guitar Solo/ Electric
Funeral/ N.I.B./ Gypsy/ Paranoid/ Children Of The
Grave
R: G-Vg. Audience.   S: Olympen In Lund,
Sweden Apr. 21 '77.   C: Japanese CD. Dcc.
'Autographs' on disc. Time 71:58.

CD - THE RAY GILLEN YEARS
BONDAGE MUSIC BON 025
Danger Zone/ War Pigs/ Heart Like A Wheel/
Sweet Leaf/ Black Sabbath/ Neon Knights/ Glory
Ride/ Lost Forever/ Eternal Idol/ The Shining/
Ancient Warrior/ Born To Lose
R: Tracks 1-6 G-Vg. Tracks 7-13 G. Soundboard.

S: Tracks 1-6 San Antonio, Texas '86. Tracks 7-13
'The Eternal Idol' demos '87.   C: Japanese CD.
Pic CD. Time 74:01.

BLIND FAITH

CD - THE MORGAN REHEARSALS
BL 121391-1/2
CD1: Tracks 1-9 Instrumental Jams, African
Chant/ (vocals on track 5 y Ginger Baker)/ Track
10 'Well Alright' (take 1)
CD2: Tracks 1-6 'Well Alright' (takes 2-7)/ Tracks
7-8 'Hey Joe'/ Track 9 Instrumental Jam/ Tracks
10-11 'Well Alright' (takes 8 and 9)/ Tracks 12-17
Instrumental Jams
R: Ex. Soundboard.   S: The Morgan Studios,
London '69.   C: Japanese CD. Dcc. Mini poster
of Clapton. Time CD1 75:37. CD2 73:58.

CD - SUNSHINE OF YOUR LOVE
EC IN PERSON EIP022
Well Alright/ Can't Find My Way Home/ Had To
Cry Today/ Sleeping In The Ground/ Crossroads/
Presence Of The Lord/ Sea Of Joy/ Do What You
Like/ Sunshine Of Your Love
R: Good audience recording.   S: Hemisfair
Arena, San Antonio, Texas Aug. 20 '69.
C: Japanese CD.

BLIND MELON

CD - CLIMBING THE CLOUDS
OXYGEN OXY 033
2 x 4 (4:25)/ Toes Across The Floor (3:05)/ Tones
Of Home (4:58)/ Wilt (2:48)/ Vernie (3:21)/ No
Rain (4:28)/ Walk (2:44)/ Lemonade (2:57)/ Time
(4:40)/ St. Andrew's Fall (3:59)/ Skinned (2:31)/
Change (3:33)/ All Go Away (3:22)/ The Duke
(3:42)/ Galaxie 92:43)/ Car Seat (God's Presents)
(2:57)/ Galaxie (2:48)/ Walk (2:37)/ Change
(6:02)/ No Rain (5:40)
R: Exs. Soundboard.   S: Tracks 1-16 The
Commodore Ballroom, Vancouver, Canada Oct. 3
'95. Tracks 17-18 acoustic session, BBC Studios,
London Sept. 17 '95. Tracks 19-20 acoustic session, Vara Studios', Hilversum, Holland Nov.10
'93.   C: ECD. Dcc. Pic CD.

BLUE MURDER

CD - PLEASE DON'T LEAVE ME FOR WEST -
TRIBUTE TO PHIL LYNOTT
WYVERN BMW-521F1/2
CD1: Riot/ Dance/ Cry For Love/ Runaway/ Cold
Sweat/ Drums Solo/ Billy/ She Know/ Save My
Love
CD2: Jelly Roll/ We All Fall Down/ I Need An
Angel/ Blue Murder/ Please Don't Leave Me/
Dancin' In The Moonlight/ Still Of The Night
R: Vg. Audience.   S: Osaka Dec. 5 '93.

BLUR

CD - BLURED
BLACK ADDER BA1
Sunday Sunday/ Jubilee/ Tracy Jacks/ She's So High/ Girls And Boys/ London Loves/ Trouble In The Message Centre/ Chemical World/ Pop Scene/ To The End/ Advert/ End Of A Century/ Parklife (featuring Phil Daniels)/ There's No Other Way/ For Tomorrow/ Bank Holiday/ This Is A Low
R: Exs. Soundboard.   S: Shepherds Bush Empire May 26 '94.   C: ECD. Dbw. Time 74:00.

CD - BLURRED VISION
HOME RECORDS HR5995-0
Sunday Sunday (1:52)/ Jubilee (2:38)/ Tracy Jacks (4:25)/ Magic America (4:00)/ End Of A Century (3:15)/ Pop Scene (3:46)/ For Tomorrow (5:03)/ Chemical World (4:39)/ There's No Other Way (4:16)/ To The End (4:19)/ Advert (4:33)/ Parklife (3:29)/ I Was A Heineken Super Shopper (2:44)/ Girls & Boys (4:57)/ Bank Holiday (2:22)/ This Is A Low (5:54)
R: Ex. Audience.   S: Live '94.   C: ECD. Dcc.

CD - BLURRED VISIONS
OXYGEN OXY 018
Intro - Popscene (0:41)/ End Of A Century (2:53)/ Jubilee (2:46)/ Parklife (3:18)/ For Tomorrow (4:53)/ She's So High (4:47)/ Presentation - Country House (5:35)/ End Of A Century - Interview (4:37)/ Parklife (3:28)/ End Of A Century (2:47)/ This Is A Low (2:59)/ Girls & Boys (2:38)/ To The End (2:28)/ Intro - Top Man (4:53)/ Charmless Man (3:29)/ Country House (4:23)/ Globe Alone (2:02)/ Pop Scene (3:11)/ She's So High (4:37)/ The Universal (4:04)
R: Exs. Soundboard.   S: Tracks 1 plus 12-13 excerpt from 'MTV Blur-Ology' in concert '95. Tracks 2-6 acoustic radio session, WNNX, Atlanta, Georgia Nov. 18 '94. Tracks 7-9, acoustic radio session, WNEW, New York City Sept. 27 '95. Tracks 12-13 from MTV's 'Most Wanted' studio session '95. Tracks 14-18 BBC Radio Theatre, Broadcasting House, London Sept. 7 '95. Track 19 'Basement Tapes' session '90. Track 20 MTV European Music Awards, Le Zenith, Paris Nov. 23 '95.   C: ECD. Dcc. Pic CD.

CD - ENTERTAINMENT
MOONRAKER 030/31
CD1: The Great Escape/ Charmless Man/ Jubilee/ Popscene/ End Of A Century/ Tracy Jacks/ Mr, Robinsons' Quango/ Instrumental/ To The End/ Fade Away/ It Could Be You/ Stereotypes/ Supra Shoppa/ Girls & Boys/ Advert/ Bank Holiday/ Country House/ This Is A Low CD2: Entertain Me/ He Thought Of Cars/ Parklife/ Can I/ Globe Alone/ The Universal Bonus/ Charmless Man/ To The End/ Stereotypes/ Supra Shoppa/ Girls & Boys/ Country House/ This Is A Low/ Entertain Me/ Parklife/ The Universal
R: Vg. Audience. CD2 tracks 7-16 Exs. Soundboard.   S: The Docks, Hamburg Oct. 23

'95. CD2 tracks 7-16 Stockholm Oct. 19 '95.
C: ECD. Dcc. Time CD1 64:05. CD2 70:10

CD - THE MOD SQUAD
BLUE MOON RECORDS BMCD30
Lot 105/ Sunday, Sunday/ Jubilee/ Tracy Jacks/ Magic America/ End Of A Century/ Trouble In The Message Centre/ She's So High/ For Tomorrow/ Chemical World/ Badhead/ There's No Other Way/ Advert/ Supershopper/ Mr. Robinson's Quango/ Parklife/ Girls And Boys/ Bank Holiday Centre, Birmingham Oct. 5 '94.   C: ECD. Dcc.
R: Exs. Soundboard.   S: Ashton Villa Leisure

BODY COUNT

CD - COP KILLER
Cop Killer/ Bitch Meets Evil Dick (Chief Mix)/ Cop Killer (Death Zone Mix)/ Colors/ Dog 'n' The Wax/ 6 In The Morning/ Iceapella/ Ya Don't Quit/ Cop Killer (Terminator Mix)
R: Exs. Soundboard.   S: Track 1 is the original version from the first edition of 'Body Count'. Tracks 3 and 9 are the special remixes for this edition. Track 4 is the title song of the film 'Colors'. Tracks 5-8 are the legendary I-Party songs by Ice-T.   C: ECD. Dcc. Pic CD. Time 48:07.

BOLAN, MARC AND JOHN'S CHILDREN

LP - BEYOND THE RISING SUN
CAMBRA SOUND CR115
S1: Mustang Ford/ Jasmine '49/ Jagged Time Lapse*/ Killer Ben*/ Let Me Know*/ Observations S2: Cat Black/ Black And White Incident/ Charlie/ You're A Nothing*/ Leave Me Alone*/ The Perfumed Garden Of Gulliver Smith S3: You Scare Me To Death/ I'm Weird/ Smash Blocked*/ Hippy Gumbo/ Strange Affair*/ Not The Sort Of Girl*/ The Wizard S4: Beyond The Rising Sun/ Eastern Spell/ Just What You Want, Just What You'll Get*/ You've Got The Power/ Cold On Me
R: Vg-Ex. Stereo.   S: Studio. *John's Children - unknown live source.   C: UK boot from '84.

BON JOVI

CD - ACOUSTIC
KISS THE STONE KTS 409
Love For Sale (3:00)/ I'll Sleep When I'm Dead (4:32)/ Blood On Blood (6:36)/ Fever (1:44)/ Bed Of Roses (7:54)/ Keep The Faith (5:21)/ Never Say Goodbye (5:46)/ Livin' On A Prayer (5:08)/ Wanted Dead Or Alive (4:59)/ Bed Of Roses (5:37)/ Drift Away (5:34)/ Never Say Goodbye (5:23)
R: Exs. Soundboard.   S: Tracks 1-9 The Virgin Megastore, Melbourne, Australia Oct. 10 '93. Tracks 10-12 Live in Australia.   C: ECD. Dcc. Pic CD.

CD - AT POWERSTATION
ROCKET SOUND RS-1001
Runaway/ She Don't Know Me/ Shot The Heart/
Heartbreak Eye/ Love Lies/ Hollywood Dream/
What Do You Want/ Talking In Your Heart/ No
Action/ Open Your Heart/ This Woman Is
Dangerous/ Don't Do That To Me Any More/
Stringin' A Lie/ Slippin' Away/ Head Over Heels/
Don't Keep Me Wonderin'/ Charlene/ Don't Leave
Me Tonight/ Bubblious Girl
C: Poor soundboard recording.   S: Powerstation
demos, New York '81.

CD - BED OF ROSES
SPLAT CAT MUSIC SCM 002
Love For Sale/ I Sleep When I'm Dead/ Blood On
Blood/ Fever/ Bed Of Roses/ Keep The Faith/
Never Say Goodbye/ Living On A Prayer/ Wanted
Dead Or Alive/ Bed Of Roses/ Drift Away/ Never
Say Goodbye
R: Exs. Soundboard.   S: Virgin Megastore,
Melbourne, Australia Oct. 10 '93.   C: ECD. Dcc.
Pic CD.

CD - COVERAND
BUGSY BGS 039
With A Little Help From My Friends (6:20)/ Brother
Louie (5:55)/ Fever (1:51)/ It's My Life (3:05)/ We
Gotta Get Out Of This Place (3:38)/ Can't Help
Falling In Love (1:53)/ Midnight Rider (2:41)/ Walk
This Way (5:05)/ Bed Of Roses (4:27)/ Never Say
Goodbye (5:21)/ Dry County (12:04)/ It's Only
Rock 'N' Roll (5:13)/ Waltzing Matilda (4:50)/
Stranger In This Town (6:40)/ Blood Money (2:24)/
Keep The Faith (6:29)
R: Exs. Soundboard.   S: Live during '93 world
tour.   C: ECD. Dcc. Pic CD.

CD - COVERING' EM
OCTOPUS OCTO 089
Walk This Way (jam with Steve Tyler and Joe
Perry, Milton Keynes Bowl, UK Aug. 19 '89)
(5:17)/ Help (Milton Keynes Bowl, UK Sept. 18
'93) (3:02)/ With A Little Help From My Friends
(New York City, Oct. 29 '92) (5:52)/ Midnight
Rider, Wanted Dead Or Alive (Richie Sambora's
solo tour, San Diego, CA Jan. 10 '92) (7:35)/ It's
Only Rock 'N' Roll (Count Basie Theater, Red
Bank, NJ Dec. 20 '93) (5:05)/ Shout (Milton
Keynes Bowl, UK Sept. 18 '93) (3:11)/ Backdoor
Santa (Nassau Coliseum, Uniondale, NY Dec. 18
'87) (3:59)/ Shooting Star (Hammersmith Odeon,
London, UK Jan. 10 '90) (6:02)/ Drift Away
(Cincinnati Gardens Mar. 19 '87) (3:54)/ Bang
Bang (Wembley Arena, London, UK Jan. 2 '90)
(1:36)/ Fever, It's My Life, We Gotta Get Out Of
This Place (New York City Oct. 29 '92) (8:24)/
Johnny Be Good (5:12)/ Get Back (3:45)/ We're
An American Band (5:36)/ Helter Skelter (4:48)/
Travellin' Band (jam with Scorpions and
Cinderella, Olympia Halle, Munich, German Dec.
19 '88) (4:28)
R: Ex. Soundboard/Audience.   C: ECD. Dcc.
Pic CD.

CD - GET READY
BONDAGE BON 039
Tokyo Road/ Breakout/ Only Lonely/ She Don't
Know Me/ Shot Through The Night/ Guitar Solo,
In And Out Of Love/ Runaway/ Home, Get Ready/
Burn For Love
R: Exs. Soundboard.   S: Summerfest,
Milwaukee, Wisconsin June 29 '85.
C: Japanese CD. Dcc. Pic CD. Time 62:43.

CD - HAPPY HOUR
OCTOPUS OCTO 199/200
CD1: Wild In The Streets (5:35)/ Keep The Faith
(7:19)/ Blood On Blood (5:36)/ Always (7:17)/ I'd
Die For You (4:53)/ Blaze Of Glory (5:45)/
Runaway (4:49)/ Dry Country (11:54)/ Lay Your
Hands On Me (9:48)/ I'll Sleep When I'm Dead,
Jumping Jack Flash (9:48)
CD2: Bad Medicine, Shout (9:09)/ Bed Of Roses
(9:04)/ Hey God (6:14)/ These Days (6:30)/
Rockin' All Over The World (5:36)/ I Don't Like
Monday's (5:02)/ Wanted Dead Or Alive (8:01)/
Stranger In This Town (6:19)/ Someday, I'll Be
Saturday Night (8:11)/ This Ain't A Love Song
(7:39)
R: Exs. Soundboard.   S: Wembley Stadium,
London June 25 '95.   C: ECD.

CD - HIDDEN TREASURES
OXYGEN OXY 048
Borderline (4:03)/ Edge Of A Broken Heart (4:00)/
Too Much Too Soon (4:19)/ Game Of The Heart
(3:46)/ Lonely Is The Night (4:06)/ Deep Cuts The
Nife (3:14)/ Love Is War (4:30)/ Let's Make It
Baby (6:00)/ Judgement Day (3:57)/ River Of
Love (4:11)/ Now And Forever (5:27)/ Growing Up
The Hardway (4:41)/ Does Anyone Really Fall In
Love Anymore? (4:24)/ Rosie (3:53)/ Backdoor To
Heaven (5:12)/ Love Hurts (4:14)/ Starting All
Over (3:43)
R: Exs. Soundboard.   S: Tracks 1-2 'Slippery
When Wet' outtakes, USA '86. Tracks 3-6
'Slippery When Wet' rough demos, USA '86.
Tracks 7-16 'New Jersey' rough demos, USA '88.
'Keep The Faith' outtake USA '92.   C: ECD.
Pic CD.

CD - KEEP THE FAITH - NEW JERSEY
OUTTAKES
BONDAGE MUSIC BON 022
Love Is War/ Let's Make It Baby/ Judgment Day/
River Of Love/ Now And Forever/ Growing Up
The Hard Way/ Does Anybody Really Fall In Love
Anymore/ Rosie/ Wild Is The Wind/ Living In Sin/
Blood On Blood/ Backdoor To Heaven/
Homebound Train/ Love Hurts/ Stick To Your
Guns
R: Ex. Soundboard.   S: Outtakes '88-'92.
C: Japanese CD. Dcc. Pic CD. Time 73:32.

CD - MADE IN JAPAN
THE SWINGIN' PIG TSP 192
Tokyo Road/ Breakout/ Only Lonely/ She Don't
Know Me/ Shot Through The Heart/ Silent Night/

Runaway/ Burning For Love/ Get Ready
R: Exs. Soundboard.   S: Shibuya Public Hall,
Tokyo, Japan Apr. 28. '85.   C: ECD.

CD - NOW AND FOREVER
KISS THE STONE KTS 464/65
CD1: Wild In The Street/ Keep The Faith/ Blood
On Blood/ Always/ I Die For You/ Blaze Of Glory/
Runaway/ Dry County/ Lay Your Hands On Me/ I'll
Sleep When I'm Dead/ Jumping Jack Flash
CD2: Bad Medicine/ Shout/ Bad Of Roses/ Hey
God/ These Days/ Rockin' All Over The World/ I
Don't Like Mondays?/ Wanted Dead Or Alive/ No
Stranger In This Town/ Someday I'll Be Saturday
Night/ This Ain't A Love Song
R: Exs. Soundboard.   S: Wembley Stadium,
London, June 25 '95.   C: ECD. Dcc. Pic CD.

CD - THE RETURN OF THE JERSEY BOY
OCTOPUS OCTO 178
Love For Sale (3:26)/ I'll Sleep When I'm Dead
(4:40)/ Living On A Prayer (5:46)/ With A Little
Help From My Friends (6:00)/ Lay Your Hands On
Me (4:55)/ Blaze Of Glory (5:20)/ Shout (6:00)/
Bed Of Roses (8:40)/ Fever (1:40)/ We've Got To
Get Out Of This Place (6:38)/ Wanted Dead Or
Alive (8:07)/ I'll Sleep When I'm Dead (4:56)/ Bad
Medicine (5:48)/ Keep The Faith (6:34)
R: Exs. Soundboard.   S: Tracks 1-3, Hard Rock
Cafe, NYC Oct. 28 '92. Tracks 4-14 MTV Studios,
NYC Oct. 10 '92.   C: ECD. Dbw. Pic CD.

CD - ROCKIN' ALL OVER THE WORLD
MIDNIGHT BEAT MB CD 051/52
CD1: Livin' On A Prayer (6:34)/ You Give Love A
Bad Name (3:40)/ Wild In The Streets (5:33)/
Keep The Faith (7:12)/ Blood On Blood (5:57)/
Always (6:57)/ I'd Die For You (5:19)/ Blaze Of
Glory (5:31)/ Dry Country (11:30)/ Lay Your Hands
On Me (9:42)
CD2: I'll Sleep When I'm Dead, Jumpin' Jack
Flash (8:50)/ Bad Medicine (7:52)/ Shout, Reprise
Bad Medicine (4:21)/ Rockin' All Over The World
(3:37)/ Someday I'll Be Saturday Night (8:13)/
With A Little Help From My Friends (9:43)/
Acoustic Guitar Solo (3:34)/ Wanted Dead Or
Alive (5:35)/ This Ain't A Love Song (7:03)
R: Exs. Soundboard.   S: Weser Stadium,
Bremen, Germany May 27 '95.   C: ECD. Dcc.
Pic CD.

CD - SLIPPERY WHEN WET OUTTAKES
BONDAGE MUSIC BON 008
You Give Love A Bad Name/ Without Love/ Wild
In The Streets/ Wanted Dead Or Alive/ Raise Your
Hands/ Never Enough/ Edge Of A Broken Heart/
Borderline/ Give My Heart/ I'd Die For You/ Let It
Rock/ Social Disease/ Livin' On A Prayer/ Lonely
In The Night/ Dick After Night/ Never Say
Goodbye
R: Poor soundboard. Hiss.

CD - UNWIRED
OCTOPUS OCTO 101
Diamond Ring (previously unreleased) (3:49)/
Wanted Dead Or Alive (4:43)/ Living On A Prayer
(4:35)/ Ride Cowboy Ride (2:53)/ Blood Money
(3:00)/ I'll Be There For You (2:33)/ Little Wing
(1:32)/ Wanted Dead Or Alive (7:59)/ Love For
Sale (3:36)/ I'll Sleep When I'm Dead (4:32)/
Blood On Blood (6:40)/ Fever (1:41)/ Bed Of
Roses (7:55)/ Keep The Faith (5:31)/ Never Say
Goodbye (6:10)/ Living On a Prayer (5:15)/ Now
And Forever (previously unreleased) (5:28)
R: Ex. Soundboard and Audience.   S: Tracks 1-
3 Rockline Studios, London Dec. 14 '92. Track 4
Tokyo Dome Dec. 31 '88. Track 5 Rotterdam Apr.
9 '93. Tracks 6-8 Wembley, London May 16 '93.
Tracks 9-16 Virgin Megastore, Melbourne,
Australia Oct. 10 '93. Track 17 outtake from 'Keep
The Faith' sessions '92.   C: ECD. Dcc.

BOSTON

CD - CHERRY BLOSSOM TOUR
CBCD-790420A/B
CD1: Rock'N Roll Band/ Peace Of Mind/ Feelin'
Satisfied/ Don't Look Back/ The Journey/ More
Than A Feeling/ A Man I'll Never Be
CD2: Smokin'/ Bach (Pipe Organ Solo)/ Smokin'/
Tom Scholz Solo/ Something About You/ Party
R: Vg audience recording.   S: Apr. 20 '79.
Cover lists wrong source

BOWIE, DAVID

CD - A CRASH COURSE FOR THE RAVERS
GOLD STANDARD DB01 62294XK1
Queen Bitch/ Bombers/ The Superman/ Looking
For A Friend/ Almost Grown/ Kooks/ Song For
Bob Dylan/ Andy Warhol/ It Ain't Easy/ Changes/
Andy Warhol/ The Superman/ Ziggy Stardust/
Five Years/ Waiting For The Man/ White Light,
White Heat/ Rock And Roll Suicide/ Starman/
Drive In Saturday/ Janine
R: Ex. Soundboard.   S: BBC Radio - Tracks 1-9
June 20 '71. Track 10 May 22 '72. Tracks 11-12
Oct. 4 '71 with Ronson. Tracks 13-15 Feb. 7 '72
with Spiders. Tracks 16-17 June 19 '72 with
Spiders. Track 18 '72 with Spiders. Track 19 '73
with Spiders. Track 20 Oct. 26 '69 with Junior's
Eyes.   C: Dcc. Pic CD. Time 75:33.

CD - ANOTHER STAGE
BLACK EAGLE BE 003/004
CD1: Warszawa/ Heroes/ What In The World?/ Be
My Wife/ The Jean Genie/ Blackout/ Sense Of
Doubt/ Speed Of Life/ Breaking Glass/ Fame/
Beauty And The Beast/ Five Years/ Soul Love/
Star/ Hang On To Yourself/ Ziggy Stardust/
Suffragette City
CD2: Art Decade/ Alabama Song/ Station To
Station/ Stay/ TVC 15/ Rebel Rebel/ Heroes (a)/
Sound And Vision (b)/ Fame (b)
R: Vg. Audience. (a) Ex. Audience. (b) Vg.
Soundboard.   S: The Scandinavium,

Gothenburg 4/6/78 except (a) Falkoner Theatre, Copenhagen 3/5/78 and (b) Earl's Court Arena, London 1/7/78.   C: CD1 72:37. CD2 50:12.

CD - LIVE INSIDE
KISS THE STONE KTS 502/503
CD1: Outside (4:31)/ Scary Monsters (5:36)/ Reptile (5:04)/ Hallo Spaceboy (5:10)/ Hurt (6:09)/ Look Back In Anger (5:03)/ I'm Deranged (5:44)/ The Hearts Filthy Lesson (5:08)/ The Voyeur Of Utter Destruction (5:24)/ I Have Not Been To Oxford Town (4:19)
CD2: Outside (4:43)/ Andy Warhol (3:45)/ Breaking Glass (3:40)/ The Man Who Sold The World (3:41)/ We Prick You (4:24)/ Joe The Lion (4:31)/ A Small Plot Of Land (6:09)/ Nite Flights (5:51)/ Band Introduction (0:44)/ Under Pressure (4:00)/ Teenage Wildlife (7:23)/ Strangers When We Meet (4:53)
R: Exs. Soundboard.   S: USA '95.   C: ECD.

CD - OPEN THE DOG
MOONRAKER 033/34
CD1: The Motel/ Look Back In Anger/ The Hearts Filthy Lesson/ Scary Monsters/ The Voyeur Of Utter Destruction/ I Have Not Been To Oxford Town/ Outside/ Andy Warhol/ The Man Who Sold The World/ A Small Plot Of Land/ Introductions/ Boys Keep Swinging
CD2: Strangers When We Meet/ Hallo Spaceboy/ Breaking Glass/ We Prick You/ Nite Flights/ My Death/ D.J./ Teenage Wildlife/ Under Pressure/ Moonage Daydream
R: Vg-Ex. Audience.   S: Wembley Arena, London Nov. 15 '95.   C: ECD. Time CD1 55:40. CD2 52:02.

CD - PIERROT IN TURQUOISE
CLOWN IQ-001
When I Live In My Dream/ Columbine/ The Mirror/ Threepenny Pierrot/ When I Live In My Dream/ Right On Mother/ I'm Waiting For The Man/ Little Toy Soldier/ Space Oddity/ That's A Promise/ Silly Boy Blue/ London Bye Ta-Ta/ In The Heat Of The Morning
R: Vg-Ex. Soundboard.   S: Studio demos and outtakes '66 - '71.   C: Most tracks from acetates. Time 36:21.

CD - VAMPIRES OF HUMAN FLESH
MIDNIGHT BEAT MB CD021
Scream Like A Baby/ Because You're Young/ Kingdom Come Up The Hill Backwards/ It's No Game/ Is There Life After Marriage?/ Up The Hill Backwards/ Teenage Wildlife/ Kingdom Come/ Scary Monsters
R: Vg sound.   S: Demos. Alternative versions.

BRAND X

CD - OPERATION 'X'
ALL OF THE WORLD AOTW-94010
Dance Of The Illegal Aliens/ Don't Makes Waves/ Malaga Vergen/ Ancl So To F/ Access To Data

R: Poor-G.   S: Park West, Chicago Sept. '79.

BROTHERS JOHNSON, THE

CD - FUNKY BROTHERS
SHOW COMPANY SC-9447-4
Free Yourself Be Yourself/ Mr. Quincy Jones/ Right On Time/ Get The Funk Out Ma Face/ Ain't We Fuckin' Now/ The Real Thing/ We Supply/ Drum Solo And Bass Solo/ Stomp
R: Ex sound.   S: Tracks 1-5 '78. Tracks 6-9 '81.

BROWN, JAMES

CD - FUNKY WONDERLAND
WET LIP PRODUCTION WLP940606
Hot Pants Road/ Boogie Wonderland/ It's Too Funky In Here/ Bodyheat/ Try Me/ Georgia On My Mind/ Please, Please, Please/ Jam/ Nature/ It's Too Funky In Here (Reprise)
R: Vg sound.   S: Forum, Inglewood, CA '79.

CD - LIVING IN AMERICA 1991
WET LIP PRODUCTION WLP940607
Living In America/ We're Gonna Have A Funk Good Time/ It's A Man's Man's World/ Get On The Good Foot/ Sex Machine/ I Got You (I Feel Good)/ Please, Please, Please/ Jam/ Living In America (Reprise)
R: Poor audience recording.   S: USA '91.

BROWNE, JACKSON

CD - EVERYWHERE I GO
JB-001/2
CD1: Doctor My Eyes/ I'm Alive/ Rosie/ World In Motion/ Everywhere I Go/ My Problem Is You/ Take It Easy, Our Lady Of The Well/ Your Bright Blues/ In The Shape Of Heart/ Love Needs A Heart/ Late For The Sky/ i Am a Patriot
CD2: Too Many Angels/ Jamaica Say You Will/ Rock Me On The Water/ For Every Man/ Boulevard/ Sky Blue And Black/ Pretender/ Running On Empty/ The Lord Out, Stay/ Somebody's Baby
R: Vg. Audience.   S: Kose Nenkin Hall, Tokyo Apr. 24 '94.   C: Japanese CD.

CD - I AM ALIVE
SILVER RARITIES SIRA 136/137/138
CD1: Doctor My Eyes/ I'm Alive/ World In Motion/ Soldier Of Plenty/ Everywhere I Go/ My Problem Is You/ In The Shape Of A Heart/ Late For The Sky/ Rock Me On The Water/ Your Bright Baby Blues/ Take It Easy/ Our Lady Of The Well
CD2: Lives In The Balance/ 2 Of Me, 2 Of You/ Miles Away/ Too Many Angels/ For Everyman/ Boulevard/ That Girl Could Sing/ For A Dancer/ These Days/ Sky Blue And Black/ The Pretender/ Running On Empty
CD3: The Load Out/ Stay/ I Am A Patriot/ Rosie/ Linda Paloma/ Somebody's Baby/ Nothing But Time/ All Good Things/ Miles Away/ For Everyman
R: Ex. Audience.   S: Royal Albert Hall, London

June 12-14 '94.   C: ECD. Dcc.

CD - INNER COURTYARD FOUNTAIN
TS RRC 027
That Girl Could Sing/ Fountains Of Sorrow/
Boulevard/ Doctor My Eyes/ Running On Empty/
Sleep's Dark And Silent Gate/ The Pretender/
Hold On Hold Out/ The Load Out-Stay/ The Road
And The Sky/ Late For The Sky/ The Crow On
The Cradle
R: Exs. Soundboard.   S: Montreux July 18 '82.
C: Time 75:10.

CD - ROCK ME ON THE WATER
DYNAMITE STUDIO DS94A069/70
CD1: Jamaica Say You Will/ Rock Me On The
Water/ Come All Ye Fair A Tender Ladies, Take It
Easy, Our Lady Of The Well/ Song For Adam/
Ready Or Not/ Walkin' Slow
CD2: Fountain Of Sorrow/ For Everyman/ Doctor
My Eyes, These Days/ The Road And The Sky/
Before The Deluge
R: Vg. Radio broadcast.   S: Caldeone Music
Hall Mar. '75.   C: Japanese CD.

CD - SKY BLUE AND BLACK
JB 003/4
CD1: Doctor In My Eyes/ I'm Alive/ World In
Motion/ Everywhere I Go/ My Problem Is You/ In
The Shape Of A Heart/ Late For The Sky/ Your
Bright Baby Blues/ Miles Away/ Too Many Angels/
For Everyman
CD2: Blue Bird/ Unknown/ Sky Blue And Black/
Introduce The Musician/ Pretender/ Running On
Empty/ The Loadout, Stay/ Linds Paloma/
Interview/ Two Of Me, Two Of You (Studio)
R: Exs. Soundboard.   S: Oregon Mar. '94.
C: Japanese CD.

CD - TAKE IT EASY
DYNAMITE STUDIO DS94M073/74
CD1: Take It Easy/ The Fuse/ Fountain Of
Sorrow/ Here Come Those Tears Again/ Before
The Deluge/ You Bright Baby Blues/ Rock Me On
The Water/ Cocaine/ Rosie/ For A Dancer
CD2: Doctor My Eyes/ These Days/ Walkin' Slow/
Running On Empty/ Love Needs A Heart/ The
Pretender/ The Load Out/ Stay/ The Road And
The Sky
R: G.   S: Nashville Feb. 22 '78.   C: Japanese.

BRUCE, JACK

CD - FEATURING FIVE AXEMEN
ALL OF US AS20
White Moon (6:56)/ Smiles & Grins (4:11)/ Blues
Saraceno's Guitar Solo (3:52)/ Keep It Down
(9:23)/ Spoonful (with Jeff Healy at Pistoia Blues
'92 - 14:34)/ Theme From An Imaginary Western
(with Chris Spedding in Holland '71 - 6:59)/ Sitting
On Top Of The World (with Gary Moore in Koln
Nov. '93 - 6:45)/ Sunshine Of Your Love (with
Clem Clempson in New York Mar. '80 - 7:57)
R: Exs. Soundboard.   S: Tracks 1-4 with Blues

Saraceno at Pistoia Blues '92.   C: ECD. Dcc.

CD - THE RETURN OF A SUPER GROUP
ROCK CALENDAR RECORDS RC 2111
Tales Of Brave Ulysses (4:21)/ White Room
(5:24)/ Sitting On Top Of The World (4:40)/ I'm So
Glad (8:49)/ Rollin' And Tumblin' (6:12)/ Sweet
Wine (14:36)/ Politician (6:21)/ Born Under A Bad
Sign (7:28)/ Sunshine Of Your Love (5:58)
R: Vg-Ex.   S: Tracks 1-6 Cream, San Jose,
Civic Auditorium May 25 '68. Track 7 Jack Bruce
Band, Passaic, Capitol Theater '89. Tracks 8-9
Jack Bruce Band, Bottom Line, NYC '89.
C: ECD. Dcc.

BRUFORD, BILL

CD - CONFUSION
CANTERBURY DREAM CTD-011/012
CD1: Hell's Bells/ Sample And Hold/ Fainting In
Coils, Back To The Begging/ Fainting In Coils/
Forever Until Sunday/ Joe Frazir/ Travels With
Myself, And Someone Else
CD2: Untitled/ Beelzebub/ the Sahara Of Snow
Part 1/ The Sahara Of Snow Part 2/ Five/ Feels
Good To Me
R: Vg-Ex sound.   S: Toad's Place, New Haven,
Conn. July 18 '79.

BUCKLEY, JEFF

CD - DREAM BROTHER
OXYGEN OXY 006
Lover (7:51)/ So Real (5:14)/ Last Goodbye
(5:09)/ Grace (6:08)/ Eternal Life (6:31)/ Dream
Brother (6:19)/ Kick Out The Jams (4:03)/
Hallelujah (7:31)/ Mojo Pin (12:18)/ What Will You
Say (7:44)
R: Exs. Soundboard.   S: Tracks 1-5 The
Nighttown, Rotterdam, Holland Feb. 25 '95.
Tracks 6-8 The Roskilde Festival, Denmark June
30 '95. Tracks 9-10 Frankfurt, Germany '95.
C: ECD. Pic CD.

BUCKLEY, TIM

CD - RETURN OF THE STARSAILOR
NIXED RECORDS NIX 005
Intro, Vocal Warm-Up/ Nighthawkin'/ Dolphins/
Get On Top/ Devil Eyes/ Buzzin' Fly/ Sweet
Surrender/ Honey Man/ Tijuana Moon/ Sally Go
Round The Roses/ Helpless/ Who Could Deny
You/ Song To The Siren
R: Tracks 1-12 audience recordings.   S: Tracks
1-8 Knebworth Festival, Hertfordshire, UK July
'74. Tracks 9-12 Detroit June '75. Track 13 'The
Monkees' TV show Dec. 22 '67.

BUSH

CD - THE JEKYLL IN YOU
OXYGEN OXY 044
Monkey (4:46)/ Body (5:35)/ Greedy Fly
(Unreleased Song) (2:06)/ X-Girlfriend (0:38)/

Little Things (5:00)/ Glycerine (3:32)/ Everything Zen (5:21)/ Swim (5:16)/ Everything Zen (5:29)/ Comedown (5:34)/ Wild Horses (Rolling Stones cover) (5:34)/ X-Girlfriend (2:16)/ Glycerine (4:22)/ Machine Head (4:03)/ Bomb (5:33)/ Little Things (5:57)
R: Exs. Soundboard.   S: Tracks 1-8 Roxy Theatre, Hollywood, CA Feb. '95. Tracks 9-13 APC Studios, Atlanta, GA Oct. 13 '95. Tracks 14-16 Splash Club, London, UK Mar. '95.   C: ECD. Pic CD.

BUTTHOLE SURFERS

CD - THE HOLE TRUTH AND NOTHING BUTT!
TOTONKA CD PR08
Butthole Surfer (3:10) ('83 demo)/ Something (5:00) ('83 demo)/ Moving To Florida (4:02) (The Cameo Club, San Antonio Sept. 21 '85)/ Hurdy Gurdy Man (2:43) (The Cameo Club, San Antonio Sept. 21 '85)/ Come Together (0:52) (The Cameo Club, San Antonio Sept. 21 '85)/ Cherub (6:08) (The Cameo Club, San Antonio Sept. 21 '85)/ Graveyard (3:03) (Mabuay Gardens, San Francisco Jan. 18 '86)/ USSA (4:46)/ (Mabuay Gardens, San Francisco Jan. 18 '86)/ Lady Sniff (3:32) (Mabuay Gardens, San Francisco Jan. 18 '86)/ John E. Smoke (7:09) (The I-Beam, San Francisco Oct. 24 '88)/ 1401 (2:43)/ (The I-Beam, San Francisco Oct. 24 '88)/ Psychedelic (9:57) (The Underground, Phoenix Feb. 4 '89)/ Bon Song (3:15) (Lollapalooza, Irvine, CA July 23 '91)/ The Wooden Song (3:32) (Castaic Lake, CA July 23 '93)/ Pittsburgh To Lebanon (3:26) (Castaic Lake, CA July 23 '93)/ The Shah Sleeps In Lee Harvey's Grave (6:09) (Castaic Lake, CA July 23 '93)/ WNYU Interview (5:28) (radio interview, New York July 28 '87)
R: Ex. Soundboard. Some Vg. Audience.
C: ECD.

BYRDS, THE

CD - IN THE STUDIO
CAPRICORN CR-2006
Mr. Tambourine Man/ I Know I'd Want You/ It's Now Use/ The Bells Of Rhymney/ I'll Feel A Whole Lot Better/ It's All Over Now, Baby Blue/ The World Turns All Around Her/ It's All Over Now Baby Blue/ It Won't Be Long/ Satisfied Mind/ Set You Free This Time/ Stranger In a Strange Land/ Wait And See/ 5D (Fifth Dimension)
R: Vg-Ex sound.   S: Columbia Studios Jan. 20 '65 - May 24 '66.

BYRNE, DAVID

CD - THIS SENSUOUS WORLD
OCTOPUS OCTO 063
Long Time Ago (3:52)/ Tiny Town (5:00)/ God Child (4:20)/ My Love Is You (2:44)/ And She Was (3:29)/ This Must Be The Place (4:45)/ Crash (4:56)/ Lilies Of The Valley (5:21)/ Government (3:16)/ Sad Song (3:22)/ Nothing At All (5:03)/

Back In The Box (4:41)/ Marching Through The Wilderness (4:48)/ Once In A Lifetime (5:06)/ Angels (4:37)/ Buck Naked (3:40)/ Psychokiller (5:23)/ Moonlight In Glory (4:28)
R: Exs. Soundboard.   S: Europe '94.
C: ECD. Dcc.

C

CAMEL

CD - ECHOES
DYNAMITE STUDIO DS94M083/84
CD1: Medley: Earthrise, First Light/ Rhayder/ Uneven Song/ song Within A Song/ The Sleeper Supertwister/ Nimrodel, The Procession/ The White Rider/ Tell Me/ Extract From 'The Snow Goose'
CD2: The Rainbow's End/ Echoes/ Never Let Go/ One Of These Days I'll Get An Early Night/ Lunar Sea
R: Vg. Audience.   S: Kouseinenkin Hall, Tokyo, Japan Jan. 23 '79.   C: Japanese CDs.

CAN

CD - FUTURE DAYS AND PAST NIGHTS
KEEP AN EYE OUT SONGS KAEOS CD001
Chain Reaction/ Bel Air/ Dizzy Dizzy/ Pinch Of Sky/ One More Night/ Meadowsweet
R: Exs. Soundboard.   S: University Of Essex, England May 17 '75.   C: ECD. Dcc. Time 74:38.

CANDLEBOX

CD - A LIGHT YOU'LL NEVER FORGET
KTS OF AUSTRALIA-006-A/B
CD1: Dancing Queen Intro/ Don't You/ Change/ Mother's Dream/ Arrow/ Anything/ No Sense/ Blossom/ Everybody Wants You/ No Way/ To Kill You/ Cover Me/ You
CD2: Road House Blues/ Far Behind, Voo Doo Child/ Recorded Live On Tour With Rush Apr. 24, '94: Don't You/ Mother's Dream/ Change/ Arrow/ Far Behind/ You/ Rockline Interview 2-7-'94/ Pull Away (unreleased track)
R:G-Vg. Audience.   S: Live 11/10/94.
C: Australian CD. Dcc.

CAPTAIN BEEFHEART

CD - CRAZY LITTLE THINGS
TRIANGLE PYCD 080
Mirror Man/ Upon The My-O-My/ Crazy Little Things/ Full Moon Hot Sun/ Sugar Bowl/ This Is The Day/ Keep On Rubbing/ Be Your Dog/ Sweet Georgia Brown/ Abba Zabba/ Peaches/ Peaches
R: Vg. Soundboard.   S: Cowtown, Kansas City Apr. 22 '74.   C: ECD. Time: 64:53

CD - THE ORIGINAL BAT CHAIN PULLER
CBCD 514
Bat Chain Puller/ Seam Crooked Sam/ Harry Irene/ Poop Hatch/ A Carrot Is Close As A Rabbit Gets To A Diamond/ Brickbats/ Floppy Boot Stomp/ Flavour Bud Living/ Carson City (Owned T' Alex)/ Odd Jobs/ 1010th Day Of The Human Totem Pole/ Apes Ma/ Bass Solo/ Alice In Blunderland/ Abba Zabba/ Click Clack/ My Human Gets Me Blues/ I'm Gonna Boogalize You Baby/ Golden Birdies
C: Vg sound.   S: Studio, tracks 13-19 Paris '73.

CAPTAIN BEYOND

CD - BEYOND THE PURPLE
ZA26
I Can't Feel Nothin'/ Dancing Madly Backwards/ Dancing Madly Backwards/ Thousand Days Of Yesterdays/ Mesmerization Eclipse
R: Tracks 1-2 G. Soundboard. Tracks 3-5 Poor. Audience.   S: Tracks 1-2 Montreux Sept. 18 '71. Tracks 3-5 New York July 17 '72.
C: Japanese. CD. Time 50:20.

CARAVAN

CD - LONG WALK DESERT
CANTERBURY DREAM CTD-014
The Show Of Our Lives/ Memory Lane, Hugh/ Headloss/ The Dabsong Conshirtoe a) The Mad Dabsong b) Ben Karratt Rides Again c) Pro's And Ladders d) Wraiks And Ladders e) All Sorts Of Unmentionable Things/ The Love In Your Eye, To Catch Me Brother, Subsultus
R: Vg sound.   S: Reading Festival '75.

CAST

CD - PRIME TIME
OXYGEN OXY 039
Follow Me Down (4:17)/ Back Of My Mind (3:11)/ Sandstorm (3:02)/ Will I Ever Get Out (3:42)/ Finetime (3:14)/ Free From This World (3:13)/ Alright (3:49)/ History (4:49)/ Two Of A Kind (8:17)/ Back Of My Mind (3:09)/ Sandstorm (2:45)/ Finetime (3:05)/ Follow Me Down (3:14)/ Four Walls (3:16)/ Sandstorm (2:46)/ Finetime (3:06)/ Reflection (3:00)/ Alright (3:27)/ Follow Me Down (3:30)/ Sandstorm (3:03)
R: Exs. soundboard.   S: Tracks 1-9 Melkweg, Amsterdam, Holland Dec. 19 '95. Tracks 10-12 BBC acoustic session Oct. '95. Tracks 13-14 BBC electric session July '95. Tracks 15-18 BBC electric session Aug. '95. Tracks 19-20 Auditorium Flog, Firenze, Italy Nov. '95.   C: ECD. Pic CD.

CAVE, NICK

7" - 500 MILES
S1: 500 miles
S2: Helpless/ Sonny
R: Ex. Soundboard.   S: Live radio broadcast.
C: USA. Limited edition of 1,000.45 RPM.

CHAIN CARPENTER, MARY

CD - PASSIONATE KISSES FROM AUSTIN
RSM 33 SQ
Never Had It So Good/ You Win Again/ Going Out Tonight/ How Do/ Rhythm Of The Blues/ Passionate Kisses/ Read My Lips/ Only A Dream/ Come On Come On/ He Thinks He'll Keep Her/ The Moon And St. Christopher/ I Feel Lucky/ Never Had It So Good
R: Exs. Soundboard.   S: Austin, Texas '92.
C: ECD. Time 59:54.

CHARLES, RAY AND B.B. KING

CD - LIVE IN MILANO
FU 206/2
C: See listing under KING, B.B. AND RAY CHARLES.

CLAPTON, ERIC

CD - ALL INSPIRATION
SILVER RARITIES SIRA AF010/11
CD1: Motherless Child/ Malted Milk/ How Long Blues/ Kidman Blues/ The Call Of Gin/ The Fourtyfour/ Blues All Day Long/ Standin' Round Crying/ Hoochie Coochie Man/ It Hurts Me Too/ Blues Before Sunrise/ Third Degree/ So Long/ Sinner's Prayer/ I Can't Judge Nobody/ Someday After Awhile
CD2: I'm Tore Down/ Blues Leave Me Alone/ Crosscut Saw/ Five Long Years/ Born Under The Bad Sign/ Crossroad/ Runover Blues/ Ain't Nobody's Business
R: Ex. Audience.   S: Bradley Center, Milwaukee, WI Oct. 24 '94.   C: ECD. Dcc.

CD - ANOTHER JUST ONE NIGHT
BLUES POWER 005/006
CD1: Tulsa Time/ Early In The Morning/ Lay Down Sally/ Wonderful Tonight/ If I Don't Be There By Morning/ Worried Life Blues/ Double Trouble
CD2: All Our Past Times/ Blues Power/ Knockin' On Heaven's Door/ Setting Me Up/ Rambling On My Mind/ Have You Ever Loved A Woman/ Further On Up The Road
R: G-Vg audience recording.   S: Budokan Hall, Tokyo Dec. 12 '79.   C: Japanese CD.

CD - BACK FROM THE EDGE
SILVER RARITIES SIRA 179/180
CD1: Tulsa Time/ I Shot The Sheriff/ Lay Down Sally/ Worried Life Blues/ Let It Rain/ Double Trouble/ Sweet Little Lisa/ After Midnight/ The Shape You're In
CD2: Wonderful Tonight/ Blues Power/ Ramblin' On My Mind/ Have You Ever Loved A Woman/ Cocaine/ Layla/ Further Up The Road
R: Exs. soundboard.   S: Standthalle, Bremen Apr. 20 '83 (not Mar. as listed on the cover).
C: ECD. Dcc.

CD - BEST OF TOUR '74
WHOOPY CAT WKP-0021/22
CD1: Smile/ Let It Grow/ Can't Find My Way
Home/ I Shot The Sheriff/ Layla/ Ramblin' On My
Mind/ Have You Ever Loved A Woman/ Willie And
The Hand Jive/ Get Ready/ Blues Power/ Little
Wing
CD2: Badge/ Presence Of The Load/ Tell The
Truth/ Crossroads/ Little Queenie/ Key To The
Highway/ Easy Now/ Let Rain/ Baby Don't Do It
C: Gs. Hiss.   S: Capital Center, Largo, MD July
14 '74. CD 2 track 6 Providence, RI July 10 '74.
CD2 track 7 Long Beach, CA July 20 '74. CD2
tracks 8-9 Atlanta, GA Aug. 1 '74.   C: Japanese.

CD - BIG BAND
BLACKIE 14/15
CD1: Crossroads/ White Room/ I Shot The
Sheriff/ Bell Bottom Blues/ Lay Down Sally/
Wonderful Tonight/ Wanna Make Love To You/
After Midnight/ Can't Find My Way Home
CD2: Forever Man/ Sam Old Blues/ Tearing Us
Apart/ Cocaine/ A Remark You Made/ Layla/
Behind The Mask/ Sunshine Of Your Love
R: Vg-Exs audience recording.   S: Royal Albert
Hall, London Jan. 28 '89.   C: CD1 tracks 8-9
with Carole King.

CD - THE BLUES CONCERT
KISS THE STONE KTS 457-58
CD1: Blues Leave Me Alone/ Standin' Round
Crying/ 44/ It Hurts Me Too/ Five Long Years/
Crossroads/ Malted Milk/ Motherless Child/ How
Long Blues/ Reconsider Baby/ Sinner's Prayer/
Everyday I Have The Blues
CD2: Someday After A While/ Crosscut Saw/
Have You Ever Loved A Woman/ I'm Tore Down/
Groaning The Blues/ Ain't Nobody's Business If I
Do/ Early In The Morning/ Driftin'/ Hoochie
Coochie Man/ Born Under A Bad Sign
R: Exs. Soundboard.   S: The Fillmore, San
Francisco Aug. 9 '94. CD2 tracks 9-10 New York
Sept. 28 '94.   C: ECD. Dcc. Pic CDs.
Time CD1 47:05. CD2 50:07.

CD - CRADLE MUSIC
SILVER RARITIES SIRA 181/182
CD1: Motherless Child/ Malted Milk/ From Four
Till Late/ How Long/ Kingdom Blues/ Gonna Cut
Your Hair/ Forty Four/ Blues All Day Long/ Stand
Around Crying/ Hoochie Coochie Man/ It Hurts
Me To/ Blues Before Sunrise/ The Third Degree/
Reconsider/ 2 more tracks
CD2: Early In The Morning/ Can't Judge Nobody/
Someday After While/ Tore Down/ Have You Ever
Loved A Woman/ Cross Cut Saw/ Have Ever
Been Mistreated/ Crossroads/ Got My Mojo
Workin'/ 1 more track
R: G-Vgs. Audience.   S: Royal Albert Hall Feb.
20 '95.   C: ECD. Dcc.

CD - DRIFTIN' BLUES REVISITED
BGS 1993-7RE
CD1: Smile/ Easy Now/ Let It Grow/ I Shot The

Sheriff/ Layla/ Little Wing/ Willie And The Hand
Jive/ Get Ready/ Badge/ Can't Find My Way
Home
CD2: Drifting Blues/ Rambling On My Mind/ Let It
Rain/ Presence Of The Lord/ Crossroads/ Steady
Rollin' Man/ Little Queenie/ Blues Power/
Pretending/ Running On Faith
R: Vgs.   S: Long Beach Arena July 20 '74. CD2
tracks 9-10 Royal Albert Hall '91.   C: Japanese.

CD - FOUR PIECE 1989
BLACKIE 03/04
CD1: Crossroads/ White Room/ I Shot The
Sheriff/ Bell Bottom Blues/ After Midnight/
Wonderful Tonight/ Can't Find My Way Home
(Nathan East on vocal)/ Forever Man/ Same Old
Blues
CD2: Knockin' On Heaven's Door/ Easy Lover
(Phil Collins on vocal)/ Tearing Us Apart/ Cocaine/
A Remark You Made/ Layla/ Behind The Mask/
Sunshine Of Your Love
R: Poor audience recording.   S: Royal Albert
Hall, London Jan. 21 '94.

CD - GENUINE CROSSROADS
STONEWALL CD 3139/3140
CD1: Lawdy Mama (a)/ N.S.U. (b)/ Can't Find My
Way Home (c)/ Cold Turkey (d)/ Well Alright (e)/
Sea Of Joy (e)/ Sleeping In The Ground (e)/
Under My Thumb (e)/ It's Too Late (f)/ Got To Get
Better In A Little While (f)
CD2: Matchbox (3 takes) (f)/ Blues Power (f)/ Key
To The Highway (g)/ Crossroads (g)/ Dobro Jam
#1 (h)/ Dobro Jam #2 (h)/ Please Be With Me (h)/
Meet Me (h)/ Blues Instrumental (h)/ It's Too Late
(h)/ Fool Like Me (i)
R: Ex. Soundboard.   S: (a) CREAM: Atlantic
Studios, NYC June '67. (b) CREAM: Fillmore
West, San Francisco Mar. '68. (c) BLIND FAITH:
Morgan Studios, London Feb. - Mar. '69. (d)
PLASTIC ONO BAND: Abbey Road Studios,
London Sept. '69. (e) BIG FAITH: Hyde Park,
London June 7 '69. (f) DEREK & THE DOMINOS:
Johnny Cash Show, Ryman Auditorium, Nashville
Nov. 5 '70. (g) Rainbow Theatre, London Jan. 13
'73. (h) Criteria Studios, Miami Apr. - May '74. (i)
Dynamic Sound Studios, Kingston Sept. 8 '74.
C: CD1 61:28. CD2 58:08.

CD - GOD IS GOOD
ARMS 24PR
Well All Right/ Sea Of Joy/ Sleeping On The
Ground/ Crawling Up A Hill/ Crocodile Walk/ Bye
Bye Bird/ Instrumental Jam
R: Tracks 1-3 Vgs. Tracks 4-7 Vgm.   S: Tracks
1-3 Hyde Park, London June 7 '69. Tracks 4-6
BBC Studios, London Apr. 24 '65. Track 7 jam
with Peter Green at the Boston Tea Party Feb. 10
'70.   C: Japanese CD.

CD - HOW MANY TIMES MUST I TELL YOU, BABY
EC RARITIES ECR-016/7
CD1: Motherless Children/ I Shot The Sheriff/

Same Old Blues/ White Room Tangled In Love/ Steppin' Out/ Wonderful Tonight/ Double Trouble
CD2: She's Waiting/ She Love You/ Badge/ Let It Rain/ Cocaine/ Layla/ Forever Man/ Further On Up The Road
R: Vgs hiss.   S: Garden State Arts Center, Holmdel, NJ June 28 '85.

CD - IT HURTS ME TOO
EC 94001/2
CD1: Motherless Child/ Malted Milk/ How Long Blues/ Kidman Blues/ Country Jail Blues/ '44' Blue Leave Me Alone/ Gon' Away Baby/ Standin' Round Crying/ Hoochie Coochie Man/ It Hurts Me Too/ Blues Before Sunrise/ Third Degree/ Reconsider Baby/ one other track
CD2: I Can't Judge Nobody/ Someday After A While/ I'm Tore Down/ Have You Ever Loved A Woman/ Crosscut Saw/ Five Long Years/ Born Under A Bad Sign/ Groaning Blues/ Crossroads/ two other tracks
R: Ex audience recording.   S: Madison Square Garden, NY Oct. 9 '94.

CD - THE LAST REHEARSAL '94
EC 94003
Hoochie Coochie Man/ I'm Tore Down/ Sinner's Player/ Motherless Child/ Malted Milk/ Born Under A Bad Sign/ Someday After A While/ It Hurts Me Too/ '44'/ Five Long Years/ Crossroad/ Ain't Nobody's Business/ I'm Tore Down Five Long Years
R: Exs.   S: New York City Sept. 28 '94. Tracks 13-14 Saturday Night Live '94.

CD - THE LONDON HOWLIN' WOLF SESSIONS OUTTAKES
ARMS 22PR
Who's Been Talking/ The Killing Floor/ The Red Rooster/ Poor Boy/ Built For Comfort/ Do The Do/ Highway 49/ Worried About My Baby/ What A Woman/ Wang-Dang-Doodle
R: Vg.   S: Olympic Sound Studios, London Apr. '70.   C: Japanese CDs. With Bill Wyman, Charlie Watts, and Ringo Starr.

CD - LOST JAMS
KISS THE STONE KTS 453
Behind The Mask (5:24)/ Layla (6:51)/ Wonderful Tonight (5:42)/ Before You Accuse Me (5:29)/ Sweet Home Chicago (5:23)/ Before You Accuse Me (5:29)/ Tearing Us Apart (7:09)/ Runaway Train (5:11)/ Tears In Heaven (4:44)/ Tears In Heaven (4:40)/ The Weight (6:55)/ I'm Tore Down (3:12)/ Five Long Years (4:48)/ Matchbox (3:13)
R: Ex. Soundboard.   S: Tracks 1-2 Princes' Trust June '88. Track 3 Nelson Mandela Tribute June 11 '88 with Dire Straits. Tracks 4-5 International Rock Awards June 6 '90. Tracks 6-7 Knebworth June '90. Track 8 NYC Aug. 22 '92 with Elton John. Track 9 MTV Awards, LA Sept. '92. Track 10 Grammy Awards, LA Feb. 24 '93. Track 11 Rock And Roll Hall Of Fame NYC Jan. '94 with The Band. Tracks 12-13 Saturday Night

Live Sept. 24 '94. Track 14 LA Oct. '86 with Carl Perkins and The Ringo Starr Band.   C: ECD. Dcc. Pic CD.

CD - MILWAUKEE TIME
SILVER RARITIES SIRA 187/188
CD1: Tulsa Time/ I Shot The Sherrif/ Worried Life Blues/ Lay Down Sally/ Let It Rain/ Double Trouble/ Sweet Little Lisa/ Blow Wind Blow/ The Shape Your In
CD2: Late In The Evening/ Blues Power/ Don't Say You Don't Love Me/ Have You Ever Loved A Woman/ Ramblin' On My Mind/ Cocaine/ Layla/ Further Up The Road
R: Ex. Soundboard.   S: Milwaukee Festival, Milwaukee July 10 '83.   C: ECD. Dcc. Time CD1 53:03. CD2 48:27.

CD - NO REASON TO CRY SESSIONS
EC IN PERSON EIP 012
Hello Old Friend/ Sign Language/ Black Summer Rain/ Carnival/ Last Night/ Beautiful Thing/ Hungry/ All Our Past Times/ Country Jail/ Double Trouble
R: Poor sound. Loud hiss.   C: Japanese CD. Bob Dylan and Robbie Robertson on some tracks.

CD - NUDE GIRLS AND STUFF LIKE THAT
TEDDY BEAR TB 62
Sign Language (4:01)/ Further Up The Road (7:15)/ Knocking On Heaven's Doors (5:30)/ Stormy Monday Blues (12:15)/ Tell The Truth (10:45)/ Key To The Highway (8:40)/ Nobody Knows You When You Are Down And Out (3:40)/ Layla (7:36)
R: Vg. Audience.   S: Falconer Theatre, Copenhagen June 9 '77.   C: ECD. Dcc.Pic CD.

CD - PRIVATE GIG 1976
UNAUTHORIZED REPRO 76729
Hello Old Friend/ All Our Past Times/ Double Trouble/ Tell The Truth/ Knockin' On Heaven's Door/ Can't Find My Way Home/ Layla/ I Shot The Sheriff/ Key To The Highway
R: G-Vg stereo.   S: Hemel Hempstead Pavilion, England July 29 '76.

CD - RAINBOW CONCERT
ARMS 19/17PR
CD1: Badge/ Nobody Knows You When You Are Down And Out/ Roll It Over/ Why Does Love Got To Be So Sad/ Little Wing/ Bottle Of Red Wine/ After Midnight/ Bell Bottom Blues
CD2: Presence Of The Road/ Tell The Truth/ Pearly Queen/ Key To The Highway/ Let It Rain/ Crossroads
R: Good stereo recording. Hiss.   S: Rainbow Hall, London Jan. 13 '73.   C: Japanese CD.

CD - ROYAL ALBERT HALL 1994
BLACKIE 01/02
CD1: Terraplane Blues/ Come On In My Kitchen/ Malted Milk/ How Long/ Kidman/ County Jail/

Forty Four/ Standing Around Crying/ Goin' Away Baby/ Blues All Day Long/ Hoochie Coochie Man/ It Hurts Me Too/ Blues Before Sunrise/ Someday After A While/ one other track
CD2: White Room/ Badge/ Wonderful Tonight/ Stone Free/ Circus Left Town/ Tears In Heaven/ Five Long Years/ Tearing Us Apart/ Crossroads/ Groaning The Blues/ Layla/ T'Ain't Nobody's Business If I Do
R: Good audience recording.   S: Royal Albert Hall, London Feb. 20 '94.

CD - SINGIN' THE BLUES
YELLOW CAT YC 016
Alberta/ The Sky Is Crying/ Singin' The Blues/ Little Rachel/ Worried Life Blues/ Steady Rollin' Man/ Stormy Monday/ Little Queenio/ Have You Ever Loved A Woman?
R: Vg soundboard.   S: Various '70s tours.

CD - SPLENDOR
VINTAGE RARE MASTERS VRM-001/2
CD1: Layla/ Further On Up The Road/ I Shot The Sheriff/ Make It Through Today/ Keep On Growing/ Can't Find My Way Home/ Driftin' Blues/ Sunshine Of Your Love/ Motherless Children/ Mean Old World
CD2: Teach me To Be Your Woman/ Bell Bottom Blues/ Badge/ Knockin' On Heaven's Door/ Tell The Truth/ Eyesight to The Blind/ Why Does Love Got To Be So Sad
R: Vg. Audience.   S: Civic Center, Providence, RI, USA June 25 '75.   C: Japanese CDs.

CD - TELL THE BLUES
IT'S ITS-1002
Smile/ Let It Grow/ Let It Rain/ Willie And The Hand Jive, Get Ready/ Badge/ Tell The Truth/ Have You Ever Loved A Woman/ Little Queenie/ Crossroads
R: Vg. Audience recording.   S: Roosevelt Stadium July 7 '74.

CD - THE UNRELEASED LIVE ALBUM
EC IN PERSON EIP023
Crossroads/ White Room/ Farther On Up The Road/ Farther On Up The Road (Robert Cray)/ Layla/ Hung Up On Your Love/ Holy Mother/ Miss You/ Wonderful Tonight/ Tearing Us Apart/ Badge, Let IT Rain
R: Vgs. Slight hiss.   S: Live '86-'87.
C: Japanese CD.

CD - THE UNRELEASED SESSIONS
CAPRICORN RECORDS CR-2048
It's Too Late (4:11)/ Meet Me (6:52)/ Jamine (7:39)/ Dobro Jam (3:28)/ Dobro Jam (2:32)/ B Minor Jam (6:57)/ B Minor Jam (3:58)/ Give Me Strength (3:29)/ Blues Instrumental (4:21)/ Jamine (8:00)/ Give Strength (2:23)/ Jam (3:54)/ Fool Like Me (5:05)*/ Burial (3:57)*
R: Exs. Soundboard.   S: Dynamic Studios, Jamaica Aug. 29 - Sept. 18 '74. *Criteria Studios, Miami Apr. - May '74.   C: Time 66:35.

CD - WE ALL CAME DOWN TO MONTREAUX
JOKER JOK-002-B/C
CD1: Crossroads/ White Room/ I Shot The Sheriff/ Wanna Make Love To You/ Run/ Miss You/ Same Old Blues/ Tearing Us Apart
CD2: Holy Mother/ Behind The Mask/ Badge/ Cocaine/ Layla/ Sunshine Of Your Love/ Further Up The Road/ Let It Rain
R: Exs. Soundboard.   S: Montreaux Casino Dec. 17 '86.   C: Australian CD. Dcc.

CD - 'WONDERFUL NIGHT'
CUTTLEFISH RECORDS CFR 007/08
CD1: Pretending/ Running Faith/ I Shot The Sheriff/ White Room/ Before You Accuse Me/ Old Love
CD2: No Alibis/ Tearing Us Apart/ Wonderful Tonight/ Layla/ Crossroads/ Sunshine Of Your Love
R: Exs. Soundboard.   S: Royal Albert Hall, London, England Feb. 7 '90.   C: Japanese CD. Dcc. Pic CDs

CD - WONDERFUL TONIGHT
THE SWINGIN' PIG TSP 196-6
CD1: Peaches And Diesel/ Wonderful Tonight/ Lay Down Sally/ Next Time You See Her/ The Core/ We're All The Way/ Rodeo Man/ Fool's Paradise/ Cocaine/ Badge/ Double Trouble
CD2: Nobody Knows You When Your Down And Out/ Let It Rain/ Knockin' On Heavens Door/ Last Night/ Goin' Down Slow/ Layla/ Bottle Of Red Wine/ You'll Never Walk Alone
CD3: Tulsa Time/ I Shot The Sheriff/ Say Down Sally/ Worried Life Blues/ Let It Rain/ double Trouble/ Sweet Little Lisa/ After Midnight
CD4: The Shape Your In/ Wonderful Tonight/ Blues Power/ Rambling On My Mind/ Have You Ever Loved A Women/ Cocaine/ Layla/ Further On Up The Road
CD5: Tulsa Time/ Motherless Children/ I Shot The Sheriff/ Same Old Blues/ Blues Power/ Tangled In Love/ Behind The Sun/ Wonderful Tonight/ Steppin' Out/ Never Make You Cry/ She's Waiting
CD6: Something Is Wrong/ Say Down Sally/ Badge/ Let It Rain/ Double Trouble/ Cocaine/ Layla/ Forever Man/ Further On Up The Road
R: Exs. Soundboard.   S: CD1-2 Civic Auditorium, Santa Monica Feb. 11 '78. CD3-4 Stadthalle, Bremen Apr. 20 '83. CD5-6 Coliseum, Richmond, VA Apr. 22 '85.   C: ECD. Box set.

CLAPTON, ERIC WITH JIMMY VAUGHAN

CD - GROANING THE BLUES
TRES HOMBRES RECORDINGS EC 94004/5
CD1: Intro/ Hey Yeah/ Just Like Putty/ Just Some Old Song/ Six Strings Down/ Some Other Song/ Boom Babba Boom/ Motherless Child/ Malted Milk/ How Long How Long Blues/ Kid Man Blues/ Country Jail Blues/ Forty Four/ Blues All Day Long/ Standin Round Cryin'/ (I'm Your) Hoochie Coochie Man/ It Hurts Me Too

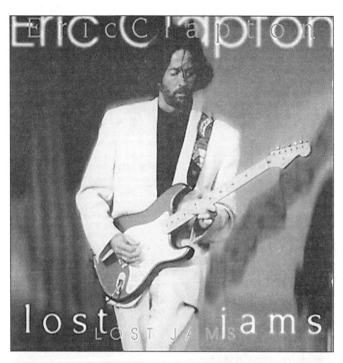

CD2: Blues Before Sunrise/ Third Degree/ So
Long/ Sinner's Prayer/ I Can't Judge Nobody/
Someday After A While (You'll Be Sorry)/ I'm Tore
Down/ Have You Ever Loved A Woman/ Cross
Cut Saw/ Five Long Years/ Crossroads/ Groaning
The Blues/ 'Tain't Nobody's Bizness If I Do/ Sweet
Home Chicago (with Jimmy Vaughan)
R: G. Audience.   S: Tracks 1-7 Jimmy Vaughan.
CD1 tracks 8-17 and CD2 Eric Clapton. San Jose
Event Arena Nov. 4 '94.   C: Japanese CD. Dcc.
Time CD1 74:06. CD2 74:24.

CLASH, THE

CD - LIVE AT MONT DE MARSAN
RED HOT RH-014
London's Burning/ Capital Radio/ Complete
Control/ Pressure Drop/ The Prisoner/ I'm So
Bored With The USA/ Cheat/ Hate & War/ Clash
City Rockers/ Remote Control/ Career
Opportunities/ Janie Jones/ White Riot/
Garageland/ 1977/ What's My Name/ Complete
Control/ Protex Blue/ London's Burning
R: Poor analogue, scratchy noise.   S: Mont De
Marsan, France Aug. 5 '77.

CD - THIS IS LIVE CLASH - CHICAGO 1979
WEEPING GOAT WG-004
Jimmy Jazz/ I'm So Bored With The USA/
Complete Control/ London Calling/ Clampdown/
White Man In Hammersmith Palace/ Koka Koka/ I
Fought The Law/ Jail Guitar Doors/ Police And
Thieves/ Stay Free/ Clash City Rockers/ Safe
European Home/ Capitol Radio/ Janie Jones/
Garageland/ Armagideon Time/ Career
Opportunities/ White Riot
R: Ex. Soundboard.   S: Chicago, Nov. 14 '79.
C: Japanese CD. Dbw. Time 63:51.

COCKER, JOE

LP - LIVE IN LA
CUBE RECORDS 853011
Dear Landlord/ Early In The Morning/ Didn't You
Know You've Got To Cry Sometime/ St. James
Infirmary/ Hitchcock Railway/ Midnight Rider/
What Kind Of Man Are You?/ High Time We
Went/ Love The One You're With
R: Exs. Soundboard.   S: Hollywood Bowl '72.
Long Beach Arena '72.   C: US boot from '76.

COHEN, LEONARD

CD - THE HOUSEWIFE, THE REFEREE AND
THE UNDERTAKER
TEDDY BEAR TB 80
Dance Me To The End Of Love (6:11)/ The Future
(7:42)/ Bird On The Wire (6:40)/ Anthem (6:20)/
Chelsea Hotel (3:56)/ Democracy (8:07)/ Joan Of
Arc (6:59)/ Closing Time (7:28)/ Take This Waltz
(7:50)/ Hallelujah (7:35)/ So Long Marianne (5:44)
R: Exs. Soundboard.   S: Congresshalle, Zurich
May 21 '93.   C: ECD. Dcc. Pic CD.

COLLECTIVE SOUL

CD - ATLANTA'S BRIGHTEST SONS
OCTOPUS OCTO 097
Goodnight, Good Guy (3:35)/ Another Little Thing
(For Me) (4:30)/ Breathe (3:07)/ Wasting Time
(3:38)/ Sister, Don't Cry (4:34)/ Goodnight, Good
Guy (3:15)/ Scream (3:22)/ Shine (6:03)/ Bleed
(4:11)/ Simple (3:18)/ Gel (3:11)/ Reach (4:17)/
The World I Know (4:13)/ Untitled (4:20)/
Heaven's Already Here (2:59)/ Where The River
Flows (4:05)/ See The Colors (4:17)/ Leaves
(3:28)/ Waiting (6:34)
R: Tracks 1-13 Exs. Soundboard. Tracks 14-19
Vg. Audience.   S: Track 1 Jon Stewart Show
Sept. 28 '94. Tracks 2-9 South Street Seaport,
NYC Aug. '94. Tracks 10-13 The Roxy, Hollywood
'94. Tracks 14-19 Heritage Festival, West Palm
Beach, FL Nov. 10 '94.   C: ECD. Dcc.

COLLINS, PHIL

CD - MISTER NICE GUY
OXYGEN RECORDS OXY 021
Drum Solo Introduction (4:08)/ I Don't Care
Anymore (5:57)/ Another Day In Paradise (5:37)/
One More Night (4:43)/ Separate Lives (6:08)/
Both Sides Of The Story (8:12)/ In The Air Tonight
(6:19)/ Hang In Long Enough (4:45)/ Something
Happened On The Way To Heaven (5:10)/
Medley: You Can't Hurry Love, Two Hearts,
Sussudio (12:47)/ Take Me Home (10:06)
R: Exs. Soundboard.   S: Fukuoka Dome,
Fukuoka, Japan May 7 '95.   C: ECD. Dbw.

COODER, RY

CD - BORDERLINE
DYNAMITE STUDIO DS94M089/90
CD1: Viva Seguin/ Do Re Mi/ Goodnight Irene/
Traditional Track #1/ He'll Have To Go/ How Can
A Poor Man Stand Such Time And Live/ Harder
Chicken Night/ Smoke Dab In The Middle
CD2: Alimony/ Stand By Me/ The Dark End Of
The Street/ Ditty Wah Ditty/ Traditional Track #2/
Instrumental/ Traditional Track #3/ Traditional
Track #4/ Jesus On The Mainline
R: Good audience recording. Hiss.
S: Concertgebouw, Amsterdam Jan. 23 '77.
C: Japanese CD.

CD - STAND BY ME
VINTAGE RARE MASTERS VRM-004
Stand By Me/ Tattler/ Dark End Of The Street/
Ditty Wah Ditty/ F.D.R. In Trinidad/ One Meat Ball/
Fool For A Cigarette/ Tamp 'Em Up Solid/ He'll
Have To Go/ Mexican Divorce/ Jesus On The
Mainline/ How Can A Poor Man Stand Such
Times/ Ditty Wah Ditty/ Fool For A Cigarette
R: Ex. Soundboard.   S: Tracks 1-10 San
Francisco Dec. '76. Tracks 11-13 Cambridge Folk
Festival, UK '75. Track 14 Pennsylvania '72.
C: Japanese CD. Dcc. Time 68:57.

COODER, RY AND FLACO JIMENEZ

CD - CONJUNTO IN AMSTERDAM
MAIN STREET MST 109
Alimony/ Stand By Me/ ...The Best That You Can/ Dark End Of The Street/ Diddy Wah Diddy/ One Meat Ball/ Hawaiian Song/ Fool About A Cigarette/ Down In The Boondocks/ Jesus On The Mainline/ Do-Re-Mi/ Goodnight Irene
R: Exs. Soundboard.   S: Amsterdam '77.
C: ECD. Dcc. Time 54:11.

COODER, RY AND DAVID LINDLEY

CD - LIVE IN OSAKA 1979
COLLECTORS DREAM DREAM 002
CD1: Alimony/ Go Home Girl/ Mexican Divorce/ F.D.R. In Trinidad/ Ax Sweet Mama/ Billy The Kid/ Denomination Blues/ One Meat Ball
CD2: Travellin' Man/ If Walls Could Talk/ How Can A Poor Man Stand Such Times And Live?/ Jesus On The Mainline/ The Tattler/ Blue Suede Shoes/ The Bourgeois Blues
R: Vg. Audience.   S: Osaka '79.
C: Time CD1 45:39. CD2 46:05.

CD - OSAKA 79
COLLECTORS DREAM DREAM 002
CD1: Alimony/ Go Home Girl/ Mexican Divorce/ F.D.R. In Trinidad/ Ax Sweet Mama/ Billy The Kid/ Denomination Blues/ One Meat Ball
CD2: Travellin' Man/ If Walls Could Talk/ How Can A Poor Man Stand Such Times And Live/ Jesus On The Mainline/ The Tattler/ Blue Suede Shoes/ Burgeois Blues
R: Vg audience recording.   S: Osaka May '79.

COP SHOOT COP vs HELMUT

7" - PREVIOUSLY UNRELEASED TRACKS
C: See listing under 'Helmut'.

COPE, JULIAN

CD - RARITIES
THE MUSIC'S OVER FOX-111-TMO
Starsbourg/ Death Mask (Quizmaster)/ Head Hang Love/ Blaze Star/ Holy Love/ Bill Drummond Said/ Mik Mak Mok/ The Bloody Assizes/ The Greatness And Perfection Of Love/ Sunspots/ I Went On A Chourney/ Mik Mak Mok/ Land Of Fear/ Umpteenth Unnatural Blues/ Non Alignment Pact/ Transporting/ Disaster/ Mock Turtle/ Warwick The Kingmaster/ Eve's Volcano! Vulcano Lungo! (Covered In Sin)
R: Poor sound.   S: Demos, re-mixes & others.

COSTELLO, ELVIS

CD - JESUS, THIS IS ELVIS
KISS THE STONE KTS 454
Remove The Staff/ Hidden Charms/ Everybody Is Crying Mercy (But Nobody Knows The Meaning Of The Word)/ I've Been Wrong Before/ Runnin'

Outta Fools/ Leave My Kitten Alone/ The Very Thoughts Of You/ Pouring Water On A Drowning Man/ Must You Throw That In My Face?/ Ram A Lam, Bam A Lou/ Why Don't You Love Me (Like You Used To Do)/ Allison, My Aim Is True/ Pump It Up/ Bam A Lam, Bam A Lou*
R: Exs. Soundboard.   S: Sheppards Bush, London May 17 '95. *David Letterman Show May 16 '95.   C: ECD. Dcc. Pic CD. With The Attractions. Time 58:37.

CD - PLUGGING THE GAPS
TONE-2CD 001
Allison/ Miracle Man/ Neat Neat Neat/ Blame It On Caine/ Mystery Dance/ Cry Cry Cry/ Wondering/ Blues Keep Calling/ Honky Tonk Girl/ Stranger In The House/ Don't Get Above Your Raising/ Psycho/ The Imposter/ Town Cryer/ Tomorrow's Just Another Day/ Party Party/ Don't Let Me Be Misunderstood/ Many Rivers To Cross/ St. Stephen's Day Murders/ Mischievous Ghost/ Ship Of Fools
R: Vg. Some surface noise.   S: Studio outtakes.

CD - SO LIKE CANDY
RAG DOLL MUSIC RDM-942014A/B
CD1: No Action/ High Fidelity/ The Beat/ Beyond Belief/ Sulky Girl/ London's Brilliant Parade/ Deep Dark Truthful Mirror/ You Tripped At Every Step/ Pony St./ New Lace Sleeves/ Clown Strike/ Kinder Murder/ Shabby Doll/ Rocking Horse Road
CD2: Still Too Soon To Know/ So Like Candy/ Man Out Of Time/ Watching The Detectives/ You Belong To Me/ 13 Steps Lead Down/ Radio Radio/ Lipstick Vogue/ Party Girl/ Allison/ Tracks Of My Tears/ three other tracks
R: Vg. Audience.   S: Northrup Auditorium, Minneapolis, Minn. May 27 '94.   C: Japanese CD. With The Attractions.

CD - STIFFED AGAIN
PLANET RECORDS 0871-20
Third Rate Romance/ Living In Paradise/ Radio Soul/ Radio Soul #2/ Pay It Back/ Imagination Is A Powerful Deceiver/ Imagination Is A Powerful Deceiver #2/ Imagination Is A Powerful Deceiver #3/ Knockin' On Heaven's Door/ I'm Packing Up/ I'm Packing Up #2/ Don't Stop The Band/ Red Shoes/ Blame It On Cain/ The Beat/ You Belong To Me/ Radio Radio/ Just Don't Know What To Do With Myself/ Stranger In The House/ Pump It Up/ Beaten To The Punch/ High Fidelity/ B Movie
R: Ex. Soundboard.   S: Tracks 1-12 demo recordings for Stiff Records. Tracks 13-23 recordings for The BBC '77-'80.   C: ECD. Dcc. 75:55.

CD - UNDER THE INFLUENZA
KISS THE STONE KTS 386
I Want You/ There's No Answer/ My Science Fiction Twin/ Watching The Detectives/ Deep, Dark, Truthful Mirror/ Complicated Shadows/ London's Brilliant Parade/ Allison/ Pump It Up/ Shipbuilding/ London's Brilliant Parade
R: Exs. Soundboard.   S: Live on tour '94.

C: ECD. Dcc. Pic CD. Time 48:24

COSTELLO, ELVIS AND JERRY GARCIA

CD - SWEETWATER
MOONLIGHT ML 9503
Accidents Will Happen/ Deep Dark Truthful Mirror/
Mystery Dance/ Poisoned Rose/ God's Comic/
The Angels Wanna Wear My Red Shoes/ New
Lace Sleeve/ Pads, Paws And Claws/ Radio
Sweetheart, Jackie Wilson Said/ Peace Love And
Understanding/ Only Daddy That'll Walk The Line/
Leave My Kitten Alone/ You Win Again/ Tonight
The Bottle Let Me Down/ Why Don't You Love Me
Like You Used To Do/ CC Rider/ Lovelight
R: G. Audience recording from boot video.
S: 'Sweetwater' Mill Valley, CA Apr 29 '89.

COW, HENRY

CD - RUINS
CANTERBURY DREAMS CTD-025/026
CD1: Unreleased Title 1/ Unreleased Title 2/ Nine
Funerals Of Citizen King 1/ Nirvana For Mice/
Nine funerals Of Citizen King 2/ Unreleased Title
3
CD2: Beautiful As The Moon, Terrible As An Army
With Banners/ Nirvana For Mice/ Ottawa Song/
Gloria Gloom/ Ruins/ Beautiful As The Moon
Reprise
R: Vgs.   S: CD1 demos. CD2 NDR Jazz Work
shop, Hamburg Mar. 26 '76.   C: Japanese CD.

CRANBERRIES, THE

CD - FRUITS OF OUR LABOUR
KTS OF AUSTRALIA 008 A
How (4:29)/ Sunday (3:32)/ Pretty (2:20)/
Dreaming My Dreams (5:08)/ Linger (5:05)/
Wanted (2:10)/ Daffodil Lament (5:19)/ I Can't Be
With You (3:21)/ Liar (2:55)/ Yeat's Grave (3:10)/
Ode To My Family (5:30)/ I Just Shot John
Lennon (2:45)/ Ridiculous Thoughts (5:10)/
Waltzing Back (4:15)/ Zombie (5:44)/ No Need To
Argue (3:21)/ Empty 4:02)/ Dreams (4:46)
R: Vg. Audience.   S: The Beacon Theater, New
York Dec. 17 '94.   C: Australian CD. Dcc.

CD - SONGS AGAINST WAR
OCTOPUS OCTO 087
How (3:08)/ Sunday (3:19)/ Linger (5:13)/
Dreaming My Dreams (4:13)/ Daffodil Lament
(4:46)/ I Can't Be With You (3:08)/ Wanted (2:27)/
I Don't Need (3:47)/ Ode To My Family (5:00)/
Ridiculous Thoughts (4:51)/ Sorry (4:28)/ So Cold
In Ireland (4:41)/ Empty (3:31)/ Dreams (4:09)
R: Exs. Soundboard.   S: Live Europe '94.
C: ECD. Dcc.

CD - STRANGE FRUITS
OXYGEN OXY 028
Sunday/ Zombie/ Wanted/ Linger/ Dreaming My
Dreams/ Dreaming My Dreams/ Linger/ I Can't Be
With You/ The Icicle Melts/ Dreams/ Zombie/ Ode

To My Family/ Linger/ Ave Marie/ Free To Decide
(unreleased)/ John Lennon Died (unreleased)
R: Ex.   S: Tracks 1-5 acoustic set, WNNX
Studio, Atlanta, GA Aug. 19 '94. Tracks 6-12
Mayflower, Newcastle, UK Oct. 12 '94. Tracks 13-
14 Parco Novi Sad, Modena, Italy Sept. 12 '95.
Tracks 15-16 Utrect, Holland Feb. 8 '95.
C: ECD. Dbw. Pic CD.

CD - UNWIRED
OCTOPUS OCTO 189
Dreaming My Dreams (4:33)/ Ode To My Family
(5:54)/ Linger (5:19)/ Empty (4:07)/ Zombie (4:25)/
Put Me Down (4:22)/ Ode To My Family (5:30)/
Wanted (2:36)/ Sunday (3:47)/ Empty (4:01)/
Linger (5:16)/ I Can't Be With You (3:28)/
Dreaming My Dreams (3:57)/ Waltzing Back
(4.27)/ No Need To Argue (2:57)/ Sunday (4:00)/
False (2:30)
R: Exs. Soundboard.   S: Tracks 1-5 'Unplugged'
session, NYC Apr. 18 '95. Tracks 6-15 Fleadh
Festival, Finsbury Park, London June 11 '94.
Tracks 16-17 LA Dec. 11 '93.   C: ECD.

CREAM

CD - KLOOKS KLEET '66
CAPRICORN RECORDS CR-2042
Lawdy Mama (take 2)/ Rollin' And Tumblin' (take
2)/ Sweet Wine (take 1)/ Cat's Squirrel (take 1)/
Coffee Song (take 1)/ Toad (take 1)/ You Make
Me Feel (take 2)/ Wrapping Paper (take 1)/ I Feel
Free (basic track)/ Falstaff Beer (take 1)/ Steppin'
Out (live)/ Sweet Wine (live)/ Meet Me At The
Bottom (live)/ N.S.U. (live)/ Lawdy Mama (live)/
Crossroads (live)
R: Exs. Soundboard. Tracks 11-17 G.   S: Track
1 Atlantic Studios, NY May 8-19 '67. Tracks 2-9
Chalk Farm Studios and Mayfair Studios, London
July thru Aug. '66. Track 10 IBC Studios, London
Aug. '67. Tracks 11-17 Klooks Kleet, West
Hampstead, London Aug. 2 and Nov. 15 '66.
C: Dcc. Time 59:57.

CD - THE RETURN OF A SUPER GROUP
ROCK CALENDAR RECORDS RC 2111
Tales Of Brave Ulysses (4:21)/ White Room
(5:24)/ Sitting On Top Of The World (4:40)/ I'm So
Glad (8:49)/ Rollin' And Tumblin' (6:12)/ Sweet
Wine (14:36)/ Politician (6:21)/ Born Under A Bad
Sign (7:28)/ Sunshine Of Your Love (5:58)
R: Vg-Ex.   S: Tracks 1-6 San Jose, Civic
Auditorium May 25 '68. Track 7 Jack Bruce Band,
Passaic, Capitol Theater '89. Tracks 8-9 Jack
Bruce Band, Bottom Line, NYC '89.   C: ECD.
Dcc.

CD - TIP TOP CONDITION
ARMS 25PR
Steppin' Out/ Train Time/ Toad/ Crossroads/
Sunshine Of Your Love/ Spoonful
R: G-Vg. Tracks 1-3 audience. Tracks 4-6 sound-
board.   S: Tracks 1-3 San Francisco, Mar. '68.
Tracks 4-6 Oakland Oct. '68.   C: Japanese CD.

CREEDENCE CLEARWATER REVIVAL

CD - MIDNIGHT ON THE BAY
GREAT DANE GDR CD9403
Born On The Bayou/ Green River/ Tombstone Shadow/ It Came Out Of The Sky/ Travelin' Band/ Who'll Stop The Rain/ Bad Moon Rising/ Proud Mary/ Fortunate Son/ Commotion/ Midnight Special/ The Night Time Is The Right Time/ Us Around The Bend/ Keep On Chooglin'
R: Ex.   S: Oakland Coliseum, Oakland, CA Jan. 31 '70.

CROSBY, STILLS, NASH AND YOUNG

CD - ALL ALONG THE NAVAJO TRAIL
F*!#IN' UP FUPCD-3009/10/11
CD1: Love The One You're With/ Wooden Ships/ Immigration Man/ Traces/ Cowgirl In The Sand/ Grave Concern/ Black Queen/ Ohio/ three other tracks
CD2: Carry Me/ For Free/ The Lee Shore/ Prison Song/ It's Alright/ Our House/ Long May You Run/ Only Love Can Break Your Heart/ three other tracks
CD3: You Can't Catch Me, Word Game/ Can't Be Denied/ Deja Vu/ Pre-Road Downs/ First Thing First/ Long Time Gone/ Revolution Blues/ three other tracks
R: Vg. Audience.   S: Oakland Coliseum, Oakland, CA July 13 '74.   C: Japanese CD.

CD - BRING ME SADNESS
F*!#IN'UP FUPCD 2020/21
CD1: Suite: Judy Blue Eyes/ Blackbird/ Helplessly Hoping/ Guinnevere/ Lady Of The Island/ Black Queen/ Birds/ I've Loved Her So Long/ You Don't Have To Cry/ So Begins The Task
CD2: Pre-Road Downs/ Long Time Gone/ Bluebird Revisited/ Sea Of Madness/ Wooden Ships/ Down By The River/ On The Way Home/ Black Queen/ 49 Bye-Bye, American Children (includes For What It's Worth)/ So Begins The Task
R: G-Vg. Soundboard. Static.   S: Live '69.
C: Japanese CD. Dcc. CD1 38:46. CD2 51:34.

CD - DETROIT EXPERIENCE
MAIN STREET MST 108
Suite Judy Blue Eyes/ Black Bird/ On The Way Home/ Teach Your Children/ Triad/ Guinevere/ Hour House/ Country Girl/ Helpless/ Black Queen/ Pre-Road Down/ And So Begins The Task/ Long Time Gone/ Woodstock
R: Ex. Soundboard.   S: Detroit Dec. 16 '69.
C: ECD. Dcc. Time 76:17.

CROW, SHERYL

CD - ACOUSTIC
KISS THE STONE KTS 427
Leaving Las Vegas (5:46)/ Strong Enough (3:13)/ All I Wanna Do (5:05)/ The Na Na Song (3:48)/ D'yer Mak'er (4:03)/ All I Wanna Do (3:59)/ Can't Cry Anymore (4:54)/ Leaving Las Vegas (5:58)/ Strong Enough (3:37)/ The Na Na Song (4:55)/ All I Wanna Do (4:45)
R: Exs. Soundboard.   S: Tracks 1-5 The Brooklyn Academy Of Music Feb. '95. Track 6 The Grammy Awards Mar. 1 '95. Tracks 7-11 Disney World, FL Jan. '95.   C: ECD. Dcc. Pic CD.

CD - AS THE CROW FLIES
CAPRICORN RECORDS PF-900
Easy Good Thing/ Leaving Las Vegas/ The Na Na Song/ All I Want To Do/ Can't Cry Anymore/ Shattered/ Easy Good Thing/ Solidify/ The Na Na Song/ Strong Enough/ Leaving Las Vegas/ All I Want To Do/ I Shall Believe
R: Exs. Soundboard. Tracks 5-13 Ex. Audience.
S: Tracks 1-4 Los Angeles 12/10/94. Tracks 5-13 San Diego Nov. '94.   C: Dbw. 71:07.

CD - EVEN ANGELS ROCK
OCTOPUS OCTO 161
Wake Me Up When You Are Over (4:46)/ Can't Cry No More (4:56)/ Run Baby, Run (5:54)/ The Na-Na Song (7:43)/ Strong Enough (4:04)/ No One Said It Would Be Easy (6:56)/ Leaving Las Vegas (6:47)/ What Can I Do For You (7:18)/ I Shall Believe (7:17)/ Live With Me (4:18)
R: Tracks 1-9 Exs. Soundboard. Track 10 Ex. Audience.   S: Tracks 1-9 Shepherd Bush Empire, London July 7 '94. Track 10 Joe Robbie Stadium Nov. 25 '94.   C: ECD. Dcc. Pic CD.

CD - I FEEL HAPPY
ZA-46-47
CD1: Factory Girl (Rolling Stones recorded intro)/ Leaving Las Vegas/ Love Is A Good Things/ Can't Cry Anymore/ Run, Baby, Run/ Hard To Make A Stand/ Keep On Growing/ Solidify/ The Na-Na Song/ All I Wanna Do/ Coffee Shop/
CD2: Strong Enough/ D'Yer Mak'er/ What I Can Do For You/ All I Wanna Do/ I Shall Believe/ I'm Gonna Be A Wheel Someday/ I Feel Happy/ Keep On Growing*/ D'Yer Mak'er*/ All I Wanna Do/ I Feel Happy*
R: Vg-Ex. Audience.   S: Tokyo Liquid Room, Tokyo Apr. 13 '95. *Apr. 14' 95.   C: Japanese CD. Dcc.

CD - UNWIRED
OCTOPUS OCTO 191
Leaving Las Vegas (5:45)/ Strong Enough (3:07)/ All I Wanna Do (4:54)/ The Na Na Song (3:46)/ D' Yer Mak'Er (3:53)/ I Can't Cry Anymore (5:01)/ Leaving Las Vegas (6:03)/ Strong Enough (3:35)/ The Na Na Song (5:09)/ All I Wanna Do (4:46)/ Run Baby Run (5:35)/ What Can I Do For You (5:51)/ Love Is A Good Thing (6:01)/ Live With Me (4:13)
R: Exs. Soundboard.   S: Tracks 1-5 'Unplugged' sessions New York City '95. Tracks 6-10 Las Vegas '94. Tracks 11-12 The House Of Blues, Los Angeles Jan 27 '95. Track 13 The Universal Amphitheatre, Los Angeles Dec. 11 '94. Track 14

Joe Robbie Stadium, Miami Nov. 25 '94.
C: ECD.

D

CULT, THE

CD - CEREMONIA
NR 03
Nirvana/ Lil' Devil/ Coming Down/ The Witch/ In
The Clouds/ Rain/ Eddie/ Fire Woman/ Stars/
Wild Flower/ Sun King Baby/ Love Removal
Machine/ She Sells Sanctuary/ Love/ Be Free/
Earth Mofo
R: Vg-Ex. Audience.   S: Buenos Aires,
Argentina Mar. '95.   C: ECD. Dcc. Time 73:53.

CURE, THE

CD - ALTERNATIVE MEDICINE
CHELSEA CFD026
Lament (free with Flexipop magazine No. 22)/ All I
Had To Do Is Kill Her ('Pornography' tour, Paris
L'Olympia '82)/ Splintered In Her Head
('Pornography' tour, Paris L'Olympia '82)/ Birdmad
Girl (studio demo '84)/ Throw Your Foot (studio
demo '84)/ Happy Birthday Simon (Brussels,
Belgium '80)/ Caterpillar (rare acoustic version,
MTV '91)/ Caterpillar ((studio demo '84)/ Close To
Me (demo for 'The Head On The Door' sessions)/
A Reflection (Stokvishal, Netherlands May 24
'80)/ Pornography ('Pornography' tour, Paris
L'Olympia '82)/ I Dig You* (rare live performance)/
Desperate Journalist (BBC Radio sessions Oct.
'79)/ The Blood (acoustic version, MTV '91)/
Aerial (unreleased track '79-'80)/ Accuracy (Peel
Session '79)/ Hello I Love You (Rubaiyat compila-
tion album)/ Purple Haze (live Hendrix tribute)/ I
Dig You (B-Side of rare Cult Hero single '79)/ I'm
A Cult Hero (A-Side of rare Cult Hero single '79)
R: Ex. Soundboard. Live material G-Vg. *G.
C: ECD. Dcc. Time 77:24.

CD - DRESSING UP FOR A DAY OUT
KISS THE STONE KTS 466
Pictures Of You/ Lullaby/ Just Like Heaven/
Jupiter Crash/ High/ The Walk/ Let's Go To Bed/
Dressing Up/ A Strange Day/ Push/ Mink Car/
Friday I'm In Love/ In Between Days/ From The
Edge Of The Deep Green Sea/ Shiver And
Shake/ Disintegration/ End
R: Exs. Soundboard.   S: Glastonbury Festival
June 26 '95.   C: ECD. Dcc. Pic CD. Time 78:35.

CD - HAPPINESS IN SADNESS
OCTOPUS OCTO 194
Pictures Of You (7:37)/ Lullaby (4:30)/ Just Like
Heaven (3:38)/ Drift To Press (4:35)/ High (3:31)/
The Walk (3:30)/ Let's Go To Bed (3:42)/ Dressing
Up To Kiss (2:56)/ Stay (4:43)/ Nick Car (3:46)/
Friday I'm In Love (3:43)/ Inbetween Days (3:14)/
From The Edge Of The Deep Green Sea (8:24)/
Shame (4:05)/ Disintegration (8:20)
R: Exs. Soundboard.   S: Glastonbury Festival ,
UK June 25 '95.   C: ECD.

DALTRY, ROGER

CD - SUMMERTIME BLUES
THAT'S LIFE TL 930024
Substitute (3:29)/ Pictures Of Lily (2:51)/ Behind
Blue Eyes (2:28)/ 5:15 (6:09)/ After The Fire
(3:51)/ Under A Raging Moon (7:25)/ Let Me
Down Easy (4:34)/ Giving It All Away (3:43)/ Won't
Get Fooled Again (7:42)/ Free Me (6:19)/
Summertime Blues (1:21)/ C' Mon Everybody
(1:51)
R: Exs. Soundboard.   S: Orpheum Theatre,
Boston '85 not '89 as cover claims.   C: ECD.
Dcc. Time 51:53.

DEAD CAN DANCE

CD - THE HIDDEN TREASURE
SWINDLE RECORDS SWN 030
Awakening (2:03)/ Reached From Above (3:04)/
In Power We Entrust - The Love Advocated
(4:02)/ To The Shore (3:37)/ Alone (3:57)/ Pray
For Dawn (6:08)/ Lartormento (2:29)/ The Night
We Were Lost (4:30)/ Lyndra (4:46)/ Isabella
(2:20)/ Tune For Sheba (5:12)/ Cyndrill (2:50)/
The Serpent's Army (2:10)/ They Don't Even Cry
(3:05)/ Eyeless In Gaza (3:34)/ The Endless
Longing Of Sea Doves (20:30)
R: Ex. Audience.   S: Live during '94 world tour.
C: ECD. Pic CD.

DEAD KENNEDYS

7" - COLD FISH
S1: Cold Fish (previously unreleased)/ Forward
To Death
S2: Holiday In Cambodia
S: Demos '78.   C: USA. Yellow/green cover.
Black type. Clear yellow vinyl. Limited edition of
1,500.

7" - DEAD KENNEDYS
S1: Give It
S2: Meantime Oven
S: Live '92.

DEEP PURPLE

CD - A NIGHT OF THE MACHINE
TNT STUDIO TNT-940150/ 151
CD1: Highway Star/ Smoke On The Water/
Strange Kind Of Woman/ Child In Time
CD2: Lazy, The Mule/ Space Trackin'/ Black Night
R: Vg audience recording.   S: Osaka, Japan
June 27 '73.   C: Japanese CDs.

CD - BLACK NIGHT IN DENMARK
BABY CAPONE BC 020/2
CD1: Highway Star (7:47)/ Strange Kind Of
Woman (9:07)/ Child In Time (17:30)/ The Mule

(9:36)/ Lazy (10:41)/ Fireball (4:16)
CD2: Space Truckin' (22:13)/ Lucille (6:44)/ Black
Night (5:15)/ Smoke On The Water (6:41)/ Never
Before (4:24)/ Maybe I'm A Leo (5:07)
R: Exs. Soundboard.   S: Denmark Jan. 3 '72.
C: ECD. Dcc. Pic CDs.

CD - BLACKLESS MORSEMANIA
DP 95-A/B
CD1: Fireball (4:15)/ Black Night (7:45)/ The
Battle Rages On (6:38)/ Take The Mechanic
(4:34)/ Woman From Tokyo (6:12)/ The
Perpendicular Walls (5:46)/ When A Blind Man
Cries (6:58)/ Perfect Strangers (7:00)
CD2: Anyone's Daughter (4:45)/ Child In Time
(9:05)/ Anya (10:42)/ Soon Forgotten (5:33)/ Lazy
(10:10)/ Speed King (6:15)/ Highway Star (6:48)/
Smoke On the Water (8:22)
R: Ex. Audience.   S: The Musical Theatre,
Sunrise, FL Mar. 4 '95.   C: ECD. Dcc.

CD - BURNING PURPLE
BONDAGE MUSIC BONO 20/21
CD1: Burn/ Black Night (includes Long Live
Rock'N Roll, Child In Time)/ Truth Hurts/ The Cut
Runs Deep (includes Hush)/ Perfect Strangers/
Fire In the Basement (includes Bass Solo)/ Love
Conquers All
CD2: Difficult To Cure (includes Keyboards Solo)/
Knockin' At The Back Door/ Lazy/ Highway Star/
Smoke On The Water (includes Drum Solo,
Woman From Tokyo)
R: Ex soundboard recording.   S: Tower Theater,
Philadelphia, Pennsylvania Apr. 20 '91.

CD - DESTROYED THE ARENA
TNT STUDIO TNT-940139/40
CD1: Highway Star/ Smoke On The Water/
Strange Kind Of Woman/ Child In Time
CD2: Lazy, Drum Solo/ The Mule/ Space Truckin'
R: Poor. Audience recording.   S: Budokan,
Tokyo, Japan June 25 '73.   C: Japanese CD.

CD - EMPTINESS, EAGLES AND SNOW
MIDNIGHT BEAT MB CD 032/33
CD1: Speaker Intro, World Tour Intro (1:04)/
Highway Star (7:28)/ Ramshackle Man (6:14)/
Maybe I'm A Leo (5:11)/ Fireball (4:16)/ Perfect
Strangers (6:27)/ Pictures Of Home (5:49)/
Keyboard Solo (3:54)/ Knocking At Your
Backdoor, Guitar Solo (9:29)/ Child In Time
(9:32)/ Anya, Guitar Solo (10:01)/ When A Blind
Man Cries (6:13)
CD2: Lazy, Drum Solo (6:32)/ Satch Boogie
(3:47)/ Woman From Tokyo (3:37)/ Paint It Black
(4:05)/ Smoke On The Water (7:43)/ Outro,
Fireworks (2:36)/ Anyone's Daughter (3:43)/ The
Battle Rages On (6:12)/ Space Truckin' (2:26)/
Woman From Tokyo (2:38)/ Paint It Black (5:40)/
Hush (encore) (4:20)/ Black Night (encore) (7:27)/
Smoke On The Water (with Leslie West) (encore)
(8:17)/ Speed King (encore) (4:38)

R: Vg-Ex. Audience.   S: CD1 and CD2 tracks 1-
6 Festpladsen GL. Vardevej, Esbjerg 'Rock
Festival', Denmark 4-6-'94. CD2 tracks 7-14
Bellevueparken, Karlshamn 'Summer Festival',
Sweden 10-6-'94. CD2 track 15 Heden, Goteborg
'All Star Festival', Sweden 11-6-'94.   C: ECD.
Dcc.

CD - FIRE IN THE SKY
DPCD-41533
Guitar Solo, Smoke On The Water/ Strange Kind
Of Woman/ God Save The Queen Introduction,
Mary Long/ Organ Solo, Lazy, Drums Solo, The
Mule/ Space Truckin'/ Smoke On The Water
R: Poor-G. Audience recording.   S: Long Beach
Arena Apr. 15 73. Track 6 'The Rock & Blues
Band' featuring Jon Lord and Ian Paice.

CD - FIREBALL OVER SWITZERLAND
KIWI RECORDS KIWI 1001
Ramshakle Man (6:20)/ Maybe I'm A Leo (5:20)/
Fireball (4:40)/ Perfect Stranger (6:40)/ Pictures
Of Home (10:40)/ Knocking At Your Backdoor
(9:20)/ The Battle Rages On (6:20)/ When A Blind
Man Cries (6:20)/ Speed King (7:00)/ Smoke On
The Water (9:00)
R: Vg. Audience.   C: Australian CD. Dcc.

CD - IN FLAME
ZA 53/54
CD1: Burn/ Lay Down Stay Down/ Mistreated/
Smoke On The Water/ You Fool No One, Drum
Solo, The Mule
CD2: Space Truckin'/ Smoke On The Water
R: Vg. Audience.   S: Madison Square Garden,
NYC Mar. 13 '74. CD2 track 2 San Diego Apr. 9
'74.   C: Japanese CD. Dcc. Pic CD.

CD - MARY LONG
DP-1003
Highway Star, Guitar Improvisation/ Smoke On
The Water/ Strange Kind Of Woman/ Mary Long/
Organ Improvisation, Lazy, Drum Solo
R: Ex FM recording.   S: Palais Des Sports,
Lyon Mar. 16 '73.

CD - OUT
STARQUAKE SQ-08
John Stew/ Blood Sucker/ Wring That Neck/ Child
In Time/ Into The Fire/ No, No, No/ Hey Joe/
Emmeretta/ Lalena/ Painter/ Ricochet/
Emmeretta/ Speed King
R: Vg. Soundboard. Some hiss. Some surface
noise.   C: Japanese CD. Dcc. Time 57:25

CD - PRESNAKE
GERMAN RECORDS 034
Burn/ Might Just Take Your Life/ Mistreated/
Smoke On The Water/ You Fool No One/ The
Mule/ Space Trucking
R: G-Vg. Soundboard.   S: California Jam,
Ontario Motor Speedway Apr. 6 '74.   C: ECD.
Dcc. Digi-pack. Time 72:42.

CD - PURPLE SUNSHINE
NIGHTLIFE N-032/033
CD1: Fire Ball/ Black Night/ The Battle Rages On/
Ken The Mechanic/ Woman From Tokyo/ The
Perpendicular Waltz/ When A Blind Man Cries/
Perfect Strangers/ Pictures Of Home, Jon Lord
Solo/ Knocking At Your Backdoor/ Anyone's
Daughter
CD2: Child In Time/ Anya/ Lazy, Ian Paice Solo/
Speed King/ Highway Star/ Smoke On The Water/
Black Night/ Child In Time/ The Highlander
R: Ex. Audience. CD2 tracks 7-11 radio broad-
cast.   S: Sunrise Theater, Ft. Lauderdale, FL
Mar. 4 '95. CD2 tracks 7-11 acoustic set, South
Africa Apr. '95.

CD - THE SATURATION POINT
TNT STUDIO TNT-940164/165
CD1: Highway Star/ Smoke On The Water/
Strange Kind Of Woman/ Child In Time
CD2: Lazy, The Mule/ Space Truckin'/ Black Night
R: Poor audience recording.   S: Kohkaido,
Hiroshima, Japan June 23 '73.   C: Japanese.

CD - THE STORY OF A LOSER (IT COULD BE YOU)
TNT STUDIO TNT-940143/144
CD1: Highway Star/ Smoke On The Water/
Strange Kind Of Woman/ Child In Time
CD2: Keyboard Solo, Lazy, Drum Solo, The Mule/
Space Truckin'/ Black Night
R: Poor.   S: Nagoya, Japan June 23 '73 (?).
C: Japanese CD.

CD - WELCOME JOE
ALL OF US AS 29/2
CD1: Intro/ Highway Star/ Ramshackle Man/
Maybe I'm A Leo/ Fireball/ Perfect Strangers/
Pictures Of Home/ Jon Lord Solo/ Knockin' At
Your Backdoor/ Anyone's Daughter/ Anya
CD2: The Battle Rages On/ When A Blind Man
Cries/ Lazy/ Satch Boogie/ Space Truckin'/
Woman From Tokyo/ Paint It Black/ Speed King/
Smoke On The Water
R: Vg sound.   S: Expo Genova June 22 '94.
C: ECD.

DEFF LEPPARD

CD - ONE MAN BAND
BABY CAPONE BC 005
Stagefright (4:10)/ Rock! Rock! (3:32)/ Women
(6:14)/ Too Late For Love (5:51)/ Hysteria (7:24)/
Gods Of War (6:38)/ Die Hard The Hunter (6:55)/
Bringin' The Heartbreak (6:15)/ Foolin' (5:06)/
Armageddon It (5:31)/ Animal (4:54)/ Pour Some
Sugar On Me (4:50)/ Guitar Solo (3:08)/ Rock Of
Ages (8:52)
R: Exs. Soundboard.   S: Tampa during '88
world tour.   C: ECD. Dcc. Pic CD.

DELANEY, BONNIE AND FRIENDS

CD - ALL FRIENDS ARE COMING
MAIN STREET MST 110
I Wanna Go Home/ Alone Together/ My Man/ 12
Bar Blues/ Come Into My Kitchen/ Goin' Down
The Road Feelin' Bad/ Poor Elijah/ The Ghetto
R: Vgs.   S: New York '71.

DENNY, SANDY

CD - DARK THE NIGHT
NIXED RECORDS NIXED 006
Green Grow The Laurels (4:00)/ Fhir A Bhata
(The Boat Man) (4:58)/ Blues Run The Game
(3:25)/ Milk And Honey (3:38)/ Soho (3:10)/ In
Memory (Tender You) (2:28)/ It Ain't Me Babe
(3:37)/ East Virginia (3:22)/ My Dear Geordie
(3:21)/ Until The Real Thing Comes Along (3:58)/
Whispering Grass (3:38)/ Dark The Night (3:59)/
Solo (4:22)/ It Suits Me Well (4:17)/ The Music
Weaver (3:05)/ Bushes And Briars (2:31)/ It'll Take
A Long Time (3:54)/ Man Of Iron (7:30)/ Here In
Silence (3:31)
R: Ex. Soundboard.   S: Tracks 1-2 'Cellarful Of
Folk' BBC World Service Nov. 7 '66. Tracks 3-9
home demos '66. Tracks 10-13 BBC 'Sounds Of
The Seventies' Nov. 14 '73. Tracks 14-17 BBC
'Sounds Of The Seventies' Oct. 25 '72. Tracks 18-
19 'Pass Of Arms' film soundtrack '72.   C: ECD.
Dcc.

CD - ONE LAST REFRAIN
NIXED RECORDS NIXED 002
Solo/ The North Star/ Nothing More/ Gold Dust/
the Sea/ Tomorrow Is A Long Time/ The Lady/
Wretched Wilbur/ Stranger To Himself/ For Shame
Of Doing Wrong/ One More Chance/ Who Knows
Where The Time Goes/ Water Mother/ What Will I
Do With Tomorrow/ Are The Judges Sane/ I Need
You
R: Vg-Ex. Soundboard. Some hiss. Tracks 13-16
Exs. Soundboard.   S: Tracks 1-12 Sandy
Denny's last concert, Sound Circus, The Royalty
Theatre, Kingsway, London Nov. 27 '77. Tracks
13-16 'Swedish Fly Girls' soundtrack '72.
C: ECD. Dcc. Pic CD. Time 69:43.

DEREK AND THE DOMINOES

CD - LAYLA AND OTHER ASSORTED UNRE-LEASED SONGS
YELLOW DOG YD 040
Layla (out of tune version)/ Nobody Loves You
When You're Down And Out/ Key To The
Highway/ Little Wing/ Nobody Loves You When
You're Down And Out/ It's Too Late/ Got To Get
Better In A Little While/ Son Of Apache/ Snake
Lane Blues/ High/ Untitled Instrumental/ One
More Chance
R: Ex soundboard recording.   S: '70 studio out-
takes.   C: ECD.

CD - LITTLE WING
BLACKIE 12/13
CD1: Why Does Love Got To Be So Sad/ Tell The
Truth/ Key To The Highway/ Got To Get Better In
A Little While/ Mean Old World/ Little Wing
CD2: Blues Power/ Have You Ever Loved A
Woman/ Let It Rain/ Chuck Berry Medley
R: Poor audience recording.   S: Berkeley
Community Theatre, CA Nov. 19 '70.

CD - STORMY MONDAY
TMQ-71082CD
Derek's Boogie/ Blues Power/ Stormy Monday/
Tell The Truth
R: Good audience recording.   S: Santa Monica
Civic Auditorium Nov. 20 '70.   C: Japanese CD.

DINOSAUR

7" - RADIO RUCUS
S1: Chunks
S2: Freak Scene
R: Vg.   C: USA. Dbw. Red type. 45 RPM.

DIRE STRAITS

CD - HIGH FALLS
BABY CAPONE BC 022/2
CD1: Ride Across The River (9:54)/ Expresso
Love (6:58)/ One World (5:10)/ Romeo And Juliet
(10:46)/ Private Investigations (8:35)/ Sultan Of
Swing (9:35)/ Why Worry (5:26)/ Walk Of Life
(4:26)
CD2: Two Young Lovers (5:06)/ Money For
Nothing (8:22)/ Wild West End (8:46)/ Tunnel Of
Love (17:23)/ Solid Rock (4:30)/ Brothers In Arms
(8:04)/ Going Home (4:35)
R: Exs. Soundboard.   S: Cuyahoga Falls, USA
Aug. '85.   C: ECD. Dcc. Pic CD.

DIXIE DREGS

CD - SEX, DREGS & ROCK 'N' ROLL
ALL OF US AS 24
Patch Work (4:52)/ Night Of The Living Dregs
(3:58)/ Night Meets Light (8:52)/ Punk Sandwich
(3:15)/ Cruise Control (14:36)/ Take It Off The Top
(4:25)/ Disco Rhythm (3:13)/ Gina Lola
Breakdown (4:36)/ Odyssey (4:38)
R: Exs. Soundboard.   S: 'My Father's Place',
New York June 19 '79.   C: ECD. Dcc.

DR. JOHN

CD - SUCH A FUNKY NIGHT!
MAIN STREET MST 115
Loop Garoo/ Walk On Gilded Splinters/ Dansee
Kalinda Ba Doom/ Stag-A-Lee/ Hard Judgment/
Travelling Mood/ Mother/ Put A Little Love
In Your Heart/ Tipitina/ Mess Around/ Talking/ I've
Been HooDood/ Such A Night/ Right Place Wrong
Time/ Let The Good Times Roll/ Wang Dang
Doodle/ Mama Roux/ Qualified
R: Ex. Soundboard.   S: Ultrasonic Studios, NYC

Nov. 6 '73.

DOOBIE BROTHERS, THE

CD - DOOBY BROTHERS
UNFORGOTTEN JEWELS UJ 94006
Jesus Is Just Alright/ Long Train Running/ Sweet
Maxine/ It Keeps You Running/ Echoes Of Love/
Neals Fandango/ What A Fool Believes/ Disciple/
Take Me In Your/ Don't Stop To Watch The
Wheels/ Steamer Lane Breakdown/ China Girl
R: Exs. Soundboard.   S: USA '87.   C: ECD.
Dcc. Pic CD. Time 46:59.

CD - LISTEN TO THE DOOBIES
RSM 018
Dangerous (5:39)/ Rockin' Down The Highway
(3:10)/ Jesus Is Just Alright (4:48)/ Little Darling, I
Need You (3:31)/ Dependin' On You (4:40)/
Echoes Of Love (2:48)/ The Doctor (4:05)/ Take
Me In Your Arms (3:58)/ It Keeps Me Runnin'
(5:13)/ South City Midnight Lady (5:54)/ Minute
By Minute (4:30)/ What A Fool Believes (3:45)/
China Grove (3:14)/ Takin' It To The Streets
(4:01)/ Long Train Running (6:08)/ Listen To The
Music (4:55)
R: Exs. Soundboard.   S: Concorde Pavilion, CA
'94.   C: ECD. Dcc.

CD - LIVE WILD WEST COAST '79
LAM 7901
Jesus Is Just Alright/ Without You/ Sweet Maxine/
It Keeps You Running/ Take Me In Your Arms/
Open Your Eyes/ What A Fool Believes/ Neal's
Fandango/ Echoes Of Love/ Your Made That
Way/ Black Water/ September Lane Breakdown/
Road Angel/ China Grove/ Takin' It To The Street/
Listen To The Music
R: Vg FM recording.   S: Japan '79.

CD - REUNION
KISS THE STONE KTS 402
Dangerous/ Rockin' Down The Highway/ Jesus Is
Alright/ Li'l Darlin'/ Depending On You/ Echoes Of
Love/ Doctor/ Take Me In Your Arms/ It Keeps You
Runnin/ South City Midnight Lady/ Minute By
Minute/ What A Fool Believes/ China Grove/
Takin' It To The Streets/ Long Train Running/
Listen To The Music
R: Exs. Soundboard.   S: The Concord Pavilion,
Concord CA '94.   C: ECD. Dcc. Time 70:24.

DOORS, THE

CD - THE BLACK ANGEL'S DEATH SONG
BLACK ANGEL RECORDS BA 597604
Get Off My Life, Rock Me Baby, Crawling King
Snake (San Francisco Mar. 7 '67)/ I'm A King Bee
(San Francisco Mar 10 '67)/ Hitler (Seattle June 5
'70)/ You Need Meat, Don't Go No Further, The
Journey/ Who Scared You (New Orleans Dec. 12
'70)/ Back Door Man, Five To One (Los Angeles
July 5 '68)/ Little Red Rooster (USA '68 with
Albert King)/ Who Do You Love (San Francisco

Mar 10 '67)/ Whiskey, Mystics And Men ('Rock Is Dead' session)/ Roadhouse Blues (New York '70)/ Love Me Two Times (Miami Mar. 1 '69)/ Rock Is Dead (rehearsal session Dec. 8 '70)/ Love Me Tender ('Rock Is Dead' session)
R: Ex.   C: ECD. Dcc. Time 78:46.

CD - BLUES BEFORE SUNRISE
BLACK ANGEL RECORDS BA 597604
Get Off My Life (San Francisco 7-3-'67)/ Rock Me Baby (San Francisco 7/3/67)/ Crawling King Snake (San Francisco 7/3/67)/ I'm A King Bee (San Francisco 10/3/67)/ Hitler (Seattle 5-6-'70)/ You Need Meat, Don't Go No Further (New Orleans 12/12/70)/ Back Door Man (Los Angeles 5/7/68)/ Little Red Rooster (USA '68 with Albert King)/ Who Do You Love (San Francisco 10/3/67)/ Whiskey, Mystics And Men ('Rock Is Dead' session)/ Roadhouse Blues (New York '70)/ Love Me Two Times (Miami 1/3/69)/ Rock Is Dead (Doors rehearsal session 8/12/70)/ Love Me Tender ('Rock Is Dead' session)
R: Vg-Ex.   C: ECD. Dcc.

CD - FURTHER ADVENTURES WITH THE MOJO WIRE
RHP 456
Moonlight Drive (7:06)/ Get Out Of My Life (4:04)/ I'm A King Bee (3:47)/ Back Door Man (5:19)/ Sittin' And Thinkin' (3:24)/ Rock Me Baby (5:01)/ Woman Is A Devil (6:05)/ Love In Vain (Different Lyrics) (3:54)/ Love Me (Boogie Theme) (5:23)/ Rock Is Dead (10:11)/ Someday Soon (2:47)/ The End (12:25)
R: Vg-Ex.   S: Tracks 1-6 rehearsals in San Francisco Feb. and Mar. '67. Tracks 7-11 rehearsals in Los Angeles Feb.-May '69. Track 12 Copenhagen - Danish TV Show Sept. '68.
C: ECD. Dcc.

CD - LIBERATION
STRANGE DAYS SDCD 001
Build Me A Woman/ Wild Child/ Wintertime Love/ Wishful, Sinful/ The Soft Parade/ The Wasp/ Love Me Two Times/ Alabama Song/ When The Music's Over/ The Unknown Soldier/ Mystery Train/ Someday Soon/ Frederick/ Not To Touch The Earth/ The End
R: Ex.Soundboard. Tracks 13-15 G. Hiss.
S: Alternate studio versions and unreleased songs recorded between '65 and '70.   C: ECD. Dcc. Pic CD.

CD - LIVE IN SEATTLE 1970
TRADE MARK OF QUALITY TMOQ 01
Back Door Man, Love Hides, Back Door Man/ Roadhouse Blues/ When The Music's Over/ People Get Ready, Baby Please Don't Go/ Mystery Train-Crossroads/ Break On Through/ Someday Soon
R: Vg. Soundboard.   S: Seattle Coliseum June 5 '70.   C: Japanese CD. Cardboard sleeve with photo-copy insert. No relation to the original TMOQ. Time 70:01.

CD - NO FUTURE
TEDDY BEAR TB 24
Roadhouse Blues (5:33)/ Peace Frog (3:37)/ Medley: Alabama Song, Backdoor Man, Five To One (10:08)/ The Celebration Of The Lizard (19:03)/ Soul Kitchen (7:01)/ Light My Fire (10:46)/ Build Me A Woman (3:39)/ When The Music's Over (12:07)
R: Vg-Ex.   S: Felt Forum, New York City Jan. 18 '70.   C: ECD.

CD - SNEAKING OUT THE BACKDOOR
THE LAST BOOTLEG RECORDS LBR SP 001/7
CD1: My Eyes Have Seen You (3:24)/ Soul Kitchen (6:06)/ I Can't See Your Face In My Mind (3:18)/ People Are Strange (2:19)/ When The Music's Over (12:12)/ Money (3:27)/ Who Do You Love (4:43)/ Moonlight Drive (6:08)/ Summer's Almost Gone (3:52)/ I'm A King Bee (4:30)/ Gloria (5:56)/ Break On Through (4:53)/ Summertime (8:48)/ Back Door Man (5:35)/ Alabama Song (3:22)
S: The Matrix, San Francisco Mar. 7 and 10 '67.
CD2: Light My Fire (8:48)/ The End (14:49)/ Get Off My Life (4:28)/ Close To You (3:49)/ Crawling King Snake (6:01)/ The Crystal Ship (3:19)/ 20th Century Fox (3:02)/ Unhappy Girl (4:06)/ Rock Me Baby (8:34)/ Bleeding Heart (12:20)/ Morrison's Lament (5:13)/ Tomorrow Never Knows (3:28)
S: Tracks 1-9 The Matrix, San Francisco Mar. 7 and 10 '67. Tracks 10-12 Jim Morrison with Jimi Hendrix and Johnny Winter at The Scene Club NYC '68.
CD3: When The Music's Over (12:58)/ Alabama Song (Whiskey Bar) (1:56)/ Back Door Man (2:34)/ 5 To 1 (2:47) Moonlight Drive (3:25)/ Horse Latitudes (1:58)/ A Little Game (1:50)/ The Hill Dwellers (7:21)/ Spanish Caravan (1:51)/ Wake Up (1:50)/ Light My Fire (extended version) (9:34)/ The Unknown Soldier (4:40)/ The End (17:16)/ Love Street (3:13)/ A Little Game (1:54)/ The Hill Dwellers (2:45)
S: Tracks 1-13 Hollywood Bowl on '68 tour. Tracks 14-16 Concerthuset, Stockholm Sept. 20 '68.
CD4: 5 To 1 (5:58)/ Mack The Knife, Alabama Song (3:00)/ Back Door Man (4:18)/ You're Lost, Little Girl (3:13)/ Love Me Two Times (3:32)/ When The Music's Over (13:15)/ Wild Child (2:27)/ Money (4:00)/ Wake Up (1:51)/ Light My Fire (2:23)/ The End (12:22)/ Unknown Soldier (4:59)
S: Concerthuset, Stockholm Sept. 20 '68.
CD5: Mother (2:25)/ Unknown Soldier (3:06)/ The River Knows (2:32)/ Gloria (2:56)/ 5 To 1 (4:24)/ Let It Bleed (2:19)/ Who Do You Love (4:20)/ Money (1:53)/ Petition The Lord Rock With Prayer (1:54)/ Sunday Soon (2:50)/ Jim Morrison Interview (1:58)/ Rock Is Dead (2:24)/ Light My Fire (2:57)/ Who Do You Love (8:05)/ Light My Fire (17:42)/ The End (16:46)
S: Tracks 1-13 Live and unreleased. Tracks 14-16 Vancouver, Canada '70 with Albert King.
CD6: 1 To 5 (6:11)/ Back Door Man (7:10)/

Roadhouse Blues (5:30)/ When The Music's Over
(19:53)/ People Get Ready (1:53)/ Train I Ride
Part 1 (3:41)/ Baby Please Don't Go (3:34)/ Train
I Ride Part 2 (13:49)/ Bullfrog Blues (3:12)/ Break
On Through (5:17)/ Someday Soon (6:13)
S: Track 1 Vancouver, Canada '70 with Albert
King. Tracks 2-11 Live in Canada '70.
CD7: Roadhouse Blues (7:23)/ Someday Soon,
Harvest Moon (3:40)/ Train Coming Round The
Bend (6:00)/ Break On Through (5:12)/ 5 To 1
(6:09)/ Back Door Man (7:08)/ The End (16:14)/
When The Music's Over 12:25)
R: As with any collection of this size, quality
varies. Generally speaking Vg-Ex. Some G-Vg.
S: Seattle June 5 '70.   C: ECD. Box set. Book.
Pic CDs.

CD - SOMEWHERE IN AMERICA
JOKER JOK-004-A
When The Music's Over/ Peace Frog/ Build Me A
Woman/ Get Out Of My Life Woman/ Crawling
King Snake/ The Celebration Of The Lizard/ You
Make Me Real/ Soul Kitchen/ The End/ Wild
Child/ Touch Me/ Light My Fire
R: Vg-Ex.   S: Live USA '67.   C: Australian
CD. Time 72:21.

DREAM THEATRE

CD - DREAM IN PROGRESS
DTJL 931/932
CD1: Metropolis Part 1 (The Miracle And The
Sleeper)/ Mission: Impossible/ Afterlife/ Under A
Glass Moon/ Wait For Sleep/ Surrounded/ Ytse
Jam (includes Drum Solo)/ Puppies On Acid (The
Mirror)/ Take The Time
CD2: To Live Forever, Improvised Jam/ A Fortune
In Lies/ Another Day/ Pull Me Under/ Eve/
Learning To Live
R: Exs.   S: Sun Plaza, Japan Aug. 25 '93.

CD - MIND CONTROL
KISS THE STONE KTS 416/17
CD1: Pull Me Under/ 6.00/ Take The Time/
Caught In A Web/ Lifting Shadows Off A Dream/
The Mirror, Lie
CD2: Another Day/ Erotomania/ Voices/ The
Silent Man/ Metropolis Part 1/ Tears/ The Silent
Man
R: Vg-Ex.   S: Urawa City Hall, Saitama, Japan
Jan. 24 '95. CD2 Tracks 6-7 Europe Feb. '95
(acoustic).   C: ECD. Dcc. Pic CDs.
Time CD1 66:34. CD2 43:29.

CD - MISSION IMPOSSIBLE
WYVERN DT104WV 1/2
CD1: Metropolis/ Mission: Impossible/ Afterlife/
Under A Glass Moon/ Wait For Sleep/
Surrounded/ Ytse Jam (includes Drum Solo)/
Puppies On Acid/ Take The Time
CD2: To Live Forever/ Improvised Jam (Guitar
Solo)/ A Fortune In Lies/ Another Day/ Pull Me
Under/ Eve/ Learning To Live
R: Exs audience recording.   S: Osaka Festival

Hall Aug. 28 '93.   C: Japanese CD.

CD - WAKE UP!
OCTOPUS OCTO 080-081
CD1: Pull Me Under (9:20)/ 6:00 (5:45)/ Take The
Time (14:28)/ Caught In A Web (9:26)/ Lifting
Shadows Off A Dream (5:54)/ Instrumental (5:27)
CD2: Instrumental (3:24)/ The Mirror (6:46)/ Lies
(6:51)/ John Myung's Happy Birthday (1:14)/
Another Day (4:44)/ Erotomania (6:43)/ Voices
(12:06)/ The Silent Man (4:12)/ Metropolis (Part
One) (10:41)
R: Ex.   S: Japan '95.   C: ECD. Dcc. Pic CDs.

DURAN DURAN

CD - IN CONCERT
ALL OF US AS 01
Breath Under Breath (with Milton Nascimento -
first version) (6:40)/ Planet Earth (6:08)/ Hungry
Like A Wolf (7:30)/ Ordinary World (6:03)/ Come
Undone (8:14)/ Crystal Ship (3:12)/ Girls On Film
(6:14)/ Notorious (6:11)/ Too Much Information
(7:21)/ Save A Prayer (8:23)/ Wild Boys (2:23)/
Rio (7:38)
R: Exs. Soundboard.   S: Buenos Aires, Velez
Stadium Apr. 30 '93.   C: ECD. Dcc.

CD - THE MEDICINE
MIDNIGHT BEAT MB CD 034
I Am The Medicine (3:46)/ I Am The Medicine
(2nd verse insert) (0:45)/ I Believe (alternate chorus) (2:15)/ Nick-Simon (instrumental) (5:03)/
Bomb (instrumental) (4:50)/ Bomb (with vocals)
(4:28)/ Do You Believe In Faith (alternate-different
lyrics) (4:11)/ Too Late For Marlene (alternate 1 -
different lyrics) (5:16)/ Too Late For Marlene
(alternate 2 - different lyrics) (5:15)/ All She Wants
Is (alternate - different lyrics) (5:19)/ Welcome To
The Edge (acoustic rehearsals) (2:49)/ Welcome
To The Edge (electric rehearsals-different lyrics)
(4:43)/ Pressure (piano chorus) (1:24)/ A View To
Kill (rehearsal) (8:38)/ A View to Kill (rough take)
(14:07)
R: Exs. Soundboard.   C: ECD. Dcc.

DYLAN, BOB

CD - A MILLION FACES AT FEET
TUFF BITES TB 95 1019
CD1: Crash On The Levee (Down In The Flood)/
If Not For You/ All Along The Watchtower/ Just
Like A Woman/ Tangled Up In Blue/ Queen Jane
Approximately/ Mr. Tambourine Man/ Boots Of
Spanish Leather
CD2: Maggie's Farm/ Like A Rolling Stone/ It Ain't
Me Babe/ Man In The Long Black Coat*/ God
Knows*/ She Belongs To Me*/ My Back Pages
Masters Of War*/ Disease Of Conceit*
R: Vg-Ex. Audience.   S: Vorst National,
Brussels, Belgium Mar. 23 '95. *USA '94.

CD - AND THE NEVER ENDING TOUR BAND
P 910053/54
CD1: Rainy Day Woman #12 & 35 (5:35)/ If Not
For You (5:27)/ All Along The Watchtower (6:20)/
Tangled Up In Blue (11:32)/ Shelter From The
Storm (8:05)/ Stuck Inside Of Mobile With The
Memphis Blues Again (10:32)/ It Takes A Lot To
Laugh, It Takes A Train To Cry (6:09)/ Tomorrow
Night (4:56)
CD2: Mr. Jones (7:43)/ Mr. Tambourine Man
(8:05)/ It's All Over Now, Baby Blue (6:07)/ Cats
In The Well (6:08)/ I And I (7:38)/ Knockin' On
Heavens Door (7:23)/ Highway 61 Revisited
(8:04)/ What Good Am I? (6:50)/ It Ain't Me Babe
(9:11)
R: Ex. Audience.   S: Florida Nov. '92.
C: ECD.

CD - AT THE FLOOD
DYNAMITE STUDIOS DS94MO85/86
CD1: Most Likely You Go Your Way/ Lay Lady
Lay/ Rainy Day Woman #12&35/ It Ain't Me,
Babe/ Ballad Of A Thin Man/ Stage Fright/ King
Harvest/ The Night They Drove Old Dixie Down/
When You A Wake/ I Shall Be Released/ Up On
Cripple Creek
CD2: All Along The Watchtower/ Highway 61
Revisited/ Knockin' On Heavens' Door/ Endless
Highway/ The Shape I'm In/ The Weight/ Highway
61 Revisited/ Like A Rolling Stone/ Heart Of Mine/
Death Is Not The End
R: G-Vg. Soundboard. Hiss.   S: Various loca-
tions on tour with The Band '74. CD2 track 9
'Shot Of Love' outtake. CD2 track 10 'Infidel' out-
take.   C: Japanese CD. Blue/white cover with
pink and orange type. CD1 43:53. CD2 44:56.

CD - THE BANJO TAPE AND NYC TOWN HALL
YELLOW DOG YD 058
Lonesome River Edge (0:43)/ Back Door Blues
(1:42)/ Bob Dylan's Dream (3:43)/ You Can Get
Her (1:00)/ Farewell (2:39)/ All Over You (3:51)/
Masters Of War (5:57)/ Instrumental (1:35)/ Keep
Your Hands Of Her (1:46)/ Honey Babe (0:52)/
Going Back To Rome (1:33)/ Stealin' (1:28)/
Ramblin' Down Through The World (2:30)/ Bob
Dylan's Dream (4:38)/ Tomorrow's A Long Time
(3:10)/ Bob Dylan's New Orleans Rag (3:23)/
Masters Of War (5:25)/ Walls Of Red Wing (5:47)/
Hero Blues (2:58)/ Who Killed Davey Moore?
(4:04)/ With God On Our Side (6:10)
R: Ex. Soundboard.   S: Tracks 1-12 New York
City with Happy Traum Feb. 8 (?) '63. Tracks 13-
21 New York City Town Hall Apr. 12 '63.
C: ECD. Dcc.

CD - BEACON BLUES AGAIN
WANTED MAN MUSIC WMM 68
Seeing The Real You At Last/ I'll Remember You/
It Takes Alot To Laugh/ Most Of The Time/ Dead
Man Dead Man/ What Good I Am/ Man Of Peace/
Queen Jane Approximately/ Everything Is Broken/
Masters Of War/ Precious Memories/ Simple
Twist Of Fate/ Memphis Blues Again/ Like A
Rolling Stone
R: Ex. Audience.   S: The Beacon Theatre, New
York Oct. '89.   C: ECD. Dcc. Time 74:34

CD - BLUE EYED BOSTON BOY
THE RAZOR'S EDGE RAZ 012/13
CD1: Jokerman/ Senor/ All Along The
Watchtower/ Queen Jane Approximately/ Tangled
Up In Blue/ Most Likely You Go Your Way/ 4 other
tracks
CD2: You're A Big Girl Now/ One Too Many
Mornings/ Two Soldiers (Orpheum Theatre,
Boston Oct. 9 '94)/ Rainy Day Women Numbers
12 & 35, Highway 61 Revisited (Roseland, News
York Oct. 20 '94)
R: Vg. Audience recording.   S: CD1 Orpheum
Theatre, Boston Oct. 8 '94.   C: ECD.
Times CD1 74:18. CD2 75:31.

CD - BRIXTON BLUES
KISS THE STONE KTS 435/36
CD1: Crash On The Levee (Down In The Flood)
(5:10)/ Senor (Tales Of Yankee Power) (5:18)/ All
Along The Watchtower (6:11)/ I Don't Believe You
(She Acts Like We Never Have Met) (6:23)/
Tombstone Blues (8:01)/ Shelter From The Storm
(6:37)/ Mr. Tambourine Man (6:48)/ Lonesome
Death Of Hattie Carroll (6:34)/ It's All Over Now
Baby Blue (7:48)
CD2: Highway Revisited (6:45)/ In The Garden
(8:31)/ Joey (9:52)/ Like A Rolling Stone (7:51)/
My Back Pages (8:17)/ I Shall Be Released
(5:35)/ Rainy Day Women 12 & 35 (4:19)
R: Ex. Audience.   S: The Brixton Academy,
London '95.   C: ECD. Dcc. Pic CDs.

CD - BRUCE SPRINGSTEEN AND
BOB DYLAN: FOREVER YOUNG
GAMBLE RECORDS BSGR-09
C: See listing under 'Various Artists'.

CD - THE CRITICS CHOICE VOL. 7
WANTED MAN MUSIC 69
She Belongs To Me (Aug. 2 '88)/ Hallelujah,
Driftin' Too Far From The Shore, I'll Be Around
(Aug. 4 '88)/ Don't Think Twice It's Alright,
Knockin' On Heaven's Door (Aug. 6 '88)/
Leopard-Skin Pill Box Hat, Shelter From The
Storm, Big River (Aug. 7 '88)/ We Three (Aug. 6
'88)/ Trail Of The Buffalo (Aug. 2 '88)/ I'm In The
Mood For Love, Visions Of Johanna (Aug. 3 '88)
R: Vg-Ex.   C: ECD. Dcc. Time 59:31.

CD - THE CRITICS CHOICE VOL. 8
WANTED MAN MUSIC WMM 70
I Don't Believe You, Subterranean Homesick
Blues (Sept. 3 '88)/ Rank Strangers (Sept. 4 '88)/
Bob Dylan's 115th Dream, With God On Your
Side, Wagoner's Lad (Oct. 14 '88)/ My Dear La
La (May 28 '89)/ Confidential To Me (May 30 '89)/
Congratulations (June 6 '89)/ Ballad Of Hollis
Brown (June 8 '89)/ Lonesome Town (June 7 '89)/
In The Garden (June 8 '89)
R: Vg-Ex.   C: ECD. Dcc. Time 54:50.

CD - DON'T DREAM YOUR LIFE...
DIAMONDS IN YOUR EAR
Jokerman/ Gates Of Eden/ It's All Over Now Baby Blue/ God Knows/ Man In The Long Black Coat/ I'll Remember You/ Maggie's Farm/ What Good Am I?/ It Ain't Me Babe/ Under The Red Sky/ Mama You Been On My Mind
R: G. Audience.   S: Chicago Apr. 17 and 18 '94.
C: ECD. Time 78:42.

CD - DYNAMIC LIVE
APPLE HOUSE
The Times They Are A-Changing/ Man Of Peace/ I'll Be Your Baby Tonight/ John Brown/ I Want You/ Ballad Of A Thin Man/ Stuck Inside Of Mobile/ Queen Jane Approximately/ Chimes Of Freedom/ All Along The Watchtower/ Knockin' On Heaven's Door/ With God On Our Side, It Ain't Me Babe (Philharmonic Hall, NY Oct. 31 '64)
R: Ex.   S: Foxboro, Mass. July 4 '87.

CD - THE EARLY YEARS VOL. I
WINGED WHEEL WW 9425
Railroad Billy/ Will The Circle Be Unbroken/ Man Of Constant Sorrow/ Pretty Polly/ Railroad Boy/ Jame Alley Blues/ Why'd You Cut My Hair/ This Land Is Your Land/ Two Trains Running/ Wild Mountain Thyme/ How Did You/ Car Car/ Don't You Push Me Down/ Come See/ I Want It Now/ San Francisco Bay Blues/ A Long Time Growin'/ Devilish Mary/ (As I Go) Ramblin' Round/ Death Don't Have No Mercy/ It's Hard To Be Blind/ This Train Is Bound For Glory/ Harmonica Solo/ Talking Fish Blues/ Pasture Of Plenty
R: Ex.   S: Minnesota May '62.   C: ECD. Dcc cardboard sleeves. CDs look like records.

CD - THE EARLY YEARS VOL. II
WINGED WHEEL WW 9426
Candy Man/ Baby Please Don't Go/ Stealin'/ Poor Lazarus/ I Ain't Got No Home/ It's Hard To Be Blind/ Dink's Song/ Man Of Constant Sorrow/ Naomi Wise/ Made In The Water/ I Was Young When I Left Home/ In The Evening/ Baby Let Me Follow You Down/ Sally Girl/ Gospel/ Long John/ Cocaine/ Medley: VD Blues, VD Waltz, VD City/ VD Gunners Blues/ See That My Grave Is Kept Clean/ (As I Go) Ramblin' Round/ Blackcross
R: Ex.   S: Minnesota Dec. '61.   C: ECD. Dcc cardboard sleeves. CDs look like records.

CD - THE EMMETT GROGAN ACETATES
CAPRICORN RECORDS CR2055
I Don't Believe You (4:29)/ Chimes Of Freedom (7:21)/ Motorpsycho Nitemare (4:35)/ Mr. Tambourine Man (6:52)/ All I Really Want To Do (4:33)/ Black Crow Blues (3:46)/ I Shall Be Free (5:21)/ All I Really Want To Do (Live) (4:03)/ Bonus Tracks: Denise (2:57)/ California (3:05)/ Bob Dylan's New Orleans Rag (1) (1:03)/ East Lorado Blues (3:09)/ That's All Right Mama, Sally Free And Easy (3:13)/ New Orleans Rag (2) (3:21)/ Hero Blues (3:44)
R: Ex. Soundboard.   S: All tracks 'Another Side

Of Bob Dylan Sessions' recorded June 9 '64. Track 8 Newport Folk Festival July 26 '64.
C: Dcc.

CD - FAREWELL BLOOMFIELD
CUTTLEFISH RECORDS
CD1: Gotta Serve Somebody/ I Believe In You/ Like A Rolling Stone*/ Man Gave Names To The Animals, Simple Twist Of Fate/ Ain't Gonna Go To Hell/ Girl From The North Country/ Slow Train/ Abraham Martin And John/ Let's Keep It Between Us
CD2: Mary From The Wild Moor/ Covenant Women/ Solid Rock/ Just Like A Woman/ Groom's Still Waiting At The Alter*/ When You Gonna Wake Up/ In The Garden/ Blowin' In The Wind/ City Of Gold
R: Exs. Soundboard.   S: Fox Warfield, San Francisco Nov. 15 '80.   C: Japanese CDs. *With Mike Bloomfield. Time CD1 49:21. CD2 43:03.

CD - FLAGGING DOWN THE DOUBLE E'S
THE RAZOR'S EDGE
CD1: When I Paint My Masterpiece/ It Ain't Me Babe/ The Lonesome Death Of Hattie Carroll/ Tonight I'll Be Staying Here With You/ It Takes A Lot To Laugh/ Romance In Durango/ Isis/ The Times They Are A-Changin/ Dark As A Dungeon/ Never Let Me Go/ I Dreamed I Saw St. Augustine/ I Shall Be Released/ It's All Over Now Baby Blue/ Love Minus Zero-No Limit/ Simple Twist Of Fate/ Oh Sister/ Hurricane
CD2: One More Cup Of Coffee, Sara, Just Like A Women, Knockin On Heaven's Door, This Land Is Your Land (Maple Leaf Gardens, Toronto Dec. 1 '75)/ A Hard Rain's A Gonna Fall, Blowin In The Wind, Wild Mountain Thyme, Mama You Been On My Mind, Mr Tambourine Man, Tangled Up In Blue (Maple Leaf Gardens, Toronto Dec. 2 '75)/ I Don't Believe You (Bangor, Maine Nov. 27 '75)/ With God On Our Side (Providence, Rhode Island Nov. 4 '75 afternoon)/ It's Alright Ma (I'm Only Bleeding) (Providence, Rhode Island Nov. 4 '75 evening)
R: Ex. Audience.   S: CD1 Maple Leaf Gardens, Toronto Dec. 1 '75.   C: ECD.

CD - FOXBORO
YELLOW CAT YC 040
The Times Are A-Changing/ Man Of Peace/ I'll Be Your Baby Tonight/ John Brown/ I Want You/ Ballad Of A Thin Man/ Stuck Inside Of Mobile With The Memphis Blues Again/ Queen Jane Approximately/ Chimes Of Freedom/ Slow Train/ Joey/ All Along The Watchtower
R: Exs. Soundboard.   S: Sullivan Stadium, Foxboro, Mass. July 4 '87.   C: ECD. Dcc. With the Grateful Dead. Time 71:03.

CD - FRIEND OF THE DEVIL
WANTED MAN MUSIC WMM 64/65
CD1: Everything Is Broken/ Friend Of The Devil/ All Along The Watchtower/ Under The Red Sky/ Just Like A Woman/ It Takes Alot To Laugh/ I

Believe In You/ I'll Be Your Baby Tonight/ Ballad Of Hollis Brown/ Hard Rain/ To Ramona/ It's All Over Now, Baby Blue
CD2: Visions Of Johanna/ Every Grain Of Sand/ If Not For You/ I And I/ Idiot Wind/ Lenny Bruce/ To Be Alone With You/ What Good Am I/ Highway 61/ It Ain't Me Babe
R: Vg. Audience.   S: Minneapolis Aug./Sept. '92.   C: ECD. Dcc. CD1 72:12. CD2 72:49.

CD - FROM THE MOUNTAINS OF MADRID
THE RAZOR'S EDGE RAZ 011
It Takes A Lot To Laugh.../ Tangled Up In Blue/ Heart Of Mine/ Why Do I Have To Choose?/ Forever Young/ To Ramona/ With God On Our Side/ The Death Of Hattie Carroll/ Man Of Peace/ Just Like Tom Thumb's Blues/ When You Gonna Wake Up?/ I Shall Be Released/ Love Minus Zero, No Limit/ Shelter From The Storm/ All Along The Watchtower
R: Poor audience recording.   S: Europe May 28-July 8 '84.

CD - F*** THE PLAY LIST! BRIXTON II
STERLING SOUNDS SSCD-BD01/02
CD1: Crash In The Levee (5:15)/ If You See Her, Say Hello (6:37)/ All Along The Watchtower (5:49)/ Jokerman (7:38)/ Every Grain Of Sand (8:10)/ Positively Fourth Street (6:32)/ Mr. Tambourine Man (acoustic) (6:32)/ Masters Of War (acoustic) (5:28)/ Love Minus Zero, No Limit (acoustic) (6:35)/ God Knows (5:56)
CD2: Stuck Inside Of Mobile (with Memphis Blues Again) (9:53)/ Band Introductions (0:30)/ I Believe In You (7:00)/ Like A Rolling Stone (7:51)/ The Times They Are-A-Changin' (6:21)/ I Shall Be Released (featuring Elvis Costello) (6:22)/ I Want You (4:21)/ Just Like A Woman (5:26)/ It Takes A Lot To Laugh (7:04)/ Boots Of Spanish Leather (7:25)/ Don't Think Twice It's Alright (5:35)
R: Ex. Audience.   S: The Academy Theatre, Brixton, London Mar. 30 '95. CD2 tracks 7-11 The Academy Theatre, Brixton, London Mar. 29 '95. C: ECD. Dcc. Pic CD.

CD - GET LOUD!
CUTTLEFISH RECORDS CFR 013/14
CD1: She Belongs To Me/ 4th Time Around/ Visions Of Johanna/ It's All Over Now, Baby Blue/ Desolation Low/ Just Like A Woman/ Mr. Tambourine Man
CD2: Tell Me Mama/ I Don't Believe You/ Baby Let Me Follow You Down/ Just Like Tom Thumb's Blues/ Leopard Skin Pill-Box Hat/ One Too Many Mornings/ Ballad Of A Thin Man/ Like A Rolling Stone
R: G. Audience.   S: Bristol Colston Hall, London, England May 10 '66.   C: Japanese CD.

CD - GETTING HARDER AND HARDER TO SEE A NEW SUNRISE
RED SKY RECORDS CD1007/1008
CD1: To Be Alone With You/ Shelter From The Storm/ My Back Pages/ I Believe In You/ Love

Minus Zero - No Limit/ It's All Over Now Baby Blue/ Under The Red Sky/ TV Talking Song/ Shooting Star/ All Along The Watchtower/ Knockin' On Heaven's Door/ Like A Rolling Stone/ Song To Woody/ To Ramona/ One Too Many Mornings/ Tight Connection/ Dark As A Dungeon
CD2: Silvio/ She Belongs To Me/ Visions Of Johanna/ My Head's In Mississippi/ Buckets Of Rain/ Every Grain Of Sand/ Oxford Town/ One Too Many Mornings/ John Brown/ Absolutely Sweet Marie/ Moon River/ Friend Of The Evil/ I've Been All Around This World/ Detroit City/ Shelter From The Storm/ Dock Of The Bay/ Man Of Constant Sorrow/ Willing/ Lakes Of Pontchartrain
R: Vg audience recording.   S: Various US locations Aug. - Nov. '90.   C: ECD.

CD - HARD TIMES IN MARSEILLE
MOONLIGHT ML9510/11
CD1: Hard Times (Come Again No More)/ Stuck Inside Of Mobile With The Memphis Blues Again/ All Along The Watchtower/ Just Like a Woman/ Tangled Up In The Blue/ Shelter From The Storm/ Watching The River Flow/ Little Moses/ Tomorrow Night
CD2: It's All Over Now Baby Blue/ Desolation Row/ Cat's In The Well/ Highway 61 Revisited/ My Back Pages/ Maggie's Farm/ Rainy Day Woman #12 & 35/ It Ain't Me Babe
R: G-Vg. Soundboard.   S: Marseille, France June 29 '93.

CD - HEARTS OF FIRE SESSIONS
COUNTDOWN FACTORY CDF-941003
The Usual 1/ The Usual 2/ Had A Dream About You, Baby 1/ Had A Dream About You, Baby 2/ Had A Dream About You, Baby 3, Had A Dream About You, Baby 4
R: Vg.   S: Townhouse Studios, London Aug. 27-28 '86.

CD - IF NOT FOR YOU
BD-005/6
CD1: Jokerman/ If Not For You/ All Along The Watchtower/ Ring Them Bells/ Tangled Up In Blues/ Under The Red Sky/ Tomorrow Night/ Mr. Tambourine Man
CD2: Don't Think Twice, It's Alright/ Series Of Dreams/ I And I/ Maggies Farm/ Ballad Of A Thin Man/ It Ain't Me Babe
R: Exs. Audience recording.   S: Osaka-Jo Hall, Osaka, Japan Feb. 12 '94.

CD - IN CONCERT
CAPRICORN COL.CL-2302 CS-9102
Ramblin Through The World/ Bob Dylan's Dream/ Tomorrow Is A Long Time/ Bob Dylan's New Orleans Rag/ Masters Of War/ Walls Of Red Wing/ Hero Blues/ Who Killed Davey Moore?/ With God On Our Side/ Dusty Old Fairgrounds/ John Brown/ You've Been Hiding Too Long/ Lay Down Your Weary Tune/ When The Ship Comes In/ Percy's Song/ Seven Curses
R: G-Vg.   S: Town Hall, New York Apr. 12 '63.

Tracks 14-16 Carnegie Hall, NYC Oct. 26 '63.

CD - IN THE STUDIO
COUNTDOWN FACTORY
Medicine Sunday/ Can You Please Crawl Out
Your Window/ I Wanna Be Your Lover/ Number
One/ Visions Of Johanna/ She's Your Lover Now/
You're Gonna Make Me Lonesome When You Go/
Simple Twist Of Fate/ Going Going Gone
R: Poor.   S: Tracks 1-6 Studio Sessions 30 Nov.
1 - Dec. 66. Tracks 7-9 tour rehearsals Jan. '78.

CD - IT'S ALL RIGHT, BABE
JOKERMAN JKM-001/2
CD1: A Hard Rain's A-Gonna Fall/ Love Her With
A Feeling/ Mr. Tambourine Man/ I Threw It All
Away/ Shelter From The Storm/ Love Minus Zero-
No Limit/ Girl From The North Country/ Ballad Of
A Thin Man/ Maggie's Farm/ I Don't Believe You
CD2: One More Cup Of Coffee/ Blowin' In The
Wind/ I Want You/ Don't Think Twice, It's All Right/
Just Like A Woman/ Oh, Sister/ To Ramona/ All
Along The Watchtower/ The Man In Me
R: Poor. Audience.   S: Sportsground, Sydney,
Australia Apr. 1 '78.

CD - LAKE COMPOUNCE FESTIVAL PARK
AUDIFON
Subterranean Homesick Blues/ I Don't Believe
You/ Just Like Tom Thumbs Blues/ Ballad Of A
Thin Man/ Had A Dream About You Baby/ Simple
Twist Of Fate/ Highway 61 Revisited/ Rank
Strangers To Me/ Don't Think Twice Its Alright/
Knockin On Heavens Door/ Silvio/ I Shall Be
Released/ Like A Rolling Stone/ It Ain't Me Babe/
Masters Of War/ Maggie's Farm
R: Vg.   S: Bristol, Connecticut 4 Sept. '88.
C: ECD.

CD - LIFE TAKES LIVE TAKES
DIAMONDS IN YOUR EAR DIYE 37
Simple Twist Of Fate/ Enough Is Enough/ Every
Grain Of Sand/ To Ramona/ With God On Your
Side/ It's All Over Now Baby Blue/ Tupelo Honey/
Leopard Skin pill Box/ Blowin' In The Wind/ Mr.
Tambourine man/ Knockin' On Heavens Door/
Shelter From The Storm/ Just Like A Woman
R: Vg soundboard recording.   S: Live outtakes.
Tracks 6-7 with Van Morrison on vocals.

CD - LIVE
MAINLINE MUSIC
Tell Me Momma/ I Don't Believe You/ Baby Let
Me Follow You Down/ Just Like Tom Thumbs
Blues/ Leopard Skin Pill-Box/ One Too Many
Mornings/ Ballad Of A Thin Man/ Like A Rolling
Stone
S: Manchester, England May 17 '66.   C: ECD.

CD - LIVE ADVENTURES
SOUND ALIVE
C: See 'Luck Old Sun' (Pipeline) for songs and
source.

CD - LIVE AT THE WAREHOUSE
YELLOW CAT YC 038/39
CD1: Mr. Tambourine Man/ Love Minus Zero, No
Limit/ Vincent Van Gogh/ Maggie's Farm/
Mozambique/ Diamonds And Rust/ Railroad Boy/
I Pity The Poor Immigrant/ Shelter From The
Storm/ Stuck Inside Of Mobile With The Memphis
Blues Again/ You're A Big Girl Now/ Rita May/ Lay
Lady Lay
CD2: Idiot Wind/ Knocking On Heavens Door/
Gotta Travel On/ Hurricane/ Oh Sister/ Simple
Twist Of Fate
R: Ex. Soundboard.   S: Evening show, The
Warehouse In New Orleans On May 3 '76. CD2
Tracks 4-6 are from the TV show 'World Of John
Hammond' recorded in Chicago Sept. 10 '75.
C: ECD.

CD - LJUBLJANA '91
RED SKY RECORDS CD 1006
New Morning/ Ballad Of A Thin Man/ All Along
The Watchtower/ Shelter From The Storm/ Gotta
Serve Somebody/ Love Minus Zero, No Limit/
Don't Think Twice, It's Alright/ It Ain't Me, Babe/
Rainy Day Women Nos. 12 & 35/ Just Like A
Woman/ Knocking On Heaven's Door/ I Shall Be
Released/ Like A Rolling Stone/ The Times They
Are A-Changing
R: Poor audience recording.   S: Ljubljana '91.

CD - LONESOME TOWN VOL. 2
FLAMINGO RECORDS FR-19
Ballad Of A Thin Man/ Refugee/ Rainy Day
Woman/ Seeing The Real You At Last/ Across
The Borderline/ I And I/ Like A Rolling Stone/ In
The Garden/ Blowin' In The Wind/ Rock 'Em
Baby, Rock 'Em Dead/ Knockin' On Heaven's
Door
R: Ex audience recording.   S: Hoffman Estates,
Illinois June 29 '86.   C: ECD. With Tom Petty.

CD - LUCKY OLD SUN
PIPELINE
Positively 4th Street/ All Along The Watchtower/
Masters Of War/ I'll Remember You/ I Forgot
More/ Just Like A Women/ Blowin In The Wind/
Lucky Old Sun/ Like A Rolling Stone/ Knockin On
Heavens Door
R: Exs. Soundboard.   S: Westwood One radio
broadcast Nov. 11 '86.   C: ECD.

CD - MASTERS OF WAR
BD-003/4
CD1: Joker Man/ Shelter From The Storm/ All
Along The Watchtower/ She Belongs To Me/
Tangled Up In Blue/ Watching The River Flow/
Tomorrow Night/ Masters Of War
CD2: Don't Think Twice, It's Alright/ Series Of
Dreams/ I And I/ Maggie's Farm/ Man In The
Long Black Coat/ It Ain't Me Babe
C: Exs. Audience recording.   S: Hiroshima-
Kouseinekin Hall Feb. 16 '94.

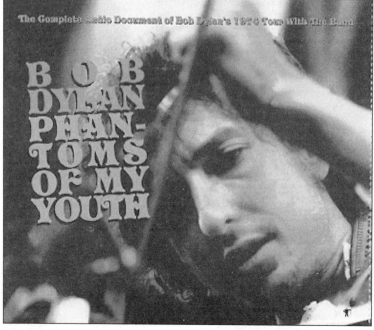

CD - MERAN 92
77000-1/2
CD1: 2x2/ Pretty Peggy-o/ Maggie's Farm/ Every Grain Of Sand/ Seeing The Real you At Last/ I Dreamed I Saw St. Augustine/ I'll Be Your Baby Tonight/ To Ramona/ Girl Of The North Country/ Mr. Tambourine Man
CD2: Don't Think Twice, It's Alright/ Everything Is Broken/ Shelter From The Storm/ The Times They Are A-Changing/ Like A Rolling Stone/ What Good Am I ?/ All Along The Watchtower/ Blowing In The Wind
R: Ex audience recording.   S: Meran July 7 '92.

CD - 1965 REVISITED
GREAT DANE RECORDS GDR
9419/1/2/3/4/5/6/7/8/9/10/12/13/14
CD1: I'll Keep It With Mine 1 (mono mix with intro)/ It's All Over Now Baby Blue 1 (mono mix)/ Subterranean Homesick Blues 1 (mono mix)/ Farewell Angelina (mono mix)/ You Don't Have To Do That (mono mix)/ She Belongs To Me 1 (mono mix)/ Love Minus Zero, No Limits 1 (mono mix)/ If You Gotta Go, Go Now 1 (original mono mix)/ If You Gotta Go, Go Now 1 (mono acetate mix)/ If You Gotta Go, Go Now 2 (mono mix with intro)/ If You Gotta Go, Go Now 2 (stereo mix without intro)/ I'll Keep It With Mine 2 (instrumental) (stereo acetate mix)/ It's All Over Now Baby Blue/ Interview/ It's All Right Ma (It's Life And Life Only)
R: Ex. Soundboard.   S: 'Bringing It All Back Home' outtakes Columbia Studio A, New York City. Tracks 1-5 Jan. 13. Tracks 6-12 Jan. 15. Tracks 13-15 The Les Crane Show, ABC TV Studios, New York City Feb. 17.   C: Time 70:32.
CD2: To Ramona/ Gates Of Eden/ If You Gotta Go, Go Now/ It's All Right Ma (I'm Only Bleeding)/ Love Minus Zero, No Limit/ Mr. Tambourine Man/ Don't Think Twice - It's All Right/ With God On Your Side (incomplete)/ She Belongs To Me/ It Ain't Me Babe (incomplete)/ The Lonesome Death Of Hattie Carroll (incomplete)/ All I Really Want To Do/ It's All Over Now Baby Blue
R: G-Vg. Audience.   S: Santa Monica Civic Auditorium, Santa Monica, CA Mar. 27.
C: Time 53:01.
CD3: The Times They Are A-Changin'/ To Ramona/ Gates Of Eden/ If You Gotta Go, Go Now/ It's All Right Ma (It's Life And Life Only)/ Love Minus Zero, No Limit (incomplete)/ Interview Snippets From The '65 Tour: A: London Airport, Apr. 26: Arrival Area, Interview, Press Conference/ B: Sheffield City Hall, Apr. 30: Back Stage After Concert (interview with Jenny DeYong and Peter Roche for The Paper 'Darts', Sheffield University/ C: London, Savoy Hotel, May 9: Horace Judson Interview For 'Time Magazine' (unpublished)/ The Times They Are A-Changin', To Ramona (Sheffield, The Oval City Hall, Apr. 30)/ The Lonesome Death Of Hattie Carroll (Leicester, De Montfort Hall, May 2)/ Lost Highway, I'm So Lonesome I Could Cry (hotel room, England May 3 or 4)/ Piano Tune (hotel room, Newcastle May 6)/ Don't Think Twice It's All Right (incomplete),

Don't Think Twice It's All Right (City Hall, Newcastle May 6)/ It's All Over Now Baby Blue (Savoy Hotel, London May 8)/ Piano, Harmonica Tune (backstage, Royal Albert Hall, London May 9)/ Medley: The Times They Are A-Changing, Talkin' World War III Blues, It's All Right Ma (I'm Only Bleeding), Gates Of Eden, Love Minus Zero-No Limits, All I Really Want To Do (Royal Albert Hall, London May 9)/ Sales Convention Speech 1 & 2/ If You Gotta Go, Go Now
R: Ex.   S: Tracks 1-6 The Oval City Hall, Sheffield, England Apr. 30. Tracks 7-10 interview snippets from the '65 tour. Tracks 11-21 live. Tracks 22-23 Miami sales convention speech, Levi's Recording Studio, London May 12.
C: Time 67:00.
CD4: The Times They Are A-Changing/ To Ramona/ Gates Of Eden/ If You Gotta Go, Go Now/ It's All Right Ma (I'm Only Bleeding)/ Love Minus Zero - No Limit/ Mr. Tambourine Man/ Talkin' World War III Blues/ Don't Think Twice, It's All Right/ With God On Our Side/ She Belongs To Me/ It Ain't Me Babe/ The Lonesome Death Of Hattie Carroll/ All I Really Want To Do/ It's All Over Now Baby Blue
R: Ex. Soundboard.   S: Free Trade Hall, Manchester, England May 7.   C: Time 75:55.
CD5: The Times They Are A-Changin'/ To Ramona/ Gates Of Eden/ If You Gotta Go, Go Now/ It's All Right Ma (I'm Only Bleeding) (incomplete)/ Love Minus Zero-No Limit/ Mr. Tambourine Man/ Talkin' World War III Blues/ Don't Think Twice - It's All Right/ With God On Our Side/ She Belongs To Me/ It Ain't Me Babe/ The Lonesome Death Of Hattie Carroll/ All I Really Want To Do/ It's Al Over Now Baby Blue
R: Poor-G. Audience.   S: Royal Albert Hall, London, England May 9.   C: 67:51.
CD6: Ballad Of Hollis Brown/ Mr. Tambourine Man/ Gates Of Eden/ If You Gotta Go, Go Now/ The Lonesome Death Of Hattie Carroll/ It Ain't Me Babe/ Love Minus Zero - No Limit/ One Too Many Mornings/ Boots Of Spanish Leather/ It's All Right Ma (I'm Only Bleeding)/ She Belongs to Me/ It's All Over Now Baby Blue
R: Vg. Soundboard.   S: BBC Television Theatre, London, England June 1.   C: 66:07.
CD7: Sitting On A Barbed Wire Fence (mono mix with intro)/ Sitting On A Barbed Wire Fence 1 (stereo mix)/ Sitting On A Barbed Wire Fence 2 (stereo acetate No. 86444 titled 'Over The Cliffs')/ It Takes A Lot To Laugh, It Takes A Train To Cry 1 (mono mix with intro)/ It Takes A Lot To Laugh, It Takes A Train To Cry 1 (stereo mix 1 from acetate No. 86445 titled 'Phantom Engineer')/ It Takes a Lot To Laugh, It Takes A Train To Cry 1 (stereo mix 2)/ Like A Rolling Stone (warm up) (stereo mix)/ Can You Please Crawl Out Your Window? 1 (mono mix)/ Can You Please Crawl Out Your Window? 2 (mono mix)/ Positively 4th Street (mono mix)/ It Takes A Lot To Laugh, It Takes a Train To Cry (mono mix)/ Tombstone Blues (mono mix)/ From A Buick 6, #1 (mono mix)/ From A Buick 6, #2 (mono acetate mix)/ From A Buick 6,

#2 (stereo mix)
R: Ex. Soundboard.   S: 'Highway 61 Revisited'
Outtakes, Columbia Studio A, New York City.
Tracks 1-8 June 15. Tracks 9-10 June 16. Tracks
11-13 June 29. Tracks 14-16 July 30.   C: 64:02.
CD8: Desolation Row 1 (mono mix)/ Queen Jane
Approximately (mono mix)/ Highway 61 Revisited
(mono mix)/ Ballad Of A Thin Man (mono mix)/
Just Like Tom Thumb's Blues (mono mix)/ All I
Really Want To Do (workshop area)/ Maggie's
Farm/ Like A Rolling Stone/ It Takes A Lot To
Laugh, It Takes a Train To Cry/ It's All Over Now
Baby Blue/ Mr. Tambourine Man
R: Tracks 1-5 and 7-11 Ex. Soundboard. Track 6
Vg.   S: 'Highway 61 Revisited' Outtakes,
Columbia Studio A, New York City. Tracks 1 July
30. Tracks 2-4 Aug. 2. Track 5 Aug. 4. Tracks 6-
11 Newport Folk Festival, Newport, Rhode Island,
July 24* and 25 (main stage).   C: Time 72:02.
CD9: Introduction/ She Belongs To Me/ To
Ramona/ Gates Of Eden/ Love Minus Zero - No
Limit/ Desolation Row/ It's All Over Now Baby
Blue/ Mr. Tambourine Man/ Intermission
Comments/ Tombstone Blues/ I Don't Believe
You/ From A Buick 6/ Just Like Tom Thumb's
Blues
R: Poor-G. Audience.   S: Forest Hill Tennis
Stadium, New York City Aug. 28 (Pt. 1).
C: Time 68:50.
CD10: Maggie's Farm/ It Ain't Me Babe/ Ballad Of
A Thin Man/ Like A Rolling Stone/ Can You
Please Crawl Out Your Window 3 (mono mix)/
Can You Please Crawl Out Your Window 4 (mono
mix)/ Can You Please Crawl Out Your Window 4
(stereo acetate No. 87184)/ I Wanna Be Your
Lover 1 (mono mix)/ I Wanna Be Your Lover 2
(mono mix)/ Jet Pilot (stereo mix)/ Medicine
Sunday (mono mix)/ Number One Instrumental
(mono mix)/ Freeze Out (stereo acetate No.
88581)
R: Tracks 1-4 Poor-G. Audience. Tracks 5-13 Ex.
Soundboard.   S: Tracks 1-4 Forest Hill Tennis
Stadium, New York City Aug. 28 (Pt. 2). Tracks 5-
10 'Blonde On Blonde' outtakes, Columbia Studio
A, New York City Oct. 20. Tracks 8 and 9 possibly
from the Nov. 30-Dec. 1 session.   C: 56:55.
CD11: Allen Stone interview, Cobo Hall, Detroit,
Michigan Oct. 24 broadcast by WATM radio sta-
tion, Detroit/ Nat Hentoff interview for 'Playboy'
magazine (unpublished) Columbia office, New
York City Oct. or Nov. (Pt. 1)
R: Ex.   C: Time 65:46.
CD12: Nat Hentoff interview for 'Playboy' maga-
zine (unpublished) Columbia office, New York City
Oct. or Nov. (Pt. 2)
R: Ex.   C: Time 75:22.
CD13: San Francisco Press Conference/
Tombstone Blues/ I Don't Believe You/ Baby Let
Me Follow You
R: Track 1 Vg-Ex. Tracks 2-4 G-Vg. Audience.
S: Track 1 KQED TV Studios, San Francisco Dec.
3. Tracks 2-4 Berkeley Community Theatre,
Berkeley Dec. 4 (Pt. 1).   C: 66:13.
CD14: Just Like Tom Thumb's Blues/ Long

Distance Operator/ It Ain't Me Babe/ Ballad Of A
Thin Man/ Positively 4th Street/ Like a Rolling
Stone/ Los Angeles Press Conference
R: Tracks 1-6 G-Vg. Audience.   S: Tracks 1-6
Berkeley Community Theatre, Berkeley Dec. 4
(Pt. 2). Track 7 Columbia Records press room,
Los Angeles Dec.17.   C: Time 66:20.
C: Another masterpiece from Italy's GREAT
DANE. The 14 CDs come housed in a large box
with a well illustrated book with great documenta-
tion. If only the legitimate record industry would
take note of items such as this, Great Danes'
Beatles BBC box and BIG Music's Beatles
'Artifacts' series for the way things should be pre-
sented. Wake up guys, this is what we want!

CD - NO TIME TO THINK
RED SKY RECORDS CD1009/1010
CD1: Stuck Inside Of Mobile/ Maggie's Farm/
Shooting Star/ God Knows/ Gates Of Eden/ Don't
Think Twice/ Shelter From The Storm/ You're A
Big Girl Now/ Ballad Of A Thin Man/ Blowin' In
The Wind/ New Morning/ Tonight I'll Be Staying
Here With You/ Trail Of The Buffalo
CD2: Delia/ If Not For You/ It's All Over Now Baby
Blue/ Idiot Wind/ When I Paint My Masterpiece/
Shelter From The Storm/ Love Minus Zero/No
Limit/ Little Moses/ Desolation Row/ It Ain't Me
Babe/ Cat's In The Well/ Absolutely Sweet Marie/
The Lady Of Carlisle/ The Times They Are A-
Changin'
R: Vg-Ex. Audience and soundboard.   S: CD1
Tracks 1-8 Wolf Trap, Vienna, USA Sept. 9 '93.
Rest various locations, Australia Apr. '92.
C: ECD.

CD - OVER THE BROKEN GLASS
CRACKER CR-1
Maggie's Farm/ I And I/ License To Kill/ A Hard
Rain's A-Gonna Fall/ Tangled Up In Blue/ To
Ramona/ It's Alright Ma (I'm Only Bleeding)/
Shelter From The Storm/ Mr Tambourine Man/ It
Ain't Me Babe/ Times They Are A-Changing/ It's
All Over Now Baby Blue/ Knockin' On Heaven's
Door
R: Good.   S: Tracks 1-8 Slane Castle, Ireland
July 8 '84. Tracks 9-13 Parc De Sceaux, Paris,
France July 1 '84.   C: Time 72:02.

CD - PHANTOMS OF MY YOUTH
CAPRICORN RECORDS CR 2039/40/41
CD1: Hero Blues (5:25)/ Most Likely You Go Your
Way (And I'll Go Mine) (5:42)/ Rainy Day Woman
#'s 12 & 55 (2:42)/ Lay Baby Lay (2:59)/ It Takes
A Lot To Laugh, It Takes A Lot To Cry (5:20)/ Just
Like Tom Thumb's Blues (6:02)/ Tough Mama
(4:17)/ It Ain't Me Babe (5:12)/ As I Went Out One
Morning (5:21)/ I Don't Believe You (5:28)/ One
Too Many Mornings (4:26)/ Ballad Of A Thin Man
(5:40)/ Leopard-Skin Pill-Box Hat (4:02)/ All Along
The Watchtower (2:56)/ Mr. Tambourine Man
(4:28)/ Ballad Of Hollis Brown (4:00)/ Knockin On
Heavens Door (4:11)
CD2: The Times They Are A-Changin' (2:54)/

Blowin' In The Wind (2:42)/ Song To Woody
(2:48)/ 4th Time Around (3:43)/ Don't Think Twice,
It's All Right (3:58)/ Visions Of Johanna (6:02)/
Wedding Song (2:56)/ Girl Of The North Country
(3:01)/ She Belongs To Me (2:40)/ Gates Of Eden
(4:58)/ A Hard Rain's A-Gonna Fall (5:28)/ To
Ramona (3:49)/ It's Over Now, Baby Blue (4:34)/
The Lonesome Death Of Hattie Carroll (5:05)/
Mama, You Been On My Mind (2:15)
CD3: Just Like A Woman (4:06)/ Desolation Row
(8:30)/ Nobody 'Cept You (2:38)/ Love Minus
Zero: No Limit (3:50)/ Mr. Tambourine Man (4:37)/
It's Alright Ma (I'm Only Bleeding) (4:53)/ Forever
Young (4:47)/ Something There Is About You
(4:29)/ Highway 61 Revisited (4:29)/ Like A
Rolling Stone (6:33)/ Most Likely You Go Your
Way (And I'll Go Mine) (Reprise) (3:15)/ Maggie's
Farm (3:50)/ Blowin' In The Wind (4:29)
R: As with any recording with this number of
sources the quality varies from G-Ex audience
and soundboard.   S: Various locations on
Dylan's '74 tour with The Band.   C: Dcc. A ver-
sion of every song played on the tour. The discs
say 'See booklet for track listings' (and sources?)
but there was nothing with the copy we received.

CD - PHOENIX
TYPHOON TYN 007
World Gone Wrong/ I Want You/ All Along The
Watchtower/ Tears Of Rage/ Silver And Gold/
Tangled Up In Blue/ Someone Who Is Hanging
On His Mind/ One Too Many Mornings/ Band
Intro/ Seen The Real You At Last/ Rainy Day
S: The Phoenix Festival July 14 '95.   C: ECD.

CD - PILL-BOX
TNT STUDIO TNT-940157/158
CD1: She Belongs To Me/ Fourth Time Around/
Visions Of Johanna/ It's all Over Now, Baby Blue/
Desolation Row/ Just Like A Woman
CD2: Tell Me Mama/ I Don't Believe You/ Baby,
Let Me Follow You Down/ Just Like Tom Thumb's
Blues/ Leopard-Skin Pill-Box Hat/ One Too Many
Mornings/ Ballad Of a Thin Man/ Like A Rolling
Stone
R: Good audience recording.   S: ABC Hall,
Dundee University, Edinburgh, Scotland May 20
'66.   C: Japanese CDs.

CD - PITTSBURGH '94
RED SKY
Jokerman/ Senor/ All Along The Watchtower/
Positively 4th Street/ Cats In The Well/ In The
Garden/ Maggies Farm/ A Hard Rains A Gonna
Fall/ Under The Red Sky/ To Ramona (Cleveland
Aug. 20 '94)
R: Vg. Audience.   S: Pittsburgh Aug. 19 '94.

CD - REAL LIVE OUTTAKES 1984
YELLOW CAT YC 022
Just Like A Woman (5:41)/ When You Gonna
Wake Up? (4:57)/ Senor (5:14)/ The Times They
Are A' Changing (5:48)/ Knocking On Heavens
Door (5:31)/ Shelter From The Storm (5:43)/ To

Ramona (4:25)/ With God On Our Side (4:36)/ It's
All Over Now, Baby Blue (5:24)/ Tupelo Honey
(4:25)/ Leopard-Skin Pill-Boxed Hat (4:58)/
Blowin' In The Wind (5:05)/ Mr. Tambourine Man
(5:45)/ Enough Is Enough (3:34)
R: Ex.   C: ECD. Dcc.

CD - THE REAL VOICE OF AMERICA
TUFF BITES TB.94.1011
CD1: Jokerman/ Senor/ All Along The
Watchtower/ Born In Time/ Tangled Up In Blue/ I
Don't Believe You/ Master Of War/ Mama You've
Been On My Mind/ Mr. Tambourine Man/ Silvio/ I
And I
CD2: Tears Of Rage/ Maggie's Farm/ Ballad Of A
Thin Man/ It Ain't Me Babe/ You're A Big Girl Now/
Simple Twist Of Fate/ Under The Red Sky/ Lady
Came From Baltimore/ It's All Over Now, Baby
Blue/ two other tracks
R: Poor audience recording, hiss.   S: Topeka,
Kansas Apr. 28. '94. CD2 tracks 5-11 Peoria, Ill.
Apr. 13 '94.

CD - ROSELAND
WANTED MAN MUSIC WMM 66/67
CD1: Jokerman/ If You See Her Say Hello/ All
Along The Watchtower/ I'll Be Your Baby Tonight/
Tangled Up In Blue/ Man In The Long Black Coat/
Mr. Tambourine Man/ Masters Of War
CD2: Don't Think Twice It's Alright/ Knocking On
Heaven's Door/ God Knows/ Tears Of Rage/
Maggie's Farm/ Ballad Of A Thin Man/ My Back
Pages
R: Vg. Audience.   S: The Roseland Ballroom,
New York Oct. 18 '94.   C: ECD. Dcc.
Time 57:28. CD2 55:02.

CD - SAN RAFAEL REHEARSALS VOL 1
YELLOW CAT
The Times They Are A-Changin'/ When I Paint My
Masterpiece/ Man Of Peace/ I'll Be Your Baby
Tonight/ Ballad Of Ira Hayes/ I Want You/ Ballad
Of A Thin Man, Dead Man/ Queen Jane
Approximately/ Boy In The Bubble/ The French
Girl/ In The Summertime/ Man Of Peace/ Union
Sundown
S: Dylan/Dead rehearsals Mar. - Apr. '87.
C: ECD.

CD - SAN RAFAEL REHEARSALS VOL 2
YELLOW CAT
It's All Over Now Baby Blue/ If Not For You/ Joey/
Slow Train Coming/ Tomorrow Is A Long Time/
Gotta Serve Somebody/ Gonna Change My Way
Of Thinking/ Maggie's Farm/ Chimes Of Freedom/
All I Really Wanna Do/ John Brown/ Heart Of
Mine/ Rollin' In My Sweet Baby's Arms
S: Dylan/Dead rehearsals Mar. - Apr. '87.
C: ECD.

CD - SKIPPIN' REELS OF RHYME
CD1: Down In The Flood/ If You See Her, Say
Hello/ All Along The Watchtower/ Jokerman/
Every Grain Of Sand/ Positively 4th Street/ Mr.

Tambourine Man/ Masters Of War/ Love Minus Zero/ God Knows/ Stuck Inside Of Mobile
CD2: I Believe In You/ Like A Rolling Stone/ The Times They Are A Changing/ I Shall Be Released (with Elvis Costello)/ Down In The Flood/ I Want You/ Just Like A Woman/ Tangled Up In Blue/ It Takes A Lot To Laugh, It Takes A Lot To Cry/ Boots Of Spanish Leather/ Stuck Inside Of Mobile/ Don't Think Twice It's Alright
R: Vg-Ex. Audience.   S: CD1 and CD2 tracks 1-4 The Brixton Academy, London Mar. 30 '95. CD2 tracks 5-12 The Brixton Academy, London Mar. 29 '95.   C: ECD. Dcc. CD1 74:45. CD2 75:32.

CD - SOUNDS INSIDE MY HEAD
THE RAZOR'S EDGE RAZ 018
Drifter's Escape/ I Want You/ All Along The Watchtower/ Tears Of Rage/ Silvio/ Tangled Up In Blue/ Mamma You Been On My Mind/ One Too Many Mornings/ Seeing The Real You At Last/ Rainy Day Women
R: Ex. Audience.   S: Phoenix Festival, Long Marston Airport, Stratford Upon Avon, Warwickshire, England July 14 '95.   C: ECD. Time 77:48.

CD - STUDS TERKEL'S WAX MUSEUM
YELLOW DOG YD 057
Introduction (0:46)/ Farewell (8:50)/ A Hard Rain's A-Gonna Fall (18:34)/ Bob Dylan's Dream (6:31)/ Boots Of Spanish Leather (10:56)/ John Brown (11:16)/ Who Killed Davey Moore? (6:00)/ Blowin' In The Wind (2:37)
R: Ex. Soundboard.   S: Studs Terkel's Wax Museum, Chicago May 3 '63. Broadcast at a later date by WFMT Radio.   C: ECD. Dcc.

CD - STUMBLIN' ALONG
HAWK
You're Gonna Quit Me Baby/ Stuck Inside Of Mobile/ All Along The Watchtower/ Born In Time/ Silvio/ I And I/ Jim Jones/ Gates Of Eden/ Don't Think Twice/ God Knows/ Maggie's Farm
R: Ex.   S: Hollywood Bowl Oct. '93.   C: ECD. Pic CD.

CD - TRUE STORIES
METEOR
Ballad Of A Thin Man/ In The Summertime/ Shot Of Love/ Walk Around Heaven All Day/ The Times They Are A-Changin'/ Let's Begin/ Lenny Bruce/ Saved/ I Believe In You/ Like A Rolling Stone/ 'till I Get It Right/ Man Gave Names To All The Animals/ Maggie's Farm/ Girl From The North Country
R: Ex. Soundboard.   S: Palace Des Sports, Avignon, France July 26 '80.   C: ECD. 57:51.

CD - 12/- A POUND
CD1: Down In The Flood/ If Not For You/ All Along The Watchtower/ Just Like A Woman/ Tangled Up In Blue/ Watching The River Flow/ Mr. Tambourine Man/ Boots Of Spanish Leather/ Its All Over Now Baby Blue/ Man In A Long Black

Coat/ God Knows
CD2: Maggies Farm/ Shelter From The Storm/ It Ain't Me Babe/ Down In The Flood/ I Don't Believe In You/ Just Like A Woman/ Tangled Up In Blue/ Watching The River Flow/ Desolation Row/ Ballad Of A Thin Man
R: Vg. Audience.   S: Prague Mar. 11 '95. CD2 tracks 4-10 Prague Mar. 12 '95.   C: Japanese CD. Dcc. Time CD1 72:07. CD2 69:30.

CD - VISIT TO ISLAEL
CUTTLEFISH RECORDS CFR 010/11
CD1: Maggies Farm/ I'll Be Your Baby Tonight/ Senor/ Highway 61 Revisited/ I And I/ Watching The River Flow/ Simple Twist Of Fate
CD2: Stuck Inside Of Mobile With The Memphis Blues Again/ In The Garden/ Joey/ Dead Man Dead Man/ I'll Remember You/ Tangled Up In Blue/ All Along The Watchtower/ Knockin' On Heaven's Door/ Blowin' In The Wind
R: G-Vg. Audience.   S: Hayarkon Park, Tel-Aviv, Israel Sept. 5 '87.   C: Japanese CDs. Dcc. Pic CD. Title miss-spelled. CD1 44:15. CD2 43:38.

CD - WHAT'S REAL
TNT STUDIO TNT-940154/155/156
CD1: Highway 61 Revisited/ Jokerman/ All Along The Watchtower/ Just Like A Woman/ Maggie's Farm/ I And I/ License To Kill/ Just My Imagination/ two other tracks
CD2: It's Alright, Ma/ Simple Twist Of Fate/ Masters Of War/ Enough Is Enough/ Ever Grain Of Sand/ Like A Rolling Stone/ Mr. Tambourine Man/ two other tracks
CD3: Leopard-Skin Pill-Box Hat/ It's All Over Now, Baby Blue/ Tombstone Blues/ Senor/ The Times They Are A-Changin'/ Blowin' In The Wind/ one other track
C: Good audience recording.   S: Wembley Stadium, London July 7 '84.   C: Japanese CDs. CD3 with Eric Clapton, Carlos Santana, Van Morrison and Chrissy Hinde.

CD - WILD CATHEDRAL EVENING
TSP GRUNT 001
The Times They Are A-Changing/ Like A Rolling Stone/ Maggie's Farm/ Senor/ I Want You/ Pledging My Time/ Simple Twist Of Fate/ Seeing The Real You At Last/ I Shall Be Released/ Tomorrow Is A Long Time/ Dead Man, Dead Man/ In The Garden/ Chimes Of Freedom/ Knockin' On Heaven's Door
R: Vg audience recording.   S: International Arena, National Exhibition Centre, Birmingham, England Oct. 10 '87.   C: Japanese CD. With Tom Petty.

CD - WOODSTOCK 1994
WOOD 99407/08
CD1: Jokerman/ Just Like A Woman/ All Along The Watchtower/ Ridin' On The A-Train/ Don't Think Twice, It's All Right/ Masters Of War/ It's All Over Now, Baby Blue/ God Knows
CD2: I Shall Be Released/ Highway 61 Revisited/

Rainy Day Women #12 & 35/ It Ain't Me, Babe/ Stuck Inside Of Mobile With The Memphis Blues Again/ Tangled Up In Blue/ Cat's In The Well
R: Exs. Soundboard. CD2 tracks 5-7 Ex audience recording.   S: Woodstock, Aug. 14 '94. CD2 tracks 5-7 American 'Good As I Been To You' tour.
C: Time CD1 52:52. CD2 55:49.

E

EAGLES, THE

CD - THE BOYS OF SUMMER
GREAT DANE GDR 9414/ABCD
CD1: Take It Easy/ How Long/ Tequila Sunrise/ Witchy Woman/ Peaceful Easy Feelin' A Good Day In Hell/ Already Gone/ James Dean/ Midnight Flyer/ Twenty-One/ Ol' 55/ Your Bright Baby Blues/ Desperado/ Doolin' Dalton, Desperado (reprise)/ Take It Easy
CD2: Chug All Night/ Outlaw Man/ Train Leaves Here This Morning/ Journey Of The Sorcerer/ Too Many Hands/ You Never Cry Like A Lover/ Seven Bridges Road/ Lyin' Eyes/ Desperado/ One Of These Nights/ Hotel California/ Victim Of Love/ Take It To The Limit
CD3: Train Leaves Here This Morning/ A Moment Of Time/ The Boys Of Summer/ New Kid In Town/ The Best Of My Love/ Hotel California/ Life In The Fast Lane/ Life's Been Good/ Take It To The Limit/ Desperado/ I Can't Tell You Why/ Peaceful Easy Feelin'/ Medley: Lyin' Eyes, Part Of You, Part Of Me, Take It Easy/ Lover's Moon/ Desperado
CD4: Hotel California/ Wasted Time/ The Girl From Yesterday/ One Of These Nights/ Tequila Sunrise/ Help Me Make It Through The Night/ The Heart Of The Matter/ Love Will Keep Us Alive/ Learn To Be Still/ Life's Been Good/ Pretty Maids All In A Row/ Smuggler's Blues/ Desperado/ Take It Easy
R: Vg-Ex.   S: CD1 '72-'74. Tracks 6-15 Jackson Brown on vocals. Track 12 Linda Ronstadt on vocals. CD2 '75-'79. Track 6 Osaka, 7 with Steve Young. CD3 '77. CD4 audience recording, two nights in California '94.   C: ECD. Book-style digi-pack.

CD - DOOLIN DOLTON
DYNAMITE STUDIO DS94A075/76
CD1: Take It Easy/ Outlaw Man/ Doolin Dalton, Desperado/ Train Leaves Here This Morning/ Peaceful Easy Feeling/ Desperado/ Ol '55/ One Of These Nights/ Bernie Leadon Solo/ Midnight Flyer/ Journey Of The Sorcerer
CD2: Too Many Hands/ Already Gone/ Good Day In Hell/ James Dean/ Witch Woman/ Chug All Night/ Best Of My Love/ Tequila Sunrise
R: Good.   S: Civic Center May 15 '75.
C: Japanese CD.

CD - EASTERN TOUR 1976
GOLD RUSH GR001-2
CD1: Take It Easy/ Outlaw Man/ Doolin' Dalton, Desperado/ Turn To Stone/ Lyin' Eyes/ You Never Cry Like A Lover/ Take It To The Limit/ Desperado/ Midnight Flyer
CD2: One Of These Nights/ Already Gone/ Too Many Hands/ Good Day In Hell/ Witchy Woman/ Rocky Mountain Way/ James Dean/ Best Of My Love/ Funk #49/ Carol
R: Vg-Ex. Soundboard.   S: Feb. '76.
C: Japanese CD. Sepia tone cover.
Time CD1 60:17. CD2 62:01.

CD - THE GRAND RESUMPTION
HOME RECORDS HR5965/66
CD1: Hotel California (6:49)/ Victim Of Love (5:00)/ New Kid In Town (5:03)/ Wasted Time (6:04)/ The Girl From Yesterday (4:09)/ I Can't Tell You Why (5:04)/ New York Minute (7:35)/ Ordinary Average Guy (4:59)/ Lyin' Eyes (6:47)/ One Of These Nights (4:16)/ Tequila Sunrise (4:19)/ Help Me Through The Night (4:24)/ Forgiveness (5:48)
CD2: Love Will Keep Us Alive (4:30)/ Learn To Be Still (4:41)/ You Belong (7:20)/ Boys Of Summer (5:12)/ Life's Been Good (8:05)/ All She Wants To Do Is Dance (5:22)/ Heartache Tonight (4:28)/ Life In The Fast Lane (5:15)/ Get Over It (3:40)/ Rocky Mountain Way (7:16)/ Already Gone (4:46)/ Desperado (4:50)/ Take It Easy (4:17)
R: Vg-Exs. Audience.   S: Irvin Meadows, CA May '94.   C: ECD. Dcc. Pic CD.

CD - HIGH NOON
TNT STUDIO TNT 940159/160
CD1: Hotel California/ Victim Of Love/ Doolin Dalton, Desperado/ Lyin' Eyes/ Wasted Time/ Take It To The Limit/ New Kid In Town
CD2: Desperado/ Already Gone/ Life In The Fast Lane/ Rocky Mountain Way/ James Dean/ The Best Of My Life/ Take It Easy
R: G. Audience.   S: Wembley Arena Apr. 9 '77.
C: Japanese CD. Dcc. CD1 46:25 CD2 39:16

CD - HUNGRY COWBOY
TEDDY BEAR TB 59
Peaceful Easy Feeling (4:48)/ Midnight Flyer (4:20)/ Twenty One (2:31)/ Ol' 55 (4:35)/ James Dean (3:40)/ Doolin' Dalton (5:47)/ Desperado (2:57)/ Take It Easy (5:43)/ Already Gone (5:00)/ Hotel California (6:30)/ New Kid In Town (4:53)/ Wasted Time (5:30)/ The Girls From Yesterday (3:58)/ Tequila Sunrise (4:23)/ Heartache Tonight (4:25)/ Desperado (4:05)
R: Ex. Soundboard.   S: Tracks 1-9 NYC '74. Tracks 10-16 California '94.   C: ECD. Dcc. Pic CD. Tracks 10-16 with Jackson Brown and Linda Ronstadt on backing vocals.

CD - L.A. FORUM 1980
GOLD RUSH GR-003-4
CD1: Hotel California/ Already Gone/ In The City/ King Of Hollywood/ The Sad Cafe/ Lyin' Eyes/ I

Can't Tell You Why
CD2: Those Shoes/ Heartache Tonight/ One Of
These Nights/ Turn To Stone/ The Long Run/
Life's Been Good/ Life In The Fast Lane
R: Vg. Soundboard. Low level.   S: LA Forum
Mar. 4 '80.   C: Japanese CD. Dbw.
Time CD1 41:46. CD2 43:02.

CD - OUTLAW MAN
RAG DOLL MUSIC RDM-942003A/B
CD1: Take It Easy/ Outlaw Man/ Doolin Dalton,
Desperado (reprise)/ Train Leaves Here This
Morning/ Peaceful Easy Feeling/ Desperado/ Ol'
55/ One Of These Night/ Instrumental/ Midnight
Flyer/ Instrumental
CD2: Too Many Hands/ Already Gone/ Good Day
In Hell/ James Dean/ Witchy Woman/ Chug All
Night/ The Best Of My Love/ Oh Carol/ Tequila
Sunrise
R: G. Audience.   S: Spectrum, Philadelphia, PA
May 17 '75.   C: Japanese CD. Time CD1 59:17.
CD2 49:47.

CD - TALES OF FRONTIERS
MA-82274
Take It Easy/ Outlaw Man/ Already Gone/ Doolin
Dalton/ Desperado/ Peaceful Easy Feeling/
Midnight Flyer/ Pie Berry Blossom/ Tryin'/ Witchy
Woman/ Chug All Night/ Tequila Sunrise
R: G-Vg. Audience.   S: Lenox, MA Aug. 22 '74.

CD - THE UNFORGIVEN
TNT STUDIO TNT-940166
Take It Easy/ Tell Me How Long/ Doolin Dalton/
Bitter Creek/ Peaceful Easy Feeling/ Desperado/
Twenty-One/ Earlybird/ Certain Kind Of Fool/
Outlaw Man/ Witchy Woman/ Lazy Day/ Tryin/
Out Of Control/ Tequila Sunrise
R: Vg audience recording.   S: Curtis Hickson
Hall, Tampa, FL June 7 '73.   C: Japanese CD.

CD - WANTED
MAIN STREET MTS 102
Take It Easy/ How Long/ Doolin' Dalton/ Bitter
Creek/ Peaceful Easy Feeling/ Desperado/
Twenty-One/ Earlybird/ Instrumental/ Certain Kind
Of Fool/ Outlaw Man/ Witchy Woman/ Lazy Days/
Trying/ Tequila Sunrise
R: Vg. Audience.   S: Berkeley Community
Theater June 16 '73.   C: ECD. Time 74:44.

CD - WITCHY WOMAN
RAG DOLL MUSIC RDM-942004A/B
CD1: Hotel California/ Walk Away/ Victim Of Love/
Doolin' Dalton, Desperado/ Lyin' Eyes/ One Of
These Nights/ Turn To Stone
CD2: Already Gone/ Witchy Woman/ Life's Been
Good/ Life In The Fast Lane/ Rocky Mountain
Way/ Take It Easy/ James Dean/ Tequila Sunrise
R: Poor audience recording.   S: Comiskey Park,
Chicago Aug. 19 '78.   C: Japanese CD.

EDMUNDS, DAVE

CD - STILL ROCKIN'
HOME RECORDS HR6036-4
I Knew The Bride/ Shoots And Ladders/ Standing
On The Crossroads/ Queen Of Hearts/ The Race
Is On/ Half Way Down/ The Clock/ Here Comes
The Weekend/ Lady Madonna/ I Got The Will/
Girls Talk/ Doesn't Matter At All/ Teenage Rock N'
Roller/ I Hear You Knocking/ Crawling From The
Wreckage/ Rocking N' Rolling Until Tomorrow
Night/ Instrumental
R: Vg. Audience.   S: Boston, Mass. Sept. 13'
94.   C: ECD. Dcc.

ELASTICA

ANGELS WITH DIRTY FACES
PSEUDO INDIE LABEL PIL08
Spastica/ Connection/ Line Up/ 2-1/ See That
Animal/ S.O.F.T./ Car Song/ Rockunroll/ Never
Here/ Stutter/ Vaseline/ Connection/ Car Song/
S.O.F.T./ Never Here/ Hold Me Now/ Work So
Hard/ Waking Up/ In the City/ 2-1/ Connection/
Four Wheeling/ Vaseline/ Stutter/ Brighton Rock/
Blue/ Happy Birthday/ Vaseline
R: Ex. Soundboard. Tracks 25-27 G. Audience.
S: Tracks 1-10 Zap Club, Brighton, UK Sept. 9
'94. Tracks 11-13 'Later', UK TV show Nov. 19
'94. Tracks 14-24 radio sessions and demos
'93/'94. Tracks 25-27 Hultsfred and Reading
Festival Aug. '94.   C: ECD. Dcc. Pic CD.

CD - PERKY PUNK NOISE
PRINT 006
Connection/ In The City (Unreleased)/ 2:1/
Waking Up/ Never Here/ Car Song/ Hold Me Now/
Ba Ba Ba (Unreleased)/ Connection/ Vaseline/
Car Song/ Spastica (Unreleased)/ Rock Un Roll
(Unreleased)/ Line Up/ Connection/ S.O.F.T./
Waking Up/ 18. 2:1/ See That Animal/ Vaseline/
Stutter/ Waking Up
R: Exs. Soundboard.   S: Tracks 1-3 BBC
Session Apr. '94. Tracks 5-8 BBC Session, July
'94. Tracks 9-11 BBC TV, Dec. '94. Tracks 12-22
Lille, France Mar. 31 '94.   C: ECD. Dcc. 56:55.

CD - POORER IS BETTER
OCTOPUS OCTO 198
Gloria (3:08)/ Rock 'N Roll Is Dead (2:19)/ Line
Up (3:13)/ Annie (1:29)/ Car Song (2:24)/ Never
Here (4:22)/ Stutter (2:32)/ 2:1 (2:17)/ See That
Animal (2:30)/ Waking Up (3:21)/ S.O.F.T. (3:47)/
Connection (2:17)/ Blue (2:36)/ Vaseline (1:34)/
Hold Me Now (2:22)/ Work So Hard (2:30)/ Four
Wheeling (2:22)/ Never Here (3:40) Gloria (2:57)/
I Wanna Be King Of Orient (2:00)/ Black Dogs
(3:09)/ Blue (2:19)/ Connection (2:16)/ Line Up
(3:17)/ Stutter (2:25)
R: Exs. Soundboard.   S: 1-14 The Sound City
Festival, Bristol, UK Apr. 18 '95. Tracks 15-22
BBC Sessions, UK July '94. Tracks 23-25 The
Brighton Rock Festival UK Sept. '94.   C: ECD.

CD - THE VASELINE GANG
KISS THE STONE KTS 438
Gloria/ Rockunroll/ Line Up/ Annie/ Car Song/
Never Here/ Stutter/ 2:1/ See That Animal/
Waking Up/ S.O.F.T./ Connection/ Blue/ Vaseline/
Spastica/ Connection/ Line Up/ 2:1 (Instrumental)/
See That Animal/ S.O.F.T./ Car Song/ Rockunroll/
Never Here/ Stutter/ Car Song/ Connection/ Line
Up
R: Ex.   S: Europe. Tracks 1-14 Apr. 18 '95.
Tracks 15-24 Sept. 6 '94. Tracks 25-27 Apr. 7 '95.
C: ECD. Dcc. Pic CD. Time 72:29.

CD - WEEKEND SWINGERS
PINK FRAG PF154
Spastica/ Rockunroll/ Line Up/ Soft/ Connection/
Never Here/ Car Song/ Stutter/ Waking Up/
Brighton Rock/ 2:1/ See That Animal/ Hold Me
Now/ Blue/ Vaseline/ Never Me Now/ Four-
Wheeling/ Hold Me Now/ Bar Bar Bar/ All For
Gloria/ King Of Orient/ Cleochristmas/ Blue/ Line
Up/ In The City/ Vaseline
R: Ex.   S: Tracks 1-15 Hultsfred Rock Festival,
Sweden '94. Tracks 16-23 John Peel Sessions
'94. Track 24 'The Word' TV show '94. Tracks 25-
26 '94 demos.   C: ECD. Pic CD. Time 66:47.

ELECTRIC LIGHT ORCHESTRA

CD - STRANGE MAGIC
CHAPTER ONE CO 25141
Poker (4:30)/ Nightrider (4:18)/ On The Third Day,
a) Ocean Break-Up, b) King Of The Universe, c)
On The Third Day, d) Bluebird Is Dead, e) New
World Rising (13:50)/ Showdown (4:48)/ Can't
Get It Out Of My Head (6:02)/ Illusion In G-Major
(2:42)/ Strange Magic (5:17)/ 10538 Overture, Do
Ya (5:40)/ Evil Woman (4:35)
R: Exs. Soundboard. Some surface noise.

EMERSON, LAKE AND PALMER

CD - NUTROCKER '72
MY PHENIX CO. ZA 72/73
CD1: Hoedown/ Tarkus, Eruption, Stone Of Years,
Iconoclast, Mass, Manticore, Battlefield Including
Epitaph, Aquatarkus/ The Endless Enigma Pt. 1/
Fugue/ The Endless Enigma Pt. 2/ Unknown
Unreleased Song/ The Sheriff/ Take A Pebble/
Lucky Man
CD2: Take A Pebble (Reprise)/ Pictures At An
Exhibition, Promenade, The Hutop Babayaga,
The Curse Of Babayaga, The Great Gates Of
Kiev/ Nutrocker, Drum Solo, Rondo (Encore)
R: G-Vg. Audience.   S: London Nov. 26 '72.
C: Japanese CD. Dcc. Time CD1 47:39.
CD2 53:06.

ENO, BRIAN

CD - DALI'S CAR
GERMAN LUBEK 001
The Paw Negro Blow Torch/ Fever/ The Fat Lady
Of Limbourg*/ Third Uncle*/ Baby's On Fire/ I'll

Come Running
R: Exs. Soundboard. *Vg. Audience.   S: BBC
'Top Gear' radio session Feb. 26 '74. *Reading
Festival Aug. 26 '76.   C: ECD. Digi-pack. With
The Winkies. *with 801. Time 30:57.

ETHERIDGE, MELISSA

CD - ACOUSTIC
KISS THE STONE KTS 415
Come To My Window/ Ain't It Heavy/ If I Wanted
To/ Bring Me Some Water/ Maggie Ma/ Yes I Am/
Thunder Road/ I'm The Only One/ Like The Way I
Do/ Piece Of My Heart/ Happy Xmas-Give Peace
A Chance/ All American Girls/ Honky Tonk
Woman
R: Exs. Soundboard.   S: The Brooklyn
Academy Of Music Feb. '95. Track 10 'Rock 'N'
Roll All Of Fame' New York City Jan. '95. Track 11
Los Angeles Dec. '94. Track 12 New York City
Oct. '94. Track 13 Los Angeles June '94.
C: ECD. Pic CD. Time 60:21.

CD - ALL I WANNA DO
KTS OF AUSTRALIA 009 B
What I Can Do For You (6:29)/ I Feel Happy
(5:06)/ All I Wanna Do (5:10)/ New Song (Untitled)
(2:50)/ I Shall Believe (7:44)/ Interview (6:50)/
Leaving Las Vegas (6:20)/ Interview (3:55)/ On
The Outside (Demo) (4:47)/ Interview (1:47)/ All I
Wanna Do (4:37)/ Interview (:44)/ Run Baby Run
(5:254)/ Interview (:25)/ Strong Enough (3:10)/
Closing (1:42)
S: Oct. 17 '94. Tracks 6, 8, 9, 10, 11 and 12 K-
Rock WXRK NYC with Al Kopper 3/6/94.
C: Australian CD.

CD - BEING SENSITIVE
ETHEL 01
A Lot Like You (4:30)/ Somewhere In The City
(5:16)/ Occasionally (vibro groove mix) (3:20)/
Dancing In The Fire (6:13)/ You And I Know
(3:38)/ Watching You (Take 1) (5:57)/ Meet Me In
The Back (3:42)/ Don't You Need (4:44)/ No
Guarantee (3:07)/ Whispers In My Heart (4:50)/
Santa Claus Is Coming To Town (2:26)/ Don't You
Need (solo version) (4:42)/ Out Of My Mind
(5:22)/ Watching You (5:35)/ Occasionally (solo)
(2:50)/ American Girl (5:06)
R: Ex. Soundboard.   S: Private demos '86 - '93.
C: ECD. Dcc. Pic CD.

CD - EVEN ANGELS ROCK
BACK STAGE BKCD 093
Wake Me Up When You Are Over (4:46)/ Can't
Cry No More (4:56)/ Run Baby, Run (5:54)/ The
Na-Na Song (7:43)/ Strong Enough (4:04)/ No
One Said It Would Be Easy (6:56)/ Leaving Las
Vegas (6:47)/ What Can I Do For You (7:18)/ I
Shall Believe (7:17)/ Live With Me (4:18)
S: Tracks 1-9 Europe '94. Track 10 USA '94.
C: ECD.

CD - I WISH I WAS YOUR LOVER
OXYGEN OXY 030
Your Little Sweet (5:01)/ Bring Me Some Water
(with Joan Osborne - 5:03)/ Sing To Lisa (with
Joan Osborne - 5:22)/ Occasionally (with Paula
Cole - 3:46)/ Watch The Woman's Hands (with
Paula Cole - 4:56)/ You Can Sleep When I Drive
(with Jewel - 3:41)/ Foolish Games (with Jewel -
4:57)/ I Wish I Was Your Lover (with Sophie B.
Hawkins - 5:49)/ Love And Affection (5:55)/ An
Unusual Kiss (5:51)/ Nowhere To Go (6:01)/ I
Could Have Been You (with Joan Osborne, Jewel,
Paula Cole and Sophie B. Hawkins - 6:07)/ I'm
The Only One (6:38)/ Your Little Secret (4:14)
R: Exs. Soundboard.   S: Tracks 1-9 'Doheny
Mansion', Los Angeles Oct. 10 '95. Tracks 10-14
Roma, Italy Oct. '95.   C: ECD. Dcc. Pic CD.
This is one of those CDs that makes listening to
the dregs worth it... excellent performances and
excellent sound.

CD - LAS VEGAS
KTS OF AUSTRALIA 009 A
Button Down Shirt (4:55)/ Can't Cry Anymore
(5:20)/ Love Is A Good Thing (7:04)/ Leaving Las
Vegas (6:25)/ Run, Baby, Run (6:21)/ Solidify
(5:02)/ The Na-Na song (7:20)/ D'yer Mak'er
(5:11)/ Strong Enough (4:30)/ Rodeo (6:26)
S: Oct. 17 '94.   C: Australian CD.

CD - LET'S GET IT ON
KISS THE STONE KTS 408
Come To My Window (4:00)/ No Souvenirs (5:05)/
Similar Features (4:29)/ Dance Without Sleeping
(5:28)/ The Weakness In Me (5:28)/ Me And
Bobby McGee (4:42)/ Bring Me Some Water
(4:49)/ Maggie Mae (6:01)/ I'm The Only One
(5:15)/ Come To My Window (3:29)/ I'm The Only
One (4:36)/ You Can Sleep While I Drive (4:07)/
Come To My Window (3:40)/ Let's Get It On
(5:12)
R: Exs. Soundboard.   S: Tracks 1-9 NYC '94.
Track 10 NYC July 5 '94. Tracks 11-13 The
Beacon Theatre NYC June '94. Track 14 Chicago
Dec. 15 '92.   C: ECD. Pic CD.

CD - MELISSA VOLUME 1
KTS OF AUSTRALIA 015 A
If I Wanted To (4:30)/ No Souvenirs (5:10)/ Yes I
Am (7:00)/ You Used To Love (8:40)/ Don't You
Bleed (6:27)/ Close Your Eyes (4:42)/ Dance
Without Sleeping (5:20)/ Ain't It Heavy (6:47)/ I'm
Lonely (4:13)/ Ready To Love (5:49)
R: Vg. Audience.   S: Live 12/11/94.
C: Australian CD.

CD - MELISSA VOLUME 2
KTS OF AUSTRALIA 015 B
Chrome Plated Heart (6:53)/ All American Girl
(5:20)/ Silent Legacy (10:23)/ 2001 (6:22)/ Come
To My Window (4:13)/ I'm The Only One (11:00)/
Must Be Crazy For Me (10:49)/ Pink Cadillac
(8:42)

R: Vg. Audience.   S: Live 12/11/94.
C: Australian CD.

CD - MELISSA VOLUME 3
KTS OF AUSTRALIA 015 C
Bring Me Some Water (8:00)/ Piece Of My Heart
(11:39)/ Like The Way I Do (17:31)/ I'd Take You
With Me (8:18)/ All American Girl (4:18)/ Happy
Xmas War Is Over, Give Peace A Chance (4:23)/
Interview with Jay Leno (1:51)
R: Ex. Soundboard.   S: 'The Late Show' Nov.
16 '94. Tracks 6 and 7 'The Tonight Show' Dec.
20 '94.   C: Australian CD.

CD - SET YOURSELF FREE
HOME RECORDS HR 6007-6
Come To My Window/ I'm The Only One/ Like I
Do/ You Can Sleep While I Drive/ Bring Me Some
Water/ Like I Do/ Try, Just A Little Bit Harder/ Cry
Baby/ Ball And Chain/ Piece Of My Heart
R: Exs. Soundboard.   S: Tracks 1-3 Aids
Benefit Concert, The Beacon Theater, New York
City June '94. Tracks 4-10 Woodstock Aug. 14
'94.   C: ECD. Pic CD. Time 53:03.

CD - TEN YEARS OF COVERS
KISS THE STONE KTS 470
Moondance/ Chuckie's In Love/ You Can't Always
Get What You Want/ I'm On Fire/ Me And Bobby
McGee/ Let's Get It On/ Maggie Mae/ Honkey
Tonk Woman/ The Weakness In Me/ Burning
Love/ Pink Cadillac/ Happy Xmas (War Is Over),
Give Peace A Chance/ Piece Of My Heart/
Thunder Road (with Springsteen)
R: Vg-Ex.   S: Various dates '85 to '95.
C: ECD. Dcc. Pic CD. Time 68:21.

CD - WHEN I WAS A CHILD
OCTOPUS OCTO 107
Come To My Window (4:15)/ Ain't It Heavy (4:46)/
If I Wanted To (3:21)/ Bring Me Some Water
(4:21)/ Maggie Mae (4:27)/ Yes I Am (7:04)/
Thunder Road (with Bruce Springsteen - 4:37)/
I'm The Only One (4:37)/ Like The Way I Do
(6:17)/ Come To My Window (4:19)/ If I Wanted
To (5:10)/ Silent Legacy (6:10)
R: Exs. Soundboard.   S: Tracks 1-9 Unplugged,
NYC Mar. 21 '95. Tracks 10-12 Woodstock
Festival Aug. 13 '94.   C: ECD. Dcc.

EXTREME

CD - CAUGHT IN THE ACT
HOME RECORDS HR5954-5
It's A Monster/ Warheads/ Kid Ego/ Do You
Wanna.../ Rest In Peace/ Am I Ever Gonna
Change/ Drum Solo/ Cupid's Death/ Guitar Solo/
More Than Words/ Decadence Dance/ Makin'
What You Like When You Get Makin'/ Get The
Funk Out
R: Vg FM stereo, some background noise.
S: Monsters Of Rock, Donnington Park, UK

June 4 '94.   C: ECD.

CD - HIP TODAY, HERE TOMORROW
CRACKER CR-17
Get The Funk Out/ Hip Today/ Tell Me Something
I Don't Know/ Cupid's Dead/ Midnight Express/
Am I Gonna Change/ Cynical/ The Rhythm
Method/ Play With Me/ Unconditionally, Stop The
World, Rest In Peace, Tragic Comic, More Than
Words/ Hole Hearted/ Naked
R: Audience.   S: Sacramento, CA Apr. 15 '95.

CD - PLAY WITH ME
METEOR BANG 1-017
Kid Ego/ It's A Monster/ Rest In Peace/
Pornograffiti/ Suzie/ The Midnight Express
(Acoustic Guitar Show-Case)/ More Than Words/
Hole-Hearted/ Naked/ Play With Me/ Cupid's
Dead/ Get The Funk Put/ Mutha (Don't Wanna Go
To School Today)
R: Ex audience recording.   S: Sea Bright, New
Jersey Aug. 11 '93.

F

FACES

CD - TELL ME A STORY
TNT STUDIO TNT-940149
It's All Over Now/ Miss Judy's Farm/ Maybe I'm
Amazed/ Too Bad/ Memphis/ Love In Vain/ Stay
With Me/ That's All You Need (includes Gasoline
Alley)/ I Feel So Good
R: Poor audience recording.   S: Tampa
Stadium, FL Apr. 30 '72.   C: Japanese CD.

FAIRPORT CONVENTION

CD - A CHRONICLE OF SORTS, 1967-9
NIXED RECORDS NIX 003
Chelsea Morning/ Lay Down Your Weary Tune/
Let's Get Together/ One Sure Thing/ Violets Of
Dawn/ If (Stomp)/ If I Had A Ribbon Bow/ Morning
Glory/ Time Will Show The Wiser/ Reno, Nevada/
Marcie/ Night In The City/ You Never Wanted Me/
Eastern Rain/ Fotheringay/ Book Song/ Dear
Landlord/ Si Tu Dois Partir/ Cajun Woman/
Autopsy/ The Lady Is A Tramp/ Light My Fire
R: G-Vg. Soundboard.   S: Tracks 1-4 BBC 'Top
Gear' Nov. 24 '67. Tracks 5-7 BBC 'Top Gear'
Feb. 6 '68. Tracks 8-10 Bouton Rouge, French TV
Show Apr. 27 '68. Tracks 11-12 'David Symonds
Show' June 18 '68. Track 13 BBC 'Top Gear' May
28 '68. Tracks 14-15 BBC 'Top Gear' Aug. 26 '68.
Track 16 'David Symonds Show' Dec. 27 '68.
Track 17 studio outtake, London mid '68. Tracks
18-20 BBC 'Top Gear' Mar. 18 '69. Track 21 BBC
'Top Gear' Sept. 23 '69. Track 22 BBC 'Top Gear'
Dec. 9 '68.   C: ECD. Dbw. Pic CD. Time 76:18.

FAITH NO MORE

CD - EVIDENCE
KISS THE STONE KTS 424
Digging A Grave/ I Started A Joke/ Ricochet/
Evidence/ Get Out/ What A Day/ A Small Victory/
Easy/ Caffeine/ Be Aggressive/ Midlife Crisis/
R.V./ Epic/ Everythings Ruined/ Midlife Crisis/
Epic/ R.V.
R: Exs. Soundboard.   S: Tracks 1-6 Europe
7/3/95. Tracks 7-13 Phoenix, Arizona July '93.
Tracks 14-17 Europe 4/12/92.   C: ECD. Dcc.
Pic CD. Time 65:44.

CD - FEROCIOUS NEUROSIS
OCTOPUS OCTO 197
Digging The Grave (3:13)/ Be Aggressive (4:02)/
Midlife Crisis (3:23)/ Land Of Sunshine (3:43)/
Epic (4:53)/ Evidence (4:56)/ What A Day (2:37)/
We Care A Lot (4:03)/ I'm Easy (3:03)/ Introduce
Yourself (1:42)/ Get Out (2:35)/ Acoustic Groove
(8:25)/ Ricochet (4:18)/ From Out Of Nowhere
(4:11)/ Zombie Eaters (6:09)/ Medley: Zombie,
Enter The Sandman (1:56)/ Take This Bottle
(4:18)/ Caffeine (4:53)
R: Exs. Soundboard.   S: The Sentrum Scene,
Oslo, Norway Mar. 20 '95.   C: ECD.

CD - NO MORE
LAST BOOTLEG RECORDS LBR 017
Falling To Pieces (4:10)/ Land Of Sunshine (3:39)/
Midlife Crisis (3:52)/ Be Aggressive (3:46)/ Easy
(2:57)/ Crack Hitler (5:11)/ We Care A Lot (3:57)/
Epic (4:54)/ As The Wurms Turns (2:34)/ RV
(3:56)/ Real Thing (7:44)/ Underwater Love
(3:36)/ Woodpecker From Mars (5:46)/ Surprise
You're Dead! (2:31)/ War Pigs (8:21)/ From Out
Of Nowhere (3:10)
R: G. Audience.   S: Hollywood Palladium Apr.
26 '93.   C: ECD. Dcc.

FEAR

7" - BUDWEISER
S1: Budweiser
S2: Hank Williams Was Queer/ Fear Anthem
R: Vg-Ex. Audience.   S: S1 Los Angeles, CA.
'85. S2 Eugene, Oregon '82.   C: USA. Dbw.
Red type. Red vinyl. 45 RPM.

FERRY, BRYAN

CD - LOVE ME MADLY AGAIN
ARCHIVIO ARC012
Let's Stick Together (2:55)/ Love Is A Drug (3:50)/
A Hard Rain's A Gonna Fall (4:25)/ This Is
Tomorrow (3:28)/ Shame, Shame, Shame (3:25)/
In Your Mind (4:42)/ All Night Operator (3:03)/ You
Go To My Head (3:00)/ Love Me Madly Again
(8:31)/ Casanova (3:20)/ Tokyo Joe (3:40)
R: Exs. Soundboard. Some buzz.   S: Australia
July 7 '79.   C: ECD. Dbw.

FLAMIN' GROOVIES, THE

CD - OH, HOW GROOVY!
DISCURIOS DIS 126
Teenage Head/ Call Me Lightning/ Feel A Whole
Lot Better/ I Can't Hide/ Million Miles Away/ Step
Up/ Stay Away/ Way Over My Head/ Milkcow
Blues/ Shake Some Action/ Slow Death/ In The
USA/ Baby Please Don't Go/ Jumpin' In The
Night/ Slow Down/ Kicks/ Bittersweet
R: G-Vg. Audience.   S: Salle De Faubourg,
Geneva, Switzerland Oct. 8 '87.   C: ECD. 71:36.

FLEETWOOD MAC

CD - LIVE AT MARQUEE CLUB 1967
ROCKET SOUND RS-1004
Talk To Me Baby (I Can't Hold Out)/ Held My
Baby Last Night/ My Baby Sweet/ Looking For
Somebody/ Long Grey Mare/ Got To Move/ Got
No Place To Go/ Love That Woman/ Mighty Long
Time/ Dust My Broom/ I Need You/ Shake Your
Money Maker
R: G. Audience.   S: Marquee Club, London '67.
C: Japanese CD. Dcc. Time 53:08.

FLYING BURRITO BROTHERS, THE

CD - THE HIGH LONESOME SOUND OF THE FLYING BURRITO BROTHERS
GOLD STANDARD 95-BUR-04-05
Close Up The Honky Tonks/ Dark End Of The
Street/ Sweet Mental Revenge/ The Image Of Me/
Christine's Tune/ Sin City/ Man In A Fog/ Wake
Up Little Susie/ You Win Again/ We've Got To Get
Ourselves Together/ She Thinks I Still Care/
Sweet Dreams Baby/ Lucille/ Take A Message To
Mary/ Train Song/ Lazy Day/ 100 Years Ago/ My
Uncle/ High Fashion Queen/ Cody Cody/ Wild
Horses
R: G. Audience.   S: Tracks 1-15 Seattle Pop
Festival, Woodenville, WA July 27 '69. Tracks 16-
21 Wynona, Minn. May '70.   C: Dcc.

FOCUS

CD - FOCAL DISTANCE
TNT STUDIO TNT-940145/146
CD1: Focus III/ Answers? Questions! Questions?/
Answers!/ Focus II/ Sylvia/ Harem Scarem/ Love
Remembered/ Tommy (Eruption)
CD2: House Of The Kings/ Birht/ Hocus Pocus/
Hamburger Concerto/ Untitled/ Hocus Pocus
R: Poor sound.   S: Kouseinekin Kaikan, Osaka,
Japan, June 2 '74.   C: Japanese CDs.

FOO FIGHTERS

CD - ENTER THE DRAGON
RED SUN RSCD 006
C: ECD. Dcc. See 'X-Static' (Typhoon TYN 003)
for songs and source.

CD - FRENZY!
OXYGEN RECORDS OXY 036
This Is A Call (4:18)/ Winnebago (2:58)/
Wattershed (2:15)/ For All The Cows (3:38)/
Weenie Beanie (3:24)/ Butterflies (3:21)/ I'll Stick
Around (3:52)/ Podunk (3:09)/ Alone + Easy
Target (5:16)/ Exhausted (6:26)/ Floaty (5:28)/ My
Hero (Unreleased Track) (4:00)/ Down In The
Park (Unreleased Track) (4:26)/ Alone + Easy
Target (4:22)/ Floaty (5:17)/ How I Miss You
(5:57)/ Up In Arms (Unreleased Track) (2:07)/
Gas Chamber (0:55)
R: Exs. Soundboard.   S: Tracks 1-13 The
'Circus', Stockholm, Sweden Oct. 16 '95. Tracks
14-18 'BBC Evening Session', London Nov. '95.
C: ECD.

CD - FIGHTING THE 'N' FACTOR
OXYGEN OXY 031
Enough Space (2:39)/ This Is A Call (4:08)/
Winnebago (2:57)/ Wattershed (2:07)/ For All The
Cows (3:31)/ Weenie Beanie (2:59)/ Big Me
(2:27)/ I'll Stick Around (3:51)/ Alone + Easy
Target (5:02)/ Up In Arms (1:39)/ Gas Chamber
(1:18)/ Exhausted (7:48)/ Winnebago (2:58)/
Wattershed (2:02)/ Marygold (3:08)/ Heart
Shaped Box (Take 1) (6:05)/ Heart Shaped Box
(Take 2) (4:49)/ Rape Me (2:57)/ Serve The
Servants (3:27)/ Dumb (2:34)
R: Exs. Soundboard.   S: Tracks 1-12 Brixton
Academy, London Nov. 15 '95. Tracks 13-14 BBC
Studios, London Nov. 16 '95. Track 15 Dave
Grohl - acoustic demo, Upland Studios, Arlington,
VA Dec. 23 '90. Tracks 16-18 Nirvana -
rehearsals for 'Saturday Night Live' TV Show,
NYC '94. Tracks 19-20 Nirvana - 'Tunnel TV
Show', Rome, Italy Feb. 23 '94.   C: ECD. Dcc.
Pic CD.

CD - ON THE AIR
MOONRAKER 038
Enough Space/ This Is A Call/ Winne Bago/
Wattershed/ For All The Cows/ Weenie Beenie/
Big Me/ I'll Stick Around/ Alone + Easy Target/ Up
In Arms/ Gas Chamber/ Exhausted/ Interview/ I'll
Stick Around*/ For All The Cows*
R: Exs. Soundboard.   S: Brixton Academy,
London Nov. 14 '95. *Saturday Night Live, NYC
Dec. 2 95.   C: ECD. Dcc. Time 51:37.

CD - TUNEFUL CHAOS
OXYGEN OXY 007
Big Me (2:18)/ This Is A Call (4:23)/ Weenie
Beenie (3:11)/ For All The Cows (3:48)/ My Hero
(3:53)/ Oh, George (3:07)/ Watershed (2:46)/ Big
Me (2:32)/ This Is A Call (3:55)/ Weenie Beenie
(3:09)/ For All The Cows (3:45)/ Exhausted (6:19)/
I'll Stick Around (4:18)/ Winnebago (3:26)/ Butter
Lies (3:24)/ Podunk (3:35)/ Good Grief (4:44)/ X-
Static (5:05)/ Alone, Easy Target (4:09)
R: Tracks 1-12 Exs. Soundboard. Tracks 13-19
Vg. Audience.   S: Tracks 1-6 The Lowlands
Festival, Holland Aug. 27 '95. Tracks 7-12 The
Reading Festival, UK Aug. 26 '95. Tracks 13-19

The King's College, London June 3 '95.
C: ECD. Dcc. Pic CD.

CD - WEENIE BEENIE
MOONRAKER 027
Enough Space/ This Is A Call/ Winne Bago/
Wattershed/ For All The Cows/ Weenie Beenie/
Butterflies/ Big Me/ I'll Stick Around/ Oh, George/
Good Grief/ Podunk/ Alone + Easy Target/
Exhausted/ Floaty/ My Hero/ Down In The Park
R: Ex. Audience.   S: Cirkus, Stockholm Oct. 16
'95.   C: ECD. Dcc. Time 67:20.

CD - X STATIC
TYPHOON TYN 003
This Is A Call (4:47)/ I'll Stick Around (4:18)/
Podunk (2:57)/ Weanie Beany (2:58)/ For All The
Cows (4:13)/ Winnebago (3:15)/ X Static (3:25)/
Big Me (2:24)/ Watershed (3:30)/ Good Grief
(4:59)/ Butterflies (5:14)/ Alone And Easy Target
(5:12)/ Exhausted (6:15)
R: Vg. Audience.   S: King's College, London
June 3 '95.   C: ECD. Dcc. Pic CD.

4 NON BLONDES

CD - WHAT'S UP!?
ROCKET RECORDS ROCKET 889
Train/ Pleasantly Blue/ Nevermind/ What's Up/
Spaceman/ Morphine And Chocolate/ Old Mr.
Heffer/ No Place Like Home/ Superfly/ In My
Dreams/ Drifting/ Need It Bad/ Mary's House
R: Poor-G. Audience.   S: Live in the USA.
C: ECD. Dcc. Time 45:51.

FREE

CD - JAKE THE RIPPER
TNT STUDIO TNT-940161
Be My Friend/ The Stealer/ Woman/ Ride On
Pony/ Walk In The Shadow/ Moonshine/ Song Of
Yesterday/ All Right Now/ Come Together In The
Morning/ Seven Angels/ Heartbreaker/ Travelling
In Style/ The Stealer
R: Tracks 1-8 Vg audience recording. Tracks 9-13
poor sound.   S: Kouthestad, Vienna, Austria
Nov. 23 '70. Tracks 9-13 'Heartbreaker' outtakes
'72.   C: Japanese CD.

CD - REVENGE OF HEARTBREAKER
PICARESQUE SOUND PS-003
Heartbreaker/ I'm On The Run/ Soldier Boy/
Child/ Everyday I Have The Blues (incomplete)/
Come Together In the Morning/ Wishing Well/
Seven Angels/ Alright Now/ The Hunter (incom-
plete)
R: Good sound.   S: Portsmouth '73.

CD - SONGS FROM YESTERDAY
DISCURIOS DIS 118
The Stealer/ Fire & Water/ Ridin' On A Pony/
Heavy Load/ Woman/ I Love You So/ Allright
Now/ Broad Daylight/ Waiting On You/ Be My
Friend/ The Stealer/ Woman

R: Vg. Soundboard. Some hiss.   C: ECD. Dcc.
Time 59:16.

CD - TWO YEARS FREE
DYNAMITE STUDIO DS94J099/100
CD1: Fire And Water/ Ride On Pony/ I'm A Mover/
Be My Friend/ The Stealer/ Heavy Load/ The
Highway Song/ My Brother Jake/ Soon I Will Be
Gone/ All Right Now/ Mr. Big/ The Hunter
CD2: Fire And Water/ Woman/ Ride On Pony/ I'm
A Mover/ Be My Friend/ Mr. Big/ Walk In My
Shadow/ I'll Be Creeping/ All right Now/ The
Hunter
R: CD1 Vg audience recording, CD2 G sound-
board recording.   S: CD1 Sankei Hall, Tokyo,
Japan May 1-2 '71. CD2 Municipal Auditorium,
Aachen, Germany July 10 '70.   C: Japanese.

FRIPP, ROBERT

CD - KAN-NON POWER
PLUTO RECORDS PLR CD 9324
Sound Scape/ Yamanashi Blues/ Melrose
Avenue/ Kan-Non Power/ Firescape/ Any Easy
Way/ Moving Force/ Asturias/ Walk. Don't Run/
Chromatic Fantasy/ Contrapunctus/ Eye Of The
Needle/ Blockhead/ Hope/ Urban Scape/ Pipeline/
Kan-Non Power
R: Ex. Soundboard.   S: TFM Hall, Tokyo, Japan
Nov. 11 '92.   C: ECD. Dbw. Time 74:11.

FUNKADELIC

CD - RED HOT MAMA IN RICHMOND 1976
WEEPING GOAT WG-016
Cosmic Slop/ Red Hot Mama/ Let's Take It To The
Stage, Take Your Dead Ass Hole/ Do That Stuff/
Undisco Kidd/ Mothership Connection/ Swing
Down, Sweet Chariot/ Tear The Roof Off The
Sucker Medley/ Undisco Kidd/ Undisco Kidd
R: G-Vg soundboard.   S: Tracks 1-8 Richmond,
Virgina '76. Tracks 9-10 Denver, Colorado '76.
C: Japanese CD.

G

GABRIEL, PETER

CD - ONE OF US
CRYSTAL CAT CC 318/319
CD1: Come Talk To Me/ Steam/ Games Without
Frontiers/ Across The River/ Shakin' The Tree/
Blood Of Eden/ San Jacinto/ Love Town/ Only Us
CD2: Kiss That Frog/ Washing Of The Water/
Solsbury Hill/ Digging In The Dirt/ Sledgehammer/
Secret World/ In Your Eyes/ Biko
R: Vg. Audience.   S: Stockholm Apr. 13 '93.
C: ECD. Time CD1 67:37. CD2 69:14.

CD - SECRET WORLD
PG-001/002
CD1: Opening/ Come Talk To Me/ Steam/ Games

Without Frontiers/ Across The River/ Shaking The Tree/ Blood Of Eden/ San Jacinto/ Lovetown/ Shock The Monkey
CD2: Solsbury Hill/ Digging In The Dirt/ Sledgehammer/ Secret World/ In Your Eyes/ Biko/ Across The River/ Shaking The Tree/ Biko
R: Ex audience recording.   S: Budokan, Tokyo, Japan Mar. 8 '94. CD2 tracks 7-8 promo only edit versions. CD2 track 9 Blossom Music Center, Cleveland July 27 '87.

GALLAGHER, RORY

CD - 'ON THE WESTERN PLAINS'
TMOQ 0017
CD1: Continental Op (6:17)/ Moon Child (5:39)/ Don't Start Me Talking (4:39)/ I Wonder Who (7:34)/ The Loop (2:31)/ Tattoo'd Lady (6:17)/ Bad Penny (4:53)/ Shin Kicker (3:29)/ Off The Handle (7:37)/ Heaven's Gate (5:01)
CD2: A Million Miles Away (6:57)/ Laundromat (3:16)/ Going Down To Eli's (5:56)/ Out On The Western Plain (5:16)/ Walkin' Blues (7:05)/ Empire State Express (5:36)/ Shadow Play (5:19)/ Messing With The Kid (6:39)
R: Exs. Soundboard.   S: Radio Show, Cleveland '91.   C: Japanese CD.
Time CD1 65:56. CD2 46:06.

LP - TAKE IT EASY BABY
SPRINGBOARD SPB-4056
Wee Wee Baby/ Worried Man/ Norman Invasion/ How Many More Years/ Take It Easy Baby/ Pardon Me Mister/ You've Got To Pay
R: Ex.   S: Studio. Source and year unknown.
C: US boot from '76.

GARBAGE

CD - THE 'G' FILES
OXYGEN OXY 032
Stupid Girl (4:41)/ My Lover's Box (3:43)/ As Heaven Is Wide (5:30)/ Queer (4:35)/ Subhuman (5:06)/ A Stroke Of Luck (5:02)/ Fix Me Now (4:49)/ Trip My Wire (4:39)/ Only Happy When It Rains (4:20)/ Not My Idea (3:36)/ Vow (5:47)
R: Exs. Soundboard.   S: Melkweg, Amsterdam, Holland Nov. 25 '95.   C: ECD. Dcc. Pic CD.

GARCIA, JERRY

CD - FLOODED AWAY
TEDDY BEAR TB 68
Simple Twist Of Fate (10:55)/ Knockin' On Heaven's Door (12:27)/ Mission In The Rain (8:28)/ How Sweet It Is (6:07)/ Mississippi Moon (11:22)/ Tangled Up In Blue (8:35)/ Dear Prudence (9:56)/ Midnight Moonlight (7:45)
R: Ex. Audience.   S: Track 1 June 25 '81. Tracks 2-4 Nov. 25 '77. Tracks 5-8 June 26 '81.   C: ECD. Pic CD.

CD - JERRY'S HOME
KISS THE STONE KTS 478/79

CD1: Man Of Constant Sorrow - Take 1 (5:14)/ Man Of Constant Sorrow - Take 2 (5:11)/ Luis Collins - Take 1 (5:11)/ Luis Collins - Take 2 (5:33)/ Shady Grove - Take 1 (0:43)/ Improvisation Jam (3:28)/ Shady Grove - Take 2 (4:25)/ Improvisation Jam (4:19)/ Shady Grove - Take 3 (3:48)/ Summertime (7:21)
CD2: Long Black Veil - Take 1 (0:40)/ Long Black Veil - Take 2 (2:36)/ Rosa Lee McFall - Take 1 (3:12)/ Rosa Lee McFall - Take 2 (3:46)/ Drifting Too Far From The Shore - Take 1 (0:18)/ Drifting Too Far From The Shore - Take 2 (4:51)/ Long Black Veil - Take 3 (4:40)/ Amazing Grace (3:10)/ Little Sadie (3:51)/ Knockin' On Heaven's Door (5:36)/ Improvisation Jam (1:14)/ So What (5:32)/ House Of The Rising Sun (3:22)
R: Ex. Soundboard.   S: Recorded at Jerry's home in the spring of '95 with David Grisman and Tony Rice.   C: ECD. Dcc. Pic CDs.

GARCIA, SAUNDERS AND KREUTZMAN

CD - BLUES FOR NO ONE
MAIN STREET MST 113/2
CD1: It Takes A Lot To Laugh A Train To Cry/ Expressway To Your Mind/ That's The Touch I Like/ The Wheel/ Imagine
CD2: That's Allright Mama/ Blues For Everyone/ When I Paint My Masterpiece/ I Was Made For Love Her/ Lonely Avenue/ How Sweet It Is
R: Exs. Soundboard.   S: Ksan Pacific High Studios May '73.   C: ECD. Time CD1 47:35. CD2 54:22.

GENESIS

CD - APOCALYPSE
GHOST RECORDS GHOST 0101/0102
CD1: Dance On A Volcano/ Behind The Lines/ Follow You Follow Me/ Dodo/ Abacab/ Supper's Ready/ Misunderstanding/ Man On The Corner
CD2: In The Cage/ Afterglow/ Turn It On Again/ Drum Duet, Los Endos/ The Lamb Lies Down On Broadway, Watcher Of The Skies (Closing Selection)/ I Know What I Like
R: G.   S: Rome Sept. 7 '82.

CD - THE CARPET CRAWLERS
CHAPTER ONE CO 25134
Watcher Of The Skies (7:46)/ Cuckoo Cuckoo (2:23)/ Back In The New York City (7:45)/ Hairless Heart (Counting Out Time) (6:42)/ The Carpet Crawlers (5:32)/ Lillywhite Lilith (2:40)/ The Waiting Room (9:35)/ Anyway (3:34)/ Ravine (4:42)/ The Light Dies Down On Broadway (3:34)/ Riding The Scree (4:14)/ In The Cage (6:47)/ It (4:16)
R: Ex. Soundboard.   S: Wembley Empire Pool, London Apr. 15 '75.   C: ECD. Dcc.

CD - CONNECTICUT '75
SPIRAL 006-7
CD1: The Lamb Lies Down On Broadway/ Fly On A Windshield/ Broadway Melody Of 1974/ Cuckoo

Cocoon/ In The Cage/ The Grand Parade Of Lifeless Packaging/ Back In NYC/ Hairless Heart/ Counting Out Time/ Carpet Crawl/ The Chamber Of 32 Doors
CD2: Lilywhite Lilith/ The Waiting Room/ Here Comes The Supernatural Anaesthetist/ The Lamia/ Silent Sorrow In Empty Boats/ The Colony Of Slippermen/ The Arrival, A Visit To The Doctor, The Raven/ Ravine/ The Light Dies Down On Broadway/ Riding The Scree/ In The Rapids/ It/ The Musical Box
R: Vg-Ex. Soundboard.   S: Palace Theater, Connecticut Apr. 12 '75.   C: Japanese CD. Dcc. Time CD1 45:08. CD2 54:47.

CD - 'FIRTH OF FIFTH'
ALEGRA CD 9031
Dancing With The Moonlight Knight (6:32)/ Firth Of Fifth (8:44)/ The Musical Box (9:30)/ I Know What I Like (4:57)/ Suppers' Ready (24:31)
R: Vg.   S: London '72. Track 3 Basel '72.
C: ECD. Dcc.

CD - GENUINE GENESIS LIVE
GGI-2/73
Watcher Of The Skies/ The Musical Box/ Get 'Em Out By Friday/ The Knife/ Supper's Ready
R: Poor-G.   S: Free Trade Hall, Manchester and De Montofort Hall, Leicester, England Feb. '73.

GENTLE GIANT

CD - GIANT STEPS FORWARD
REEL TAPES RTCD002
Introduction, Giant, Cogs In Cogs, Proclamation (9:32)/ Funny Ways (8:13)/ The Runaway, Keyboard Solo, Experience (9:51)/ Knots, Guitar Acoustic Duet Solo, The Advent Of Panurge, Recorder Quartet Solo (13:20)/ Nothing At All, Plain Truth (27:38)
R: Vg.   S: Rome Nov. 26 '74.   C: ECD. Dcc.

GRATEFUL DEAD, THE

CD - APRIL FOOL'S DAY
KISS THE STONE KTS BX 012
CD1: Picasso Moon (6:59)/ Deal (10:56)/ Wang Dang Doodle (7:27)/ Dire Wolf (3:21)/ Black Throated Wind (6:16)/ Bird Song (13:34)
CD2: China Cat Flower, I Know Your Rider (14:18)/ Box Of Rain (5:53)/ Estimated Prophet (13:58)/ He's Gone (11:41)/ That Would Be Something (2:42)
CD3: Drums-Space (32:56)/ The Other One (7:08)/ Wharf Rat (10:02)/ Turn On Your Lovelight (6:47)/ Broken Down Palace (4:47)
R: Ex.   S: The Omni, Atlanta, Georgia Apr. 1 '94.   C: ECD. Box set. Full color poster. Pic CDs.

CD - BERLIN 1990
LIVE STORM LSCD 52527
CD1: You Have Step Uptown (6:08)/ Toodeloo (7:53)/ Walking The Blues (5:43)/ Friend Of The

Devil (7:56)/ Black Throated Wind (5:53)/ Checkeroo (4:40)/ Let It Flow, Let It Grow (15:26)/ Box Of Rain (4:57)/ Eyes Of The World (11:12/
CD2: Samson And Delilah (7:07)/ Ship Of Fools (7:14)/ Dark Star (14:13)/ Drum Solo (10:47)/ Guitar Solo (10:47)/ Throwing Stones (9:46)/ Not Fade Away (8:58)/ One More Saturday Night (5:03)
R: Ex. Audience.   S: International Congress Centrum, Berlin Oct. '90.   C: ECD.

CD - CLOUDS OF DEW
SILVER RARITIES SIRA 176
Ship Of Fools/ Promised Land/ Dark Star/ Morning Dew/ Not Fade Away, Going Down The Road Feeling Bad, Not Fade Away/ It's All Over Now Baby Blue
R: Vg-Ex. Soundboard. Slight hiss.
S: Winterland, San Francisco Feb. 24 '74.
C: ECD. Dcc. Time 75:56.

CD - COMES A TIME FOR ALL
KISS THE STONE KTS 422/23
CD1: Jack Straw/ Sugaree/ Walkin' Blues/ Candyman/ Memphis Blues/ Tennessee Jed/ The Music Never Stopped/ Scarlet Begonias Fire On The Mountain
CD2: Truckin'/ Smokestack Lightning/ He's Gone/ Drums/ Space/ Comes A Time/ Goin' Down The Road Feelin' Bad/ Good Lovin'/ Baby Blue (Encore)
R: Exs. Soundboard.   S: Sandstone, Kansas June 25 '91.   C: ECD. Dcc. Pic CDs.
Time CD1 79:36. CD2 79:10.

CD - THE DEAD DON'T HAVE NO MERCY
BIG MUSIC BIG100-01
CD1: Morning Dew/ Good Morning, Little School Girl/ Don't That Rag/ King Bee/ Love Light/ Cryptical Envelopment/ Drums/ That's It For The Other One/ Cryptical Envelopment
CD2: Dark Star/ St. Stephen/ The Eleven/ Death Don't Have No Mercy/ Alligator/ Drums/ Alligator/ Caution/ And We Bid You Goodnight
R: Vg soundboard recording.   S: Fillmore West, San Francisco Feb. 28 '69.

CD - THE DEAD IN BLOOM
HOME RECORDS HR6010/11
CD1: I Will Survive/ Beat It On Down The Line/ Round And Round/ Little Red Rooster/ Lazy River Road/ Don't Murder Me/ Black Throated Wind/ Bird Song/ Box Of Rain/ Shakedown Street
CD2: Seabirds/ Going Down The Road Feeling Bad/ Drums/ Space/ The Wheel/ You Dreamed Of Me/ Round And Round/ Rock My Soul
R: G-Vg. Audience.   S: Boston Garden, Boston Mass. Oct. 3 '94.   C: ECD. Dcc.

CD - FALLIN' STARS
CAPRICORN CR-2017
Weather Report Suite, Dark Star, China Doll
R: Vg soundboard.   S: Second set Addams Field House, Mazula, Montana May 14 '74.

CD - GRATEFUL DEAD AND BRANFORD MARSALIS
AUDIF N DEUTSCHLAND AF001
Estimated Prophet/ Dark Star/ Drums/ Dark Star (return)/ Throwing Stones (Ashes Ashes)/ Lovelight
R: Ex soundboard recording.   S: Second set, Nassau Coliseum, New York Mar. 29 '90.

CD - GOIN' EAST
METEOR FRONT ROW FM 2104/5/6
CD1: Intro (2:14)/ Jackstraw (5:44)/ Jack A Aow (5:32)/ It's All Over Now (6:04)/ Stagger Lee (7:24)/ Queen Jane (7:33)/ Candyman (7:05)/ Easy Answers (6:45)/ Deal (10:43)
CD2: Samson And Delilah (21:35)/ Iko-Iko (13:21)/ Playin' The Band (7:53)/ Uncle's John's Band (12:59)/ Drumz (14:53)
CD3: Space (16:25)/ The Other One (6:32)/ Morning Dew (14:51)/ Johnny B Goode (4:52)
R: G-Vg. Audience.   S: Nassau Coliseum, New York '94.   C: ECD. Pic CD.

CD - HARDLY AGED A DAY
SILVER RARITIES SIRA 174/175
CD1: Spanish Jam*/ Turn On Your Lovelight*/ Dancing In The Streets/ China Cat Sunflower-I Know You Rider/ High Time
CD2: Dire Wolf/ Alligator/ Drums/ Me And My Uncle/ Not Fade Away/ Mason's Children/ Caution/ Feedback/ We Bid You Goodnight
R: Vg. Soundboard.   S: Fillmore East Feb. 14 '70. *Fillmore East Feb. 11 '70.   C: ECD.

CD - HEARTLESS EXCURSION
CAPRICORN RECORDS CR 2049/50
CD1: Dark Star/ Death Letter Blues/ Jam/ The Eleven/ Death Don't Have No Mercy
CD2: Jam/ Prisoner Blues/ Jam/ Dark Star Jam
R: Exs. Soundboard.   S: The Matrix, San Francisco Dec. 30 '68.   C: Dcc.

CD - LIVE AT THE ICE PALACE
HAIGHT STREET RECORDS
Morning Dew/ Good Morning Little School Girl/ Doin' That Rag/ Dark Star/ St. Steven/ The Eleven/ Turn On Your Lovelight
R: Poor soundboard. Hiss.   S: Ice Palace, Las Vegas, Nevada Mar. 29 '69.   C: Japanese CD.

CD - LIVE AT THE ORPHEUM THEATRE
SWINGIN' PIG SARL 1202080
Lazy Lightning/ Supplication/ Weather Report Suite/ Loser/ Space/ The Other One/ St. Stephen/ The Wheel/ The Other One (Reprise)/ Stella Blue/ Johnny B. Good
R: Exs. Soundboard.   S: Orpheum Theatre, San Francisco July 10 '76.   C: ECD.

CD - MELKWEG BIRTHDAY BASH
CAPRICORN RECORDS CR 2044
Dire Wolf/ Monkey And Engineer/ Bird Song/ Cassidy/ Ain't No Lie/ The Race Is On/ Ripple/ Gloria/ Lovelight/ GDTRFB/ Playin' In The Band/ Black Peter/ Sugar Magnolia
R: Exs. Soundboard.   S: Melkweg, Amsterdam, The Netherlands Oct. 16 '81.   C: Tracks 1-7 acoustic set. Tracks 8-13 electric set. Time 65:39.

CD - 'NOTHIN' BUT THE BEST ...'
WONDER MINNOW RECORDS WM01-101
Cold Rain And Snow (6:08)/ Me And Bobby McGee (6:08)/ Loser (8:11)/ Easy Wind (9:05)/ Playin' In The Band (5:16)/ Me And My Uncle (4:39)/ Tuning, False Start (2:57)/ Ripple (4:34)/ Tuning (1:00)/ Next Time (4:00)/ Sugar Magnolia (6:48)/ Tuning, Bob's Excuses (1:50)/ Greatest Story Ever Told, Johnny B. Goode (7:29)
R: Exs. Soundboard.   S: Capitol Theatre, Port Chester, NY Feb. 21 '71.   C: ECD. Dcc.

CD - OH BOY!
HAIGHT STREET RECORDS HS012
Bertha/ Beat It On Down The Line/ It Hurts Me, Too/ Me And Bobby McGee/ Dire Wolf/ I'm A Hog For You, Baby/ In The Midnight Hour/ Mama Tried/ Cumberland Blues/ Casey Jones
R: Ex. Soundboard.   S: The Manhattan Center, NYC Apr. 6 '71.   C: ECD. Dcc. Time 58:29.

CD - PLAY DEAD
KISS THE STONE KTS 430/31
CD1: Might As Well/ Jack Straw/ Dire Wolf/ Looks Like Rain/ Loser/ El Paso/ Ramble On Rose/ Minglewood Blues/ It Must Have Been Roses/ Let It Grow/ Bertha/ Good Lovin'
CD2: Friends Of The Devil/ Estimated Prophet/ Eyes Of The World/ Space/ St. Stephen/ Drums-Not Fade Away/ Black Peter/ Sugar Magnolia/ Sunshine Daydream/ One More Saturday Night
R: Exs. Soundboard.   S: The Evans Field House, Northern Illinois University, Decalb, IL Oct. 29 '77.   C: ECD. Dcc. Pic CD. Time CD1 79:32. CD2 79:18.

CD - RESURRECTION
AMERICAN FLY HF001-02
CD1: Let The Good Times Roll/ Jack Straw/ Althea/ Queen Jane Approximately/ Deal/ It's All Over Now/ Tennessee Jed/ Let It Grow/ Truckin/ One Way Or Another
CD2: Way To Go Home/ Corinna/ Uncle John's Band/ Drums/ Space/ I Go Time/ I Need A Miracle/ Standing On The Moon/ Sunshine Daydream/ Us Blues/ Sugar Magnolia
R: Ex audience recording.   S: Franklin County Airport, Highgate, VT July 13 '94.   C: ECD.

CD - SOUNDCHECK '73
FLASHBACK 05.94.0229
Promised/ Sugaree/ Mexicali Blues/ Bird Song/ Big River/ Tennessee Jed/ Improvisation/ The Other One/ Merry Go Round Broke Down
R: Good soundboard recording.   S: Grand Prix Racecourse, Watkins Glen, New York July 27 '73.   C: ECD.

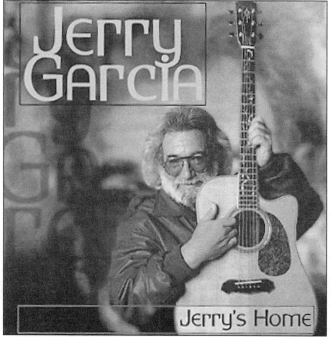

CD - STANDING ON THE CORNER
HAIGHT STREET RECORDS
Viola Lee Blues/ Don't Ease Me In/ Pain In My Heart/ All New Minglewood Blues/ Sitting On Top Of The World/ You Don't Have To Ask/ Gold Rain And Show/ Good Morning Little Schoolgirl/ It's All Over Now, Baby Blue/ Big Boss Man/ Standing On The Corner/ Beat It On Down The Line/ In The Pines/ Cardboard Cowboy/ Nobody's Fault But Mine/ Next Time You See Me
R: Vg soundboard recording.   S: Fillmore West, July 16 '66. Tracks 10-16 July 17 '66.
C: Japanese CD.

CD - THIS BETTER BE GOOD
MOONLIGHT RECORDS ML 9504/5
CD1: Bertha/ Truckin'/ It Hurts Me Too/ Loser/ Medley: Pump Man, Johnny B. Goode/ Mama Tried/ Hard To Handle/ Medley: Dark Star, Wharf Rat, Dark Star, Me And My Uncle
CD2: Casey Jones/ Playin' In The Band/ Me And Bobby McGee/ Candy Man/ Big Boss Man/ Sugar Magnolia/ Medley: St. Stephen, Not Fade Away, Goin' Down The Road, Not Fade Away, Uncle John's Band
R: Vg soundboard recording.   S: The Capitol Theatre, Port Chester, New York Feb. 18 '71.
C: ECD. Black cover, red type.

CD - TO THE SKY: JERRY GARCIA'S FINAL SHOW
JGCD 909-1/2/3
CD1: Touch Of Grey/ Little Red Rooster/ Lazy River Land/ Masterpiece/ Childhood's End/ Cumberland Blues/ Promised Land/ Shakedown Street
CD2: Samson And Delilah/ So Many Roads/ Samba In The Rain/ Corrina, Drumz
CD3: Space/ Unbroken Chain, Sugar Magnolia/ Black Muddy River/ Box Of Rain/ Fireworks/ Star Spangled Banner
R: Vg. Audience.   S: Soldier Field, Chicago 7-9-'95.   C: Japanese CD. Dcc. Time CD1 58:46. CD2 48:45. CD3 57:55.

CD - 12:00 O'CLOCK CURFEW
CAPRICORN CR-2026
Dark Star/ St. Stephen, The Eleven/ Death Don't Have No Mercy/ Cryptical Envelopment, Drums, The Other One, Cryptical Envelopment, New Potato Caboose
R: Poor. Hiss.   S: Avalon Ballroom, San Francisco Oct. 13 '68.   C: KPFA-Berkeley FM broadcast.

GREEN DAY

CD - ATTACK OF INSOMNIA
MOONRAKER 013
Going To Pasalacqua/ Welcome To Paradise/ Chump/ Longview/ Stuck With Me/ Geek Stink Breath/ 2,000 Light Years Away/ Knowledge/ Basket Case/ She/ F.O.D./ Burnout/ Paper Lanterns/ Eye Of The Tiger/ My Way/ Paper Lanterns II/ All By Myself/ Dominated Love Slave/ When I Come Around/ Road To Nowhere
R: Vg-Ex. Audience.   S: Stockholm Sept. 2 '95.
C: ECD. Dcc. Time 57:18.

CD - EATING MY BUGERS
RAZOR BLADE RB508
2000 Light Years Away (2:43)/ One Of My Lies (2:25)/ Only Of You (3:07)/ At The Library (2:37)/ Welcome To Paradise (3:43)/ Christie Road (3:36)/ Going To Pasalacqua (3:47)/ Same Old Shit (4:05)/ 16 (5:57)/ Paper Lanterns (2:42)/ Dominated Love Slave (2:59)/ Long View (3:37)/ Better Not Come Around (2:47)/ Don't Leave Me (2:37)
R: Exs. Soundboard.   S: Live in Italy '93.
C: ECD. Dcc. Pic CD. Time 46:48.

CD - EGOCENTRIC PLASTIC MEN
METAL CRASH MECD 119
Welcome To Paradise (3:46)/ What Are My Lies (2:25)/ Chump (2:28)/ Burn Out (2:00)/ Only Of You (2:47)/ When I Come Around, 2000 Light Years Away (5:28)/ Basket Case (2:50)/ Dominated Love Slave (1:44)/ Christy Road (3:26)/ Going To Passalacqua (Infatuation) (4:43)/ Chump (2:36)/ Long View (3:38)/ Burn Out (2:00)/ When I Come Around (2:56)/ Welcome To Paradise (3:33)/ Coming Clean (2:32)/ Knowledge (3:31)/ Dominated Love Slave (3:10)/ 2000 Light Years Away (3:11)/ The Disappearing Boy (4:11)/ F.O.D. (2:21)/ Paper Lanterns (9:44)
R: Tracks 1-9 Vg-Ex. Audience. Tracks 10-23 G-Vg. Audience.   S: Tracks 1-9 Europe June '94. Tracks 10-23 USA Dec. '94.   C: ECD. Dcc. Pic CD.

CD - FUCK YOU
KTS OF AUSTRALIA 011 A
Far Away (4:50)/ Chump (3:37)/ Long View (3:34)/ Burnout (2:19)/ When I Come Around (3:45)/ Welcome To Paradise (3:45)/ Coming Clean (3:28)/ All The Girls (3:58)/ Basket Case (3:56)/ All By Myself (3:18)/ 2000 Light Years (4:40)/ Disappearing Boy (2:20)/ Bon Jour, Sweet Home Alabama, General Fucking Around (4:25)/ F.O.D. (2:37)/ Paper Lanterns (9:28)/ Christy Road (4:25)/ She (3:43)
R: G-Vg. Audience.   S: Mullen Center, University Of Massachusetts, Amherst, Mass. Nov. 28 '94.   C: Australian CD. Dcc.

CD - GREENDAZE
OCTOPUS OCTO 102
Welcome To Paradise (4:19)/ Chump (2:37)/ Long View (3:31)/ Burnout (2:47)/ Christie Road (3:56)/ 2000 Light Years Away (3:19)/ Basket Case (2:56)/ She (2:42)/ Paper Lanterns (8:56)/ Welcome To Paradise (4:02)/ One Of My Lies (2:19)/ Going To Pasalacqua (4:09)/ Chump (2:35)/ At The Library (2:42)/ 2000 Light Years Away (3:16)/ Who Wrote Holden Caulfield? (2:55)/ Knowledge (2:23)/ Disappearing Boy (1:57)/ She (2:09)/ Road To Acceptance (6:42)

R: Ex.   S: Tracks 1-9 Goteborg, Sweden Oct. 8
'94. Tracks 10-20 Munchen, Germany Oct. '94.
C: ECD. Dcc. Pic CD.

CD - THE GREENEST HITS
KTS OF AUSTRALIA 011B
Far Away (4:32)/ Chump (2:50)/ Longview (3:27)/
Burnout (2:20)/ Coming Clean (1:38)/ When I
Come Around (2:57)/ Welcome To Paradise
(3:38)/ 2000 Light Years (3:22)/ Basket Case
(2:49)/ All By Myself (1:08)/ I Love Feeling Dirty
(2:05)/ F.O.D. (2:26)/ Paper Lanterns (3:26)/
Christy Road (3:57)/ She (3:52)/ When I Come
Around (3:06)/ I Know What I Want (2:18)/ Chump
(2:46)/ Going To Pasalaqua (4:15)/ F.O.D. (2:48)/
Christy Road (3:49)
R: Exs. Soundboard.   S: Chicago Dec. '94.
Tracks 16 and 17 Saturday Night Live 12/3/94.
Tracks 18-21 Jannuf Landing, Saint Petersburg,
Florida Mar. 11 '94.   C: Australian CD. Dcc.

CD - PUNK ACADEMY
TYPHOON TYN 011
Welcome To Paradise/ Burnout/ Chump/ Long
View/ Stuck With Me/ Geek Stink Breath/ 2,000
Light Years Away/ Knowledge/ Basket Case/ She/
Coming Clean/ F.O.D./ Paper Lanterns/ All By
Myself/ Dominated Love Slave/ When I Come
Around/ I'm A Loser
S: Brixton Academy, London Sept. 9 '95.
C: ECD.

GRIFFITH, NANCI

CD - SOUND OF LONELINESS
KISS THE STONE KTS 410
From A Distance/ Say It Isn't So/ Always Will/
Across The Great Divide/ Trouble In The Fields/
Don't Forget About Me/ Southbound Train/ Time
Of Inconvenience/ Speed Of The Sound Of
Loneliness/ Tecumseh Valley/ Are You Tired Of
Me, My Darlin'?/ Going Back To Georgia/ This
Heart/ It's A Hard Life
R: Exs. Soundboard.   S: Europe 11-10-'94.
C: ECD. Pic CD. Time 62:20.

GUNS N' ROSES

CD - LIVE IN SANPLAZA-HALL 1988
OFM 0041
You're Crazy/ It's So Eazy/ Move To The City/ Mr.
Brownstone/ Out To Get Me/ Patience/ Rocket
Queen/ Welcome To The Jungle/ Knockin' On
Heaven's Door/ Sweet Child Of Mine/ Used To
Love Her/ Mama Kin/ Paradise City
R: Ex.   S: Sanplaza-Hall, Tokyo, Japan Dec. 8
'88.

CD - LONDON MOTHERFUCKERS 1987
CD 94103-1/2
CD1: It's So Easy/ Move To The City/ Out Ta Get
Me/ Mr. Brownstone/ My Michelle/ Rocket Queen/
Welcome To The Jungle/ Nightrain/ You're Crazy/
Paradise City/ Knockin' On Heaven's Door/

Reckless Life
CD2: Mama Kin/ Sweet Child O'Mine/ Whole
Lotta Rosie/ Ready Steady Go/ It's So Easy/ Mr.
Brownstone/ Nightrain/ My Michelle/ Welcome To
The Jungle/ You're Crazy/ Paradise City/ 3 other
tracks
R: Vg audience recording.   S: Hammersmith
Odeon, London Oct. 8 '87. CD2 Marquee Club,
London June 22 '87.

CD - SUCH A FUCKIN' NIGHT
FRAGILE FR-94001/002
CD1: Intro/ You're Crazy/ It's So Easy/ Mr.
Brownstone/ Move To The City/ Patience/ Blues
Jam/ Welcome To The Jungle/ Nightrain
CD2: Used To Love Her/ Knockin' On Heaven's
Door/ Sweet Child O'Mine/ Paradise City
R: Poor sound.   S: Festival Hall, Osaka Japan
Dec. 5 '88.

CD - UNPLUGGED
GURO 4732
Dead Flowers/ You Ain't The First/ You're Crazy/
Used To Love Her/ Medley: (Patience/ Imagine)/
Knockin' On Heaven's Door/ One In A Million/
Used To Love Her/ Patience/ Mr. Brownstone/
Move To The City
R: Ex.   C: ECD. Dcc. Time 58:30.

CD - UNWANTED ILLUSIONS
AXE 004
Crash Diet/ Bring It Back Home/ Sentimental
Movie/ Just Another Sunday/ Axl's Blues/ It Tastes
Good, Don't It?/ Too Fast To Live/ It's So Easy/
Scrap Bar Daze/ Booze Party/ tracks 11-13
Jumping Jack Flash/ tracks 14-15 Heartbreak
Hotel
R: Vg sound.   S: Tracks 1-4 unreleased tracks
from the 'Use Your Illusion' sessions, RS Studios,
Canoga Park, LA spring '90. Track 5 Pasadena,
Dec. '87. Track 6 Hilton Coliseum, Iowa July 27
'87. Track 8 live take June '88. Track 9 '88.
Tracks 7, 10, 11,14 studio demos. Tracks 12, 15
Hellhouse rehearsal. Track 13 acoustic demo.

LP - YOU COULD BE...
MIXING RECS.
S1: Nighttrain/ Mr. Brownstone/ Bad Obsession/
Live And Let Die/ Dust And Bones
S2: Double Talking Jive/ Civil War/ Slash Solo/
Patience
S3: You Could Be Mine/ November Rain/
Welcome To The Jungle/ Drum Solo-Matt Sorcum
S4: Godfather Theme/ Rocket Queen/ Only
Women Bleed/ Knockin' On Heavens Door
S5: Sweet Child O'Mine/ Estranged/ Paradise City
S6: Civil War/ Down On The Farm
R: Exs. S6 Gs.   S: Stockholm, Sweden Aug. 16
'91. S6 Farm Aid Apr. 7 '91.   C: Eb. Dcc. GF.

H

HALL AND OATES

CD - UPTOWN LIVE
EXX-ELLENT EXX 52513
Family Man (4:51)/ Say It Isn't So (7:19)/ Kiss On
My List (5:35)/ Everytime You Go Away (9:15)/ So
Close (5:32)/ I Can't Go For That (No Can Do)
(8:00)/ She's Gone (4:30)/ Maneater (6:21)/ Adult
Education (7:01)
R: Exs. Soundboard.   S: Live in London '90.
C: ECD. Dcc. Pic CD. Time 56:19.

HANOI ROCKS

LP - LIGHTNING BAR KIDS
METAL DISC RECS.
S1: Oriental Beat/ Mystery City/ Lost In The City/
Until I Get You/ Motorvatin'
S2: Mental Beat/ Don't Ever Leave Me/ Tragedy/
Malibu Beach Nightmare/ Taxi Driver
R: Exs.   S: Klub Foot, Hammersmith, London
Jan. 20 '83.   C: Eb. Dcc.

HARRISON, GEORGE

CD - BEWARE OF ABKCO!
STRAWBERRY STR 001
Run Of The Mill (acoustic version - 2:03)/ Art Of
Dying (acoustic version - 3:22)/ Everybody,
Nobody (acoustic version - 3:56)/ Wah-Wah (electric guitar - 4:36)/ Window, Window (acoustic version - 2:04)/ Beautiful Girl (acoustic version -
3:50)/ Beware Of Darkness (acoustic version -
4:30)/ Let It Down (acoustic version - 4:09)/ Tell
Me What Happened To You (acoustic version -
3:11)/ Hear Me Lord (electric guitar - 5:10)/
Nowhere To Go (electric guitar - 2:59)/ Cosmic
Empire (acoustic version - 3:06)/ Mother Divine
(acoustic version - 2:55)/ I Don't Wanna Do It
(acoustic version - 2:17)/ If Not For You (acoustic
version - 1:53)/
R: Ex. Soundboard. Vocal one side, instrument on
other.   S: Harrison solo studio recordings of
demos for 'All Things Must Pass'.   C: ECD.
Time 50:01.

CD - HARI AND THE HIJACK BAND
641992/93
CD1: JOE WALSH: Pretty Maids All In A Row/ In
The City/ Life In The Fast Lane/ Goin' On Down/
Rocky Mountain Way/ GARY MOORE: Walking
By Myself/ This Guy's Crying/ The Blues Is
Alright/ Still Got The Blues/ GEORGE HARRI-
SON: I Want To Tell You/ Old Brown Shoe/
Taxman/ Band Introductions/ Give Me Love/
Something
CD2: GEORGE HARRISON: What Is Life/
Piggies/ Got My Mind Set On You/ Cloud Nine/
Here Comes The Sun/ My Sweet Lord/ All Those
Years Ago/ Cheer Down/ Isn't A Pity/ Devil's

Radio, Applause/ While My Guitar Gently Weeps/
Roll Over Beethoven/ Drums And Percussion
(Solo)/ Roll Over Beethoven (Reprise)
R: Vg-Ex. Audience.   C: ECD. Dcc.
Time CD1 74:23. CD2 72:39.

CD - PIRATE SONGS
VIGOTONE VIGO 146 CD
The Pirate Song (for 'Rutland Weekend
Television' '75) (2:17)/ Bangla Desh (alternate mix
'71) (3:52)/ Deep Blue (alternate mix '71) (3:39)/
Miss O'Dell ('no laughing' version from acetate)
(2:22)/ Dark Horse (demo '74) (4:18)/ Sue Me
Sue You Blues (demo version '72) (3:01)/ Mo
(recorded in '77 and released in '95) (4:52)/ Life
Itself (demo '79) (4:21)/ Hari's On Tour (Largo,
Maryland '74) (4:47)/ For You Blue (Largo,
Maryland '74) (4:10)/ Sat Singing (remixed version '80) (4:26)/ Lay His Head (remixed version
'80) (3:50)/ Flying Hour (remixed version '78)
(4:34)/ Tears Of The World (remixed version '80)
(3:46)/ Hottest Gong In Town (recorded '86)
(3:36)/ Between The Devil And The Deep Blue
Sea (live in London from 'Mister Roadrunner', UK
documentary, recorded in '91 and aired June 6
'92) (2:36)/ Maxine ('Travelling Wilbury's Vol. 3'
outtake '90) (3:39)/ End Of The Line ('The
Traveling Wilbury's Vol. One' outtake '88) (3:09)/
My Sweet Lord (US 45 mix, recorded in '70,
released Nov. 23 '70)
R: Ex.   C: Dcc. 16 page booklet.

CD - SONGS FOR PATTI - THE MASTERTAPE
STRAWBERRY STR 004
Intro/ Wah-Wah (instrumental)/ My Sweet Lord/
Art Of Dying/ If Not For You/ Behind That Locked
Door/ Let It Down/ All Things Must Pass (false
start)/ All Things Must Pass/ Down To The River/
Wah-Wah/ Ballad Of Sir Frankie Crisp (Let It
Roll)/ Awaiting On You All (instrumental)/ Art Of
Dying (instrumental)/ What Is Life/ Isn't It A Pity/
Behind That Locked Door/ I Still Love You/ I Still
Love You/ Apple Jam
R: Ex. Soundboard.   S: 'All Things Must Pass'
outtakes.   C: ECD. Time 74:52.

HARRISON, GEORGE WITH ERIC CLAPTON

CD - HIROSHIMA 1991
GH-001/2
CD1: I Want To Tell You/ Old Brown Shoe/
Taxman/ Give Me Love/ If I Needed Someone/
Something/ What Is Life/ Dark Horse/ Piggies/
Pretending/ Old Love/ Badge/ Wonderful Tonight
CD2: Got My Mind Set On You/ Cloud 9/ Here
Comes The Sun/ My Sweet Load/ All Those Years
To Go/ Cheer Down/ Devil's Radio/ Isn't It A Pity/
While My Guitar Gently Weeps/ Roll Over
Beethoven
R: Good audience recording. Hiss.
S: Hiroshima, Japan Dec. 6 '91.

HARVEY, P.J.

CD - MY LIFE
OXYGEN OXY 042
Meet Ze Monsta (4:00)/ Working For The Man (5:23)/ My Naked Cousin (4:46)/ Teclo (6:17)/ C'Mon Billy (3:29)/ Hook (4:32)/ Long Snake Moan (5:00)/ Me Jane (3:31)/ 50 Ft Queenie (2:37)/ Goodnight (5:58)/ Walking On Water (5:49)/ C'Mon Billy (Acoustic Version) (2:59)/ The Dancer (Acoustic Version) (4:18)/ Harder (1:59)/ Long Time Coming (4:17)/ Send His Love To Me (4:23)/ Down By The Water (3:33)
R: Exs. Soundboard.   S: Tracks 1-11 Glastonbury Festival, UK June 24 '95. Tracks 12-15 BBC 'Evening Session', London, UK July '95. Tracks 16-17 'Later With Jools Holland', London, UK '95.   C: ECD. Pic CD.

CD - PRETTY POLLY
MOONRAKER 035/36
CD1: Hook/ Harder/ Long Snake Moan/ Dress/ Driving/ I Think I'm A Mother/ Lying In The Sun/ One Time Too Many/ Meet Ze Monster/ C'Mon Billy/ To Bring You My Love/ Send His Love To Me/ Me Jane/ Soft Queenie
CD2: Legs/ Down By The Water/ Naked Cousin/ Working For The Man/ Goodnight/ C'Mon Billy/ Send His Love To Me/ Hardly Wait
R: CD1 and CD2 tracks 1-5 Ex. Audience. CD2 tracks 6-8 Ex. Soundboard.   S: CD1 and CD2 tracks 1-5 Le Zenith, Paris Nov. 14 '95. CD2 track 6 Canal + Nov. 13 '95. Tracks 7-8 MTV Europe's Most Wanted Nov. '95.   C: ECD. Dcc. Time CD1 55:48. CD2 44:06.

HELIOS CHROME

7" - HELIOS CHROME
S1: Malavia Melenium
S2: Master Blaster/ TV As Eyes
R: Vg. Audience.   S: Live Jan. '93.   C: USA. B&w sleeve. 45 RPM.

HELMUT VS COP SHOOT COP

7" - PREVIOUSLY UNRELEASED TRACKS
MICRO RECORDS
S1: Unknown Title (first Helmut demo)
S2: Drop The Bombs (live CSC radio broadcast)
R: Vg-Ex.   C: USA. Purple/black cover. 45 RPM.

HENDRIX, JIMI

CD - BALTIMORE CIVIC CENTER, JUNE 13, 1970
STARQUAKE SQ 09
Pass It On/ Lover Man/ Machine Gun/ Ezy Rider/ Red House/ Message Of Love/ Hey Joe/ Freedom/ Hear My Train A Comin'/ Room Full Of Mirrors/ Foxy Lady/ Purple Haze/ Star Spangled Banner/ Voodoo Child (Slight Return), 'Keep On Groovin'
R: Poor-G. Audience.   S: Baltimore Civic Center June 13 '70.   C: Japanese CD. Dcc. Time 72:00.

CD - THE BIGGEST SQUARE IN THE BUILDING
Are You Experienced?/ Let Me Stand Next To Your Fire/ The Wind Cries Mary/ Tax Free/ Foxy Lady/ Hey Joe/ Spanish Castle Magic/ Red House/ Purple Haze/ Wild Thing
R: G-Vg. Audience.   S: State Fair Music Hall, Texas Feb. 16 '68.   C: Dcc. Complete and unedited recording. Time 68:42.

CD - BLUES AT MIDNIGHT
MIDNIGHT BEAT CD 037
Little Wing (9:19)/ Everything's Gonna Be Allright (8:47)/ Three Little Bears Part 1 (Jam) (15:54)/ Three Little Bears Part 2 (6:19)/ Instrumental Jam (8:45)/ Stormy Monday (8:24)/ Blues In C (19:49)*
R: Vg-Ex. *G-Vg.   S: The Cafe A Go Go, Greenwich Village, New York Apr. 17 '68. Track 7 The Generation Club, New York Apr. 15 '68.
C: ECD. Dcc. Pic CD. Some song fade-in at beginning and out at end.

CD - BURNING AT FRANKFURT
MIDNIGHT BEAT MB CD 040
Come On Part 1 (6:40)/ Fire (4:15)/ Red House (12:34)/ I Don't Live Today (10:03)/ Little Wing (3:52)/ Foxy Lady (5:32)/ Sunshine Of Your Love (11:41)/ Hey Joe (4:32)/ Purple Haze (4:30)
R: G-Vg. Audience.   S: The Jahrhunderthalle, Frankfurt, Germany Jan. 17 '69.   C: ECD. Dcc. Pic CD.

CD - CAT'S SQUIRREL
CSO 01/2
CD1: Voodoo Chile (Slight Return)/ Foxy Lady/ Red House/ Sunshine Of Your Love/ I Don't Live Today/ Hear My Train A' Coming
CD2: Spanish Castle Magic/ Purple Haze/ The Star Spangled Banner/ Sgt. Pepper's Lonely Hearts Club Band/ Fire/ Hey Joe/ Catfish Blues/ The Wind Cries Mary/ Purple Haze/ Spanish Castle Magic/ Wild Thing
R: Poor audience recording.   S: Lorensberg Circus, Gothenberg, Sweden Jan. 8 '69. CD2 4-11 Tivolis Koncersal, Copenhagen Jan. 7 '68.

CD - COME ON STOCKHOLM 1970
JH-001/002
CD1: Here Comes Your Lover Man/ Catfish Blues/ Race With The Devil/ Ezy Ryder/ Red House/ Come On/ Room Full Of Mirrors/ Hey Baby (The Land Of The New Rising Sun)/ Drum Solo
CD2: Message To Love/ Machine Gun/ Voodoo Child (Slight Return)/ In From The Storm/ Purple Haze/ Foxy Lady, Star Spangled Banner
R: Good audience recording.   S: Stora Scenen Grona Lund, Stockholm, Sweden Aug. 31 '70.

CD - THE COMPLETE BBC SESSION AND...
THE LAST BOOTLEG RECORDS LBR 036/2
CD1: Radio One Theme (1:57)/ Catfish Blues
(5:23)/ Interview At BBC '67 During Hey Joe
Session (1:54)/ Hey Joe (4:03)/ Foxy Lady (2:47)/
Stone Free (3:30)/ Love Or Confusion (2:54)/
Look Over Yonder (Mr. Bad Luck) (2:58)/ Purple
Haze (3:03)/ Killing Floor (2:29)/ Fire (2:41)/ The
Wind Cries Mary (3:06)/ Wild Thing (1:54)/ Ma
Pouppee Qui Fait No (3:42)/ The Burning Of The
Midnight Lamp (3:44)/ Jam # 1 With Steve
Wonder (3:24)/ Jam #2 With Steve Wonder
(5:06)/ Little Miss Lover (2:57)/ Drivin South
(4:47)/ Experience The Blues (5:29)/ Hound Dog
(2:44)/ All Along The Watchtower (3:46)
CD2: Can You Please Crawl Out Your Window
(3:34)/ Hoochie Koochie Man (5:35)/ Spanish
Castle Magic (3:22)/ Day Tripper (3:22)/ Sgt.
Pepper's Lonely Hearts Club Band (1:58)/ Getting
My Heart Back Together (4:57)/ Wait Until
Tomorrow (2:55)/ Hey Joe (demo) (2:59)/ Purple
Haze (unreleased demo) (2:46)/ Red House (vari-
ous takes) (10:55)/ I Don't Live Today (various
takes) (16:19)/ Fire (instrumental) (2:36)/ The
Wind Cries Mary (instrumental) (3:41)/ Gloria
(9:03)/ Hound Dog (acoustic) (2:29)
R: Ex. Soundboard.   S: CD1 BBC Studios dur-
ing '67 sessions, Except Tracks 8 And 13. CD2:
Recorded Live At BBC Studios During '67
Sessions, Except Tracks 5,14, And 15.
C: ECD. Dcc. Pic CDs.

CD - CROSSTOWN TRAFFIC
Dear Mr. Fantasy/ Rock Me Baby/ Foxy Lady/ I
Don't Live Today/ Hey Joe/ Fire/ Red House/
Purple Haze/ Wild Thing
R: Vg. Audience.   S: Moody Coliseum,
Southern Methodist University, Dallas, Texas Aug.
3 '68.   C: Dcc. Complete and unedited record-
ing. Time 63:48.

CD - ELECTRIC ANNIVERSARY JIMI
MIDNIGHT BEAT MB CD 024
Pride Of Man (Valleys Of Neptune Jam) (3:43)/
World Traveler (8:06)/ It's too Bad (10:44)/
Cherokee Mist (different mix) (5:38)/ You Make
Me Feel (4:30)/ Jungle Jam (5:58)/ All Devil's
Children (basic version) (4:17)/ Little Drummer
Boy, Silent Night (4:53)/ Auld Lang Syne (with
background choir) (2:30)/ Instrumental Jams:
Sending My Love To Linda, Live And Let Live,
Valleys Of Neptune Arising (9:43)/ Message From
Nine To The Universe (15:51)
R: Vg. Soundboard.   S: The Record Plant
Studios, New York between '69/'70. Tracks 1, 5
and 6 The Hit Factory Studios, New York. Track 7
TTG Sunset Highland Studios '68.   C: ECD.
Dcc. Pic CD.

CD - EXPERIENCE THE VOODOO SESSIONS
VC 2568
The Slight Return Session: Yours Truly (guitar,
vocal), Bob Dylan's Grandmother (bass), Queen
Bee (drums) (Record Plant May 3 '68)/ The The

Blues Session: Yours Truly (guitar, vocal), Pooneil
(bass), Queen Bee (drums), Mr. Fantasy (organ)
(Record Plant May 2 '68)
R: Ex. Soundboard.   C: ECD. Dcc. Time 73:48.

CD - EYES AND IMAGINATION
TSD 18970
Backward Experiment/ Freedom/ Lover Man/
Jungle Beginning/ Bleeding Heart/ Bleeding
Heart/ Earth Blues/ Astro Man Jam/ Ezy Rider/
Room Full Of Mirrors/ Captain Coconut/ Valleys
Of Neptune/ Arriving/ Once I Had A Woman/ Dolly
Dagger
R: Ex. Soundboard.   S: Tracks 1, 2, 5-11 and
13 at The Record Plant, NYC. Tracks 3 and 12 at
Electric Lady Studios, NYC. Tracks 4, 12 and 15
at The Hit Factory, NYC.   C: ECD. Dcc.
Time 61:57.

CD - 51ST ANNIVERSARY (THE STORY OF LIFE...)
JMH RECORDS 001-008
CD1: Collage (3:53)/ Hey Joe (demo London '66 -
2:56)/ Jimi Interview (1:54)/ How Would You Feel
(Kurtis Knight and Jimi, NY '65 - 2:55)/ Love Or
Confusion (unreleased live version '76 - 2:49)/
Sgt. Pepper's Lonely Hearts Club Band (Sweden
Sept. '67 - 1:56)/ All Along The Watchtower (unre-
leased demo, Olympic Studio, London '68 - 3:45)/
Little Wing (Royal Albert Hall, London Feb. '69 -
3:01)/ Electric Church Red House (studio jam, LA
'68 - 6:43)/ Spanish Castle Magic (Top Gear '76 -
3:06)/ Hear My Train A Comin' (unreleased live
version, London '67 - 4:32)/ Rock'N'Roll Band
(with Eire Apparent '68 - 3:22)/ Stepping Stone
Band Of Gypsies (unreleased studio version '69 -
4:08)/ Gloria (unreleased live session '67 - 8:44)/
My Diary (Rosa Lee books '62 - 2:20)/ Utee
(Rosa Lee books '62 - 2:00)/ The Burning Of The
Midnight Lamp (Tivoli Garden, Stockholm Sept.
11 '67 - 4:31)/ Little Miss Lover (unreleased studio
version, Olympic Studios, London '67 - 2:19)/
Foxy Lady (3:18), Catfish Blues (Vitus Studio,
Holland Sept. 10 '67 - 7:46)/ Slow Walkin' Talk
(3:00) (With Robert Wyatt, T.T.G. Studios,
Hollywood Oct. '68)
CD2: Traffic Jam (5:28), Hey Baby Jam (New
Rising Sun) (14:46), Jazz Jam (5:31), Moonlight
Jam (4:50) (unreleased studio jam with Traffic)/
Studio Catastrophe (1:58), Valley Of Neptune
(Take 2) (5:50) ('Valley Of Neptune' session late
'69)/ Rainy Day Super Jam (Electric Ladyland
outtakes, M. Finningan on keyboards spring '68 -
5:22)/ Nervous Breakdown (take 2, jam with Fat
Mattress, late '69 - 3:52)/ Captain Coconut And
Cherokee Mist Jam MLK (studio Jam) (6:27),
Crash Landing (outtake) (4:29) (Electric Ladyland
late '69)
CD3: #7 Man (Electric Ladyland sessions late '69
- 7:32)/ Voodoo Chile (unreleased studio version
with Lee Michaels on keyboards spring '68 -
20:45)/ Somewhere Over The Rainbow (first version, TTG Studios '68 - 3:37)/ Red House (jam,
Electric Ladyland spring '68 - 7:30)/ Angel (voice

and guitar) (3:23), 1983 (voice and guitar) (4:00) (Jimi's home, New York '69)/ First Jam (Jimi with John Mc Laughin, NY late '69 - 15:49)
CD4: 7 Dollars In My Pocket (Late '69 - 15:09)/ Devil Jam (studio jam late '69 - 9:31)/ Lover Man (hard studio version late '69 - 4:58)/ Midnight Lightning (acoustic version late '69 - 4:35)/ Further On Up The Road (live in the studio late '69 - 1:54)/ The Things I Used To Do (live in the studio with Johnny Winter late '69 - 7:09)/ Once I Had A Woman (take 2 late '69 - 5:36)/ Machine Gun (first studio version late '69 - 8:25)/ Lord I Sing The Blues For Me And You (with Gipsy Sun And Rainbow Band live in studio Sept. 9 '69 - 4:15)/ Country Blues (Plant Studios, NY with Band Of Gypsies Jan 23 '70 - 6:33)/ Stop (Band Of Gypsies rehearsal, Fillmore East, NY Dec. 31 '69 - 4:41)
CD5: Midnight Lightning (outtakes '69 - 6:31)/ Lower Alcatraz (unreleased track '69 - 3:41)/ There Goes Ezy Rider. Dollars In My Pocket (studio improvisation '69 - 11:38)/ Heavy Rider Jam (studio jam '69 - 9:29)/ Easy Blues (studio improvisation '69 - 7:47)/ Gypsy Boy (outtake, take 2 '70 - 3:15)/ Peace In Mississippi (outtake '70 - 4:26)/ Bluesiana Jam (private tape Mar. '69 - 17:03)/ BB King Slow Instrumental Jam (Generation, NYC May 18 '69 - 19:46)
CD6: Two Guitars Jam (10:19), San Francisco Bay Blues (8:12) (Woodstock session with Steve Stills Sept. '69)/ Gypsy Eyes (Electric Ladyland outtake Oct. '68 - 4:24)/ Cherokee Mist (studio jam NY '68) (7:11)/ The Street Things (outtake, 'Buddy Miles Express' sessions - 5:12)/ In From The Storm (outtake, 'Cry Of Love' sessions - 3:42)/ Freedom (outtake, 'Cry Of Love' sessions - 3:29)/ Somewhere Over The Rainbow II (outtake, 'Cry Of Love' sessions - 3:37)/ Belly Button Window (instrumental outtake, 'Cry Of Love' sessions - 4:48)/ Captain Coconut II, Cherokee Mist (outtake, take 5 'First Rays Of New Rising Sun' sessions - 6:17)/ Rider Blues (outtake, 'First Rays Of New Rising Sun' sessions - 11:38)/ Electric Ladyland Theme (instrumental outtake, 'First Rays Of New Rising Sun' sessions - 4:33)/ Jazzy Jamming (studio jam, 'First Rays Of New Rising Sun' sessions - 4:55)
CD7: She's So Fine (outtake - 2:47), Axis Bold As Love (outtake - 3:32), EXP (outtake - 1:56), Up From The Skies (outtake - 2:56), Love Jam (with Brian Jones - 13:09), Electric Ladyland Jam (instrumental outtake - 6:19) (Sotheby Auction Tape, Olympic Studios Sept. '67)/ Pass It On (7:30), Hey Baby (New Rising Sun) (6:06), Stone Free (4:08), Hey Joe (4:53), Freedom (5:12), Red House (7:55), Ezy Rider (6:37) (Berkeley Community Centre May 30 '70)/ New Rising Sun Theme (instrumental, Maui Hawaii July 30 '70 - 4:51)
CD8: Fire (3:45), Getting My Heart Back Together Again (7:02) (Miami Pop Festival, Hallandale, Florida May 18 '68)/ Spanish Castle Magic (2nd show, Winterland, San Francisco Oct. 11 '68 - 9:44)/ Purple Haze (2nd show, Capital Theatre,

Ottawa, Canada Mar. 18 '68 - 7:20)/ Tax Free (LA Forum Apr. 26 '69 - 14:21)/ Message To Love (rehearsal, Woodstock '69 - 4:00)/ Red House (Woodstock '69 - 5:14)/ Voodoo Chile (Slight Return) (5:36), Machine Gun (10:55) (Isle Of Wight '70)/ Hey Baby (KB Hallen, Copenhagen Sept. 3 '70 - 7:19)
R: As with any collection of this size, quality varies. The thing to keep in mind is the amount of rare material found on this set. C: ECD. This set comes in a large box with an extensive book (in Italian) and a video (PAL system). Very impressive.

CD - HAVE MERCY ON ME BABY!
MIDNIGHT BEAT MB CD 038
Killing Floor (1:19)/ Have Mercy (4:06)/ Can You See Me (4:28)/ Like A Rolling Stone (8:36)/ Rock Me Baby (3:15)/ Catfish Blues (9:01)/ Stone Free (3:31)/ Hey Joe (4:16)/ Wild Thing (8:10)/ I Don't Live Today (8:16)/ Hear My Train A Comin' (8:56)/ Spanish Castle Magic (6:31)
R: G. Audience. Tracks 10-12 Poor-G. Audience. S: The Flamingo Club, London Feb. 4 '67. Tracks 10-12 The Philharmonic Hall, New York Nov. 28 '68. C: ECD. Dcc. Pic CD. Jimi introduces his new band 'The Experience'.

CD - HISTORIC CONCERT
MIDNIGHT BEAT MB CD 017
Intro, Are You Experienced/ Fire/ Red House/ I Don't Live Today/ Foxy Lady/ Like A Rolling Stone/ Purple Haze/ The Star Spangled Banner/ Hey Joe/ Wild Thing
R: Poor audience recording. S: New York Rock Festival, Singer Bowl, Flushing Meadow Park, Queens, New York Aug. 23 '68. C: ECD. Dcc. Pic CD.

CD - JIMI A MUSICAL LEGACY (THE DEFINITIVE COLLECTION OF UNRELEASED RARITIES 1963 -1970)
KISS THE STONE KTS BX 010
CD1: Goodbye Bessie Mae/ Soul Food (That's What I Like) (Jimi's first recording Philadelphia Sept. '63)/ My Diary, Utee (Jimi on Lee Brooks single Los Angeles Jan. '64)/ Testify (Isley Brothers single New York City Mar. '64)/ Whole Lotta Shakin', Hound Dog (with Little Richard Los Angeles July '65)/ I'm A Man, Strange Things, How Would You Feel? (with Curtis Knight and The Squires New York City Oct. '65)/ Free Spirit, House Of The Rising Sun (with Curtis Knight, George's Club Hackensack, New Jersey Jan. '66)/ Hey Joe (vocal reference tape, De Lane Studios, London Oct. 23 '66)/ Red House (original take, London Dec. 13 '66)/ I Don't Live Today (alternate take), Purple Haze (monitor mix), Fire (alternate take), The Wind Cries Mary (instrumental), Are You Experienced? (backward take) (London Feb. '67/ Purple Haze (acetate London Feb. '67)
CD2: Room Full Of Mirrors, Shame Shame Shame (early attempts, London May 4 '67)/

Catfish Blues (Vitus Studios, Holland Sept. 10 '67)/ She's So Fine, Axis: Bold As Love (Olympic Studios, London Sept. '67)/ EXP, Up From The Skies (outtakes Sept. '67)/ Little One (take 1, Olympic Studios, London Oct. 5 '67)/ Love Or Confusion (London Feb. 13 '67)/ Gloria (TTG Studios, London Oct. 2 '67)/ Burning Of The Midnight Lamp, Sergeant Pepper's Lonely Hearts Club Band (Stockholm Sept. 5 '67)/ Like A Rolling Stone (Saville Theatre, London Aug. 27 '67)/ The Stars That Play With Laughing Sam's Dice (unreleased take, New York July 18 '67)/ Dream, Dance (Olympic Studios, London Dec. 20 '67)/ Electric Ladyland (alternate take, London Oct. 25 '67)/ Ain't Too Proud To Beg Jam (recorded for BBC's 'Top Gear', London Oct. 6 '67)/ Getting My Heart Back Together Again (BBC outtake, London Dec. 15 '67)/ Castles Made Of Sand (reversed original with what would become the backwards guitar track, London Oct. '67)
CD3: All Along The Watchtower (alternate take, Olympic Studios, London Jan. 28 '68)/ 1983...(A Merman I Should Turn To Be) (home demo, London Feb. '68)/ Somewhere (Sound Centre Studios, New York City Mar. '68)/ Morrison's Lament - Tomorrow Never Knows (jam with Jim Morrison, The Scene, New York City Mar. 7 '68)/ Wild Thing (Atwood Hall, Clark University, Worcester, Mass. Mar. 15 '68)/ Angel (reference tape), Gypsy Eyes (outtake), Cherokee Mist (outtake) (New York City Apr. and Oct. '68)/ God Save The Queen (summer '68)/ Three Little Bears (The Record Plant, New York City May 2 '68)/ Voodoo Child (home recording, New York City May '68)/ Traffic Jam (a jam with 3 members of Traffic and Jack Cassady, London June '68)/ Duelling Guitars (Jimi and Beck? or Stills? summer '68)/ Spanish Castle Magic (Winterland, San Francisco Oct. 11 '68)
CD4: Jimi Comments, Voodoo Child, Hey Joe - Sunshine Of Your Love (Lulu's BBC TV show, London Jan. 4 '69)/ Jimi - Jimmy Jam (jam with John McLaughlin, New York City Mar. 25 '69)/ Ships Passing In The Night (embryonic version of 'Night Bird Flying', New York City Apr. 14 '69)/ Message To Love, Lord I Sing The Blues (rehearsal for Woodstock, Shokan, New York Aug. '69)/ Little Drummer Boy, Silent Night, Taps, Auld Lange Syne (The Record Plant, New York City Dec. '69)/ Earth Blues (Baggies, New York City Dec. 20 '69)/ Gypsy Boy, Alcatraz, Captain Coconut II - Cherokee Mist, Bleeding Heart (unreleased tracks, The Record Plant, New York City early '70)/ Killin' Floor, Voodoo Child (Love And Peace Festival, Fehmarn, Germany Sept. 6 '70. Jimi's last concert appearance)
C: ECD. Another excellent chronological collection from the people who gave you the (forget 'Anthology' and buy this) Beatles 'Artifacts' box sets. Four pic CDs in a digi-book with a full color book containing material sources, photos and interview transcripts. Time CD1 70:58. CD2 74:06. CD3 75:58. CD4 75:36.

CD - JIMI IN DENMARK
DYNAMITE STUDIOS DS95J356
Catfish Blues (9:24)/ Tax Free (11:49)/ Master James And Co. (23:32)/ Fire (4:01)/ Voodoo Child (Slight Return) (7:24)/ Foxy Lady (4:54)/ Spanish Castle Magic (9:31)/ Freedom (4:02)
R: Ex. Audience.   C: Japanese CD. Dcc.

CD - JIMI PLAYS BERKELEY
JMH 005/2
CD1: Rehearsal: Blue Suede Shoes (4:30)/ Power Of Soul (2:50)/ Machine Gun (7:30)/ Message Of Love (5:37)/ Room Full Of Mirrors (1:50)/ Freedom (4:35)/ First Show: Johnny B Goode (4:45)/ Hear My Train A Coming (12:09)/ Freedom (5:24)/ Red House (7:58)/ Ezy Rider (6:36)
CD2: Pass It On (8:30)/ Hey Babe (New Rising Sun) (5:40)/ Lover Man (3:00)/ Stone Free (4:32)/ Hey Joe (5:15)/ I Don't Live Today (5:32)/ Machine Gun (11:23)/ Foxy Lady (6:31)/ The Star Spangled Banner (Traditional) (2:29)/ Purple Haze (4:00)/ Voodoo Child (10:16)/ Rehearsal Jam (9:08)
R: Ex. Soundboard.   S: Berkeley Community Center, May 30 '70 (Memorial Day).   C: ECD. Dcc. Pic CDs.

CD - LET'S DROP SOME LUDES AND VOMIT WITH JIMI - RECORD PLANT JAMS VOL. 2
MIDNIGHT BEAT MB CD 026
Drivin' South, Everything's Gonna Be Allright (instrumental jam) (23:54)/ Drone Blues (5:55)/ Easy Blues (7:52)/ Strato Strut (8:51)/ I'm A Man (instrumental) (6:25)/ I'm A Man (with vocals) (15:20)/ Instrumental Jam (embryonic version of 'Tomorrow Never Knows') (9:00)
R: Vg. Soundboard.   S: Record Plant Studios, NYC '69 - '70. Track 4 Electric Lady Studios.
C: ECD. Dcc. Pic CD.

CD - LIVE AT AT FLAMINGO CLUB, LONDON
MY PHENIX ZA 25
Killin' Floor (fades in)/ Have Mercy Baby/ Can You See Me/ Like A Rolling Stone/ Rock Me Baby/ Catfish Blues/ Stone Free/ Hey Joe/ Wild Thing
R: Poor-G. Audience.   S: The Flamingo Club, London 2-4-'67.   C: Japanese CD. Dbw. Purple background with yellow type. Time 42:03.

CD - THE LIVE WITHDRAWN
BABY CAPONE BC 077
Are You Experienced (13:28)/ Voodoo Chile (Slight Return) (5:45)/ Like A Rolling Stone (11:48)/ Spanish Castle Magic (9:42)/ Villanova Junction Blues, Fire (3:11)/ Guitar Improvisation (4:47)/ Villanova Junction Blues (2:54)/ Freedom (5:09)/ Red House (7:48)/ Ezy Rider (7:01)/ Hey Baby (New Rising Sun) (4:47)
R: Ex. Soundboard.   S: Tracks 1-4 Winterland, San Francisco Oct. 10, 11 and 12, '68. Tracks 5-7 Woodstock Festival Aug. 18 '69. Tracks 8-10 1st concert, Berkeley Community Center May 30 '70. Track 11 First show, Haleakala Crater, Maui,

Jimi a musical legacy

Jimi Hendrix

The Definitive Collection of Unreleased Rarities
1963-1970

Hawaii July 30 '70.   C: ECD. Dcc. Pic CD.

CD - LIVING REELS VOL. 1
JMH 011
Castle Made Of Sand (Olympic Studios Oct. 25 '67 - 3:04)/ Spanish Castle Magic (instrumental, Olympic Studios Oct. 27 '67 - 2:51)/ South Saturn Delta I (Olympic Studios Oct. 16 '67 - 4:58)/ Wait Until Tomorrow (Olympic Studios Oct. 26 '67 - 3:31)/ Ain't No Telling (Olympic Studios Oct. 26 '67 - 1:57)/ One Rainy Wish (Olympic Studios Oct. 6 '67 - 4:00)/ She's So Fine (Olympic Studios Oct. 30 '67 - 2:42)/ Axis: Bold As Love (Olympic Studios Oct. 29 '67 - 3:39)/ Up From The Skies (Olympic Studios Oct. 29 '67 - 3:02)/ Jam #I (Olympic Studios Sept. 28 '67 - 5:13)/ Little Wing (Olympic Studios Oct. 27 '67 - 2:31)/ Unknown (Olympic Studios Sept. 22 '67 - 3:38)/ Axis: Bold As Love II (Olympic Studios Oct. 29 '67 - 3:34)/ EXP (Olympic Studios May 5 '67 - 1:56)/ Up From The Skies II (Olympic Studios Oct. 29 '67 - 2:57)/ Jam #II (Olympic Studios Sept. 28 '67 - 13:11)/ Sitar Song (Olympic Studios May 26 '67 - 3:19)/ Hey Joe (D.L.L. Studios Oct. 23 '66 - 3:29)/ I Don't Live Today (D.L.L. Studios Feb. 15 '67 - 2:21)/ Fire (Olympic Studios Mar. 2 '67 - 2:42)/ Foxy Lady (CBS Studios Dec. 13 '66 - 3:11)
R: Ex. Soundboard.   C: ECD. Dcc. Pic CDs.

CD - LIVING REELS VOL. II
JMH 012/2
CD1: Tax Free (Record Plant Studios Jan. 5 '68 with Steve Winwood on keyboards - 5:10)/ Three Little Bears (Record Plant Studios Feb. 5 '68 - 5:06)/ Gypsy Eyes (Record Plant Studios Apr. 5 '68 - 4:28)/ Cherokee Mist (Record Plant Studios Feb. 5 '68 - 7:09)/ Little Rock 'N' Roll Jam (Record Plant Studios Apr. 5 '68 - 1:56)/ Little Wing (Cafe Au Gogo, New York Mar. 17 '68 - 9:46)/ Rock Me Baby (Cafe Au Gogo, New York Mar. 17 '68 - 7:11)/ Voodoo Chile Session (Record Plant Studios, NY Feb. 3 '68 - 27:10)/ Look Over Yonder (TTG Studios Oct. 22 '68 - 2:35)/ Rainy Day Jam (Record Plant Studios '68 - 5:34)
CD2: Somewhere I (Cen Studios Mar. 13 '68 - 3:42)/ Peace In Mississippi #1 (TTG Studios Oct. 24 '68 - 5:41)/ Jimi And Mitch Jam (TTG Studios Oct. 27 '68 - 5:40)/ Somewhere II (Cen Studios Mar. 12 '68 - 3:40)/ My Friend (Cen Studios Mar. 13 '68 - 4:22)/ 1983 (A Mermaid I Should Never Be) (Plant Studios Apr. 24 '68 - 3:57)/ Electrical Ladyland (Plant Studios Apr. 5 '68 - 6:31)/ Are You Experienced (17:46), Voodoo Chile (Slight Return) (7:33)/ Red House (11:00) (Winterland Arena, San Francisco Oct. 11 '68)/ Fire (Miami Pop Festival May 18 '68 - 2:54)
R: Ex. Soundboard.   C: ECD. Dcc.

CD - PHILHARMONIC PLUS
BRCD1901
I Don't Live Today/ Getting My Heart Back Together/ Spanish Castle Magic/ Interview/ Lover Man/ Hey Joe/ Hound Dog/ Voodoo Chile/ Getting My Heart Back Together/ Dolly Dagger
R: G-Vg.   S: Tracks 1-3 Philharmonic Hall, NYC Nov. 28 '68. Tracks 4-5 Tonight Show July 19 '69. Tracks 6-9 afternoon rehearsals, Royal Albert Hall Feb. 24 '69. Track 10 breakdown mix with Eddie Kramer.   C: ECD. Dcc. Time 71:27.

CD - POWER OF SOUL
STARQUAKE SQ-10
Power Of Soul/ Lover Man/ Hear My Train A Comin'/ Them Changes/ Izabella, Machine Gun/ Stop/ Ezy Ryder/ Bleeding Heart/ Earth Blues/ Burning Desire
R: G. Audience.   S: The complete first show, Fillmore East Dec. 31 '69.   C: Japanese CD. Dbw. With The Band Of Gypsys. Time 70:46.

CD - RAINBOW BRIDGE 2
JMH 003/2
CD1: Rainbow Band: It's A Beautiful Day (1:53)/ Chuck Wein Introduction (2:19)/ Jimi Hendrix - Cry Of Love Band: Spanish Castle Magic (4:43)/ Lover Man (2:34)/ Hey Baby (4:36)/ In From The Storm (5:00)/ Message To Love (4:49)/ Foxy Lady (4:45)/ Hear My Train A-Comin' (9:08)/ Voodoo Chile (Slight Return) (7:16)/ Fire (3:51)/ Purple Haze (4:17)/ Dolly Dagger (5:09)/ Villanova Junction Blues (5:27)/ Ezy Rider (4:55)
CD2: Red House (6:45)/ Freedom (4:21)/ Jam Back The House (6:59)/ Land Of The Rising Sun (4:46)/ Dolly Dagger (Isle Of Wight '70) (5:34)/ Hey Baby (Isle Of Wight '70) (7:17)/ Hear My Train A-Comin' (Berkely '70) (11:11)/ Message Of Love (Fillmore '69) (4:32)/ Ezy Rider (Fillmore '69) (4:54)/ Room Full Of Mirrors (B.O.G. '69) (3:03)/ Stepping Stone (B.O.G. '69) 4:09)/ Earth Blues (B.O.G. '69) (4:20)/ Hey Baby (C.O.L.B. '70) (6:00)
R: Ex. Soundboard.   S: Haleakala Crater, Maui, Hawaii July 30 '70.   C: ECD. Dcc. Pic CDs.

CD - REMEMBER THE ALAMO
Sgt. Pepper's Lonely Hearts Club Band/ Can You Please Crawl Out Of Your Window/ The Wind Cries Mary/ Let Me Stand Next To Your Fire/ Cat Fish Blues/ Foxy Lady/ Hey Joe/ Purple Haze/ Wild Thing
R: Vg. Audience.   S: Will Rogers Auditorium, Fort Worth, Texas Feb. 17 '68.   C: Dbw with red type. Complete and unedited recording. Time 55:54.

CD - 'SCUSE ME WHILE I KISS THE SKY
SONIC ZOOM SZ1001
Are You Experienced/ Fire/ Wind Cries Mary Tax Free, Drum Solo/ Foxy Lady/ Hey Joe/ Spanish Castle Magic/ Improvisation/ Purple Haze/ Wild Thing/ Star Spangled Banner/ Hey Joe/ Guitar Improvisation/ Purple Haze/ Wild Thing
R: G-Vg audience recording.   S: Tracks 1-11 Memorial Auditorium, Dallas, Texas Feb. 16 '68. Tracks 12-15 Will Rogers Auditorium, Fort Worth, Texas Feb. 17 '68.

CD - SHOKAN SUNRISE

Izabella/ Instrumental/ Beginnings, If 6 Was 9/
Shokan Sunrise/ Izabella (2nd Version)/ Flute
Instrumental/ Jimi's March/ African Instrumental/
Message Of Love/ Beginnings (2nd Version)/
Jimi's March (Live Version)
R: Poor sound, hiss.   S: New York Aug. '69.

CD - SYMPHONY OF EXPERIENCE

THIRD STONE DISCS TSD-24966
Hey Joe/ Purple Haze/ Are You Experienced?/
She's So Fine/ Little Miss Lover/ Drivin' South/
Instrumental Jam, Ain't Too Proud To Beg/ Can
You Please Crawl Out your Window?/ Drivin'
South/ Wait Until Tomorrow/ Castles Made Of
Sand/ Spanish Castle Magic/ Bold As Love/
Getting My Heart Back Together Again/ Dream/
Dance/ Drivin' South, Sergeant Pepper's Lonely
Hearts Club Band/ All Along The Watchtower/
Little One/ Little One
R: Vg. Soundboard.   S: Studio outtakes.

CD - TWO DAYS AT NEWPORT

JMH 007/2
CD1: Stone Free (4:05)/ Drum Solo (2:00)/ Are
You Experienced (6:25)/ Stone Free (1:50)/
Sunshine Of Your Love (6:00)/ Fire (3:10)/ Hear
My Train A Comin (14:00)/ Like A Rolling Stone
(5:04)/ Voodoo Child (Slight Return) (5:15)/ Drum
Solo (2:52)/ Purple Haze (3:51)/ Red House
(7:10)/ Foxy Lady (4:30)
CD2: Power Of Soul, Jam Improvisation (2:20)/
Hear My Train A Comin (9:39)/ Voodoo Child,
Slight Return, Rock 'N' Roll Jam (10:42)/ Come
On (4:59)/ Star Spangled Banner (5:31)/ We
Gotta Live Together (18:31)/ The Things We Used
To Do (2:43)/ Keep On Movin (11:45)*/ The Sweet
Things (5:17)*
R: Ex. Soundboard.   S: Newport Pop Festival.
CD1 June 20, CD2 June 22 '69 with Buddy Miles
Express. *Record Plant Studios, Nov. 14 '69 with
Buddy Miles Express.   C: ECD. Dcc. Pic CDs.

CD - THE WARM HELLO OF THE SUN

CD1: Spanish Castle Magic/ Killin' Floor/ Getting
My Heart Back Together Again/ Message Of Love/
Hey Baby, The Land Of The New Rising Sun/ In
From The Storm
CD2: Hey Joe/ Foxy Lady/ Red House/ Room Full
Of Mirrors/ Straight Ahead/ Purple Haze/ Voodoo
Chile (Slight Return)
R: G. Audience.   S: Stora Scenen, Liseberg,
Goteborg, Sweden Sept. 1 '70.   C: Japanese
CD. Dbw. Red/yellow type. Time CD1 45:52.
CD2 46:02.

CD - WELCOME TO THE ELECTRIC CIRCUS

MIDNIGHT BEAT MB CD 016
Fire/ Foxy Lady/ Tax Free/ Spanish Castle Magic/
Red House/ Sunshine Of Your Love/ I Don't Live
Today, Star Spangled Banner/ Purple Haze
R: G-Vg audience recording.   S: Falkoner
Centret, Copenhagen, Denmark Jan. 10 '69.
C: ECD. Dcc. Pic CD.

CD - WELCOME TO THE ELECTRIC CIRCUS VOL. 2

MIDNIGHT BEAT MB CD 018
Freedom/ Message To Love/ Land Of The Rising
Sun, Drum Solo/ Hey Baby/ All Along The
Watchtower/ Ezy Rider/ Red House/ In From The
Storm/ Purple Haze/ Voodoo Chile (Slight
Return)/ Hey Joe/ Fire
R: Good audience recording.   S: Tracks 1-3
Vejiby Risskov Hallen, Arhus, Denmark Sept. 2
'70. Tracks 4-12 The KB Hallen, Copenhagen,
Denmark Sept. 3 '70.   C: ECD. Dcc. Pic CD.

CD - WIGHT

JMH 006/2
CD1: The Queen (Traditional) (2:40)/ Sgt.
Pepper's Lonely Hearts Band Club (1:50)/
Spanish Castle Magic (4:38)/ All Along The
Watchtower (5:00)/ Machine Gun (22:11)/ Lover
Man (3:10)/ Freedom (4:24)/ Red House (11:33)/
Dolly Dagger (6:00)/ Midnight Lightning (6:50)
CD2: Foxy Lady (9:07)/ Message To Love (6:10)/
Hey Baby (New Sun Rising) (7:24)/ Ezy Rider
(3:59)/ Hey Joe (3:25)/ Purple Haze (8:23)/
Voodoo Child (7:43)/ In From the Storm (6:12)/
Bonus Outtakes: Trying To Be A Jam (7:39)/
Lover Man (5:15)/ Message To Love (3:29)/
Freedom (4:07)
R: Ex. Soundboard.   S: The Isle Of Wight Pop
Festival (East Afton Farm) Aug. 30, '70.
C: ECD. Dcc. Pic CDs.

CD - THE WINK OF AN EYE

WHOPPY CAT RECORDS WKP 0033/34
CD1: Tax Free/ Getting My Heart Back Together/
Fire/ Spanish Castle Magic/ Red House/ Foxy
Lady/ Star Spangled Banner/ Purple Haze/
Spanish Castle Magic
CD2: Killing Floor/ Spanish Castle Magic/ All
Along The Watchtower/ Hey Joe/ Land Of The
Rising Sun/ Message To Love/ Foxy Lady/ Red
House/ Ezy Rider/ Freedom/ Roomful Of Mirrors/
Purple Haze/ Voodoo Child (Slight Return)
R: Poor-G. Audience.   S: CD1 tracks 1-8
Denver Pop Festival, Mile High Stadium June 29
'69. CD1 track 9 MSG May 18 69. CD2 Love And
Peace Festival, Isle Of Fehmarn Sept. 6 '70.
C: Japanese CD. Dbw. Time CD1 75:14.
CD2 77:24.

CD - THE WOODSTOCK REHEARSALS 1969

MIDNIGHT BEAT MB CD 039
Lover Man (4:19)/ Hear My Train A Comin' (8:33)/
Spanish Castle Magic (4:47)/ Izabella (4:31)/
Message Of Love (5:31)/ Instrumental Jam I
(11:38)/ Instrumental Jam II (2:23)/ Jam Back At
The House 1 (6:18)/ Instrumental Jam III (4:37)/
Jam Back At The House II (4:23)/ Jam Back At
The House III (5:37)/ If Six Was Nine (1:29)/ Sun
Dance (5:43)/ Free Form Blues (6:16)
R: G-Vg. Tracks 13-14 Poor-G.   S: At Jimi's
house, Traver Hollow, Shokan, New York Aug. 14
'69. Tracks 13-14 Tinker Street Cinema,

Woodstock, New York Aug. 10 '69.   C: ECD.
Dcc. Pic CD.

HOLDSWORTH, ALLAN

CD - LIVE SECRETS EUROPEAN TOUR 1992
ALL OF US AS 07
Funnels (7:30)/ Mr. Berwell (11:10)/ Pud Wud
(9:54)/ Devil Take The Hindmost (11:46)/ Sea
Hawks (4:48)/ Lesson Of Love (9:25)/ 54 Duncan
Terrace (10:52)/ Tell Me (5:14)/ City Heights
(6:35)
R: Vg. Audience.   S: European Tour '92.
C: ECD.

HOLE

CD - ASKING FOR IT
KISS THE STONE KTS 456
Miss World/ Best Sunday Dress/ Asking For It/
Drown Soda/ He Hit Me (And It Felt Like A Kiss)/
Doll Parts/ Sugar Coma/ Old Age/ Closing Time
R: Ex. Audience.   S: Apr. 25 '95.   C: ECD.
Dcc. Pic CD. Time 50:21.

CD - BRING ME THE HEAD OF LYNN HIRSCHBERG
KROQ3
Plump/ Never Go/ Miss World/ Asking For It/ Doll
Parts/ Violet/ Plump/ Never Go/ Beautiful Son/
Miss World/ Jennifer's Body/ Asking For It/
Gutless/ Softer; Softer/ I Think That I Could Die/
Credit In A Strange World/ Teenage Whore/ Doll
Parts/ Violet/ Never Go/ Pale Blue Eyes/ Rock
Star*/ Talk To Me*
R: Vg-Ex. Soundboard. *Vg. Audience.
S: Tracks 1-6 KROQ Christmas Party Dec. 10 '94.
Tracks 7-20 The Reading Festival Aug. 26 '94.
Track 21 Los Angeles '91. Track 22 Los Angeles
'93. Track 23 Nijmegan '91.   C: ECD. Dcc. Pic
CD. Time 73:46.

CD - COURTNEY ACT
PSEUDO INDIE LABEL PIL07
Beautiful Son/ Credit In The Straight World/
Teenage Whore/ Do It Clean/ Pennyroyal Tea/
Olympia/ She Walks On Me/ The Void/ P-Girl/ Old
Age/ Gutless/ Over The Edge/ Violet/ Chocolate
Boy/ Forming/ Drown/ Soda/ Doll Parts/ Dicknail/
Burn Black/ Turpentine/ Retard Girl/ Phonebill
Song/ Where Did You Sleep Last Night?/
Skinhead Girl
R: Vg- Ex. Soundboard.   S: Tracks 1-5 Phoenix
Festival, UK July 16 '93. Tracks 6-11 Studio
Sessions, London Mar. '93. Tracks 12-17 Studio
Sessions, London Dec. '91. Tracks 18-20 Studio,
Seattle Oct. '90. Track 21 Boston Nov. '91. Track
22 London July '93.   C: ECD. Dcc. Time 72:30.

CD - DISSED
KTS OF AUSTRALIA 013 A
Plump (3:14)/ My Beautiful Son (3:57)/ Miss
World (3:11)/ Jennifer's Body (5:31)/ Asking For It
(5:36)/ Put On My Best Sunday Dress (2:30)/

Gutless (2:35)/ Softer Softest (4:32)/ I Think That I
Would Die (5:10)/ Pretty On The Inside Real
World (5:28)/ Teenage Whore (2:40)/ Doll Parts
(5:50)/ Violet (6:37)/ I'm So High (4:23)/ Hungry
Like A Wolf (1:45)/ Rock Star (3:57)
R: G-Vg. Audience.   S: Live 10/08/94.
C: Australian CD. Dcc.

CD - THE GIRL WITH THE MOST CAKE
PRINT 004
Plump/ My Beautiful Sun/ Miss World/ Drum
Soda/ No, No, No/ Asking for It/ Miss World/ Best
Sunday Dress/ Softer, Softest/ Drum Soda/ He Hit
Me (And It Felt Like A Kiss)/ Asking For It/ You've
Got No Right (unreleased Kurt Cobain song)/ Old
Age/ Hungry Like A Wolf/ Doll Parts/ Sugar Coma
R: Ex. Soundboard.   S: Tracks 1-6 Amsterdam
Apr. 24 '95. Tracks 7-17 'MTV Unplugged' New
York Feb. '95.   C: ECD. Dcc.

CD - GOOD SEX
HOME RECORDS HR 6042-7
Plump (2:42)/ Beautiful Son (3:49)/ Jennifer's
Body (3:37)/ Miss World (2:46)/ Asking For It
(4:37)/ Gutless (4:15)/ I Think That I Would Die
(6:07)/ Hungry Like A Wolf (1:58)/ Pretty On The
Inside (1:21)/ Credit In The Straight World (2:39)/
Sunday Dress (2:22)/ Teenage Whore (2:27)/
Love Away (3:28)/ Doll Parts (1:00)/ Take
Everything (3:33)/ I Will Stay (2:52)/ I'm So High
(Unreleased) (2:53)/ She Walks On Me (3:25)/
Stay Awhile (3:34)/ Rockstar (3:29)
R: Vg. Audience.   S: Live USA Oct. 23 '94.
C: ECD. Dcc. Pic CD.

7" - HIT ME PLEASE
S1: He Hit Me (And It felt Like A Kiss)
S2: Doll Parts
R: Ex. Soundboard.   S: Live radio broadcast.
C: USA. B&w sleeve. Yellow type. 45 RPM.

CD - MISS WORLD LIVE 1994
DEAD DOG RECORDS SE-465
Miss World/ Gutless/ Softer, Softest/ Doll Parts/
Beautiful Son/ Credit In The Straight World/
Teenage Whore/ Pennyroyal Tea/ Violet/ Beautiful
Son/ Miss World/ Jennifer's Body/ Asking For It/
Softer, Softest/ Credit In The Straight World/ P-
Girl/ Doll Parts
R: G-Vg. Audience.   S: Madison Square
Garden, New York 5/12/94.   C: ECD.
Time 66:25.

CD - THE PRINCESS OF LOVE
BANZI BZCD 066
Miss World/ Best Sunday Dress/ Softer, Softest/
Drown Soda/ He Hit Me (And I Felt Like A Kiss)/
Asking For It/ You're Got No Right/ Old Age/
Hungry Like A Wolf/ Doll Parts/ Sugar Come
R: Ex. Audience.   S: The Brooklyn Academy Of
Music, New York Feb. '95.   C: ECD. Dcc. Pic
CD. Time 46:20.

CD - RIOT GIRLS
OCTOPUS OCTO 184
Plump (2:53)/ Beautiful Son (4:23)/ Miss World (3:25)/ Jennifer's Body (4:00)/ Credit In The Straight World (2:51)/ Teenage Whore (2:39)/ Doll Parts (4:08)/ Violet (3:53)/ Plump (4:15)/ Beautiful Son (2:59)/ Miss World (3:17)/ Drown Soda (6:25)/ No No No (3:53)/ Asking For It (6:42)
R: Exs. Soundboard.   S: Tracks 1-8 The Palace, Melbourne, Australia Jan. '13 '95. Tracks 9-14 The Paradiso, Amsterdam, Holland Apr. 24 '95.   C: ECD. Dcc. Pic CD.

CD - ROCK'S BITCH
HOME RECORDS HR 6045-0
Plump (3:15)/ Beautiful Son (4:03)/ Miss World (2:59)/ Jennifer's Body (3:51)/ Asking For It (4:48)/ Gutless (5:07)/ Softer, Softest (3:37)/ I Think That I Would Die (3:56)/ Sunday Dress (2:22)/ Pretty On The Inside (4:13)/ Credit In The Straight World (2:34)/ Teenage Whore (3:35)/ Doll Parts (4:00)/ Violet (2:37)/ I Will Stay (3:24)/ In This Town (2:54)/ I'm So High (unreleased) (3:20)/ I Can't Live Without You (unreleased) (3:13)/ Crawl (unreleased) (4:00)
R: Ex. Audience.   S: The Orpheum, Boston, Mass. Dec. 4 '94.   C: ECD. Dcc. Pic CD.

CD - UGLY DEMENTED WORLD
OCTOPUS OCTO 069
Plump (2:38)/ Beautiful Son (3:49)/ Miss World (3:07)/ Jennifer's Body (3:55)/ Asking For It (4:26)/ Gutless (2:37)/ Softer, Softest (4:00)/ I Think That I Would Die (3:38)/ Credit In The Straight World (2:40)/ Teenage Whore (2:38)/ Doll Parts (3:50)/ Violet (3:49)/ Never Go Away (2:12)/ So High (3:25)/ Unreleased Track (2:57)/ Rock Star (5:31)/ Garbage Man (3:32)/ Baby Doll (8:48)
R: Ex. Audience.   S: Tracks 1-13 Europe '94. Tracks 14-16 Rendon Inn, New Orleans Oct. 29 '94. Tracks 17-18 California '91.   C: ECD. Dcc. Pic CD.

CD - UNPLUGGED AND UNLOVED
DALMATION RECORDS SPOT 002
Miss World/ Best Sunday Dress/ Softer, Softest/ Drown Soda/ He Hit Me (And It Felt Like A Kiss)/ Asking For It/ You've Got No Right/ Old Age/ Hungry Like A Wolf/ Doll Parts/ Sugar Coma/ Doll Parts/ He Hit Me (And It Felt Like A Kiss)/ Miss World/ Doll Parts/ Dicknail/ Burn Black/ Turpentine
R: Ex. Soundboard.   S: Tracks 1-11 MTV 'Unplugged' Feb. 14 '95. Tracks 12-14 'Later With Jools Holland'. Track 15 TOTP. Tracks 16-18 'Studio '90'.   C: ECD. Dbw. Red type. 75:24.

CD - UNWIRED
OCTOPUS OCTO 190
Miss World (3:17)/ Best Sunday Dress (3:11)/ Softer, Softest (3:47)/ Drown Soda (5:55)/ He Hit Me (And It Felt Like A Kiss) (3:30)/ Asking For It (5:03)/ You've Got No Right (4:32)/ Old Age (5:28)/ Hungry Like The Wolf (1:51)/ Doll Parts

(4:11)/ Sugar Coma (5:04)/ Plump (2:53)/ Sugar Coma (1:23)/ Miss World (3:49)/ Asking For It (5:45)/ Doll Parts (4:37)/ Violet (4:02)
R: Exs. Soundboard.   S: Tracks 1-11 The Brooklyn Academy Of Music, New York City Feb. 14 '95 during the 'Unplugged Session'. Tracks 12-17 The Universal Amphitheatre, Los Angeles, CA. Dec. 12 '94.   C: ECD.

CD - WHITE STEEL ROSE
FLASHBACK 05.95.0261
Plumb (2:34)/ Beautiful Son (3:44)/ Jennifer's Body (3:32)/ Miss World (2:42)/ Asking For It (4:30)/ Softer, Softest (3:34)/ Gutless (2:31)/ I Think That I Would Die (3:21)/ Hungry Like A Wolf (3:14)/ Credit In The Straight World (2:35)/ Best Sunday Dress (2:11)/ Teenage Whore (2:24)/ Love Away (3:25)/ Doll Parts (3:49)/ Violet (3:08)/ Sugar Coma (2:50)/ Old Age (2:51)/ She Walks On Me (3:22)/ Little While (2:33)/ Rock Star (4:21)
R: Ex. Audience.   S: Corey's Bar & Grill, Crystal, MN Oct. 23 '94.   C: ECD.

HOOTIE AND THE BLOWFISH

CD - BLOW FISH BLOW
PRINT 011/012
CD1: Hanna Jane/ Hey Little Girl/ I Go Blind/ Let Her Cry/ If You're Going My Way/ Not Even The Trees/ Fine Line In Between Right And Wrong/ Happy Birthday Mark Zeno/ Look Away/ Running From An Angel/ Motherless Child/ I'm Going Home/ When I Get To Heaven
CD2: Drowning/ Let My People Go/ Use Me/ Only Wanna Be With You/ Time/ Ziggy Stardust/ Mandy/ Hold My Hand/ Goodbye/ Love The One You're With
R: Exs. Soundboard.   S: Wetlands, New York City Nov. 30 '94.   C: ECD. Dcc.

CD - BLUE MIRAGE
OXYGEN OXY 001/2
CD1: Hanna Jane (3:47)/ You Got Me Screaming (4:14)/ I Go Blind (4:04)/ Let Her Cry (6:12)/ If You're Going My Way (3:48)/ Not Even The Trees (5:07)/ A Fine Line (5:13)/ Look Away (2:41)/ Running From An Angel (4:41)/ Motherless Child, I'm Going Home (6:32)/ The Old Man And Me (6:43)/ Drowning (7:52)/ Let My People Go (2:55)
CD2: Use Me (6:46)/ Only Wanna Be With You (4:11)/ Time (9:06)/ Ziggy Stardust (3:32)/ Mandy (1:06)/ Hold My Hand (8:52)/ Goodbye (6:01)/ Love The One You're With (9:58)/ Hannah Jane (3:29)/ Only Wanna Be With You (4:01)/ I'm Going Home (4:30)/ Hold My Hand (5:35)
R: Exs. Soundboard.   S: CD1 and CD2 Tracks 1-8 The Wetlands Theatre, NYC Sept. 30 '94. CD2 Tracks 9-12 The House Of Blues, Los Angeles Jan. 27 '95.   C: ECD. Dcc. Pic CD.

CD - ON THE LEFT COAST
KISS THE STONE KTS 407
Hannah Jane/ Only Wanna Be With You/ I'm Going Home/ Hold My Hand/ I Go Blind/ Let Her

Cry/ Look Away/ Time Drowning/ Acoustic Set:
Hannah Jane/ Hold My Hand/ Only Wanna Be
With You
R: Exs. Soundboard.   S: Tracks 1-4 The House
Of Blues, Los Angeles '94. Tracks 5-9 The Coast
House, San Juan Capistrano, CA Nov. 12 '94.
Tracks 10-12 acoustic live studio session.
C: ECD. Dcc. Pic CD. Time 50:54

HOT TUNA

CD - CATCHING TUNA IN NEW YORK
WONDER MINNOW WN1002
Invitation/ Bar Room Crystal Ball/ I Can't Be
Satisfied/ I Am The Light Of This World/ Serpent
Of Dreams/ It's So Easy/ Walkin' Blues/ Genesis/
Come Back Baby
R: Poor-G. Audience.   S: New York Queens
College, Queens, NY Nov. 11 '76.

CD - ROCK ME BABY
MAIN STREET MST 117
Intro Of The Band/ That'll Never Happen No
More/ How Long Blues/ Candyman/ Start/ Keep
Your Lamps Trimmed And Burning/ Uncle Sam
Ain't No Woman/ Something Cookin'/ Rock Me
Baby/ I Want You To Know/ Rider
R: Ex. Soundboard.   S: Fillmore West July 3
'71.   C: ECD. Dbw. Red type. Time 73:22.

HUMBLE PIE

CD - ROUTE 66
DYNAMITE STUDIO DS94J101/102
CD1: I Don't Need No Doctor/ In Fatuation/ 30
Days In A Hole/ Fool For a Pretty Face
CD2: Route 66/ Be Bop A Lula/ Tulsa Time/ Four
Day Creep/ Stone Cold Fever/ C'mon Everybody/
I Don't Need No Doctor
R: Vgs.   S: Country Club, Reseda, CA June 23
'73. CD2 4-7 Philadelphia '73.   C: Japanese.

INDIGO GIRLS

CD - DAYS OF WINE AND ROSES
TEDDY BEAR TB 65
The Wood Song (4:13)/ World Falls (3:38)/
Virginia Wolf (4:56)/ Dead Man's Hill (4:02)/
Power Of Two (4:38)/ Reunion (3:29)/ Language
Of The Kiss (5:12)/ Least Complicated (3:58)/
This Train Revised (3:51)/ Ghost (5:20)/ Kid Fears
(4:42)/ Gallies (4:19)/ Southern Man (5:25)/
Closer To Me (4:13)
R: Vg. Audience.   S: Radio City Music Hall,
NYC June 28 '94.   C: ECD. Dcc. Pic CD.

INFEST

7" - NOT OVER YET
S1: Sick Of Talk/ Life's Hault/ The End

S2: Dirty Dope Dealer/ Son Of The Sun/ Going
R: G. Audience.   C: USA. Black/white/red
sleeve. 45 RPM.

INSTEAD

7" - WE'LL BE REMEMBERED
S1: It's Up To You/ Your Choice/ Never Last/
United
S2: Proud Youth/ Keep The Faith/ Don't Give Up
R: Vg-Ex. Soundboard.   S: Demos.   C: USA.
Yellow/black sleeve. Limited edition of 600 on
blue and yellow vinyl. 33 RPM.

IRON MAIDEN

CD - ECATOMBE
BABY CAPONE 007/2
CD1: Moonchild (6:30)/ The Evil That Me Do
(4:42)/ Prisoner (5:39)/ Still Life (4:29)/ Die With
Your Boots On (6:32)/ Infinite Dreams (5:49)/
Killers (5:30)/ Can I Play With Madness (5:30)/
Heaven Can Wait (3:58)/ Wasted Years (4:53)/
The Clairvoyant (6:11)/ Seventh Son Of A 7th Son
(10:32)/ The Number Of The Beast (4:27)
CD2: Hallowed Be Thy Name (7:35)/ Iron Maiden
(4:37)/ Aces High (5:31)/ Two Minutes To Midnight
(6:27)/ Trooper (4:46)/ Revelations (6:14)/ Flight
Of Icarus (5:38)/ Rime Of The Ancient Mariner
(5:02)/ Powerslave (8:27)/ Run To The Hills
(3:53)/ Running Free (9:44)/ Sanctuary (6:31)
R: Exs. Soundboard.   S: Live USA and Japan
during '88 world tour.   C: ECD. Dcc. Pic CD.

CD - THE ETERNAL FLAME
OXYGEN OXY 029
Man On The Edge (4:15)/ Wrathchild (2:49)/
Heaven Can't Wait (7:33)/ Lord Of The Flies
(5:27)/ Afraid To Shoot Strangers (6:45)/ The Evil
That Men Do (5:26)/ The Aftermath (3:06)/ Sign
Of The Cross (9:36)/ Iron Maiden (3:19)/ Man On
The Edge (4:06)/ Wrathchild (2:46)/ Heaven Can
Wait (8:18)/ Fortunes Of War (7:10)
R: Exs. Soundboard.   S: Tracks 1-9 The Karen,
Gothenburg, Sweden Nov. 1 '95. Tracks 10-13
The 'Barrowlands', Glasgow, Scotland Nov. 5 '95.
C: ECD. Dcc. Pic CD.

CD - HEAVY USERS OF POWER
BANG! BANG-016
Wrathchild/ Purgatory/ Sanctuary/ Remember
Tomorrow/ Another Life, Drum Solo/ Genghis
Kahn/ Killers/ Innocent Exile/ Twilight Zone/
Strange World/ Murders In The Rue Morgue/
Phantom Of The Opera/ Iron Maiden/ Running
Free/ Transylvania, Guitar Solo/ Drifter
R: Good.   S: Sun Plaza Hall, Tokyo, Japan
May 24 '81.

THE METAL YEARS: 1978-1983
KOBRA RECORDS KRHM 003
Iron Maiden/ Invasion/ Prowler/ Iron Maiden/
Running Free/ Transylvania/ Sanctuary/ Women
In Uniform/ I've Got The Fire/ Twilight Zone/

Wrathchild/ Killers/ The Trooper/ Revelations/ Flight Of Icarus/ 22, Acacia Avenue/ The Number Of The Beast
R: Ex. Soundboard. Tracks 10-12 Vg. Soundboard.   S: Tracks 1-3 demos, Spaceward Studios, Cambridge, England Dec. 30 '78 - issued as a limited edition 7" called 'The Soundhouse Tapes'. Tracks 4-7 BBC Sessions, London, England Dec. 14 '79. Tracks 8-9 'Top Of The Pops', London, England Feb. 10 '80. Tracks 10-12 first demo-tape with Bruce Dickinson, London, England Sept. '81. Tracks 13-17 'H.M. For X-Mas Festival', Dortmund, Germany Dec. 18 '83.
C: ECD. Dcc. Time 69:05.

IVEY'S, THE

CD - SOMEDAY WE'LL BE KNOWN - 1968 DEMO TAPE
SPANK RECORDS SP 142 CD
I Believe (version 1)/ The French Song (In A Taxi)/ Harmonizing/ 'I Hope You Win Something On Bingo'/ Man Without A Heart/ The Girl Next Door In A Miniskirt/ Turn On Your Lovin' Mood/ It Takes So Long/ Unknown Title (acoustic guitar)/ Handsome Malcolm/ Hey Baby/ The Leaves (acoustic version 1)/ The Leaves (acoustic version 2)/ The Leaves (acoustic version 3)/ The Leaves (piano version 1)/ The Leaves (piano version 2)/ The Leaves (piano version 3)/ Mr. Strangeways/ I'll Kiss You Goodnight/ Sausage And Egg/ Handsome Malcolm/ Another Day/ I Believe (version 2)/ Love Hurts/ For My Sympathy (acetate)/ Maybe Tomorrow (mono single mix)/ And Her Daddy's A Millionaire/ Dear Angie/ No Escaping Your Love/ Storm In A Teacup (mono EP mix)/ Sali Boo (with Wah-Wah guitar intro)
R: G-Vg.   S: Tracks 1-24 Ivey's demos '68. Track 26 demo acetate ' 68. Tracks 26 and 27 Apple single Jan. '69. Tracks 28 and 29 Apple single July '69. Track 30 is from Wall's Ice Cream EP July '69. Track 31 from Apple LP July '69.
C: Time 59:13.

J

JAGGER, MICK

CD - STONE ALONE
TNT STUDIO TNT-940141/42
CD1: Honky Tonk Woman/ Throwaway/ Bitch/ Let's Spend The Night Together/ Lonely At The Top/ Beast Of Burden/ Tumblin' Dice/ Miss You/ Ruby Tuesday/ Just Another Night/ War Baby/ 4 other tracks
CD2: Party Doll/ You Can't Always Get What You Want/ Radio Control/ Shoot Off Your Mouth/ Simon Phillips Drum Solo/ Gimme Shelter/ Start Me Up/ Brown Sugar/ It's Only Rock'N'Roll/ Jumpin' Jack Flash/ 2 other tracks
R: Poor audience recording.   S: Osaka-Jo Hall, Osaka, Japan Mar. 15 '88. CD1 tracks 13-14 and

CD2 tracks 10-12 Mar. 18 '88.   C: Japanese.

CD - THROUGH THE YEARS
THE SWINGIN' PIG TSP 191
Deep Down Under (tour rehearsals '88)/ Around And Around (Paard van Troje Club, Den Haag '82 with George Thorogood)/ Let It Rock-Back In The USA, Lonely At The Top (Live Aid Concert, Philadelphia '85)/ Just Another Night, Miss You, State Of Shock-It's Only Rock'n'Roll, Honky Tonk Women (tour rehearsals Los Angeles '87 with Jeff Beck)/ Sympathy For The Devil, Dead Flowers, Shine A Light, Little Red Rooster, Memory Motel (solo recording '89)/ No Expectations (live with Lenny Kravitz '91)/ Sweet Thing (Saturday Night Live TV Show '93)/ Don't Tear Me Up, Stomp (tour rehearsals '88)
R: Ex.   C: ECD.

CD - WEBSTER HALL 1993
IDOL MIND PRO. IMP-CD-028
Wired All Night/ Out Of Focus/ Sweet Thing/ Use Me/ Don't Tear Me Up/ Evening Gown/ Angel In My Heart/ Introductions/ Wandering Spirit/ Put Me In the Trash/ Think/ Mother Of A Man/ Rip This Joint/ Live With Me/ Have You Seen Your Mother, Baby, Standing In The Shadow?
R: Poor audience recording.   S: Webster Hall, New York Feb. 9 '93.   C: Japanese CD.

JAM, THE

CD - BORED WITH THE U.S.A.
AMERICAN FLY AF009
Saturdays Kids (3:00)/ Burning Sky (3:06)/ Thick As Thieves (3:46)/ It's Too Bad (2:53)/ Going Underground (3:10)/ Mr. Clean (3:40)/ The Butterfly Collector (3:12)/ Private Hell (3:38)/ Smithers - Jones (3:03)/ The Dreams Of Children (2:43)/ To Be Someone Must Be A Wonderful Thing (3:50)/ The Eton Rifles (3:50)/ Strange Town (3:40)/ When You're Young (2:58)/ Down To The Station At Midnight (4:26)/ Girl On The Phone (2:47)/ All Mod Cons (1:35)/ David Watts (3:41)/ 'A' Bomb In Wardour Street (2:47)/ Boy About Town (1:58)/ Monday (2:48)/ Pretty Green (2:53)/ A Man In The Corner Shop (3:20)/ Start (2:26)
R: Exs. Soundboard.   S: USA '79.   C: ECD. Dcc. Pic CD.

CD - DAVID WATTS AND POLKADOTS
HEATWAVE RECORDS HEAT 021
Modern World/ Sounds From The Street/ Away From The Numbers/ All Mod Cons/ To Be Someone/ It's Too Bad/ Mr. Clean/ Billy Hunt/ In The Street Today/ Standards/ Tonight At Noon/ Down At The Tube Station/ News Of The World/ Weekend/ Bricks & Mortar/ Batman Theme/ The Place I Love/ David Watts/ Heatwave/ 'A' Bomb In Wardour Street
R: Vg-Ex.   S: Reading University, UK Feb. 16 '79.   C: ECD. Dcc. Time 59:12.

CD - SET THE SKIES ABLAZE
KISS THE STONE KTS 387
Dreamtime/ Thick As Thieves/ Boy About Town/
Going Underground/ Pretty Green/ The Man In
The Cornershop/ Set The House Ablaze/ Private
Hell/ Liza Radley/ Dreams Of Children/ The
Modern World/ Little Boy Soldiers/ But I'm
Different Now/ Start/ Scrape Away/ Strange Town/
When You're Young/ In The City/ To Be Someone/
David Watts/ Eton Rifles/ Down In The Tube
Station At Midnight
R: Exs. Soundboard.   S: 'Sound Affects'
European tour Nov. '80'.   C: ECD. Dcc. Pic CD.
Time 73:05.

JANE'S ADDICTION

CD - INVITATION TO DREAM
BABY CAPONE BC 048/2
CD1: Been Caught Stealing (remix) (4:22)/ Had A
Dad (demo - unreleased) (3:51)/ LA Medley: LA
Woman, Nausea, Lexicon Devil, (Jacksonville,
Florida '91) (3:43)/ Had A Dad (Jacksonville '91)
(4:58)/ I Would For You (demo - unreleased)
(3:26)/ Jane Says (demo - unreleased) (4:52)/ No
One's Leaving (Indianapolis '91) (3:15)/ Ain't No
Right (Indianapolis '91) (3:08)/ No One's Leaving
(Irvine Meadows '91) (3:55)/ Ain't No Right (Irvine
Meadows '91) (2:58)/ Three Days (Irvine
Meadows '91) (12:33)/ Been Caught Stealing
(Irvine Meadows '91) (4:24)/ Had A Dad (Irvine
Meadows '91) (5:08)/ Trip Away (Irvine Meadows
'91) (4:26)/ Of Course (Irvine Meadows '91)
(8:42)/ Classic Girl (Irvine Meadows '91) (4:45)
CD2: Up The Beach (5:09)/ Whores (4:13)/
Standing In The Shower, Thinking (3:21)/ Ain't No
Right (5:18)/ Three Days (12:05)/ Been Caught
Stealing (4:27)/ Obvious (6:08)/ Trip Away (4:36)/
Then She Did (9:53)/ Mountain Song (4:21)/ Stop!
(5:23)/ Jane Says (6:29)/ Chip Away (3:31)
R: Ex.   S: CD2 live '91.   C: ECD. Dcc.
Pic CDs.

CD - SEX 'N' DRUGS 'N' ROCK 'N' ROLL
BLUE MOON BMCD36
Up The Beach/ Whores/ Standing In The
Shower...Thinking/ Ain't No Right/ Summertime
Rolls/ Been Caught Stealing/ 1%/ Chip Away/
Ted, Just Admit It/ Thank You Boys/ Three Days/
Mountain Song/ Stop!
R: Ex. Soundboard.   S: Lollapalooza,
Washington, DC Aug. 16 '91.   C: ECD. 74:02.

JEFFERSON AIRPLANE, THE

CD - GLIDIN' OVER FILLMORE EAST
MAIN STREET MST 107
New Song For Morning/ Man's Fate/ Have You
Seen The Saucers?/ 3/5 Of A Mile In Ten
Seconds/ We Can Be Together/ Volunteers/
Somebody To Love/ Wooden Ships/ Mexico/
Uncle Sam's Blues/ Emergency/ Crown Of
Creation Total
R: Ex. Soundboard.   S: Fillmore East May 15

'70.   C: ECD. Dcc. Time 73:37.

JESUS AND MARY CHAIN

CD - FEEDBACK
LAST BOOTLEG RECORDS LBR012
In A Hole (3:12)/ The Hardest Walk (2:37)/ Fall
(2:52)/ Some Candy Talking (4:33)/ Cherry Came
Too (3:50)/ Everything's Alright When You Are
Down (2:42)/ Just Like Honey (2:58)/ Happy
When It Rains (4:00)/ Deep One Perfect Morning
(2:56)/ Nine Million Rainy Days (4:35)/ April Skies
(4:16)/ Kill Surf City (3:50)/ Bo Diddley Is Jesus
(2:30)
R: Ex. Soundboard.   S: Live '87.   C: ECD.
Dcc. Pic CD. Time 45:00.

JETHRO TULL

CD - A NEW DAY YESTERDAY
GOLD STANDARD JT-24-94-08
So Much Trouble/ Song For Jeffrey/ My Sunday
Feeling/ Beggar's Farm/ Love Story/ Stormy
Monday/ Dharma For One/ Living In The Past/ A
New Day Yesterday/ Fat Man/ Nothing Is Easy/
Bouree/ Witches Promise/ Nothing Is Easy/ For A
Thousand Mothers/ Back To The Family/ Sweet
Dreams/ Instrumental 1968
R: Ex. Soundboard.   S: Tracks 1-3 BBC 'Top
Gear' Sept. 22 '68. Tracks 4-6 BBC 'Top Gear'
Nov. 5 '68. Tracks 8-10 BBC 'Top Gear' June 22
'69. Tracks 11-13 BBC 'Top Of The Pops' '69.
Tracks 14, 16 Newport Pop Festival June 21 '69.
Track 15 Fillmore East '70. Tracks 17-18 BBC
Radio '68.   C: Dcc. Time 73:58.

CD - OUT OF EGYPT
ALL OF THE WORLD AOTW94001/002
CD1: Opening/ Sweet Dream/ Thick As A Brick/
Queen And Country/ Passion Play/ Skating Away
On The Thin Ice Of The New Day
CD2: My God, God Rest Merry Gentleman,
Bouree, Keyboard Solo/ Cross Eyed Mary/ For A
Thousand Mothers/ Drum Solo/ Aqualung/
Backdoor Angels/ Locomotive Breath.
R: G. Audience.   S: Osaka Aug. 21 '74.

CD - UTRECHT 1993
BLACK EAGLE BE 001/2
CD1: Intro/ My Sunday Feeling/ For A Thousand
Mothers/ Instrumental/ Living In The Past/
Bouree/ So Much Trouble/ With You There To
Help Me/ Instrumental/ Black Sunday/ Sossity,
You're A Woman/ Reasons For Waiting/ Songs
From The Wood/ Later That Same Evening/ Life
Is A Long Song/ Thick As A Brick/ Andy Giddin's
Parrot
CD2: Budapest/ A New Day Yesterday/
Instrumental/ Farm On The Freeway/ This Is Not
Love/ Aqualung/ Locomotive Breath/ Cross-Eyed
Mary (encore)/ Dharma For One (encore)
R: G. Audience.   S: Vredenburg, Utrech June
17 '93.   C: ECD. Dcc. Pic CD.

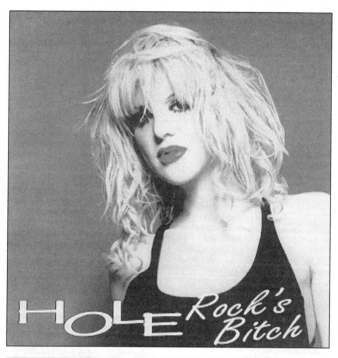

JETT, JOAN AND THE BLACK HEARTS

CD - BLACK LEATHER
NOW ROSE 003
Bad Reputation/ (I'm Gonna) Run Away/ Woolly Bully/ Bits And Pieces/ You Don't Know What You've Got/ Love Is Pain/ I Love Playing With Fire/ Wait For Me/ Victim Of Circumstance/ Oh Woe Is Me/ You're Too Possessive/ I Love Rock N' Roll/ Nag/ Black Leather/ Do You Wanna Touch Me/ Star Star/ Shout/ Rebel Rebel
R: Exs. Soundboard.   S: Tokyo NHK Hall Dec. 4 '82.

JOHN, ELTON

CD - EUROPE 1993
GOLDEN STARS GSCD 2308
CD1: Take Me To The Pilot (4:13)/ Empty Garden (4:53)/ Simple Life (5:40)/ The One (6:08)/ Come Down In Time (3:20)/ Sorry Seems To Be the Hardest Word (4:10)/ Captain Fantastic And The Brown Dirt Cowboy (6:03)/ The Last Song (3:42)/ Loves Lies Bleeding (10:28)/ Rocket Man, I Think It's Going To Be A Long, Long Time (12:08)
CD2: Bennie And The Jets (9:19)/ Sad Song (12:57)/ The Show Must Go On (3:55)/ Saturday Night Is Alright For Fighting (6:01)/ Don't Let The Sun Go Down On Me (5:29)/ Jumpin' Jack Flash (5:30)/ Your Song (4:21)/ Sacrifice (5:14)/ Candle In The Wind (4:15)
R: Ex.   S: Earl Court Arena, London '93.
C: ECD.

CD - FIRST VISIT 1971
M-9501/2
CD1: You Need To Turn It/ Your Song/ Rock Me When He's Gone/ Come Down In Time/ Skyline Pigeon/ Rotten Peaches/ In Sunset/ Introduction/ Ballad Of A Well Known Gun/ Friends/ King Must Die/ Holiday Inn/ Can I Put You On/ Country Comfort/
CD2: Honky Tonk Women/ Life Is Sometimes Very Difficult/ Mad Man Across The Water/ Amoreena/ Take Me To The Pilot/ Piano Solo/ My Baby Left Me/ Instrumental/ Whole Lotta Shakin' Goin' On
R: Ex. Soundboard.   S: Oct. 11 '71.
C: Japanese CD. Dcc.

CD - LORD CHOC ICE GOES MENTAL
EXX-ELLENT EXX 52514-2
CD1: Highlander (2:00)/ Tonight (7:01)/ One Horse Town (5:51)/ Better Off Dead (3:02)/ Rocket Man (5:46)/ Honky Cat (5:45)/ Burn Down The Mission (5:39)/ Someone Saved My Life Tonight (6:51)/ The Bitch Is Back (3:42)/ Medley: Song For You, Blue Eyes, I Guess That's Why They Call It The Blues (8:01)/ Restless (5:32)/ Passengers (4:26)/ Bennie And The Jets (6:28)
CD2: Sad Songs (Say So Much) (7:16)/ Shoot Down The Moon (5:01)/ This Town (4:17)/ Nikita (5:54)/ I'm Still Standing (5:33)/ Your Song (4:03)/ Wrap Her Up (5:08)/ Candle In The Wind (4:51)/

Can I Get A Witness? (3:50)
R: Ex. Audience.   S: Wembley Arena, London Dec.14 '85.   C: ECD. Dcc.

CD - 21 YEARS OF FUN
JAG 003/2
CD1: Funeral Of A Friend (4:48)/ Love Lies Bleeding (7:13)/ Candle In The Wind (4:28)/ Hercules (8:40)/ Rocket Man (5:26)/ Bernie And The Jets (5:57)/ Daniel (4:09)/ Honky Cat (7:30)/ Goodbye Yellow Brick Road (3:18)
CD2: All The Young Girls Love Alice (7:40)/ Crocodile Rock (4:34)/ Elderberry Wine (5:33)/ Lucy In The Sky With Diamonds (5:32)/ Don't Let The Sun Go (5:30)/ Skyline Pigeon (4:00)/ Your Sing (4:21)/ Saturday Night's Alright For Fighting (8:06)/ Concert Rehearsal: This Song Has No Title (2:41)/ Ballad Of Danny Bailey (6:34)/ Instrumental (1:53)/ I've Seen That Movie Too (5:38)/ Lady Samantha (BBC Session '69 - 3:04)
R: Exs. Soundboard.   S: Hammersmith Odeon, London Dec. 22 '73.   C: ECD. Dcc. Pic CD.

JUDAS PRIEST

CD - GENOCIDE
BONDAGE MUSIC BON 037
White Heat, Red Hot/ Victim Of Changes/ Beyond The Realms Of Death/ Genocide/ Tyrant/ White Heat, Red Hot/ Starbreaker/ Beyond The Realms Of Death
R: Vg-Ex. Soundboard.   S: Kosei-Nenkin Hall, Tokyo July 7 '78. Tracks 6-8 Cleveland, Ohio '78. C: Japanese CD. Dcc. Pic CD. Time 58:22.

K

KING, B.B. AND RAY CHARLES

CD - LIVE IN MILANO
FU 206/2
CD1: B.B. KING: Intro/ When Love Comes Into Town (5:10)/ Wake Up This Morning (8:10)/ Please Send Me Someone To Love (4:10)/ Since I Meet You Baby (4:13)/ Don't Be Untreated Baby (2:32)/ Ain't Nobody's Business If I Do (2:56)/ Sweet Sixteen (8:40)/ The Thrill Is Gone (4:42)/ Crew For The Bus, Peace To The World (9:15)
CD2: RAY CHARLES: Intro/ Let The Good Time Roll (2:55)/ Busted (2:18)/ Georgia On My Mind (5:30)/ I'm Gonna Move To The Outskirt Of Town (2:53)/ Just For A Thrill (6:00)/ Teardrops From My Eyes (3:38)/ Ellie, My Love So Sweet (5:10)/ Gotta Move (7:20)/ I Can't Stop Loving You (3:35)/ What'd I Say (4:25)/ RAY CHARLES & B.B. KING: Intro/ It's Time For Me To Close The Show/ I Get The Blues/ Outro (9:18)
R: Ex. Audience.   S: Palatrussardi, Milano Nov. 8 '90.   C: ECD. With Philip Morris Superband.

KING CRIMSON

CD - CELEBRATION OF THE LIZARD
GOLD STANDARD KC-21-94-05
Introduction/ Pictures Of A City/ Formentara Lady/
The Devils Triangle/ Cirkus/ Panaemonia/ 21st
Century Schizoid Man/ Celebration Of The Lizard/
Cadence And Cascade
R: Vg.   S: The Orpheum Theatre, Boston
Mar. 27 '72.

CD - COMPLETE WOLVERHAMPTON
ZA 57/58
CD1: Pictures Of A City/ Cirkus/ Formentera
Lady/ Sailor's Tale/ The Letters/ Cadence And
Cascade
CD2: Ladies Of The Road/ Groon, Drum Solo/
21st Century Schizoid Man/ Devil's Triangle
R: G. Audience.   S: Wolverhampton, UK Sept.
10 '71.   C: Japanese CD. Dcc.

CD - DARK KINGDOM
TARANTURA TUDCD 001
Picture Of City/ Cadence And Cascade/ Groon/
21st Century Schizoid Man/ Walli In K.F.L./ The
Sailors Tale
R: Vg sound, some background noise.   S: KFL
Studio, Denver, Colorado Mar. 13 '72.
C: Japanese CD.

CD - THE DEATH SEED
KC-007
The Great Deceiver/ Doctor Diamond/ Exiles/
Lament/ Easy Money/ Fracture/ Starless/ The
Talking Drum Lark's Tongues In Aspic, Part Two/
21st Century Schizoid Man
R: Good sound.   S: Hollywood Sportatorium,
Miami, FL Apr. 20 '74.

CD - FRACTURE
GOLD STANDARD ZA 31
Fracture/ Easy Money/ Improvisation/ The
Nightwatch/ Dr. Diamond/ Starless/ The Talking
Drum/ Lark's Tongue In Aspic 2/ 21st Century
Schizoid Man
R: Vg. Audience.   S: The Felt Forum, NYC May
1 '74.   C. Japanese CD. Dcc. Time 66:04.

CD - INDIE VROOM
KC 201/2
CD1: Vroom/ Code: Marine 475/ Frame By
Frame/ Dinosaur/ One Time/ Red/ B'Boom/
Thrack/ Matte Kudasai/ Sex Sleep Eat Drink
Dream/ People/ Vroom Vroom/ Indiscipline
CD2: Elephant Talk/ B'Bish (Unreleased Track)/
Talking Drum/ Lark's Tongues In Aspic Part Two/
Dinosaur/ Walking On Air/ Yamahashi Blues/
Melrose Avenue/ Train To Lamy Suite/ Punta
Patri/ The Good The Bad The Ugly/ Untitled/
Toccata And Fugue In D Minor
R: Vg-Ex. Audience.   S: Italy May 2 '95.
C: ECD. Dcc. Time CD1 71:25. CD2 62:42.

CD - LADY SUPERMARKET IN SAN FRANCISCO
ZA-15
Lark's Tongue In Aspic Part 1 (9:50)/ Easy Money
(5:52)/ The Night Watch (3:58)/ Lament (4:09)/
Cat Food (4:27)/ Exiles (5:53)/ Fracture (12:38)/
Lark's Tongue In Aspic Part 2 (6:14)/ 21st Century
Schizoid Man (9:07)
R: G. Audience.   S: Cow Palace Theater, San
Francisco June 13 '74.   C: Japanese CD. Dcc.
Time 62:14.

CD - LIVROOM
K-IN-G 001/002
CD1: Vroom/ Frame By Frame/ Dinosaur/ One
Time/ Red/ B'Boom, Thrak/ Matt'e Kudasai
CD2: Sex, Sleep, Eat, Drink, Dream/ People Are
The Mainspring/ Vroom/ Elephant Talk/
Indiscipline/ B'Bish, Talking Drum/ Lark's Tongue
In Aspic/ Walking On Air
R: Ex. Audience.   S: Royal Albert Hall, London,
England May 17 '95.   C: ECD. Time CD1 47:45.
CD2 51:24.

CD - MIAMI BOUND
ZA-50
Pictures Of A City/ Formentara Lady/ Sailor's
Tale/ Cirkus/ Ladies Of The Road/ Groon Part 1/
Groon Part 2, Drum Solo/ 21st Century Schizoid
Man/ Miami Bound/ Cadence And Cascade
R: Poor. Audience.   S: Malibu Beach Feb. 5 '72.
C: Japanese CD.

CD - THE MINCER - FROM NY TO DETROIT
KC-001/002
CD1: Doctor Diamond/ Lark's Tongues In Aspic,
Part 1/ Easy Money/ Improvisation/ Exiles/ Book
Of Saturday/ Talking Drum Lark's Tongues In
Aspic, Part 2/ 21st Century Schizoid Man
CD2: Lark's Tongues In Aspic, Part 1/ Easy
Money/ Improvisation, Drum Solo, Talking Rhythm
Box/ Book Of Saturday/ The Talking Drum/ Lark's
Tongues In Aspic, Part 2, 21st Century Schizoid
Man
R: Vg sound.   S: CD1 Academy Of Music, NY
Apr. 28 '73. CD2 Masonic Temple, Detroit
May 8 '73.

CD - NEURO-SURGEONS
KC-009
Doctor Diamond/ Lark's Tongues In Aspic, Part
One/ Easy Money/ Improvisation/ Exiles/
Improvisation/ The Talking Drum/ Lark's Tongues
In Aspic, Part Two/ 21st Century Schizoid Man
R: Vg audience recording.   S: Palace Theatre,
Waterbury, Conn. May 6 '73.

CD - PRISM SHIP
KC-011
21st Century Schizoid Man/ Get My Bearing/ In
The Court Of The Crimson King/ Travel Weary
Capricorn/ Mars
R: Vg-Ex.   S: Plumpton Festival, England
Aug. 9 '69.

CD - THE ULTIMATE LIVE RARITIES VOL. 1
MY PHENIX ZA 21
Book Of Saturday/ Improvisation 1/ Exiles/ Easy
Money/ Improvisation 2/ The Talking Drum/ Lark's
Tongue In Aspic Part 2/ 21st Century Schizoid
Man
R: Poor-G. Audience.   S: Portsmouth, UK Dec.
15 '72.   C: Japanese CD. Time 63:21.

CD - THE ULTIMATE LIVE RARITIES VOL. 2
MY PHENIX ZA 22
Lark's Tongue In Aspic Part 1/ Dialogue/ Book Of
Saturday/ Improvisation/ Exiles/ Improvisation*
R: Poor. Audience.   S: Oxford, UK Nov. 25 '72.
*Bremen, Germany Oct. 17 '72.   C: Japanese
CD. Time 69:30.

KISS

CD - CARNIVAL
HOME RECORDS HR6013-5
Creature Of The Night (4:48)/ Deuce (3:29)/
Parasite (3:37)/ Fire House (4:34)/ Dr. Love
(3:07)/ Take It Off (5:40)/ Domino (4:05)/ Love
Gun (4:25)/ Lick It Up (4:12)/ Love It Loud (3:13)/
Detroit Rock City (4:59)/ Heavens On Fire (5:26)
R: Ex. Soundboard.   S: Sao Paul, Brazil July 28
'94.   C: ECD. Dcc.

CD - COMIN' HOME TO NEW YORK CITY 95
MASQUERADE RECORDS
Comin' Home/ Plaster Caster/ Goin' Blind/
Domino/ Nothin' To Loose/ Sure Know Something/
Calling Dr. Love/ Take Me/ Mr. Speed/ C'Mon And
Love Me/ Spit/ I Still Love You/ God Of Thunder/
Christeene Sixteen/ Love Theme From Kiss/ See
You Tonight/ Goodbye/ 100,00 Years/ Two Times/
Hard Luck Woman/ Surprise Bonus Track I (Live
USA)/ Surprise Bonus Track II (Live USA)
R: G-Vg. Audience.   S: New York City July 30,
'95.   C: ECD. Dcc. Pic CD. Time 78:27.

CD - DEMOS 1981-1983
BOLD MOVE RECORDS BM-CD2953
Boys Wanna Rock/ It's So Pretty/ Gypsy In Her
Eyes/ Back On The Streets/ I'm In Love/ Your
Baby/ The Unknown Force (Instrumental)/
Heaven/ Young And Restless/ A World Without
Heroes/ The Council Of The Elder/ Don't Run/
You/ Lick It Up/ Young And Wasted/ Fits Like A
Glove/ Fits Like A Glove/ A Million To One/ Exciter
(instrumental)
R: Poor-G. Some G-Vg. Soundboard.
S: Demos '81-'83. Tracks 1-6, 9 and 13 feature
vocals by Vinnie Vincent. Tracks 1-2, 5-6, 9, 13-
19 from 'Lick It Up' demos '83. Tracks 3-4 from
'Creatures Of The Night' demos '82. Tracks 7-8,
10-12 from 'Music From The Elder Demos' '81.
C: ECD. Dcc. Pic CD. Time 67:19.

CD - DIE-HARD
OXYGEN OXY 014
Coming Home (2:58)/ Plaster Easter (3:51)/ Do
You Love Me? (3:45)/ Goin' Blind (3:56)/ Black
Diamond (3:47)/ Hide Your Heart (4:57)/ Domino
(4:10)/ Sure Know Something (4:26)/ God Of
Thunder (2:14)/ Strange Ways (1:33)/ Shock Me
(2:16)/ World Without Heroes (3:14)/ Hard Luck
Woman (3:29)/ Calling Dr. Love (3:16)/ Rock
Bottom (3:30)/ Charisma (2:34)/ C'Mon And Love
Me (3:23)/ Everytime I Look At You (4:59)/ Take
Me (3:18)/ Let's Put The X In Sex (4:06)/ Lady
(3:53)
R: Exs. Soundboard.   S: Acoustic set,
Monroeville Expo Market, Pittsburgh Aug. 1 '95.
C: ECD. Dcc. Pic CD.

CD - FUEGO EN BUENOS AIRES
OCTOPUS OCTO 066/067
CD1: Intro, Love Gun (4:26)/ Deuce (4:00)/
Parasite (5:14)/ Unholy (3:40)/ 100,00 Years
(5:23)/ Cold Gin (5:45)/ Watchin' You (3:40)/
Firehouse (4:26)/ I Want You (6:48)/ I Was Made
For Lovin' You (4:37)/ Calling Dr. Love (3:06)/
Makin' Love (3:33)/ Domino (3:58)/ Tears Are
Falling (4:03)/ War Machine (4:14)
CD2: Lick It Up (6:10)/ Forever (4:02)/ Creature
Of The Night (4:23)/ I Love It Loud (4:08)/ Detroit
Rock City (5:22)/ Strutter (4:19)/ She (5:51)/ Soy
Kissero (3:10)/ La Bamba (1:20)/ Black Diamond
(7:22)/ Heaven's On Fire (4:19)/ Rock And Roll All
Nite (6:04)
R: Ex. Audience.   S: Argentina Sept. 16 '94.
C: ECD. Dcc. Pic CDs.

LP - KISS OF DEATH
PAX GERMANIC RECS.
S1: Cold Gin, Bang Bang You (11:00)/ Heavens
On Fire (4:09)/ Whole Lotta Love (9:57)/ Detroit
Rock City (4:06)
S2: Creatures Of The Night (4:08)/ Fits Like A
Glove (4:58)/ Thrills In The Night (4:38)/ Guitar
Solo, Under The Gun, War Machine (8:50)
R: Exs.   S: St. Paul Dec. 1 '87.   C: Eb. Dbw.
Red vinyl.

CD - 'MAMA WEER ALL CRAZZE NOW'
PLAIN OLD STEREO KR 9047
Mama Weer All Crazee Now (Slade - fades in)/
Detroit Rock City/ Take Me/ Let Me Go Rock N'
Roll/ Ladies Room/ Firehouse/ Makin' Love/ I
Want You/ Cold Gin/ Do You Love Me/ Nothin' To
Lose/ God Of Thunder/ Rock And Roll All Nite/
Shout It Out Loud/ Beth/ Black Diamond
R: Poor-G.   S: Budo Kan Hall, Tokyo Apr. 1 '77.
C: Japanese CD. Dcc. Time 65:43.

CD - PETER GENE PAUL AND ACE
INSECT RECORDS IST 26/2
CD1: Deuce (3:36)/ Strutter (3:15)/ She (6:14)/
Firehouse (4:19)/ Nothin' To Loose (4:31)/ Cold
Gin (3:44)/ 100 000 Years (5:18)/ Black Diamond
(6:00)/ Let Me Go, Rock N' Roll (5:02)/ Deuce
(3:50)/ Strutter (4:19)/ She (6:15)
CD2: Firehouse (4:35)/ Love Theme From Kiss
(2:34)/ You're Much Too Young (3:19)/ Let Me
Know (3;22)/ Black Diamond (5:49)/ Let Me Go,
Rock N' Roll (6:41)/ Deuce (3:52)/ Nothin' To

Loose (3:59)/ She (6:36)/ Firehouse (4:03)/ Strutter (5:35)/ 100 000 Years (4:45)/ Black Diamond (4:47)
R: G-Vg.   S: CD1 tracks 1-9 Detroit Apr. 7 '74. CD1 tracks 10-12 and CD2 tracks 1-6 Washington DC July 14 '74. Tracks 7-13 Long Beach, CA May 3 '74.   C: ECD. Dcc.

CD - ROCK AND ROLL PARTY 1978
CACKER CR-9-1-2
CD1: I Stole Your Love/ King Of The Night Time World/ Ladies Room/ Firehouse/ Love Gun/ Let Me Go Rock 'N' Roll/ Makin' Love/ Christine Sixteen/ Shock Me-Guitar Solo/ I Want You/ Calling Dr. Love/ Shout
CD2: God Of Thunder, Drum Solo/ Rock And Roll All Nite/ Detroit Rock City/ Beth/ Black Diamond/ Do You Love Me/ Flaming Youth/ God Of Thunder (Instrumental Version)/ None Of Your Business/ Great Expectations
R: Live - Poor-G. Audience. Studio - Poor-G. Soundboard. Hiss.   S: CD1 and CD2 tracks 1-5 Mar. 31 '78. CD2 tracks 6-10 'Destroyer' demo. C: Japanese CD. Dcc. Time CD1 55:35. CD2 52:51.

CD - ROCKIN' IN CHILE
KISS THE STONE KTS 411/12
CD1: Creatures Of The Night/ Deuce/ Parasite/ Unholy/ I Stole Your Love/ Cold Gin/ Watching You/ Firehouse/ Calling Dr. Love/ Making Love/ War Machine/ I Was Made For Lovin You
CD2: I Want You/ Domino/ Love Gun/ Lick It Up/ God Of Thunder/ I Love It Loud/ Detroit Rock City/ Black Diamond/ Heaven's On Fire/ Rock And Roll All Night
R: Exs. Soundboard.   S: Santiago, Chile Sept. 1 '94.   C: ECD. Dcc. Pic CDs. Time CD1 51:28. CD2 56:28.

LP - SHOUT IT OUT LOUD
BUD RECS.
S1: Deuce/ Strutter/ C'Mon And Love Me/ Hotter Than Hell/ Fire House
S2: She/ Guitar Solo/ Ladies In Waiting/ Nothing To Lose/ 100,000 Years/ Drum Solo/ Black Diamond
R: Poor-Gs.   S: Alive-Tour, Detroit '76.
C: Dcc. Cover says Casablanca.

CD - UNPLUGGED
KISS THE STONE KTS 400/01
CD1: Strutter/ Goin' Blind/ Shandy/ Rock Bottom/ I Still Love You/ Domino/ I Love It Loud/ Got To Choose/ Black Diamond/ Hillbilly Jam/ Hard Luck Woman/ I Was Made For Lovin' You
CD2: A World Without Heroes/ Take Me/ Room Service/ Do You Love Me/ Unholy/ Shout It Out Loud/ Forever/ Love Her All I Can/ Nothin' To Loose/ Comin' Home/ Sure Know Something/ Lick It Up
R: Vg-Ex. Audience   S: Melbourne, Australia Feb. 7 '95.   C: ECD. Dcc. Pic CD. Time CD1 50:13. CD2 48:21.

CD - UNPLUGGED
SWINDEL RECORDS SWN 033
Detroit Rock City (4:33)/ Hard Luck Woman (3:45)/ Cold Gin (4:53)/ Lick It Up (3:54)/ I Still Love You (2:54)/ Calling Dr. Love (1:52)/ Detroit Rock City (4:43)/ Every Time I Look At You (2:03)/ Goin' Blind (2:43)/ Cold Gin (1:56)/ Acoustic Medley (6:39)/ Rock 'N' Roll All Nite (1:52)/ Beth (1:48)
R: Vg-Ex. Soundboard.   S: Track 1 Feb. 25 '93. Tracks 2-4 July 1 '93. Tracks 5-7 May 15 '93. Track 8 May '92. Track 9 Mar. 3 '94. Tracks 10-12 '90. Track 13 Jan. 12 '85.   C: ECD. Dcc. Pic CD.

CD - UNWIRED
OCTOPUS OCTO 094
Detroit Rock City (4:31)/ Hard Luck Woman (3:12)/ Cold Gin (4:53)/ Lick It Up (3:58)/ I Still Love You (2:58)/ Calling Dr. Love (1:33)/ Detroit Rock City (4:43)/ Every Time I Look At You (1:48)/ Goin' Blind (2:49)/ Help (1:49)/ Forever (3:28)/ Rock 'N' Roll All Nite (1:18)/ Cold Gin (0:57)/ When Two Hearts Collide (4:26)/ Don't Let Go (3:39)/ Hide Your Heart (4:05)/ Best Man For You (4:12)/ Time Traveller (4:36)/ Give It To You Easy (Unreleased Track) (2:04)/ Ring Ding Do (Gene's song '68) (2:53)/ I Stole Your Love (Demo '77) (2:43)
R: Vg-Ex. Some G-Vg. Soundboard.   S: Tracks 1-13 acoustic versions various locations USA '90-'94. Tracks 14-18, Paul Stanley's demos for an unreleased solo album in '90.   C: ECD. Dcc.

CD - 'WORLD TOUR 1984'
KISS 3
Intro/ Creatures Of The Night/ Detroit Rock City/ Cold Gin/ Fits Like A Glove/ Firehouse/ Gimme More/ Vinnie Vincent Guitar Solo/ War Machine/ Gene Simmons Bass Solo/ I Love It Loud/ I Still Love You/ Eric Carr Drum Solo/ Young And Wasted/ Love Gun
R: Poor-G. Audience.   S: Long Beach Arena Jan. 27 '84.   C: Japanese CD. Time 73:01.

KRAFTWERK

CD - THE REMIX
ON IT MUSIC CD 049
Computerwelt (Razormaid Mix) (10:00)/ Das Model (Razormaid Edit) (2:26)/ Sex Objekt (Razormaid Mix) (7:41)/ Pocket Calculator (Mix-It Remix) (6:33)/ The Telephone Call (Razormaid Mix) (6:48)/ The Mix-Medley (Razormaid Mix) (13:18)/ Re-Werked (Music Factory Master Mix) (4:39)/ Sex Object (Techno Pop Version) (4:02)/ Tour De France (Disconnect Remix) (5:33)/ Electric Cafe (Mix-It Remix) (5:06)/ Technopop (Demo) (4:19)
R: Exs. Soundboard.   C: ECD. Dcc. Time 70:40.

CD - SCHONE NEUE WELT
PING PONG 9401
Electric Cafe (Mixx-It-Remix)/ Die Roboter (US Rap Mix)/ Sex Objekt (Demo Mix)/ Computerwelt

(US DJ Promo Mix By Razormaid)/ Powerwork
Megamix/ Telephone Mix/ Re-Worked (US DJ
Promo Mix By Razormaid)/ Razormaid - Gridlock
Mix Medley/ Sex Objekt/ Housephone/ The
Telephone Call (Re-Mix)
R: Exs. Soundboard.   S: Re-mixes.   C: ECD.
Dcc. Pic CD. Time 78:33.

KRAVITZ, LENNY

CD - FLOWER CHILD
JOKER JOK-037-B
Mr. Cabdriver/ Freedom Train/ Be/ Flower Child/
Cold Turkey/ If Six Where Nine/ Let Love Rule/
Let Me Be/ Blues For Sister Someone/ My
Precious Love/ Does Anybody Out There Even
Care?
R: Ex. Audience.   S: Amsterdam '93.
C: Australian CD. Dcc. Time 54:57

CD - IF 6 WAS 9
BABY CAPONE 006
Flower Child (4:23)/ Mr. Cab Driver (4:15)/
Freedom Train (4:28)/ Be (4:50)/ My Precious
Love (5:30)/ Cold Turkey (7:09)/ If Six Was Nine
(5:53)/ Fear (5:53)/ Let Love Rule (10:29)
R: Exs. Soundboard.   S: Live in Europe during
'90 world tour.   C: ECD. Dcc. Pic CD.

CD - PLUGGELECTRIC
SWINDLE RECORDS SWN 031
ACOUSTIC SET: Are You Gonna Go My Way
(6:19)/ Believe (4:58)/ Rosemary (5:37)/ Just Be A
Woman (3:52)/ Sister (7:165)/ Always On The
Run (3:57)/ ELECTRIC SET: Sister (7:27)/ Are
You Gonna Go My Way (3:36)/ Let Love Rule
(9:33)/ Always On The Run (6:25)/ Believe (6:14)/
It Ain't Over 'Til It's Over (4:18)/ My Precious Love
(5:53)
R: Exs. Soundboard.   S: Live USA '94.
C: ECD. Dcc. Pic CD.

CD - STILL WALKING ON THIN ICE
OXYGEN OXY 013
Tunnel Vision (9:01)/ Stop Draggin' Around (3:39)/
Circus (5:20)/ Beyond The 7th Sky (6:28)/ Can't
Get You Off My Mind (5:29)/ Fields Of Joy (4:25)/
What The Fuck Are We Sayin' (6:54)/ Mr. Cab
Driver (4:02)/ Let Love Rule (9:37)/ It Ain't Over
Till It's Over (8:05)/ Are You Gonna Go My Way
(4:14)/ Rock And Roll Is Dead (5:30)
R: Exs. Soundboard.   S: The E-Werk, Cologne,
Germany Oct. 7 '95.   C: ECD. Dcc. Pic CD.

LANG, K.D.

CD - CONSTANT CRAVING
GRAPEFRUIT GRA-008-A
Save Me (4:38)/ The Mind Of Love (3:35)/ Still
Thrives This Love (3:26)/ Don't Let The Stars Get

In Your Eyes (2:52)/ Luck In My Eyes (5:21)/
Outside Myself (5:51)/ Wash Me Clean (4:03)/
Miss Chatelaine (4:41)/ Ridin' The Rails (2:58)/
Big Big Love (3:15)/ Pullin' Back The Reins
(5:29)/ Constant Craving (4:40)/ Big Boned Gal
(5:06)/ Trail Of Broken Hearts (3:25)/ Constant
Craving (#2) (4:25)/ Big Big Love (#2) (3:01)/
Crying (4:11)
R: Exs. Soundboard.   S: Toronto, Canada '93.
C: Australian CD.

LED ZEPPELIN
(also see pages 228 and 229)

CD - A RIOT GOING ON
POT 006/007
CD1: Dazed And Confused/ Heartbreaker/ White
Summer, Black Mountain Side/ Since I've Been
Loving You/ Organ Solo, Thank You/ Moby Dick
CD2: How Many More Times/ Whole Lotta Love/
Communication Breakdown/ C'Mon Everybody/
Something Else/ Bring It On Home/ Long Tall
Sally
C: Fair. Audience.   S: KB Hallen, Copenhagen
Feb. 28 '70.   C: Japanese CD.
Time CD1 71:37. CD2 62:05.

CD - ALL MY LOVE
TRANTULRA NO. 16000
Carouselambra/ Untitled/ Wearing And Tearing/
Fool In The Rain/ Hot Dog/ In The Evening/ South
Bound Saurez/ Darlene/ Fool In The Rain/
Carouselambra/ All My Love/ All My Love
R: Ex. Soundboard.   S: Polar Studios In
Stockholm, Sweden '78.   C: Japanese CD.
Limited edition of 300 copies with 6 different cov-
ers in brown paper envelopes. Each cover denot-
ed by a sticker (A, B, C, D, E or F) on envelope.

CD - ARABESQUE AND BAROQUE
ANTRABATA ARM 17575-1/2/3
CD1: Intro/ Rock And Roll/ Sick Again/ Over The
Hills/ In My Time Of Dying/ The Song Remains
The Same/ The Rain Song/ Kashmir
CD2: No Quarter/ Tangerine/ Going To California/
That's The Way/ Bron Y Aur Stomp/ Trampled
Underfoot/ Trampled Underfoot
CD3: Moby Dick/ Dazed And Confused/ Stairway
To Heaven/ Whole Lotta Love/ Black Dog
R: G. Audience.   S: Earl's Court, London May
17 '75.   C: Japanese CD. Full color box. Time
CD1 54:38. CD2 60:33. CD3 70:53.

CD - AT THE BEEB 1971
CUTTLEFISH RECORDS CFR 009
Immigrant Song/ Heartbreaker/ Black Dog/ Going
To California/ That's The Way/ What Is And What
Should Never Be/ Communication Breakdown/
Stairway To Heaven/ Whole Lotta Love Medley:
Whole Lotta Love, Boogie Mama, Minnesota
Blues, My Baby Left Me/ Mess Of Blues/ The
Lemon Song/ Whole Lotta Love
R: Exs. Soundboard.   S: Paris Theatre, London,
England Apr. 1 '71 for BBC Radio 1's 'John Peel

Sessions'. C: Japanese CD. Time 64:17.

CD - BIRTH OF THE GODS
BALBOA BP-0001
I Can't Quit You/ Dazed And Confused/ You
Shook Me/ How Many More Times/
Communication Breakdown/ I Can't Quit You/
Heartbreaker/ Dazed And Confused/ How Many
More Times Medley
R: Tracks 1-4 Ex. Soundboard. Tracks 5-9 G.
Audience.   S: Tracks 1-4 Fillmore West Jan. 11
'69. Tracks 5-9 Kansas Nov. 5 '69.
C: Japanese CD. Time 75:02.

CD - BLAZE
IMMIGRANT IM 40-42
CD1: Rock And Roll/ Sick Again/ Over The Hills/
In My Time Of Dying/ Song Remains The Same/
Rain Song/ Kashmir
CD2: No Quarter/ Trampled Underfoot/ Moby Dick
CD3: Dazed And Confused/ Stairway To Heaven/
Whole Lotta Love/ Black Dog
R: Vg. Audience.   S: Baton Rouge Feb. 28 '75.
C: Japanese CD. Time CD1 49:38. CD2 53:49.
CD3 53:48.

CD - BLOW-UP
IMMIGRANT IM-029/30
CD1: Good Times Bad Times, Communication
Breakdown/ I Can't Quit You Baby/ Heartbreaker/
Dazed And Confused/ White Summer, Black
Mountain Side/ What Is & What Should Never Be
CD2: Moby Dick/ How Many More Times/ C'mon
Everybody/ Something Else
R: Poor-G. Audience.   S: Winterland Ballroom,
San Francisco Nov. 6 '69.   C: Japanese CD.
Dbw. Red/blue type. Time CD1 47:22. CD2 43:13.

CD - BLUEBERRY HILL
COBLA STANDARD SERIES 005
CD1: Immigrant Song/ Heartbreaker/ Dazed And
Confused/ Bring It On Home/ That's The Way/
Bron-Y-Aur/ Since/ Organ Solo/ Thank You
CD2: What Is And What Should Never Be/ Moby
Dick/ Whole Lotta Love Medley/ Communication
Breakdown Medley/ Out On The Tiles/ Blueberry
Hill
R: Ex. Audience.   S: Inglewood Forum, Los
Angeles Sept. 4 '70.   C: Japanese CD.
Time CD1 69:44. CD2 59:55.

CD - BLUEBERRY HILL 1 AND 2
ROUND PIN PRODUCTIONS LZCD522/1 &
LZCD522/2
CD1: Immigrant Song (5:22)/ Heartbreaker (4:54)/
Dazed And Confused (17:31)/ Bring It On Home
(10:12)/ That's The Way (7:30)/ Bron-Y-Aur Stomp
(3:33)/ Since I've Been Loving You (8:01)/ Organ
Solo - Thank You (9:31)/ What Is And What
Should Never Be (4:26)
CD2: Whole Lotta Love Medley: Boogie Mama,
I'm Movin' On, I've Got A Girl, Some Other Guy,
Think It Over, Honey Bee, Lemon Song (17:23)/
Communication Breakdown Medley: Good Times

Bad Times, For What It's Worth, I Saw Her
Standing There (11:19)/ Out On The Tiles (4:20)/
Blueberry Hill (3:17)/ How Many More Times
Medley: Bolero, The Hunter, Hi-Fi Mama, Lemon
Song (20:57)*
R: Vg. Audience.   S: Inglewood Forum, Los
Angeles Sept. 4 '70. *Dusseldorf, Germany Mar.
12 '70.   C: ECD. Dcc. Picture on front from
Australia '72 (?).

CD - BONZO'S BIRTHDAY PARTY
COBLA STANDARD SERIES 002
CD1: Rock And Roll/ Celebration Day/ Black Dog/
Over The Hills And Far Away/ Misty Mountain
Hop/ Since I've Been Loving You/ No Quarter
CD2: The Song Remains The Same/ The Rain
Song/ Dazed And Confused/ Stairway To Heaven
CD3: Moby Dick/ Happy Birthday Song/
Heartbreaker/ Whole Lotta Love/ Communication
Breakdown/ The Ocean
R: Vg. Audience.   S: Inglewood Forum, LA May
31 '73.   C: Japanese CD. Cardboard sleeve
with 'pig in the cake' LP cover and a simulated
rubber stamp on the back. Cardboard card with
track listings inside. Time CD1 47:15.
CD2 55:07. CD3 47:41.

CD - BONZO'S 25TH BIRTHDAY
ARMS 31/32/33PR
CD1: Rock And Roll/ Celebration Day/ Bring It On
Home Intro, Black Dog/ Over The Hills And Far
Away/ Misty Mountain Hop/ Since I've Been
Loving You/ No Quarter/ The Song Remains The
Same/ The Rain Song
CD2: Dazed And Confused (includes San
Francisco)/ Stairway To Heaven
CD3: Moby Dick/ Happy Birthday/ Heartbreaker/
Whole Lotta Love (includes Boogie Woogie)/ The
Ocean
R: G-Vg. Audience.   S: Inglewood Forum, LA
May 31 '73.   C: Japanese CD. Dcc.
Time CD1 57:21. CD2 38:27. CD3 37:11.

CD - BRING IT ON HOME
POT 008/009
CD1: Since I've Been Loving You/ Black Mountain
Side/ Dazed And Confused/ Bring It On Home/
White Summer, Black Mountain Side/ Since I've
Been Loving You
CD2: Organ Solo, Thank You/ What Is And What
Should Never Be (fades in)/ Moby Dick/ How
Many More Times/ Whole Lotta Love
R: G. Audience.   S: CD1 tracks 1-3 Dusseldorf,
Germany Mar. 12 '70. Rest from Curtis Hickson
Hall, Tampa Apr. 9 '70.   C: Japanese CD. Dcc.
Time CD1 64:29. CD2 65:23.

CD - BUDOKAN OCT 2, 1972
PATRIOT
CD1: Introduction/ Rock And Roll/ Over The Hills
And Far Away/ Black Dog/ Misty Mountain Hop/
Since I've Been Loving You/ Dancing Days/ Bron-
Y-Aur Stomp/ The Song Remains The Same/ The
Rain Song

CD2: Stairway To Heaven/ Whole Lotta Love Medley/ Heart Breaker/ Immigrant Song/ Communication Breakdown
R: Vg. Audience.   S: Budokan, Japan Oct. 2 '72.   C: Japanese. CD1 73:39. CD2 52:25.

CD - CALIFORNIA'69
LEMON SONG LS-7206/07
CD1: As Long As I Have You (includes 'Fresh Garbage')/ I Can't Quit You Baby/ Dazed And Confused/ Babe, I'm Gonna Leave You/ Communication Breakdown/ You Shook Me/ White Summer/ The Train Kept A Rollin'/ Pat's Delight
CD2: How Many More Times (includes 'The Hunter')/ Killing Floor (includes 'The Lemon Song')/ The Train Kept A Rollin'/ You Shook Me/ Communication Breakdown/ As Long As I Have You (includes 'Fresh Garbage')
R: Vg.   S: San Francisco. Jan. 12 '69 Fillmore West. CD2 tracks 3-6 Apr. 25 '69 Winterland.
C: Japanese CD. Time CD1 57:56. CD2 44:28.

CD - CANADA DRY
TARANTURA
Rock And Roll/ Celebration Day/ Black Dog/ Over The Hills And Far Away/ Misty Mountain Hop/ Since I've Been Loving You/ No Quarter/ Dazed And Confused
R: G-Vgm. Audience.   S: PNE Coliseum, Vancouver, Canada July 18 '73.   C: Japanese CD. Dcc. Time 49:00.

CD - CUSTARD PIE
COBLA STANDARD SERIES 001
CD1: Rock And Roll/ Over The Hills And Far Away/ Black Dog/ Misty Mountain Hop/ Since I've Been Loving You/ Bron-Y-Aur Stomp/ The Song Remains The Same/ The Rain Song/ Dazed And Confused
CD2: Stairway To Heaven/ Whole Lotta Love, Everybody Needs Someone To Love, Let That Boogie, Baby I Don't Care, Let's Have A Party, I Can't Quit You, The Lemon Song, Whole Lotta Love/ Heart Breaker/ Kashmir
R: Good-Vg.   S: Offenbach Mar. 24 '73.
C: Japanese CDs.

CD - THE DEFINITIVE KINGDOM
WHOLE LOTTA LIVE WLL020/21
CD1: Walk Don't Run (2:07)/ Immigrant Song (4:15)/ Heartbreaker (7:03)/ Since I've Been Loving You (8:10)/ Black Dog (5:56)/ Dazed And Confused (21:35)/ Stairway To Heaven (9:33)/ Celebration Day (4:40)/ That's The Way (6:22)
CD2: What Is And What Should Never Be (5:15)/ Moby Dick (17:26)/ Whole Lotta Love (23:36)/ Communication Breakdown (8:22)/ Organ Solo (5:19)/ Thank You (7:47)
R: G. Audience.   S: The Forum, LA Aug. 22 '71.
C: ECD. Dcc. Limited edition of 500.

CD - DESTROYER II
SILVER RARITIES SIRA 197/8/9

CD1: Song Remains The Same/ Sick Again/ Nobody's Fault But Mine/ In My Time Of Dying/ Since I've Been Loving You/ No Quarter
CD2: Ten Years Gone/ Battle Of Evermore/ Going To California/ Black Country Woman/ Bron-Y-Aur Stomp/ White Summer/ Kashmir
CD3: Moby Dick/ Guitar Solo/ Achilles Last Stand/ Stairway To Heaven/ Rock And Roll/ Trampled Underfoot
R: Vg-Exs. Audience.   S: Cleveland Apr. 28 '77.
C: ECD. Dcc. Time CD1 59:14. CD2 41:02. CD3: 58:09.

CD - DON'T DO IT
HOLY GRAIL HG CD105
CD1: Immigrant Song/ Heartbreaker/ Celebration Day/ Black Dog/ Since I've Been Loving You/ Stairway To Heaven/ Going to California/ That's The Way/ Tangerine/ Bron-Y-Aur Stomp
CD2: Dazed And Confused/ What Is And What Should Never Be/ Moby Dick/ Whole Lotta Love/ Rock And Roll/ Communication Breakdown
C: Good audience recording, hiss.
S: Coliseum, Charlotte, NC June 9 '72.
C: Japanese CD. CD1 74:31. CD2 64:46.

CD - THE DRAG QUEEN
TARANTURA DQ 001/2/3
CD1: Rock And Roll/ Celebration Day/ Black Dog/ Over The Hills/ Misty Mountain Hop/ Since/ No Quarter/ Song Remains The Same/ Rain Song
CD2: Dazed And Confused/ Stairway To Heaven/ Moby Dick
CD3: Heartbreaker/ Whole Lotta Love/ Communication Breakdown
R: Ex. Soundboard.   S: New Orleans May 14 '73.   C: Japanese CD. Time CD1 60:13. CD2 61:26. CD3 27:48.

CD - ELVIS PRESLEY HAS JUST LEFT THE BUILDING
LZ 6837-281
Baby I Don't Care/ Let's Have A Party/ I Can't Quit You/ Going Down Slow/ Whole Lotta Love/ Heartbreaker/ The Ocean/ Dazed And Confused/ Whole Lotta Love/ Everybody Needs Somebody To Love/ Whole Lotta Love/ Boogie Woogie/ Baby I Don't Care/ Blue Suede Shoes/ Let's Have A Party/ I Can't Quit You/ Going Down Slow/ Whole Lotta Love/ Drum, Mellotron Tuning/ Love Me Tender/ Frankfurt Special/ King Creole/ Love Me Tender
R: Ex. Soundboard.   S: Tracks 1-7 Liverpool Empire Jan. 14 '73. Tracks 8-18 St. George Hall Bradford Jan.18 '73. Tracks 19-23 Southampton University Jan. 20 '73.   C: Japanese CD. Dcc. Time 76:23.

CD - THE END OF 69
WHOLE LOTTA LIVE WLL007/8
CD1: Opening/ Good Times Bad Times/ Communication Breakdown/ I Can't Quit You/ Heartbreaker/ Dazed And Confused/ White Summer-Black Mountain Side

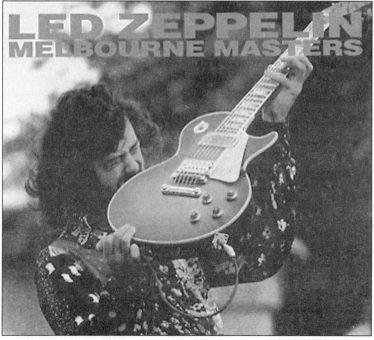

CD2: What Is And What Should Never Be/ Moby Dick/ Introduction-How Many More Times/ C'mon Everybody/ Something Else
S: Winterland Ballroom, San Francisco Nov. 6 '69.
C: ECD. Dcc. 500 made. CD1 49:34. CD2 45:13.

CD - ESSEN 1973
SAVAGE BEAST MUSIC SBM-7-1/2
CD1: Rock And Roll/ Over The Hills And Far Away/ Black Dog/ Misty Mountain Hop/ Since I've Been Loving You/ Dancing Days/ Bron-y-aur Stomp
CD2: The Song Remains The Same/ The Rain Song/ Dazed And Confused (includes San Francisco)/ Stairway To Heaven (incomplete)
R: G. Audience.   S: Grugahalle, Essen, Germany Mar. 22 '73.   C: Japanese CD. Dcc. Time CD1 42:15. CD2 46:47.

CD - 56,800 IN THE OCEAN
SILVER RARITIES SIRA 166/167
CD1: Rock'n'Roll/ Celebration Day/ Black Dog/ Over The Hills And Far Away/ Misty Mountain Hop/ Since I've Been Loving You/ No Quarter/ The Songs Remain The Same/ The Rain Song
CD2: Dazed And Confused/ Stairway To Heaven/ Moby Dick/ Heartbreaker/ Whole Lotta Love/ The Ocean/ Communication Breakdown
R: Vg. Audience.   S: Tampa 5 May '73.
C:-ECD. Time CD1 53:43. CD2 69:40.

CD - FILLMORE WEST 1969
LZ 01/2
CD1: Train Kept A Rollin/ I Can't Quit You/ As Long As I Have You/ You Shook Me/ How Many More Times Medley
CD2: Killing Floor/ Babe I'm Gonna Leave You/ Sittin' And Thinkin/ Moby Dick/ Dazed And Confused/ Communication Breakdown
R: Ex. Soundboard.   S: Fillmore West Apr. 27 '69.   C: ECD. Time CD1 57:34. CD2: 45:57.

CD - THE FINAL STATEMENT
ANTRABATA REFERENCE MASTER ARM
040970/280773/270477
CD1: Immigrant Song/ Heartbreaker/ Dazed And Confused/ Bring It On Home/ That's The Way/ Bron-Y-Aur/ Since I've Been Loving You/ Organ Solo/ Thank You
CD2: What Is And Should Never Be/ Moby Dick/ Whole Lotta Love/ Communication Breakdown/ Out On The Tiles/ Blueberry Hill
CD3: Rock N Roll/ Celebration Day/ Black Dog/ Over The Hills And Far Away/ Misty Mountain Hop/ Since I've Been Loving You/ No Quarter/ The Song Remains The Same/ Rain Song
CD4: Dazed And Confused/ Stairway To Heaven/ Moby Dick
CD5: Heart Breaker/ Whole Lotta Love/ The Ocean
CD6: The Song Remains The Same/ The Rover, Sick Again/ Nobody's Fault But Mine/ In My Time Of Dying/ Since I've Been Loving You/ No Quarter
CD7: Ten Years Gone/ The Battle Of Evermore/

Going To California/ Black Country Woman/ Bron-Yr-Aur-Stomp/ White Summer - Black Mountain Side/ Kashmir/ Out On The Tiles, Moby Dick
CD8: Guitar Solo/ Achilles Last Stand/ Stairway to Heaven/ Rock N Roll/ Trampled Underfoot
R: CD1-2 Ex. Audience. CD3-8 Exs. Soundboard.
S: CD1-2 Inglewood Forum, Los Angeles Sept. 4 '70. CD3-5 Madison Square Garden, NYC July 28 '73. CD6-8 Cleveland Apr. 27 '77.
C: Japanese. Each CD comes in a full color sleeve. These are bound between two blue vinyl-clad book-boards. The group's name is stamped in silver while the title is in gold. Limited edition of 325 with a certificate of authenticity. From master or first generation tapes. Time CD1 69:34.
CD2 52:59. CD3 64:16. CD4 72:05. CD5 28:04.
CD6 58:57. CD7 62:07. CD8 44:23.

CD - FINAL TOUR - EUROPEAN DAZE 1980
PATRIOT 003
CD1: Train Kept A Rollin/ Nobody's Fault/ Black Dog/ In The Evening/ Rain Song/ Hot Dog/ All My Love/ Trampled Underfoot/ Since I've Been Loving You/ Achilles Last Stand
CD2: Stairway To Heaven/ Rock And Roll/ Whole Lotta Love
R: Vg-Ex. Soundboard.   S: Zurich June 29 '80.
CD2 Berlin July 7 '80.   C: Japanese CD.
Time CD1 71:24. CD2 67:14.

CD - V 1/2
COBLA STANDARD SERIES 007
CD1: Intro/ Rock And Roll/ Celebration Day/ Black Dog/ Over The Hills/ Misty Mountain Hop/ Since I've Been Loving You/ No Quarter
CD2: Song Remains The Same/ Rain Song/ Dazed And Confused/ Stairway To Heaven
CD3: Moby Dick/ Heartbreaker/ Whole Lotta Love/ The Ocean
R: Ex. Audience.   S: Seattle July 17 '73.
C: Japanese CD. Time CD1 51:54. CD2 62:58.
CD3 62:05.

CD - FOOTSTOMPING GRAFFITI
CD1: Rock And Roll/ Sick Again/ Over The Hills/ In My Time Of Dying/ Song Remains The Same/ Rain Song/ Kashmir
CD2: No Quarter/ Trampled Underfoot/ Moby Dick/ How Many More Times Medley/ Stairway To Heaven/ Whole Lotta Love/ Black Dog/ Communication Breakdown
R: Fair-Good.   S: Greensboro Jan. 29 '75.
C: Japanese CD. Time CD1 76:34. CD2 54:53.

CD - FOR BADGE HOLDERS ONLY
ARMS 28/29/30PR
CD1: The Song Remains The Same/ The Rover Intro, Sick Again/ Nobody's Fault But Mine/ Over The Hills And Far Away/ Since I've Been Loving You/ No Quarter
CD2: Ten Years Gone/ The Battle Of Evermore/ Going To California/ Black Country Woman/ Bron-Yr-Aur Stomp/ White Summer/ Black Mountain Side/ Kashmir

CD3: Out On The Tiles, Moby Dick (fade out)/ Guitar Solo (includes Star Spangled Banner)/ Achilles Last Stand/ Stairway To Heaven/ Whole Lotta Love
R: Vg-Ex audience recording.   S: LA Forum, LA June 23 '77.   C: Japanese CD.

CD - FOR BADGE HOLDERS ONLY
BALBOA BP-95007/8/9
CD1: Since I've Been/ No Quarter/ Ten Years Gone/ Battle Of Evermore/ Going To California/ Bron-Y-Aur Stomp
CD2: White Summer/ Kashmir/ Trampled Underfoot/ Moby Dick/ Guitar Solo/ Achilles Last Stand
CD3: Stairway To Heaven/ Whole Lotta Love/ Rock And Roll/ No Quarter*/ Ten Years Gone*/ Battle Of Evermore*
R: Ex. Audience. *Ex. Soundboard.   S: LA Forum June 23 '77. *New York June 11 '77.
C: Japanese CD. Time CD1 73:16. CD2 72:25. CD3 64:27.

CD - THE FUCKIN' P.A. SYSTEM
TARANTURA OK-001-3
CD1: The Song Remains The Same/ The Rover Intro, Sick Again/ Nobody's Fault But Mine/ In My Time Of Dying/ Since I've Been Loving You/ No Quarter
CD2: Ten Years Gone/ Battle Of Evermore/ Going To California/ Black Country Woman/ Bron-Yr-Aur Stomp/ White Summer/ Black Mountain Side/ Kashmir
CD3: Over The Top (Moby Dick)/ Guitar Solo/ Achilles Last Stand/ Stairway To Heaven/ Rock And Roll/ Trampled Underfoot
R: Vgs. Audience.   S: The Myriad, Oklahoma City, OK Apr. 3 '77.   C: Japanese CD. 300 numbered copies in a small carrying case.
Time CD1 64:14. CD2 53:13. CD3 63:55.

CD - FUCKING T.Y.
TATTYTURA TAK 001/2/3
CD1: Intro/ Song Remains The Same/ Sick Again/ Nobody's Fault But Mine/ In My Time Of Dying/ Since I've Been Loving You/ No Quarter/ Ten Years Gone
CD2: Battle Of Evermore/ Going To California/ Black Country Woman/ Bron-Y-Aur Stomp/ White Summer/ Kashmir/ Moby Dick
CD3: Guitar Solo/ Achilles Last Stand/ Stairway To Heaven/ Rock And Roll/ Trampled Underfoot/ Song Remains The Same*/ Sick Again*/ Nobody's Fault But Mine*
R: G-Vg.   S: Oklahoma Apr. 3 '77. *Tampa June 3 '77.   C:ECD. Time CD1 75:21. CD2 61:24. CD3 63:07.

CD - GET LOOSE
HOLY GRAIL HG CD100
CD1: Immigrant Song/ Heartbreaker/ Dazed And Confused/ Bring It On Home/ That's The Way/ Bron-Yr-Aur/ Since I've Been Loving You
CD2: Organ Solo/ Thank You/ What Is And What

Should Never Be/ Moby Dick/ Whole Lotta Love/ Communication Breakdown/ Good Times Bad Times/ The Train Kept A Rollin'/ Blueberry Hill/ Long Tall Sally
R: G. Audience.   S: Oakland, CA Sept. 2 '70.
C: Japanese CD. Time CD1 60:08. CD2 65:06.

CD - GOING TO CALIFORNIA II
TARANTURA T2CD-17-1,2
CD1: Immigrant Song/ Heartbreaker/ Since I've Been Loving You/ Black Dog/ Dazed And Confused/ Stairway To Heaven/ Celebration Day/ That's The Way/ Going To California
CD2: What Is And What Should Never Be/ Moby Dick/ Whole Lotta Love/ Communication Breakdown
R: Ex. Audience.   S: Berkely Community Center Sept. 13 '71.   C: Japanese CD. 'Dumbo' cover. Original release with a blue cover. Second with a red cover. Time CD1 74:02. CD2 55:45.

CD - GONZAGA '68
CAPRICORN CR-2031E
Train Kept A Rollin'/ I Can't Quit You Baby/ As Long As I Have You Medley: Fresh Garbage, Shake, Hush/ Dazed And Confused/ White Summer/ How Many More Times (includes 'The Hunter')/ Pat's Delight
R: Good audience recording.   S: The Gymnasium, Gonzaga University, Spokane, WA Dec. 30 '68.   C: Dcc. Limited numbered edition of 500. Time 59:30.

CD - GRANDILOQUENCE
ANTRABATA REFERENCE MASTER ARM 17773/27773/6773
CD1: Introduction/ Rock N Roll/ Celebration Day/ Black Dog/ Over The Hills And Far Away/ Misty Mountain Hop/ Since I've Been Loving You/ No Quarter
CD2: Song Remains The Same/ Rain Song/ Dazed And Confused
CD3: Stairway To Heaven/ Moby Dick/ Heartbreaker/ Whole Lotta Love/ The Ocean
CD4: Introduction/ Rock N Roll/ Celebration Day/ Black Dog/ Over The Hills And Far Away/ Misty Mountain Hop/ Since I've Been Loving You/ No Quarter/ Song Remains The Same/ Rain Song
CD5: Dazed And Confused/ Stairway To Heaven
CD6: Stairway To Heaven/ Moby Dick/ Heartbreaker/ Whole Lotta Love/ The Ocean
CD7: Rock N Roll/ Celebration Day/ Black Dog/ Over The Hills And Far Away/ Misty Mountain Hop/ Since I've Been Loving You/ No Quarter/ Song Remains The Same, Rain Song
CD8: Dazed And Confused/ Stairway To Heaven
CD9: Moby Dick/ Heartbreaker/ Whole Lotta Love/ Communication Breakdown
R: CD1-3 Ex. Audience. CD4-9 Exs. Soundboard.
S: CD1-5 Seattle July 17 '73. CD6 Madison Square Gardens July 27 '73. CD7-9 Chicago July 6 '73.   C: Japanese. Each CD comes in a full color sleeve. These are bound between two burgundy-clad book boards. The group's name is

stamped in silver while the title is in gold. Limited edition of 325 with a certificate of authenticity. From master or first generation tapes.
Time CD1 52:01. CD2 51:53. CD3 74:57. CD4 66:24. CD5 49:07. CD6 58:28. CD7 60:15. CD8 40:47. CD9 53:42.

CD - HARD COMPANY
ZA 13/14
CD1: Immigrant Song/ Heartbreaker/ Since I've Been Loving You/ Black Dog/ Dazed And Confused/ Stairway To Heaven/ Celebration Day, That's The Way
CD2: Going To California/ What Is And What Should Never Be/ Moby Dick/ Whole Lotta Love (includes - Just A Little Bit, Boogie Woogie, My Baby Left Me, That's Alright, Mess O'Blues, You Shock Me)/ Communication Breakdown/ Organ Solo, Thank You/ Rock And Roll
R: Poor-G. Audience.   S: Madison Square Garden, NYC Sept. 3 '71.   C: Japanese CD. Dcc. Time CD1 71:07. CD2 67:56.

CD - IT'LL BE ZEP
SILVER RARITIES SIRA 171/172/173
CD1: Crowd Anticipation/ The Song Remains The Same/ Sick Again/ Nobody's Fault But Mine/ In My Time Of Dying/ Since I've Been Loving You
CD2: No Quarter Ten Years Gone/ Going To California/ Black Country Woman/ Bron-Y-Aur Stomp/ White Summer/ Black Mountainside/ Kashmir
CD3: Moby Dick/ Jimmy's Solo/ Achilles Last Stand/ Stairway To Heaven/ Whole Lotta Love/ It'll Be Me
R: G-Vg. Audience.   S: Fort Worth, Texas 22 May '77.   C: ECD.

CD - KNEBWORTH FESTIVAL
TARANTURA KNEB 04-1-3 KNEB 11-3
CD1: The Song Remains The Same/ Celebration Day/ Black Dog/ Nobody's Fault But Mine/ Over The Hills And Far Away/ Misty Mountain Hop/ Since I've Been Loving You/ No Quarter
CD2: Ten Years Gone/ Hot Dog/ The Rain Song/ White Summer/ Black Mountain Side/ Kashmir/ Trampled Underfoot/ Sick Again/ Achilles Last Stand
CD3: Jimmy's Solo/ In The Evening/ Stairway To Heaven/ Rock And Roll/ Whole Lotta Love/ Heartbreaker
CD4: The Song Remains The Same/ Celebration Day/ Black Dog/ Nobody's Fault But Mine/ Over The Hills And Far Away/ Misty Mountain Hop/ Since I've Been Loving You/ No Quarter
CD5: Hot Dog/ The Rain Song/ White Summer/ Black Mountain Side/ Kashmir/ Trampled Underfoot/ Sick Again/ Achilles Last Stand
CD6: Jimmy's Solo/ In The Evening/ Stairway To Heaven/ Rock And Roll/ Whole Lotta Love/ Communication Breakdown
R: Ex. Audience.   S: Knebworth Festival CD1-3 Aug. 4 '79. CD4-6 Aug. 11 '79.   C: Japanese. Discs are housed in large hardback book-style

cover. Full color pictures front and back. There is also a book of B&w photos from the concerts. Limited edition of 150 sets.

CD - THE LAST DAY IN MANNHEIM
WHOLE LOTTA LIVE WLL024/025
CD1: The Train Kept A Rollin'/ Nobody's Fault But Mine/ Black Dog/ In The Evening/ The Rain Song/ Hot Dog/ All My Love/ Trampled Underfoot/ Since I've Been Loving You
CD2: Achilles Last Stand/ White Summer/ Black Mountain Side/ Kashmir/ Stairway To Heaven// Communication Breakdown/ Rock And Roll
R: Soundboard.   S: Eisstadion, Mannheim, Germany July 3 '80.   C: ECD. Dcc. 500 made. Time CD1 63:09. CD2 47:32.

CD - LED ASTRAY
SILVER RARITIES SIRA 194/195/196
CD1: Introduction/ Rock And Roll/ Sick Again/ Over The Hills And Far Away/ In My Time Of Dying/ The Song Remains The Same/ Rain Song/ Kashmir
CD2: No Quarter/ Trampled Underfoot/ Moby Dick
CD3: Dazed And Confused/ Stairway To Heaven/ Whole Lotta Love/ Black Dog
R: Exs. Audience.   S: Louisiana State University, Baton Rouge Feb. 28 '75.   C: ECD. Dcc.

CD - THE LEGENDARY END
SILVER RARITIES SIRA 206/207/208
CD1: The Song Remains The Same/ Sick Again/ Nobody's Fault But Mine/ Over The Hills And Far Away/ Since I've Been Loving You/ No Quarter
CD2: Ten Years Gone/ The Battle Of Evermore/ Going To California/ Just Can't Be Satisfied/ Black Country Woman/ Bron-Y-Aur Stomp/ Dancing Days/ White Summer, Black Mountain Side/ Kashmir/ Trampled Underfoot
CD3: Moby Dick/ Guitar, Bow Solo/ Achilles Last Stand/ Stairway To Heaven/ Whole Lotta Love/ Rock & Roll
R: Exs. Audience.   S: LA Forum June 27 '77. C: ECD. Dcc. CD1 75:16 CD2 71:06. CD3 72:22.

CD - LET ME GET BACK TO 1972
H-BOMB - 95R01/2/3
CD1: Rock And Roll/ Black Dog/ Over The Hills/ Misty Mountain Hop/ Since I've Been Loving You/ Dancing Days/ Song Remains The Same/ Rain Song
CD2: Dazed And Confused/ Stairway To Heaven/ Moby Dick
CD3: Whole Lotta Love/ Stand By Me/ Immigrant Song
R: Vg-Ex. Audience.   S: Osaka, Oct. 9 '72. C: Japanese CD. Copy of 'Tapes From The Darkside' on the same label. Time CD1 46:41. CD2 55:10. CD3: 40:21.

CD - LISTEN TO THIS EDDIE
SILVER RARITIES MASTER SERIES SIRA 161/62/63

CD1: The Song Remains The Same (6:20)/ Sick Again (6:10)/ Nobody's Fault But Mine (8:40)/ Over The Hills And Far Away (6:50)/ Since I've Been Loving You (9:00)/ No Quarter (29:50)
CD2: Ten Years Gone (9:25)/ Battle Of Evermore (6:50)/ Going To California (6:45)/ Black Country Woman (2:25)/ Bron-Y-Aur Stomp (6:55)/ White Summer - Black Mountainside (9:10)/ Kashmir (9:13)/ Out On The Tiles - Moby Dick (18:25)
CD3: Heartbreaker (9:25)/ guitar solo (16:20)/ Achilles Last Stand (9:15)/ Stairway To Heaven (12:55)/ Whole Lotta Love (2:23)/ Rock n' Roll (4:17)
R: Exs. Audience. From first generation copies of master tape.　S: Forum, Inglewood, CA June 21 '77.　C: ECD. Simulated rubber-stamp cover.

CD - LIVE AT LEEDS 1971
ZA61
Immigrant Song/ Heartbreaker/ Since I've Been Loving You/ Black Dog/ You Shook Me/ Whole Lotta Love/ Organ Solo/ Thank You
R: G-Vg.　S: Rochester Sept. 11 '71 - Not Leeds.　C: Japanese CD. Time 47:55.

CD - LIVE IN NAGOYA
SMILE TOE 001
CD1: Rock And Roll/ Black Dog/ Over The Hills/ Misty Mountain Hop/ Since/ Dancing Days/ Bron-Y-Aur Stomp/ Song Remains The Same/ Rain Song
CD2: Dazed And Confused/ Stairway To Heaven/ Whole Lotta Love Medley/ Organ Solo/ Thank You
R: Poor. Audience.　S: Nagoya, Japan Oct. 5 '72.　C: Japanese CD. CD1 45:06. CD2 53:41.

CD - LZ RIDER
TARANTURA. LZ-1,2
CD1: Rock And Roll/ Celebration Day/ Black Dog/ Over The Hills And Far Away/ Misty Mountain Hop/ Since I've Been Loving You/ No Quarter/ The Song Remains The Same/ The Rain Song
CD2: Dazed And Confused/ Stairway To Heaven/ Moby Dick/ Heartbreaker/ Whole Lotta Love/ The Ocean
R: Vg. Audience.　S: Civic Center, Providence, Rhode Island July 21 '73.　C: Japanese CDs. Time CD1 59.36. CD2 72:08.

CD - MAD SCREAMING GALLERY
LEMON SONG.LS-7203/04/05
CD1: Immigrant Song/ Heart Breaker/ Since I've Been Loving You/ Black Dog/ Dazed And Confused
CD2: That's The Way/ Going To California/ What Is And What Should Never Be/ Moby Dick
CD3: Organ Solo/ Thank You/ Rock And Roll/ Celebration Day/ That's The Way/ Going To California/ What Is And What Should Never Be/ Moby Dick
R: G-Vg. Audience. CD3 tracks 4-8 G. Audience. S: Madison Square Garden, New York Sept. 3 '71. CD3 tracks 4-8 War Memorial Auditorium, Rochester Sept. 14 '71.　C: Japanese CD. Fold-

out cardboard sleeve. Dcc. Time CD1 70:42. CD2 65:21. CD3 71:58.

CD - MAGICK
TARANTURA
CD1: Heartbreaker/ Black Dog/ Since I've Been Loving You/ Rock And Roll/ Stairway To Heaven/ Going To California/ That's The Way
CD2: Dazed And Confused/ What Is And What Should Never Be/ Celebration Day/ Moby Dick/ Whole Lotta Love
R: Gm. Audience. Some hiss.　S: Empire Pool, Wembley, London 11/20/71.　C: Japanese CD. Dcc. Cover is a copy of the 'Electric Magic' poster. Total time 100 minutes.

CD - MELBOURNE MASTERS
IMMIGRANT IM-035-36
CD1: Immigrant Song/ Heartbreaker/ Black Dog/ Since I've Been Loving You/ Stairway To Heaven/ Going To California/ That's The Way/ Tangerine/ Bron-Y-Aur Stomp
CD2: Dazed And Confused/ Rock And Roll/ Whole Lotta Love Medley: Let That Boy Boogie, Let's Have A Party/ Interview*
R: G-Vg. Audience. *Vg-Ex.　S: Kooyong Tennis Courts, Melbourne Feb. 20 '72. CD2 track 4 Radio Perth, West Australia Feb. 16 '72. C: Japanese CDs. Dcc. CD1 53:18. CD2 53:54.

CD - MISSING SAILOR
IMMIGRANT IM 031-32
CD1: Immigrant Song/ Heartbreaker/ Dazed And Confused/ Bring It On Home/ That's The Way/ Since I've Been Loving You
CD2: Organ Solo, Thank You/ What Is And What Should Never Be/ Moby Dick/ Whole Lotta Love Medley: Boogie Woogie, I've Got A Girl, Killing Floor, Two And One To Three, Crosscut Saw, Honey Bee, Lemon Song, Needle Blues, Since My Babe's Been Gone, Lawdy Miss Clawdy/ Communication Breakdown
R: Poor-G. Audience.　S: San Diego Sports Arena, San Diego, CA Sept. 3 '70.
C: Japanese CD. Time CD1 57:26. CD2 61:23.

CD - NASTY MUSIC
TARANTURA
CD1: Rock And Roll/ Over The Hills And Far Away/ Black Dog/ Misty Mountain Hop/ Since I've Been Loving You/ Dancing Days/ Bron-Yr-Aur Stomp/ The Song Remains The Same/ The Rain Song
CD2: Dazed And Confused/ Stairway To Heaven
CD3: Whole Lotta Love, Everybody Needs Somebody To Love, Boogie Woogie, Baby I Don't Care, Let's Have A Party/ I Can't Quit You, Lemon Song/ Heartbreaker/ Communication Breakdown/ The Ocean
R: Vg soundboard recording.　S: Various locations Jan. '73 UK and Berlin '73.　C: Japanese CD. 300 numbered copies in a small carrying case. Time CD1 52:59. CD2 37:47. CD3 42:21.

CD - THE 9TH US TOUR
WHOLE LOTTA LIVE WLL004/05/06
CD1: Opening/ Rock And Roll/ Celebration Day/ Black Dog/ Over The Hills And Far Away/ Misty Mountain Hop/ Since I've Been Loving You/ No Quarter/ The Song Remains The Same/ The Rain Song
CD2: Dazed And Confused/ Stairway To Heaven/ Moby Dick
CD3: Heartbreaker/ Whole Lotta Love/ The Ocean
R: Soundboard. S: Madison Square Gardens, New York July 28 '73. C: ECD. Dcc. 500 made. Time CD1 63:36. CD2 70:31. CD3 29:13.

CD - NO LICENSE, NO FESTIVAL
SILVER RARITIES SIRA 164/165
CD1: Introduction - Announcements/ Immigrant Song/ Black Dog/ Dazed And Confused/ Bring It On Home/ That's The Way/ Bron-Y-Aur/ Since I've Been Loving You
CD2: Thank You/ What Is And What Should Never Be/ Moby Dick/ Whole Lotta Love/ Communication Breakdown
R: G. Audience. S: Boston Sept. 9 '70.
C: ECD. Dcc. Time CD1 60:16. CD2 52:52.

CD - PHYSICAL VANCOUVER FAREWELL
TARANTURA PV-001-6
CD1: Rock And Roll/ Sick Again/ Over The Hills And Far Away/ In My Time Of Dying/ The Song Remains The Same/ Kashmir
CD2: No Quarter/ Trampled Underfoot/ Moby Dick
CD3: Dazed And Confused (Incomplete)
CD4: Rock And Roll/ Sick Again/ Over The Hills And Far Away/ In My Time Of Dying/ The Song Remains The Same/ The Rain Song/ Kashmir
CD5: No Quarter/ Trampled Underfoot/ Moby Dick
CD6: Dazed And Confused/ Stairway To Heaven/ Whole Lotta Love/ Heartbreaker
R: Vgs. Audience. S: PNE Coliseum, Vancouver, Canada. CD1-3 Mar. 19 '75. CD4-6 Mar. 20 '75. C: Japanese CD. Each disc in its own sleeve with a color photo on it.
Time CD1 54:40. CD2 35:54. CD3 38:31. CD4 52:40. CD5 36:14. CD6 73:25.

CD - PURE NOSTULGIA
NEPTUNE
CD1: Train Kept A Rollin'/ Nobody's Fault But Mine/ Black Dog/ In The Evening/ The Rain Song/ Hot Dog/ All My Love/ Trampled Underfoot/ Since I've Been Loving You
CD2: Achilles Last Stand/ White Summer, Black Mountain Side/ Kashmir/ Stairway To Heaven/ Rock And Roll/ Communication Breakdown
R: Vg-Ex soundboard recording. S: Sporthalle, Cologne, Germany June 18 '80. C: Japanese CD. Time CD1 53:52. CD2 45:28.

CD - RETURN TO BLUEBERRY HILL
IMMIGRANT IM 033-34
CD1: Immigrant Song/ Heartbreaker/ Dazed And Confused/ Bring It On Home/ That's The Way/ Bron-Y-Aur Stomp/ Since I've Been Loving You/ Organ Solo/ Thank You
CD2: What Is And What Should Never Be/ Moby Dick/ Whole Lotta Love Medley: Boogie Woogie, Some Other Guy/ I've Got A Girl, I'm Movin' On, Think It Over, Honey Bee, Lemon Song/ Communication Breakdown Medley: Good Times Bad Times, For What It's Worth, I Saw Her Standing There/ Out On The Tiles/ Blueberry Hill
R: Vg-Ex. Audience. S: Inglewood Forum, Los Angeles Sept. 4 '70. C: Japanese CD.
Time CD1 68:23. CD2 51:36.

CD - RIOT HOUSE
COBLA STANDARD SERIES 006
CD1: Rock And Roll/ Over The Hills And Far Away/ Black Dog/ Misty Mountain Hop/ Since I've Been Loving You/ Dancing Days/ Bron-Y-Aur Stamp/ The Song Remains The Same/ The Rain Song/ Stairway To Heaven
CD2: Dazed And Confused/ Whole Lotta Love, Everybody Needs Somebody To Love, Boogie Woogie, Let's Have A Party, Heartbreak Hotel, I Can't Quit You/ Immigrant Song/ Heartbreaker/ Mellotron Solo, Thank You
R: G-Vgm. Audience. S: Alexandra Palace, London Dec. 22 '72. C: Japanese CD. Total time 140 minutes.

CD - RIP IT UP
SILVER RARITIES SIRA 200/1/2
CD1: The Song Remains The Same/ Sick Again/ Nobody's Fault But Mine/ In My Time Of Dying/ Since I've Been Loving You/ No Quarter
CD2: Ten Years Gone/ Battle Of Evermore/ Going To California/ Black Country Woman/ Bron-Y-Aur Stomp/ White Summer/ Kashmir/ Trampled Underfoot
CD3: Moby Dick/ Guitar Solo/ Achilles Last Stand/ Stairway To Heaven/ Whole Lotta Love/ Communication Breakdown
R: Vg-Exs. Audience. S: LA Forum June 25 '77. C: ECD. Dcc. Time CD1 68:03. CD2 57:06. CD3 67:55.

CD - ROYAL ALBERT HALL
Whole Lotta Love/ Communication Breakdown/ C'Mon Everybody/ Something Else/ Bring It On Home/ How Many More Times Medley
R: Vg-Ex. Soundboard. S: Royal Albert Hall Jan. 9 '70. C: Japanese CD. Dbw.

CD - ROYAL DRAGON
TARANTURA RAH-1, 2
CD1: Whole Lotta Love/ Communication Breakdown/ C'mon Everybody/ Something Else/ Bring It On Home/ How Many More Times Medley
CD2 : We're Gonna Groove/ I Can't Quit You/ White Summer, Black Mountain Side/ Whole Lotta Love/ Communication Breakdown/ C'mon Everybody/ Long Tall Sally Medley
R: CD1 Vg-Ex. Soundboard. CD2 G from video. S: Royal Albert Hall Jan. 9 '70. C: Japanese CD. Box set with poster. Pic CDs.

Time CD1 50:10. CD2 47:11.

CD - THE 7TH AMERICAN TOUR
WHOLE LOTTA LIVE WLL022/023
CD1: Immigrant Song/ Heartbreaker/ Since I've Been Loving You/ Black Dog/ Dazed And Confused/ Stairway To Heaven/ That's The Way/ Going To California
CD2: What Is And What Should Never Be/ Whole Lotta Love/ Weekend/ Rock And Roll/ Communication Breakdown/ Organ Solo/ Thank You
R: G. Audience.   S: Forum, Los Angeles Aug. 21 '71.   C: ECD. Dcc. 500 made.
Time CD1 65:43. CD2 59:13.

CD - SONG OF THE SOUTH
CAPRICORN CR-2036
Moby Dick/ Guitar Solo/ Achilles Last Stand/ Stairway To Heaven/ Whole Lotta Love/ Rock And Roll/ It'll Be Me
R: Vg-Ex. Stereo.   S: Fortworth, Texas May 22 '77.   C: Time 60:37. Limited numbered edition of 1,000.

CD - STAIRWAY TO HEAVEN SESSIONS 1970 - 1971
ZOSO'S COMPANY ZOSO 9301/2
CD1: Stairway To Heaven (version 1) (3:42)/ Untitled 1 (3:56)/ Untitled 2 (1:52)/ Black Dog (6:46)/ No Quarter (5:01)/ Stairway To Heaven (version 2) (5:51)/ Untitled 3 (1:03)/ Stairway To Heaven (version 3) (6:01)/ Stairway To Heaven version 4) (8:08)/ Stairway To Heaven (live) (8:39)/ Friends (4:29)
CD2: Immigrant Song (2:35)/ Out On The Titles (3:39)/ I Wanna Be Her Man (1:39)/ Acoustic Jam 1 (2:40)/ Acoustic Jam 2 (6:01)/ Acoustic Jam 3 (2:09)/ Acoustic Jam 4 (6:17)/ Acoustic Jam (4:11)/ Acoustic Jam (11:24)/ Down By The Seaside 1 (3:19)/ Down By The Seaside 2 (2:16)/ Down By The Seaside 3 (1:42)/ Acoustic Jam 7 (2:01)/ Bron-Y-Aur Stomp (1:39)/ Poor Tom (2:48)/ Hey Hey, What Can I Do (1:39)
R: G-Vgs. Some hiss.   C: Japanese CD. Dcc.

CD - SUMMER OF '69
RUBBER DUBBER RD-001
Train Kept A Rollin'/ I Can't Quit You Baby/ I Gotta Move/ Dazed And Confused/ White Summer/ You Shook Me/ How Many More Times
R: G-Vg audience recording.   S: The Swing Auditorium, San Bernadino, CA Aug. 8 '69.
C: Japanese CD. Time 54:46. Limited edition of 750 numbered copies.

CD - SUNDAZED
SILVER RARITIES SIRA203/4/5
CD1: Song Remains The Same/ Sick Again/ Nobody's Fault But Mine/ Over The Hills/ Since I've Been Loving You/ No Quarter/ Ten Years Gone
CD2: The Battle Of Evermore/ Going To California/ That's Alright/ Black Country Woman/ Bron-Y-Aur Stomp/ White Summer/ Kashmir/ Moby Dick
CD3: Guitar Solo/ Achilles Last Stand/ Stairway To Heaven/ It'll Be Me
R: Vg-Exs. Audience.   S: LA Forum June 26 '77.   C: ECD. Time CD1 77:14. CD2 51:34. CD3 50:26.

CD - THE 10TH US TOUR
WHOLE LOTTA LIVE WLL01/0203
CD1: Rock And Roll/ Sick Again/ Over The Hills And Far Away/ In My Time Of Dying/ The Song Remains The Same/ The Rain Song/ Kashmir
CD2: No Quarter/ Trampled Underfoot/ Moby Dick
CD3: Dazed And Confused/ Stairway To Heaven/ Whole Lotta Love/ Black Dog/ Heartbreaker
R: G-Vg. Audience. Warble. Hum.   S: Madison Square Gardens, New York Feb. 12 '75.
C: ECD. Dcc. 500 made. Time CD1 52:45. CD2 45:46. CD3 61:50.

CD - TOCCATA & FUGUE
TARANTURA TF 001/2
CD1: We're Gonna Groove/ I Can't Quit You/ Dazed And Confused/ Heartbreaker/ White Summer/ Since/ Organ Solo/ Thank You
CD2: Moby Dick/ How Many More Times/ Whole Lotta Love
R: G. Audience.   S: Helsinki Feb. 21 '70.
C: Japanese CD. Time CD1 58:42. CD2 49:16.

CD - TRAMPLED UNDER JIMMY'S FOOT
SILVER RARITIES SIRA 168/169/170
CD1: Rock 'N' Roll/ Sick Again/ Over The Hills And Far Away/ In My Time Of Dying/ The Song Remains The Same/ The Rain Song/ Kashmir
CD2: No Quarter/ Trampled Underfoot/ Moby Dick
CD3: Dazed And Confused/ Stairway To Heaven/ Whole Lotta Love/ Heartbreaker
R: G. Audience.   S: Long Beach Mar. 12 '75.
C: ECD. Dcc. CD1 55:23. CD2 46:50. CD3 74:49.

CD - TWO DAYS AFTER
IMMIGRANT IM-037-039
CD1: Rock And Roll/ Celebration Day/ Bring It On Home, Black/ Over The Hills And Far Away/ Misty Mountain Hop/ Since I've Been Loving You/ No Quarter
CD2: The Song Remains The Same/ The Rain Song/ Dazed And Confused/ Stairway To Heaven
CD3: Moby Dick/ Heartbreaker/ Whole Lotta Love Medley: The Crunge, Boogie Woogie/ Communication Breakdown/ The Ocean
R: G.   S: Kezar Stadium, San Francisco June 2 '73.   C: Japanese CDs.

CD - VOODOO DRIVE
TARANTURA T2CD-16-1,2
CD1: Opening/ Immigrant Song/ Heartbreaker/ Black Dog/ Since I've Been Loving You/ Stairway To Heaven/ Going To California/ That's The Way/ Tangerine/ Bron-Y-Aur Stomp
CD2: Moby Dick/ Dazed And Confused/ Whole Lotta Love Medley

R: Vg. Audience.   S: Adelaide, Australia Feb. 19
'72.   C: Japanese CD. Vinyl gatefold sleeve
with photos from gig. CD1 52:56. CD2 43:44.

CD - WIZARDRY
JOKER JOK 008 A
Rock And Roll/ Celebration Day/ Bring It On
Home/ Black Dog/ Over The Hills And Far Away/
Misty Mountain Top/ Since I've Been Loving You/
No Quarter
R: Exs. Soundboard.   S: Madison Square
Garden, NY July 28 '73.   C: Australian CD.

CD - YOU GOTTA BE COOL
WHOLE LOTTA LIVE
CD1: Intro/ Immigrant Song/ Heartbreaker/ Dazed
And Confused/ Bring It On Home/ That's The
Way/ Bron-yr-Aur/ Since I've Been Loving You
CD2: Organ Solo/ Thank You/ What Is And What
Should Never Be/ Moby Dick/ Whole Lotta Love/
Communication Breakdown
R: G-Vg. Audience.   S: Tulsa, Oklahoma Aug.
21 '70.   C: ECD. Dcc. 500 made.
Time CD1 72:25. CD2 65:54.

LENNON, JOHN

CD - FREE AS A BIRD
FAB 1
Free As A Bird (Take 1 - 3:25)/ Free As A Bird
(Take 3 - 2:41)/ Real Love (Take 1 - 3:45)/ Real
Love (Take 4 - 3:56)/ Real Love (Take 5 - 2:46)/
Real Love (Take 6 - 2:19)/ Real Love (unknown
source - 3:08)/ Real Love (take that preceded the
Imagine film and video - 1:28)/ Oh My Love
(rehearsals for 'Working Class Hero' - 32:05)/
Starting Over (12" promo version - taken from
vinyl - 4:17)/ I Need Your Loving ('Ready Steady
Go' - 2:13)/ Open Your Box (demo - 3:32)/
Greenfield Morning (demo - 5:30)/ Don't Let Me
Down (home demo 2:09)
R: Tracks 1-8 Vg. Tracks 9-14 G.   C: Dcc. 70:00.

CD - IMAGINE...ALL THE OUTTAKES
VIGOTONE VT-118/119/120
CD1: Imagine/ Crippled Inside/ Jealous Guy/ It's
So Hard/ I Don't Wanna Be A Soldier Mama, I
Don't Wanna Die/ Gimme Some Truth/ Oh My
Love/ How Do You Sleep?/ How?/ Oh Yoko!/ 'Just
A Little Story...'/ Well (Baby Please Don't Go)
CD2: Tracks 1-4 Imagine/ Crippled Inside/ Tracks
6-8 Jealous Guy/ Tracks 9-10 I Don't Wanna Be A
Soldier Mama, I Don't Wanna Die/ Tracks 11-12
Oh My Love/ Tracks 13-15 How?/ Oh Yoko!/ I'm
The Greatest/ Imagine/ San Francisco Bay Blues
CD3: How Do You Sleep?/ Oh My Love/ How?/
People Get Ready, How?/ Medley: How?, Child
Of Nature, Oh Yoko!/ Oh Yoko!/ It's So Hard/ I
Don't Wanna Be a Soldier Mama, I Don't Wanna
Die/ How Do You Sleep?
R: Ex.   S: CD1 alternate album. CD2 outtakes.
CD3 tracks 1-8 sessions. Tracks 9-15 demos.
Tracks 16-18 overdub session.   C: 34 page
booklet included.

CD - THE MAN AND HIS MUSIC VOL. IV
NIGHTLIFE N-008
Don't Let Him Slip Away (version 1)/ Look What
The Wind Blew In/ Return Of The Farmer's Son/
Going Down/ Dublin/ Things Ain't Working Out
Down On The Farm/ It's Only Money/ Little
Darling/ Still In Love With You/ Jailbreak/ Thunder
And Lightning/ Rosalie/ Hate/ Don't Let Him Slip
Away (version 2)
R: Poor-Vg sound.   S: Tracks 1, 13, 14 studio
takes. Tracks 2-6 studio recordings. Tracks 7-9
BBC sessions. Tracks 10-12 '83 tour.

CD - S.I.R. JOHN WINSTON ONO LENNON
MOONLIGHT ML 9506
Roll Over Beethoven (2:30)/ Honey Don't (3:05)/
Ain't That A Shame (2:34)/ My Babe, Not Fade
Away (2:30)/ Send Me Some Lovin' (2:49)/ Yoko
Jam (2:21)/ Whole Lotta Shakin' Goin' On (5:29)/
Honey Hush (2:13)/ Don't Be Cruel, Hound Dog
(4:27)/ Caribbean (3:09)/ Honky Tonk (3:11)/ Mind
Train (8:07)/ Come Together (7:00)/ We're All
Water (11:04)
R: Exs. Soundboard.   S: Rehearsals at S.I.R.
Studios Aug. 21 and 22 '72.   C: ECD. Dcc.

CD - WINSTON O'BOOGIE
BAG RECORDS BAG 5072
Move Over MS. L (1)/ Mover Over MS. L (2)/
Move Over MS. L (3)/ Surprise, Surprise (Sweet
Bird Of Paradox) (1)/ Whatever Gets You Through
The Night (1)/ Whatever Gets You Through The
Night (2)/ Move Over MS. L (4)/ Surprise,
Surprise (Sweet Bird Of Paradox) (2)/ Going
Down On Love/ Beef Jerky/ Whatever Gets You
Through The Night (3)/ Steel And Glass/ Scared/
Old Dirty Road/ Nobody Love You When (Your
Down And Out)/ Bless You/ What You Got/ No. 9
Dream (1)/ No. 9 Dream (2)
R: Ex. Soundboard.   S: Studio.   C: ECD.
Time 69:02.

LENNOX, ANNIE

CD - GOLDEN LADY
KISS THE STONE KTS 433
You Have Placed A Chill In My Heart (5:21)/ Why
(5:12)/ Cold (4:43)/ No More 'I Love You's' (4:56)/
Here Comes The Rain Again (5:17)/ Train In Vain
(5:00)/ Don't Let It Bring You Down (5:05)/ No
More 'I Love You's' (5:02)*/ Train In Vain (3:43)*
R: Exs. Soundboard.   S: Toronto Mar. 13 '95.
*New York City Mar. 25 '95.   C: ECD. Dcc. Pic
CD.

LITTLE VILLAGE

CD - ON THE BORDER
BABY CAPONE BC 011
Solar Sex Panel (7:53)/ The Action (4:09)/ Fool
Who Knows (4:02)/ Do You Want My Job (6:04)/
She Runs Hot (4:57)/ Don't Think About Her
When You're Trying To Drive (5:15)/ Memphis In
The Meantime (6:10)/ Cryin' In My Sleep (4:53)/

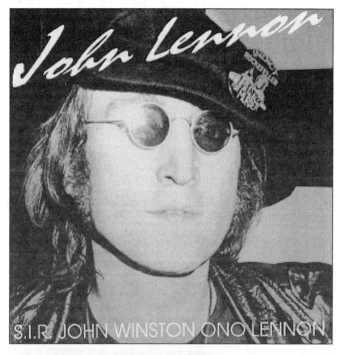

Big Love (8:47)/ Little Sister (3:39)/ Half A Boy
And A Man (3:44)/ Thing Called Love (6:07)/
Lipstick Sunset (5:27)
R: Exs. Soundboard.   S: Warfield Theatre, San
Francisco Dec. 12 '92.   C: ECD. Dcc. Pic CD

LIVE

CD - SELLING THE DRAMA
PRINT 007
All Over You/ Selling The Drama/ Lightning
Crashes/ I Alone/ All Over You/ Stage/ Shit Town/
Selling The Drama/ Supernatural/ I Alone/
Operation Spirit/ Selling The Drama/ All Over You/
Beauty Of Grey/ T.B.D./ I Alone/ Lightning
Crashes/ White Discussion
R: Exs. Soundboard.   S: Tracks 1-4 'Unplugged'
session for Studio Hilversum Feb. 20 '95. Tracks
5-10 Melkweg, Amsterdam Feb. 11 '95. Tracks
11-18 'MTV Unplugged', New York Feb. '95.
C: ECD. Dcc. Time 76:35.

CD - SHIT TOWN
KISS THE STONE KTS 437
Operation Spirit/ Selling The Drama/ All Over You/
Beauty Of Grey/ T.B.D/ I Alone/ Supernatural/
Lightning Crashes/ White, Discussion/ All Over
You/ Stage/ Shit Town/ Selling The Drama/
Supernatural/ I Alone/ Waitress/ Iris
R: Ex.   S: Tracks 1-9 acoustic show The
Brooklyn Academy, New York City Nov. '94.
Tracks 10-17 electric show Amsterdam, Holland
11/2/95.   C: ECD. Dcc. Pic CD. Time 77:14.

CD - STAGE
PRINT 008
The Dam At Otter Creek/ All Over You/ Selling
Drama/ Rain Lies On The Riverside/ Iris/ Pillar Of
Davidson/ We're Breaking Up/ I Alone/ Take My
Anthem/ Waitress/ Lightning Crashes/ T.B.D./ Hit
Towne/ Road Crew Introduction: White Discussion
R: Ex. Audience.   S: Bethlehem, PA Mar. 14
'95.   C: ECD. Dbw. Red type. Time 77:04.

CD - SUPERNATURAL
KISS THE STONE KTS 449
Selling The Drama (3:26)/ All Over You (4:21)/
Beauty Of Gray (4:38)/ Shit Town (4:20)/ Top
(3:10)/ Supernatural (3:30)/ Pain Lies On The
Riverside (4:18)/ Iris (4:43)/ Lightning Crashes
(5:30)/ I Alone (5:39)/ 10,000 Years (5:46)/ White,
Discussion (5:01)/ All Over You (4:05)/ Selling The
Drama (3:26)/ Lightning Crashes (5:19)/ I Alone
(3:49)
R: Ex. Soundboard.   S: Tracks 1-12 The
Academy Theater, New York City Nov. '94. Tracks
13-16 acoustic session.   C: ECD. Dcc. Pic CD.

CD - UNWIRED
OCTOPUS OCTO 192
Operation Spirit (4:47)/ Selling Drama (3:50)/ All
Over You (5:02)/ The Beauty Of Grey (4:44)/
T.B.D.(4:39)/ I Alone (5:13)/ Supernatural (3:34)/
Lightning Crashes (5:24)/ White Discussion

(5:21)/ Stage (3:01)/ Shit Town (4:17)/ Selling The
Drama (3:48)/ Supernatural (3:58)/ Iris (4:09)/ I
Alone (6:09)/ Waitress (6:09)
R: Exs. Soundboard.   S: Tracks 1-9 'Unplugged'
sessions, New York City Apr. '95. Tracks 10-16
Melkweg, Amsterdam, Holland Feb. 11 '95.
C: ECD.

CD - YORKSTERS IN BOSTON
HOME RECORDS KR 6035-8
Selling The Drama (3:21)/ All Over You (4:08)/
The Beauty Of Grey (4:54)/ Shit Towne (5:06)/
Top (2:51)/ Pillar Of Davidson (7:18)/
Supernatural (4:01)/ Pain Lies On The Riverside
(4:35)/ Stage (3:08)/ Iris (4:14)/ Waitress (4:49)/
Lightning Crashes (6:02)/ I Alone (4:12)/ 10,000
Years (Peace Is Now) (7:15)/ Friend (Unreleased)
(6:07)/ White, Discussion (5:55)
R: Vg. Audience.   S: Orpheum Theater, Boston
Nov. 22 '94.   C: ECD. Dcc.

LOFGREN, NILS

CD - BACK IT UP
THE SWINGIN' PIG TSP 194
Cry Tough/ It's Not A Crime/ For Your Love/ Goin'
Back/ Share A Little/ Incidentally...It's Over/ You're
The Weight/ Take You To The Movies/ Back It Up/
Keith Don't Go (Ode To The Glimmer Twin)/ Rock
And Roll Crook
R: Exs. Soundboard.   S: Tower Theatre,
Philadelphia '76.   C: ECD.

L7

7" - L7
S1: Death Wish/ Cat 'O Nine Tails
S2: Mr. Intercity/ Shove
R: G. Audience.   S: International Pop Festival
Underground Convention, Olympia, WA Aug. 20-
25 '91.   C: USA. Green/black sleeve. Limited
edition of 1000 on yellow vinyl. 45 RPM.

LYNOTT'S, PHIL GRAND SLAM

CD - LIVE & DEMOS
BONDAGE MUSIC BON 012
Yellow Pearl/ Nineteen/ Sisters Of Mercy/ Harlem/
Parisienne Walkways/ Crime Rate Is Going Up/
Breakdown/ Here We Go/ Gay Boys/ Can't Get
Away/ Military Man/ Crime Rate Is Going Up/
Breakdown
R: G-Vg. Soundboard.   S: Tracks 1-8 Glasgow
'84. Tracks 9-13 demos '84.   C: Japanese CD.
Dbw. Time 72:51.

LYNYRD SKYNYRD

CD - ATLANTA 1993
SWINGIN' PIG TSP-CD-209
Al Kooper Introduction/ Workin' For MCA/
Saturday Night Special/ What's Your Name/
Simple Man/ Gimme Three Steps/ That Smell/
Good Lovin's Hard To Find/ Outta Hell In My

Dodge/ The Last Rebel/ Don't Misunderstand Me/ Sweet Home Alabama
S: The Fox Theatre, Atlanta Feb. 19 '93.
C: ECD.

M

MACHINE HEAD

CD - PRESSURE POINT
KISS THE STONE KTS 455
A Thousand Lies/ Blood For Blood/ Old/ Alan's On Fire/ Davidian/ My Mystery/ Old/ None But My Own/ Davidian/ A Thousand Lies/ The Rage To Overcome/ Blood For Blood/ Old/ Alan's On Fire/ Block
R: Exs. Soundboard.   S: On tour Nov. '94.
C: ECD. Dcc. Pic CD. Time 78:38.

MADONNA

CD - CLOWNING AROUND
JOKER JOK-009-C
Material Girl/ Cherish/ Into The Groove/ Like A Virgin/ Like A Prayer/ Live To Tell/ Oh! Father/ Papa Don't Preach/ Express Yourself/ Open Your Heart/ Holiday/ Vogue
R: Exs. Soundboard.   S: Live Europe '90.
C: Australian CD. Dcc. Time 60:25.

CD - EMMY AND THE EMMYS FEATURING MADONNA
TOTONKA. CD PRO 11
Best Girl/ Hot House Flower/ Bells Ringing/ Simon Says/ Nobody's Fool/ No Time For Love/ Drowning/ Love For Tender/ Love Express/ Drowning*
R: Poor. Audience.   S: Club date. *First studio demo.

CD - THE GIRLIE SHOW
BLACK SUN MUSIC BSM 002/3
CD1: Erotica (6:37)/ Fever (4:52)/ Vogue (5:31)/ Rain, Just My Imagination (9:29)/ Express Yourself (5:04)/ Deeper And Deeper (6:29)/ Why Is It So Hard? (5:32)/ In This Life (7:46)/ The Beast Within (Remix) (6:00)
CD2 Live A Virgin, Falling In Love Again (5:55)/ Bye Bye Baby (4:37)/ Going Bananas (2:11)/ La Isla Bonita (6:11)/ Holiday (11:32)/ Justify My Love (8:52)/ Everybody Is A Star, Everybody (10:58)
R: Exs. Soundboard.   S: Live '93.   C: ECD. Dbw. Pic CDs.

CD - LIVE VOL. 1
JOKER JOK-009-A
Like A Virgin, Can't Help Myself/ Where's The Party?/ Live To Tell/ Into The Groove/ La Isla Bonita/ Who's That Girl?/ Holiday
C: Australian CD.

CD - LIVE VOL. 2
JOKER JOK-009-B
Open Your Heart/ Lucky Star/ True Blue/ Papa Don't Preach/ White Heat, Perry Mason Theme/ Causing A Commotion/ The Look Of Love/ Dress You Up/ Material Girl
C: Australian CD.

CD - SPECIAL DJ REMIXES
Justify My Love (The Justified XXX-Rated Remix) (7:30)/ Vogue (The Bette Davis Pose 12" Version) (10:08)/ Into The Groove (D.M.C. Remix) (6:13)/ Holiday (Rap Mix) (8:40)/ Like a Prayer (12" Extended Dance Club Remix) (9:30)/ Rescue Me (Special Edit Remix) (11:26)/ Promise To Try (Willing To Dance Mix) (3:34)/ Dear Jessie (Joyeux Noel Mix) (4:35)/ Prayer-Dance Megamix (Including: Love Song, Like A Prayer, Express Yourself, Holiday, Think Of Me, Into The Groove, Lucky Star, Like A Virgin, True Blue, Everybody, Papa Don't Preach, Angel, Material Girl) (16:55)
R: Exs. Soundboard.   C: ECD. Dcc.

CD - TOTAL SATISFACTION MIXES
BS 06951
Rescue Me (Houseboat Mix) (7:12)/ Vogue (12" Version) (8:16)/ Express Yourself (Shep's Re-Mix) (4:01)/ Like A Prayer (Club Version) (6:38)/ Causing A Commotion (Silver Screen Mix) (6:40)/ Deeper And Deeper (John's Classic 12" Version) (7:25)/ Like A Virgin (Extended Dance Remix) (6:06)/ La Isla Bonita (Chris' Extended Dance Remix) (5:26)/ Erotica (Woolen-Willy-Warmers Remix) (6:10)/ Fever (Late Night Mix) (2:12)/ Bedtime Story (Orbital Remix) (7:42)/ Bye Bye Baby (Erotic Saxy Remix) (4:00)/ Take A Bow (Steve's Sweaty Soul Remix) (6:21)
R: Exs. Soundboard.   C: ECD. Dcc. Pic CD.

MALMSTEEN, YNGWIE

CD - HEAVEN TONIGHT 14
WYVERN WYM-35F1/2
CD1: Never Die/ Bed Room Eyes/ Rising Force/ Bad Blood/ Guitar Solo/ Far Beyond The Sun/ Forever One/ Pyramid Of Cheops/ Drum Solo/ Seventh Sign/ Guitar Solo
CD2: Spasebo Blues/ Guitar Solo/ You Don't Remember I'll Never Forget/ Keyboard Solo, Brothers/ Crash And Burn/ Heaven Tonight/ Black Star/ Hendrix Medley: Spanish Castle Magic, Foxy Lady/ Purple Haze/ Highway Star
R: Ex audience recording.   S: Osaka Mar. 14 '94.   C: Japanese CD.

CD - HIGHWAY STAR
NIGHTLIFE N-030/031
CD1: Intro, Liar/ Queen In Love/ Fury/ For Beyond The Sun/ Fire/ Keyboard Solo/ Soldier Without Faith/ I Am A Viking/ Guitar Solo/ You Don't Remember, I'll Never Forget
CD2: On The Run Again/ Trilogy Suite Op:5/ I'll See The Light, Tonight/ Blues Jam/ Black Star/

Too Young To Live, Too Drunk To Die/ Highway Star
R: Exs. Audience.   S: Festival Hall, Osaka Nov. 14 '86.   C: Japanese CD.

CD - LITTLE SAVAGE
YMS-0524
As Above, So Below/ Far Beyond The Sun/ On The Run Again/ Little Savage/ Kree Nakoorie/ Guitar Solo/ Anguish And Fear/ Disciples Of Hell/ Black Star/ Magic Mirror/ As Above, So Below/ Anguish And Fear/ Motherless Child/ I Surrender
R: Ex. Live - audience. Demos - soundboard. S: Tracks 1-9 Stockholm, Sweden May 24 '85. Tracks 10-13 'Rising Force' demos. Track 14 Manchester, England Nov. 17 '88.   C: With Rising Force.

CD - SOMETHING ELSE
CRYSTAL SOUND CS-013
Merlin Castle/ Birth Of The Sun/ Dyin' Man/ Suite Opus No. 3/ Something Else/ Burn/ Smoke On The Water/ Highway Star/ Woman From Tokyo/ Jimi Hendrix Medley
C: Vg. Surface noise.   S: Tracks 1-4 demos. Track 5 Nagoya '84. Track 6 Tokyo '94. Track 7 Tokyo '88. Track 8 Osaka '86. Tracks 9-10 Hyogo '92.

CD - SWEDISH GOD
BONDAGE MUSIC BON 011
Intro, As Above, So Below/ I'll See The Light, Tonight/ Far Beyond The Sun/ Icarus' Dream Suite Opus 4/ I Am A Viking/ On The Run Again/ Little Savage, Guitar Solo/ Anguish And Fear, Drum Solo/ Disciples Of Hell/ Acoustic Solo, Black Star/ Hiroshima Mon Amour
R: Ex. FM recording.   S: Milwaukee July 6 '85. C: Japanese CD. With Rising Force.

MARILLION

CD - BRAVE TOUR
BANZAI BZCD 015/16
CD1: Bridge/ Living With The Big Lie/ Runaway/ Goodbye To All That, Wave, Mad, The Opium Den, The Slide, Standing In The Swing/ Hard As Love/ The Hollow Man/ Alone Again In The Lap Of Luxury, Now Wash Your Hands/ Paper Lies/ Brave/ The Great Escape, The Last Of You, Fallin' From The Moon/ Made Again
CD2: Cover My Eyes/ Slainte Mhath/ Easter/ Garden Party/ Waiting To Happen/ Hooks In You/ Sugar Mice/ Freaks/ Gimme Some Lovin'/ Substitute/ Eric
R: Ex. Audience.   S: Teatro Verdi, Sestri Ponente, Genova, Italy Apr. 15 '94. CD2 Track 7 Milwaukee Feb. 23 '90. Tracks 8-9 live at Tivoli, Utrecht, Sept. 22 '90. Track 10 live in Cologne, June 1 '91. Track 11 London Dec. 22 '90.
C: ECD. Dcc.

CD - CHILDHOOD REHEARSALS
PAPER CORN MUSIC PC 010

Intro by Richard Skinner/ Garden Party (7:17)/ Cinderella Search (6:08)/ Jigsaw (7:48)/ Misplaced Childhood (Alternate Version) (16:34)/ Incubus (8:40)/ Chelsea Monday (8:11)
R: Ex.   S: Hammersmith Odeon Dec. 13, 14 and 15 '84.   C: ECD. Dcc.

CD - HEAVEN & HELL
BABY CAPONE BC 029
Garden Party (4:48)/ Freaks (4:20)/ Assassin (6:22)/ Misplaced Childwood I Medley: Pseudo Silk Kimono, Kaileigh, Bittersuite, Heart Of Lothian (18:52)/ Misplaced Childhood II Medley: Waterhole, Lords Of The Backstage, Blind Curve, Misplaced Childhood Finale (17:33)/ White Feather (6:50)/ Forgotten Song (8:27)/ Market Square Heroes (8:25)
R: Ex. Audience.   S: Live in Europe '86. C: ECD. Dcc. Pic CD.

MARLEY, BOB

CD - FROM THE INSIDE
SWINDLE SWN 026
Slave Driver ('73 BBC session) (3:08)/ Concrete Jungle ('73 alternate studio) (3:57)/ Get Up, Stand Up ('73 studio demo) (3:47)/ Talkin' Blues ('74 studio demo) (4:33)/ Amadu ('73 alternate studio) (3:20)/ Jah Live ('75 studio demo) (2:38)/ Smile Jamaica Dub ('76 alternate studio) (2:22)/ Turn Your Lights Down Low ('77 studio demo) (3:49)/ Exodus ('77 studio demo) (8:01)/ Runnin' Away ('78 studio demo) (4:31)/ Who Colt The Game ('78 studio demo) (3:15)/ I Know A Place ('78 studio demo) (4:00)/ Ride Natty Ride ('79 Tuff Gong rehearsal) (11:07)/ Give Thanks And Praises ('80 studio demo) (3:38)/ Chant Down Babylon ('80 studio demo) (4:48)/ Babylon Feel Dis One ('80 studio demo) (2:15)/ Zion Train ('80 Tuff Gong rehearsal) (3:56)/ I Shot The Sheriff ('80 Tuff Gong rehearsal) (2:56)/ Redemption Song ('80 Essex House Hotel, NY) (2:29)
R: Ex. Soundboard.   C: ECD.

CD - OFFICIAL LIVE BOOTLEG
THE LAST BOOTLEG RECORD LBR 007/2
CD1: Positive Vibration (5:55)/ Wake Up And Live (5:27)/ Them Belly Full (3:31)/ Concrete Jungle (5:23)/ I Shot The Sheriff (4:36)/ Running Away (3:12)/ Crazy Baldheads (4:47)/ Ambush In The Night (3:58)/ Heathen (5:08)/ War (4:49)/ No More Trouble (2:15)/ Ride Natty Ride (4:32)/ Africa Unite (4:31)/ One Drop (4:15)/ Jammin' (6:55)/ In This Love (3:35)/ Natty Dread (3:49)
CD2: Exodus (4:42)/ Get Up, Stand Up (5:47)/ Rebel Music (6:03)/ I Shot The Sheriff (12:42)/ Natty Dread (8:23)/ Slave Driver (4:27)/ Trenchtown Rock (6:03)/ Concrete Jungle (6:00)/ Midnight Ravers (6:37)/ Talkin' Blues (6:22)
R: Ex. Soundboard.   S: CD1 and CD2 tracks 1-2 The Civic Centre, Santa Cruz, Dec. 2/12/'79. CD2 tracks 3-10 Quiet Knight Club, Chicago June 10 '75.   C: ECD. Pic CDs.

CD - SOUL REBEL
BABY CAPONE BC 016
Conquering Lion (5:00)/ Natural Mystic (4:50)/
Trenchtown Rock (6:38)/ Natty Dread (6:06)/
Rastaman Vibration/Jah Love (7:40)/ War (6:04)/
Jammin' (9:12)/ Jah Live (4:40)
R: Exs. Soundboard.   S: Kingston, Jamaica Apr.
22 '78.   C: ECD. Dcc. Pic CD.

CD - WELCOME TO NEW YORK
THE SWINGIN' PIG TSP 207
Trenchtown Rock/ Burnin' And Lootin'/ No Woman
No Cry/ Kinky Reggae/ Stir It Up/ Lively Up
Yourself/ I Shot The Sheriff/ Get Up, Stand Up
R: Exs. Soundboard.   S: New York '76.
C: ECD.

MATTHEWS, DAVE BAND

CD - EAT, DRINK AND BE MERRY
KISS THE STONE KTS 473
What Would You Say/ Ants Marching/ Jimi Thing/
All Along The Watchtower/ Tripping Billies/
Granny Dancing Nancies/ Drive In Drive Out/ Two
Step Song That Jane Likes/ Help Myself/ Rhyme
And Reason
R: Exs. Soundboard.   S: On tour '93 and '95.
C: ECD. Dcc. Pic CD. Time 70:14.

CD - RIDING THE RHYTHM
OCTOPUS OCTO 185/186
CD1: One Sweet World (9:45)/ Satellite (5:49)/
Trippin' Billies (4:52)/ The Best Of What's Around
(6:27)/ Quick Lay And Say Goodbye (5:41)/
Warehouse (8:55)/ Dancing Nancies (8:57)/ Jimi
Thing (10:08)/ Typical Situation (9:50)
CD2: The Song Jane Likes (5:39)/ Rhyme And
Reason (5:28)/ All Along The Watchtower (8:20)/
Pay For What You Get (6:35)/ Ants Marching
(7:02)/ No. 36 (8:17)/ Warehouse (9:29)/ Trippin'
Billies (4:39)/ Rhyme And Reason (5:23)/ What
Would You Say (3:28)
R: Exs. Soundboard.   S: The Irving Plaza, NYC
July 28 '94. CD2 Tracks 6-8 The Roxy Club,
Amsterdam, Holland Nov. 2 '94. Track 9 The
House Of Blues, Los Angeles Mar. 10 '95. Track
10 The Roseland Theatre, NYC Feb. 24 '95.
C: ECD. Dcc. Pic CD.

MAYALL, JOHN AND THE BLUESBREAKERS

CD - BULLDOGS FOR SALE
TEDDY BEAR TB 73
Crawling Up A Hill (2:16)/ Crocodile Walk (2:24)/
Bye Bye Bird (2:53)/ I'm Your Witchdoctor (2:13)/
Cheating Woman (2:05)/ Nowhere To Run (1:49)/
On Top Of The World (2:36)/ Key To Love (2:50)/
Riding On The L And N (2:24)/ Sitting In The Rain
(2:57)/ Leaping Christine (1:55)/ Parchman Farm
(14:26)/ Time Has Come (6:45)
R: Ex. Soundboard.   S: Tracks 1-11 BBC
'65/'67. Tracks 12-14 Bremen, Germany '68.
C: ECD. Dcc.

CD - LIVE IN MILAN
FU 204
My Time After Awhile (5:23)/ Time To Hide (5:14)/
Oh Pretty Woman (7:58)/ Shakin On My Baby
(9:13)/ Catfish Blues (10:44)/ I Should Know
Better (8:36)/ Have You Heard (8:22)/ The
Stumble (4:19)/ Room To Move (10:39)/ Baby
What You Want Me To Do (9:15)
R: G-Vg. Audience.   S: Rolling Stone, Milan
Nov. '82.   C: ECD. Dcc. Pic CD. Featuring Mick
Taylor.

McLAUGHLIN, JOHN

CD - LIVE IN EUROPE 1991
ALL OF US AS 05
1 Nite Stand (8:04)/ Baba (7:02)/ Florianapolis
(19:30)/ Willows (5:50)/ Belo Horizonte (9:01)/
Jozy (5:25)/ Are You The One? (Part 1-3) (14:10)
R: Vg. Audience.   S: Europe '91.   C: ECD.
Pic CD.

CD - MAHAVISHNU ORCHESTRA: MC LAUGH-LIN, JOHN
ALL OF US AS 27
Spoken Presentation (1:14)/ Meeting Of The
Spirits (14:01)/ You Know You Know (7:30)/ The
Dance Of Maya (12:31)/ Awakening (includes
drum solo) (6:25)/ Dawn (12:43)/ The Noonward
Race (9:56)/ A Lotus On Irish Stream (7:09)
R: G. Audience.   S: Syracuse University, New
York 12/5/72.   C: ECD.

McCARTNEY, PAUL

CD - A ROYAL PERFORMANCE
STRAWBERRY RECORDS STR 005 CD
Introduction By Paul McCartney/ A Leaf/ Paul
Introducing Willard White/ The Drinking Song,
From Movement VI Work/ Long Time Ago/ The
Dodger/ Willard Introducing Sally Burgess/ Tres
Conejos, From Movement II, School/ Do You
Know Who You Are? From Movement VII, Crisis/
Can't Help Lovin' Dat Man/ Harold In Islington/
Paul Introducing Elvis Costello/ The Birds Will Still
Be Singing (Elvis Costello and the Brodsky
Quartet)/ One After 909 (McCartney and
Costello)/ Mistress And Maid (McCartney and
Costello)/ For No One (McCartney and the
Brodsky Quartet)/ Eleanor Rigby (McCartney and
the Brodsky Quartet)/ Yesterday (McCartney and
the Brodsky Quartet)/ Speech By Prince Charles/
Lady Madonna (McCartney and the Brodsky
Quartet)
R: Exs.   S: Complete performance, St. James
Palace, London Mar. 23 '95. Tracks 1-11 include
excerpts from 'The Liverpool Oratorio'.   C: ECD.
Dcc. McCartney with Elvis Costello and the
Brodsky Quartet. Time 66:21.

CD - BALLROOM DANCING
ORANGE 021
Ballroom Dancing (4:15) Old Man Lovin' (4:10)/
Reggae Instrumental #1 (3:10) Instrumental #1

(4:22)/ Crackin' Up (2:26)/ Nature Is Calling Me
(3:50)/ Instrumental #2 (2:22)/ Instrumental #3
(2:34)/ Reggae Instrumental #2 (2:18)/ Takin' On
A Woman (3:10)/ Instrumental #4 (4:05)/
Instrumental #5 (1:57) Instrumental #6 (3:00)/
Instrumental #7 (3:35)/ Instrumental #8 (2:06)/
Instrumental #9 (6:00)/ Instrumental #10 (8:49)/
Paul's Jazz Experiment (4:13)
C: ECD. Dcc. Time 66:24.

CD - GOOD TIMES COMIN'
VIGOTONE VT-121
Rock Show (Intro)/ Suicide/ Improvisation 1
(1980)/ Improvisation 2 (1980)/ Blackpool/ Twenty
Flight Rock/ Peggy Sue/ I'm Gonna Love You
Too/ Sweet Little Sixteen/ Loving You/ We're
Gonna Move/ Matchbox/ Cut Across Shorty/ Blue
Moon Of Kentucky/ Sally G./ Country Dreamer/
On The Wings Of A Nightingale/ Hanglide/ Press/
Yvonne/ Good Time Comin', Feel the Sun/ Rock
Show (Outro)
R: Vg. Tracks 5-12, 16 surface noise.   S: '73-
'86 studio takes. Tracks 5-12, 16 '74 studio takes.

CD - LIVE VOL. 1
JOKER JOK-038-A
Figure Of Eight/ Jet/ Got To Get You Into My Life/
Band On The Run/ We Got Married/ Let 'Em In/
The Long And Winding Road/ The Fool On The
Hill/ Sgt. Peppers Lonely Hearts Club Band/ Good
Day Sunshine/ Can't Buy Me Love/ Put It There/
Things We Said Today/ Eleanor Rigby/ This One/
My Brave Face/ Back In The USSR/ I Saw Her
Standing There
C: Australian CD.

CD - LIVE IN VENEZIA
FU 205/2
CD1: Presentation/ Venus And Mars, Rock Show,
Jet/ Let Me Roll It/ Spirit Of Ancient Egypt/
Medicine Jar/ Maybe I'm Amazed/ Call Me Back
Again/ Lady Madonna/ The Long And Winding
Road/ Live And Let Die/ Picasso Last Words,
Richard Cory/ Bluebird
CD2: I've Just Seen A Face/ Blackbird/ Yesterday/
You Gave Me The Answer/ Magneto And Titanium
Man/ My Love/ Listen To What The Man Said/ Let
'Em In/ Time To Hide/ Silly Love Song/ two other
tracks
R: Vg audience recording.   S: Venezia, Piazza
San Marco Sept. 25 '76.

CD - LIVERPOOL LIVE!
AYATOLLAH REC. ARC-011-50CD
Got To Get You Into My Life/ Getting Closer/
Every Night/ Again And Again And Again/ I've Had
Enough/ No Words/ Old Siam Sir/ Maybe I'm
Amazed/ The Fool On The Hill/ Let It Be/ Hot As
Sun/ Spin It On/ Twenty Flight Rock/ Go Now/
Arrow Through Me/ Wonderful Christmastime/
Coming Up/ Goodnight Tonight/ Yesterday/ Mull
Of Kintyre/ Band On The Run
R: Good audience recording. Static.
S: Liverpool Nov. 25 '79.

CD - OOBU JOOBU PART 1 AND 2
YELLOW CAT RECORDS
CD1: Oobu Joobu Intro (unreleased - 1:57)/ Take
It Away (outtake - 3:28)/ Talk About The
Radioshow (4:15)/ Biker Like An Icon (sound-
check - 3:55)/ Oobu Joobu (rehearsal - 1:54)/
Oobu Joobu, Good Rockin' Tonight (partial plus
chat - 3:34)/ Lucille (Paul and Little Richard ver-
sions edited together - 2:25)/ Little Richard's
Story, Tutti Frutti (3:51)/ Oubu Joobu, Cook Of
The House (Linda's Recipe - 2:13)/ New Orleans,
Oobu Joobu (unreleased Linda McCartney song -
2:20)/ Oobu Joobu, I Wanna Be Your Man (Paul
talks about 1st Stones single - 1:48)/ I Wanna Be
Your Man (soundcheck Giant Stadium - 2:35)/
Oobu Joobu, Story About Paul's Father (1:42)/
Flight Of The Bumblebee (Brenford Marcalls -
1:19) We Can Work It Out (soundcheck/rehearsal
- 2:57)/ Oobu Joobu Superman Jingle, Reggae
Story (chat - 1:53)/ Buttercup (Winston Scott from
7" single - 2:25)/ Ou Est Le Soleil? (home record-
ing and finished version - 3:32)/ Atlantic Ocean
(unfinished song - 1:48)/ Bonus track: A Fairy Tale
- Paul At The Piano Telling A Story To His
Children (mid seventies - 6:46)
CD2: Welcome Back, About Alan Crowder (jam -
1:32)/ Oobu Joobu, Don't Get Around Much
Anymore (studio outtake - 4:34)/ Papa's Got A
Brand New Bag (James Brown record - 2:04)/
They Call My Baby Baby (soundcheck jam -
4:35)/ Boil Crisis, Oubu Joobu Jingle (part of an
unreleased song from 'The Rude Corner' - 1:00)/
C-Moon (rehearsal - 4:12)/ Put It There (rehearsal
- 3:19)/ My Dad (from TV show, Chet Atkins -
4:07)/ Oobu Joobu Jingle, Paul About Buddy
(chat - 1:27)/ That'll Be The Day (Buddy Holly
record - 2:21)/ It's Now Or Never (jam - 1:46)/
(part of) Green Sleeves, Talk About Rainforests
(Jeff Beck, chat - 1:43)/ Once In A Lifetime
(Talking Heads record - 4:07)/ Cumberland Gap
(improvisation - 1:59)/ Chants (2 women from the
Burundi Tribe - 1:06)/ Oobu Joobu Intro, Ebony
And Ivory (rehearsal with Stevie Wonder - 7:03)/
Oobu Joobu Outro, Tutti Frutti (soundcheck -
2:30)/ Bonus tracks: It Seems Like Old Times #1
(home demo - 4:02) It Seems Like Old Times #2
(home demo - 3:47)
R: Ex.   S: Debut of Westwood One's 'Oobu
Joobu Radio Chronicles'. Broadcast the weekend
of May 27 '95.   C: ECD. Dcc. A program creat-
ed, directed and presented by DeeJay Paul
McCartney.

CD - OOBU JOOBU PART 3
YELLOW CAT RECORDS
Intro (2:00) Ain't That A Shame (outtake - 3:12)/
Intro, I'm In Love Again (Fats Domino, Paul sings
along - 2:20)/ Back In The USSR (studio outtake,
probably '89 - 3:35)/ Intro, Ain't She Sweet
(Jonathan and Darlene Edwards - 2:27)/ Lovers
That Never Were (Paul and Elvis Costello, part of
demo and part of regular - 3:08)/ This Sad
Burlesque (Elvis Costello and The Brodsky
Quartet - 4:19) Be Bop A Lula (soundcheck,

Kansas City - 3:55)/ Intro, The Joker (Steve Miller Band - 3:48)/ Hey Jude (rehearsal, mock version - 5:28)/ Linda's Recipe, Sugertime (Linda sings lead, Paul on backing vocals - 4:40)/ Intro, Spies Like Us (demo - 4:25)/ Let 'Em In (reggae version by Shinehead -2:40)/ Can't Buy Me Love (soundcheck - 3:58)/ Bonus Tracks: Oobu Joobu (demo - 5:54)/ Instrumental Jam (2:15)
R: Ex.   S: Broadcast the weekend of May 29 '95.   C: ECD. Dcc.

CD - OOBU JOOBU PART 4
YELLOW CAT RECORDS
Intro, Oobu Joobu (2:40)/ I Love This House (unfinished track with David Gilmour - 1:42)/ Knock On Wood (Eddy Floyd single - 3:03)/ Blue Moon Of Kentucky, Oobu Joobu Jingle (4:35)/ We're Gonna Move (Aka 'There's A Leak'), Oobu Joobu Jingle (rehearsal - 1:33)/ Reggae Intro, No Sun Will Shine (Bob Marley single - 3:53)/ We Got Married (demo - 4:07)/ Got To Get You Into My Life (rehearsal - 3:32)/ Oobu Joobu, Radio Play (chat - 3:16)/ Virginia Plain (Roxy Music single - 3:43)/ Blackbird (chat, rehearsal (1:03)/ Linda's Recipe, Cook Of The House (2:28)/ White Coated Man (Linda McCartney outtake - 2:40)/ Welcome Back, Oobu Joobu Time, Introduction (chat and jam - 1:20) Singin' The Blues (Toronto soundcheck - 2:45)/ Happy Jack (The Who single - 2:08)/ Pete Townsend (chat - 2:45)/ Rock Island Line (rehearsal by Paul - 2:04)/ Oobu Joobu Closing Theme (0:59)/ Bonus track: Long Instrumental (jam - 4:50)
R: Ex.   S: Broadcast the weekend of June 5 '95.   C: ECD. Dcc. Cover has an additional track (Oobu Joobu Jam) listed but it's not on the CD.

CD - OOBU JOOBU PART 5
YELLOW CAT RECORDS
Intro, Oobu Joobu (1:17)/ Love Mix (unfinished song - 2:44)/ Stop, You Don't Know Where She Came From (short demo from 'Rude Corner' - 0:26)/ Intro, Tipitina (song by Professor Longhair - 4:25)/ Fool On The Hill, O.J. Jingle (tour rehearsal - 4:38)/ Intro, New Moon Over Jamaica (mix of Paul's demo and Johnny Cash version - 4:31)/ Intro, Buladance (The Baki Tribe - 1:42)/ Bring It On Home (Minneapolis soundcheck - 6:57)/ Dance Of The Cossacks (from Nutcracker Ballet by The Royal Philharmonic Orchestra - 1:15)/ Linda's Recipe, Cook Of The House (1:57)/ You Know You Are Such An Incredible Thing (jam - 4:30)/ Fixing A Hole, O.J. Outro (tour rehearsal - 3:56)/ Intro, I Lost My Little Girl (soundcheck - 2:12)/ Gimme Some Loving (Spencer Davis Group single -2:49)/ Comedy (chat - 0:58)/ Let It Be (mock version - 0:37)/ Let It Be (rehearsal - 3:53)/ Oobu Joobu (outro jingle - 1:16)/ Bonus Tracks: Oobu Joobu Jingle Act 1: Right (from the animation film 'Daumier's Law' - 2:25)/ Act 2: Wrong (from the animation film 'Daumier's Law' - 2:03)
R: Ex.   S: Broadcast the weekend of June 12 '95.   C: ECD. Dcc.

CD - OOBU JOOBU PART 6
YELLOW CAT RECORDS
Intro, Welcome To Oobu Joobu (2:51)/ Looking For Changes (Las Vegas soundcheck - 2:41)/ Peace In The Neighbourhood (Las Vegas soundcheck - 5:13)/ Oobu Joobu Jingle, Hold A Candle To This (Pretenders single - 4:02)/ Message Of Chrissie Hynde (chat - 0:58)/ Wildlife (chat and music - 5:32)/ Oobu Joobu Jingle, I Can See Clearly Now (Johnny Nash single - 3:21)/ Introduction To 'Mother Nature's Son' (1:12)/ Mother Nature's Son (soundcheck - 3:05)/ Off The Ground (soundcheck - 4:31)/ Cook Of The House, Linda's Recipe (2:27)/ Cow (Linda McCartney and Carla Lane - 4:34)/ How Many People (rehearsal - 5:18)/ We All Stand Together (original demo - 4:01)/ Oobu Joobu Introductions (jingles - 0:16)/ Bonus Tracks: Act 3: Justice (from the animation film 'Daumier's Law' - 2:58)/ Act 4: Punishment (from the animation film 'Daumier's Law' - 2:33)
R: Ex.   S: Broadcast the weekend of June 19 '95.   C: ECD. Dcc.

CD - OOBU JOOBU PART 7
YELLOW CAT RECORDS
There's No Business Like Show Business, Oobu Joobu (3:41)/ Twenty Flight Rock (rehearsal - 2:58)/ The Girl Can't Help It (1:12)/ Summertime Blues (Eddy Cochran single - 1:57)/ Summertime (soundcheck - 4:15)/ Reggae Tunes And Highlights (studio - 2:24)/ Deacon Blues (Steely Dan single - 6:19)/ Drive My Car (rehearsal - 2:27)/ Oobu Joobu Jingle, You Know My Name, Intro About Brian Jones (Beatles' track, chat - 6:05)/ Cook Of The House, Linda's Recipe (1:50)/ Wild Prairie (Paul and Linda outtake - 4:33)/ Doing It All Day Long (film music - 1:17)/ Oobu Joobu (jingle - 1:14)/ Oobu Joobu, Introduction (1:27)/ Courtly Dancers (Julian Breem from 'Gloriana' - 1:25)/ Give Us A Chord, Roy (partial outtake From 'Rude Corner' - 0:54)/ Oh Mama, Eh Papa (soundcheck - 4:36)/ Oobu Joobu Outro, Soon You're Singing 'Round With Me (1:57)/ Bonus Tracks: Act 5: Payment (from the animation film 'Daumier's Law' - 3:32)/ Act 6: Release (from the animation film 'Daumier's Law' - 0:45)
R: Ex.   S: Broadcast the weekend of June 26 '95.   C: ECD. Dcc.

CD - OOBU JOOBU PART 8
YELLOW CAT RECORDS
Intro, Oobu Joobu (1:35)/ Two Instrumental Tracks (from 'Rude Corner' - 1:55)/ No I Never (jam - 2:52)/ Sneaking Up Behind You (instrumental by The Brecker Brothers - 4:38)/ Oobu Joobu Welcome Back (chat - 0:54)/ Crackin' Up (soundcheck - 4:24)/ Loui, Loui (Toots and The Maytells - 5:50)/ Daytime, Night-time Suffering (Wings' B-Side - 3:29)/ Intro To Bill Haley (chat - 1:40)/ Rock Around The Clock (Bill Haley and His Comets - 2:22)/ Intro To Fanclub Xmas Discs (chat - 1:14)/ If I Ever See Another Banjo (part of a X-mas flexi - 1:42)/ Introduction To Love In The Open Air (chat - 1:58)/ Love In The Open Air (Family Way

soundtrack - 1:04)/ Cook Of The House, Linda's Recipe (1:15)/ Hot Soup, Jam And Fools (improvisation - 2:41)/ Midland Two Step (Dusee Cajun Band - 3:42)/ San Francisco Bay Blues (Detroit soundcheck - 2:25)/ After You've Gone (demo from 'The Rude Corner' - 1:17)/ Oobu Joobu Outro (1:02)/ Yellow Submarine (rehearsal - 1:19)/ Bonus Tracks: Rupert Song #1 (4:04)*/ Tippi Tippi Toes (2:56)*/ Parents Theme, Flying Horses (2:29)*
R: Ex.   S: Broadcast the weekend of July 3 '95. C: ECD. Dcc. *Bonus songs are from the 'Rupert The Bear' animation film, which was never released. Only four acetates with the complete soundtrack were made for Paul and the members of Wings. The songs on this CD have been digitally declicked and denoised and were taken from Steve Holly's acetate.

CD - OOBU JOOBU PART 9
YELLOW CAT RECORDS
Intro, Oobu Joobu (1:19)/ Jet (rehearsal - 3:51)/ Keep Under Cover (demo and outtake with Stanley Clark - 3:11)/ Johnny B Goode (Chuck Berry record - 3:03)/ Oobu Joobu, Get Out Of My Way (St. Louis soundcheck - 5:25)/ Apology (unknown artist, Jamaica - 3:01)/ Three Cool Cats (rehearsal - 4:04)/ Don't Break The Promises (demo and Eric Stewart version - 7:23)/ Cook Of The House, Linda's Recipe - 1:32)/ Peacocks (unreleased song - 3:48)/ I've Just Seen A Face (tour rehearsal - 2:46)/ Music For Glass Harmonica (from the rehearsal studio - 2:27)/ Winedark Open Sea (rehearsal - 6:39)/ Welcome To Oobu Joobu (1:17)/ Bonus Tracks: Cohen The Wind Is Blowing (3:54)*/ The Castle Of The King Of The Birds (1:44)*/ Sunshine Something (3:34)*
R: Ex.   S: Broadcast the weekend of July 10 '95.   C: ECD. Dcc. *Bonus songs are from the 'Rupert The Bear' animation film, which was never released

CD - ROCKESTRA SESSION
ORANGE 024
Intro, Rockestra (Paul on piano - 3:30)/ EMI Studio's Music Gallery (various artists - 2:40)/ Obscure And Oblique Introductions (Pete Townshend - 1:53)/ Tuning And Testing (3:25)/ Rockestra: Paul's Demo (3:21)/ Rockestra (pre-recorded demo - 2:15)/ Rockestra (guitar practicing - 5:39)/ Rockestra (drums practicing - 2:49)/ Rockestra (riffs and more drums - 2:40)/ Rockestra (full version - 2:53)/ So Glad To See You Here (Paul's demonstration - 2:17)/ So Glad To See You Here (practice - 2:08)/ So Glad To See You Here (full version - 3:20)/ After The Ball (video outro - 1:12)/ So Glad To See You Here, Rockestra (rough vocal version - 1:22)/ Outro, Rockestra Tune (2:18)
C: ECD. Dcc. Time 43:44.

CD - UNSURPASSED MASTERS VOL. 1
STRAWBERRY RECORDS STR 002
Big Barn Bed/ The Mess/ When The Night/ Single

Pigeon/ Thank You Darling/ Mary Had A Little Lamb/ Loup/ Tragedy/ Seaside Woman/ Wild Life/ Little Woman Love, C Moon/ Maybe I'm Amazed/ My Love/ Live And Let Die
R: Ex. Soundboard.   S: 'Red Rose Speedway' outtakes. Tracks 9-14 Newcastle.   C: ECD. Dcc. Time 62:48.

CD - UNSURPASSED MASTERS VOL. 2
STRAWBERRY RECORDS STR 003
Bridge Over The River Suite/ Back Seat Of My Car/ Best Friend/ Momma's Little Girl/ Hey Diddle/ A Love For You/ Would Only Smile/ Tragedy/ Long Haired Lady, Live Is Long/ Sunshine, Sometime/ Rode All Night/ Night Out/ Seaside Woman
R: Ex. Soundboard.   S: 'Cold Cuts' outtakes. C: ECD. Dcc. Time 57:12.

CD - WINGS OVER AMERICA II
DYNAMITE STUDIO DS94J056/7
CD1: Venus And Mars, Rock Show, Jet/ Let Me Roll It/ Spirits Of Ancient Egypt/ Medicine Jar/ Maybe I'm Amazed/ Call Me Back Again/ Lady Madonna/ The Long And Winding Road/ Live And Let Die Picasso's Last Words (Drink To Me)/ Richard Corey/ Bluebird
CD2: You Gave Me The Answer/ Magneto And Titanium Man/ Go Now/ My Love/ Listen To What The Man Said/ Let 'Em In/ Time To Hide/ Silly Love Songs/ Beware My Love/ Letting Go/ Band On The Run
R: G. Audience. Hiss.   S: The Forum, Inglewood, CA June 23 '76.   C: Japanese CDs.

MEATLOAF

CD - CAUGHT IN THE ACT
LAST BOOTLEG RECORDS LBR 005
I'd Do Anything For Love (12:26)/ You Took The Words (8:54)/ Two Out Of Three Ain't Bad (8:40)/ Life Is A Lemon (10:29)/ Objects In The Rearview Mirror (12:18)/ Bat Out Of Hell (11:53)/ Paradise By The Dashboard Light (15:32)
R: Exs. Soundboard.   S: Hudson Theatre, Broadway, NYC Sept. 18 '93.   C: ECD. Dcc. Pic CD.

CD - THE HELL ON THE HILL
BABY CAPONE BC 023
Bolero (3:00)/ Bat Out Of Hell (10:26)/ You Took The Words Right Out Of My Mouth (5:36)/ All Revved Up With No Place To Go (8:00)/ Paradise By The Dash-Board Light (21:56)/ Two Out Of Three Ain't Bad (8:00)/ River Deep Mountain High (5:00)/ I'm Gonna Love Her For Both Of Us (7:47)/ Deadringer Of Love (6:19)
R: Exs. Soundboard.   S: The Music Hall, Cleveland Apr. 19 '78.   C: ECD. Dcc. Pic CD.

CD - IT'S LIVE FOR YOU (AND THAT'S THE TRUTH)
KISS THE STONE KTS 499
You Took The Words Right Out Of My Mouth/

Where The Rubber Meets The Road/ Amnesty/ I'd Lie For You (And That's The Truth)/ Life Is A Lemon And I Want My Money Back/ Like A Bat Out Of Hell
R: Exs. Soundboard.   S: Toronto, Canada Nov. 9 '95.   C: ECD. Dcc. Pic CD.

MEGADETH

CD - DE KUIP, ROTTERDAM
HAMMERJACK HJ 012
Intro/ Holy Wars/ Skin O' My Teeth/ Wake Up Dead/ Countdown To Extinction/ Sweating Bullets/ In My Darkest Hour/ The Conjuring/ Ashes In You Mouth/ Symphony Of Destruction/ Peace Sells But Who's Buying?/ Anarchy
R: G. Audience.   S: De Kuip, Rotterdam Dec. 6 '93.   C: ECD. Dcc. Time 55:25.

CD - THE OTHER SIDE
OXYGEN OXY 008
Killing Road (3:54)/ The Conjuring, Wake Up The Dead (3:35)/ Reckoning Day (4:33)/ This Was My Life (3:42)/ Peace Sells... But Who's Buying (4:38)/ Skin O' My Teeth (3:43)/ Train Of Consequences (4:02)/ Hangar 18 (5:06)/ A Tout Le Monde (4:36)/ In My Darkest Hour (6:18)/ Angry Again (3:45)/ Tornado Of Souls (5:22)/ Holy Wars (7:09)/ Symphony Of Destruction (5:49)/ Hook In Mouth (4:27)/ Anarchy In The UK (3:09)
R: Exs. Soundboard.   S: Tracks 1-5 The Brixton Academy, London Mar. 20 '95. Tracks 6-16 Buenos Aires, Argentina Sept. '94.   C: ECD. Dcc. Pic CD.

CD - YOUTH IN JAPAN TOUR 1995
CD1: Skin O'My Teeth/ Hanger 18/ Wake Up Dead/ Reckoning Day/ This Was My Life/ Countdown To Extinction/ Angry Again/ Foreclosure Of A Dream/ A Tout Le Monde/ In My Darkest Hour/ Train Of Consequences
CD2: The Killing Road/ Tornado Of Souls/ Holy Wars...The Punishment Due/ Sweating Bullets/ Mechanix/ Symphony Of Destruction/ Peace Sells/ Anarchy In The UK Intro/ Anarchy In the UK
R: G-Vgs. Audience.   S: Tokyo May 30 '95.

MELLENCAMP, JOHN COUGAR

CD - WILD AT NIGHT
KISS THE STONE KTS 403
When Jesus Left Birmingham (6:53)/ I Need A Lover (4:49)/ Dance Naked (3:06)/ Jack And Diana (5:45)/ Lonely Ol' Night (4:52)/ Wild Night (4:21)/ Paper In Fire (6:05)/ Small Town (5:11)/ What If I Came Knockin' (5:05)/ Crumblin' Down (5:39)/ Authority Song (7:17)/ Pink Houses (8:00)/ Check It Out (5:08)/ Wild Night (3:49)
R: Ex. Audience.   S: The World Music Theater, Chicago Aug. 27 '94. Track 14 NY June 25 '94.   C: ECD. Dcc. Pic CD.

MERCURY, FREDDIE

CD - MR. BAD GUY (SPECIAL EXTENDED VERSION)
ROYAL MUSIC RMCD 006
Let's Turn It On/ Made In Heaven/ I Was Born To Love You/ Foolin' Around/ Your Kind Of Lover/ Mr. Bad Guy/ Man Made Paradise/ There Must Be More To Life Than This/ Living On My Own/ My Love Is Dangerous/ Love Me Like There's No Tomorrow/ Let's Turn It On (12" version)/ I Was Born To Love You (12" version)/ Living On My Own (12" version)/ She Blows Hot And Cold (extended 12" Mix)/ Love Me Like There's No Tomorrow (extended 12" mix)/ Made In Heaven (extended 12" mix)
R: Exs. Soundboard.   S: Special edition with additional mixes.   C: ECD. Dcc. Pic CD. 74:02.

METALLICA

CD - COVERING 'EM
BKCD079
So What/ Stone Cold Crazy/ Last Caress/ Little Wing/ Heavy Mixed Medley: Smoke On The Water, Black Night, Symptom Of The Universe, Run To The Hill, The Adams Family, Hell's Bells, Back In Black/ Mistreated/ Am I Evil/ Helpless/ Sow What (Extended)/ Let It Loose/ The Killing Time/ Hit The Lights/ The Mechanix/ Motorbreath/ Seek And Destroy/ Metal Militia/ Jump In The Fire/ Phantom Lord
R: Ex. Soundboard and audience.   S: Tracks 1-11 live. Tracks 12-18 'Life 'Til Leather' demos.

CD - COVERING 'EM
OCTOPUS OCTO 088
Breadfan (Woodstock Festival, Saugerties, NY, Aug. 13 '94) (4:08)/ Blitzkrieg (Aardshok Festival, Zwolle, Holland Feb. 8 '87) (4:58)/ Stone Cold Crazy (Freddy Mercury Tribute, Wembley Stadium, London Apr. 20 '92) (2:56)/ Medley: London Dungeon, Last Caress, Green Hell (jam with Danzig, World Amphitheater, Chicago July 3 '94) (6:32)/ The Heavy Joke #2 (Frolundaborg, Goteborg, Sweden Feb. 13 '87) (3:28)/ La Grange (Wembley Arena, London, Oct. 25 '92) (1:43)/ Crash Course In A Brain Surgery (3:09), The Small Hours (6:53), The Wait (6:19), Helpless (6:08) (secret gig at The 100 Club, London Aug. 20 '87)/ Breadfan (unfinished mix without complete vocals USA '88) (5:38)/ *The Frayed Ends Of Sanity (complete instrumental version) (7:23)/ *Eye Of The Beholder (early version with different lyrics) (6:13)/ *Blackened (early version) (5:48)/ Whip Lash (performed by Pantera, Civic Center, Santa Monica, CA May 2 '94) (4:40)
R: Vg-Ex. Some G-Vg. Audience/Soundboard.   S: *Instrumental demos from the '...And Justice For All' '88 sessions.   C: ECD. Dcc. Pic CD.

CD - ENTER HELL
METEOR FRONT ROW FM 1103/4
CD1: Intro - Breadfan (5:59)/ Master Of Puppets

(3:43)/ Wherever I May Roam (7:39)/ Harvester Of Sorrow (6:49)/ Sanitarium (7:15)/ God That Failed (6:48)/ Old Shit Medley: Ride The Lightning, No Remorse, Four Horsemen, Phantom-Lord, Fight Fire With Fire/ For Whom The Bell Tolls (7:28)/ Disposable Heroes (7:19) CD2: Seek And Destroy (13:32)/ Nothing Else Matters (6:06)/ Creepin' Death (8:04)/ Fade To Black (7:59)/ Whiplash (7:25)/ Sad But True (5:40)/ One (11:23)/ Enter Sandman (6:28)/ So What! (3:11)
R: Vg.   S: Jones Beach, Wantaugh, Long Island, New York June 8 '94.   C: ECD. Black cover, silver type.

CD - ESCAPE FROM THE STUDIO '95
OCTOPUS OCTO 216
Master Of Puppets (3:59)/ Wherever I May Roam (6:58)/ Two By Four (unreleased) (5:45)/ Harvester Of Sorrow (includes excerpts from 'Remember Tomorrow' and 'The Unforgiven') (7:29)/ Nothing Else Matters (7:24)/ Sad But True (5:42)/ One (10:48)/ Enter Sandman (6:55)/ Welcome Home (Sanitarium) (6:55)/ Seek And Destroy (6:39)/ And Justice For All (5:09)
R: Exs. Soundboard.   S: Tracks 1-8 The Donnington Festival, UK Aug. 26 '95. Tracks 9-11 The Hammersmith Odeon, London, UK Oct. 10 '88.   C: ECD.

CD - FROM THE STORM
SWINDLE SWN 024
Enter Sandman (4:53)*/ Unforgiven (6:02)*/ Nothing Else Matters (5:39)*/ Wherever I May Roam (5:24)*/ Sad But True (4:43)*/ Holier Than Thou (3:40)*/ Nothing Else Matters (6:05)*/ Disposable Heroes (5:53)**/ Battery (3:12)**/ Master Of Puppets (4:44)**/ Welcome Home (4:57)**/ Blackened (studio demo) (5:48)/ ...And Justice For All (studio demo)/ 8:04)/ Dyers Eve (studio demo) (5:30)
R: Ex. Soundboard.   S: *Demos for 'Metallica'. **Demos for 'Master Of Puppets'.   C: ECD. Dcc. Pic CD.

CD - THE GOOD, THE BAD METALLICA
ROCKWROK RW3307/3308
CD1: Enter Sandman (5:50)/ Creeping Death (6:49)/ Harvester Of Sorrow (6:19)/ Wherever I May Roam (6:24)/ The Four Horsemen (4;56)/ Bass Guitar Solo (8:13)/ Through The Never (3:28)/ The Unforgiven (6:26)/ ...And Justice For All (8:40)/ Drum Solo (7:49)
CD2: Mistreated (7:53)/ For Whom The Bell Tolls (5:13)/ Welcome Home (6;44)/ Whiplash (4:16)/ Master of Puppets (3:30)/ Seek And Destroy (12:02)/ One (8:17)/ Last Caress (3:16)/ Am I Evil (2:40)/ Battery (4;50)/ Breadfan (3:32)
R: G-Vg.   S: Sacramento, CA, Jan. 10-11 '92.

CD - LIVE VOL. 1
JOKER JOK-010-A
Master Of Puppets/ Of Wolf And Man/ Wherever I May Roam/ The Thing That Should Not Be/ Orion/

To Live Is To Die/ The Call Of Ktulu/ Four Horsemen/ Fade To Black/ Battery/ Welcome Home (Sanitarium)/ Last Caress/ One/ Nothing Else Matters/ Enter Sandman
C: Australian CD

CD - LIVE VOL. 2
JOKER JOK-010-B
Master Of Puppets/ For Whom The Bell Tolls/ Welcome Home Sanitarium/ Ride The Lightning/ Whiplash/ No Remorse/ Fade To Black/ Creeping Death/ Am I Evil?/ Motor Breath/ Phantom Lord/ Four Horsemen
C: Australian CD

CD - LIVE VOL. 3
JOKER JOK-010-C
Intro/ Enter Sandman/ Creeping Death/ Harvester Of Sorrow/ Wherever I May Roam/ Four Horsemen/ Through The Never/ The Unforgiven/ Medley: Eye Of The Beholder, Blackened, Frayed Ends Of Sanity, And Justice For All/ Blackened/ Peter Gunn
R: Vg. Audience.   S: Sacramento, CA '92 part 1.   C: Australian CD. Dcc.

CD - LIVE VOL. 4
JOKER JOK-010-D
Mistreated/ For Whom The Bells Tolls/ Fade To Black/ Whiplash/Cat Scratch Fever/ Master Of Puppets/ Seek And Destroy/ One/ Last Caress/ Am I Evil?/ Battery/ Breadfan
R: Ex. Audience.   C: Australian CD

CD - LOUD BUT SECRET
TYPHOON TYN 005/06
CD1: Breadfan/ Master Of Puppets/ Wherever I May Roam/ The God That Failed/ Fade To Black/ 2 X 4/ Medley: Ride The Lightning, No Remorse, Hit The Lights/ For Whom The Bell Tolls/ Devil Dance/ Creeping Death
CD2: Welcome Home (Sanitarium)/ Harvester Of Sorrow/ Nothing Else Matters/ Sad But True/ One/ Last Caress/ Seek And Destroy/ Enter Sandman/ So What?
S: London, England Aug. 23 '95.   C: ECD.

CD - THE MANIACS RETURN
Hit The Lights/ The Mechanics/ Phantom Lord/ Jump In The Fire/ Motor Breath/ No Remorse/ Seek And Destroy/ Whiplash/ Am I Evil/ Metal Militia
S: Old Waldorf Nov. 29 '82.   C: Japanese CD. Limited edition of 500 copies.

CD - MIDDLE SHIT 1994
BONDAGE MUSIC BON 018/19
CD1: The Good, The Bad, The Ugly/ Breadfan/ Master Of Puppets/ Wherever I May Roam/ Harvester Of Sorrow/ Welcome Home (Sanitarium)/ The God That Failed/ Pile Of Shit Part 2, Medley: Ride The Lightning, No Remorse, The Four Horsemen, Phantom Lord/ Fight Fire With Fire/ For Whom The Bell Tolls/ Disposable

Heroes
CD2: Seek And Destroy/ Nothing Else Matters/
Creeping Death/ Fade To Black/ Whiplash/ Sad
But True/ One/ Enter Sandman/ So What
R: Exs. Soundboard.   S: Middle Town, NY June
17 '94.   C: Japanese CD. Dcc.

CD - NEW SKULLS FOR THE OLD CEREMONY
(THE COVER VERSIONS)
SWINDLE SWN 012
Breadfan (5:35)/ The Prince (4:30)/ So What
(3:09)/ Stone Cold Crazy (2:17)/ Helpless (6:40)/
The Small Hours (6:47)/ Killing Time (3:04)/ The
Wait (4:55)/ Crash Course In Brain Surgery
(3:12)/ Last Caress (1:30)/ Green Hell (1:45)/
Enter Sandman (LA '92) (5:44)/ Harvester Of
Sorrow ('92) (6:05)/ For Whom The Bell Tolls ('91)
(4:59)/ Jarnia: Wherever I May Roam (Live '92)
(5:41)/ Prowler, Run To The Hills, Trash ('88)
(6:24)
R: Exs. Soundboard. Some audience.   S: All
songs recorded live in the US '88-'92.   C: ECD.
Pic CD.

CD - PILE OF SHIT
KISS THE STONE KTS 365/66
CD1: Breadfan/ Master Of Puppets/ Wherever I
May Roam/ Harvester Of Sorrow/ Welcome Home
(Sanitarium)/ The God That Failed/ Pile Of Shit
Part Two: Ride The Lightning, No Remorse, Fight
Fire With Fire/ Loud Jam, For Whom The Bell
Tolls/ Disposable Heroes/ Seek And Destroy/ The
Unforgiven, Nothing Else Matters
CD2: Creeping Death/ Fade To Black/ Whiplash/
Sad But True/ One/ Enter Sandman/ So What?/
London Dungeon, Last Caress, Green Bell/ So
What?, Suicidal Tendencies
R: G-Vg. Audience.   S: Orange County
Speedway, Middletown, New York June 17 '94.
CD2 tracks 8-9 Chicago World Amphitheatre July
3 '94.   C: ECD. Dcc. Pic CDs.

CD - ROAMING IN SWEDEN 921212
CKR 001/002
CD1: Enter Sandman/ Creeping Death/ Harvester
Of Sorrow/ Welcome Home/ Sad But True/
Wherever I May Roam/ The Unforgiven/ And
Justice Medley/ Solos Bass, Guitar/ Through The
Never
CD2: For Whom The Bell Tolls/ Fade To Black/
Master Of Puppets/ Seek And Destroy/ Whiplash/
Nothing Else Matters/ Am I Evil/ Last Caress/
One/ Battery/ Stone Cold Crazy
R: Vg audience.   S: Sweden Dec. 12 '92.

CD - SECRET DEMOS (1985 -1988)
NADCD001
Battery (4:48)/ Welcome Home (4:58)/ Orion
(4:05)/ Disposable Heroes (Take 1) (5:54)/
Disposable Heroes (take 2) (3:15)/ The Frayed
Ends Of Insanity (&:23)/ Eye Of The Beholder
(6:17)/ Blackened (5:48)/ One (7:03)/ Sad But
True (4:45)/ Holier Than Thou (3:47)
R: G-Vg.   S: Tracks 1-5 instrumental demos

July 4 '85. Tracks 6-8 instrumental demos Nov.
13 '87. Track 9 demo with different lyrics Nov. 15
'87. Tracks 10-11 demos Aug. 12 '90.   C: ECD.
Dcc.

CD - TOTAL DESTRUCTION
SWINDLE SWN 020
So What (2:55)/ Stone Cold Crazy (3:08)/ Last
Caress (1:58)/ Little Wing (3:31) Smoke On The
Water Medley (5:29)/ Mistreated (6:44)/ Am I Evil?
(5:59)/ Helpless (4:05)/ So What (3:45)/ La
Grange (1:56)/ Prowler (1:58)/ Bread Fan (4:05)/
Halloween II (3:09)/ Stone Cold Crazy (3:05)/
Killing Time (2:36)/ Let It Loose (3:10)/ The
Mechanics (4:29)/ Hit The Lights (4:18)/ The Four
Horsemen (4:26)/ Motorbreath (3:16)
R: Vg-Ex. Some G. Soundboard and audience.
S: Live during '93 and '94 tours.   C: ECD. Dcc.
Pic CD.

CD - USE IT OR LOSE IT
ROCK CALENDAR RECORDS RC 2114/15
CD1: Enter Sandman (5:54)/ Creeping Death
(6:51)/ Harvester Of Sorrow (6:32)/ Welcome
Home (Sanitarium) (6:28)/ Sad But True (5:08)/
Wherever I May Roam (6:30)/ Bass-Guitar Solo
(7:02)/ The Unforgiven (6:30)/ ...And Justice For
All (6:44)/ Blackened (2:06)/ Drum Solo (5:47)
CD2: Mistreated (8:44)/ Nothing Else Matters
(5:44)/ For Whom The Bell Tolls (5:22)/ Fade To
Black (6:52)/ Whiplash (4:30)/ Boogie (2:10)/
Master Of Puppets (3:29)/ Seek And Destroy
(5:41)/ One (8:40)/ Last Caress (2:39)/ Am I Evil
(3:07)/ Battery (5:01)
R: Poor-G. Audience.   S: Bison Sports Arena,
Fargo May 15 '92.   C: ECD. Dcc.

CD - WHITE ALBUM
THE LAST BOOTLEG RECORDS BR 032
Helpless (6:37)/ The Small Hours (6:39)/ The Wait
(4:51)/ Crash Course In Brain Surgery (3:08)/
Last Caress - Green Hell (3:28)/ Stone Cold
Crazy (2:17)/ Killing Time (2:59)/ Enter Sandman
(demo) (5:04)/ The Unforgiven (demo) (6:12)/
Nothing Else Matters (demo) (5:52)/ Wherever I
May Roam (demo) (5:35)/ Sad But True (demo)
(4:51)/ One (demo) (7:03)/ Nothing Else Matters
(elevator version) (6:30)/ So What (3:04)
R: Ex. Soundboard.   S: Recorded and mixed at
A&M Conway, LA, CA '87.   C: ECD. Dcc.
Pic CD.

CD - WOODSTOCK WHIPLASH 1994
BMCD 23
Intro/ Breadfan/ Master Of Puppets/ Wherever I
May Roam/ Harvester Of Sorrow/ Fade To Black/
For Whom The Bell Tolls/ Seek And Destroy/
Nothing Else Matters/ Creeping Death/ Whiplash/
One/ So What
R: Exs. Soundboard.   S: Woodstock '94 Aug. 13
'94.   C: Time 77:40.

METHENY, PAT

CD - AUTUMN LEAVES
OXYGEN RECORDS OXY 035
Have You Heard (6:10)/ And Then I Knew (7:37)/
Here To Stay (6:48)/ First Circle (8:34)/ Scrap
Metal (5:17)/ Farmer's Trust (6:17)/ Episode
D'Azur (10:42)/ Third Wind (6:17)/ This Is Not
America (3:33)/ Minuano (Six-Eight) (6:32)/
Stranger In Town (6:04)
R: Exs. Soundboard.   S: Gotanda Youport Hall,
Tokyo, Japan Oct. 8 '95.   C: ECD.

MISFITS, THE

CD - 'BEWARE AND THE REST'
We Are 138/ Bullet/ Hollywood Babylon/ Attitude/
Horror Business/ Teenagers From Mars/ Last
Caress/ Cough Cool/ She/ Teenagers From Mars,
Children In Heat/ Rat Fink/ Horror Hotel/ Who
Killed Marilyn/ Spook City USA/ Halloween I/
Halloween II/ Return Of The Fly
C: Black/white cover. Our copy came with the
wrong disc - Rancid 'Demos From The Pit'.

CD - BEYOND EVIL
HALLOWEEN RECORDS
Children In Heat (2:12)/ Rat Fink (1:56)/
Halloween II (2:14)/ Nike A Go-Go (2:34)/ We Are
138 (1:47)/ Teenagers From Mars (2:53)/ Come
Back (5:00)/ Angel Fuck (1:24)/ Spook City USA
(2:14)/ Demonomania (:52)/ Halloween III (1:30)/
Theme For A Jackal (3:18)/ Who Killed Marilyn
(2:02)/ Where Eagles Dare (2:07)/ Return Of The
Fly (1:40)/ Devil's Whore House (1:49)/ Devil Lock
(1:25)/ Green Hell (1:57)/ Last Caress (2:06)/
Hybryde Moments 91:50)/ Attitude (1:36)/
Hollywood Babylon (2:22)
R: G-Vg. Some poor-G.   S: Demos and out-
takes '77-'80.   C: ECD. Dbw/purple cover.

MISSING PERSONS

CD - I LIKE BOYS
LDLA-8235CD
Mental Hopscotch/ Noticeable One/ Words/ Tears/
It Ain't None Of Your Business/ Bad Streets/
Windows/ Here And Now/ Walking In LA/ No Way
Out/ I Like Boys/ Destination Unknown/ US Drag/
Here And Now/ I Like Boys/ Walking In LA/
Destination Unknown/ Words/ No Way Out
R: Exs.   S: Track 1-12 London '82. Tracks 13-
15 Long Beach Arena '83. Tracks 16-19 LA '85.

MOODY BLUES

CD - LIVE VOL. 1
JOKER JOK-029-A
Lovely To See You/ Tuesday Afternoon/ Bless The
Wings (That Bring You Back)/ Lean On Me
(Tonight)/ Say It With Love/ I'm Just A Singer (In A
Rock And Roll Band)/ Nights In White Satin/
Legend Of A Mind/ Question/ Ride My See Saw
C: Australian CD.

CD - THE STORY IN YOUR EYES
RAG DOLL MUSIC RDM-942008A/B
CD1: Higher And Higher/ After You Came/ The
Story In Your Eyes/ One More Time To Love/
Tuesday Afternoon/ Legend Of A Mind/ Watching
And Waiting/ Melancholy Man
CD2: Are You Sitting Comfortably/ The Dream/
Have You Heard Part 1/ The Voyage/ Have You
Heard Part 2/ Nights In White Satin/ I'm Just A
Singer (In A Rock And Roll Band)/ Question/ Ride
My See-Saw
R: Poor audience recording.   S: Osaka Jan. 22
'74.   C: Japanese CD.

MOORE, GARY

CD - HOLD ON TO LOVE
SHOW COMPANY SC-9447-14/15
CD1: Rockin' Every Night/ Murder In The Skies/
Wishing Well/ Shapes Of Things/ Cold Heated/
Don't Take Me For A Loser/ Victims Of The Future
CD2: So Far Away, Empty Rooms/ Blinder, Drum
Solo/ Guitar Solo, End Of The World/ Back On
The Street/ Hold On To Love
R: Vgs. Audience recording.   S: Japan Feb. 29
'84.

MORAZ, PATRICK AND BILL BRUFORD

CD - THE STORY OF 'Pb'
IMPROVISATION LABEL IL-3668132/14
CD1: Innings/ Blue Brains/ Hazy/ Eastern
Sundays/ Cachaca (Baiao)/ Galatea
CD2: The Drum Also Waltzes/ Impromptu, Too/
Flags/ Children's Concerto/ Machines
Programmed By Genes/ Moraz Solo From 'Time
For A Change Serenade'/ Jungles Of The World/
Temples Of Joy
R: Vg sound from FM radio.   S: Laforet
Museum, Tokyo, Japan July 4 '85.

MORISSETTE, ALANIS

CD - GOING NORTH
MOONRAKER O41
Intro/ All I Really Want/ Right Through You/ Not
The Doctor/ Hand In My Pocket/ Mary Jane/ You
Learn/ Ironic/ Forgiven/ You Oughta Know/ Wake
Up/ All I Really Want/ Hand In My Pocket/ You
Oughta Know/ Perfect
R: Ex. Audience.   S: Minneapolis July 24 '95.
Tracks 12-15 Seattle Sept. 18 '95.   C: ECD.
Dcc. Time 74:02.

CD - MISS THING
OXYGEN RECORDS OXY 037
All I Really Want (7:07)/ Right Through You
(3:39)/ Not The Doctor (7:39)/ Hand In My Pocket
(4:48)/ Mary Jane (6:24)/ Ironic (4:29)/ You Learn
(5:27)/ Forgiven (6:02)/ You Oughta Know (5:28)/
Wake Up (7:21)/ Head Over Feet (4:30)/ Perfect
(3:27)/ You Oughta Know (4:29)
R: Exs. Soundboard.   S: Tracks 1-12 Melkweg,
Amsterdam, Holland Oct. 17 '95. Track 13 'MTV'

Music Awards, Radio City Music Hall, NYC Sept. 7 '95.   C: ECD. Pic CD.

CD - TUNE IN, TURN ON, TUNE OUT
MOONRAKER 040
You Oughta Know (David Letterman Aug. 17 '95)/ All I Really Want, Hand In My Pocket/ (MTV 120 Minutes)/ You Oughta Know (MTV Video Music Awards '95)/ Wake Up, You Learn, Not The Doctor, Your House, Head Over Feet, Forgiven (Modern Rock Live Oct. 12 '95)/ Hand In My Pocket, All I Really Want (Saturday Night Live Oct. 28 '95)/ Interview (Modern Rock Live Oct. 12 '95)
R: Exs. Soundboard.   C: ECD. Dcc.
Time 73:32.

MORRISON, VAN

CD - DARK KNIGHT OF THE SOUL
MOONTUNES MOON001
Tore Down A La Rimbaud/ In The Garden/ Rave On John Donne/ Did Ye Get Healed/ Star Of The Down/ She Moved Through The Fair/ Ta Mo Chleamhnas Deanta/ Tell Me Ma/ Carrick Fergus/ Celtic Ray/ Marie's Wedding/ Boffyflow And Spike/ Goodnight Irene/ Moon Dance/ T For Texas/ When I Was A Cowboy/ Sense Of Wonder/ Celtic Ray/ In The Garden/ Raglan Road/ Send In The Clowns
R: Ex. Soundboard.   S: Tracks 1-14 Ulster Hall, Belfast Sept. 15 '88. Tracks 15-20 Colrain University, Apr. 20 '88. Track 21 Ronnie Scott's, London June '86.

CD - EDINBURGH CASTLE WITH THE BBC ORCHESTRA
KISS THE STONE KTS 490
All Right, Okay, You Win/ How Long Has This Been Going On?/ Early In The Morning/ Days Like This/ Who Can I Turn To?/ That's Life/ I Will Be There/ Vanlose Stairway/ Blues In The Night/ Haunts Of Ancient Peace/ Your Mind Is On Vacation/ Moondance
S: The Edinburgh Jazz Festival, Aug. '95.
C: ECD. Pic CD.

CD - LOST IN A FUGITIVES DREAM
MOONTUNES MOON 011/12
CD1: Sweet Thing (5:55)/ Did Ye Get Healed, It's All In The Game, Make It Real One More Time (7:36)/ I Believe To My Soul (3:25)/ Whenever God Shines His Light (3:48)/ My Name Is Raincheck (4:45)/ See Me Through, Soldier Of Fortune, Thank You Falettinme Be Mice Elf Agin (7:40)/ Ain't That Loving You Baby? (4:38)/ Stormy Monday, Going Down Slow, Baby What You Want Me To Do? (5:33)/ Real Real Gone (3:50)/ Days Like This (3:38)/ Vanlose Stairway (4:48)/ Hungry For Your Love (3:54)/ You Don't Know Me (3:58)/ Help Me (6:30)/ Tupelo Honey, Why Must I Explain? (7:16)
CD2: Moondance, Blue Moon, Fever, My Funny Valentine (8:45)/ I'll Take Care Of You, When The Clock Strikes, It's Hustle Time (8:30)/ It's A Man's, Man's, Man's World (8:42)/ Lonely Avenue, 4 O'Clock In The Morning, Be Bop A Lula, Down The Line, Nothing But The Blues (6:42)/ In The Garden, You Send Me (10:53)/ Melancholia (5:01)/ Northern Muse (Solid Ground), No Prima Donna - All Change (8:10)/ Gloria (7:47)/ Have I Told You Lately (4:17)/ Did Ye Get Healed, All In The Game, Make It Real One More Time (7:54)
R: Ex.   S: Cambridge Corn Exchange, Cambridge UK Apr. 14 '95. Disc 2 track 9 with Sinead O'Connor and The Chieftains, David Letterman Show. CD2 track 10 with The Jim Daly Blues Band, E.M.A. Awards, Belfast Apr. 13 '95.
C: ECD. Dcc.

MORRISON, VAN AND DR. JOHN

CD - AMSTERDAM'S TAPES
ARCHIVIO ARC013
Fever (4:09)/ I'll Go Crazy (3:00)/ Baby Please Don't Go (4:20)/ Santa Rosalia (4:16)/ I Just Want To Make Love To You (5:20)/ Shakin' All Over (4:17)/ I Believe, Into The Music (5:05)
R: G-Vg. Soundboard.   S: Vara Studios, Amsterdam June 24 '74.   C: ECD. Dbw.

MORRISSEY

CD - 'THAT'S NEW ENTERTAINMENT'
Angel Angel, We Go Together/ Interesting Drug/ Piccadilly Palare/ Trush/ Mute Witness/ The Last Of The Famous International Playboy/ Alsatian Cousin/ Sister I'm A Poet/ Asian Rut/ The Loop/ King Leer/ November Spawned A Monster/ Everyday Is Like Sunday/ That's Entertainment/ Cosmic Dancer/ Suedehead/ Our Frank/ Sing Your Life/ Disappointed
R: Poor. Audience.   S: Budokan, Tokyo Sept. 2 '91.   C: ECD. Dbw. Red type. Time 59:54.

MOTLEY CRUE

CD - DECADE OF EXPLOSION
WYVERN WV-3133C1/2
CD1: Hooligan's Holiday/ Live Wire/ Shout At The Devil/ Wild Side/ Power Of The Music/ Uncle Jack/ Tommy Lee's Drum Solo/ Dr. Feelgood
CD2: Misunderstood/ Kickstart My Heart/ Home Sweet Home/ Revolution/ Loveshine/ Don't Go Away Mad (Just Go Away)/ Hammered/ Primal Scream
R: Ex audience recording.   S: Osaka Oct. 3 '94.
C: Japanese CD.

CD - DECADENT LIVE
BONDAGE MUSIC BON 043
In The Beginning, Shout At The Devil/ Knock' Em Dead, Kid/ Too Young To Fall In Love/ Red Hot-Guitar Solo/ Piece Of Your Action/ Looks That Kill/ Helter Skelter/ Live Wire/ Take Me To The Top/ Looks That Kill/ Red Hot/ Starry Eyes/ Piece Of Your Action/ Merry-Go-Round/ Shout At The Devil/ Hotter Than Hell

R: Exs. Soundboard.   S: Tracks 1-8 Tucson, Arizona '83. Tracks 9-16 Pasadena, CA '82. C: Japanese CD. Dcc. Time 71:01.

CD - HELTER SKELTER
REEL MUSIC RMCD-95017
Shout At The Devil/ Knock 'Em Dead Kid/ Keep Your Eye On The Money/ Too Young To Fall In Love/ Red Hot, Guitar Solo/ City Boy Blues/ Piece Of Your Action/ Looks That Kill/ Smokin' In The Boys Room/ Live Wire/ The Seconds Till Love/ Helter Skelter/ Jailhouse Rock
R: Vg-Exs. Audience.   S: July 15 '85.

CD - THE HOT RED SPOT
INSECT IST 24
In The Beginning, Bastard/ Knock' On Dead/ Shout At The Devil/ 10 Seconds To Love/ Piece Of Your Action/ Red Hot/ Looks That Kill/ Live Wire/ Helter Skelter/ In The End/ Take It Right By Your Side/ Registration/ Girls, Girls, Girls/ Feel Good/ Anarchy In The United Kingdom
R: Poor stereo.   S: Tracks 1-9 Milan, Italy Nov. 12 '84. Tracks 10-15 Monsters Of Rock, Modena, Italy Sept. '91.

CD - SECRETS OF TONE
HOME RECORDS HR5938-1
Take Me To The Top/ Looks That Kill/ Red Hot/ Stray Eyes/ Piece Of The Action/ Merry Go Round/ Shout At The Devil/ Louder Than Hell/ Live Wire/ Knock 'Em Dead, Kid/ Live Wire/ Kickstart My Heart
R: Tracks 1-10 Vg sound. Tracks 11-12 Poor audience recording.   S: Tracks 1-10 Dallas, TX '81. Tracks 11-12 Pasadena '92.

MOTORHEAD

CD - BETTER WEAR ARMOR!
ARMONIE CELESTI RECORDS AC001
I'll Be Your Sister/ Traitor/ I'm So Bad (Baby, I Don't Care)/ Metropolis/ Bad Religion/ Stay Clean/ Hellraiser/ Just 'Cos You Got The Power/ Love Me Forever/ Drum Solo/ The One To Sing The Blues/ You Better Run/ Killed By Death/ Going To Brazil/ Overkill/ Jam/ Guitar Solos/ Catch Scratch Fewer/ Ace Of Spades
R: Vg audience recording.   S: Gtaut-Halle, Offenbach Dec. 10 '92.

THE MUMMIES

7" - THE MUMMIES
SUB POP SP257
S1: Uncontrollable Urge
S2: Girl You Want
R: G. Audience.   S: Reciprocal Recordings, Seattle.   C: USA. B&w sleeve. Limited edition of 1,000. 45 RPM.

N

NATIONAL HEALTH

CD - DREAMS WIDE AWAKE
CANTERBURY DREAM CTD 007/8
CD1: Borogoves 1/ Borogoves 2/ Clocks And Clouds 1/ Tenemos Roads/ Clocks And Clouds 2/ The Collapso
CD2: Dreams Wide Awake/ Underwater Song/ Squarer For Mand/ T.N.T.F.X.
R: CD1 G-Vg. CD2 G-Vg. Audience.   S: CD1 tracks 1-6 Virgin demo '76. Track 7 BBC '76. CD2 Bottom Line, NY '79.   C: Japanese CD. Time CD1 66:18. CD2 66:36.

NEIL, VINCE

CD - EXPOSED 1993
WYVERN EC BV WV-312B1/2
CD1: Look In Her Eyes/ Kickstart My Heart/ Set Me Free/ Can't Have Your Cake/ Gettin' Hard/ I Wanna Be Sedated/ Girls, Girls, Girls/ Same Old Situation/ Home Sweet Home/ You're Invited/ Vik Fox Drum Solo/ Fine, Fine Wine
CD2: Steve Stevens Guitar Solo/ The Edge/ Look That Kill/ Sister Of Pain/ Can't Change Me/ Dr. Feelgood
R: G. Audience.   S: Festival Hall, Osaka, Japan, Sept. 28 '93.   C: Japanese CD.

NEW BARBARIANS

CD - BLIND DATE REVISITED
SWINGIN' PIG TSP-CD-202-2
CD1: John Belushi Introduction/ Sweet Little Rock 'N' Roller/ F.U.C. Her/ Breathe On Me/ Infekshun/ I Can Feel The Fire/ Am I Grooving You/ Seven Days/ Before They Make Me Run
CD2: Prodigal Son/ Let It Rock/ Respectable/ Starfucker/ Beast Of Burden/ Just My Imagination/ When The Whip Comes Down/ Shattered/ Miss You/ Jumping Jack Flash
R: Exs. Soundboard.   S: Keith Richard's C.N.I.B. Benefit Concert, Civic Auditorium, Oshawa, Ontario, Canada Apr. 22 '79.   C: ECD.

NICKS, STEVIE

CD - LIVE VOL. 1
JOKER JOK-028-A
Outside The Rain/ Dreams/ Talk To Me/ Stand Back/ Whole Lotta Trouble/ Love's A Hard Game To Play/ Stop Draggin' My Heart Around/ Edge of Seventeen/ Landslide
C: Australian CD.

NINE INCH NAILS

CD - A DEMON POSSESSED
HOME RECORDS HR 6057-3
Terrible Lie (4:52)/ Sin (3:33)/ Sanctified (5:44)/

That's What I Get (4:27)/ Get Down, Make Love (3:23)/ Ringfinger (5:49)/ Down In It (4:30)/ Head Like A Hole (5:57)/ Terrible Lie (4:44)/ Sin (4:03)/ Down On It (3:45)/ Get Down, Make Love (2:44)/ Head Like A Hole (5:47)/ Psychical (4:50)/ Wish (4:31)
R: G-Vg. Audience.   S: Tracks 1-8 Metro, Chicago Apr. 7 '90. Tracks 9-10 Lollapalooza, Irvine, CA Oct. 16 '91. Tracks 11-13 live in the USA Sept. 1 '91. Tracks 14-15 Tipitina's, New Orleans July 11 '91.   C: ECD. Dcc.

CD - CHILDREN OF THE NIGHT
KISS THE STONE KTS 498
Terrible Lie/ March Of The Pigs/ The Becoming/ Sanctified/ Piggy/ Burn/ Closer/ Wish/ Broken Machine/ Down In It/ Eraser/ Scary Monsters, Reptile, Hurt (with David Bowie)
R: Exs. Soundboard.   S: On the '95 David Bowie tour.   C: ECD. Dcc. Pic CD. Time 70:45.

CD - I FEEL FINE
AMERICAN FLY AFO 12/13
CD1: Pinion (2:34)/ Mr. Self-Destruct (3:40)/ Sin (4:17)/ March Of Pigs (3:59)/ Piggy (4:54)/ Reptile (6:24)/ Gave Up (4:28)/ Happiness In Slavery (8:06)/ Erasure (5:06)/ Hurt (5:05)/ Wish (7:17)/ Suck (4:15)/ The Only Time (5:21)/ Down In It (4:33)/ Head Like A Hole (5:54)
CD2: Closer (6:12)/ Dead Souls (6:54)/ Something I Can Never Have (6:32)/ Twist (4:46)/ Sanctified (5:36)/ Kinda I Want To (4:43)/ Down In It (4:29)/ Supernaut (6:26)/ Head (Flood Mix) (5:49)/ Down In It (Demo) (3:58)/ Sin (DJ Edit) (3:27)/ Wish (DJ Edit) (3:56)/ Suck (Demo) (3:44)
R: G-Vg. Audience. CD2 tracks 4-13 Exs. Soundboard.   S: Toronto Dec. 1 '94. CD2 Tracks 4-7 studio demos '88. Track 8 original version with Trent Reznor on vocal. Tracks 9-13 various promo mixes.   C: ECD. Dcc. Pic CDs.

CD - LOVE IT TO DEATH
BANZAI BZCD 058
Mr. Self Destruct/ Sin/ March Of The Pigs/ Piggy/ Reptile/ Hurt/ Wish/ Suck/ Ruiner/ Down In It/ Head Like A Hole/ Closer/ They Keep Calling Me/ I Do Not Want This
R: G. Audience.   S: The Summit, Houston Oct. 31 '94.   C: ECD. Dcc. Pic CD. Time 79:21.

CD - RUSTY NAILS - THE REMIXES
BLUE MOON RECORDS BMCD 40
Closer/ Terrible Lie/ Get Down Make Love/ Kinda I Want To/ Down On It/ That's What I Get/ Twist/ Ringfinger/ Heresy/ Head Like A Hole/ Closer To God/ I Do Not Want This/ Happiness Is Slavery/ Kinda I Want To/ Underneath The Skin/ Sin/ Wish/ Memorabilia/ All Pigs Lined Up/ March Of The Pigs/ Piggy
R: Exs. Soundboard.   C: ECD. Dcc. Time 64:11.

CD - SEX, PAIN AND ROCK & ROLL
RAZOR BLADE RB507
Terrible Lies (5:05)/ Sin (4:17)/ Mr. Self Destruct

(3:32)/ Something I Can Never Have (6:36)/ Closer (5:52)/ Reptile (7:08)/ Gave Up (4:23)/ March Of Pigs (4:05)/ Erasure (5:18)/ Hurt (4:49)/ Wish (3:42)/ Burn (5:25)/ The Only Time (5:26)/ Down In It (4:33)/ Dead Souls (5:29)/ Suck (2:56)
R: Vg. Audience.   S: The Universal Amphitheater, LA Oct. 7 '94.   C: ECD. Pic CD.

CD - SYMPATHY FOR THE EVIL
FINGER PRINT PRINT 005
Terrible Lie/ Sin/ March Of The Pigs/ Something I Can Never Have/ Closer/ Reptile/ Wish/ Suck/ The Only Time/ Get Down, Make Love/ Down On It/ Big Man With Gun/ Head Like A Hole
R: G-Vg. Audience.   S: The Moore Theatre, Seattle Apr. 19 '94.   C: ECD. Dcc. Time 63:06.

CD - TIME TO SUCK
MIND THE MAGIC MTM 026
Sin/ Sanctified/ That's What I Get/ Get Down, Make Love/ The Only Time/ Down In It/ Head Like A Hole/ Now I Am Nothing, Terrible Lie/ Physical/ The Only Time/ Suck/ That's What I Get/ Something
R: G-Vg.   S: Tracks 1-7 USA '90. Tracks 8-13 USA '91.   C: ECD. Time 64:57.

NIRVANA

CD - BANG! YOU'RE DEAD
VOX 1013/14
CD1: Radio Friendly Unit Shifter (4:03)/ Drain You (3:57)/ Breed (3:38)/ Serve The Servants (3:32)/ Come As You Are (4:07)/ Smells Like A Teen Spirit/ Sliver (3:14)/ Dumb (2:59)/ In Bloom (4:22)/ About The Girl (2:59)/ Lithium (4:51)/ Penny Royal Tea (3:45)/ School (3:15)/ Polly (3:23)
CD2: Very Ape (1:55)/ Lounge Act (2:57)/ Rape Me (2:33)/ Territorial Pissings (3:51)/ The Man Who Sold The World (4:32)/ Francis Farmer Will Have Revenge On Seattle (4:05)/ Make You Happy (4:09)/ All Apologies (3:37)/ On A Plain (3:12)/ Scentless Apprentice (4:01)/ Heart Shaped Box (4:38)/ Marijuana (3:24)*/ I Want It All (2:35)*/ Make You Happy (3:31)*/ In To The Dirt (1:52)*/ Rape Me (2:43)*
R: Ex. Audience. *Soundboard.   S: Italy Mar. '94. *'In Utero' demos.   C: ECD. Dcc. Pic CDs.

CD - CRACKER
THE LAST BOOTLEG RECORDS LBR 031/2
CD1: Radio Friendly Unit Shifter (4:03)/ My Sharona (1:37)/ Drain You (3:57)/ Breed (3:38)/ Serve The Servants (3:37)/ Come As You Are (4:07)/ Smells Like Teen Spirit (4:35)/ Sliver (3:14)/ Dumb (2:59)/ In Bloom 94:22)/ About A Girl (2:59)/ Lithium (4:51)/ Penny Royal Tea (3:45)/ School (3:15)/ Polly (3:23)/ Very Ape (1:55)/ Lounge Act (2:57)/ Rape Me (2:33)/ Territorial Pissings (3:51)/ The Man Who Sold The World (4:32)
CD2: Francis Farmer Will Have A Revenge On Seattle (4:05)/ Make You Happy (4:09)/ All Apologies (3:37)/ On A Plain (3:12)/ Scentless

Apprentice (4:01)/ Heart - Shaped Box (4:38)/
Aneurysm (4:56)/ Been A Son (3:24)/ All
Apologies (3:04)/ Blew (3:16)/ Star Away (3:34)/
Floyd The Barber (2:19)/ Negative Creep (2:27)/
Love Buzz (3:17)
R: Vg. Audience.　　S: Rennes, France, Feb. 16
'94.　　C: ECD. Dcc. Pic CD.

CD - THE FIRST NIGHT
AMERICAN FLY AF 017
Drain You/ Breed/ Serve The Servants/ About A
Girl/ Heart Shaped Box/ Sliver/ Dumb/ In Bloom/
Come As You Are/ Lithium/ Pennyroyal Tea/
School/ Polly/ Milk It/ Rape Me/ Territorial Pissing/
Smells Like Teen Spirit/ All Apologies/ Shame
R: Vg. Audience.　　S: Vets Memorial Coliseum,
Phoenix, Arizona Oct. 18 '93.　　C: ECD. Dcc. Pic
CD. Time 69:01.

CD - HEART SHAPED BOX
COB 001/8
CD1: Floyd The Barber (2:18)/ Paper Cuts (4:06)/
Downer (1:52)/ Beeswax (2:47)/ Mexican Seafood
(1:52)/ Hairspray Queen (4:12)/ Aero Zeppelin
(4:38)/ Love Buzz (7" single version) (3:46)/ Big
Cheese (7" single version) (3:41)/ Spank Thru
(3:23)/ Swap Meet (3:03)/ Mr. Moustache (3:24)/
Blew (2:55)/ About A Girl (2:48)/ School (2:42)/
Negative Creep (2:55)/ Scoff (4:10)/ Sifting (5:24)/
Big Long Now (5:01)/ Do You Love Me (3:33)/
Stain (2:38)/ Been A Son (2:20)
S: Reciprocal Recording Studios, Seattle. Tracks
1-7 ? Tracks 8-9 June 11 '88. Tracks 10-19 Jan.
23 '88, June 30 '88, July 16 '88 and Sept. 27 '88.
Track 20 June 10-21 '89. Tracks 21-22 Aug. '89.
CD2: A Bureaucratic Desire For Revenge (part 1)
(7:23)/ A Bureaucratic Desire For Revenge (part
2) (6:39)/ Ouroboros Is Broken (18:39)/ Where
Did You Sleep Last Night? (3:59)/ Down In The
Dark (3:20)/ In Bloom (Early Version) (4:31)/ Dive
(3:53)/ Sliver (7" single version) (2:52)/ Turn
Around (2:21)/ D - 7 (3:48)/ Son Of A Gun (2:50)/
Molly's Lips (1:54)/ Aneurysm (4:50)/ Even In His
Youth (3:05)/ Smells Like Teen Spirit (4:34)
S: Tracks 1-3 Smegma Studios Oct. '89 by 'Earth'
with Kurt on guitar. Tracks 4 and 5 from Mark
Lanegan's solo CD Dec. '89. Track 4 has Kurt on
guitar and Chris on bass. Track 5 has Kurt on
back up vocals. Track 6 Sub Pop Video Network
Program 1, Madison, WI Apr. '90. Track 7 Smart
Studios Apr. '90. Track 8 Reciprocal Studios July
11 '90. Tracks 9-12 recorded Oct. '90 for John
Peel BBC radio show. Tracks 13-14 Music
Source, Seattle Jan. 11 '91.
CD3: If You Must (3:46)/ Downer (1:57)/ Floyd
The Barber (2:05)/ Paper Cuts (3:51)/ Spank Thru
(3:18)/ Beeswax (2:32)/ Pen Cap Chew (2:48)/
Hairspray Queen (4:19)/ Love Buzz (3:16)/ About
A Girl (2:39)/ Spank Thru (3:16)/ Polly (2:35)/
Blandest (3:39)/ Love Buzz (3:12)/ About A Girl
(2:35)/ Polly (acoustic) (2:20)/ Misery Loves
Company (acoustic) (2:21)/ Sappy (acoustic)
(2:48)/ Opinion (1:50)/ D - 7 (2:31)/ Lithium (Take
6) (2:44)/ Immodium (3:12)/ Pay To Play (3:31)/

Sappy (3:25)
S: Tracks 1-8 original uncut demo tape,
Reciprocal Recording Studios, Seattle Jan 23 '88.
Tracks 9-12 recorded for John Peel sessions.
Tracks 13-14 Reciprocal Studios June 11 '88.
Track 15 Reciprocal Studios June 30 '88. Tracks
16-18 Jan. '89. Track 19 Feb. '90. Tracks 20-25
Smart Studios, Madison, WI Apr. '90.
CD4: In Bloom (4:25)/ Immodium (Take 2) (3:08)/
Pay To Play (Take 2) (2:05)/ Polly (2:36)/ Spank
Thru (3:12)/ Lithium (4:08)/ Here She Comes Now
(4:40)/ Where Did You Sleep Last Night? (4:58)/
Junkyard (3:30)/ Help Me (3:30)/ Dazed And
Confused (4:25)/ About A Girl (2:27)/ Spank Thru
(2:57)/ Molly's Lips (2:02)/ In Bloom (4:06)/ Floyd
The Barber (2:44)/ In His Hand (3:02)/ Bullshit
Jam (1:57)/ Jesus Wants Me For A Sunbeam
(3:35)/ School (2:31)/ Drain You (3:35)/ Talk To
Me (3:20)
S: Tracks 1-6 Smart Studios, Madison, WI Apr.
'90. Tracks 7-8 outtakes Nov. '91. Track 9
England Oct. 27 '89. Track 10 Austrian radio with
TAD on guitar Nov. '89. Track 11 Italy 11 '89.
Tracks 12-14 Pine Street Theater, Portland, OR
Apr. '90. Tracks 15-17 sound check, Hollywood
Palladium, Aug. 17 '90. Tracks 18-19 Trees Club,
Dallas, TX Oct. 19 '91. Tracks 20-21 Paramount
Theatre, Seattle Oct. 31 '91. Track 22 Europe
Dec. '91.
CD5: Been A Son (1:53)/ New Wave Polly (1:56)/
Aneurysm (4:53)/ Something In The Way (3:20)/
Here She Comes Now (4:59)/ Curmudgeon
(2:58)/ Oh The Guilt (3:22)/ Return Of The Rat
(3:08)/ The Priest They Called Him (9:44)/
Interview (6:17)/ About A Girl (Live) (2:32)/
Interview (5:35)/ On A Plain (Live) (2:55)/
Interview (8:30)
S: Tracks 1-4 Mark Goodier session, BBC Nov.
'91. Track 5 Velvet Underground tribute album
Nov. '91. Tracks 6-8 Laundry Room Studios,
Seattle, WA Apr. '92. Track 9 Kurt's guitar part,
Laundry Room Studios Nov. '92. Tracks 11-16
from 'Nevermind - It's An Interview' Jan. '92.
Tracks 11, 13 and 15 Paramount Theatre, Seattle
Oct. 31 '91.
CD6: 'Nevermind - It's An Interview' continued
(3:25)/ Dumb (2:34)/ Drain You (4:00)/ Endless
Nameless (7:55)/ Rape Me (2:50)/ Scentless
Apprentice (3:47)/ Heart Shaped Box (4:40)/ Milk
It (3:54)/ Dumb (2:28)/ Radio Friendly Unit Shifter
(5:00)/ Very Ape (1:57)/ Penny Royal Tea (3:36)/
Frances Farmer (4:11)/ Tourettes (1:55)/ Serve
The Servants (3:38)/ All Apologies (3:58)/ MV
(Moist Vagina) (3:32)/ VS Chorus VS (3:24)/
Gallons Of Rubbing Alcohol Flow Thru The Strip
(7:33)
S: Tracks 2-3 BBC, London Nov. '91. Track 4 out-
take Apr. '91. Tracks 5-16 Pachyderm Studios,
Minnesota Feb. 20 '93 - Mar. 7 '93. Tracks 17-19
outtakes, Pachyderm Studios, Minnesota Feb. 20
'93 - Mar. 7 '93.
CD7: Outtakes, Unplugged And NYC, July 23,
'93: Marigold (2:33)/ I Hate Myself And Want To
Die (2:53)/ All Apologies (3:43)/ About A Girl

(3:22)/ Come As You Are (4:13)/ Jesus Wants Me For A Sunbeam (4:16)/ Dumb (3:07)/ Man Who Sold The World (4:10)/ Penny Royal Tea (3:47)/ Polly (3:16)/ On A Plain (4:08)/ Plateau (3:20)/ Lake Of Fire (2:57)/ All Apologies (3:54)/ Where Did You Sleep Last Night? (4:53)/ Serve The Servants (4:09)/ Scentless Apprentice (3:46)/ School (2:57)/ Breed (3:10)/ Lithium (4:20)
S: Track 1 'In Utero' outtake from European CD single. Track 2 'In Utero' outtake from Beavis and Butthead Experience CD. Track 3 MTV 'Unplugged' promo CD. Tracks 4-15 for MTV 'Unplugged'. Tracks 12-13 with Curt and Chris Kirkwood from the Meat Puppets. Tracks 16-20 Roseland Ballroom July 23 '93.
CD8: Come As You Are (3:55)/ Milk It (4:40)/ Drain You (3:46)/ Tourettes (1:59)/ Aneurysm (4:35)/ Very Ape (2:43)/ Blew (3:32)/ Heart Shaped Box (4:31)/ Rape Me (2:49)/ Territorial Pissings (4:19)/ All Apologies (5:25)/ Polly (2:56)/ Dumb (3:53)/ Something In The Way (3:30)/ Where Did You Sleep Last Night? (5:29)/ Smells Like Teen Spirit (4:43)/ Endless Nameless (9:17)/ Secret Song (2:34)
S: Roseland Ballroom July 23 '93.
R: As with any collection of this size, quality varies. The thing to keep in mind is the amount of rare material found on this set.   C: ECD. This set comes in a heart-shapped box with a full-color book by Paul Haus. Pic CDs.

CD - HEAVEN CAN WAIT
SWINDLE SWN 008
School (3:23)/ Floyd The Barber (2:16)/ Love Buzz (3:24)/ Dive (3:36)/ Spank Thru (3:41)/ Breed (3:12)/ Scoff (5:06)/ About A Girl (2:57)/ Molly's Lips (3:18)/ Been A Son (2:01)/ Stain (2:47)/ Negative Creep (2:55)/ Blew (3:48)/ Aneurysm (3:08)/ Drain You (3:36)/ On A Plan (2:56)/ School (2:06)
R: Ex.   S: Tracks 1-13 Raji's, Hollywood Feb. 15 '90. Tracks 14-17 Paramount Theatre, Seattle Oct. 31 '91.   C: ECD. Dcc. Pic CD. Some songs fade in.

CD - HEROES AND HEROINE
ROLLING THUNDER RECORDS RT 56004
School (2:46)/ Drain You (3:34)/ Breed (2:53)/ Sliver (2:06)/ In Bloom (4:17)/ Come As You Are (3:28)/ Love Buzz (3:33)/ Lithium (4:25)/ Polly (2:45)/ About A Girl (2:42)/ Smells Like A Teen Spirit (4:47)/ On A Plain (3:42)/ Negative Creep (2:24)/ Been A Son (2:00)/ Blew (2:57)/ Lithium (5:48)/ Scentless Apprentice (Chaotic Version) (9:34)/ Aneurysm (4:40)/ Territorial Pissings (2:20)
R: Vg.   S: USA spring '93.   C: ECD. Dcc.

CD - HOBKAN 1989
CACKER CR 12
School/ Floyd The Barber/ Love Buzz/ About A Girl/ Scoff/ Spank Thru/ Big Cheese/ Polly/ Paper Cuts/ Negative Creep/ Blew
R: G-Vg. Audience.   S: Hobkan July 13 '89.
C: Japanese CD. Dbw. Time 39:15.

CD - I HATE MYSELF AND I WANT TO DIE
BUGSY BGS 025/2
C: See 'Live And Demons' (Swindle SWN 006/2) for songs and sources.   C: ECD. Dcc.

CD - IN THE RAW
SWINDLE SWN 028
Blandest (3:51)/ Spank Thru (3:12)/ Downer (1:58)/ Hairspray Queen (1:56)/ Polly (2:50)/ Molly's Lips (2:12)/ Happy Hour (2:20)/ M.V. (3:25)/ Marigolds (2:35)/ Happy Hour (3:30)/ Oh, The Guilt (2:50)/ Lithium (4:09)/ Breed (3:03)/ In Bloom (4:24)/ Stay Away (3:13)/ Son Of A Gun (2:49)/ Talkin' (2:51)/ D-7 (4:20)
R: Vg-Ex. Soundboard.   S: Demos recorded live '87-'92.   C: ECD. Dcc. Pic CD.

CD - LIVE AND DEMONS
SWINDLE SWN 006/2
CD1: Polly (2:49), Molly's Lips (2:11), Everything And Nothing (2:18) (demos '87/ Blandest (3:50), Spank Thru (3:11), Downer (1:38), Hairspray Queen (3:57), Mexican Seawood (1:51) (demos '88)/ Marijuana (3:24)/ I Want It All (2:35)/ Make You Happy (3:31)/ Untitled Demo (2:47)/ Into The Dirt (1:52)/ Rape Me (2:43)/ Scentless Apprentice (3:42)/ Heart Shaped Box (4:33)/ Milk It 3:47)/ Radio Friendly Unit Shifter (4:43)
CD2: Love Buzz (3:55)/ Floyd The Barber (3:03)/ Scoff (4:18)/ Dive (3:49)/ About A Girl (2:36)/ Spank Through (3:44)/ Breed (3:30)/ In Bloom (4:23)/ School (3:21)/ Been A Son (1:50)/ Negative Creep (3:07)/ Blew (2:52)/ In Bloom (4:06)/ Floyd The Barber (2:44)/ Aneurysm (3:03) Polly (2:54)/ Big Cheese (3:40)/ Mr. Moustache (3:50)/ Even In This Youth (3:22)/ Never Mind (4:35)
R: Vg-Ex. Soundboard. Some G.   S: CD1 Tracks 9-18 'In Utero' demos and unreleased '93. CD2 Hollywood Palladium and soundcheck Aug. 17 '90. CD2 Tracks 13-15 soundcheck, Rose Club, Koln, Germany Nov.8 '89.   C: ECD. Dcc. Pic CD.

CD - LIVE AT HOLLYWOOD ROCK FESTIVAL
JW 1001 - 1/2
CD1: Instrumental 1 Intro, Floyd The Barber/ Drain You/ On A Plain/ Sliver/ In Bloom/ Come As You Are/ School/ Smells Like...(intro)/ Smells Like Teen Spirit/ Polly/ About A Girl/ Smells Like Teen Spirit (faster)/ On A Plain (strange version)/ Hate Me - Never Retreat
CD2: Intro/ Mexican Seawood/ Drain You/ Silence Appearance (strange version)/ Territorial Pissing/ Blandest/ Spank Thru/ Downer/ Hairspray Queen/ Mexican Seawood/ Polly/ Polly's Lips/ Everything & Nothing/ Moist Vagina (different lyrics)/ Heart Shaped Box/ Make You Happy/ Tourette's/ Lithium/ Breed/ In Bloom/ Stay Away/ Son Of A Gun/ Turn Around/ Dee Seven
R: Vg. Audience. CD2 tracks 6-24 Vg. Soundboard. Some hiss.   S: CD1 and CD2 tracks 1-5 Hollywood Rock Festival, Rio Jan. 23 '93. Tracks CD2 6-10 demos '88. CD2 tracks 11-

13 demos '87. CD2 tracks 14-17 demos '92. CD2
tracks 18-24 demos '90.   C: ECD.

CD - LOUDER
BUGSY BGS 035/2
CD1: Floyd The Barber (2:52)/ Love Buzz (4:28)/
Dive (4:07)/ Spank Through (3:22)/ Immodium
(3:29)/ About A Girl (3:38)/ Big Cheese (3:35)/
Scoff (4:54)/ Molly's Lips (3:07)/ Stain (2:33)/
Been A Son (1:59)/ Negative Creep/ Blew (3:20)/
Drain You, Aneurysm (3:43)/ School (7:07)/
Smells Like Teen Spirit (5:01)/ About A Girl (2:57)/
Polly (2:51)/ Sliver (2:01)/ Breed (3:05)
CD2: Breed (3:03)/ Drain You (3:42)/ Aneurysm
(4:54)/ School (3:11)/ Sliver (2:16)/ In Bloom
(4:31)/ Come As You Are (3:42)/ Lithium (4:19)/
Smells Like Teen Spirit (5:53)/ On A Plain (3:02)/
Been A Son (3:20)/ Mary (3:09)/ Blew (3:17)/
Dumb (2:44)/ Star Away (3:48)/ Territorial Pissing
(2:53)/ Come As You Are (3:41)/ Lithium (4:56)/
Territorial Pissing (3:30)
R: CD1 Vg. Audience. Tracks 14-20 Vg-Ex.
Soundboard. CD2 Ex. Soundboard.   S: CD1
Michigan '90. Tracks 14-20 Delmare, CA '92. CD2
Europe '92.   C: ECD. Dcc. Pic CD.

CD - MELTDOWN
CHROME HEARTS CH001
Radio Friendly Unit Shifter/ Drain You/ Breed/
Serve The Servants/ About A Girl/ Heart Shaped
Box/ Dumb/ In Bloom/ Come As You Are/ Lithium/
Pennyroyal Tea/ Polly/ Kurt Guitar Solo/
Tourettes/ Rape Me/ Territorial Pissings/ Jesus
Wants Me For A Sunbeam/ Scentless Apprentice/
Smells Like Teen Spirit
R: Ex. Audience recording.   S: Bayfront
Amphitheatre, St. Petersberg, FL Nov. 27 '93.

CD - MIXED AND UNRELEASED MATERIAL
WN 9502
Live Mix (44:02)/ Teen Spirit Mix (11:52)/ Marigold
(previously unreleased) (2:33)/ Moist Vagina (previously unreleased) (3:32)/ Even In His Youth
(previously unreleased) (4:20)/ Aneurysm (previously unreleased) (4:44)
R: Vg-Ex. Soundboard.   C: ECD. Dcc. Pic CD.
Time 69:56.

CD - THE NEEDLE & THE DAMAGE DONE:
OUTCESTICIDE II
BLUE MOON RECORDS BMCD25
C: See 'Outcesticide Vol. 2 (Kobra Records
KRCD 002) for songs and sources.   C: ECD.
Dcc. Time 74:17.

CD - OUTCESTICIDE VOL. 1
KOBRA RECORDS KRCD 001
If You Must/ Downer/ Floyd The Barber/ Paper
Cuts/ Spank Thru/ Beeswax/ Pen Cap Chew (Jan
1 '88)/ Blandest (June 11 '88)/ Polly (acoustic)
(Jan. '89)/ Misery Loves Company (Jan. '89)/
Sappy (acoustic) (Jan. '89)/ Do You Love Me
(June '89)/ Been A Son (Aug. '89)/ Junkyard (Nov.
'89)/ Opinion (Feb. '90)/ D.7 (Mar. '90)/ Imodium/

Pay To Play/ Sappy/ Here She Comes Now (Nov.
'91)/ Where Did You Sleep Last Night? (Nov. '91)/
Return Of The Rat (Nov. '91)/ Talk To Me (Dec.
'91)
R: Vg-Ex.   S: Tracks 1-7 first demo tape,
Reciprocal Recording Seattle Jan. 23 '88. Tracks
17-19 unreleased Sub Pop mini album, Smart
Studios, Madison, WI Apr. '90. All other tracks are
studio outtakes, demos and rehearsals.
C: ECD. Dbw. Red type. Time 69:52.

CD - OUTCESTICIDE VOL. 2
KOBRA RECORDS KRCD 002
In Bloom (unissued Sub Pop 7" master tape May
'90)/ Imodium (early version of 'Breed' with differ-
ent lyrics Nov. '89)/ Help Me (unreleased song
winter '89)/ Oh, The Guilt (live version Nov. '89)/
Smells Like A Teen Spirit (with Flea from The Red
Hot Chili Peppers on trumpet Jan. '93)/
Pennyroyal Tea (early version with different lyrics
Oct. '91)/ It's Closing Soon (Kurt and Courtney
date unknown)/ Heart Shaped Box (early version
with different lyrics Jan. '93)/ Scentless
Apprentice (extended experimental feedback ver-
sion Jan. '93)/ Been A Son (acoustic rehearsal
Oct. '91)/ Something In The Way (in-store
acoustic gig Oct. '91)/ Where Did You Sleep Last
Night (Kurt solo at Castaic Lake Sept. '92)/ Baba
O'Riley (Rennes Dec. '91)/ The End (Belgium
Nov. '91)/ Lithium (mix six, unreleased studio ver-
sion June '91)/ Dumb (with Melora Craeger on
cello Feb. '94)/ Molly Lips (an early attempt at
'Vaseline' Nov. '89)/ In His Hands (unreleased
song written circa summer '90)/ The Man Who
Sold The World (electric version Dec. '93)/ Smells
Like A Teen Spirit ('The Word' TV show Nov. '91)
R: Vg-Ex. Soundboard and Audience.   C: ECD.
Blue/black cover. Yellow type. Time 74:17.

CD - OUTCESTICIDE VOL. 3
KOBRA RECORDS KRCD 003
Love Buzz, About A Girl, Polly, Spank Thru
(Maida Vale Studios, London Oct. 26 '89)/ Son Of
A Gun, Molly's Lips, D-7, Turnaround (Maida Vale
Studios, London Oct. 21 '89)/ Dumb, Drain You,
Endless-Nameless (Maida Vale Studios, London
Sept. 3 '91)/ Been A Son, Punk Rock, Polly,
Aneurysm, Something In The Way (Maida Vale
Studios, London Nov. 5 '91)/ Here She Comes
Now, Where Did You Sleep Last Night (Hilversum
Studios, London Nov. 24 '91)/ Drain You, Polly,
Territorial Pissings (MTV Studios, New York Jan.
10 '92)/ Lithium (MTV Awards, Los Angeles Sept.
10 '92)
R: Exs. Soundboard.   C: ECD. Purple/black
cover. Green type. Time 72:11.

CD - OUTCESTICIDE VOL. 4
KOBRA RECORDS KRCD 004
Smells Like Teen Spirit (Gothic version USA '92)/
Marigold (demo '92)/ Oh, The Guilt (outtake '93)/
MV (Moist Vagina) (outtake '93)/ Do You Love Me
(outtake '90)/ Curmudgeon (outtake '92)/ Into The
Dirt (outtake '93)/ Return Of The Rat (outtake

'92)/ Verse Chorus Verse (outtake '93)/ I Hate Myself And I Want To Die (outtake '93)/ Frances Farmer Will Have Her Revenge On Seattle (demo '93)/ About A Girl (outtake '90)/ Breed (demo '90)/ Turn Around (outtake '89)/ Molly's Lips (Hollywood, CA Feb. 15 '90)/ Spank Thru' (Hollywood, CA Feb. 15 '90)/ Drain You (Chicago '94)/ School, Smells Like Teen Spirit, Lithium, Territorial Pissing (Rock And Environment Fest, Seattle Nov. '92)
R: Ex. Soundboard.   C: ECD. Orange/black cover. Blue type. Time 67:05.

CD - OUTCESTICIDE VOL. 5
KOBRA RECORDS KRCD 005
Rape Me, Pennyroyal Tea, Drain You ('Null Part A' French TV studios Feb. 4 '94)/ Marigold (Dave's original demo, Upland Studios, Arlington, VA Dec. 23 '90)/ Dive (early version, different lyrics June '89)/ Mr. Moustache (early version, different lyrics summer '88)/ Blandest (original scrapped B-Side of 'Love Buzz' Sub Pop 7" June 11 '88)/ Even In His Youth (early version, studio Seattle, Nov. '89)/ Smells Like Teen Spirit (MTV Studios, NY Jan. 10 '92)/ Serve The Servants, Dumb ('Tunnel', Rai Italian TV Studios Feb. 23 '94)/ The Eagle Has Landed (AKA 'Tourette's, early live version Aug. '92)/ Aneurysm (early live version, different lyrics Nov. '90)/ Oh, The Guilt (early live version, different lyrics Nov. '90)/ Dive, About A Girl (The 'Lost' Radio Session Vpro, Hilversum, Holland Nov. 5 '89)/ The Money Will Roll Right In (live cover version of a Fang song Aug. '92)/ In His Hands (live version of an unreleased song with different lyrics Nov. '90)/ Curmudgeon (only live performance from Belgium Nov. '91)/ Alcohol (only live performance Italy Oct. '89)/ Run Rabbit, Run* (rough but rare, the long forgotten set closer from '87)/ Beans (left off the 'Bleach' LP Dec. '88)
R: Vg-Ex. Some G-Vg. *G.   C: ECD. Yellow/black cover. Pink type. Time 73:25.

CD - PISSING IN ACTION
BABY CAPONE BC 045/2
CD1: Floyd The Barber (2:52)/ Love Buzz (4:28)/ Dive (4:07)/ Spank Through (3:22)/ Immodium (3:29)/ About A Girl (3:38)/ Big Cheese (3:35)/ Scoff (4:54)/ Molly's Lips (3:07)/ Stain (2:33)/ Been A Son (1:59)/ Negative Creep (3:42)/ Blew (3:20)/ Drain You, Aneurysm (3:43)/ School (7:07)/ Smells Like Teen Spirit (5:01)/ About A Girl (2:57)/ Polly (2:51)/ Sliver (2:01)/ Breed (3:05)
CD2: Breed (3:03)/ Drain You (3:42)/ Aneurysm (4:54)/ School (3:11)/ Dive (2:16)/ In Bloom (4:31)/ Come As You Are (3:42)/ Lithium (4:19)/ Smells Like Teen Spirit (5:53)/ On A Plain (3:02)/ Been A Son (3:20)/ Mary (3:09)/ Blew (3:17)/ Dumb (2:44)/ Star Away (3:48)/ Territorial Pissings (2:53)/ Come As You Are (3:410/ Lithium (4:56)/ Territorial Pissings (3:30)
R: Exs. Soundboard.   S: CD1 tracks 1-13 Michigan '90. Tracks 14-20 Delmare, CA '92. CD2 Europe '92.   C: ECD. Dcc. Pic CD.

CD - R.I.P.
VAMPIRE VR 500018
About A Girl/ Come As You Are/ Jesus Wants Me For A Sunbeam/ Pennyroyal Tea/ Polly/ On A Plain/ Plateau/ Lake Of Fire/ All Apologies/ Where Did You Sleep Last Night/ Dumb/ Man Who Sold The World/ Drain You/ Aneurysm/ School/ Been A Son/ Negative Creep/ Smells Like Teen Spirit
R: Exs. Soundboard.   S: Track 1-10 'Unplugged' sessions '94. Track 11-12 'Unplugged' club gig '93. Track 13-18 USA '93. C: ECD. Time 65:03.

CD - ROUGH TAPES (BLEEDING YEARS)
METAL CRASH MECD 1087
Turnaround (2:38)/ Molly's Lips (1:44)/ D-7 (Take 1) (3:32)/ Sliver (2:08)/ Dive (3:46)/ Lithium (2:44)/ In Bloom (Take 1) (4:25)/ Breed (Take 1) (3:08)/ Stay Away (Take 1) (2:05)/ Another Rule (3:25)/ D-7 (Take 2) (2:29)/ Love Buzz (Take 1) (3:12)/ About A Girl (Take 1) (2:35)/ Polly (2:34)/ Breed (Take 2) (3:12)/ Stay Away (Take 2) (3:31)/ Donner (1:42)/ Love Buzz (Take 2) (3:17)/ About A Girl (Take 2) (2:41)/ Polly, Spank Thru (5:48)
R: Ex. Soundboard.   S: Outtakes.   C: ECD. Pic CD.

7" - SATURDAY NIGHT LIVE
S1: Heart Shaped Box   S2: Rape Me
R: Exs. Soundboard.   S: Saturday Night Live. C: USA. Black/white sleeve. Purple and green stars. 45 RPM.

CD - SMELLS LIKE... (VOL. 1)
BANANA BAN-027-A
School (2:38)/ Scoff (3:58)/ Love Buzz (3:21)/ Floyd The Barber (2:08)/ Dive (3:42)/ Polly (2:38)/ Big Cheese (3:33)/ Spank Thru (3:08)/ About A Girl (3:14)/ Negative Creep (2:19)/ Blew (3:03)/ Love Buzz (3:25)/ Son Of A Gun (2:48)/ Turnaround (2:21)/ D7 (3:47)/ Molly's Lips (1:50)/ In Bloom (4:28)/ Stay Away (3:26)
S: Europe, USA '89/'92.   C: Australian CD.

CD - SMELLS LIKE... (VOL. 2)
BANANA BAN-027-B
Drain You (3:45)/ Aneurysm (4:26)/ School (2:45)/ Smells Like Teen Spirit (5:07)/ About A Girl (2:58)/ Polly (2:56)/ Sliver (2:03)/ Breed (3:02)/ Come As You Are (3:45)/ Lithium (4:54)/ Get Together (0:20)/ Territorial Pissings (2:45)/ Been A Son (1:59)/ Negative Creep (2:45)/ On A Plain (2:52)/ Blew (3:10)
S: Europe '91.   C: Australian CD.

CD - SUICIDE SOLUTION?
KOBRA RECORDS KRCD 006
Radio Friendly Unit Shifter/ Drain You/ Breed/ Serve The Servants/ Come As You Are/ Smells Like Teen Spirit/ Sliver/ Dumb/ In Bloom/ About A Girl/ Lithium/ Pennyroyal Tea/ School/ Polly/ Francis Farmer Will Have Her Revenge On Seattle/ Verse Chorus Verse/ Rape Me/ Territorial Pissing/ All Apologies/ On A Plain/ Scentless

Apprentice/ Heart-Shaped Box
R: Ex. Audience.   S: Palatrussardi, Milano, Italy
Feb. 25 '94 - the last complete show Nirvana
played.   C: ECD. Dcc. Pic CD. Time 78:32.

CD - TACOMA 1987
CACKER CR 14
If You Must/ Downer/ Floyd The Barber/ Paper
Cuts/ Spank Thru/ Hairspray Queen (band stops
halfway through)/ Aero Zeppelin/ Beeswax/
Mexican Seafood/ Pen Cap Chew/ Unreleased
Song #1/ Hairspray Queen/ Unreleased Song #2/
Moby Dick
R: G. Audience.   S: Tacoma, Washington
Dec. '87.   C: Japanese CD. Dbw. Time 50:50.

CD - TOUR OVER EUROPE
HOME RECORDS HR 5917-5
Radio Friendly Unit Shifter (4:05)/ Drain You
(3:37)/ Breed (3:00)/ Serve The servants (3:10)/
Come As You Are (3:22)/ Smells Like Teen Spirit
(4:34)/ Sliver (1:53)/ Dumb (2:26)/ In Bloom
(4:38)/ About A Girl (2:40)/ Scentless Apprentice
(3:30)/ Lithium (4:00)/ Pennyroyal Tea (3:28)/
School (2:29)/ Polly (3:22)/ Very Ape 1:57)/
Lounge Act (2:48)/ Rape Me (2:40)/ Territorial
Pissing (2:25)/ All Apologies (3:19)/ On A Plain
(2:51)/ Heart Shaped Box, Closure (7:47)
R: Exs. Soundboard.   S: Rome Feb. 22 '94.
C: ECD. Dcc.

CD - VIRGIN SONGS
PAPER CORN MUSIC PC 002
Turnaround/ Molly's Lips/ Straight As An Arrow
(1)/ Never Take Me Home/ Down With Me/
Lithium/ In Bloom (1)/ Breed (1)/ Stay Away (1)/
Happy Hour (2)/ Straight As An Arrow (2)/ Love
Buzz (1)/ About A Girl (1)/ Polly (1)/ In Bloom (2)/
Breed (2)/ Stay Away (2)/ Happy Hour (2)/
Downer/ Hairspray Queen/ Love Buzz (2)/ About
A Girl (2)/ Poll (2)/ Spank Thru
R: Vg-Ex. Soundboard.   S: Studio.   C: ECD.
Dcc. Time 73:56.

7" - YOUR OPINION
POOL HALL RECORDS 1995
S1: Opinion/ Smelly Vagina
S2: Here She Comes Now
R: Ex. Soundboard.   C: Blue/white sleeve .
33 RPM.

NOFX

CD - SMASHING PUNK KINGS
OCTOPUS OCTO 188
Linoleum (2:22)/ Showerdays (2:23)/ The Longest
Line (1:56)/ Punk Guy (1:15)/ Bob (1:50)/
Everything For Free (2:14)/ Life Of Riley (2:32)/
Don't Call Me White (2:32)/ My Dick Is Burning
(2:17)/ A Perfect Government (1:59)/ Please Play
This Song On The Radio (2:17)/ Moran Brothers
(2:35)/ Straight Edge (2:28)/ Lisa & Louise (2:11)/
Dying Degree (3:07)/ The Malachi Crunch (2:51)/
Leave It Alone (2:08)/ Johnny Appleseed (2:44)/

Stickin' In My Eyes (2:26)/ Together In The Sand,
Nowhere (4:06)/ Stickin' In My Eyes (2:43)/ Bob
(2:21)/ Vanilla Sex (2:26)/ Green Corn (2:18)/
Straight Edge (3:04)/ The Longest Line (2:15)/
Soul Doubt (2:53)/ Please Play This Song On The
Radio (2:14)/ The Malachi Crunch (2:49)/ Buggley
Eye (2:00)
R: Exs. Soundboard.   S: Tracks 1-19 The
Factory, Milano, Italy Feb. 27 '95. Tracks 20-30
The Grugahalle, Essen, Germany Jan. '95.
C: ECD. Dcc. Pic CD.

CD - TOGETHER ON THE ROAD
KISS THE STONE KTS 413
Together On The Sand/ Nowhere/ Stickin' In My
Eyes/ Bob/ You Are Bleeding/ Straight Edge/ Lisa
And Louise/ Shower Days/ Kill All The White Men/
The Moron Brothers/ The Longest Line/ Soul
Doubt/ Please Play This Song On The Radio/ The
Malachi Crunch
R: Ex. Audience.   S: Live in Europe '94.
C: ECD. Pic CD. Time 37:57.

O

OASIS

CD - A YEAR IN THE LIFE
BLUE MOON RECORDS BMCD34
Cigarettes & Alcohol (4:13)/ Shakermaker (4:30)/
Bring It On Down (3:18)/ Up In The Sky (acoustic)
(3:16)/ Married With Children (2:53)/ Live Forever
(acoustic) (4:57)/ Shakermaker (acoustic) (4:12)/
Fade Away (4:22)/ Digsy's Dinner (2:29)/ Live
Forever (4:58)/ Supersonic (5:14)/ It's Good To Be
Free (3:23)/ Married With Children (2:34)/ Sad
Song (acoustic) (4:25)/ Talk Tonight (acoustic)
(3:35)/ Whatever (5:39)/ I Am The Walrus (7:09)
R: Exs. Soundboard. Audience.
S: Tracks 1-6 BBC Maida Vale Studios, London
May '94. Tracks 7-8 Royal Albert Hall, London
June 6 '94. Tracks 9-11 Glastonbury Festival,
Somerset, June '94. Track 12 New York July '94.
Tracks 13-18 Fan Club Concert, London Dec. '94.
C: ECD. Time 74:10.

CD - CIGARETTES & ALCOHOL
OCTOPUS OCTO 086
Rock 'N' Roll Stars (4:43)/ Shakermaker (4:52)/
Bring It On Down (4:10)/ Up In The Sky (4:31)/
Slide Away (5:44)/ Cigarettes And Alcohol (3:57)/
Married With Children (2:42)/ Sad Song (4:30)/
Whatever (4:12)/ I Am The Walrus (7:27)/ (It's
Good) To Be Free (3:23)/ Married With Children
(2:26)/ Sad Song (4:27)/ Talk Tonight (3:30)/
Whatever (5:34)
R: Exs. Soundboard.   S: Live Europe '94.
C: ECD. Dcc. Pic CD.

CD - DEFINITIVE!
CHELSEA RECORDS CFCD 027
Noel And Liam Gallagher Talking (0:14)/ Fade

Away (4:24)/ Digsy's Dinner (2:52)/ Live Forever (4:28)/ Cigarettes And Alcohol (4:40)/ Shakermaker (4:50)/ Digsy's Dinner (2:35)/ Live Forever (4:26)/ Cigarettes And Alcohol (4:30)/ Supersonic (5:20)/ Sad Song (4:16)/ Fade Away (4:11)/ Rock 'N' Roll Star (4:45)/ Married With Children (2:45)/ It's Good To Be Free (3:17)/ Talk Tonight (3:34)/ Whatever (5:14)/ Shakermaker (5:05)/ I Am The Walrus (3:58)/ Noel And Liam Gallagher Talking (0:18)
R:Exs. Soundboard from broadcasts.   S: Tracks 2-4 Glastonbury Festival, Somerset June '94. Track 5, demo, taken from NME's 'Mutha Of All Creation'. Tracks 6-10 Tramshed, Glasgow Apr. '94. Tracks: 11,17 and 19 'Later With Jools Holland' BBC 2 Dec. 10 '94. Track 12 'Top Live', Paris, Festival Des Inrockuptibles Nov. 3 '94. Tracks 15 and 16 BBC Maida Vale Studios, London Dec. 15 '94.   C: ECD. Time 75:44.

CD - MIRAGE
HAWK 75 (Europe)
Rock 'N' Roll (Cuts In) (4:41)/ Columbia (4:43)/ Fade Away (4:36)/ Digsy's Dinner (2:55)/ Shakermaker (5:29)/ Live Forever (4:44)/ Bring It On Down (5:05)/ Up In The Sky (4:55)/ Slide Away (5:11)/ Cigarettes & Alcohol (5:02)/ Married With Children (3:01)/ Supersonic (5:51)/ I Am The Walrus (11:27)/ Rock 'N' Roll Star (Encore) (6:10)
R: Exs. Soundboard.   S: Wetlands, New York Oct. 24 '94.   C: ECD. Time 74:59.

CD - 1996
OXYGEN OXY 041
The Swamp Song (3:15)/ Acquiesce (3:40)/ Some Might Say (4:58)/ Cigarettes And Alcohol (4:11)/ Wonderwall (acoustic version) (3:51)/ Live Forever (4:39)/ Supersonic (4:42)/ Hello (2:52)/ Roll With It (4:12)/ Whatever (acoustic version) (4:25)/ Champagne Supernova (8:55)/ Sad Song (acoustic version) (4:13)/ Whatever (with orchestra) (5:03)/ I Am The Walrus (with orchestra) (4:00)/ Fade Away (4:16)/ Some Might Say (6:33)
R: Exs. Soundboard.   S: Tracks 1-11 Vredenburg, Utrect, Holland Jan. 10 '96. Tracks 12-14 'Later With Jools Holland', London, UK Dec. 10 '94. Track 15 electric demo version Apr. '94. Track 16 demo version '95 - lead vocals by Noel.   C: ECD. Pic CD.

CD - PARIS '94 AND DEMOS
KMACD006
Rock And Roll Star (6:35)/ Shakermaker (6:17)/ Live Forever (5:09)/ Fade Away (4:30)/ Cigarettes And Alcohol (4:54)/ Supersonic (4:18)/ I Am The Walrus (11:19)/ Digsy's Dinner 2:17)/ Live Forever II (3:45)/ Shakermaker II (3:40)/ Sad Song (3:23)/ Supersonic II (2:26)/ Cigarettes And Alcohol II (3:36)/ Fade Away II (3:18)/ Whatever (3:49)/ I Am A Walrus (3:03)
R: Exs. Soundboard.   S: Tracks 1-8 Paris 2/11/94. Tracks 9-14 demos spring '94 - acoustic and electric. Tracks 15-16 TV studios with orchestra London Dec. '94.   C: ECD. Dcc.

CD - PARIS SUPERNOVA
MOONRAKER 032
The Swamp Song/ Acquiesce/ Supersonic/ Hello/ Some Might Say/ Shakermaker/ Roll With It/ Cigarettes And Alcohol/ Live Forever/ Champagne Supernova/ Wonderwall/ Cast No Shadow/ Morning Glory/ Don't Look Back In Anger/ Whatever/ I Am The Walrus
R: Ex. Audience.   S: Le Zenith, Paris Nov. 7 '95.   C: ECD. Dcc. Time 77:49.

CD - ROCK 'N' ROLL STARS
CHELSEA CFC 022
Rock 'N' Roll Star (4:54)/ Columbia (4:21)/ Fade Away (4:14)/ Digsy's Diner (3:01)/ Shakermaker (5:08)/ Live Forever (4:44)/ Bring It On Down (4:48)/ Up In The Sky (4:46)/ Slide Away (6:11)/ Cigarettes And Alcohol (4:14)/ Married With Children (3:04)/ Sad Song (Acoustic) (4:42)/ Spaceman (acoustic) (2:49)/ Supersonic (6:02)/ Whatever (5:29)/ I Am The Walrus (8:01)
R: G-Vg. Audience.   S: The Hammersmith Palais Dec. 13 '94.   C: ECD. Dcc.

CD - SUPERSONIC POP REACTION
WALRUS MUSIC WMCD001
Columbia/ Fade Away/ Digsy's Dinner/ Shaker Maker/ Live Forever/ Bring It On Down/ Up In The Sky/ Slide Away/ Cigarettes And Alcohol/ Supersonic/ I Am The Walrus/ Supersonic/ Digsy's Dinner/ Married With Children/ Live Forever/ Shaker Maker
R: Exs.   S: Astoria Theatre, London Aug. 18 '94. Tracks 12-14 radio sessions May '94. Tracks 15-16 Royal Albert Hall, London June 6 '94.

CD - SWEDISH RADIO 94 + MORE
KMA RECORDS KMACD002
Columbia (4:47)/ Shakermaker (4:47)/ Fade Away (4:27)/ Digsy's Dinner (2:57)/ Live Forever (4:10)/ Bring It On Down (4:54)/ Up In The Sky (4:42)/ Slide Away (6:22)/ Cigarettes And Alcohol (4:28)/ Supersonic (5:13)/ I Am The Walrus (8:54)/ Rock 'N' Roll Star (4:53)/ Cigarettes And Alcohol (5:03)/ Married With Children (3:21)/ Supersonic (4:57)
R: Exs. Soundboard. Tracks 12-15 Audience. S: Tracks 1-11 Hultsfred Festival, Sweden Aug. 13 '94. Tracks 12-15 Whiskey A Go Go, Los Angeles Sept. 29 '94.   C: ECD. Time 73:57.

CD - TALK TONIGHT
OCTOPUS OCTO 068
Columbia (4:57)/ Shakermaker (4:48)/ Fade Away (4:15)/ Digsy's Dinner (2:43)/ Live Forever (0:35)/ Rock 'N' Roll Star (4:50)/ Up In The Sky (4:48)/ Slide Away (6:21)/ Cigarettes And Alcohol (4:31)/ Supersonic (5:18)/ I Am A Walrus (8:14)/ (It's Good) To Be Free (3:23)/ Married With Children (2:27)/ Sad Song (4:27)/ Talk Tonight (3:30)/ Whatever (5:34)
R: Exs. Soundboard.   S: Tracks 1-11 live Europe Aug. '94. Tracks 12-16 studio sessions in Europe Dec. '94.   C: ECD. Dcc. Pic CD.

CD - UNDRUGGED: 19 ALL ACOUSTIC SONGS
OXYGEN RECORDS OXY 034
Live Forever (4:25)/ Shakermaker (4:15)/ Up In
The Sky (3:10)/ Supersonic (2:56)/ Married With
Children (2:47)/ Talk Tonight (3:54)/ Sad Song
(3:59)/ Supersonic (2:56)/ Live Forever (4:13)/
Shakermaker (4:17)/ Wonderwall (3:11)/ Don't
Look Back In Anger (1:04)/ Take Me Away (4:29)/
D'Yer Wanna Be A Spaceman? (4:40)/ Whatever
(4:17)/ Live Forever (4:16)/ Digsy's Dinner (2:24)/
You've Got To Hide Your Love Away (Unreleased
Track) (2:08)/ Wonderwall (3:08)/ Champagne
Supernova (Electric Version) (6:01)
R: Exs. Soundboard.   S: Various locations.
C: ECD.

CD - UP IN THE SKY
KISS THE STONE KTS 463
Intro/ Some Might Say/ Shakermaker/ Slide Away/
Its Good To Be Free/ Morning Glory/ Cigarettes
And Alcohol/ So Sorry/ I Am The Walrus/ Rock
And Roll Star/ Shakermaker/ Bring It On Down/
Up In The Sky/ Slide Away/ Married With
Children/ Whatever
R: Ex. Audience.   S: Tracks 1-9 The
Glastonbury Festival June 23 '95. Tracks 10-16
The Civic Hall, Wolverhampton Dec. 12 '94.
C: ECD. Dcc. Pic CD. Time 75:03.

CD - WIRED AND INSPIRED
THE BIG KAHUNA HUNA 001 (?U.S.A.)
Spirit In The Sky (3:58)/ Some Might Say (5:14)/
Shakermaker (4:42)/ Roll With It (3:53)/ Slide
Away (5:54)/ It's Good To Be Free (3:13)/ Morning
Glory (4:31)/ Cigarettes And Alcohol (4:08)/ Don't
Look Back In Anger (5:01)/ I Am The Walrus
(7:12)/ Live Forever (4:44)/ Rock 'N' Roll Star
(6:02)/ Bring It On Down (5:08)/ Up In The Sky
(4:40)/ Columbia (5:03)/ Fade Away (4:10)
R: Exs. Soundboard.   S: Tracks 1-12
Glastonbury Festival, Somerset June 23 '95.
Tracks 13-16 The Metro, Chicago June 5 '95.
C: US(?) CD. Time: 77:45.

OFFSPRING

CD - COME OUT AND STAY
SOUNDGARDEN MMR-CD9502
Bad Habit/ Get It Right/ Kill Boy Powerhead/ Burn
It Up/ Genocide/ Gotta Get Away, So Alone/ What
Are We Heading For/ What Happened To You/
Come Out And Play/ It'll Be A Long Time/ Self
Esteem/ We Are One/ Session
R: Exs. Soundboard.   S: Live USA '94.
C: ECD. Dcc. Pic CD. Time 48:52.

CD - LIVE
KTS OF AUSTRALIA 018 A
Bad Habit (3:35)/ We Are One (3:50)/ Killboy
Powerhead (2:10)/ Burn It Up (3:23)/ Genocide
(4:03)/ Gotta Get Away (3:40)/ So Alone (1:33)/
Kick Him When He's Down (3:25)/ It'll Be A Long
Time (3:35)/ What Happened To You? (2:30)/
Come Out And Play (5:40)/ Smash (2:40)/ No

Way Out (3:25)/ Nitro, Youth Energy (2:35)/ Self
Esteem (5:00)/ Session (3:40)/ Jennifer Lost The
War (unreleased - 2:40)
R: G-Vg. Audience.   S: Roseland NYC Oct. 25
'94.   C: Australian CD. Dcc.

CD - LIVE SMASH
PRINT 010
Bad Habit/ Power/ Genocide/ Gotta Get Away/
Something To Believe In/ It'll Be A Long Time/
Come Out And Play/ Self Esteem/ Bad Habit/ No
Way Out/ So Alone/ Power/ Genocide/ Gotta Get
Away/ LAPD/ It'll Be A Long Time/ Come Out And
Play/ What Happened To You/ Smash/ Nitro/
Something To Believe In/ Self Esteem
R: Tracks 1-8 Vg-Ex. Audience. Tracks 9-22 G.
Audience.   S: Tracks 1-8 Melbourne, Australia
Jan. 20 '95. Tracks 9-22 Sydney, Australia Jan.
26 '95.   C: ECD. Dbw. Red/yellow type.
Time 77:08.

CD - REBELLING TEENS
TORNADO TOR 001
Bad Habit (3:57)/ We Are One (3:42)/ Killboy
Powerhead (2:24)/ Burn It Up (3:38)/ Genocide
(3:36)/ Gotta Get Away (3:34)/ So Alone (1:22)/
Kick Him When He's Down (3:52)/ It'll Be A Long
Time (3:14)/ What Happened To You? (4:41)/
Come Out And Play (3:40)/ Smash (3:01)/ LAPD
(3:00)/ Nitro (3:52)/ Self Esteem (5:18)/ Session
(2:38)
R: Ex. Audience.   S: The Edge, Jacksonville,
Florida Nov. 11 '94.   C: ECD. Dcc. Pic CD.

CD - THE REVENGE OF THE NERDS
OCTOPUS OCTO 187
Bad Habit (3:49)/ Burn It Up (3:16)/ Genocide
(3:27)/ Gotta Get Away (3:33)/ Kick Him When
He's Down (3:18)/ It'll Be A Long Time (4:55)/
Come Out And Play (3:19)/ Self Esteem (4:39)/
Bad Habit (3:43)/ Get It Right (3:19)/ Killboy
Powerhead (3:12)/ Gotta Get Away, So Alone
(5:12)/ What Are We Waiting For (3:14)/ What
Happened To You (2:45)/ Come Out And Play
(4:00)/ It'll Be A Long Time (3:27)/ Self Esteem
(4:41)/ We Are One (4:40)/ Session (2:53)
R: Exs. Soundboard.   S: Tracks 1-8 The
Palace, Melbourne, Australia Jan. 21 '95. Tracks
9-19 The Princess Charlotte Club, Leicester, UK
Sept. 25 '94.   C: ECD. Dcc.

7" - THEY WERE BORN TO KILL
S1: Jennifer Lost The War
S2: Out On Patrol
R: Ex. Soundboard.   S: Unreleased demos.
C: USA. White/puple/black sleeve. 45 RPM.

OLDFIELD, MIKE

CD - US PREMIER OF TUBULAR BELLS 2
ALL OF US AS 02
Tubular Bells 2 (73:41)
R: Ex. Audience.   C: ECD.

OPERATION IVY

CD - UNRELEASED ENERGY
1987 Demo: Uncertain/ Trouble Bound/ Someday/
Plea For Peace/ 1988 Gilman St. Demo: Healthy
Body (extended version)/ Bombshell/ Hedgecore/
Hangin' Out/ Sarcastic (unreleased song)/ Left
Behind/ Break It Down (unreleased song)/
Steppin' Out (unreleased song)/ 1088 Energy
Demos: Artificial Life/ Freeze Up/ Sound System/
Jaded/ Take Warning/ 6 To 10 (unreleased song)/
Missionary/ Bankshot/ Unity (with horns)/ Smiling/
One Of Those Days/ Face That Screams (unre-
leased song)/ Gonna Find You/ Room Without A
Window/ Hangin' Out/ Sound System (Instro)/
Sound System (Ext.)/ Unity (Insto W/Sax)
R: Ex. Soundboard.   C: Black/white cover. Pic
CD says 'Hedge Rock'. Time 64:45.

OSBOURNE, OZZY

LP - THE BATMAN RETURNS
S1: Diary Of A Madman/ I Don't Know/ Mr.
Crowley/ Rock And Roll Rebel
S2: Bark At The Moon/ Revelation Mother Earth/
Steel Away (The Night)
S3: Suicide Solution/ Forever/ Carmen Appice
S4: Flying High Again/ Iron Man/ Crazy Train/
Paranoid
R: Exs.   S: Hammersmith Odeon, London Nov.
29 '83.   C: Dbw. Contains rare keyboard-solo
by Don Airey. Fred says 'Ozzy has a cold and
sings worse than usual'.

CD - BEAST IN THE DARKNESS
BANG-012/013
CD1: I Don't Know/ Mr. Crowley/ Rock 'N' Roll
Rebel/ Bark At The Moon/ Revelation (Mother
Earth)/ Steal Away (The Night)
CD2: Suicide Solution, Guitar Solo, Key Solo/
Centre Of Eternity, Drum Solo/ Flying High Again/
Iron Man/ Crazy Train/ Paranoid
R: Exs.   S: Japan June 29 '84.

CD - BLIZZARD OF RANDY
CRYSTAL SOUND CS-11
Radio Spot/ I Don't Know/ Crazy Train/ Believe/
Mr. Crowley/ Flying High Again/ Revelation
(Mother House)/ Steal Away (The Night)/ Solo:
Tommy Aldridge/ No More Bone Movies/ Suicide
Solution, Solo: Randy Rhoads/ Iron Man/ Children
Of The Grave, Paranoid
R: Vg-Ex sound.   S: NY Auditorium Theatre Apr.
29 '81. Track 13 Chelmsford, UK Oct. 22 '80.

LP - CRAZY TRAIN
METAL MESS RECS.
S1: Over The Mountain/ Mr. Crowley/ Crazy Train/
Suicide Solution
S2: Revelation/ Steel Away/ Good Bye To
Romance/ Iron Man/ Children Of The Grave/
Paranoid
R: Exs.   S: San Francisco '83.   C: Pic-Disc.

CD - LET THE MADNESS BEGIN
KISS THE STONE KTS 500/01
CD1: Paranoid/ Desire/ I Don't Know/ Flying High
Again/ Goodbye To Romance/ No More Tears/ I
Just Want You/ I Don't Want To Chance The
World/ Suicide Solution
CD2: Sabbath Bloody Sabbath/ Iron Man,
Children Of The Grave/ Mr. Crowley, War Pigs/
Crazy Train/ Mama I'm Coming Home/ Bark At
The Moon
R: Exs. Soundboard.   S: Santiago, Chile Sept.
9 '95.   C: ECD. Dcc. Pic CDs. Time CD1 49:15.
CD2 45:53.

LP - NEVER A DULL MOMENT
KM 11408
S1: Over The Mountain/ Mr. Crowley/ Crazy Train
S2: Suicide Solution/ Flying High Again/ Paranoid
R: Exs.   S: USA '83.   C: Canadian boot (?)
with DJ intro (radio broadcast). Dcc.

CD - OVER THE MOUNTAIN
MOTHER EARTH ME-010
Over The Mountain/ Mr. Crowley/ Crazy Train/
Revelation (Mother Earth) Steal Away (The
Night)/ Suicide Solution, Guitar Solo, Drums Solo/
Goodbye To Romance/ Believer/ Flying High
Again/ Iron Man/ Children Of The Grave/
Paranoid
R: Poor. Audience.   S: Minneapolis Jan. 15 '82.

LP - (STILL) THE WILDMAN OF ROCK AND ROLL
S1: I Don't Know/ Mr. Crowley/ Rock And Roll
Rebel/ Bark At The Moon
S2: Revelation/ Steal Away/ Suicide Solution/
Improvisations/ Forever/ Drum Solo
R: Exs.   S: Live '84.   C: Belgian boot on
green vinyl. Dbw.

P

PAGE, JIMMY

CD - STUDIO WORKS
COUNTDOWN FACTORY CDF-942001A/B
Prelude/ Carol's Theme/ The Chase/ Hypnotizing
Ways (Oh Mama)/ The Chase/ Sax, And Violence/
Shadow In The City/ Hotel Rats/ Shadow In The
City/ Jam Sandwich #1/ Jam Sandwich #2/ Jam
Sandwich #3/ Orchestra Tracks/ The Fiesta/
Fiesta Too/ The Restaurant
R: Vg. Hiss.   S: 'Death Wish II' outtakes '82.

PAGE - PLANT / PLANT - PAGE

CD - BROADCASTS
TWO SYMBOLS TS-004
In The Evening/ Black Dog/ Four Sticks/ In The
Evening/ Calling To You Medley (includes Break
On Thru, Dazed & Confused)/ Four Sticks/ In The
Evening/ Kashmir/ Since I've Been Loving You

R: Vg from video feed (muddy in places).
S: Tracks 1-3 New Orleans Mar. '95. Tracks 4-5
Luneberg, Germany June '95. Tracks 6-10
Glastonbury, UK June 25 '95.   C: Japanese CD.
Time 65:09.

CD - CELEBRATION DAY
CD1: Intro/ Wanton Song/ Bring It On Home/
Celebration Day/ Thank You/ Dancing Days/
Shake My Tree/ Lullaby/ No Quarter/ Wonderful
One/ Gallows Pole/ Nobody's Fault But Mine/
Song Remains The Same
CD2: Since I've Been Loving You/ Friends/
Calling To You (includes The Hunter, Dazed And
Confused)/ Four Sticks/ In The Evening/ Hey Hey
What Can I Do/ Black Dog/ Kashmir
R: Vg. Audience. Crowd noise.   S: Orlando Mar.
7 '95.   C: Japanese. CD1: 65:11. CD2 70:15.

CD - DANCING DAYS IN ATLANTA
JR 001-2
CD1: Immigrant Song-Wanton Song/ Bring It On
Home/ Celebration Day/ Thank You/ Dancing
Days/ Don't Shake My Tree/ Spider/ No Quarter/
Wonderful One/ Gallows Pole/ Nobody's Fault But
Mine/ The Song Remains The Same
CD2: Since I've Been Loving You/ Friends/
Calling You Medley: Riders On The Storm-Dazed
And Confused/ Four Sticks/ In The Evening/ Black
Dog/ Kashmir
R: Vg. Audience.   S: Atlanta Mar. 1 '95.
C: Japanese CD. Dcc. CD1 65:13. CD2 60:09.

CD - GLASTONBURY
KISS THE STONE KTS 462
Gallows Pole/ Since I've Been Lovin' You/ The
Song Remains The Same/ Friends/ Calling To
You (Break On Through, Dazed And Confused)/
Four Sticks/ In The Evening/ Kashmir
R: Ex.   S: The Glastonbury Festival June 25
'95.   C: ECD. Dcc. Pic CD. Time CD1 65:09.

CD - GET RID OF THE SMOKE
CD1: Immigrant Song/ Wanton Song/ Bring It On
Home/ Thank You/ No Quarter/ Hurdy Gurdy
Solo/ Gallows Pole/ Since I've Been Loving You/
The Song Remains The Same/ Friends
CD2: Calling To You/ Smokestack Lightening/
Break On Through/ Dazed And Confused/ Four
Sticks/ In The Evening/ Kashmir
S: Glastonbury Festival June 25 '95.
C: Time CD1 47:21. CD2 41:55.
CD3: Tales Of Bron Intro/ Wanton Song/ Bring It
On Home/ Ramble On/ No Quarter/ Gallows Pole/
Hurdy Gurdy Solo/ When The Levee Breaks/
Yallah (with Orchestra)/ Since I've Been Loving
You/ The Crunge Jam/ The Song Remains The
Same
CD4: Whole Lotta Love/ Theramin/ Down By The
Seaside/ Break On Through/ Dazed And
Confused/ You Need Love/ Friends/ Four Sticks/
Kashmir/ Black Dog/ In The Evening
S: SECC, Glasgow July 12 '95.
C: Time CD3 50:52. CD4 61:45.

CD5: Egyptian Violin Intro/ Wanton Song/ Bring It
On Home/ Ramble On/ Robert 'Get Rid Of The
Smoke'/ No Quarter/ Gallows Pole/ Hurdy Gurdy
Solo/ Yallah (with Orchestra)/ Since I've Been
Loving You, Tea For One/ The Song Remains The
Same
CD6: Whole Lotta Love/ Theramin/ Smokestack
Lightening/ Break On Through/ Dazed And
Confused/ You Need Love/ Friends/ Four Sticks/
Kashmir/ Louis Louis/ Black Dog/ In The Evening
S: Sheffield Arena, Sheffield July 13 '95.
C: Time CD5 47:27. CD6 65:20.
CD7: Egyptian Intro/ Whole Lotta Love With
Cutdown Theramin/ Bring It On Home/ Ramble
On/ No Quarter/ Gallows Pole/ Hurdy Gurdy Solo/
Yallah/ Since I've Been Loving You/ The Song
Remains The Same
CD8: Friends/ Calling You/ What Is And What
Should Never Be/ Unknown Jam/ Break On
Through/ Four Sticks/ Kashmir/ Blue Jean Baby
Jam/ Black Dog/ In The Evening
S: Cornwall Coliseum, St. Austell, Cornwall July
15 '95.   C: Time CD7 51:07. CD8 61:21.
CD9: Egyptian Intro/ Thank You/ Bring It On
Home/ Whole Lotta Love/ No Quarter/ Gallows
Pole/ Hurdy Gurdy Solo/ Yallah/ Since I've Been
Loving You/ Tea For One/ The Song Remains The
Same
CD10: Dancing Days/ Four Sticks/ Kashmir/ Black
Dog/ In The Evening
S: Poole Arts Centre, Poole July 16 '95.
C: Time CD9 50:20. CD10 44:00.
CD11: Egyptian Intro/ Wanton Song/ Bring It On
Home/ Ramble On/ Thank You/ No Quarter/ Battle
Of Evermore/ Hurdy Gurdy Solo/ Gallows Pole/
Since I've Been Loving You/ The Song Remains
The Same
CD12: Going To California/ Friends/ Four Sticks/
Whole Lotta Love/ Theramin/ Smokestack
Lightening/ Break On Through/ Dazed And
Confused/ Kashmir/ Black Dog/ In The Evening
S: NEC, Birmingham July 22 '95.
C: Time CD11 57:22. CD12 68:41.
CD13: Egyptian Intro/ Wanton Song/ Bring It On
Home/ Thank You/ No Quarter/ Battle Of
Evermore/ Hurdy Gurdy Solo/ Gallows Pole/
Since I've Been Loving You/ The Song Remains
The Same
CD14: Going To California/ Friends/ Four Sticks/
Whole Lotta Love/ Theramin/ Porl Solo/ Jimmy
Page Solo/ Kashmir/ Black Dog/ In The Evening
S: NEC, Birmingham July 23 '95.
C: Time CD13 52:49. CD14 62:31.
CD15: Egyptian Intro/ Wanton Song/ Bring It On
Home/ Ramble On/ Thank You/ No Quarter/ Battle
Of Evermore/ Hurdy Gurdy Solo/ Gallows Pole/
Since I've Been Loving You/ The Song Remains
The Same
CD16: Going To California/ Friends/ Four Sticks/
Whole Lotta Love/ Theramin/ Calling To You
(excerpt)/ Kashmir/ Black Dog/ In The Evening
S: Wembley Arena, London July 25 '95.
C: Time CD15 56:55. CD16 63:06.
CD17: Egyptian Intro/ Wanton Song/ Bring It On

Home/ Ramble On/ Thank You/ No Quarter/ Battle Of Evermore/ Hurdy Gurdy Solo/ Gallows Pole/ Since I've Been Loving You/ The Song Remains The Same
CD18: Going To California/ Friends/ Four Sticks/ Whole Lotta Love/ Theramin/ Smokestack Lightning, Calling To You (excerpt), Dazed And Confused (excerpt)/ In The Evening/ Candy Store Rock Jam/ Black Dog/ Kashmir
S: Wembley Arena, London July 25 '95.
C: Time CD17 57:11. CD18 62:03
CD19: Egyptian Intro/ Wanton Song/ Heartbreaker/ What Is And What Should Never Be/ Thank You/ No Quarter/ Tangerine/ Hurdy Gurdy Solo/ Gallows Pole/ Since I've Been Loving You/ The Song Remains The Same
CD20: Going To California/ Babe I'm Gonna Leave You/ Whole Lotta Love/ It's A Man's World/ Break On Through/ Dazed And Confused/ Dancing Days/ In The Evening/ Black Dog/ Kashmir
S: The Fleet Center, Boston Oct. 23 '95.
C: Time CD19 59:47. CD20 74:27.
R: Overall Exs. Audience. Some Vg-Exs.
C: Japanese set. Each picture CD comes in an envelope with the UK tour dates. There's also a 40-page full color book. This limited edition of 400 sets comes in one of three different full color gatefold packages making this a collector's nightmare.

CD - GOOD TIMES BAD TIMES
TARANTURA N0-1,2
CD1: Tales Of Bron/ The House Of The Rising Sun/ Good Times Bad Times/ Bring It On Home/ Celebration Day/ Thank Yew/ Dancing Days/ Shake My Tree/ Lullaby/ No Quarter/ That's The Way/ Gallows Pole/ When The Levee Breaks/ Ramble On
CD2: The Song Remains The Same/ Since I've Been Loving You/ Friends/ Calling To You (Includes Dazed And Confused)/ Four Sticks/ In The Evening/ Black Dog/ Kashmir
R: Vg. Audience.   S: Lakefront Arena, New Orleans Mar. 11 '95.   C: Japanese CD. Dcc. Book-style cover. Time CD1 66:49. CD2 66:44.

CD - IT'S FLYING TIME AGAIN
OZS 001/002
CD1: Celebration Day/ Dancing Days/ Shake My Tree/ Since I've Been Loving You/ Lullaby/ Achilles Last Stand/ No Quarter/ Wonderful One/ Gallows Pole/ When The Levee Breaks
CD2: Friends/ Calling To You, Medley: Season Of The Witch, Dazed And Confused/ Four Sticks/ In The Evening/ Black Dog/ Kashmir
R: Vg. Audience.   S: Atlanta, GA. Feb. 28 '95.
C: ECD. Dcc. Time CD1 56:05. CD2 55:47.

CD - LIVE AT THE SHARK TANK
THE SWINGIN' PIG TSP 197-2
CD1: Thank You/ Bring It On Home/ Ramble On/ Shake My Tree/ Lullaby/ No Quarter/ Gallows Pole/ Hurdy Gurdy Solo/ Nobody's Fault But

Mine/ Hey Hey What Can I Do/ The Song Remains The Same
CD2: Since I've Been Loving You/ Friends/ Calling To You/ Four Sticks/ In The Evening/ Black Dog/ Kashmir
R: Exs. Soundboard.   S: 'The Shark Tank', San José, CA May 20 '95.   C: ECD.
Time CD1 56:08. CD2 62:42.

CD - LIVE '95
KTS OF AUSTRALIA 010 A
The Rockline Interview (52:27)*/ John Paul Jones Interview (1:59)/ Induction Speech (3:56)/ Bring It On Home (3:17)/ No Matter How You Treat Me Baby, Please Don't Go (8:00)/ When The Levee Breaks, For What It's Worth (8:30)
R: Exs. Soundboard.   S: *Complete interview, New York City Jan. 11'95. Rest - Rock N' Roll Hall Of Fame Jan. 12 '95.   C: Australian CD. With Joe Perry, Steve Tyler and Neil Young.

CD - ON 'TOR'
Gallows Pole/ Since I've Been Loving You/ Song Remains The Same/ Calling To You (includes Smokestack Lightning, Break On Thru, Dazed And Confused)/ Four Sticks/ In The Evening/ Kashmir/ Thank You*/ Black Dog*
R: Ex. Soundboard.   S: Glastonbury June 25 '95. *San Jose May 20 '95.   C: ECD. 77:58.

CD - PARIS '95
SILVER RARITIES MASTER SERIES SIRA 183/184
CD1: Introduction/ Thank You/ Bring It On Home/ Ramble On/ Shake My Tree/ Lullaby/ No Quarter/ Gallows Pole/ Hurdy Gurdy Intro, Nobody's Fault But Mine/ Hey Hey What Can I Do/ The Song Remains The Same/ Since I've Been Loving You
CD2: Dancing Days (with orchestra)/ Calling You/ Four Sticks/ In The Evening/ Black Dog/ Kashmir
R: Exs. Audience.   S: The Palais Ominsports, Paris Bercy June 6 '95.   C: ECD. Sound improves 3 minutes and 53 seconds into 'Thank You'. Time CD1 66:39. CD2 65:02.

CD - PRESENCE NOW
RAIN RECORDS
CD1: Wanton Song/ Bring It On Home/ Celebration Day/ Thank You/ Dancing Days/ Shake My Tree/ Lullaby/ No Quarter/ Gallow's Pole/ Nobody's Fault But Mine/ The Song Remains The Same/ Since I've Been Loving You/ Friends
CD2: Dazed And Confused Medley/ Four Sticks/ In The Evening/ Black Dog/ Kashmir/ Bring It On Home*/ Long Distance Call Blues*/ Baby Please Don't Go*/ Medley: When The Levee Breaks, For What It's Worth*
R: Vg-Ex. Audience. *Ex.Soundboard.   S: The Skydome, Toronto Mar. 27 '95. *Rock And Roll Hall Of Fame induction ceremony, Waldorf Astoria Grand Ballroom, NYC Jan. 12 '95.
C: Japanese CD. Dcc. Tri-fold cardboard sleeve. Full color booklet. Time CD1 67:32. CD2 72:33.

CD - PITTSBURG

CD1: Intro/ Wanton Song/ Bring It On Home/ Ramble On/ Thank You/ Shake My Tree/ Lullaby/ No Quarter/ Gallows Pole/ Nobody's Fault But Mine/ Song Remains The Same/ Since I've Been Loving You
CD2: Friends/ Calling You (includes Light My Fire, Dazed And Confused/ Four Sticks/ In The Evening/ Black Dog/ Kashmir
R: Vg. Audience.   S: Civic Arena, Pittsburg Mar. 25 '95.   C: Japanese. CD1 66:15. CD2 57:39.

CD - PP - IRISH BOOTLEG

TARANTURA IRE-001-4
CD1: Thank You/ Bring It On Home/ Ramble On/ Whole Lotta Love/ No Quarter/ Gallows Pole/ Yallah/ Since I've Been Loving You
CD2: Song Remains The Same/ Dancing Days/ Calling You Medley (includes Light My Fire, Break On Thru, Dazed And Confused)/ Four Sticks/ Kashmir/ Black Dog/ In The Evening
CD3: Celebration Day/ Bring It On Home/ Custard Pie/ No Quarter/ Going To California/ Battle Of Evermore/ Gallows Pole/ Since I've Been Loving You/ (includes Tea For One)
CD4: Whole Lotta Love Medley (includes All Of My Love, What Is, Break On Thru, Dazed And Confused)/ Friends/ Four Sticks/ Kashmir/ Black Dog/ Song Remains The Same
R: Ex. Audience.   S: CD1-2 Dublin July 19 '95. CD3-4 Dublin July 20 '95.   C: Japanese CD. Deluxe gold-embossed four-way fold-out sleeve. CD1 51:33. CD2 70:03. CD3 46:14. CD4: 59:21.

CD - RAMBLE ON INTO THE 90'S

TWO SYMBOLS TS 003-A/B
CD1: Intro/ Thank You/ Bring It On Home/ Ramble On/ Shake My Tree/ Lullaby/ No Quarter/ Gallows Pole/ Hurdy Gurdy Solo/ Nobody's Fault But Mine/ Hey Hey What Can I Do/ Song Remains The Same
CD2: Since I've Been Loving You/ Friends/ Calling To You Medley (includes Down By The Seaside, Break On Thru, Dazed And Confused)/ Four Sticks/ In The Evening/ Black Dog/ Kashmir
R: Ex. Audience.   S: San Diego May 13 '95.
C: Japanese CD. Time CD1 57:27. CD2 65:36.

CD - RETURN TO ELECTRIC MAGIC

TWO SYMBOLS TS 001-A/B
CD1: Introduction/ Immigrant Song, Wanton Song/ Bring It On Home/ Ramble On/ Thank You/ No Quarter/ Battle Of Evermore/ Hurdy Gurdy Solo/ Gallows Pole/ Since I've Been Loving You/ The Song Remains The Same/ Going To California
CD2: Friends/ Four Sticks/ Whole Lotta Love/ Kashmir/ Black Dog/ In The Evening
R: Vg-Ex. Audience.   S: Wembley Arena, London July 25 '95.   C: Japanese CDs. Dcc.
Time CD1 61:04. CD2 60:50.

CD - RETURN TO ELECTRIC MAGIC II

TWO SYMBOLS TS 002-A/B

CD1: Introduction/ Immigrant Song, Wanton Song/ Bring It On Home/ Ramble On/ Thank You/ No Quarter/ Battle Of Evermore/ Hurdy Gurdy Solo/ Gallows Pole/ Since I've Been Loving You/ The Song Remains The Same/ Going To California/ Friends
CD2: Four Sticks/ Whole Lotta Love/ In The Evening/ Candy Store Rock, Black Dog/ Kashmir
R: Vg. Audience.   S: Wembley Arena, London July 26 '95.   C: Japanese CDs. Dcc.
Time CD1 66:20. CD2 54:59.

CD - RISE OF THE PHOENIX

TWO SYMBOLS TS 006-A/B
CD1: Intro/ Wanton Song/ Bring It On Home/ Ramble On/ Thank You/ Shake My Tree/ Lullaby/ No Quarter/ Gallows Pole/ Hurdy Gurdy Solo/ When The Levee Breaks/ Hey Hey What Can I Do/ The Song Remains The Same/ Since I've Been Loving You
CD2: Friends/ Calling To You Medley (includes Down By The Seaside, Break On Thru, Dazed And Confused)/ Four Sticks/ In The Evening/ Black Dog/ Kashmir
R: Vg-Ex. Audience.   S: Phoenix, Arizona May 10 '95.   C: Japanese CD. Time CD1 70:07. CD2 61:59.

CD - ROCK AND ROLL HALL OF FAME

KISS THE STONE KTS 404
Bring It On Home/ Long Distance Call Blues/ Baby Please Don't Go/ Medley: When The Levee Breaks, For What It's Worth/ Wonderful One/ When The Levee Breaks/ 29 Palms/ What Is And What Should Never Be/ Ship Of Fools/ Whole Lotta Love
R: Exs. Soundboard.   S: Tracks 1-3 Plant, Page, JP Jones, Jason Bonham, Steve Tyler and Joe Perry at The Rock And Roll Hall Of Fame Induction Ceremony Grand Ballroom, Waldorf Astoria Hotel, New York City Jan. 12 '95. Track 4 Plant, Page, JP Jones, M. Lee and Neil Young at The Rock And Roll Hall Of Fame induction ceremony. Tracks 5-6 Page And Plant Jools Holland taping, London Nov. 1 '94. Tracks 7-10 Robert Plant, Pink Pop Fest, Denhaag, Holland June 26 '93.   C: ECD. Dcc. Pic CD. Time 56:32.

CD - ROYAL ORLEANS

REAL LIVE PP-953101
CD1: Intro/ Wanton Song/ Bring It On Home/ Celebration Day/ Thank You/ Dancing Days/ Shake My Tree/ Lullaby/ No Quarter/ Hey Hey What Can I Do/ Gallows Pole/ Nobody's Fault But Mine
CD2: Song Remains The Same/ Since I've Been Loving You/ Friends/ Calling To You Medley (includes White Rabbit, Dazed And Confused)/ Four Sticks/ In The Evening/ Black Dog/ Kashmir/ Stairway To Heaven (acoustic version)*
R: Ex. Audience.   S: New Orleans Mar. 10 '95. *Japanese TV.   C: Australia CD. Deluxe double slip cover. Time CD1 55:14. CD2 68:02.

CD - THE SECOND COMING
OCTOPUS OCTO 195
Gallows Pole (4:52)/ Since I've Been Loving You
(8:33)/ The Song Remains The Same (6:31)/
Friends (4:20)/ Medley: Calling To You, Guitar
Solo/ Break On Through, Dazed And Confused,
Calling To You (Reprise) (13:48)/ Four Sticks
(5:13)/ Intro/ In The Evening (9:05)/ Kashmir
(14:16)
R: Exs. Soundboard.   S: Glastonbury Festival,
UK June 26 '95.   C: ECD.

CD - SHAKE MY TREE
PARTY LINE PLCD-020/1
CD1: Wanton Song/ Bring It On Home/
Celebration Day/ Thank You/ Shake My Tree/
Lullaby/ No Quarter/ Wonderful One/ Hurdy Gurdy
Solo/ Nobody's Fault But Mine/ The Song
Remains The Same
CD2: Since I've Been Loving You/ Friends/ Yallah/
Four Sticks/ In The Evening/ Black Dog/ Kashmir
R: Vg Audience.   S: Philadelphia Apr. 4 '95.
C: Japanese CD. Time CD1 55:59. CD2 58:28.

CD - SIMPLE TRUTH
KISS THE STONE KTS 450/51
CD1: Intro/ Thank You/ Bring It On Home/ Ramble
On/ Shake My Tree/ Intro/ Lullaby/ No Quarter/
Gallows Pole/ Hurdy Gurdy Solo/ Nobody's Fault
But Mine/ Hey Hey What Can I Do?/ The Song
Remains The Same
CD2: Intro/ Since I've Been Loving You/ Friends/
Calling To You (Dazed And Confused, Break On
Through)/ Four Sticks/ In The Evening/ Black
Dog/ Kashmir
R: Ex. Soundboard.   S: San Jose Arena, San
Jose, CA May 20 '95.   C: ECD. Pic CDs.
Time CD1 57:17. CD2 63:05.

CD - THE STORY SO FAR ...
OCTOPUS OCTO 162
Bring It On Home (3:32)/ You've Been Smart
(3:46)/ Baby, Please Don't Go (4:01)/ You Gotta
Move (8:43)/ Intro, Baby Please Don't Go (4:08)/ I
Can't Quit You Babe (7:03)/ I've Been Down So
Long (3:28)/ That's Why I Love You (4:26)/ Train
Kept A Rollin' (4:22)/ Thank You (6:39)/ Whole
Lotta Love (8:08)/ Over The Hills And Far Away
(5:34)/ Custard Pie, Black Dog (4:04)/ Stairway To
Heaven (9:17)
R: Ex.   S: Tracks 1-4 Rock And Roll Hall Of
Fame Jan. 12 '95. Tracks 5-9 Alexis Korner
Benefit Apr. 17 '94. Tracks 10-11 Plant at
Paradiso, Amsterdam Dec. 20 '93. Tracks 12-14
Page NYC Oct. 22 '88.   C: ECD. Dcc. Pic CD.

CD - TANGERINE
Intro/ Wanton Song/ Bring It On Home/ Ramble
On/ Thank You/ Dancing Days/ Shake My Tree/
Lullaby/ Tangerine/ Hey Hey What Can I Do/
Gallows Pole/ When The Levee Breaks/ Song
Remains The Same
CD2: Since I've Been Loving You/ Friends/
Calling To You (includes Dazed And Confused)/

Four Sticks/ In The Evening/ Black Dog/ Kashmir
R: Vg Audience.   S: Capitol Center, Landover
Mar. 23 '95.   C: Japanese. Time CD1 66:19.
CD2 64:04.

CD - TODAY, YESTERDAY ... AND SOME YEARS AGO
KOBRA RECORDS KRCR 001
Gallows Pole/ Wonderful One/ Four Sticks/
Hoochie Coochie Man/ 29 Palms/ Thank You/ I
Believe/ Medley: Tears I Cry, Light My Fire/
Kashmir/ Medley: Heartbreaker, Whole Lotta
Love/ Misty Mountain Hop/ Stairway To Heaven
R: Ex. Soundboard.   S: Tracks 1-3 Jools
Holland Show, London Nov. 1, '94. Tracks 4-8
Robert Plant Band acoustic session, Cadena 100
Estudios, Madrid, Spain June 19 '93. Tracks 9-12
Led Zeppelin reunion, Atlantic's 40th Anniversary,
NYC May 14 '88.   C: ECD. Dcc. Time 66:18.

CD - TOGETHER AGAIN III - THE MIAMI CONCERT
CD1: Opening/ Immigration Intro, Wanton Song/
Black Dog Intro, Bring It On Home/ Celebration
Day/ Thank You/ Dancing Day/ Shake My Tree,
Theremin Solo/ Lullaby/ No Quarter/ Wonderful
One/ Hey Hey What Can I Do/ Gallows Pole/
Hurdy Gurdy Intro, Nobody's Fault But Mine
CD2: Song Remains The Same/ Since I've Been
Loving You/ Egyptian Intro, Friends/ Calling You,
Dazed And Confused, The Hunter, Calling You/
Four Sticks/ Egyptian Intro, In The Evening,
Carouselambra/ Black Dog/ Kashmir (fades out 2
minutes from end due to interference)
R: Ex. Audience.   S: Miami Arena, Miami Mar. 6
'95 not Feb. 6 as listed on cover.   C: Japanese
CD. Dcc. Time CD1 61:25. CD2 61:02.

CD - TOGETHER AGAIN IV - HOME IN CALIFORNIA
JR MUSIC TRH*4-1/2
CD1: Introduction/ Immigrant Song/ Bring It On
Home/ Ramble On/ Thank You/ Shake My Tree/
Lullaby/ No Quarter/ Gallows Pole/ Hurdy Gurdy
Intro/ When The Levee Breaks/ The Song
Remains The Same
CD2: Since I've Been Loving You/ Dancing Days
(with orchestra)/ Calling To You Including Down
By The Seaside/ Break On Through/ Dazed And
Confused/ Foursticks/ In The Evening/ Black Dog/
Kashmir (with guest violin soloist Lilley Haven)
R: Vg. Audience.   S: The Great Western Forum,
Inglewood, CA May 17 '95.   C: Japanese CD.
Dcc. Track listing wrong on cover.
Time CD1 62:05. CD2 71:56.

CD - TOGETHER AGAIN V
Black Dog/ I Can't Quit You Baby/ Shake My
Tree/ Robert Speaks/ In The Evening,
Caroselambra/ Jimmy Speaks/ Out On The Tiles
Intro, Black Dog/ Kashmir/ Achilles Last Stand/
House Of The Rising Sun, Good Times Bad
Times/ That's The Way/ Yallah (The Truth
Explodes)/ Kashmir

S: Track 1 Depot Rehearsal Studio, London Jan. 25 '95. Track 2 Buxton Opera House, Derby Apr. 17 '94. Tracks 3, 5, 7, 8, 10, 11 Lakefront Arena, New Orleans Mar. 11 '95. Track 9 The Omni, Atlanta Feb. 28 '95. Track 12 Civic Arena, Pensacola Feb. 26 '95. Track 13 Miami Arena, Miami Mar. 6 '95.   C: Japanese CD. Dcc.

CD - TOGETHER AGAIN VI - 95 IN 95
CD1: Intro/ Wanton Song/ Bring It On Home/ Heartbreaker/ Ramble On/ No Quarter/ Tangerine/ Hurdy Gurdy Solo/ Gallow's Pole/ Since I've Been Loving You/ The Song Remains The Same CD2: Going To California/ Babe I'm Gonna Leave You/ Whole Lotta Love (includes In The Light, Break On Thru, Dazed And Confused)/ Four Sticks/ In The Evening/ Black Dog/ Belly Dancers/ Kashmir/ Rock And Roll
R: Vg. Audience (slightly bass heavy).
S: Madison Square Garden, NYC Oct 27 '95.
C: Japanese CD. Dcc with embossed metallic slip cover. Time CD1 50:36. CD2 79:01.

CD - WHOLE LOTTA ZEP
OCTOPUS OCTO 182/3
CD1: Intro, Thank You (8:26)/ Bring It On Home, Ramble On (6:30)/ Shake My Tree (8:32)/ Lullaby (6:30)/ No Quarter (5:20)/ Gallows Pole (5:13)/ Nobody's Fault But Mine (6:23)/ Hey, Hey What Can I Do (4:26)/ Song Remains The Same (5:55) CD2: Since I've Been Lovin' You (9:18)/ Friends (5:11)/ Medley: Calling To You, Guitar Solo, Break On Through, Dazed And Confused, Calling To You (Reprise) (12:42)/ Four Sticks (5:16)/ In the Evening (9:24)/ Black Dog (6:05)/ Kashmir (16:18)
R: Ex.   S: San Jose Arena, San Jose, CA May 20 '95.   C: ECD. Dcc. Pic CD.

PANTERA

CD - CASTLE DOMINATION 1994
OCTOPUS OCTO 020
Use My Third Arm/ Walk/ Strength Beyond Strength/ Domination (medley with Hollow)/ Fucking Hostile/ This Love/ Mouth For War/ Cowboys From Hell/ Intro, Domination/ Primal Concrete Sledge/ The Art Of Shredding/ Cowboys From Hell/ Heresy
R: Vg.   S: Castle Donnington, UK June 4 '94.

CD - DAMNATION
BABY CAPONE BC 030
Mouth For War (3:57)/ This Love (5:51)/ Walk (4:52)/ Psycho Holiday (5:20)/ Cemetery Gates (7:22)/ Cowboys From Hell (5:33)/ Domination (5:05)/ Art Of Shredding (4:26)/ Cowboys From Hell (4:17)/ Cemetery Gates (5:20)/ Heresy (4:59)
R: Exs. Soundboard.   S: Tracks 1-6 live during '92 US tour. Tracks 7-11 live during '93 US tour.
C: ECD. Dcc. Pic CD.

CD - METAL POWER AND WALK REMIXES
LAST BOOTLEG RECORDS LBR 023
Rock The World (3:34)/ Power Metal (3:52)/ We'll

Meet Again (3:54)/ Over And Out (5:06)/ Proud To Be Loud (4:02)/ Down Below (2:49)/ Death Trap (4:07)/ Hard Ride (4:15)/ Burn! (3:35)/ P*S*T*88 (2:42)/ Fucking Hostile (Biomechanical Mix) (4:15)/ Walk (Cervical Dub Extended) (6:38)/ Walk (Cervical Edit) (5:07)
R: Exs. Soundboard.   S: Live USA '93.
C: ECD. Dcc. Pic CD.

CD - SLAUGHTERED SHOW
SUPER QUALITY SERIES SQS001/2
CD1: A New Level/ Walk/ Use My Third Arm/ Strength Beyond Strength/ Slaughtered/ Domination, Hollow/ Becoming, Throes Of Rejection/ 5 Minutes Alone/ Shedding Skin CD2: Fucking Hostile/ This Love/ Jam (Stairway To Heaven, Moby Dick, Whole Lotta Love)/ Cold Gin/ Mouth For War/ Primal Concrete Sledge/ I'm Broken, By Demons Be Driven/ Cowboys From Hell
R: Exs. Soundboard.   S: Japan May '94.
C: Japanese CD. Dcc.

PARADISE LOST

CD - NORTHERN DARKNESS
INSECT IST 54
Mortal Watch The Day/ Gothic/ Your Hand In Mine/ Widow/ Shattered/ Daylight Torn/ Forgiving Sympathy/ Eternal/ Joys Of The Emptiness/ True Belief/ Pity The Sadness/ Mortals Watch The Day/ Gothic/ Widow/ Eternal
R: Ex. Soundboard.   S: The Mejeriet, Lund, Sweden Jan '94 and the Tobaksfabriken, Esberg, Denmark Jan. 28 '94.   C: ECD. Dcc. 69:26.

PARSONS, GRAM AND THE FALLEN ANGELS

CD - LEGENDARY LIVE '73
WEEPING GOAT WG-039-040
CD1: Instrumental/ Still Feeling Blue/ That's All It Took/ Big Mouth Blues/ Hearts On Fire/ Jambalaya/ Love Hurts/ Cry One More Time/ Sin City/ Medley: Hang On Sloopy, Baby What You Want Me To Do/ California Great Bound/ Love Hurts/ Sin City/ Instrumental/ We'll Sweep Out The Ashes In The Morning/ My Uncle CD2: Drug Store Truck Drivin' Man/ Street Of Baltimore/ Country Baptizing/ The New Soft Shoes/ Hearts On Fire/ Still Feeling Blue/ That's All It Took/ California Cotton Field/ Big Mouth Blues/ Love Hurts/ Sin City/ Medley: Hang On Sloopy, Baby What You Want Me To Do, Bony Moronie, Almost Grown/ How Much I Cry/ Six Days On The Road
R: G-Vg. Audience. You can hear the taper moving the mic around... the good old days of bootlegging. Demos G-Vg.   S: CD1 tracks 1-10 Olivers, Boston Mar. 19 '73. Tracks 11-13 home demo. CD1 tracks 14-16 and CD2 Olivers, Boston Mar. 20 '73.   C: Japanese CD. Dbw. Time CD1 68:37. CD2 69:16.

PAVEMENT

7" - TREBLE KICKER
S1: Brink Of The Clouds/ Orange Black/ 7+
S2: Tarter Martyr/ Random Title/ 5+
R: Ex. Soundboard.   S: Peel Session Feb. '94.
C: USA. Yellow/black cover. 45 RPM.

CD - STUFF UP THE CRACKS
PSUEDO INDIE LABEL PIL 06
Kentucky Cocktail, Here, Circa 1762, Secret
Knowledge Of Backroads (Peel Session July 10
'92)/ Rain Ammunition, Drunks With Guns, Ed
Aims, The List Of Dorms (Peel Session Dec. 14
'92)/ Brink Of The Clouds, Tartar Martyr, Pueblo
Domain, The Sutcliffe Catering Song (Peel
Session Feb. 26 '91)/ Unseen Power Of The
Picket Fence ('No Alternative' compilation)/ Haunt
You Down, Jam Kids (free single with 'Crooked
Rain')/ Who Should I Suspect? (Marquee, London
Aug. 26 '92)/ Sebadoh - Helen Stones, Dying On
The Street, Voguing To Shane McGowan
(Copenhagen, June 20 '93)/ Mother Mary, Box
Elder (Cambridge, USA May 21 '91)
R: Ex. Live Vg.   C: ECD. Dcc. Time 72:27.

PEARL JAM

CD - AUSSIE DYNAMOS
OCTOPUS OCTO 098/099
CD1: Release (5:09)/ Last Exit (2:43)/ Spin The
Black Circle (2:44)/ Tremor Christ (4:11)/
Corduroy (5:40)/ Not For You, 100 Pacer (6:37)/
Animal (3:03)/ Glorified G (3:09)/ Daughter (7:25)/
State Of Love And Trust (3:43)/ Why Go (3:25)/
Jeremy (5:36)/ Whipping (2:43)/ Immortality
(4:13)/ Rearview Mirror (6:52)/ Alive (5:04)
CD2: Black (6:23)/ Blood (7:51)/ Porch (8:43)/ Go
(2:52)/ Even Flow (6:33)/ Better Man (3:56)/ I Got
Shit (4:02)/ Indifference (5:14)/ Rockin' In The
Free World (6:53)/ Lifeless Dead (4:57)/ I Don't
Know (4:53)
R: Exs. Soundboard.   S: CD1 and CD2 tracks
1-9 Flinders Park Tennis Centre, Melbourne Mar.
17 '95. CD2 10-11 Palace during 'Self Pollution
Radio' Jan. 8 '95.   C: ECD. Dcc. Pic CD.

CD - BOUNDLESS
TORNADO TOR 003
Release/ Spin The Black Circle/ Last Exit/ Tremor
Christ/ Corduroy/ Not For You/ Daughter/ Glorified
G/ Go/ Deep/ Black/ Rearview Mirror/ Immortality/
Blood/ Indifference/ Act Of Love
R: Audience.   S: The Constitution Hall,
Washington, DC Jan. 14 '95.

CD - DEDICATED TO THE MOTHER***RS
OCTOPUS OCTO 056/57
CD1: Release (5:59)/ Go (3:06)/ Animal (3:11)/
Why Go (4:08)/ Deep (5:01)/ Jeremy (6:01)/
Glorified G (3:14)/ Daughter (6:25)/ Alive (6:03)/
Rearview Mirror (7:16)/ Blood (4:31)/ Rats (4:58)/
Once (4:41)/ Porch (6:42)/ Insane (2:51)
CD2: Sonic Reducer (7:47)/ Even Flow (8:30)/

Indifference (4:32)/ Last Exit (2:49)/ Tremor Christ
(4:55)/ Corduroy (5:58)/ Whipping (3:06)/ Not For
You (6:27)/ Satan's Bed (3:32)/ Immortality (7:35)/
Better Man (4:17)/ Spin The Black Circle (3:12)/
Redemption Song (4:02)/ Let My Love Open The
Door (5:40)
R: Ex. Soundboard and audience.   S: CD1 and
CD2 Tracks 1-3 Indio, CA Nov. 5 '93. CD2 Tracks
4-14 various US locations '95.   C: ECD. Dcc.

CD - DOWN UNDER
KISS THE STONE KTS 418/19
CD1: Release/ Last Exit/ Spin The Black Circle/
Tremor Christ/ Corduroy/ Not For You/ Animal/
Glorified G/ Daughter/ State Of Love And Trust/
Why Go/ Jeremy/ Whipping/ Immortality/
Rearviewmirror
CD2: Alive/ Black/ Blood/ Porch/ Go/Even Flow/
Betterman/ Indifference/ Rockin' In The Free
World
R: Exs. Soundboard.   S: Melbourne, Australia,
Mar. 17 '95.   C: ECD. Dcc. Pic CDs.
Time CD1 66:51. CD2 57:39.

CD - FREE WORLD
ALL OF US AS 10
Animal (3:06)/ Rockin' In The Free World (7:08)/
Footsteps (4:37)/ Alive (5:26)/ Daughter (4:03)/
Glorified G (2:26)/ Baba O'Riley (4:08)/ W.M.A.
(6:03)/ Dissidence (3:26)/ Blood (2:53)/ Blood
(2:53)/ Indifference (5:45)/ Rearview Mirror (4:22)/
Breath (3:48)/ Release (4:26)/ Dirty Frank (6:34)/
Sonic Producer (4:05)
R: Tracks 1-2 Exs. Soundboard. Tracks 3-16 G-
Vg. Audience.   S: Tracks 1-2 MTV Music
Awards Universal Amphitheatre, LA Sept. 2 '93.
Tracks 3-6 acoustic jam Mountain View, CA Nov.
1 '92. Tracks 7-16 surprise gig San Francisco
May 13 '93.   C: ECD. Dcc.

7" - IN YOUR FACE
S1: Alone   S2: Masters Of War
R: Ex.   S: Unheard jam.   C: USA.
Red/black/white sleeve. 33 RPM.

CD - LIVE FROM THE WAREHOUSE
OCTOPUS OCTO 072
Spin The Black Circle (3:22)/ Satan's Bed (3:26)/
Corduroy (4:47)/ Not For You (5:31)/ Immortality
(6:08)/ Last Exit (2:59)/ Blood (3:12)/ Tremor
Christ (5:42)/ Porch (3:51)/ Indifference (4:45)/
Daughter (5:15)/ Rearview Mirror (4:44)/
Previously Unreleased (4:37)/ Fell On Black Days
(4:05)
R: Exs. Soundboard.   S: Tracks 1-10 and 13-14
The Palace, Seattle Jan. 8 '95. Tracks 11-12
'Saturday Night Live' rehearsals '94.   C: ECD.
Dcc. Pic CD.

CD - MUDFEAST
RAZOR BLADE RB505
Deep (4:34)/ Jeremy (5:11)/ Daughter, Children
(5:50)/ Go (3:15)/ State Of Love And Trust (4:15)/
Garden (6:06)/ Blood (3:15)/ Alive (5:44)/ Black

they are the best overall
(psychomotion in corpus eight)

3/4

(5:36)/ Once (3:35)/ Porch (7:22)/ Indifference
(4:49)/ Sonic Reducer (4:53)/ Rockin' In The Free
World (6:21)/ Baba O'Reilly (6:31)
R: G-Vg. Audience.   S: Sunfest, Winnipeg,
Canada Aug. 14 '93.   C: ECD. Dcc. Pic CD.

CD - ROSELAND
KTS OF AUSTRALIA 020 F
Release Me (5:29)/ Evenflow (4:45)/ Once (3:30)/
Alive (6:05)/ Jeremy (5:10)/ Porch (5:10)/ Black
(4:29)/ Once (3:06)/ Evenflow (2:55)/ Alive (6:12)/
Jeremy (4:49)/ Why Go (3:05)/ Porch (5:14)
R: Vg. Audience.   S: The Roseland Ballroom,
New York City Nov.12 (tracks 1-6) and 15 (tracks
7-13) '91.   C: Australian CD. Dcc.

CD - ROUGH MIXES
JOKER JOK 061 A
Once (3:20)/ Why Go (3:29)/ Evenflow (4:59)/
Garden (5:27)/ Black (5:58)/ Oceans (Version 1)
(2:51)/ Release (4:34)/ Brother (4:19)/ Porch
(3:34)/ Jeremy (5:26)/ Breath (5:51)/ Deep (4:14)/
Alone (3:37)/ Alive (5:46)/ Wash (3:37)/ I've Got A
Feeling (3:44)
R: Exs. Soundboard.   S: London Bridge Studios
Jan. 29 '91 and Mar. '91. Rough Mix Finished On
Apr. 26 '91.   C: Australian CD. Dbw.

CD - SATAN'S BLACK BLOOD
DR. GIG DGCD 043-2
CD1: Release/ Last Exit/ Spin The Black Circle/
Tremor Christ/ Not For You/ Corduroy/ 100 Pager/
Dissident/ Act Of Love/ Animal/ State Of Love And
Trust/ Daughter/ Riz Rollins Dedication Song
CD2: Whippin'/ Immortality/ Go/ Kids Are Alright/
Porch/ Jack Irons Solo/ Blood/ I Don't Mind
Waiting 'Jam'/ Satan's Bed/ Rearviewmirror/ Too
Strong 'Jam'/ Act Of Love (with Neil Young)/
Black/ Better Man/ Let My Love Open The Door
R: Ex. Audience.   S: Moore Theatre, Seattle
Feb. 6 '95.   C: ECD. Dcc. Pic CD.

CD - SELF POLLUTION RADIO
KISS THE STONE KTS 398
Spin The Black Circle/ Satan's Bed/ Corduroy/
Not For You/ Immortality/ Last Exit/ Blood/ Tremor
Christ/ Porch/ Indifference/ Soundgarden Jam
Session/ Mad Season Jam Session
R: Ex. Soundboard.   S: Seattle Jan. 8 '95.
C: ECD. Dcc. Pic CD. Time 69:29.

CD - UNNECESSARY ROUGHNESS
TEDDY BEAR TB 63
Walking The Cow (3:38)/ Elderly Woman Behind
The Counter In A Small Town (3:28)/ Corduroy
(5:09)/ Daughter (4:55)/ Black (5:42)/ Footsteps
(4:11)/ Yellow Ledbetter (7:36)/ Let Me Sleep, It's
Christmas Time (2:19)/ Piece Of Crap (4:48)/
Wash (3:50)/ Masters Of War (4:35)/ By Your Side
(2:20)/ Let Me Sleep, It's Christmas Time (2:53)
R: Ex.   S: School Bridge Benefit, Mountain
View, CA Oct. 1 '94.   C: ECD. Dcc.

PFM

CD - CELEBRATION
TNT STUDIO TNT-940167/168
CD1: Celebration/ Four Holes In The Ground/
Dove...Quado/ Franco Mussida's Guitar Solo/ Out
Of The Roundabout
CD2: Mr. Nine Till Five/ Alta Loma Five Till Nine/
P.F.M.'s Arrangement Of Rossini's/ 'William Tell
Overture'/ Harlequin
R: Poor. Audience recording.   S: Sun Plaza
Hall, Tokyo, Nov. 29 '75.   C: Japanese CD.

CD - FOUR HOLES IN THE CHOCOLATE
ZA-43
Four Holes In The Ground/ Dove...Quando.../
Franco Mussida's Guitar Solo/ Out On The
Runabout/ Chocolate Kings/ Alta Loma Five Till
Nine/ Celebration/ Four Holes In The Ground
R: Poor. Audience.   S: Ravenna, Italy
July 26 '76.

PHISH

CD - FISHMEN TALES
HOME RECORDS HR5996-1
Dinner And A Movie (3:31)/ Bouncing Around The
Room (3:27)/ You Enjoy Myself (16:29)/ Fluffhead
(3:44)/ Fluff's Travel (7:06)/ Golgi Apparatus
(4:27)/ Esther (3:47)/ Big Fat Furry Creature
(3:14)/ Harry Hood (13:38)/ Fire (4:38)/ Lawn Boy
(2:30)
R: Exs. Soundboard.   S: Darien, New York Aug.
7 '93.   C: ECD.

CD - FRESH FROM THE SEA
AMERICAN FLY AF005/6
CD1: The Famous Mocking Bird (8:42)/ The Sloth
(4:47)/ Colonel Forbin's Ascent (9:14)/ The
Divided Sky (15:10)/ Rift (6:10)/ Sample In A Jar
(4:49)/ Reba (12:30)/ Jerusalem Of Gold (1:17)/
It's Ice (8:58)/ Stash (6:57)
CD2: You Enjoy Myself Jam (20:28)/
Weekapagroove (7:46)/ Fee (5:20)/ Possum
(8:38)/ Walk Away (4:00)/ The Lizards (10:18)/
Split Open And Melt (6:44)/ Take The A Train
(7:35)/ David Bowie (7:19)
R: G. Audience.   S: Great Woods, Boston July
8 '94.   C: ECD. Dcc.

CD - LIVE BAIT
KISS THE STONE KTS 468/69
CD1: Medley: The Man Who Stepped Into
Yesterday, Avenue Malkenu, The Man Who
Stepped Into Yesterday (7:40)/ Bouncing Around
The Room (3:49)/ Its Ice (9:04)/ Down With
Disease (7:47)/ Life Boy (7:40)/ Slave To The
Traffic Light (12:11)/ Horn (3:30)/ My Sweet One
(2:12)
CD1: Reba (11:13)/ Land Lady (3:25)/ Bath Tub
Gin (6:30)/ Sleeping Monkey (5:54)/ Runaway
(7:24)/ Foam (7:59)/ Loving Boulevard (4:03)/
Take A Train (4:48)/ Things Reconsidered (2:55)
R: Exs. Soundboard.   S: On tour '94.

C: ECD. Dcc. Pic CDs.

CD - PHISH ON PHISHIN' ON
TEDDY BEAR TB 39
Curtain (6:21)/ Split Open & Melt (8:10)/ My Poor
Heart (3:04)/ Guelah Papyrus (5:34)/ Maze (8:14)/
Moud (6:52)/ Fluffhead (15:02)/ Run Like An
Antelope: Blues Jam, Big Black Fuzzy Creatures
From Mars, Hawaii Vocal Jam, Lullaby, Big Black
Fuzzy Creatures From Mars, Antelope (18:19)
R: Ex.   S: Providence Mar. 13 '92.   C: ECD.
Dcc. Pic CD.

CD - SIMPLE
KISS THE STONE KTS 428
Suzie Greenberg/ Peaches En Regalia/ My Friend
My Friend/ Reba/ The Lizards/ Julius/ Mike's
Song/ Simple/ Possum/ Fire
R: Exs. Soundboard.   S: San Francisco, CA '94.
C: ECD. Pic CD. Time 70:50.

CD - TAKE COVER
TEDDY BEAR TB 75
2001: A Space Odyssey (4:08)/ Frankenstein
(4:46)/ Highway To Hell (3:32)/ Fire (4:27)/
Peaches En Regalia (3:10)/ Take The A-Train
(9:55)/ Medley: Scarlet Begonias, Fire, Fire On
The Mountain (17:49)/ Lively Up Yourself (5:38)/
Purple Rain (5:43)/ Good Times, Bad Times
(4:29)/ Free Bird (4:00)/ 2001: A Space Odyssey
(3:12)
R: G-Vg.   S: Various covers live.   C: ECD.
Dcc. Pic CD.

CD - THEY ARE THE BEST OVERALL
(PSYCHOMOTION IN CORPUS EIGHT)
MANGORECORDS MAN SP 001/8
CD1: Scarlet (6:18)/ Fire (4:01)/ Fire On The
Mountain (7:24)/ Slave To The Traffic Light (6:32)/
Mc Gruff (4:11)/ Dude Of Life (4:28)/ Big Fat Furry
Creatures (4:29)/ The Gala Event (8:56)/Dinner
And A Movie (3:52)/ Bouncin' Round The Room
(3:46)/ Llama (4:43)/ Squirming Coil (4:17)/ Oh
Kee Pa Ceremony (3:36)/ Suzy Greenburg (5:13)/
Magilla (5:43)
CD2: Foam (8:33)/ Runaway Jim (6:19)/ You
Enjoy Myself (16:28)/ Good Times Bad Times
(4:58)/ Fluffhead (5:38)/ Fluff's Travel (8:58)/
Landlady (3:49)/ Mike's Song (8:45)/ Wikipah
Groove (5:45)/ Hall And Solace (3:05)/ Stash
(7:21)
S: Tracks 1-6 Nectars, VT Dec. 1 '84. Tracks 7-8
private party '87. CD1 Tracks 9-15 and CD2
Boulder Theatre, Boulder, Colorado Nov. 3 '90:
CD3: Fee (5:35)/ Uncle Ben (4:30)/ Horn (3:59)/
Reba (9:21)/ Col. Forbin (4:32)/ Famous Mocking
Bird (8:10)/ Golgi Apparatus (4:33)/ Possum
(8:51)/ Tweezer (7:41)/ Manteca (5:37)/ Divided
Sky (7:18)/ No Good Tryin' (6:29)
CD4: Don't Get Me Wrong (8:51)/ Funky Bitch
(5:31)/ Encores: Bouncin' Round The Room
(3:58)/ Highway To Hell (3:39)/ Man Who Stepped
(7:26)/ Bathtub Gin (6:27)/ Curtain (6:06)/ Rocky
Top (2:36)/ Run Like An Antelope (9:44)/ Guelah

Papyrus (5:35)/ My Sweet One (2:29)/ Split Open
And Melt (7:46)/ Buried Alive (3:21)
S: CD3 tracks 1-2 Boulder Theatre, Boulder,
Colorado Nov. 3 '90. CD3 tracks 3-12 and CD4
tracks 1-4 The Marquee, NYC Dec. 28 '90. CD4
tracks 5-13 Breckenridge, CO Mar. 16 '91.
CD5: Runaway Jim (6:54)/ Sparkle (4:06)/ Rift
(6:32)/ My Friend (7:00)/ All Things Reconsidered
(3:14)/ Uncle Pen (4:05)/ Syd Barrett I Love You
(9:38)/ Dinner And A Movie (3:35)/ Baby Elephant
Walk (9:34)
CD6: Harpua (14:00)/ Poor Heart (2:25)/ Maze
(9:21)/ Bouncin' Round The Room (3:36)/ It's Ice
(8:29)/ Wedge (6:19)/ Mississippi Delta Home
(3:30)/ 2001(Also Sprach Zarathustra) (2:11)/
Slave To The Traffic Light (9:45)/ My Friend My
Friend (6:29)/ Chalkdust Torture (6:46)/ You Enjoy
Myself (6:24)
S: CD5 tracks 1-6 Arts Centre, Stowe, VT July 25
'92. CD5 tracks 7-12 Grainville, Ohio, Dec. 1 '92.
CD6 Red Rocks Amphitheatre Aug. 20 '93.
CD7: Wierd Talk (14:22)/ Purple Train (6:56)/
Cavern (5:42)/ Encores: Mango Song (7:21)/
Freebird (4:24)/ Frankenstein (4:44)/ Simple
(8:22)/ Lulius (7:55)/ Silent In The Morning (6:41)/
Golgi (5:04)/ David Bowie (8:47)
CD8: Speak To Me (1:58)/ Back In The USSR
(2:34)/ Dear Prudence (3:57)/ Glass Onion (2:09)/
Obla Di Obla Da (3:52)/ Bungalow Bill (2:43)/
While My Guitar Gently Weeps (6:02)/ Happiness
Is A Warm Gun (2:37)/ Martha (2:15)/ So Tired
(2:03)/ Blackbird (2:18)/ Piggies (1:57)/ Rocky
Racoon (3:39)/ Don't Pass Me By (3:10)/ Do It In
The Road (1:52)/ Julia (2:46)/ Birthday (2:12)/ Yer
Blues (3:39)/ Mother Natures Son (2:37)/ Me And
My Monkey (3:11)/ Sexy Sade (2:56)/ Helter
Skelter (4:24)/ Long (2:31)/ Revolution (5:32)/
Honey Pie (2:31)/ Savoi Truffle (2:43)/ Cry Baby
Cry (2:20)
S: CD7 tracks 1-5 Red Rocks Amphitheatre Aug.
20 '93. CD7 tracks 6-11 and CD8 Glens Falls, NY
Oct. 31 '94.
R: Ex. Soundboard/Audience. CD7 tracks 6-11
and CD8 Glens Falls, NY Oct. 31 '94 Vg.
Audience.   C: ECD. Four double slimlines make
up this great set. Excellent musicians with a
sense of humor.

PIG BAG

CD - SEVEN PIGGIES
BRANDNEWBEAT BNB-941010
Big Bean/ Six Of One/ Week At The Needs/
Getting Up/ Wiggling/ Papas Got A Brand New
Pig Bag
R: Vgs. FM recording.   S: Sun Plaza Hall,
Tokyo July 23 '92.

PIG PEN

CD - AIN'T IT CRAZY
HAIGHT STREET RECORDS 95-PP-04-03
Next Time You See Me (Sunny, Cortland, NY Apr.
18 '71)/ Chinatown Shuffle (Winterland, San

Francisco Jan. 31 '71)/ Kingbee (The Manhattan Center, NYC Apr. 5 '71)/ Turn On Your Lovelight (The Euphoria Club, San Raphael, CA July 14 '70 with Janis Joplin)/ Empty Pages (Gaelic Park, Bronx, NY Aug. 26 '71)/ Ain't It Crazy (Fillmore East, NYC Apr. 28 '71)/ Alligator Caution Alligator (O'Keefe Center, Toronto, Canada Aug. 4 '76)/ Down So Long There Is Something On Your Mind (3rd set Matrix Club, San Francisco Feb. '66)/ Hey Jude (Fillmore West, San Francisco Mar. 1 '69)
R: Vg-Ex. Some G.   C: Dcc. With the Grateful Dead. Time 70:50.

CD - BRING ME MY SHOTGUN
CAPRICORN RECORDS CR-2051
Two Women (1)/ Michael/ Katie Mae (1)/ New Orleans, That Train/ Instrumental/ Bring Me My Shotgun (1)/ C.C. Rider/ Katie Mae (2)/ Hitchiking Woman/ Two Women (2)/ When I Was A Boy/ Bring Me My Shotgun (2)/ I Believe/ She's Mine/ No time/ Sweet Georgia Brown, Dupree's Diamond Blues
R: Vg-Ex. Some G.   S: Tracks 1-12 4-track apartment demos '66. Tracks 13-15 Pigpens final recordings Mar. 9 '73. Track 16 Pigpen and Jorma '64.   C: Time 64:29.

PINK FLOYD

CD - A MOMENTARY LAPSE OF REASON LIMITED EDITION TRANCE REMIX
940669 #1
Sign Of Life/ Learning To Fly/ The Dogs Of War/ One Slip/ On The Turning Away/ Yet Another Movie/ A New Machine Part 1, Terminal Frost (Medley)/ A New Machine Part 2, Sorrow Medley
R: Exs. Soundboard.   C: ECD. Dcc. Pic CD. Time 72:23.

CD - ANIMALS LIMITED EDITION TRANCE REMIX
TIERE 0001 #1
Pigs On The Wing 1/ Dogs/ Pigs (Three Different Ones)/ Sheep/ Pigs On The Wing 2
R: Exs. Soundboard.   C: ECD. Dcc. Pic CD. Time 71:56.

CD - ATOM HEART MOTHER LIMITED EDITION TRANCE REMIX
AHM 001
Atom Heart Mother/ If/ Summer '68/ Fat Old Sun/ Alan's Psychedelic Breakfast
R: Exs. Soundboard.   C: ECD. Dcc. Pic CD. Time 72:18.

CD - BRAIN DAMAGE
CAPRICORN RECORDS CR 1001
Speak To Me/ Breathe/ On The Run/ Time/ The Great Gigs In The Sky/ Money/ Us And Them/ Any Colour You Like/ Brain Damage/ Eclipse
R: Exs. Soundboard.   S: Empire Pool, Wembley, London Nov. 14-17 '74.   C: Dbw. Time 52:36.

CD - THE COLD SIDE OF THE BOW
TIME MACHINE TM-2-1,2
CD1: Speak To Me/ Breathe/ On The Run/ Time/ Breath, The Great Gig In The Sky/ Money/ Us And Them/ Any Colour You Like/ Brain Damage/ Eclipse/ Breaks/ Careful With That Axe, Eugene
CD2: Echoes/ Atom Heart Mother
R: Poor. Audience.   S: Nakanoshima Sports Center, Sapporo, Hokkaido, Japan Mar. 13 '72.

CD - DARK NIGHT IN ATLANTA
WHOOPY CAT WKP-0031
Speak To Me/ Breathe/ On The Run/ Time/ The Great Gig In The Sky/ Money/ Us And Them/ Any Colour You Like/ Brain Damage/ Eclipse
C: Poor soundboard recording. Hiss.   S: Atlanta Mar. 24 '73.   C: Japanese CD.

CD - DARK SIDE OF THE MOON LIMITED EDITION TRANCE REMIX
ODY 020 #1
Speak To Me, Breathe/ On The Run/ Time/ Great Gig In The Sky/ Money/ Us And Them/ Any Colour You Like/ Brain Damage
R: Exs. Soundboard.   C: ECD. Dcc. Pic CD. Time 72:42.

CD - ENJOY THE SILENCE
WORLD PRODUCTIONS WPOCM 1190 D 066-2
Atom Heart Mother (24:33)/ Fat Old Sun (11:25)/ Cymbaline (9:13)
R: Poor-G. Audience.   S: Santa Monica Oct. '70.   C: ECD.

CD - THE FILM
The Little Boy That Santa Claus Forgot/ When The Tigers Broke Free, Part 1 / In The Flesh?/ The Thin Ice/ Another Brick In The Wall, Part 1/ Goodbye Blue Sky/ The Happiest Days Of Our Lives/ Another Brick In The Wall, Part 2/ Mother/ Empty Spaces/ Young Lust/ One Of My Tears/ Don't Leave Me Now/ Another Brick In The Wall, Part 3/ Goodbye Cruel World/ Is There Anybody Out There?/ Nobody Home/ Vera/ Bring The Boy Back Home/ Comfortably Numb/ In The Flesh/ Run Like Hell/ Waiting For The ?/ The Trial/ Outside The Wall
R: Exs. Soundboard.   S: Unreleased versions from 'The Wall' movie.   C: ECD. Dcc. Pic CD. Time 76:59.

CD - FOREVER AND EVER
PF-001/2
CD1: Astronomy Domine/ Learning To Fly/ What Do You Want From Me/ Poles Apart/ Sorrow/ Take It Back/ Lost For Words/ Keep Talking/ On the Turning Away/ Shine On You Crazy Diamond
CD2: Breathe In The Air/ Time/ Breathe In The Air Reprise/ High Hopes/ Wish You Were Here/ One Of These Days/ The Great Gig In The Sky/ Us And Them/ Money/ Comfortably Numb/ Hey You/ Run Like Hell
R: Poor audience recording.   S: San Antonio Apr. 2 '94.

CD - HOME AGAIN
TOP/PF 72010D
CD1: The Dark Side Of The Moon
CD2: One Of These Days/ Careful With That Axe,
Eugene/ Echoes
R: Poor-G. Audience.   S: Kyoto Taikukan, Kyoto
Mar. 10 '72.   C: Japanese CD. Dcc. Comes with
a 45 minute VHS video with 'Atom Heart Mother'
(Hakone 'Aphrodite' Aug. '71), 'Cymbaline'
(Fillmore West, San Francisco Oct. '70) and 'The
Other Side Of The Wall' (making of 'The Wall'
film). Time CD1 47:05. CD2 49:45.

CD - LONG TIME GONE
SWINDLE SWN 022
Careful With That Axe, Eugene (13:14)/
Cymbaline (13:05)/ Atom Heart Mother (31:49)/ A
Saucerful Of Secrets (21:09)
R: Ex. Audience.   S: The Montreux Jazz
Festival, Switzerland Sept. 18-19 '71.   C: ECD.
Dcc. Pic CD.

CD - MADE IN JAPAN
SWINDLE SWN 007
Learning To Fly (5:24)/ Yet Another Movie/ Round
And Round (6:53)/ Sorrow (9:28)/ The Dogs Of
War (7:11)/ On The Turning Away (7:36)/ One Of
These Days (6:08)/ Time (5:14)/ Us And Them
(7:18)/ Money (9:53)/ Another Brick In The Wall
Part II (5:17)/ Comfortably Numb (7:09)
R: G. Audience.   S: Tokyo, Japan '88.
C: ECD. Dcc. Pic CD.

CD - METEORA
BABY CAPONE BC 001
Shine On You Crazy Diamond (12:00)/ Brain
Damage (7:13)/ Wish You Were Here (5:53)/ Lost
Paradise (13:26)/ Money (12:29)/ Comfortably
Numb (9:00)/ Another Brick In The Wall (7:43)/
Run Like Hell (6:52)
R: Ex.   S: Knebworth, UK June 6 '90.
C: ECD. Dcc. Pic CD.

CD - MOON WALK
BABY CAPONE BC 026
Speak To Me, Breathe (2:55)/ On The Run (6:10)/
Time (6:32)/ Breathe (Reprise) (1:53)/ The Great
Gig In The Sky (4:23)/ Money (7:52)/ Us And
Them (2:18)/ Any Colour You Like (4:37)/ Brain
Damage (3:51)/ Eclipse (1:54)/ Biding My Time
(5:12)
R: Ex.   S: Rainbow Theatre, London Feb. 20
'72.   C: ECD. Dcc. Pic CD.

CD - OAKLAND COLISEUM
STONEHENGE STCD 2016/2017
CD1: Sheep (11:11)/ Pigs On The Wing (Part 1)
(2:14)/ Dogs (18:28)/ Pigs On The Wing (Part 2)
(2:23)/ Pigs (Three Different Ones) (17:18)/ Shine
On You Crazy Diamond (Part 1) (14:18)
CD2: Welcome To The Machine (8:01)/ Have A
Cigar (6:37)/ Wish You Were Here (6:08)/ Shine
On You Crazy Diamond (Part 2) (22:00)/ Money
(10:22)/ Us And them (7:38)/ Careful With That

Axe, Eugene (9:55)
R: Vg-Ex. Some hiss.   S: May 9 or 10 '77
'Animals' World Tour.   C: ECD. Pic CD.

CD - REVERSION OR REVALORIZATION
WORLD PRODUCTIONS WPOCM 0690 D 054-2
ROTTERDAM June 28 '70: Careful With That
Axe, Eugene (10:42)/ Cymbaline (8:22)/ PLUMP-
TON FESTIVAL Aug. 8 '69: Set The Controls For
The Heart Of The Sun (8:19)/ Intersteller
Overdrive (6:00)/ ESSEN Oct. 11 '69: Astronomy
Domine (8:02)/ Green Is The Colour (9:41)
R: Poor-G. Audience.   C: ECD.

CD - VARIATIONS ON A THEME OF ABSENCE
CD COMPANY DIA 001/2, 003/4, 005/6, 007/8,
1995
CD1: Remember A Day (4:30), Astronomy
Domine (4:08), Interstellar Overdrive (3:05),
Apples And Oranges (3:01), It Would Be So Nice
(3:42), Candy And A Currant Bun* (2:42), Scream
Thy Last Scream* (4:45), See Emily Play (2:55),
Flaming (2:48), Paintbox (3:31), Heart Beat, Pig
Meat (3:10), Crumbling Land (4:11), Careful With
That Axe Eugene (4:57), Point Me At The Sky
(3:36), Biding My Time (5:16), Embryo (4:38),
Mademoiselle Knobs* (1:50), Julia Dream (4:58),
Come In Number 51, Your Time Is Up (4:58),
Oenone (6:00).
R: Tracks 1-6, 8-20 Ex. Track 7 G. Most tracks
stereo, *mono.   S: Studio outtakes May 1967-
November 1970 (single and unreleased
versions/tracks. Tracks 11, 12 and 19 from
'Zabriskie Point' soundtrack. Track 17 from 'Live
At Pompeii' soundtrack.
CD2: Let There Be More Light* (3:31), Point Me
At The Sky* (4:13), Murderistic Woman* (sic)
(2:12), Julia Dream* (2:06), The Embryo* (2:56),
A Saucerful Of Secrets* (6:35), The Narrow Way*
(4:21), Green Is The Colour* (6:01), Fingal's Cave
(1:56), Rain In The Country (7:03), On The Run*
(3:21), Brain Damage* (2:02), Us And Them*
(7:08), Granchester Meadows* (6:39), Astronomy
Domine* (9:22), Cymbaline* (8:00).
R: Tracks 1-8 Vg, 9-13 Ex, 14-16 Vg. Most tracks
stereo, *mono.   S: Tracks 1-8 BBC Radio 1969-
1970. Tracks 9-10 Studio outtakes unreleased.
Tracks 11-13 'Live At Pompeii' soundtrack (studio
rehearsals). Tracks 14-16 recorded at Winterland,
San Francisco May 1970 (not October 21 as indicated on CD).
CD3: The Embryo (10:14), Green Is The Colour
(4:11), If (4:25), Atom Heart Mother (24:50), Fat
Old Sun (14:15), One Of These Days (6:52), Set
The Controls For The Heart Of The Sun* (14:50).
R: Tracks 1-6 Ex Soundboard. Track 7 Ex audi-
ence. Most tracks stereo, *mono.   S: Tracks 1-4
BBC Radio broadcast from performance at Paris
Theatre (not recorded on Dec. 12, 1970 as indi-
cated). Tracks 5-6 BBC Radio broadcast from
performance at Playhouse Theatre (not recorded
on May 15 1971 as indicated). Track 7 live at
Montreux Jazz Festival Sept. 18 or 19 1971.
CD4: Echoes* (24:25), Speak To Me-Breathe

(2:55), On The Run (6:10), Time (6:32), Breathe (Reprise) (1:53), The Great Gig In The Sky (4:23), Money (7:52), Us And Them* (7:16 not 2:56 as listed on CD), Any Colour You Like* (4:37), Brain Damage* (4:41), Eclipse* (4:53), A Saucerful Of Secrets (9:40).
R: Track 1-11 Ex audience.Track 12 Ex soundtrack. Most tracks stereo, *mono.   S: Track 1 Live at Montreux Jazz Festival Sept. 18 or 19 1971. Tracks 2-7 Live at Rainbow Theatre, London Feb. 20, 1972. Tracks 9-11 Live in Japan March 1972 (not at Sapporo, Japan Dec. 3, 1972 as indicated on CD). Track 12 'Live At Pompeii' soundtrack. Song edits on 'Time' from source tape not fault of CD.
CD5: Shine On You Crazy Diamond 1/5 (13:45), Welcome To The Machine (8:29), Sheep (10:52), Pigs On The Wing 1 (2:12), Dogs (18:26), Pigs On The Wing 2 (2:14), Pigs (Three Different Ones) (17:18), Have A Cigar (6:42).
R: Tracks 1-2, Ex audience. Tracks 3-8 Vg-Ex audience. Most tracks stereo, *mono.   S: Tracks 1-2 Madison Square Garden, New York City July 1, 2, 3 or 4 1977 (not July 22 1975 as indicated on CD). Tracks 3-8 Oakland Coliseum, Oakland, California May 9 or 10 1977.
CD6: In The Flesh (3:45), The Thin Ice (2:49), Another Brick In The Wall 1 (4:59), The Happier Days Of Our Lives (sic) (1:52), Another Brick In The Wall 2 (6:28), Mother (8:44), Goodbye Blue Sky (4:03), What Shall We Do Now (4:35), Young Lust (5:32), One Of My Turns (4:08), Don't Let My Now (sic) (2:19), Empty Spaces (2:00), Another Brick In The Wall 3 (6:10), Goodbye Cruel World (1:54), Hey You (4:57), Is There Anybody Out There (3:17), Nobody Home (3:37), Vera (2:08), Bring The Boys Back Home (1:45), Waiting For The Worms (5:10).
R: Vg audience. Most tracks stereo, *mono.
S: Live at Nassau Coliseum, Long Island, New York February 24, 25, 26, 27 or 28 1980 (not April 20 1980 as listed on CD).
CD7: Until We Sleep (6:23), All Lovers Are Deranged (5:01), Love On The Air (6:16), Short And Sweet (7:55), You Know I'm Right (8:04), Signs Of Life (3:54), Yet Another Movie (7:35), A New Machine 1 (1:52), Terminal Frost, A New Machine 2 (6:39), Sorrow (9:57) (not listed on CD but is actual track 10), Powers That Be (4:00), Another Brick In The Wall 1, Happiest Days Of Our Lives (both not listed on CD), Another Brick In The Wall 2 (10:18).
R: Tracks 1-5 Ex soundboard. Tracks 6-10 Vg-G audience. Tracks 11-12 Ex soundboard. Most tracks stereo, *mono.   S: Tracks 1-5 Radio broadcast of performance Bethlehem, Pennsylvania July 12 1984 (not October 8, 1984 as listed on CD). Tracks 6-10 live in Chicago, Illinois Sept. 25, 26, 27 or 28 1987 (not Sept. 18 as listed on CD). Tracks 11-12 Radio broadcast performance in Quebec City, Quebec, Canada recorded November 7 1987 (not May 22 1987 as listed on CD).
CD8: Learning To Fly (5:24), The Dogs Of War

(7:17), Sorrow (7:45), Run Like Hell (7:10), Shine On You Crazy Diamond (11:07), Comfortable Numb (8:44), High Hopes (8:15), Take At Back (sic) (5:59), Coming Back To Life (6:48), Keep Talking (7:35).
R: Tracks 1-2 G-Vg. Tracks 3-10 Ex soundboard. Most tracks stereo, *mono.   S: Tracks 1-2 Japan March 2, 3, 4, 5, or 6 1988 (not Oct. 19 1988 as listed). Tracks 3-4 Pay per view broadcast, Venice, Italy July 15 1989 (not August 30, 1989 as listed on CD). Tracks 5-6 radio broadcast Knebworth Festival, Knebworth, England June 30 1990 (not June 6 as listed on CD). Tracks 7-10 Pay per view broadcast concert at Earl's Court, London, England October 20 1994 (not Knebworth 1994 as listed on CD).
C: ECD deluxe box set, comes in a large circle package with moon over sun on cover. Includes T-shirt (with screen of box cover on front of shirt), video (PAL format) of Madison Square Garden, New York City, New York, USA concert October 5 1987 (first half of show - 'Shine On' and 'Momentary Lapse Of Reason' material - but generally poor sound and video) and soft cover booklet (features discography and bootlist lists). Nice attempt but ultimately a failure as definitive box set. Most material available separately elsewhere. And why some song choices and not others? (CD6 features 'Wall' material just up to 'Comfortably Numb' yet does not include this song with both Waters and Gilmour). Why so many source errors and typos? Pictures on CDs do not match appropriate years for songs and other CD cover inserts rudimentary. T-shirt poor quality. Video poor. Book not too bad but also some errors and does not relate any information about tracks found on the box set. Full points for clean up of sound however. Generally excellent sound throughout considering range of years. CD1/2 stand out. (review by Keith - see page 20)

CD - WATER'S GATE
TNT STUDIO TNT 940147/148
CD1: Dark Side Of The Moon: Speak To Me/ Breathe/ On The Run/ Time/ The Great Gig In The Sky/ Money/ Us And Them/ Any Colour You Like/ Brain Damage/ Eclipse
CD2: Atom Heart Mother/ Careful With That Axe, Eugene/ Echoes
R: Poor. Audience. Hiss.   S: Tokyo-Taiikukan, Tokyo, Japan Mar. 6 '72.   C: Japanese CD. Dcc. Time CD1 46:09. CD2 57:08.

PIXIES, THE

CD - ROUGH DIAMONDS
BLUE MOON BMCD32
Hey/ Levitate Me/ Wild Honey Pie/ Caribou/ In Heaven/ Dead/ Tame/ There Goes My Gun/ Manta Ray/ Down To The Well/ Into The White/ Surf Of Mutilation/ Monkey Gone To Heaven/ Allison/ Wave Of Mutilation/ Ana/ Palace Of The Brine/ Letter To Memphis/ Motorway To Roswell/ Subbacultcha/ Build High/ I Can't Forget/ Born In

Chicago/ Velouria/ Hang On To Your Ego/ Is She Weird/ Gigantic/ River Euphrates/ Tame/ Down To The Well/ Rock-A-My-Soul
R: Ex. Soundboard.   S: Tracks 1-5 Maida Vale Studio 4, London 3/5/88. Tracks 6-9 Hippodrome Studio, London 9/10/88. Tracks 1-12 Maida Vale Studio 3, London Apr. 16 '89. Tracks 13-16 Maida Vale Studio 5, London Aug. 18 '90. Tracks 17-20 Maida Vale Studio 3, London June 23 '91. Tracks 21-22 Master Control Studio, Burbank Sept. '91. Track 23 Recording Co. Studio, Chicago July '90. Tracks 24-26 Portastudio Demo, Los Angeles June '90. Tracks 27-28 Blackwing Studio, London 2/5/'88. Tracks 29-31 Fort Apache Studio, Boston Mar. '87.   C: ECD. Dcc. Time 73:37.

PLANT, ROBERT

CD - PROMISED LAND
INSECT RECORDS INT 19
Ramble On/ I Believe/ 29 Palms/ Bluebird/ If I Were A Carpenter/ Going To California/ Promised Land/ Call It To Ya/ What Is And What Should Never Be/ Ship Of Fools/ Whole Lotta Love
R: G. Background noise.   S: Perugia Blues Festival, summer '93.

POISON

LP - LET IT PLAY
BUD RECS.
S1: Intro/ Look What The Cat Dragged In/ Look But Not Touch/ Poor Boy Blues/ Unskinny Bop/ Every Rose Has It's Thorn
S2: Ride The Wind/ Let It Play/ Fallen Angel/ Nothing But A Good Time/ Talk Dirty
R: Exs.   S: Globe Arena, Stockholm Aug. 21 '90.   C: Dcc.

POLICE, THE

CD - MESSAGE IN A BOTTLE (VOL. 1)
BANANA BAN-025-A
Message In A Bottle (5:08)/ King Of Pain (7:06)/ Driven To Tears (4:50)/ Every Breath You Take (5:10)/ Roxanne (4:44)/ Invisible Sun (featuring Bono on vocals) (5:17)/ I Shall Be Released (performed by The Amnesty Allstars) (7:55)/ Can't Stand Losing You (4:53)/ So Lonely (6;04)/ Fall Out (2:34)/ Here In My Life (4:05)/ Truth Hits Everybody (2:32)/ Peanuts (3:43)/ Roxanne (6:59)/ Next To You (2:18)
S: USA '79, '86.   C: Australian CD. Dcc.

CD - MESSAGE IN A BOTTLE (VOL. 2)
BANANA BAN-025-B
Don't Stand So Close To Me (3:16)/ Walking On The Moon (5:13)/ Deathwish (4:16)/ Fall Out (2:42)/ Bring On The Night (4:51)/ De Do Do Do, De Da Da Da (4:35)/ Truth Hits Everybody (2:30)/ The Bed's Too Big Without You (7:23)/ Driven To Tears (3:40)/ When The World Is Running Down, You Make The Best Of What's Still Around (3:15)/ Message In A Bottle (4:28)/ Roxanne (5:47)/ Can't Stand Losing You (6:53)/ Next To You (2:04)
S: USA '81.   C: Australian CD. Dcc.

CD - MESSAGE IN A BOTTLE (VOL. 3)
BANANA BAN-025-C
Don't Stand So Close To Me (3:49)/ Walking On The Moon (4:53)/ Death Wish (3:32)/ Fall Out (2:37)/ Man In A Suitcase (2:18)/ Bring On The Night (5:38)/ De Do Do Do, De Da Da Da (5:55)/ Truth Hits Everybody (227)/ Shadows In The Rain (7:47)/ When The World Is Running Down, You Make The Best Of What's Still Around (3:00)/ The Beds Too Big Without You (6:48)/ Driven To Tears (2:56)/ Message In A Bottle (3:24)/ Roxanne (7:07)/ Can't Stand Losing You (7:18)/ So Lonely (4:19)
S: Europe '81.   C: Australian CD. Dcc.

POP, IGGY

CD - THE BEAT OF THE LIVING DEAD
MIND THE MAGIC MTM 035
Raw Power/ The Shadow Of Your Smile/ TV Eye/ Hate/ Real Wild Child/ Loose/ I Wanna Be Your Dog/ No Fun/ Search And Destroy/ The Passenger/ Fucking Alone/ Johanna/ Lust For Life/ I'm Sick Of You/ Wild America/ Home/ Louie Louie
R: Ex. Soundboard.   S: Leysin July '93.
C: ECD. Time 78:27.

CD - THE COMPLETE CHANNEL TAPES
SWINGIN' PIG TSP-CD-212
Instinct/ Kill City/ 1969/ Penetration/ Power And Freedom/ Your Pretty Face/ High On You/ 5 Foot 1/ Johanna/ Easy Rider/ Tuff Baby/ 1970/ Winners, Losers Scene Of The Crime/ Search And Destroy/ Cold Metal/ Squarehead/ No Fun/ I Wanna Be Your Dog
S: The Channel, Boston July 19 '88.   C: ECD.

CD - THE LEGENDARY BREAKING POINT TOUR '83
KLONDYKE KR 25
CD1: Fire Engine/ Loose/ Penetration/ Fortune Teller/ Five Foot One/ No Fun, I'm Waiting For The Man/ I'm Bored/ One For My Baby And One More For The Road/ Run Like A Villain/ Louie Louie/ 96 Tears/ I'm A Conservative/ The Villagers/ The Passenger/ Mass Production
CD2: Home*/ Down On The Street*/ Butt Town*/ I Won't Crap Out*/ Down On The Street**/ The Passenger**/ I Won't Crap Out**/ Brick By Brick**
S: Seaview Hotel Ballroom, Melbourne July 3 '83. *WBCN radio session, Boston June 10 '90. **BBC radio session London Sept. 17 '90.   C: ECD. Time CD1 63:06. CD2 28:43.

PORTISHEAD

CD - NOBODY LOVES ME!
KISS THE STONE KTS 452
Intro/ Glory Box/ Uncertainty/ Wandering Star/ Reaching Out/ Sour Times/ Uncertainty/ Sour

Times/ Glory Box/ Wandering Star
R: Ex.   S: Live on tour Apr. '95.   C: ECD. Pic
CD. Time 43:22.

PRESLEY, ELVIS

CD - ELVIS MEETS THE BEATLES
TEDDY BEAR TB 69
Blue Suede Shows (2:21)/ I Got A Woman (3:00)/
I'm All Shook Up (3:21)/ Love Me Tender (3:05)/
Jailhouse Rock, Don't Be Cruel (2:13)/
Heartbreak Hotel (4:03)/ Hound Dog (2:10)/
Memories (3:59)/ Mystery Train, Tiger Man (4:16)/
Life Story (Dialogue) (4:40)/ Baby, What'd You
Want Me To Do (2:27)/ Are You Lonesome
Tonight (3:13)/ Yesterday (2:29)/ Hey Jude (2:36)/
Band's Introduction (4:09)/ In The Ghetto (3:11)/
Suspicious Minds (8:01)/ What Did I Say (4:28)/ I
Can't Help Falling In Love (2:20)
R: Vg. Audience.   S: The Las Vegas
International Hotel Aug. 1 '69.   C: ECD. Pic CD.

CD - THE KING OF ENTERTAINMENT
Opening Riff - See See Rider/ I Got A Woman -
Amen Medley/ Love Me/ Trying To Get To You/
And I Love You So/ All Shook Up - Teddy Bear -
Don't Be Cruel Medley/ Hound Dog/ I'm Leavin'/
You Gave Me A Mountain/ Polk Salad Annie/ Just
Pretend/ How Great Thou Art/ Softly, As I Leave
You/ America/ Sweet Sweet Spirit/ Little Sister/
One Night/ Until It's Time For You To Go/ The
First Time Ever I Saw Your Face/ Mystery Train -
Tiger Man Medley/ O Sole Mio/ It's Now Or Never
R: G-Vg. Audience.   S: Hilton Hotel, Las Vegas
Dec. 14 '75.   C: ECD. Dcc. Time 77:52.

CD - THE UNRELEASED COLLECTION
AGLER MUSIC EP100
Need Your Love Tonight (takes 1-15 RCA Studios
Nashville June 10 '58 - 22:03)/ Milky White Way
(takes 1-15 RCA Studios Nashville Oct. 30 '60 -
6:41)/ His Hand In Mine (takes 1-5 RCA Studios
Nashville Oct. 30 '60 - 10:07)/ Echoes Of Love
(takes 2, 7, 9 RCA Studios Nashville May 26 '63 -
8:22)/ Please Don't Drag That String Around
(takes 1-4 RCA Studios Nashville May 26 '63 -
5:50)/ U.S. Male (takes 1, 2, 3, 4 RCA Studios
Nashville Jan. 17 '68 - 7:43)/ Wings Of An Angel
(jam version Jan. 17 '68 - 1:06)/ Tomorrow Night
(unreleased version - 3:05)/ Shake Rattle And
Roll (unreleased version - 2:41)/ King Creole
(unreleased promo - 2:23)/ My Little Friend (unreleased version - 2:52)/ Make The World Go Away
(live - Las Vegas Aug. 8 '73 - 2:03)
R: Ex. Soundboard. *Poor. Audience.   C: ECD.
Dbw. Gold type.

CD - WINGS OF AN ANGEL
GERMAN RECORDS GM 042
U.S. Male/ Blue Suede Shoes/ Pocketful Of
Rainbows/ Guitar Man/ Wings Of An Angel/
Follow That Dream/ What's She Really Like/ What
A Wonderful Life/ A Whistling Tune/ Milky White
Way/ Wooden Heart/ Tonight Is Right For Love/

Frankfort Special/ I Need Your Love Tonight/ Stay
Away/ Shoppin' Around/ G.I. Blues/ Please Don't
Drag That String Around/ Echoes Of Love
R: Ex. Soundboard.   S: Live USA '69 - '70.
C: ECD. Dcc. Time 45:49.

PRETENDERS, THE

CD - THE ADULTRESS
CHAPTER ONE CO 25158
Room Full Of Mirrors (5:37)/ Message Of Love
(3:28)/ The Adultress (3:56)/ Time The Avenger
(4:36)/ Kid (4:07)/ Light Of The Moon (5:23)/ My
Baby (3:34)/ Private Life (7:28)/ Hymn To Her
(5:57)/ Back On The Chaingang (4:31)/ My City
Was Gone (5:58)/ Up The Neck (4:51)/ Bad Boys
Get Spanked (8:39)/ Middle Of The Road (4:03)
R: Ex.   S: Exhibition Centre, Chicago July 15
'87.   C: ECD. Dcc.

CD - LIVE VOL. 1
JOKER JOK-031-A
The Wait/ Message Of Love/ The Adultress/ Time
The Avenger/ My City Was Gone/ Show Me/ Kid/ I
Go To Sleep/ Thin Line Between Love And Hate/
Waste Not Want Not/ Thumbelina/ Back On The
Chain Gang/ Mystery Achievement/ Middle Of
The Road/ Stop Your Sobbing/ Talk Of The Town/
Brass In Pocket/ Up The Neck/ Precious
C: Australian CD.

PRIMAL SCREAM

CD - CREAM DE LA SCRAM
HOME RECORDS HR5934-6
Rocks/ Movin' On Up/ Don't Fight It, Feel It/ I'm
Losing More Than I'll Ever Have/ Damaged,
Stoned In Love With You/ Funky Jam/ Call On
Me/ Come Together/ (I'm Gonna) Cry Myself
Blind/ Give Out But don't Give Up/ Higher Than
The Sun, Our Love Secret, Soul Train/ Loaded
R: Vgs. Audience.   S: Rolling Stone, Milan, Italy
May 1 '94

CD - SO SAD ABOUT US
3D REALITY 3D-PS-005
Lost Dogs/ Jailbird/ Rocks/ Movin' On Up/ Slip
Inside This House/ Know Your Rights/ I'm Losing
More Than I'll Ever Have/ Cry Myself Blind/ Keep
On Tryin'/ Call Me/ Funky Jam/ Loaded/ So Sad
About Us/ Jailbird/ Jail Guitar Doors
R: G-Vg Audience.   S: Rock 'N' Roll Circus Feb.
12 '95.

PRINCE, THE ARTIST FORMERLY KNOWN AS

CD - THE ASTORIA
NEWPOWER ZOUNDS NP150-2
The Glam Slam Boogie/ Sweet Thing/ U Got The
Love/ Love...Thy Will Be Done/ Funky/ 18 And
Over/ I Believe In U/ The Ride/ Get Wild/ Gold
R: Ex. Audience recording.   S: Astoria, London
Mar. 8 '95. Track 10 studio recording.   C: With
George Benson and Chaka Kan.

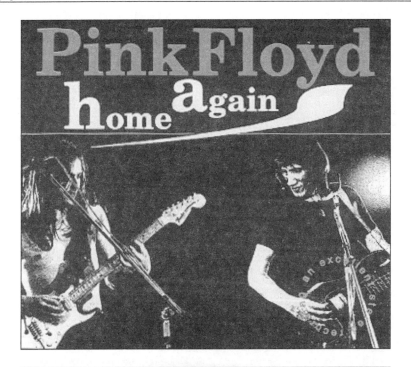

CD - B4 I STEP 2 THE STAGE
MAD 7
Instrumental 1/ Instrumental 2/ Witness/ Expert
Lover/ Sensitivity/ Step 2 The Stage/ Madhouse
#17/ Madhouse #18/ Madhouse #19/ Madhouse
#20/ Computer Blue/ Electric Chair #2/ Electric
Chair #3/ 51 Hours/ Purple Rain
R: Vg.   C: With Carlos Santana.

CD - BLUE
NB-804/05
CD1: I Here Your Voice/ Come/ Endorphine
Machine/ Deuce And A Quarter/ 2 Gether/ Tender
Heart/ Race/ I Need Love/ This Groove/
Allegiance/ Johnny
CD2: Goldie's Parade/ The Voice/ Space/ Making
It Easy/ Black Motherfucker/ Gold Nigga/
Pheromone/ We Can Funk '92/ Booty/ 51 Hours/
Insatiable/ The Lost 'Love Symbol' Segues
R: Vg.   S: Outtakes.

CD - CHICKENGREASE
MIDNIGHT BEAT MB CD027
Miss You/ Just My Imagination/ I Believe/ Love
And Happiness, I Want To Take You Higher/
What'd I Say?/ Unchain My Heart/ Outside Help/
Now's The Time/ Honky Tonk Women/ Cold
Sweat/ Villanova Junction/ A Case Of You/
Carwash/ Don't Make Me Pay For Your Mistakes/
Whole Lotta Shakin' Goin' On
R: Vg audience recording.   S: Tracks 1-11
Minneapolis Aug. '83. Tracks 12-15 '94.

CD - ESTANDARD
NB 806/807
CD1: The Sacrifice Of Victor/ Black M.F./ Race/
The Ride/ Honky Tonk Women/ Jailhouse Rock/
Come/ Endorphine Machine/ Peach
CD2: The Undertaker/ Sing A Simple Song-You
Can Make It If You Try/ House In Order/ Johnny/
Race*/ Johnny*
R: Vg. Audience. *G-Vg. Audience.
S: Aftershow gigs - Club Estandard, Barcelona
Aug. 23 '93. *Gothenburg Aug. 8 '93.
C: Time CD1 49:19. CD2 51:49.

CD - 4AM JAM
FREE MUSIC 003
Instrumental Jam (includes: I'm In The Mood,
Glam Slam Boogie)/ Sweet Thing - Sticky Wicked/
U Got The Love/ Love... Thy Will Be Done/ Let's
Get Funky - Get Loose!/ Come (18 And Over)/ I
Believe In U/ The Ride/ Get Wild
R: Poor-G.   S: The London Astoria Mar. 9 '95.
C: ECD. Dcc. With the N.P.G. Time 64:38.

CD - GET WILD
ALL OF US AS 38/2
CD1: Gold/ The Jam/ Endorphine Machine/
Space/ Days Of Wild/ Now/ The Most Beautiful
Girl In The World
CD2: Billy Jack Bitch/ Papa/ Love Sign/ Shhh/
Oh, Mary Don't You Weep/ Get Wild
R: Poor-G. Audience.   S: Club Palladium, New
York June 14 '94.   C: ECD. Dcc. Pic CDs. With
the N.P.G.

CD - HIDE THE BONE
#123
Drum Solo - Intro/ Soul Sacrifice/ 319/ Hide The
Bone/ Ripopgodazippa/ Get Wild/ Johnny
R: Vg-Ex. Soundboard.   S: Club Glam Slam
East, Miami June 9 '94.   C: ECD. Dcc. Limited
numbered edition of 1,000. With the N.P.G.
Time 57:57.

CD - HOLD ME
PCD-013
Come/ Endorphine Machine/ Space/ Pheromone/
Race/ I Hear Your Voice/ Hold Me/ Allegiance/
Your Love Is So Hard/ The Voice/ Rebirth Of The
Flesh/ Play In The Sunshine/ The Ball, Crystal
Ball/ Joy In Repetition
C: Ex.   S: Outtakes.

CD - I'LL DO ANYTHING
BAMBI 005
The Rest Of My Life/ Make Believe/ I'll Do
Anything/ Don't Talk To Strangers/ Everytime I
Pop A Pill/ Empty Room/ There Is Lonely/ Be My
Mirror/ The Ryde/ Poor Goo/ Honky Tonk Women/
Bambi/ The Undertaker/ Docphine/ Get Wild
R: Ex.

CD - IN THE FLESH
PURPLE TRACKS CD PT01
Come (3:55)/ Endorphine Machine (3:54)/ Space
(4:41)/ Pheromone (4:04)/ Race (4:15)/ I Hear
Your Voice (4:11)/ Hold Me (4:20)/ Allegiance
(3:35)/ Your Love Is So Hard (5:01)/ The Voice
(4:53)/ Rebirth Of The Flesh (4:59)/ Play In The
Sunshine (5:11)/ The Ball, Crystal Ball (15:27)/
Joy In Repetition (5:24)
R: Vg-Ex.   S: Previously unreleased outtakes.
C: ECD. Dcc. Pic CD.

CD - JUNE VII
MOONRAKER 003/4/5/6
CD1: Endorphinmachine/ The Jam/ Shhh!/ Days
Of Wild/ Now/ Sex Machine/ Funky Stuff/ The
Most Beautiful Girl In The World/ Pussy Control/
Letitgo/ Pink Cashmere/ Loose!
CD2: Count The Days/ The Return Of The Bump
Squad/ 7/ Get Wild/ Johnny/ Billy Jack Bitch/
Gold/ Bonus - Mayte's Opening Act: Children Of
The Sun/ The Rhythm Of Your Heart/ Baby Doll
CD3: Carlos Santana Medley (including Jungle
Strut, Soul Sacrifice and Toussaint L'Overture)/ I
Love U In Me/ Peach/ The Ride/ 7/ Instrumental/
Get Wild/ Big Fun/ Count The Days/ The Return
Of The Bump Squad
CD4: Pussy Control/ Asswoop/ Mary Don't You
Weep/ Skintight/ Brickhouse/ Sex Machine/ The
Glam Slam Boogie/ The Most Beautiful Girl In The
World/ Race Flashlight
R: Ex. Audience.   S: Birthday party for TAFKAP.
Glam Slam, Miami. CD1-2 June 7 '95. CD3-4
June 8 '95.   C: ECD. Box set with Dcc. Four

single CDs with Dcc. Full color book with pictures of gig, tickets and posters. Time CD1 60:38. CD2 69:10. CD3 70:07. CD4 54:12.

CD - JUST ANOTHER AFTERSHOW
PCD-003
Positivity/ The Ballad Of Dorothy Parker/ Four/ Housequake/ Just My Imagination/ I'll Take You There/ I Wish You Heaven (Part 3)/ Cold Sweat/ Prince On The Drums/ Percussion Solo (Sheila E.)/ Love Sexy/ Eighties Melody/ Chain Of Fools/ It's Gonna Be A Beautiful Night
C: Good sound.   S: Aftershow jam, San Francisco Nov. 10 '88.

CD - LE BATACLAN
LGB002
CD1: Gold/ The Jam/ I Believe In U/ Interactive/ Days Of Wild/ Now/ The Ride
CD2: Acknowledge Me/ Dark/ Instrumental/ A Capella/ Race/ Peach/ Drum Solo/ Endorphinemachine
R: Ex audience recording.   S: Club Le Bataclan, Paris, May 6 '94. CD2 track 8 French TV-Canal Plus May 5 '94.

CD - LOVE SIMPLE'S INTERACTIVE NIGHT
Interactive/ Face Of Wild/ Now/ The Ride/ The Jam/ I Believe In You/ Ssssh/ What I Say/ Peter Technic/ Marsha Law/ None Of Your Business/ Acknowledge Me/ Three-Nineteen/ Veramon
R: Ex.   S: Paisley Park Studios, Minneapolis Feb. 12 '94. Tracks 12-14 studio outtakes.

CD - THE MUTANT
BABY CAPONE BC 037/2
CD1: Intro (4:24)/ Thunder (4:13)/ Daddy Pop (7:00)/ Diamond And Pearls (6:32)/ Let's Go Crazy (2:23)/ Kiss (4:53)/ Jug Head (6:32)/ Purple Rain (8:42)/ Live 4 Love (6:41)/ Willing And Able (6:30)/ Damn U (7:16)/ Sexy Motherfucker (5:32)/ Insatiable (6:17)
CD2: Thieves In The Temple (10:43)/ Solo Instrumental (2:30)/ Get Off (6:13)/ Get Off II (3:24)/ Turn This Mother Out (5:26)/ Cream (5:52)/ Dr. Feelgood (5:48)/ 1999, Baby I'm A Star, Push (8:55)/ Instrumental (2:41)/ Play In The Sunshine (4:29)/ Housequake (3:47)/ Slow Love (4:45)/ I Could Never Take The Place Of Your Man (8:29)/ Hot Thing (5:48)
R: Vg. Audience.   S: Rotterdam, Holland, May 28 '92.   C: ECD. Dcc. Pic CD.

CD - THE PARK VOLUME ONE
MOONRAKER 009/10/11/12
CD1: Endorphinmachine/ Shhh!/ Days Of Wild/ The Most Beautiful Girl In The World/ P Control/ Waterfalls/ Letitgo/ Pink Cashmere/ 7/ Now/ Funky Stuff/ Skintight/ Johnny/ The Cross
CD2: The Return Of The Bump Squad/ Count The Days/ The Good Life/ Cherry Cherry/ Get Wild/ The Purple Medley/ Santana Medley/ The Ride
CD3: Sometimes It Snows In April/ A Case Of You/ Peach/ 7/ Dolphin/ Lannalee/ Bambi/ Tender

Surrender/ The Ride/ Mary, Don't You Weep/ Race/ Girls And Boys/ Superhero/ Dark
CD4: Billy Jack Bitch/ I Hate You/ 319/ Gold Intro/ Mad/ Days Of Wild/ In Time/ Bonus: Intermission/ I Love You/ Wishing Well/ Passion/ High Fashion/ Mutiny/ Rich Man
R: Ex. Audience. CD2 Vg-Ex. Audience.
S: Paisley Park's Love 4 One Another. CD1 Aug. 5 '95. CD2 Aug. 12 '95. CD3-4 Aug 26 '95.
C: ECD. Dcc. Time CD1 61:15. CD2 55:48. CD3 64:48. CD4 73:21.

CD - THE PARK VOLUME TWO
MOONRAKER 020/21
CD1: Shy/ People Get Ready/ The Jam/ U Got The Love/ Instrumental Jam/ Sweet Thing/ Heaven Must Be Like This/ Hide The Bone/ Funky Design/ Santana Medley/ The Undertaker/ Instrumental/ Sometimes It Snows In April
CD2: Lannalee/ The Ride/ Voodoo Child/ Honky Tonk Women/ The Girl Can't Help It/ Que Sera Sera/ The Jam/ I Believe In U/ Instrumental Jam/ Johnny/ Skintight/ Sweet Thing
R: Ex. Audience.   S: Paisley Park's Love 4 One Another. CD1 Sept. 8 '95. CD2 Sept. 16 '95.
C: ECD. Dcc. Time CD1 72:15. CD2 48:41.

CD - RED
AB-9404
Come Outside And Play/ Oobey Doop/ Thieves In The Temple Blues/ God Is Standing At Your Side/ Bays Will Be Boys/ Goodbye/ Brand New Boy/ Good Man/ My Tree/ Eliminate The Negative/ Tony's Iggnant Mix/ Love...Thy Will Be Done/ Juice/ The Ryde Dyvine/ Thunder
R: Vg sound.   S: Outtakes.

CD - ROADHOUSE
RDH-1 070684
17 Days/ Our Destiny/ Roadhouse/ 17 Days/ Our Destiny/ Roadhouse/ All Day, All Night/ Free/ Erotica City, All The Critics Love U In New York/ Something In The Water (Doesn't Compute)/ Irresistible Bitch/ When Doves Cry/ Possessed
R: Audience.   S: Matinee, First Avenue, Minneapolis June 7 '84.

CD - SEXUALITY
SULY-211181
Second Coming/ Sexuality/ Why You Wanna Treat Me So Bad/ Jack U Off/ When You Were Mine/ I Wanna Be Your Lover/ Head/ Annie Christian/ Dirty Mind/ Do Me, Baby/ Let's Work/ Controversy
R: Ex. Soundboard recording.   S: Warner Theatre, Washington Nov. 21 '81.

CD - STARS & BARS
LGB001
CD1: Intro/ The Ride/ Come/ Endorphinemachine/ Space/ Interactive/ Days Of Wild/ Now/ Acknowledge Me
CD2: Dark/ Instrumental/ Race/ The Jam/ I Believe In You/ I'm In The Mood/ Peach

R: Good audience recording.   S: Club Stars And Bars, Monte Carlo May 4 '94.

CD - SUPER HERO
SPO -1 180395
CD1: Purple Medley/ Endorphine Machine/ The Jam/ Shh/ Days Of Wild/ Now/ It Takes Two/ The Most Beautiful Girl In The World/ Pussy Control/ Letitgo/ Pink Cashmere/ Lemme See Your Body (Get Loose)
CD2: I Love You In Me/ Peach/ Instrumental - Mayte's Sword Dance/ '7'/ Get Wild/ Gold/ Bonus Tracks (7-10)
R: Vg. Audience.   S: Birmingham, UK Mar. 18 '95.   C: ECD. Dcc. Time CD1 59:46. CD2 62:09.

CD - THUNDER
TRN-1/2 240692
CD1: Intro/ Thunder/ Daddy Pop/ Diamonds And Pearls/ Let's Go Crazy/ Kiss/ Jughead/ Dead On It/ Purple Rain/ Live 4 Love/ Willing And Able/ Damn U/ Sexy M.F.
CD2: Oriental Intro/ Thieves In The Temple/ It/ A Night In Tunisia/ Strollin' (Instrumental)/ Insatiable/ Get Off/ The Flow/ Cream/ Chain Of Fools/ Bonus Track: Erotic City '92
R: Ex.   S: Earl's Court, London June 24 '92. C: ECD. Dcc. With NPG.

PRONG

CD - ENTER NIGHTMARE
OCTOPUS OCTO 052
Beg To Differ (4:20)/ Lost And Found (4:09)/ Whose Fist Is This Anyway? (6:07)/ Cut Rate (4:43)/ I'll Give You Hell If I Could (5:18)/ Broken Peace (3:24)/ Another Worldly Device (3:28)/ Prove You Wrong (7:59)/ Home Rule (4:34)/ Unconditional (7:13)/ Snap Your Fingers, Snap Your Neck (5:39)
R: Exs. Soundboard.   S: Live Europe June '94. C: ECD. Dcc.

PSYCHEDELIC FURS

CD - FORBIDDEN
BEECH MARTEN RECORDS BM 094
Merry-Go-Round (4:17)/ Run And Run (4:14)/ Love My Way (3:52)/ No Easy Street (5:23)/ Angels (4:20)/ Danger (2:28)/ Goodbye (4:58)/ Pretty In Pink (4:01)/ She Is Mine (3:42)/ Sister Europe (5:08)/ Into You Like A Train (5:05)
R: Exs. Soundboard.   S: The Hammersmith Odeon, London '82.   C: ECD. Dcc.

PUBLIC IMAGE LIMITED

CD - BOXING DAY
RAG DOLL MUSIC RDM-951020
Theme/ Low Life/ Belsen Was A Gas/ Annalisa/ Public Image/ Sod In Heaven/ Attack/ Public Image Good-Byeee
R: Poor audience recording. Hiss.   S: Debut live

performance, Rainbow Theatre, London Dec. 25 or 26 '78.   C: Japanese CD.

PULP

CD - CAFE' CONCERTO
OXYGEN OXY 043
Do You Remember The First Time? (5:00)/ Pencil Skirt (4:08)/ I Spy (6:30)/ Driving On A Saturday Night (3:55)/ Sorted For E's And Wizz (3:59)/ Live Bed Show (4:45)/ Acrylic Afternoons (6:02)/ Babies (4:25)/ Disco 2000 (5:55)/ Mis-Shapes (3:40)/ F.E.E.L.I.N.G.C.A.L.L.E.D.L.O.V.E. (5:23)/ Underwear (4:51)/ Common People (7:30)
R: Exs. Soundboard.   S: Melkweg, Amsterdam, Holland Dec. 8 '95.   C: ECD. Pic CD.

CD - MADE IN FRANCE
MOONRAKER 037
Intro/ Sorted For E's And Wizz/ Do You Remember The First Time?/ I Spy/ Underwear/ Live Bed Show/ Acrylic Afternoons/ Babies/ Disco 2000/ Common People/ Common People (Canal + Nov. 16 '95)*
R: Ex. Audience. *Exs. Soundboard.   S: Le Zenith, Paris Nov. 14 '95.   C: ECD. Dbw. Time 52:25

Q

QUATRO, SUZIE

CD - YOUR MAMA WON'T LIKE ME
REEL TAPES RTCD001
Soundcheck Instrumental 1 (4:42)/ Soundcheck Instrumental 2 (3:06)/ Your Mama Won't Like Me (3:25)/ House Announcer (0:33)/ All Shook Up (4:18)/ Medley: 48 Crash, G-Men, Too Big (4:32)/ The Wild One (3:06)/ Your Mama Won't Like Me (Reprise) (3:23)/ You Can Make Me Want You (But You Can't Make Me Love You) (3:31)/ I May Be Too Young (3:03)/ Cat Size (3:57)/ Glycerine Queen (3:26)/ Shakin' All Over (8:00)/ Instrumental Rhythm & Blues (4:56)/ Can The Can (4:59)/ Devil Gate Drive (4:36)/ Keep A Knockin' (4:22)
R: G-Vg. Audience.   S: Rimini 'L'Altro Mondo' Aug. 15 '75.   C: ECD.

QUEEN

CD - A NIGHT AT THE COURT
TARANTULA TNT 007/8
CD1: Procession/ Tie Your Mother Down/ Ogre Battle/ White Queen/ Somebody To Love/ Killer Queen/ Good Old Fashioned Lover Boy/ Millionaire Waltz/ You're My Best Friend/ Bring Back That Leroy Brown/ Death On Two Legs/ Brighton Rock/ 39/ You Take My Breathe Away/ White Man/ Prophet's Song
CD2: Bohemian Rhapsody/ Stone Cold Crazy/ In The Lap Of The Gods Revisited/ Now I'm Here/

Liar/ Lucille/ Jail House Rock/ Stupid Cupid/ Be Bop A Lula/ God Save The Queen/ Procession/ Father To Son/ Son And Daughter/ Ogre Battle/ Hangman/ Keep Yourself Alive (Cut) R: Vg. Soundboard. Some wobble.   S: Earls Court, London June 6 '77. CD2 tracks 11-16 Town Hall, Birmingham, England, Nov. 21 '73 - opening act for Mott The Hoople.   C: ECD. Dcc.

CD - REINA DE IPANEMA
BABY CAPONE BC 008
Tie Your Mother Down (4:56)/ Seven Seas Of Rhye (1:53)/ Keep Yourself Alive (2:47)/ Liar (1:54)/ It's A Hard Life (4:22)/ Now I'm Here (5:42)/ Is This The World We Created? (3:03)/ Love Of My Life (4:25)/ Brighton Rock (3:08)/ Hammer To Fall (4:56)/ Bohemian Rhapsody (5:16)/ Radio Gaga (6:12)/ I Want To Break Free (3:23)/ We Will Rock You (2:29)/ We Are The Champions (4:07)/ God Save The Queen (1:57) R: Exs. Soundboard.   S: Rio De Janeiro, Brazil Jan. 11 85.   C: ECD. Dcc. Pic CD.

CD - THE ULTIMATE QUEEN BACK CATALOGUE VOLUME 1
Doing Alright/ April Lady/ Polar Bear/ Earth/ Step On Me/ I Can Hear Music/ Goin' Back/ Mad The Swine/ See What A Fool I've Been/ Misfire/ A Human Body/ Soul Brother/ Go Crazy/ Thank God It's Christmas/ Man On The Prowl/ Keep Passing The Open Windows/ One Vision/ Blurred Vision R: Vg.   S: Outtakes.

CD - ZOOM
LLX-1/2
CD1: Bohemian Rhapsody/ Ogre Battle/ Sweet Lady/ White Queen (As It Began)/ Flick Of The Wrist/ Bohemian Rhapsody/ Killer Queen/ The March Of The Black Queen, Bohemian Rhapsody/ Bring Back That Leroy Brown/ Brighton Rock/ Son And Daughter/ The Prophet's Song/ Stone Cold Crazy
CD2: Doing All Right/ Lazing On A Sunday Afternoon/ Keep Yourself Alive/ Liar/ In The Lap of The Gods/ Now I'm Here/ Rock And Roll Medley/ God Save The Queen R: Vg audience recording.   S: Kouseinenkin Hall, Osaka, Japan Mar. 29 '76.

QUEENSRYCHE

CD - ASTORIA THEATRE '94
ONE OFF MUSIC Q1000
Empire (4:34)/ Anarchy X/ Revolution Calling (6:13)/ Damaged (5:40)/ Promised Land (8:03)/ Disconnected (5:25)/ The Killing Words (4:09)/ Della Brown (7:03)/ Bridge (4:19)/ Silent Lucidity (6:31)/ The Lady Wore Black (6:11)/ My Empty Room Real World (6:52)/ I Don't Believe In Love (5:29)/ Eyes Of A Stranger (7:20) R: Vg-Exs. Soundboard.   S: The Astoria Theatre, London, England Oct. 20 '94.   C: ECD. Dcc. Pic CD.

CD - THE DAYS BEFORE THE EMPIRE
GREAT MUSIC HISTORY DREAM 003
Waiting For The Kill Prophecy/ Child Of Fire/ Before The Storm/ Sanctuary/ The Warning/ Roads To Madness/ Scarborough Fair/ Walk In The Shadow
R: Good. Hiss.   S: Tracks 1-7 'The Warning' demos. Tracks 8-9 'Myth' demos.

CD - SAINTS AND SINNERS
KISS THE STONE KTS 460/61
CD1: 9.28 A.M./ I Am I/ Damaged/ Bridge/ Screaming In Digital NM 156/ My Global Mind/ Neue Regel/ I Remember Now Anarchy X Revolution Calling/ Operation Mindcrime/ Spreading The Disease/ The Mission/ I Don't Believe In Love/ My Empty Room
CD2: Eyes Of A Stranger/ Empire/ Jet City Woman/ Promised Land/ Dis-Con-Nec-Ted/ Lady Jane/ Out Of Mind/ One More Time/ Silent Lucidity/ Take Hold Of The Flame/ Someone Else R: Exs. Soundboard.   S: The San Jose Arena, San Jose, CA May 5 '95.   C: ECD. Dcc. Pic CD. Time CD1 60:32. CD2 63:32.

CD - STATE OF ART
OXYGEN OXY 016/017
CD1: 9.28 A.M. (1:48)/ I Am I (3:52)/ Damaged (4:06)/ Bridge (3:31)/ Screaming In Digital (2:38)/ NM 156 (2:59)/ My Global Mind (4:15)/ Neue Regel (2:58)/ I Remember Now (1:01)/ Anarchy X (1:27)/ Revolution Calling (4:58)/ Operation Mindcrime (4:12)/ Spreading The Disease (5:07)/ The Mission (5:50)/ I Don't Believe In Love (4:24)/ Waiting For 22 (1:13)/ My Empty Room (2:48)/ Real World (3:14)/ Eyes Of A Stranger (7:52)
CD2: Empire (5:26)/ Jet City Woman (5:14)/ Promised Land (8:13)/ Disconnected (4:43)/ Lady Jane (5:31)/ Out Of Mind (4:46)/ One More Time (5:32)/ Silent Lucidity (5:42)/ Take Hold Of The Flame (5:47)/ Someone Else? (4:44)/ Bridge (3:28)/ Silent Lucidity (5:40)/ The Lady Wore Black (4:54)
R: Exs. Soundboard.   S: San Jose Arena, San Jose, CA May 24 '95. CD2 Tracks 11-12 acoustic session, Rock FM Studio, Milano, Italy Oct. 28 '94. CD2 Track 13 acoustic session, Vara Studio, Hilversum, Holland Nov. '94.   C: ECD. Dcc. Pic CD.

CD - UNPLUGGED AND OTHER STORIES
OCTOPUS OCTO 165
I Will Remember (acoustic) (4:00)/ The Killing Words (3:57)/ Della Brown (acoustic) (5:53)/ Silent Lucidity (acoustic) (5:26)/ The Lady Wore Black (acoustic) (5:20)/ Prophecy (3:49)/ Blinded (4:27)/ The Lady Wore Black (electric) (3:29)/ Queen Of The Reich (7:01)/ Deliverance (3:45)/ Child Of Fire (4:43)/ En Force (5:40)/ Warning (5:23)/ Take Hold Of My Flame (5:01) R: Exs. Soundboard.   S: Tracks 1-5 MTV Unplugged. Tracks 6-9 NYC Oct. '83. Track 10 Budokan, Tokyo '85.   C: ECD. Dcc. Pic CD.

QUICKSILVER MESSENGER SERVICE

CD - SUMMER OF'68
BLUE KNIGHT BKR 033
Light Your Windows/ Dino's Song/ The Fool/ Who Do You Love?/ Mona-Maiden Of The Cancer Moon/ Smokestack Lightning*/ Codine*/ Back Door Man*/ Acapulco Gold And Silver*
R: Ex. Soundboard.   S: Fillmore East, New York June '68. *Pacific High Studios '68.   C: ECD. Time 78:01.

QUIET RIOT

CD - DEMOS FOR NEVER RELEASED 3RD LP 1979
DEMONIC SOUNDS
Unknown/ Mighty Quinn/ Unknown/ Gonna Have A Riot/ Breaking Up Is A Heartache/ Picking Up The Pieces/ One In A Million/ Gonna Be A Shake Down/ Unknown/ Slick Black Cadillac/ One In A Million/ Picking Up The Pieces
R: Poor soundboard. Hiss.   S: Tracks 10-12 Whisky A Go Go '78.

R

RAGE AGAINST THE MACHINE

CD - LIVE
THE SWINGIN' PIG TSP-CD-173
Killing In The Name/ Township Rebellion/ Know Your Enemy/ Bullet In The Head/ Bombtrack/ Wake Up/ Settle For Nothing/ Freedom/ Fistful Of Steel
R: Exs. Soundboard.   S: Tracks 1-5 Campingflight Festival, Dongen, NL Aug. 29 '93. Tracks 6-8 Melkweg, Amsterdam, NL Feb. 17 '93. Track 9 Pinkpop Festival, Landgraaf, NL May 31 '93.   C: ECD. Dcc. Time 49:07.

RAINBOW

CD - CAPTURED LIVE
RBW-3412/13
CD1: Spotlight Kid/ Miss Mistreated/ Fool For The Night/ I Surrender/ Can't Happen Here/ Difficult To Cure
CD2: Death Alley Driver/ Catch The Rainbow/ Drinkin' With The Devil/ Power/ Blues/ Stargazer/ Stranded/ All Night Long/ Maybe Next Time/ Since You Been Gone/ Long Live Rock'N'Roll
R: Ex.   S: Cardiff Sept. 14 '83.

CD - DANGEROUS EXPRESS
CRYSTAL SOUND CS10
CD1: Land Of Hope And Glory, Count Down, Over The Rainbow/ Eyes Of The World/ Love's No Friend/ Richie Blackmore Solo/ Since You've Been Gone, Over The Rainbow/ all Night Long/ Catch The Rainbow
CD2: Don Airey Solo (Part 1)/ Lost In Hollywood/

Richie Blackmore Solo, Difficult To Cure, Don Airey Solo (Part 2)/ Cozy Powell Solo/ 1812 Festival Overture, Op. 49/ Lost In Hollywood (Reprise)/ Lazy/ Man On The Silver Mountain, Blues/ Will You Still Love Me Tomorrow
R: Vg audience recording.   S: Stockholm Jan. 18 '80.

CD - #9
RACD-111179
Intro: Over The Rainbow, Eyes Of The World/ Love's No Friend/ All Night Long/ Lost In Hollywood, Beethoven's Symphony No. 9, Keyboard Solo, 1812 Overture/ Man On The Silver Mountain, Blues/ Long Love Rock'N'Roll
R: Ex audience recording.   S: Santa Monica, CA Nov. 11 '79.

CD - ON LINE
NIGHTLIFE N-021
Land Of Hope And Glory, Count Down, Over The Rainbow/ Eyes Of The World/ Love's No Friend/ Since You've Been Gone, Over The Rainbow/ Stargazer/ Man On The Silver Mountain/ Catch The Rainbow/ Keyboard Solo, Lost In Hollywood, Guitar Solo, Difficult To Cure, Keyboard Solo (Singing In The Rain)/ End (Somewhere Over The Rainbow)
R: Vg-Ex audience recording.   S: Malmo, Sweden Aug. 9 '80.   C: Japanese CD.

CD - ON STAGE IN DOWN UNDER 1976
MN52-9321/22
CD1: Over The Rainbow/ Kill The King/ Mistreated/ 16th Century Green Sleeves/ Catch The Rainbow/ Man On The Silver Mountain, Blues/ Keyboard Solo
CD2: Stargazer/ Still I'm Sad, Drum Solo '1812'/ Long Live Rock'N'Roll (rough take)/ LA Connection (rough take)/ Gates Of Babylon (rough take)
R: G-Vg. Audience and studio takes.   S: Sidney, Australia Nov. 11 '76. CD2 tracks 2-5 'Long Live Rock'N'Roll' outtakes.

CD - MIXED EMOTIONS
BABY CAPONE BC 021/2
CD1: Over The Rainbow (1:54)/ Spotlight Kid (4:56)/ Miss Mistreated (4:38)/ Can't Happen Here (4:09)/ Tearing Out My Heart (9:42)/ All Night Long (6:52)/ Power (4:31)/ Blues Interlude (2:32)/ Difficult To Cure (2:41)/ The Ninth (6:30)
CD2: Beethoven Ninth (3:25)/ Ode To Joy (3:55)/ Drums Solo (5:21)/ Long Live Rock 'N' Roll (12:19)/ Instrumental (1:52)/ Smoke On The Water (3:28)/ Bonus Extra Tracks: Bad Girl (4:55)/ Since You've Been Gone (5:05)/ I Surrender (3:38)/ Man On The Silver Mountain (3:17)/ Blackmore Solo (1:50)/ Blues Forever (1:55)/ Man On the Silver Mountain (Reprise) (2:14)/ Lazy, Woman From Tokyo (1:58)/ Smoke On Water II (5:01)
R: Exs. Soundboard.   S: Texas '82.   C: ECD. Dcc. Pic CDs.

CD - OVER MELBOURNE
RED HOT RH-010/011
CD1: Intro, Kill The King/ Mistreated/ 16th
Century Greensleeves/ Catch The Rainbow/ Man
On Silver Mountain/ Stargazer/ Still I'm Sad
(includes Drum Solo and 1812 Overture)
CD2: Do You Close Your Eyes, Taped Outro/
Interview - Ritchie Blackmore
R: Vg-Ex audience recording.   S: Festival Hall,
Melbourne, Australia Nov. 9 '76. CD2 track 2
Melbourne, Australia Nov. 21 '76.

CD - ROGER'S BIRTHDAY PARTY
BONDAGE MUSIC BON 010
Intro: Over The Rainbow, Eyes Of The World/
Love's No Friend/ Since You Been Gone/ All Night
Long/ Lost In Hollywood, Beethoven's 9th,
Keyboard Solo, Drum Solo/ Man Of The Silver
Mountain, Blues, Long Live Rock'N'Roll, Over
The Rainbow
R: Vg. Some hiss.   S: Calderone Hall, New York
Nov. 30 '79.   C: Japanese CD.

RAITT, BONNIE

CD - STORM WARNING
KISS THE STONE KTS 425
Longing In Their Hearts/ Circle Dance/ I'm In The
Mood/ Come To Me/ Fear Of Falling/ Storm
Warning/ Love Sneakin' Up On You/ Falling In
Love Is Wonderful/ Oklahoma/ Thing Called Love/
I Can't Make You Love Me/ Love Sneakin' Up On
You
R: Ex.   S: The Arlington Theatre, Santa
Barbara, CA '94. Track 10 Los Angeles Feb. 20
'90. Track 11 New York Feb. 25 '92. Track 12 Los
Angeles Mar. 1 '95.   C: ECD. Dbw. Pic CD.
Time 55:50.

RAMONES

CD - GABBA GABBA HEY
WEEPING GOAT WG-017
Teenage Lobotomy/ Psycho Therapy/ Blitzkrieg
Bop/ Do You Remember Rock'N'Roll Radio/
Ranger Zone/ Gimmie Gimmie Shock Treatment/
Rock'N'Roll High School/ I Wanna Be Sedated/
Beat On The Brat/ I'm Affected/ Too Tough To Die/
Chinese Rock/ Wart Hog/ Rockaway Beach/
Surfin' Bird/ Cretin' Hop/ California Sun/ Today
Your Love, Tomorrow The World/ Pinhead
R: G.   S: Ritz, NYC Dec. 27 '84.
C: Japanese CD.

RANCID

CD - BURN THE CITY DOWN
PITCHFORK RECORDS PF1100
The Sentence/ I'm Not The Only One/ To Hell/
Media Controller/ Battering Ram/ Idle Hands/
Unwritten Rules/ Trenches/ Opposition/ Inhalation/
Animosity/ Borderline/ Rats In The Hallway/
Institution/ Moonlight/ Situation/ Whirlwind/ Bad
Police Man/ Trenches/ Unwritten Rules Take You/

The Line/ Burn The City Down
R: Ex. Soundboard.   S: Studio Demos.
C: Time 52:25.

CD - DEMOS FROM THE PIT
The Sentence/ I'm Not The Only One/ To Hell
(unreleased)/ Media Controller/ Battering Ram/
Idle Hands/ Unwritten Roles/ Trenches/
Opposition (unreleased)/ Inhalation (unreleased)/
Animosity/ Borderline (unreleased)/ Rats In The
Hallway/ Institution (unreleased)/ Moonlight (unre-
leased)/ Situation (unreleased)/ Whirlwind/ Bad
Policeman (unreleased)/ Trenches/ Unwritten
Rules/ Take You (unreleased)/ The Line (unre-
leased)/ Burn The City Down (unreleased)
R: Ex. Soundboard.   C: Red/black cover. White
type. Pic CD says 'Kaos Kids'. Time 52:28.

R.E.M.

CD - ADHESION
KISS THE STONE KTS 471/72
CD1: What's The Frequency Kenneth?/ Crush
With Eyeliner/ Drive/ Turn You Inside Out/ Try Not
To Breathe/ I Took Your Name/ Undertow/ Bang
And Blame/ I Don't Sleep, I Dream/ Strange
Currencies/ Revolution/ Tongue/ Man On The
Moon
CD2: Country Feedback/ Half A World Away/
Losing My Religion/ Pop Song '89/ Finest
Worksong/ Get Up/ Star 69/ Let Me In/ Everybody
Hurts/ Band Introductions/ Fall On Me/ Departure/
It's The End Of The World As We Know It (And I
Feel Fine)
R: Vg-Ex. Audience.   S: Milton Keynes July 30
'95.   C: ECD. Dcc. Pic CD.

CD - ANEURYSM '95
KISS THE STONE KTS 447/48
CD1: What's The Frequency Kenneth? (4:21)/
Circus Envy (4:30)/ Crush With Eyeliner (4:58)/
Drive (3:54)/ Me In Honey (4:10)/ Try Not To
Breathe (4:17)/ I Don't Sleep, I Dream (4:26)/
Strange Currencies (4:54)/ Revolution (3:26)/
Tongue (5:02)/ Man On The Moon (5:56)/ Country
Feedback (5:52)
CD2: Monty Got A Raw Deal (4:02)/ Losing My
Religion (4:59)/ So. Central Rain (4:10)/ Star Me
Kitten (3:43)/ I Took Your Name (3:41)/ Star 69 (2:52)/ Get Up (6:00)/ Let Me In
(3:53)/ Everybody Hurts (7:23)/ Pop Song '89
(3:24)/ Bang And Blame (4:59)/ It's The End Of
The World As We Know It (5:19)
R: Vg-Ex. Audience.   S: The Shoreline
Amphitheater, Mountain View, CA May 15 '95.
C: ECD. Blue/black/red cover. Pic CD.

CD - BALLROOM DANCING
HOME RECORDS HR6043-5
Femme Fatale/ Radio Free Europe/ Gardening At
Night/ 9-9/ Windout/ Letters Never Sent/ Sitting
Still/ Driver 8/ South Central Rain/ 7 Chinese
Brothers/ Harbor Coat/ Hyena/ Pretty Persuasion/
Little America/ Second Guessing/ Don't Go Back,

To Rockville/ What's The Frequency, Kenneth?/ Bang And Blame/ I Don't Sleep, I Dream/ Hello In There
R: Ex. Soundboard.   S: Aragon Ballroom, Chicago July 7 '84. Tracks 17-19 'Saturday Night Live', New York City Nov. 12 '94. Track 20 Scotland '90 with Natalie Merchant and Billy Bragg.   C: ECD. Dcc. Time 70:32.

CD - HERE BE MONSTERS
SOS-008
What's The Frequency, Kenneth?/ Circus Envy/ I Took Your Name/ Drive/ You/ Revolution/ Try Not To Breath/ Tongue/ Man On The Moon/ I Don't Sleep, I Dream/ Bang And Blame/ Star 69/ Let Me In/ Everybody Hurts/ Crush With Eyeliner
R: Ex.   S: '95.

CD - MONSTER RADIO
MOONRAKER 023/24
CD1: I Took Your Name/ What's The Frequency, Kenneth?/ Crush With Eyeliner/ Me In Honey/ Bang And Blame/ Near Wild Heaven/ Undertow/ Welcome To The Occupation/ You/ Strange Currencies/ Revolution/ Tounge/ Man On The Moon/ Country Feedback
CD2: Losing My Religion/ Pop Song 89/ Finest Worksong/ Get Up/ Star 69/ Let Me In/ Everybody Hurts/ So. Central Rain/ Departure/ Tusk, Ghost Riders/ It's The End Of The World As We Know It (And I Feel Fine)/ Wake Up Bomb*
R: Exs. Soundboard.   S: The Monster Tour, Berlin, Germany Aug. 1 '95. *MTV Video Music Awards, NYC '95.   C: ECD. Dcc. Time CD1 68:23. CD2 61:22.

CD - PLUGGELECTRIC
SWINDLE RECORDS SWN SP 002
Half A World Away (3:52)/ Disturbance At The Heron House (4:00)/ Radio Song (4:31)/ Low (5:04)/ Perfect Circle (4:16)/ Fall On Me (3:24)/ Belong (4:37)/ Love Is All Around 'Reg Presley (3:40)/ It's The End Of The World As We Know It (And I Feel Fine) (4:57)/ Losing My Religion (5:12)/ Pop Song (3:29)/ Instrumental (La La La) (3:16)/ The One I Love (3:32)/ These Days (3:47)/ Corporation (4:15)/ Intro-Feeling The Gravity's Pull (6:24)/ Get Up (3:14)/ It's The End Of The World As We Know It (And I Feel Fine) (4:25)
R: Exs. Soundboard.   S: Tracks 1-13 MTV Unplugged, New York Oct. 1 '94. Tracks 14-18 '93 US Tour.   C: ECD. Dcc.

CD - RISING
SPQR03CD
Wolves, Lower/ Moral Kiosk/ Laughing/ Pilgrimage/ Moon River/ There She Goes Again/ 7 Chinese Brothers/ Talk About The Passion/ Sitting Still/ Harbourcoat/ Pretty Persuasion/ Gardening At Night/ 9-9/ Just A Touch/ West Of The Fields/ Radio Free Europe/ We Walk/ 1,000,000/ Carnival Of Sorts
R: Exs. Soundboard.   S: Larry's Hideaway,

Toronto July 9 '83.   C: ECD. Dcc. Time 72:02.

CD - ROUGH
SUGARCANE RECORDS SC 52015
Laughing/ Pilgrimage/ There She Goes Again/ Seven Chinese Brothers/ Talk About The Passion/ Sitting Still/ Harbour Coat/ Catapult/ Gardening At Night/ 9-9/ Just A Touch/ West Of The Fields/ Radio Free Europe/ We Walk/ 1,000,000.
R: G-Vg. Soundboard.   S: Claims to be Rhythmic Studios Sept. 11 '93 however some experts think it's from a US club gig in '83.
C: Tracks fade in and out. Time: 50:52

CD - SLEEPING SONGS
DYNAMITE STUDIO DS94J105
Finest Worksong/ Welcome To The Occupation/ Exhuming McCarthy/ Disturbance At The Heron House/ Pop Song 89/ It's The End Of The World As We Know It (And I Feel Fine)/ Orange Crush/ Fireplace/ Lightnin' Hopkins/ I Remember California/ Oddfellows Local/ Get Up/ You Are The Everything
R: Vgs.   S: 'Green' and 'Document' outtakes.
C: Japanese CD.

CD - UNPLUGGED COMPLETELY
KMACD008
Half A World Away (3:34)/ Disturbance At The Heron House (4:00)/ Radio Song (4:31)/ Low (5:01)/ Don't Give It Up (4:16)/ Fall On Me (3:26)/ Belong (4:30)/ Love Is All Around (3:42)/ It's The End Of The World (4:55)/ Losing My Religion (4:53)/ Should We Talk About The Weather (3:18)/ The One I Love (4:30)/ Welcome To The Occupation (2:45)/ Disturbance At The Heron House II (3:40)/ Finest Worksong (3:38)/ Maps And Legends (3:40)/ Harpers (1:10)/ Dark Globe (2:20)/ One (4:24)/ Moon River (2:28)*
R: Ex. Soundboard. *Ex. Audience.   S: Tracks 1-11 MTV Unplugged Apr. '91. Tracks 12-17 McCabes Guitar Shop May 24 '87. Track 18 Milan May 15 '89. Track 19 Washington Jan. 20 '93 with Larry Mullen and Adam Clayton. Track 20 Borderline, London May 15 '91.   C: ECD. Dcc.

CD - WELCOME TO THE FREAK SHOW
OCTOPUS OCTO 201/202
CD1: What's The Frequency, Kenneth?/ Crush With Eyeliner/ Driver/ Turn Your Inside-Out/ Try Not To Breathe/ I Took Your Name/ Undertow/ Bang And Blame/ I Don't Sleep, I Dream/ Strange Currencies/ Revolution/ Tongue
CD2: Man On The Moon/ Country Feedback/ Half A World Away/ Losing My Religion/ Should We Talk About The Weather/ Finest Worksong/ Get Up/ Star 69/ Let Me In/ Everybody Hurts/ Fall On Me/ Baby Come/ It's The End Of The World As We Know It (And I Feel Fine)
R: Exs. Soundboard.   S: The National Bowl, Milton Keynes, UK July 29 '95.   C: ECD. Dcc.

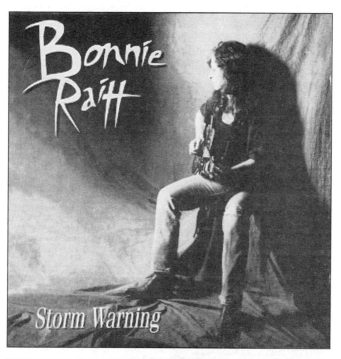

RED HOT CHILI PEPPERS, THE

CD - ONE HOT GLOBE
MOONRAKER 025/26
CD1: Give It Away/ Suck My Kiss/ Pippi
Longstockings/ Aeroplane/ Warped/ Walkabout/
Come As You Are/ Backwoods/ My Friends/
Coffee Shop/ Sound And Vision/ Higher Ground/
Transcending
CD2: Pea/ One Big Mob/ Under The Bridge/ The
Power Of Equality/ Deep Kick/ Me And My
Friends/ Bonus: Aeroplane/ Warped/ Walkabout/
Backwoods/ Coffee Shop/ Suffragette City/
Warped
R: Vg-Ex. Audience.   S: Globe Arena,
Stockholm Oct. 14 '95.   C: ECD. Dcc.
Time CD1 52:54. CD2 66:02.

CD - PORNO ZOMBIE
BABY CAPONE BC 050/2
CD1: Out In LA (2:12)/ Stone Bush (3:47)/
Standing (1:57)/ Pretty (2:29)/ Higher Ground
(3:28)/ Knock Me Down (4:06)/ Castles Made Of
Sand (3:45)/ Me And My Friends (2:45)/ Funky
Crime (3:12)/ Nobody Weird Like Me (5:02)/ If
You Have To Ask (4:24)/ Stone Cold Bush (3:54)/
Blood Sugar Sex Magic (4:27)/ Me And My
Friends (2:55)/ Nobody Weird Like Me (4:01)/ Tiny
Dancer (2:03)/ Pussy You Sure Look Good To Me
(4:50)/ Higher Ground (3:43)/ Mummy Where's
Daddy (4:24)/ Knock Me Down (4:02)
CD2: Love Trilogy (3:45)/ Organic Anti Beat Box
(4:11)/ Bullet Proof (2:05)/ Suck My Kiss (3:24)/
Black Eyed Blonde (2:25)/ Funky Crime (2:52)/
Give It Away (4:22)/ Nobody (4:37)/ If You Have
To Ask (4:38)/ Stone Cold Bush (3:26)/ Blood
Sugar Sex Magic (4:00)/ Magic Johnson (1:56)/ I
Could Have Lied (4:22)/ Subway To Venus (4:12)/
Funky Time Turtle (2:39)/ Crosstown Traffic (2:39)
R: Exs. Soundboard.   S: CD1 Tracks 1-8
Phoenix, Arizona Dec. 23 '90. CD1 Tracks 9-20
Rotterdam '92. CD2 NY Dec. 24 '91.   C: ECD.
Dcc. Pic CD.

CD - SLAP HAPPY
OXYGEN OXY 023
Give It Away (7:33)/ Suck My Kiss (4:06)/
Aeroplane (4:48)/ Warped (5:34)/ Walkabout
(6:08)/ Backwoods (Including Excerpt From:
Come As You Are) (5:15)/ My Friends (5:23)/
Sweet Home Alabama (1:05)/ Coffee Shop (3:27)/
Higher Ground (Including Excerpt From: Sound
And Vision) (4:39)/ Hey Joe (0:53)/ Transcending
(5:36)/ Pea (2:02)/ Under The Bridge (5:29)/ Deep
Kick (7:02)/ Suffragette City (4:48)
R: Exs. Soundboard.   S: Ahoy, Rotterdam,
Holland Oct. 16 '95.   C: ECD. Dbw. Gold type.
Pic CD.

CD - WHAT LIVE ALBUM?
THE SWINGIN' PIG TSP-CD-174
Love Trilogy/ Hollywood/ Bullet Proof/ Suck My
Kiss/ Blackeyed Blonde/ Do What I Wanna Do/
Give It Away/ Nobody Weird Like Me/ If You Have
To Ask/ Stone Cold Bush/ Blood Sugar Sex
Magic/ I Could Have Lied/ Subway To Venus/ Me
And My Friends
R: Exs. Soundboard.   S: O'Brien Pavilion, Del
Mar Fairgrounds, CA '92.   C: ECD. Dcc.
Time 54:47.

REED, LOU

CD - PHANTOM ANIMAL
THE GOLD STANDARD SRE-8
Intro, Sweet Jane/ How Do You Think It Feels?/
Caroline Says/ I'm Waiting For The Man/ Satellite
Of Love/ Walk On The Wild Side/ Oh Jim/ Heroin/
Rock And Roll/ White Light White Heat/ Vicious
R: G-Vg. Audience.   S: Copenhagen Sept. 19
'73.   C: Time 72:10.

CD - WAITING FOR THE GLITTERING MAN
TEDDY BEAR TB 77
Introduction (0:26)/ White Light, White Heat
(3:45)/ Vicious (3:08)/ I'm Waiting For The Man
(6:57)/ Walk And Talk It (3:48)/ Sweet Jane (4:36)/
Heroin (8:22)/ Satellite Of Love (3:26)/ Walk On
The Wild Side (5:57)/ I'm So Free (3:31)/ Berlin
(5:41)/ Rock And Roll (5:05)
R: Exs. Soundboard.   S: Hampstead Dec. 26
'72.   C: ECD. Dcc. Pic CD.

REVELATION

CD - THE EARLY YEARS 1987- 1988
War Between Race/ Always, A Friend For Life/
Will You Ever Come Back/ Take A Stand/ Wound
Up/ Under 18/ We're The Crew/ As One/ Better
Than You/ Talk Is Cheap/ Together/ My Life/
Violence To Fade/ Searchin For The Light/ It's
Clobberin' Time, Just Lies/ Pete's Sake/ Friends
Like You/ Bullshit Justice/ Pay The Price/ Pushed
To Far, Give Respect/ The Deal/ N.S./ My
Revenge/ High Hopes/ Big Mouth/ No Reason
Why/ GM2/ Hold Your Ground/ Breaking Free/
Finish What You Started/ Backfire/ My Life To
Live/ Living A Lie/ Look Back/ You're Only Young
Once/ Friends/ Side By Side/ Just Say No/ You
Laugh/ When Will It End?/ Without Reason/ Liar/
About Face
R: Ex. Soundboard. Some surface noise.
C: Gray/white cover. Blue type. Disc says 'Jazz
Masters Vol 5'. 44 tracks. Time 67:03.

RODGERS, PAUL

CD - PAUL RODGERS IN CONCERT
HQ 02
Muddy Water Blues/ Can't Get Enough/ Good
Morning Little School Girl/ Standing Around And
Crying/ Rollin' Stone/ Little Wing/ All Right Now/
Feel Like Making Love/ Can't Be Satisfied/
Louisiana Blues/ The Hunter/ Rock Me Baby/
Crossroads
R; Exs. Soundboard.   S: The Great American
Music Hall, San Francisco May 19 '93.
C: ECD. Digi-pack.

ROLLING STONES, THE

CD - A STICKY SYDENHAM RACECOURSE '73
R-187-22-7A
Brown Sugar/ Bitch/ Rocks Off/ Gimme Shelter/
Happy/ Tumbling Dice/ Love In Vain/ Sweet
Virginia/ You Can't Always Get What You Want/
Honky Tonk Women/ All Down The Line*/
Midnight Rambler*/ Little Queenie*/ Rip This Joint
R: G-Vg. Soundboard. *G. Soundboard.
S: Royal Randwick Racecourse, Sydney Feb. 26
'73.   C: Time 67:18.

CD - ACOUSTIC
TYPHOON TYN 001/02
CD1: Not Fade Away/ It's All Over Now/ Live With
Me/ Let It Bleed/ Beast Of Burden/ Angie/ Wild
Horses/ Sweet Virginia/ Dead Flowers/ Still A
Fool/ Down In A Bottom/ Shine A Light/ Like A
Rolling Stone
CD2: Jump On Top Of Me/ Connection/ Band
Intro/ Before They Make Me Run/ Slippin' Away/
Monkey Man/ Can't Get Next To You/ All Down
The Line/ Street Fightin' Man/ Rip This Joint/
Respectable
R: Poor-G. Audience.   S: Amsterdam, Holland
May 27 '95.   C: ECD.

CD - AIN'T TOUCHED A DRINK ALL NIGHT
WEEPING GOAT WG-007
Bitch/ Rocks Off/ Gimme Shelter/ Happy/
Tumbling Dice/ Love In Vain/ Sweet Virginia/ You
Can't Always Get What You Want/ Midnight
Rambler/ Band Introduction/ Bye Bye Johnny/ Rip
This Joint/ Jumpin' Jack Flash/ Street Fighting
Man
R: Poor-G. Audience.   S: Tucson, Arizona June
11 '72.   C: Japanese CD. Dbw. Red type.
Time 67:24.

CD - ALL HALLOW'S EVE
THE SWINGIN' PIG TSP 195-2
CD1: Intro/ Not Fade Away/ Tumbling Dice/ You
Got Me Rocking/ Shattered/ Rocks Off/ Sparks
Will Fly/ (I Can't Get No) Satisfaction/ Beast Of
Burden/ Out Of Tears/ Doo Doo Doo Doo Doo
(Heartbreaker)/ Love Is Strong/ It's All Over Now/
I Go Wild
CD2: Miss You/ Band Introduction/ Honky Tonk
Women/ Before They Make Me Run/ The Worst/
Sympathy For The Devil/ Monkey Man/ Street
Fighting Man/ Start Me Up/ It's Only Rock'n'Roll/
Brown Sugar/ Jumping Jack Flash
R: Exs. Soundboard.   S: Alameda Stadium,
Oakland, CA Oct. 31 '94.   C: ECD.

CD - ALL RIGHT RESERVED
SHAVED DISC TSD014/15
Let It Rock/ All Down The Line/ Honky Tonk
Women/ Starfucker/ When The Whip Comes
Down/ Beast Of Burden/ Lies/ Miss You/
Shattered
CD2: Respectable/ Far Away Eyes/ Love In Vain/
Tumbling Dice/ Happy/ Sweet Little Sixteen/

Brown Sugar/ Jumpin' Jack Flash/ Satisfaction
R: Poor audience recording.   S: Oakland
Coliseum July 26 '78.

CD - ANDREW'S BLUES
DRAGONFLY RECORDS IMP-1126
Andrew's Blues/ Cocksucker Blues/ Everybody
Needs Somebody To Love/ Around And Around/
Off The Hook/ Time Is On My Side/ Carol/ It's All
Over Now/ Little Red Rooster/ Route 66/
Everybody Needs Somebody To Love/ The Last
Time/ I'm Alright/ Hey Crawdaddy/ You Can't
Always Get What You Want/ Sympathy For The
Devil/ Salt Of The Earth
R: Vg. Soundboard.   S: Track 1 Regent Sound
Studios, London Feb. 4 '64. Track 2 Olympic
Sound Studios and Mobile Recording Unit
Newbury May 9 - Aug. '70. Tracks 3-14 live
Olympia, Paris on Apr. 18 '65. Tracks 15-17
Intertel Studios, London Dec. 10-12 '68.
C: Japanese CD. Dcc. Time 59:57.

CD - AT THE MAX
ATM 1
Intro/ Start Me Up/ Sad Sad Sad/ Tumbling Dice/
Ruby Tuesday/ Rock And A Hard Place/ Honky
Tonk Woman/ You Can't Always Get What Wou
Want/ Happy/ Street Fighting Man/ Introduction/
It's Only Rock'N'Roll (But Like It)/ Brown Sugar/ I
Can't Get No Satisfaction
R: Exs.   S: London Aug. 25 '90.   C: Poster
included.

CD - BATON ROUGE 75
IDOL MIND PRODUCTIONS IMP-CD 018/19
CD1: Honky Tonk Women/ All Down The Line/ If
You Can't Rock Me, Get Off My Cloud/ You Gotta
Move/ Rocks Off/ Ain't Too Proud To Beg/ Star
Star/ Gimme Shelter/ Band Introduction/ Happy
CD2: Luxury/ Fingerprint File/ Angie/ That's Life/
Outta Space/ Midnight Rambler/ Dance Little
Sister/ Brown Sugar/ It's Only Rock'N'Roll/
Jumpin' Jack Flash/ Rip This Joint/ Street Fighting
Man
R: G-Vg audience recording.   S: First show,
Louisiana State University, Baton Rouge June 1
'75.   C: Japanese CD.

CD - BEAST OF BELGIUM / WERCHTER 1995
THE SWINGIN' PIG TSP 190-4
CD1: Intro/ Not Fade Away/ Tumbling Dice/ You
Got Me Rocking/ It's All Over Now/ Rocks Off/
Sparks Will Fly/ (I Can't Get No) Satisfaction/ Let
It Bleed/ Angie/ Like A Rolling Stone/ Doo Doo
Doo Doo Doo (Heartbreaker)/ Gimme Shelter/ I
Go Wild
CD2: Miss You/ Band Introduction/ Honky Tonk
Women/ Before They Make Me Run/ Slipping
Away/ Sympathy For The Devil/ Street Fighting
Man/ Start Me Up/ It's Only Rock'n'Roll/ Brown
Sugar/ Jumping Jack Flash
CD3: Intro/ Not Fade Away/ Tumbling Dice/ You
Got Me Rocking/ It's All Over Now/ Live With Me/
Sparks Will Fly/ (I Can't Get No) Satisfaction/

Beast Of Burden/ Angie/ Like A Rolling Stone/ Doo Doo Doo Doo Doo (Heartbreaker)/ Monkey Man/ I Go Wild
CD4: Miss You/ Band Introduction/ Honky Tonk Women/ Happy/ The Worst/ Sympathy For The Devil/ Street Fighting Man/ It's Only Rock'n'Roll/ Brown Sugar/ Jumping Jack Flash
R: Ex. Audience.   S: CD1-2 Werchter Festival Ground June 24 '95. CD3-4 Werchter Festival Ground June 25 '95.   C: ECD. Box set.

CD - BEAT BEAT BEAT
MULTI COLOR SHADES MCS-101
Mercy Mercy/ She Said Yeah/ Play With Fire/ Not Fade Away/ The Spider And The Fly/ That's How Strong My Love Is/ Get Off Of My Cloud/ 19th Nervous Breakdown/ Satisfaction/ The Last Time/ Paint It Black/ 19th Nervous Breakdown/ Lady Jane/ Get Off Of My Cloud/ Yesterday's Papers/ Ruby Tuesday/ Let's Spend The Night Together/ Going Home/ Satisfaction
R: Tracks 1-9 poor radio recording. Tracks 10-19 poor audience recording.   S: Tracks 1-9 1st show, Showground, Sydney, Australia Feb. 18 '66. Tracks 10-19 Hautreust Hall, Haag, Holland Apr. 15 '67.

CD - BIRMINGHAM ODEON 1973
OH BOY 1-9168
Brown Sugar/ Gimme Shelter/ Happy/ Tumbling Dice/ Starfucker/ Dancing With Mr. D./ Angie/ You Can't Always Get What You Want/ Midnight Rambler/ Honky Tonk Women/ All Down The Line/ Rip This Joint/ Jumping Jack Flash/ Street Fighting Man
R: G-Vg. Audience.   S: Odeon Theatre, Birmingham Aug. 19 '73.   C: Time 73:11.

CD - BORN IN THE CROSSFIRE HURRICANE
SONIC ZOOM SZ1002
Jumping Jack Flash/ Carol/ Sympathy For The Devil/ Stray Cat Blues/ Prodigal Son/ You Gotta Move/ Love In Vain/ I'm Free/ Under My Thumb/ Midnight Rambler/ Live With Me/ Little Queenie/ Satisfaction/ Honky Tonk Women/ Street Fighting Man
R: Vg audience recording.   S: 2nd show, Inglewood Forum, LA Nov. 8 '69.

CD - BRIXTON
TYPHOON TYN 008/09
CD1: Honky Tonk Woman/ Tumbling Down/ You Got Rocking/ Live With Me/ Black Limousine/ Dead Flowers Sweet Virginia/ Faraway Eyes/ Travelling Man/ Meet Me At The Bottom/ Shine A Light/ Like A Rolling Stone/ Monkey Man
CD2: I Go Wild/ Miss You/ Band Intro/ Connection/ Slipping Away/ Midnight Rambler/ Rip This Joint/ Start Me Up/ Brown Sugar/ Jumping Jack Flash
S: Brixton, England July 19 '95.   C: ECD.

CD - THE BURNING OUT
BLACK N' BLUE RSBB-2008/009
CD1: Let It Rock/ All Down The Line/ Honky Tonk Women/ Starfucker/ When The Whip Comes Down/ Beast Of Burden/ Lies/ Miss You/ Just My Imagination
CD2: Shattered/ Respectable/ Far Away Eyes/ Love In Vain/ Tumbling Dice/ Happy/ Sweet Little Sixteen/ Brown Sugar/ Jumpin' Jack Flash
C: G-Vg audience recording.   S: Anaheim Stadium, Anaheim, CA July 23 '78.

CD - BUFFALO '81
DANDELION 94006/7
CD1: Under My Thumb/ When The Whip Comes Down/ Let's Spend The Night Together/ Shattered/ Neighbours/ Black Limousine/ Down The Road Apiece/ Just My Imagination/ Twenty Flight Rock/ She's So Cold/ Time Is On My Side/ Beast Of Burden
CD2: Let It Bleed/ You Can't Always Get What You Want/ Tops/ Tumbling Dice/ Little T&A/ Let Me Go/ Hang Fire/ Start Me Up/ Miss You/ Honky Tonk Women/ All Down The Line/ Brown Sugar
R: Vg. Audience.   S: Buffalo, New York Sept. 27 '81.   C: Japanese CD. Dcc.

CD - CATCH YOUR DREAMS (BEFORE THEY SLIP AWAY)
BLACK LIGHT BL 1001
Jumping Jack Flash/ Carol/ Sympathy For The Devil/ Stray Cat Blues/ Midnight Rambler/ Under My Thumb/ Prodigal Son/ Love In Vain/ I'm Free/ Little Queenie/ Gimme Shelter/ Satisfaction/ Honky Tonk Women/ Street Fighting Man
R: Poor audience recording. Too fast.   S: State University, Fort Collins, CO Nov. 7 '69.

CD - COLOGNE 1970
A VINYL GANG PRODUCT VGP-049
Jumping Jack Flash/ Roll Over Beethoven/ Sympathy For The Devil/ Stray Cat Blues/ Love In Vain/ Dead Flowers/ Midnight Rambler/ Live With Me/ Little Queenie/ Brown Sugar/ Honky Tonk Women/ Street Fighting Man/ Jimmy Saville Introduction/ Not Fade Away/ I Just Wanna Make Love To You/ I'm Alright
R: G-Vg.   S: Sporthalle, Cologne, Germany Sept. 18 '70. Tracks 13-16 NME Poll-Winners Concert, Empire Pool, Wembley Apr. 26 '64.

CD - DA'LAPA INCIDENT / LISBOA '95
SWINGIN' PIG TSP-CD-201-2
CD1: Intro/ Not Fade Away/ Tumbling Dice/ You Got Me Rocking/ It's All Over Now/ Live With Me/ Sparks Will Fly/ (I Can't Get No) Satisfaction/ Beast Of Burden/ Angie/ Like A Rolling Stone/ Doo Doo Doo Doo Doo (Heartbreaker)/ Gimme Shelter/ I Go Wild
CD2: Miss You/ Band Introduction/ Honky Tonk Women/ Happy/ Slipping Away/ Sympathy For The Devil/ Street Fighting Man/ Start Me Up/ It's Only Rock 'N' Roll/ Brown Sugar/ Jumping Jack Flash

S: Lisboa, Portugal July 24 '95.   C: ECD.

CD - DRIVE ME CRACKERS
BLACK N' BLUES RSBB-1001
Brown Sugar/ Bitch/ Rocks Off/ Gimme Shelter/
Happy/ Tumbling Dice/ Love In Vain/ Sweet
Virginia/ You Can't Always Get What You Want/
All Down The Line/ Midnight Rambler/ Bye Bye
Johnny/ Rip This Joint/ Jumpin' Jack Flash/ Street
Fighting Man
R: Poor recording.   S: Scope Arena, Norfork,
VA July 5 '72.

CD - EASTERN PROMISE
KISS THE STONE KTS 445/46
CD1: Intro/ Not Fade Away/ Tumblin' Dice/ You
Got Me Rocking/ Live With Me/ Rocks Off/ Sparks
Will Fly/ (I Can't Get No) Satisfaction/ Angie/
Sweet Virginia/ Rock And A Hard Place/ Love Is
Strong/ I Go Wild/ Miss You
CD2: Intro/ Honky Tonk Woman/ Before They
Make Me Run/ Slipping Away/ Sympathy For The
Devil/ Monkey Man/ Street Fighting Man/ Start Me
Up/ It's Only Rock And Roll/ Brown Sugar/
Jumping Jack Flash
R: Exs. Soundboard.   S: Tokyo Dome, Tokyo,
Japan Mar. 12 '95.   C: ECD. Dcc Pic CD.

CD - EL MOCAMBO '77
HIV INC.
Worried About You/ Crackin' Up/ Let's Spend The
Night Together/ Route 66/ Hand Of Fate/ Around
And Around/ Crazy Mama/ Little Red Rooster/
Dance Little Sister/ Route 66/ I Just Wanna Make
Love To You/ Blues Is Alright/ Let It Rock/ Back In
The U.S.A./ Around And Around
R: G-Ex audience recordings.   S: El Mocambo
Club, Toronto, Canada Mar. 3-4 '77. Tracks 11-12
London June 28 '92. Tracks 13-15 Denmark June
3 '82.

CD - GIN SOAKED BARROOM QUEEN IN BOSTON
WEEPING GOAT WG-008
Brown Sugar/ Bitch/ Rocks Off/ Gimmie Shelter/
Happy/ Tumbling Dice/ Love In Vain/ Sweet
Virginia/ You Can't Always Get What You Want/
All Down The Line/ Midnight Rambler/ Band
Introduction/ Bye Bye Johnny/ Rip This Joint/
Jumpin' Jack Flash/ Street Fighting Man
R: Poor-G. Audience.   S: Boston Garden July
19 '72.   C: Japanese CD.

CD - GLIMMER TWINS' PRIVATE TAPES - DIRTY WORK ACOUSTIC SESSIONS
WEEPING GOAT WG-020
You're Too Much/ One Hit/ Broken Hearts For Me
And You/ Don't Be Cruel/ Unknown Song/ Back
On The Streets Again/ Your Love/ Unknown
Jams/ So High
R: Poor. Hiss.   S: Hotel Room, Paris Jan. '85.
Track 9 West Side Studio's demo, London Feb.
'87.   C: Japanese CD.

CD - GRASS WIDOW
BLACK N' BLUE RSBB-1066
Brown Sugar/ Bitch/ Rocks Off/ Gimme Shelter/
Happy/ Tumbling Dice/ Love In Vain/ Sweet
Virginia/ You Can't Always Get What You Want/
All Down The Line/ Midnight Rambler/ Bye Bye
Johnny/ Rip This Joint/ Jumpin' Jack Flash/ Street
Fighting Man
R: Good audience recording.   S: RFK Stadium,
Washington, DC actually recorded on July 4 '72
not '74 as jacket.

CD - HANGBIRD DISASTER
SHAVED DISC
You're Too Much/ One Hit/ Broken Hearts For Me
And You/ Don't Be Cruel/ Unknown/ Back On The
Streets Again/ Your Love
R: G-Vg.   S: Acoustic session '85.

CD - HAVE A BEER
TEDDY BEAR TB 38
Carol (3:30)/ Gimme Shelter (3:50)/ Sympathy For
The Devil (6:10)/ I'm Free (5:13)/ Live With Me
(3:03)/ Love In Vain (4:50)/ Midnight Rambler
(7:50)/ Little Queenie (4:55)/ Honky Tonk Woman
(4:30)/ Street Fighting Man (4:05)
R: Vg. Audience.   S: Late show, Oakland
Coliseum, CA Nov. 9 '69.   C: ECD. Dcc.
Pic CD.

CD - HAVING A LAUGH IN BRIXTON
BAL 19795A/B
CD1: Honky Tonk Women/ Tumbling Dice/ You
Got Me Rocking/ Live With Me/ Black Limousine/
Dead Flowers/ Sweet Virginia/ Faraway Eyes/
Travelling Man/ Meet Me At The Bottom/ Shine A
Light/ Like A Rolling Stone/ Monkey Man
CD2: I Go Wild/ Miss You/ Band Introductions/
Connection/ Slipping Away/ Midnight Rambler/
Rip This Joint/ Start Me Up/ Brown Sugar/
Jumpin' Jack Flash
R: G-Vg. Audience.   S: The Brixton Academy,
London July 19 '95.   C: ECD. Dcc. Pic CD.

CD - HELL'S ANGELS AND MURDER AT ALTAMONT (ALTAMONT SPEED WAY)
SHAVED DISC TSD 003
Carol/ Sympathy For The Devil/ Got No Place To
Go/ Stray Cat Blues/ Love In Vain/ Under My
Thumb/ Midnight Rambler/ Live With Me/ Gimme
Shelter/ Little Queenie
R: Vg audience recording.   S: Killer Festival '69.

CD - HIP SHAKE 1978
ML001 TSP
Far Away Eyes/ Miss You/ Respectable/ Rock And
Roll Jam/ Don't Look Back/ Play With Fire/
Starfucker/ Gimme Shelter/ It's Only Rock 'N'
Roll/ All Down The Line/ Honky Tonk Woman/
Brown Sugar/ Tumbling Dice/ Cocksucker Blues/
No Expectations/ Memory Motel/ The Fat Man/
Something Else/ Hi-Heel Sneakers/ Tell Me/
Shake Your Hips
R: Soundboard.   S: Tracks 1-3 promo film

shooting, New York May 5 '78. Tracks 4-21 tour rehearsals, Bearsville, Woodstock, NY May 19 '78 onwards.   C: ECD. Dcc. Time 72:40.

CD - HOW COME YOU TASTE SO GOOD
SOUND SHELTER SS102
Brown Sugar/ Gimme Shelter/ Happy/ Tumbling Dice/ Starfucker/ Dancing With Mr. D/ Angie/ You Can't Always Get What You Want/ Midnight Rambler/ Honky Tonk Women/ All Down The Line/ Rip This Joint/ Jumping Jack Flash/ Street Fighting Man
R: Vg audience recording. Slight hiss.   S: Palais Des Sports, Antwerp, Belgium Oct. 15 '73.

CD - I'M WORKING SO HARD (TO KEEP YOU IN LUXURY)
BLACK LIGHT BL2002/2003
CD1: Honky Tonk Women/ All Down The Line/ If You Can't Rock Me, Get Off Of My Cloud/ Starfucker/ Gimme Shelter/ Ain't Too Proud To Beg/ 6 other tracks
CD2: Wild Horses/ That's Life/ Outta Space/ Brown Sugar/ Midnight Rambler/ Rip This Joint/ Street Fighting Man/ Jumping Jack Flash/ Sure The One You Need/ Luxury/ Heartbreaker
R: Good-Vg audience recording.   S: Hughes Stadium, Fort Collins, CO July 19 '75. CD2 tracks 21-23 County Coliseum, Milwaukee, WI June 6 '75.   C: Elton John on piano.

CD - JOHANNESBURG '95
THE SWINGIN' PIG TSP 185-2
CD1: Intro/ Not Fade Away/ Tumbling Dice/ You Got Me Rocking/ It's All Over Now/ Live With Me/ Sparks Will Fly/ (I Can't Get No) Satisfaction/ Out Of Tears/ Angie/ Rock And A Hard Place/ Midnight Rambler/ I Go Wild
CD2: Miss You/ Band Introduction/ Honky Tonk Women/ Happy/ Slipping Away/ Sympathy For The Devil/ Monkey Man/ Street Fighting Man/ Start Me Up/ It's Only Rock'n'Roll/ Brown Sugar/ Jumping Jack Flash
R: Exs. Soundboard.   S: Ellis Park Stakium, Johannesburg, South Africa Feb. 25 '95.
C: ECD.

CD - LIVE AT JOE ROBBIE STADIUM - MIAMI '94
THE SWINGIN' PIG TSP-CD-182-2
CD1: Not Fade Away/ Tumbling Dice/ You Got Me Rocking/ Rocks Off/ Sparks Will Fly/ Live With Me/ Satisfaction/ Angie/ Dead Flowers/ Sweet Virginia/ Heartbreaker/ It's All Over Now/ Stop Breaking Down/ Who Do You Love
CD2: I Go Wild/ Miss You/ Introduction Of The Band/ Honky Tonk Women/ Before They Make Me Run/ The Worst/ Sympathy For The Devil/ Monkey Man/ Street Fighting Man/ Start Me Up/ It's Only Rock'N'Roll/ 2 other tracks
R: Exs. Soundboard.   S: Joe Robbie Stadium, Miami Nov. 25 '94.   C: ECD.

CD - LIVE IN JAPAN
OCTOPUS OCTO 105/106
CD1: Intro, Not Fade Away (4:40)/ Tumbling Dice (4:28)/ You Got Me Rocking (3:45)/ Live With Me (4:09)/ Rocks Off (5:12)/ Sparks Will Fly (4:19)/ (I Can't Get No) Satisfaction (6:35)/ Angie (acoustic) (4:11)/ Sweet Virginia (acoustic) (4:50)/ Rock And A Hard Place (5:07)/ Love Is Strong (5:32)/ I Go Wild (6:08)
CD2: Miss You (14:28)/ Honky Tonk Women (5:16)/ Before They Make Me Run (4:18)/ Slipping Away (5:15)/ Sympathy For The Devil (7:05)/ Monkey Man (4:21)/ Street Fighting Man (6:01)/ Start Me Up (4:16)/ It's Only Rock 'N' Roll (5:08)/ Brown Sugar (7:57)/ Jumping Jack Flash (6:16)
R: Exs. Soundboard.   S: Tokyo Dome, Tokyo, Japan Mar. 3 '95.   C: ECD. Dcc. Pic CD.

CD - LONELY AT THE TOP
THE SWINGIN' PIG TSP 199
Living Is A Harder Love/ Drift Away/ Sweet Home Chicago/ Dancing Girls/ Munich Reggae/ Lonely At The Top/ Munich Hilton/ What's The Matter/ Gangster's Maul/ Hang Fire/ Claudine/ We Had It All/ Let's Go Steady
C: ECD.

CD - L.A. FORUM 75
IDOL MIND PRODUCTIONS IMP-CD 026-27
CD1: Fanfare For The Common Man/ Honky Tonk Women/ All Down The Line/ If You Can't Rock Me, Get Off My Cloud/ Star Star/ Gimme Shelter/ Ain't Too Proud To Beg/ You Gotta Move/ You Can't Always Get What You Want/ Happy/ Tumbling Dice/ Band Introduction
CD2: Doo Doo Doo Doo Doo/ Fingerprint File/ Angie/ Wild Horses/ That's Life/ Brown Sugar/ Midnight Rambler/ Rip This Joint/ Street Fighting Man/ Jumping Jack Flash/ Sympathy For The Devil
R: Vg audience recording.   S: Inglewood Forum LA July 13 '75.   C: Japanese CD.

CD - OLYMPIA
MOONRAKER 001/2
CD1: Honky Tonk Women/ Tumbling Dice/ You Got Me Rocking/ All Down The Line/ Shattered/ Beast Of Burden/ Let It Bleed/ Angie/ Wild Horses/ Meet Me In The Bottom/ Shine A Light
CD2: Like A Rolling Stone/ I Go Wild/ Miss You/ Introductions/ Connection/ Slipping Away/ Midnight Rambler/ Rip This Joint/ Start Me Up/ It's Only Rock N' Roll/ Brown Sugar/ Jumping Jack Flash
R: Vg-Ex. Audience.   S: Club gig, The Olympia, Paris July 3 '95.   C: ECD. Dcc. The audience is very much part of this show... a very 'you are there' feeling. Time CD1 53:51. CD2 73:40.

CD - OLYMPIC YEARS 1967-69
DANDELION 94003
Dear Doctor/ Sister Morphine/ Citadel (take 1)/ Citadel (take 2)/ Citadel (take 3)/ Citadel (take 4)/ You Can't Always Get What You Want/ Honky

Tonk Women/ Jumpin' Jack Flash/ No Expectations/ Gimme Shelter/ Child Of The Moon/ In Another Land/ We Love You/ Dandelion (instrumental)/ You Got The Silver/ Honky Tonk Women
R: Vg. Some poor-G. Soundboard.　　S: Olympic Studios, London '67-'69.　　C: Japanese CD. Dcc. Pic CD. Time 55:07.

CD - ON THE NEEDLE
BLACK N' BLUE RSBB-1007
Let It Rock/ Honky Tonk Woman/ Get Off My Cloud/ Mother's Little Helper/ Con Le Mie Lacrime (As Tears Go By)/ Da Doo Ron Ron/ We're Wastin' Time/ Miss You/ Everything Is Turning To Gold/ Holding Out My Love To You/ Out Of Time/ Beast Of Burden/ Memo Form Turner/ Harlem Shuffle/ (Walkin' Thru' The) Sleepy City/ Fancy Man Blues/ Oh How I'd Like To See Me On The 'B' Side/ I'm going Down/ Natural Magic/ Heart Of Stone
R: Good-Vg sound.　　S: Tracks 1-4 '71. Tracks 5-17 stereo versions. Tracks 18-20 acetate master versions.

CD - OUT FOR BLOOD
RS-1994-1/2
CD1: Not Fade Away/ Tumbling Dice/ Live With Me/ You Got Me Rocking/ Rocks Off/ Sparks Will Fly/ Shattered/ Satisfaction/ Beast Of Burden/ Out Of Tears/ Memory Motel/ All Down The Line/ Miss You
CD2: I Can't Get Next To You/ I Go Wild/ Honky Tonk Women/ Before They Make Me Run/ The Worst/ Love Is Strong/ Monkey Man/ Start Me Up/ It's Only Rock'N Roll/ Street Fighting Man/ Brown Sugar/ Jumpin' Jack Flash
R: Exs audience recording.　　S: Legion Field, Birmingham Aug. 6 '94.

CD - OUT OF JOINT
BLACK N' BLUE RSBB-2004/005
CD1: Jumpin' Jack Flash/ Prodigal Son/ You Gotta Move/ Carol/ Sympathy For The Devil/ Stray Cat Blues/ Love In Vain/ I'm Free/ Under My Thumb/ Midnight Rambler/ Live With Me/ Little Queenie/ Satisfaction/ Honky Tonk Women/ Street Fighting Man
CD2: Jumpin' Jack Flash/ Carol/ Sympathy For The Devil/ Stray Cat Blues/ Prodigal Son/ You Gotta Move/ Love In Vain/ I'm Free/ Under My Thumb/ Midnight Rambler/ Live With Me/ Gimme Shelter/ 4 other tracks
R: G-Vg audience recording.　　S: 1st & 2nd shows Oakland Coliseum, Oakland, CA Nov. 9 '69.

CD - PHILADELPHIA 81
IDOL MIND PRODUCTIONS IMP-CD 020-21
CD1: Under My Thumb/ When The Whip Comes Down/ Neighbours/ Just My Imagination/ Shattered/ Let's Spend The Night Together/ Black Limousine/ She's So Cold/ Time Is On My Side/ Beast Of Burden/ Waiting On A Friend/ Let It Bleed/ Band Introduction/ You Can't Always Get

What You Want
CD2: Tops/ Tumbling Dice/ Hang Fire/ Let Me Go/ Little T & A/ Start Me Up/ Miss You/ Honky Tonk Women/ All Down The Line/ Brown Sugar
R: Vg audience recording.　　S: JFK Stadium, Philadelphia Sept. '81.

CD - THE ROLLING STONES
ROCKSTARS IN CONCERT 6117112
Bitch (4:12)/ Brown Sugar (3:50)/ Honky Tonk Women (3:09)/ Love In Vain (6:20)/ Midnight Rambler (11:15)/ Jumpin' Jack Flash (3:23)/ (I Can't Get No) Satisfaction (5:12)/ Street Fighting Man (3:50)/ Sympathy For The Devil (6:13)/ Paint It Black (2:14)/ Lady Jane (3:04)/ Ruby Tuesday (3:16)/ Little Red Rooster (2:36)
R: Ex.　　S: Leeds Mar. 13 '71. Tracks 6 and 9 London July 5 '69. Tracks 10, 11, 12 and 13 London '64/'68.　　C: ECD.

ROLLING STONES '75 BOX
CD - BOSTON JUNE 12, '75
RS 01-02
CD1: Honky Tonk Woman/ All Down The Line/ If You Can't Rock Me Off Of My Cloud/ Starfucker/ Gimme Shelter/ Ain't Too Proud To Beg/ You Gotta Move/ You Can't Always Get What You Want/ Happy/ Tumbling Dice/ Luxury/ Heartbreaker/ Fingerprint File
CD2: Angie/ Wild Horses/ That's Lite/ Outta Space/ Brown Sugar/ Midnight Rambler/ It's Only Rock 'N' Roll/ Rip This Joint/ Street Fighting Man/ Jumpin' Jack Flash
CD - NEW YORK M.S.G. JUNE 22, '75
RS 03-04
CD3: Honky Tonk Woman/ All Down The Line/ If You Can't Rock Me Off Of My Cloud/ Starfucker/ Gimme Shelter/ Ain't Too Proud To Beg/ You Gotta Move/ You Can't Always Get What You Want/ Introduction Of The Band/ Happy/ Tumbling Dice/ It's Only Rock 'N' Roll/ Heartbreaker
CD4: Finger Print File/ Angie/ Wild Horses/ That's Lite/ Outta Space/ Brown Sugar/ Midnight Rambler/ Rip This Joint/ Street Fighting Man/ Jumpin' Jack Flash/ Sympathy For The Devil
CD - NEW YORK M.S.G. JUNE 25, '75
RS 05-06
CD5: Overture/ Honky Tonk Woman/ If You Can't Rock Me Off Of My Cloud/ Starfucker/ Gimme Shelter/ Ain't Too Proud To Beg/ You Gotta Move/ You Can't Always Get What You Want/ Tumbling Dice/ It's Only Rock 'N' Roll/ Introduction Of The Band/ Heartbreaker/ Fingerprint File
CD6: Angie/ Wild Horses/ That's Lite/ Outta Space/ Brown Sugar/ Midnight Rambler/ Rip This Joint/ Street Fighting Man/ Jumpin' Jack Flash/ Sympathy For The Devil
CD - SEATTLE JULY 18, '75
RS 07-08
CD7: Overture/ Honky Tonk Woman/ All Down The Line/ If You Can't Rock Me Off Of My Cloud/ Starfucker/ Gimme Shelter/ Ain't Too Proud To Beg/ You Gotta Move/ You Can't Always Get What You Want/ Happy/ Tumbling Dice/ It's Only

Rock 'N' Roll
CD8: Introduction Of The Band/ Fingerprint File/ Wild Horses/ That's Life/ Brown Sugar/ Midnight Rambler/ Rip This Joint/ Jumpin' Jack Flash
R: G-Vg. Audience.   C: ECD. Four double cases and a book of photos from the '75 tour come in a multi-colored book-style case. Time CD1 68:31. CD2 51:07. CD3 66:33. CD4 69:00. CD5 76:10. CD6 62:43. CD7 60:57. CD8 51:50.

CD - SECRET GIG IN TORONTO 94
DANDELION 94001/2
CD1: Live With Me/ You Got Me Rocking/ Tumbling Dice/ Shattered/ Rocks Off/ Sparks Will Fly/ Monkey Man/ No Expectations/ Love Is Strong
CD2: Brand New Car/ Honky Tonk Women/ I Go Wild/ Start Me Up/ Street Fighting Man/ Brown Sugar/ Can't Get Next To You
R: Poor-G. Audience.   S: RPM Club, Toronto July 19 '94.   C: Japanese CD.

CD - SHATTERED IN EUROPE
THE SWINGIN' PIG TSP 184 LE
Under My Thumb/ When The Whip Comes Down/ Let's Spend The Night Together/ Shattered/ Neighbours/ Black Limousine/ Just My Imagination/ Introduction Of The Band/ Little T & A/ Angle/ Tumbling Dice/ She's So Cold/ Hang Fire/ Miss You/ Honky Tonk Women/ Brown Sugar/ Start Me Up
BONUS CD: Hard Travellin'/ Hit The Road Jack/ Rock'n'Roll Jam/ He'll Have To Go/ Lonesome Whistle/ Will You Love Me Tomorrow
R: Ex. Soundboard.   S: Nice '82.   C: ECD.
First edition of 1,500 numbered copies come with a bonus CD 'The Nice Hotel Room Session' recorded in Keith's room at the Negresco Hotel.

CD - SINGING UNDER THE RAIN
JL-013
No Woman No Cry, Take The 'A' Train/ Under My Thumb/ When The Whip Comes Down/ Let's Spend The Night Together/ Shattered/ Neighbours/ Black Limousine/ Twenty Flight Rock/ Going To A Go Go/ Let Me Go/ Time Is On My Side/ Beast Of Burden/ You Can't Always Get What You Want
R: Poor-good audience recording.   S: Estadio Vincente Calderon, Madrid, Spain July 7 '82.

CD - SPEED FREAKS
BLACK N' BLUE RSBB-2002/003
CD1: Let It Rock/ All Down The Line/ Honky Tonk Women/ Starfucker/ When The Whip Comes Down/ Lies/ Miss You/ Beast Of Burden/ Just My Imagination
CD2: Shattered/ Respectable/ Far Away Eyes/ Love In Vain/ Tumbling Dice/ Happy/ Sweet Little Sixteen/ Brown Sugar/ Jumpin' Jack Flash/ Satisfaction
R: Poor audience recording.   S: Soldiers Field, Chicago July 8 '78.

CD - SOME LIKE IT HOT!
A VINYL GANG PRODUCT VGP-044
Jumping Jack Flash/ Roll Over Beethoven/ Sympathy For The Devil/ Stray Cat Blues/ Love In Vain/ Dead Flowers/ Midnight Rambler/ Live With Me/ Let It Rock/ Little Queenie/ Brown Sugar/ Honky Tonk Women/ Street Fighting Man/ Wild Horses
R: Poor-G. Track 14 Vg studio recording.
S: Palas Des Sports, Paris Sept. 23 '70. Track 14 Olympic Studios, London and Mobile Recording Unit, Newbury May 9-Aug. '70.

CD - THE SUN, THE MOON AND THE STONES
HORNY BUNGLE RECORDS HBR002
CD1: Introduction/ Not Fade Away/ Tumbling Dice/ You Got Me Rocking/ Shattered/ Rocks Off/ Sparks Will Fly/ Satisfaction/ Beast Of Burden/ Memory Motel/ Heartbreaker/ Love Is Strong/ 2 other tracks
CD2: Miss You/ Introduction Of The Band/ Honky Tonk Women/ Before They Make Me Run/ The Worst/ Sympathy For The Devil/ Monkey Man/ Street Fighting Man/ Start Me Up/ It's Only Rock'N'Roll/ Brown Sugar/ 1 other track
R: Ex audience recording.   S: Carrier Dome, Syracuse, NY Dec. 8 '94.

CD - SYDNEY LAST AFFAIR
PICARESQUE SOUND PS-001
Brown Sugar/ Bitch/ Rock Off/ Gimmie Shelter/ Happy/ Tumbling Dice/ Love In Vain/ Sweet Virginia/ You Can't Always Get What You Want/ Honky Tonk Women/ All Down The Line/ Midnight Rambler/ Little Queenie/ Brown Sugar/ Street Fighting Man
R: Good stereo, tracks 14-15 from radio.
S: Royal Randwick Race Course, Sydney, Australia Feb. 27 '73. Tracks 14-15 Europe '73.

CD - TIME TRIP VOL. 4
GOLD STANDARD RS-23-94-07
Dear Doctor/ No Expectations/ Sister Morphine/ You Got The Silver/ Gimme Shelter/ You Can't Always Get What You Want/ Jumping Jack Flash/ Child Of The Moon/ The 'Citadel' Sessions (piano and guitar riffs Take #5, Take #8, Takes #15, 16, 17, Take #24)/ In Another Session/ We Love You/ Dandelion aka Sometimes I Feel Blue/ 19th Nervous Breakdown/ Yesterdays Papers/ Connection*/ It's All Over Now*/ Carol
R: Vg-Ex. *G. Soundboard.   S: Tracks 1-4 Olympic Studios, London Mar. 6-8 '68. Track 5 Elektra Studios, Hollywood Oct./Nov. '69. Tracks 9-14 Olympic Studios, London June/Sept. '67. Track 15 Olympic Studios, London July/Aug. '67. Track 16 Olympic Studios, London Nov. '66. Track 17 RCA Studios, Hollywood Dec. '65. Track 18 Olympic Studios, London Nov./Dec. '66. Tracks 19-20 'Sunday Night At The London Palladium', BBC TV Jan. 67. Track 21 unknown location USA Nov. '69.   C: Japanese CD. Dcc. Time 75:29.

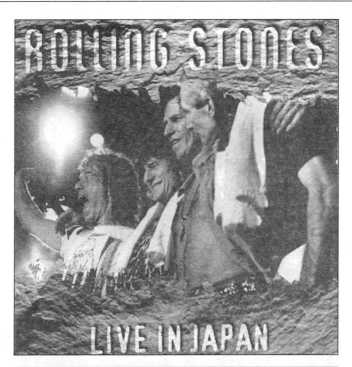

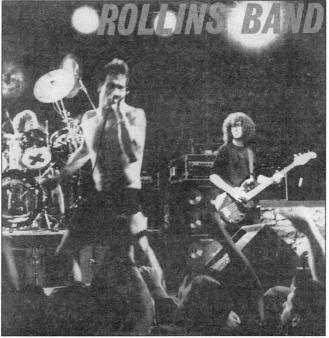

CD - TROPICAL WINDSONGS
GOLD STANDARD ZA 32
Brown Sugar/ Bitch/ Rocks Off/ Gimme Shelter/
It's All Over Now/ Happy/ Tumbling Dice/ Sweet
Virginia/ Introductions/ Dead Flowers/ You Can't
Always Get What You Want/ All Down The Line/
Midnight Gambler/ Live With Me/ Rip This Joint/
Jumpin' Jack Flash
R: Vg. Audience.   S: Second show, Honolulu,
Hawaii Jan. 21 '73.   C: Japanese CD. Dcc. Pic
CD. Time 71:49.

CD - UNPLUGGED
INVASION UNLIMITED IU 9542-1
Dear Doctor/ You Got The Silver/ Family/ No
Expectations/ Sister Morphine/ Blood Red Wine/
Country Honk/ You Can't Always Get What You
Want/ You Gotta Move/ Wild Horses/ All Down
The Line/ Cocksucker Blues/ Dead Flowers/
Angie
S: Acoustic outtakes - alternate versions and
rough mixes recorded between '68 and '73.
C: ECD.

CD - VIP DISHED JOINT
SHAVED DISC
Brown Sugar/ Bitch/ Rocks Off/ Gimme Shelter/
Happy/ Tumbling Dice/ Love In Vain/ Sweet
Virginia/ You Can't Always Get What You Want/
Honkey Tonk Women/ All Down The Line/
Midnight Rambler/ Little Queenie/ Rip This Joint/
Jumping Jack Flash/ Street Fighting Man
R: Some hiss. Plays a little fast.   S: Sydney
Feb. 26 '73.

CD - VOODOO AT HALLOWEEN
MOONLIGHT ML 9512/13
CD1: Not Fade Away/ Tumblin' Dice/ You Got Me
Rocking/ Shattered/ Rocks Off/ Sparks Will Fly/
Satisfaction/ Beast Of Burden/ Out Of Tears/ Doo
Doo Doo Doo Doo (Heartbreaker)/ Love Is
Strong/ It's All Over/ I Go Wild
CD2: Miss You/ Introduction Of The Band/
Honkey Tonk Woman/ Before They Make Me
Run/ The Worst/ Sympathy For The Devil/
Monkey Man/ Street Fighting Man/ Start Me Up/
It's Only Rock And Roll/ Brown Sugar/ Jumping
Jack Flash
R: Exs. Soundboard.   S: Oakland, CA Oct. 31
'94.   C: ECD. Dcc. Time CD1 65:01.
CD2 67:02.

CD - VOODOO CLUBBING
FRONT ROW METEOR FM 2114
Live With Me/ You Got Me Rocking/ Tumbling
Dice/ Shattered/ Rocks Off/ Sparks Will Fly/
Monkey Man/ No Expectations/ Love Is Strong/
Brand New Car/ Honky Tonk Woman/ I Go Wild/
Start Me Up/ Street Fighting Man/ Brown Sugar/
Can't Get Next To You
R: G. Audience.   S: Warm-up club gig in front of
about 300 people at The RPM Club, Toronto, July
'94.   C: ECD. Dcc. Time 78:16.

CD - WELL...COME BACK MY SWEETHEART
SHAVED DISC TSD 004/005
CD1: Under My Thumb/ When The Whip Comes
Down/ Let's Spend The Night Together/
Shattered/ Neighbours/ Black Limousine/ Just My
Imagination/ Twenty Flight Rock/ Going To A Go
Go/ Let Me Go/ 3 other tracks
CD2: Let It Bleed/ You Can't Always Get What
You Want/ Little T&A/ Tumbling Dice/ She's So
Cold/ Hang Fire/ Miss You/ Honky Tonk Women/
Brown Sugar/ Start Me Up/ Jumpin' Jack Flash/
Satisfaction
R: Ex audience recording.   S: Kansas Dec. 15
'81.   C: With Mick Taylor.

CD - WELCOME TO WASHINGTON
DANDELION 94008/9
CD1: Intro, Not Fade Away/ Undercover Of The
Night/ Tumbling Dice/ Live With Me/ You Got Me
Rocking/ Rocks Off/ Sparks Will Fly/ Shattered/
Satisfaction/ Beast Of Burden/ Out Of Tears/
Memory Motel/ All Down The Line/ Miss You
CD2: Can't Get Next To You/ Brand New Car/
Introduction Of The Band/ Honky Tonk Women/
Happy/ The Worst/ Love Is Strong/ Monkey Man/ I
Go Wild/ Start Me Up/ It's Only Rock'N'Roll three
other tracks
R: Ex audience recording.   S: RFK Stadium,
Washington, DC Aug. 3 '94.

ROLLINS BAND, THE

CD - HARD AS NAILS
INSECT RECORDS IST 71
Introduction/ Step Back/ Wrong Man/ Alien
Blueprint/ Blues Jam/ Divine Object Of Hatred/
Volume 4/ Tired/ Disconnect/ Civilized/ Liar/ Icon/
Fool
R: Vg. Audience.   S: Montfort University,
Leicester, England May 4 '94.   C: ECD. Dcc.
Pic CD. Time 68:04.

7" - ROLLINS BAND
S1: Hard   S2: Low Self Opinion
R: Ex. Soundboard.   S: Live on Request Video
July '92.   C: USA B&w sleeve. Blue type.
Limited numbered edition of 1,000 on blue vinyl.
45 RPM.

ROLLINS, SONNY

CD - THE MEETING
ALL OF US AS 40
The Meeting (21:27)/ McGhee (16:18)/ There Is
No Greater Love (14:41)/ Don't Stop The Carnival
(6:12)/ Alfie (10:39)/ St. Thomas (3:52)
R: Ex. Soundboard. Tracks 3-6 G-Vg.
Soundboard. Some hiss.   S: Tracks 1-2 Sonny
Rollins and Pat Metheny in Tokyo, Japan July 31
'83. Tracks 3-6 Sonny Rollins Quintet, Laren,
Holland Aug. 21/25 '73.   C: ECD. Dbw. Yellow
type. Pic CD.

RONSTADT, LINDA

CD - BACK IN LA
LR1003
Party Girl/ It's So Easy/ Willin'/ I Can't Help It/
Just Our Look/ Look Out For Love/ Mad Love/
Cost Of Love/ Blue Bayou/ Lies/ Faithless Love/
Hunt So Bad/ Silver Threads And Golden Needle/
Band Intro, Poor, Poor, Pitiful Me/ You're No
Good/ How Do I Make You/ Back In The USA/
Heat Wave/ Desperado
R: Vg. Audience.   S: Los Angeles Aug. 24 '80.

CD - IT'S SO EASY
COUNTDOWN FACTORY CDF-942011A/B
CD1: Lose Again/ That'll Be The Day/ Blue
Bayou/ When Will I Be In Love/ It Doesn't Matter
Anymore/ Willin/ Alison/ All That You Dream/ Love
Me Tender/ Just One Look/ Desperado/
Mohammed's Radio
CD2: It's So Easy/ Someone To Lay Down Beside
Me/ My Blue Tears, Poor Poor Pitiful Me/
Tumbling Dice/ You're No Good/ Sorrow Lives
Here/ Back in The USA
R: Exs. Soundboard.   S: Japan Mar. '79.

ROXY MUSIC

CD - FOR EUROPEANS
COUNTDOWN FACTORY CDF-942007A/B
CD1: Sentimental Fool/ The Thrill Of It All/ Love Is
The Drug/ Mother Of Pearl/ Nightingale/ She
Sells/ Street Life/ Out Of The Blue/ Whirlwind
CD2: Sea Breezes/ Both Ends Burning/ Medley:
For Your Pleasure, Diamond Head, Wild
Weekend/ Introduction/ The 'In' Crowd/ Virginia
Plain/ Medley: Re-Make Re-Model, Do The
Strand, Editions Of You/ Hard Rain's Gonna Fall
R: Ex soundboard.   S: Stockholm, Jan. 27 '76.

ROYAL TRUX

7" - ROYAL TRUX
S1: Jukebox In Brazil
S2: Get Off/ Strawberry Soda
R: Ex. Soundboard.   S: Peel Session Nov. '93.
C: USA. Yellow/green sleeve. Clear vinyl.
45 RPM.

RUSH

CD - MIRRORS
OXYGEN OXY 003/4
CD1: Intro (The Three Stooges), Force Ten
(5:52)/ Limelight (4:27)/ Freewill (4:06)/ Distant
Early Warning (4:31)/ Intro, Time Stand Still
(6:18)/ Dreamline (5:06)/ Bravado (7:02)/ Roll The
Bones (6:10)/ Intro, Show Don't Tell (6:20)/ The
Big Money (6:27)
CD2: Ghost Of A Chance (6:21)/ Subdivisions
(4:13)/ The Pass (4:54)/ Where's My Thing?
(5:16)/ The Rhythm Method (7:29)/ Closer To The
Heart (4:48)/ Xanadu (6:37)/ Superconductor
(5:09)/ Outro, Tom Sawyer (5:59)/ Medley: The

Spirit Of Radio, 2112 Overture, Finding My Way,
La Villa Stranglato, Anthem, Red Barchetta, The
Spirit Of Radio (Reprise), Cygnus X-1 (19:31)
R: Exs. Soundboard.   S: Oakland Coliseum,
Jan. 30 '92.   C: ECD. Dcc. Pic CD.

S

SAMHAIN

7" - LAST GASP
S1: Blood Feast (The Jockey Club, Cincinnati,
Ohio Oct. '85)/ To Walk The Night (The Metro,
Chicago, IL Apr. '86)
S2: Lord Of The Left Hand (from unreleased
'Samhain IV', recorded Sept. '86)/ November Fire
(alternate album version, recorded Aug. '85)
R: Ex.   C: USA. Green/black Sleeve. 45 RPM.

SATRIANI, JOE

CD - ALWAYS WITH ME
P 910124
Summer Song/ I Believe/ Satch Boogie/ Flying In
A Blue Dream/ Cryin'/ The Crush Of Love/ Tears
In The Rain/ Friends/ One Big Rush/ Always With
You, Always With Me
R: G. Soundboard.   S: USA '94.

SCAGGS, BOZ

CD - TWILIGHT HIGHWAY
COUNTDOWN FACTORY CDF-942010A/B
CD1: Lowdown/ You Make It So Hard (To Say
No)/ What Can I Say/ This Time/ Jump Street/
Slow Dancer/ It's Over/ It Seems So Long You've
Been Gone/ I Got Your Number
CD2: Breakdown Dead Ahead/ What Can I Say/
Hard Times/ You Got Some Imagination/ Georgia/
Jump Street/ Lido Shuffle/ Middle Man/ Low
Down/ Sierra/ We're All Alone
R: G-Vg.   S: CD1 live '76. CD2 Radio City
Music Hall '80.

SCHENKER, MICHAEL

CD - V
PROJECT K PKCD-94001/002
CD1: Captain Nemo/ Rock My Nights Away/ Are
You Ready To Rock/ Cry For The Nations/ On
And On/ Attack Of The Mad Axeman/ Into The
Arena/ Courvoiser Concert/ Lost Horizons/ Rock
Will Never Die
CD2: I'm Gonna Make You Mine/ Systems
Failing/ Still Love That Little Devil/ Armed And
Ready/ Rock Bottom/ Doctor Doctor
R: Poor. Audience.   S: Budokan, Tokyo
Jan. 23 '84.

CD - LIGHTS OUT IN LONDON
CRYSTAL SOUND CS-006
Theme/ Armed And Ready/ Cry For The Nations/

Natural Thing/ Feels Like A Good Thing/ Into The Arena/ Looking Out From Nowhere/ Lost Horizons/ Rock Bottom/ Tales Of Mystery/ Shoot Shoot/ Doctor Doctor/ Lights Out
R: Vg audience recording.   S: Hammersmith Odeon, London Dec. '80.

CD - STUDIO SESSION '79
BONDAGE MUSIC BON 015
Jam #1 (prototype of 'Looking Out From Nowhere')/ Jam #2/ Jam #3/ Jam #4 (prototype of 'Tales Of Mystery')/ Jam #5 (take 2 of Jam #1)/ Jam #6 (prototype of 'Feels Like A Good Thing')/ Jam #7/ Jam #8/ Jam #9 (take 2 of Jam #8)
R: Soundboard recording.   S: Studio '79.

CD - TOKYO NIGHT
CRYSTAL SOUND CS-16
Opening Set/ Armed And Ready/ Cry For The Nations/ Attack Of The Mad Axeman/ I Want More/ Victim Of Illusions/ Into The Arena/ On And On/ Cozy Powell Drum Solo/ Ready To Rock
R: Exs. Soundboard.   S: Tokyo Aug. 12 '81.

SEPULTURA

CD - BRASILIAN NIGHT
BANZAI BZCD 019
Refuse, Resist (4:29)/ Territory (4:39)/ Mark Didn't Know (2:54)/ Slave New World (3:22)/ Amen (6:35)/ Furina (2:08)/ Altered State (5:42)/ We Who Are Not As Others (4:00)/ Propaganda (3:48)/ Anti Cop (2:45)/ Murder (2:48)/ Beneath The Remains (2:11)/ Escape To The Void (1:47)/ Nomad (4:46)/ Clenched Fist (3:54)/ Biotech Is Godzilla (2:00)/ Dead Embryonic Cells (5:39)/ Crucifiction (2:16)/ Arise (3:16)/ Policia (3:05)
R: Ex. Audience.   S: Live in Brazil.   C: ECD. Dcc. Pic CD.

CD - LIVE DEGRADATION
STAY SHARP RECORDS STS70516
Refuse, Resist/ Territory/ Troops Of Doom/ Slave New World/ Medley: Amen, Innerself/ Altered State/ We Who Are Not As Others/ Propaganda/ Nomad/ Beneath The Remains/ Escape To The Void/ Anticops/ Murder/ Clenched Fist/ Biotech Is Godzilla/ Dead Embryonic Cells/ Crucificado Pelo Sistema/ Hear Nothing, See Nothing, Say Nothing/ Arise/ Policia
R: Exs.   S: Japan '93.

SETZER, BRIAN ORCHESTRA

CD - ROCK-A-BILLY'S ROOTS, O.K.!
NOW ROSE 001
Lady Luck/ Good Rockin' Daddy/ Your True Love/ A Nightingale Sang In Berkeley Square/ Brand New Cadillac/ Sittin' On It All The Time/ Stray Cat Strut/ Straight Up/ September Skies/ Route 66/ Ball And Chain/ There's A Rainbow 'Round My Shoulder/ Encore: Rock This Town/ Instrumental
R: G-Vg. Audience.   S: Kose Nenkin Hall, Tokyo 4-1-'94.   C: Japanese CD. Dcc. Time 66:17.

SIMON AND GARFUNKEL

CD - AMSTERDAM 1970
BRIDGE SONG BSCD-001
The Boxer/ Homeward Bound/ Fakin' It/ The 59th Street Bridge Song (Feelin' Groovy)/ Silver Haired Daddy/ I Am A Rock/ For Emily, Whenever I My Find Her/ Mrs. Robinson/ Scarborough Fair, Canticle/ Leaves That Are Green/ Punky's Dilemma/ America/ So Long, Frank Lloyd Wright/ Song For The Asking/ A Poem On The Underground Wall/ Bridge Over Troubled Water/ The Sound Of Silence/ Bye Bye Love/ Old Friends
R: Ex. Soundboard. Some static.   S: Kingdom Of The Netherlands, Amsterdam May 21 '70.
C: Japanese CD. Dbw. Time 74:48.

CD - BACK TO COLLEGE
YELLOW DOG YD 044
Mrs. Robinson (4:51)/ Fakin' It (3:33)/ The Boxer (5:28)/ So Long Frank Lloyd Wright (3:11)/ Why Don't You Write Me (3:38)/ Silver Haired Daddy (3:19)/ Cuba Si - Nixon No (3:27)/ Bridge Over Troubled Water (5:47)/ Sound Of Silence (4:43)/ Bye Bye Love (2:34)/ Homeward Bound (6:28)/ At The Zoo (2:18)/ America (7:19)/ Song For The Asking (1:45)/ A Poem On The Underground Wall (3:52)/ For Emily, Whenever I May Find Her (2:29)
R: Ex. Soundboard.   S: Miami University, Oxford, Ohio Nov. 11 '69.   C: ECD. Dcc.

CD - THE HARMONEY OF THE SPHERES
DYNAMITE STUDIO DS94J095
The Boxer/ Homeward Bound/ Fakin' It/ The 59 Street Bridge Song (Feelin' Groovy)/ Old Folk Song/ I'm A Rock/ Kathy's Song/ Mrs. Robinson/ Scarborough Fair/ The Leaves That Are Green/ The Lonely Living Boy In New York/ America/ So Long, Frank Loyd Wright/ Song For The Asking/ Blessed/ Bridge Over Troubled Water/ Bye Bye Love/ Old Friends
C: Vg. Radio broadcast.   S: Concertgebouw, Amsterdam May 2 '70.   C: Japanese CD.

CD - QUE VIVA BARBA!
TEDDY BEAR TB 52
R: Ex. Soundboard.   S: Miami University, Oxford, Ohio Nov. 11 '69.   C: ECD. Pic CD. See 'Back To College' for songs.

CD - VOICE OF INTELLIGENT DISSENT
VIGOTONE VIGO-124
Mrs. Robinson/ Homeward Bound/ April Come She Will/ Fakin' It/ Overs/ The 59th Street Bridge Song (Feelin' Groovy)/ America/ A Most Peculiar Man/ I Am A Rock/ At The Zoo/ Scarborough Fair, Canticle/ Bye Bye Love/ Cloudy/ Punky's Dilemma/ Benedictus/ The Dangling Conversation/ For Emily, Whenever I May Find Her/ A Poem On The Underground Wall/ Anji/ The Sound Of Silence/ Richard Cory/ Old Friends/ He Was My Brother

R: G.   S: Hollywood Bowl, CA Aug. 23 '68.

SIMPLE MINDS

CD - DON'T FORGET PARIS
OXYGEN OXY 040
She's The River (5:20)/ Up On The Catwalk
(4:48)/ See The Lights (4:55)/ The American
(5:04)/ Big Sleep (4:19)/ Love Song (6:03)/ And
The Band Played On (5:38)/ Sanctify Yourself
(6:58)/ Alive And Kicking (6:32)/ She Moved
Through The Fair (5:26)/ White Light White Heat
(3:25)/ Hypnotised (6:19)/ Don't Forget About Me
(6:48)
R: Exs. Soundboard.   S: Tracks 1-8 'L'
Olympia', Paris, France Oct. 31 '95. Tracks 9-13
'Taratata TV Show', Paris, France Oct. 10 '95.
C: ECD. Pic CD.

CD - FORM PHALLUS FUNCTION
MEN AT WORK WORK 5550-2
King Is White And In The Crowd (9:08)/ Glittering
Prize (5:13)/ Celebrate Celebrate (7:41)/ The
American (6:38)/ Colours Fly And Catherine
Wheel (4:32)/ Hunter And The Hunted (7:01)/
Promised You A Miracle (5:29)/ Someone
Somewhere In Summertime (5:39)/ Big Sleep
(6:52)/ Careful In Career (12:24)
R: Exs. Soundboard.   S: Bologna, Italy Mar. 14
'83.   C: ECD. Pic CD.

CD - PAINTING THE BLUE SKIES BLACK
OXYGEN OXY 005
She Is The River (6:09)/ The American (5:05)/
Great Leap Forward (5:47)/ Someone
Somewhere In Summertime (5:17)/ Hypnotised
(7:02)/ Let There Be Love (7:36)/ Belfast Child
(8:18)/ Medley: Waterfront, Roadhouse Blues, On
The Road Again (7:32)/ Love Song (6:04)/ Alive
And Kicking (6:18)/ Don't You (Forget About Me)
(7:06)
R: Exs. Soundboard.   S: The Royal Concert
Hall, Glasgow, Scotland Sept. 10 '95.   C: ECD.
Dcc. Pic CD.

SIMPLY RED

CD - LIVE LIFE
MOONRAKER 042/43
CD1: Sad Old Red/ Enough/ Lives And Loves/
Jericho/ A New Flame/ So Many People/ So
Beautiful/ Holding Back The Years/ You Make Me
Believe/ Never Never Love/ Come To My Aid/
Infidelity/ Hillside Avenue/ The Right Thing
CD2: Stars/ It's Only Love/ Remembering The
First Time/ Thrill Me/ Money's Too Tight (To
Mention)/ If You Don't Know Me By Now/
Something Got Me Started/ Fairground/
Fairground/ Money's Too Tight (To Mention)/
Gangsta's Paradise (featuring Coolio)/ You Make
Me Believe/ Fairground
R: CD1 and CD2 tracks 1-8 Ex. Audience. CD2
tracks 9-13 Ex. Soundboard.   S: CD1 and CD2
tracks 1-8 Hallenstadion, Zurich, Switzerland Dec.

6 '95. CD2 track 9 MTV European Awards '95.
Tracks 10-13 Taratata, French TV Dec. 10 '95.
C: ECD. Dbw. Electric blue band with red type.
Time CD1 73:39. CD2 67:43.

SIOUXSIE AND THE BANSHEES

CD - EUROPE 1993
RARITIES AND FEW RFCD 1284
Fall From Grace/ The Killing Jar/ Stargazer/ Cities
in Dust/ Hang Me High/ Nightshift/ Not Forgotten/
The Ghost In You/ Face To Face/ Kiss Them For
Me/ Peek-A-Boo/ Love Out Me/ Fear (Of The
Unknown)/ Israel/ Monitor
R: Exs. Soundboard.   S: Reading Festival Aug.
28 '93.   C: ECD. Time 75:23.

CD - SISTER MIDNIGHT
KISS THE STONE KTS 429
Tearing Apart (3:43)/ Christine (3:10)/ Kiss Them
For Me (4:54)/ Dear Prudence (4:27)/ Nightshift
(6:20)/ Cities In The Dust (3:51)/ Love Out Me
(4:45)/ Peek-A-Boo (3:19)/ Fear (Of The
Unknown) (4:13)/ Israel (4:44)/ The Ghost In You
(5:08)/ Face To Face (4:46)/ Kiss Them For Me
(5:06)/ The Killing Jar (3:55)/ Cities In The Dust
(4:14)/ Nightshift (6:24)
R: Exs. Soundboard.   S: Tracks 1-7 Europe '95.
Tracks 8-16 Europe '93.   C: ECD. Dcc. Pic CD.

SKID ROW

CD - MERCI BEAUCOUP MOTHERFUCKERS
BABY CAPONE BC 036/2
CD1: Slave To The Grind (3:47)/ Big Guns (5:38)/
Here I Am (4:04)/ Makin' A Mess (3:51)/ 18 And
Life (6:17)/ Piece Of Me (4:00)/ Sweet Little Sister
(7:20)/ Psychotherapy (2:59)/ Wasted Time (8:38)/
Psycho Love (4:03)/ Mudkicker (5:17)/ Midnight,
Tornado (3:23)
CD2: Quicksand Jesus (7:16)/ Get The Fuck Out
(10:27)/ Monkey Business (4:13)/ Riot Act (6:11)/
Train Kept A Rollin' (4:12)/ I Remember You
(3:21)/ Youth Gone Wild (6:09)/ Holidays In The
Sun (4:02)/ Blitzkrieg Bop (1:54)/ Room Service
(3:21)/ Cold Gin (4:55)/ You Really Got Me (3:25)/
Rattlesnake Shake (2:46)
R: G-Vg. Audience.   S: 'Le Zenith', Paris, Nov.
18 '91.   C: ECD. Dcc. Pic CDs.

CD - SLAVE TO THE GLIND OUTTAKES
BONDAGE MUSIC BON 014
Monkey Business/ Slave To The Glind/ Livin' On A
Chain Gang/ Mudkicker/ Beggar's Day/ Wasted
Time/ Pshyco Love/ Going Down/ You And Me/
Creep Show
R: Vg sound.   S: Demo tape.   C: Japanese
CD.

CD - THIS IS THE SUBHUMAN GIG!
CRACKER CR-18
Slave To The Grind/ Piece Of Me/ Frozen/ Here I
Am/ Bonehead/ Beat Yourself Blind/ Psycho
Therapy/ Psycho Love/ Subhuman Race/

Mudkicker/ Medicine Jar/ Into Another/ Monkey Business/ Riot Act/ Get The Fuck Out/ My Enemy/ Youth Gone Wild
R: Poor Audience.   S: Tilburg, Holland Mar. 26 '95.

SLASH'S SNAKEPIT

CD - GET IN THE PIT
SPM 1211/1212
CD1: Doin' Fine/ What Do You Want To Be/ Take It Away/ Cure Me Kill Me/ Good To Be Alive/ Lower/ Neither Can I/ Soma City Ward/ Monkey Chow
CD2: Back And Forth Again/ Jizz Da Pit/ Tijuana Jail (includes 'My Michelle')/ Be The Ball/ Begger's And Hangers On/ Shot Down In Flames
R: G-Vg. Audience.   S: Hiroshima May 21 '95.

CD - GOOD TO BE LIVE
CRACKER CR-19
Doin' Fine/ Take It Away/ Good To Be Alive/ Neither Can I/ Monkey Chow/ Soma City Ward/ Lower/ Cure Me...Or Kill Me.../ Dime Store Rock/ Back And Forth Again/ Be The Ball/ Beggars And Hangers-on/ Acid Queen/ Tie Your Mother Down
R: Vg. Audience.   S: New York City Apr. 13 '95.

SLAUGHTER

CD - PERMANENT VACATION
BABY CAPONE BC 013
Mad About You (6:03)/ Burning Bridges (4:20)/ Eye To Eye (6:59)/ Spend My Life (3:13)/ Fly To The Angels (6:45)/ Up All Night (6:10)/ Desperately (6:06)/ Loaded Gun (5:54)
R: Exs. Soundboard.   S: Electric Ladyland Studios, NYC Mar. 27 '91.   C: ECD. Dcc. Pic CDS.

SLAYER

CD - THE SICKNESS WITHIN
OXYGEN OXY 009
Chemical Warfare (5:43)/ Mandatory Suicide (3:57)/ War Ensemble (4:56)/ Divine Intervention (5:08)/ Dittohead (2:26)/ Dead Skin Mask (5:09)/ Seasons In The Abyss (6:05)/ Raining Blood (2:15)/ Angel Of Death (4:49)/ Killing Fields (4:21)/ At Dawn They Sleep (7:10)/ 213 (4:35)/ South Of Heaven (4:10)/ Raining Blood (2:30)/ Black Magic (3:43)/ Mind Control (3:33)/ Reborn (2:19)
R: Ex.   S: Tracks 1-9 Donnington Festival, UK Aug. 26 '95. Tracks 10-15 The Solnahallen, Stockholm, Sweden Dec. 16 '94. Tracks 16-17 The Brixton Academy, London, UK Nov. 9 '94.
C: ECD. Dcc. Pic CD.

SLINT

7" - STUDIO OUTAKES
S1: Title Unknown (from Tweez Sessions)
S2: Title Unknown (from Spiderland Sessions)
R: Ex. Soundboard.   C: USA. B&w sleeve.

Limited edition of 600. 45 RPM.

SLY AND THE FAMILY STONE

THANK YOU - GREATEST LIVE!
WEEPING GOAT WG-024
Love City/ Thank You/ M' Lady/ Sing A Simple Song/ Stand!/ Introduction/ Stand!/ If You Want Me To Stay/ Thank You/ Dance To The Music/ Thank You/ I Want To Take You Higher
R: Ex.   S: Track 1 Ed Sullivan Show '67. Tracks 2-5 Baarn, The Netherlands 9/10/70. Tracks 6-10 D.K.R.C. '73. Tracks 11-12 Dick Cavett Show.
C: Japanese CD.

SMASHING PUMPKINS

CD - ACOUSTIC DAZE
CHELSEA CFC 008
Cherub Rock (4:26)/ Disarm (3:19)/ Rocket (4:43)/ Spaceboy (3:02)/ Today (3:23)/ Dancing In The Moonlight (4:07)/ Mayonaise (5:18)/ Hummer (6:47)/ Obscured (5:18)/ The Honey Spiders (2:44)/ Hello Kitty Kat (4:29)/ Girl Called Sandoz (3:46)/ Lunar (3:08)/ I Am One (4:39)/ Silver Fuck (10:46)/ Rhinocerous (5:35)
R: Ex. Soundboard.   S: Tracks 1-8 live acoustic. Tracks 9-11 demos. Tracks 12-16 live '93.
C: ECD. Dcc. Time 74:18.

CD - ASTORIA '94
PUMPKIN MUSIC PM054
Rocket/ Quiet/ Today/ Disarm/ I Am One/ Hammer/ Geek USA/ Spaceboy/ Siva/ Cherub Rock/ Luna/ Starla/ Never Let Me Down Again/ Silver Fuck
R: Exs.   S: Astoria Theatre, London, England Feb. 25 '94.

CD - BLACKOUT
KISS THE STONE KTS 492
Tonight, Tonight/ Zero/ Today/ Disarm/ Fuck You (An Ode To No One)/ Thru The Eyes Of The Vast Oceans/ Bullet With Butterfly Wings/ Cherub Rock/ Mayonaise/ X.Y.U./ Baby Loves To Rock/ If You Want My Love/ Auf Wiedersehen
R: Exs. Soundboard.   S: The Riviera Theater, Chicago Oct. 23 '95.   C: ECD. Pic CD.

CD - THE CUTTING EDGE
BACKSTAGE BKCD 077
ACOUSTIC: Spaceboy (4:09)/ Dancing In The Moonlight (4:07)/ Rocket (4:20)/ Cherub Rock (4:30)/ Today (3:24)/ Disarm (3:24)/ ELECTRIC: I Am One - Disarm (4:59)/ Geek USA (6:06)/ Drown (6:41)/ I Am One (4:08)/ Cherub Rock (5:10)/ Silverfuck (10:55)/ I Am One (4:09)
R: Exs. Soundboard.   S: Tracks 1-6 VPRO Studios, Hilversum, Holland July '93. Tracks 7-13 Dronten, Belgium Aug. 27 '93.   C: ECD. 67:00.

CD - PUMPKINHEAD
MONTANA MO 10021
Clean Like Tomorrow/ White Girl/ Los Angeles/

Nausea/ Some Other Time/ Country At War/ Back To The Base/ 4th Of July/ You Wouldn't Tell Me/ Devil Doll/ Rocket/ Today/ Disarm/ Drown/ Hummer/ Soma/ Siva/ Cherub Rock
R: Exs. Soundboard.　　S: New York '94.
C: ECD. Time 75:23.

CD - STARLIGHT
MOONRAKER 028/29
CD1: Tonight, Tonight/ Jellybelly/ Zero (Take One)/ Power Failure/ Zero (Take Two)/ Today/ Disarm/ Fuck You (An Ode To No One)/ Thru The Eyes Of Ruby/ Geek U.S.A./ Porcelina Of The Vast Oceans
CD2: Bullet With Butterfly Wings/ Cherub Rock/ Mayonaise/ X.Y.U./ Baby Loves To Rock/ If You Want My Love/ Auf Wiedersehen/ Pre-Show Interview
R: Exs. Soundboard.　　S: Riviera Theatre, Chicago Oct. 23 '95.　　C: ECD.

CD - UNEREABLE
LAST BOOTLEG RECORDS LBR 018
Rocket (4:34)/ Today (3:25)/ Disarm (3:21)/ Drown (5:17)/ Hummer (6:25)/ Soma (6:53)/ Siva (5:44)/ Cherub Rock (6:08)/ Geek USA (5:06)/ Quiet (3:42)/ Bury Me (4:19)
R: Exs. Soundboard.　　S: Crosby Auditorium, Delmar, CA '93.　　C: ECD. Dbw. Red Type. Pic CD.

CD - THE WORLD IS A VAMPIRE
OXYGEN OXY 020
Tonight, Tonight (4:26)/ Jellybelly (3:53)/ Zero (5:49)/ Today (2:56)/ Fuck You -The Ode To No One (4:51)/ Thru The Eyes Of Ruby (7:09)/ Geek The USA (5:30)/ Porcelina Of The Vast Oceans (8:43)/ Bullet With Butterfly Wings (4:09)/ Cherub Rock (5:03)/ Mayonaise (6:46)/ X.Y.U. (7:23)/ If You Want My Love (3:24)/ Auf Wiedersehen (3:30)
R: Exs. Soundboard.　　S: The Riviera Theatre, Chicago Oct. 23 '95.　　C: ECD. Dcc.

SMITH, PATTI

CD - LIVE AT CBGB'S
SWINGIN' PIG TSP CD 211-2
CD1: Glass Factory/ Redondo Beach/ Song For Jim Morrison/ Kimberley/ Dancing Barefoot/ Space Monkey/ Privilege (Set Me Free)/ 25th Floor/ Cold Turkey/ For Your Love/ Revenge
CD2: Frederick/ Seven Ways Of Going/ Popples/ All Along The Watchtower/ Spider And Fly 1985/ So You Want To Be A Rock 'N' Roll Star/ 5-4-3-2-1/ Twist And Shout/ My Generation
S: CBGB'S, New York City '79.　　C: ECD.

CD - LIVE UNDERCOVER
DYNAMITE STUDIO DS94M081/82
CD1: So You Want To Be (A Rock 'N' Roll Star)/ Star Spangled Banner, Rock 'N' Roll Nigger/ Privilege (Set Me Free)/ Dancing Barefoot/ Redondo Beach/ 25th Floor/ High On Rebellion/

Revenge
CD2: Pumping (My Heart)/ Seven Ways Of Going/ Because The Night/ Frederick/ Jailhouse Rock/ Gloria/ My Generation
R: Good audience recording.　　S: Grugahalle, Essen, Germany Apr. 22 '79.　　C: Japanese CD.

CD - PHILADELPHIA ROCK
FLASHBACK 03.93.0208
Set Me Free/ Till Victory/ So You Want To Be A Rock'n'Roll Star/ Citizenship/ Redondo Beach/ Jailhouse Rock/ 25th Floor/ 5-4-3-2-1/ Be My Baby/ Because The Night/ Frederick/ Gloria/ Pumping/ My Generation
R: Vg. Soundboard.　　S: Mann Centre, Philadelphia May '79.　　C: ECD. Time 72:01.

SOFT BOYS, THE

CD - ROUT OF THE CLONES
FEG 002
Blues In The Dark/ The Bells Of Rhymney/ Sandra's Having Her Brane Out/ The Pigworker/ School Dinner Blues/ Cold Turkey/ Leppo And The Jooves/ Have A Heart Betty/ I Like Bananas/ Wading Through A Ventilator/ The Rat's Prayer/ Give It To The Soft Boys/ Hear My Brane/ Return Of The Sacred Crab/ Mystery Train/ Muriel's Hoot-Rout Of The Clones/ (I Want To Be An) Anglepoise Lamp/ Poor Will And The Jolly Hangman
R: Vg-Ex. Soundboard.　　S: Tracks 1-10 The Lady Mitchell Hall, Cambridge Nov. 27 '78. Tracks 11-14 Leicester University '78. Tracks 15-17 The Lady Mitchell Hall, Cambridge Mar. '78. Track 18 rehearsal session - date unknown.　　C: ECD. Dbw. Yellow type. Time 71:03.

SOFT MACHINE, THE

CD - FUSION
CANTERBURY DREAM CTD-013
The Floating World/ Ban-Ban Children/ Out Of Season/ Bundles/ Land Of The Bag Suake/ The Man Who Waved At Trais/ Peff
R: Vg-Ex audience recording.　　S: Reading Festival '75.

CD - HAZARD PROFILE
ZA-45
Hazard Profile Part 1, Part 2 (Toccatina), Part 3, Part 4, Part 5/ The Man Who Wave At Trains/ Peff/ Bass Solo, Bundles, Land Of The Bad Snake/ Four Gongs To Drums/ Hazard Profile
R: Vg. Audience.　　S: Howard Stains, UK Mar. 24 '74. Track 6 Montreuax Jazz Festival '74.

SONIC YOUTH

7" - NOW AND THEN
S1: Brother James (Holland '85)/ Touch Me I'm Sick (Sub Pop 7")
S2: 100% (David Letterman)/ Non Metal Dude Wearing Metal Tee (Forced Exposure 7")

R: Ex.   C: USA. Blue/yellow cover. 33 RPM.

CD - SHOOT!
LAST BOOTLEG RECORDS LBR 004/2
CD1: White Cross (8:05)/ Eric Trips (6:26)/
Cinderella's Big Score (3:01)/ Kill Your Idols
(4:45)/ Silver Rocket (5:00)/ Tunic (2:28)/ Dirty
Boots (5:34)/ Mary-Christ (4:12)/ Kool Thing
(4:25)/ My Friend Goo (7:02)/ I Wanna Be Your
Dog (8:03)/ 100% (3:24)/ Dirty Boots (4:49)/ Kool
Thing (4:37)/ Swimsuit Issue (3:06)/ Genetic
(4:00)
CD2: Theresa Soundworld (6:11)/ Tom Violence
(3:31)/ Sugar Kane (8:55)/ Schizophrenia (5:12)/
Drunken Butterfly (3:01)/ Youth Against Fascism
(3:46)/ Sugar Kane (6:06)/ J.C. (4:08)/
Schizophrenia (5:40)/ 100% (2:40)/ Kool Thing
(4:27)/ Teen Age Riot (4:37)/ Sugar Kane (7:12)/
Swimsult Issue (3:30)/ Drunken Butterfly (3:37)
R: Vg.   S: CD1 tracks 1-11 California '90. CD1
tracks 12-19 USA '92. CD2 USA '92. CD2 tracks
9-15 from 'The Big Day Out' Melbourne, Australia,
'93.   C: ECD. Dcc. Pic CD.

SOUL ASYLUM

CD - MISERY LOVES COMPANY
OXYGEN OXY 012
Hopes Up (3:40)/ Somebody To Shove (3:29)/
Shut Down (2:49)/ Bittersweetheart (3:40)/ Black
Gold (3:44)/ Eyes Of A Child (3:47)/ Promises
Broken (3:11)/ Nothing To Write Home About
(3:18)/ Misery (4:11)/ String Of Pearls (4:57)/ New
World (4:26)/ Runaway Train (4:29)/ Get Out
(3:47)/ 99% (3:58)/ Crawl (4:33)/ Caged Rat
(3:34)/ Just Like Anyone (3:32)/ To My Own
Devices (3:23)/ I Live For You (5:14)
R: Exs. Soundboard.   S: The Aragon Ballroom.
Chicago Sept. 15 '95.   C: ECD. Dcc. Pic CD.
Tracks 18-19 encore with Victoria Williams and
members of The Jayhawks.

CD - SET ME FREE
KISS THE STONE KTS 467
Caged Rat/ Black Gold/ Get On Out/ Runaway
Train/ String Of Pearls/ Just Like Anyone/ Close
To The Stars, Crawl/ Eyes Of A Child/
Bittersweetheart
R: Exs. Soundboard.   S: The Glastonbury
Festival June 23 '95.   C: ECD. Dcc. Pic CD.
Time 40:02.

SOUNDGARDEN

CD - HARDER FASTER
LAST BOOTLEG RECORDS LBR 014
Searching With My Good Eye Closed (5:14)/
Hands All Over (6:07)/ Big Dumb Sex (5:14)/
Drawing Flies (2:19)/ Incessant Mace (9:11)/ Gun
(5:29)/ Mind Riot (4:22)/ Beyond The Wheel
(7:07)/ Jesus Christ Pose (6:22)/ Somewhere
(4:05)/ Slaves And Bulldozers (16:37)
R: G-Vg. Audience.   S: Live during '92 US tour.
C: ECD. Dcc. Pic CD.

SPRINGSTEEN, BRUCE

CD - AMERICAN STYLE
FRONT ROW METEOR FM 2115
Lucky Town (4:50)/ Darkness On The Edge Of
Town (5:07)/ Chain Smoke (4:32)/ There'll Never
Be Enough Time (7:42)/ Brown Eyed Girl (5:00)/
Mustang Sally (8:15)/ Atlantic City (6:48)/ Diddie
Wa Diddie (4:30)/ Living Proof (6:37)/ Glory Days
(5:28)/ Around And Around (2:50)/ Bama Lama
Lama Loo (4:51)/ The Wanderer, Kansas City
(7:50)
C: Vg. Audience.   S: Marz American Style, Long
Branch, New Jersey Aug. 20 '94.   C: ECD.
Featuring Joe Grushecky and The Houserockers,
John Eddie and Dion.

CD - AND THE BAND PLAYED
THE SWINGIN' PIG TSP CD 051
Spirit In The Night/ The E Street Shuffle/ 4th Of
July, Asbury Park (Sandy)/ And The Band Played/
Rosalita (Come Out Tonight)/ Medley: Let The
Four Winds Blow, I'm Ready
R: Exs. Soundboard.   S: The Agora Club,
Cleveland Feb. 18 '74.   C: ECD. Time 51:43.

CD - BRUCE SPRINGSTEEN AND
BOB DYLAN: FOREVER YOUNG
GAMBLE RECORDS BSGR-09
C: See listing under 'Various Artists'.

CD - COLISEUM NIGHT
CRYSTAL CAT CC 351-353
CD1: Night/ Out In The Street/ Tenth Avenue
Freezeout/ Who'll Stop The Rain/ Darkness On
The Edge Of Town/ Factory/ Intro/ Independence
Day/ 9 other tracks
CD2: Cadillac Ranch/ Sherry Darling/ Hungry
Heart/ Merry Christmas Baby/ Fire/ Candy's
Room/ Because The Night/ 4th Of July, Asbury
Park (Sandy)/ 3 other tracks
CD3: Point Blank/ The Ties That Bind/ Ramrod/
You Can Look (But You Better Not Touch)/
Incident On 57th Street/ Rosalita (Come Out
Tonight)/ 8 other tracks
R: Ex soundboard.   S: Nassau Coliseum,
Uniondale, NY Dec. 29 '80.   C: ECD.

CD - DO YOU LOVE ME?
COUNTDOWN FACTORY CDF-953023/A/B/C
CD1: Born In The U.S.A./ Badlands/ Out In The
Street/ Johnny 99/ Seeds/ Atlantic City/ The River/
Walking On The Highway/ Trapped/ Darlington
County/ Glory Days
CD2: The Promised Land/ My Home Town/
Thunder Road/ Cover Me/ Dancing In The Dark/
Hungry Heart/ Cadillac Ranch/ Downbound Train/
I'm On Fire
CD3: Pink Cadillac/ Bobby Jean/ This Land Is
Your Land/ Born To Run/ Ramrod/ Twist And
Shout/ Do You Love Me/ Sherry Darling
R: G-Vg. Audience.   S: Giants Stadium, New
Jersey Aug. '85.   C: ECD. Dcc.
Time CD1 66:56. CD2 58:11. CD3 55:03.

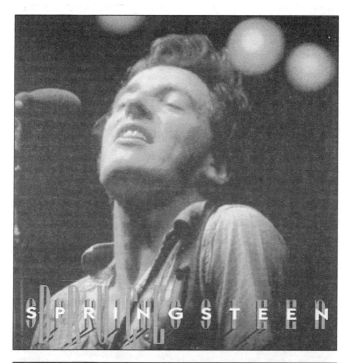

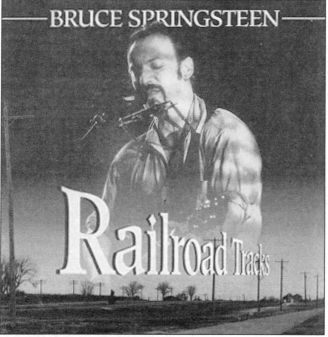

CD - DOWN IN JUNGLELAND VOL. 1
WINGED WHEEL WW9432
Night (3:12)/ Rendezvouz (3:45)/ Spirit In The Night (6:11)/ It's My Life (10:37)/ Thunder Road (6:00)/ She's The One (12:03)/ Something In The Night (4:24)/ Backstreet (7:51)/ 10th Avenue Freeze Out (4:23)
R: Exs. Soundboard. S: Springfield Aug. 22 '73. C: ECD. Dcc. Gatefold cover. Pic CD - looks like a record.

CD - DOWN IN JUNGLELAND VOL. 2
WINGED WHEEL WW9433
Jungleland (11:40)/ Rosalita (Come Out Tonight) (15:14)/ Raise Your Hand (5:24)/ 4th Of July, Ashbury Park (Sandy) (7:44)/ Quarter To Three (6:53)
R: Exs. Soundboard. S: Mobile May 11 '73. C: ECD. Dcc. Gatefold cover. Pic CD - looks like a record.

CD - EXIT THROUGH THE BACK DOOR
YELLOW CAT YC 041/42
CD1: I Just Can't Change/ All I Want To Do Is Dance/ Down To Mexico/ Bless My Soul/ Magic Kind Of Loving/ Love Is A Crazy Thing
CD2: The Band's Just Boppin' The Blues/ Down To Mexico/ Instrumental/ Bright Lights, Big City
R: G. Audience. S: The Backdoor Club, Richmond, Virginia Feb. 26-27 '72. C: ECD. Dcc. Time CD1 45:30. CD2 45:10.

CD - FIRST NIGHT IN DETROIT
MIDNIGHT BEAT MB CD 041/42
CD1: Tenth Avenue Freeze-Out (4:30)/ Spirit In The Night (7:03)/ It's Gonna Work Out Fine (8:12)/ She's The One (6:38)/ Born To Run (4:38)/ The E Street Shuffle (14:07)/ Backstreets (5:45)/ Kitty's Back (19:36)
CD2: Band Introduction (1:04)/ Jungleland (10:18)/ Rosalita (Come Out Tonight) (10:54)/ Devil With The Blue Dress Medley: Devil With The Blue Dress, Good Golly Miss Molly, CC Rider, Jenny Take A Ride (6:02)/ 4th Of July, Asbury Park (Sandy) (8:35)/ Ain't To Proud To Beg (3:38)/ Quarter To Three (7:58)/ Little Queenie (9:24)/ Twist And Shout (9:19)
R: Exs. Soundboard. S: Michigan Palace, Detroit, Michigan Oct. 4 '75. C: ECD. Dcc.

CD - GRANDE FINALE
WINGED WHEEL WW 9415/17
CD1: Born In The U.S.A(6:02)/ Badlands (5:01)/ Out In The Street (5:55)/ Johnny 99 (4:20)/ Seeds (6:40)/ Darkness On The Edge Of Town (4:46)/ The River (11:43)/ War (4:55)/ Working On The Highway (5:29)/ Trapped (5:16)/ I'm Goin' Down (4:34)/ Prove It All Night (5:57)
CD2: The Promised Land (10:01)/ My Hometown (4:51)/ Thunder Road (7:16)/ Cover Me (6:37)/ Dancing In The Dark (5:43)/ Hungry Heart (4:14)/ Cadillac Ranch (8:17)/ No Surrender (4:13)/ I'm On Fire (6:14)/ Grown' Up (13:28)
CD3: Rosalita (15:09)/ This Is Your Land (3:48)/

Born To Run (4:36)/ Bobby Jean (4:07)/ Ramrod (5:59)/ Medley: Twist And Shout, Do You Love Me? (17:24)/ Stand On It (3:20)/ Travellin' Band (3:50)/ Rockin' All Over The World (3:52)/ Glory Days (6:34)
R: G-Vg. Audience. S: LA Oct. 2 '85.
C: ECD. Box set with Dcc. B&w poster. Full color book. CDs come in B&w paper sleeve. CDs look like records.

CD - I'M A ROCKER
OTTAWA RECORDS OR-81
Sandy/ For You/ Stolen Car/ Wreck On The Highway/ Point Blank/ The Ties That Bind/ Ramrod/ Backstreets/ Rosalita/ I'm A Rocker/ Jungleland/ Born To Run/ Detroit Medley
R: Vg. Fades in and out. S: Maple Leaf Gardens, Toronto, Canada Jan. 20 '81.

CD - KILLERS IN THE SUN
WINGED WHEEL WW 9427/29
CD1: Good Rockin' Tonight (4:02)/ Badlands (4:42)/ Streets Of Fire (4:22)/ Spirit In The Night (7:27)/ Darkness On The Edge Of Town (4:35)/ It's My Life (5:08)/ Factory (5:00)/ Heartbreak Hotel (2:34)/ The Promised Land (5:50)/ Prove It All Night (11:52)/ Racing In The Street (8:19)
CD2: Thunder Road (7:17)/ Jungleland (10:07)/ Paradise By The C (5:52)/ Fire (3:19)/ Sherry Darlin' (6:29)/ I Don't Wanna Hang Up My Rock 'N' Roll Shoes (3:40)/ Candy's Room (3:15)/ Adam Raised A Cain (4:54)/ Medley: Mona, She's The One (12:26)
CD3: Growin' Up (12:45)/ Backstreet (11:23)/ Rosalita (Come Out Tonight) (10:24)/ Born To Run (5:53)/ Quarter To Three (12:07)
R: Vgs. Audience. S: Saginaw, Michigan Sept. 30 '74. C: ECD. Box set with Dcc. Full color book. CDs come in B&w paper sleeve. CDs look like records.

CD - LOOSE ENDS
KISS THE STONE KTS 406
The Tie That Bind/ Cindy/ Hungry Heart/ Stolen Car/ To Be True/ The River/ You Can Look... (But You'd Better Not Touch)/ The Price You Pay/ I Wanna Marry You/ Loose Ends
R: Exs. Soundboard. S: The Power Station, New York Sept. '79. C: ECD. Dcc. Pic CD. Time 38:41.

CD - LOST AND LIVE
KISS THE STONE KTS 426
For You (acoustic version, Amsterdam Nov. 22 '75)/ Double Shot Of My Baby's Love, Louie-Louie (South Bend, Ill. Sept. 9 '78)/ The Last Time (Cleveland Jan. 1 '79)/ No Money Down (LA Oct. 13 '80)/ This Little Girl (E. Rutherford, NJ July 3 '81 with Gary US Bonds)/ Deportee (Plane Crash At Los Gatos), Proud Mary (LA Aug. 28 '81)/ Travelin' Band, I'm Bad I'm Nationwide (Stone Pony, Asbury Park Aug. 22, '84 with La Bamba's Hupcaps)/ I'm A Rocker, Street Fighting Man, Wooly Bully (Tacoma, WA Oct. 19 '84)/ Janey

Don't You Lose Heart (Los Angeles Sept. 27 '85)/ I Can't Help Falling In Love (East Berlin July 18 '88)/ I Ain't Got No Home (Oakland Sept. 23 '88)/ Streets Of Philadelphia (MTV Awards, NYC Sept. 9 '94)/ Thunder Road (duet with Melissa Etheridge on her MTV 'Unplugged' show Feb. 15 '95)/ Murder Inc., Tenth Ave Freeze Out, Secret Garden ('Late Show With David Letterman', NYC May 5 '95 with The E. Street Band)
R: G-Vg. Some Ex. Audience. Some soundboard. C: ECD. Pic CD. Time 79:10.

CD - MOVIE OF '71
TEDDY BEAR TB 33
Send That Boy To Jail, Going Back To Georgia (19:54)/ Oh Mama Why? (4:27)/ Changin' Children (10:20)/ Medley: Dancing In The Streets, Honky Tonk Women, Dancing In The Streets (Reprise) (12:25)/ I Can't Take It No More (8:00)/ I'll Be Your Saviour (11:42)
R: Ex. Some hiss.   S: The Scene Club, Asbury Park Jan. 18 '71.   C: ECD. Dcc. Pic CD.

CD - MUSIC HALL
ALL OF US AS 45/2
CD1: Incident On 57th Street/ Tenth Avenue Freeze Out/ Spirit In The Night/ Pretty Flamingo/ Growin' Up/ It's Hard To Be A Saint In The City/ E Street Shuffle/ She's The One/ Born To Run/ Thunder Road
CD2: Kitty's Back, Nothing's Too Good For My Baby, Kitty's Back (Reprise)/ Jungleland/ Rosalita (Come Out Tonight)/ 4th Of July, Asbury Park, NJ/ Carol-Lucille-Carol/ Quarter To Three
C: Exs. Soundboard.   S: Music Hall, Houston, Texas Sept. 13 '75.   C: ECD. Dcc.

CD - OAKLAND NIGHT
CRYSTAL CAT CC 357-59
CD1: Born In The USA/ Who'll Stop The Rain/ Out In The Street/ Atlantic City/ Johnny 99/ Reason To Believe/ Mansion On The Hill/ State Trooper/ 5 other tracks
CD2: Point Blank/ Badlands/ Thunder Road/ Cover Me/ Dancing In The Dark/ Hungry Heart/ Cadillac Ranch/ Downbound Train/ I'm On Fire/ 3 other tracks
CD3: Bobby Jean/ Racing In The Street/ Rosalita (Come Out Tonight)/ Jungleland/ Follow That Dream/ Born To Run/ Devil With A Blue Dress On/ 6 other tracks
R: Vg-Ex audience recording.   S: Coliseum, Oakland, CA Oct. 21 '84.   C: ECD.

CD - PARAMOUNT NIGHT
CRYSTAL CAT CC 346-48
CD1: Good Rocking Tonight/ Badlands/ Streets Of Fire/ Spirit In The Night/ Rendezvous/ 6 other tracks
CD2: Jungleland/ The Ties That Bind/ 10 other tracks
CD3: Backstreets/ Rosalita (Come Out Tonight)/ Born To Run/ Devil With A Blue Dress On, Good Golly Miss Molly/ CC Rider, Jenny Take A Ride/

50 Dollar Insurance, Jenny Take A Ride/ Tenth Avenue Freeze-Out/ Quarter To Three/ Reprise Quarter.../ Pretty Flamingo/ The Fever
R: Ex soundboard. CD3 tracks 10-11 Ex audience recording.   S: Paramount Theatre, Portland Dec. 19 '78. CD3 tracks 10-11 Seattle Dec. 20 '78.   C: ECD.

CD - RAILROAD TRACKS
OXYGEN OXY 027
The Ghost Of Tom Joad (6:43)/ Straight Time (5:12)/ Darkness On The Edge Of Town (4:23)/ Born In the U.S.A. (4:04)/ Youngstown (4:13)/ Sinaloa Cowboys (4:27)/ Balboa Park (5:34)/ Does This Bus Stop At 82nd Street? (2:56)/ This Hard Land (4:58)/ Streets Of Philadelphia (3:18)/ The Ghost Of Tom Joad (4:42)/ Back In Your Arms Again (Take 1) (0:41)/ Back In Your Arms Again (Take 2) (3:18)/ Without You (Take 1) (1:16)/ Without You (Take 2) (3:18)/ High Hopes (2:50)/ Down By The River (5:56)/ Rocking In A Free World (5:46)
R: Exs. Soundboard. Tracks 17-18 Ex. Audience.   S: Tracks 1-10 Tower Theatre, Philadelphia Dec. 9 '95. Track 11 Jay Leno's Tonight Show, Nov. 27 '95. Tracks 12-16 live in studio with the E-Street Band, New York City Jan. '95. Tracks 17-18 Shoreline, Mountain View, CA Oct. 28 '95 with Neil Young.   C: ECD. Sepia-tone cover.

CD - THE REMIX ALBUM
COLUMBUS CSK 6969
Dancing In The Dark (Blaster Mix) (6:04)/ Dancing In The Dark (Radio) (4:50)/ Dancing In The Dark (Dub) (5:30)/ Cover Me (Undercover Mix) (6:05)/ Cover Me (Dub I) (4:02)/ Cover Me (Radio) (3:46)/ Cover Me (Dub II) (4:15)/ Born In The U.S.A. (The Freedom Mix) (7:20)/ Born In The U.S.A. (Dub) (7:36)/ Born In The U.S.A. (Radio) (6:10)/ 57 Channels (And Nothing On) (Little Steven Mix Version 1) (5:56)/ 57 Channels (And Nothing On) (Little Steven Mix Version 2) (4:45)/ 57 Channels (And Nothing On) (There's A Riot Goin' On) (8:19)/ Streets Of Philadelphia (Video Version With Live Vocals) (2:57)
R: Exs. Soundboard.   C: ECD. Dcc.

CD - ROCKS THE PLAYPEN
MOONLIGHT RECORDS ML 9501
Hey Tonight/ Suspicious Minds/ Bang A Gong (Get It On)/ Route 66/ Gloria/ Rockin' Pneumonia/ From Small Things Big Things Come/ Jersey Girl/ Glory Days/ Twist And Shout/ Message In A Bottle
R: Vg-Ex. Track 11 G.   S: Tracks 1-5 The Playpen Club, New Jersey Oct. 21 '94. Tracks 6-10 Tradewinds June 29 '93. Track 11 Madison Square Garden in '88 with Sting.   C: ECD. Dcc. Time 72:38.

CD - ROXY NIGHT
CRYSTAL CAT CC 342-44
CD1: Intro/ Rave On/ Badlands/ 9 other tracks
CD2: Paradise By The 'C'/ Fire/ Adam Raised A Cain/ Mona/ She's The One/ Growin' Up/ 4 other

tracks
CD3: Independence Day/ Born To Run/ Because
The Night/ Raise Your Hand/ Twist And Shout/
Streets Of Fire/ It's My Life/ Factory/ Jungleland/ I
Don't Wanna Hang Up My Rock'N Roll Shoes/
Candy Room/ Adam Raised A Cain
R: Ex audience recording.   S: Roxy Theatre, LA
July 7 '78. CD3 tracks 6-12 Civic Center, Saginaw
Sept. 3 '78.   C: ECD.

CD - THE ROXY ROAD
DYNAMITE STUDIO DS94A071/072
CD1: Thunder Road/ Tenth Avenue Freezeout/
Spirit In The Night/ Pretty Flamingo/ She's The
One/ Born To Run/ Sandy/ Backstreets
CD2: Kitty's Back/ Jungle Land/ Rosalita/ Going
Back/ Detroit Medley
C: Good radio broadcast. Scratchy.   S: Roxy
Oct. 17 '75.   C: Japanese CD.

CD - SMALLTOWN BOY
THE SWINGING PIG RECORDS TSP CD 037
New York City Serenade (6:23)/ Wild Billy's Circus
Story (6:02)/ Spirit In The Night (5:21)/ Does This
Bus Stop At 82nd Street? (4:41)/ Hey Santa Ana
(10:08)/ And The Band Played (7:06)/
Thundercrack (13:44)
R: Vg-Ex. Soundboard.   S: Main Point, Bryn
Mawr Apr. 24 '73.   C: ECD. Dcc.

CD - SPECTRUM NIGHT
CRYSTAL CAT CC 354-56
CD1: Intro, Prove It All Night/ 14 other tracks
CD2: Tenth Avenue Freeze-Out/ Hungry Heart/
You Can Look (But You Better Not Touch)/
Cadillac Ranch/ 6 other tracks
CD3: Born To Run/ Devil With A Blue Dress On/
Good Golly Miss Molly/ C.C. Rider, Jenny Take A
Ride/ I Hear A Train, Devil With.../ You Can't Sit
Down, Devil With.../ Sweet Soul Music/ The
Shake, Devil With.../ Johnny Bye Bye/ The River/
Joe Blon/ For You/ 2 other tracks
R: Ex audience recording.   S: The Spectrum,
Philadelphia July 15 '81. CD3 tracks 9-14 Capitol
Center, Landover Aug. 4 '81.   C: ECD.

CD - STREETS SURVIVOR
BUGSY BGS 038/2
CD1: The Lady And The Doctor (4:12)/ 4th Of
July, Asbury Park (5:40)/ Prodigal Son (6:58)/
Visitation At Fort Horn (7:43)/ Growin' Up (3:20)/
The Angel (3:28)/ Song To The Orphans (6:31)/
For You (4:46)/ Hey Santa Ana (4:59)/ Jazz
Musician (6:12)/ Camilla Horn (1:55)/ Seaside Bar
Song (3:39)/ Arabian Night (5:59)/ Family Song
(5:05)/ Evacuation Of The West (4:31)
CD2: New York City Serenade (10:07)/ Jesse
(3:07)/ Kitty's Back (7:12)/ War Nurse (2:08)/
Eloise (1:55)/ Does This Bus Stop At 82nd
Street? (2:09)/ Marie (4:45)/ Randolf Street,
Master Of Electricity (3:48)/ Local Hero (9:10)/
Growin' Up (3:17)/ The Big Muddy (4:26)/ 57
Channels, And Nothin' On (5:22)/ Glory Days
(6:53)/ Roll Of The Dice (12:06)

R: Ex. Soundboard.   S: 914 Sound Studios,
Blauvelt, NY   C: ECD. Dcc. Pic CD.

CD - SUMMERNIGHT
CRYSTAL CAT CC 363-64
CD1: Intro/ Tunnel Of Love/ Boom Boom/ Adam
Raised A Cain/ The River/ All That Heaven Will
Allow/ Seeds/ Roulette/ Cover Me/ Brilliant
Disguise
CD2: Tougher Than The Rest/ Intro/ Spare Parts/
War/ Born In The USA/ Chimes Of Freedom/
Highway Patrolman/ Downbound Train/ I'm On
Fire/ Seeds/ Rockin' All Over The World/ Street
Fighting Man
R: Vgs. CD2 tracks 7-12 Ex audience recording.
S: Stockholm July 3 '88. Track 7 London June 6
'85. CD2 tracks 8-12 London and Newcastle June
and July '85.   C: ECD.

CD - THIS AIN'T NO ROCK AND ROLL SHOW
DOBERMAN 001/002
CD1: The Ghost Of Tom Joad/ Adam Raised A
Cain/ Straight Time/ Highway 29/ Darkness On
The Edge Of Town/ Murder Incorporated/
Nebraska/ If I Should Fall Behind/ Born In The
U.S.A./ Dry Lightning/ Spare Parts/ Youngstown
CD2: Sinoloa Cowboys/ The Line/ Balboa Park/
Across The Border/ Does This Bus Stop At 82nd
Street/ This Hard Land/ Dead Man Walking/
Galveston Bay/ My Best Was Never Good
Enough
R: Exs. Audience.   S: New Brunswick, New
Jersey Nov. 21 '95.   C: UK CD. Limited edition
of 60 copies on recordable CDs. Time CD1 59:49.
CD2 46:08.

CD - USA BLUES
CRYSTAL CAT CC 320
Spirit In The Night/ For You/ Darkness On The
Edge Of Town/ If I Should Fall Behind/ The River/
Promised Land/ Born In The USA/ Mansion On
The Hill/ This Hard Land/ Point Blank/ Many
Rivers To Cross/ Thunder Road/ Satan's Jewel
Crown/ Seeds/ Adam Raised A Cain
R: Ex.   S: Acoustic in USA and Europe '92 - '93.
C: ECD. Time 73:21.

STEELY DAN

CD - AN EVENING WITH STEELY DAN
SD-001/002
CD1: Overture/ Green Earrings/ Bodhisattva/
I.G.Y./ Josie/ Hey Nineteen/ Box Of Rears/ Chain
Lightning/ Band Intros/ Green Flower Street/
Home At Last/ Black Friday
CD2: Travellin' Music/ In The Years/ Fall Of '92/
Peg/ Third World Man/ Teahouse On The Tracks/
My Old School
R: Vg audience recording.   S: Nagoya, Japan
Apr. 16. '94.

CD - AN EVENING WITH STEELY DAN JAPAN
TOUR '94
NK 41701/41702

CD1: Overture/ Green Earrings/ Bodhisattva/ I.G.Y./ Josie/ Hey Nineteen/ Book Of Liars/ Chain Lightning/ Band Introduction/ Green Flower Street/ Home At Last/ Black Friday
CD2: Travelin' Music/ Deacon Blues/ Babylon Sisters/ Reelin' In the Years/ Fall Of '92/ Peg/ Third World Man/ Teahouse On The Tracks/ My Old School/ FM
R: Vg audience recording.　　S: Tokyo Bay NK Hall Apr. 17 '94.

CD - AT THE BAY AREA: JAPAN TOUR '94
RIKKI RECORDS 001-2
CD1: The Royal Scam, Parker's Band, Aja/ Green Earrings/ Bodhisattva/ I.G.Y./ Josie/ Hey Nineteen/ Book Of Life/ Chain Lighting/ Band Introduction/ Green Flower Street/ Home At Last/ Black Friday
CD2: Jazzy Instrumental/ Deacon Blues/ Babylon Sisters/ Reelin' In The Years/ Fall Of '92/ Peg/ Third World Man/ Teahouse On The Tracks Encore/ My Old Friend/ FM
R: Ex. Audience.　　S: Tokyo Bay NK Hall Apr. 17 '94.　　C: Japanese CD. Dcc.

CD - THE KATY LIED SESSIONS & MORE
PR 1976
Daddy Don't Live In That New York City No More/ Chained Lightning/ Black Friday/ Rose Darling/ Throw Back The Little Ones/ Doctor Wu/ Your Gold Teeth II/ The Caves Of Altamira/ Do It Again/ Reeling In The Years
R: Vg-Ex. Soundboard.　　S: Tracks 1-7 outtakes and alternate versions from 'Katy Lied' sessions '74-'75. Track 8 from 'The Royal Scam' demo. Tracks 9-10 live '74.　　C: Japanese CD. Dcc. Time 39:59.

CD - MEMPHIS BLUES AGAIN
GOLD STANDARD
Bodisahtva/ Boston Rag/ Do It Again/ Brooklyn/ King Of The World/ Funky Scare Tactic Orchestra Blues/ Rikki, Don't Lose That Number/ Pretzel Logic/ Introductions/ My Old School/ Dirty Work/ Reeling In The Years/ Show Biz Kids/ This All Too Mobile Home/ East St. Louis Toodle-00
R: Exs. Soundboard.　　S: Memphis, Tenn. May '74.　　C: Japanese CD. Dcc. Time 74:19.

CD - METAL LEG
CAPRICORN RECORDS CR-2045
Do It Again/ Rikki Don't Lose That Number/ Any Major Dude Will Tell You/ King Of The World/ Barrytown/ My Old School/ Pretzel Logic/ Do It Again/ Rikki Don't Lose That Number/ Any Major Dude Will Tell You/ King Of The World/ My Old School/ Bodhisattva/ The Boston Rag
R: Exs. Soundboard.　　S: Tracks 1-7 Irvine, CA 3/10/94. Tracks 8-14 San Diego, CA 3/9/74. C: Time 73:53.

CD - SECOND ARRANGEMENT
STAM7780
Gaucho/ Second Arrangement (unreleased song)/

Glamour Profession/ My Rival/ Babylon Sisters/ Night By Night/ The Fez/ Kid Charlemagne (edited version)/ Green Earring/ My Old School/ Excerpt Of FM/ Kid Charlemagne (unedited version)
R: G-Vg.　　S: Tracks 1-5 'Gaucho' outtakes. Tracks 6-12 studio rehearsal '76.

STILLS-YOUNG BAND, THE

CD - BLIND RIVER IN 1962
F*!#IN' UP FUPCD-2012/13
CD1: Love The One You're With/ The Loner/ Helpless/ For What It's Worth/ Long May You Run/ Black Queen/ Southern Man/ Sugar Mountain/ Midnight On The Bay/ After The Gold Rush/ Word Game
CD2: 49 Bye Bye/ Circlin'/ Treetop Flyer/ Blackbird/ Heart Of Gold/ Ohio/ Buying Time/ Let It Shine/ Make Love To You/ Cowgirl In The Sand/ Mr. Soul/ Suite: Judy Blue Eyes
R: G-Vgs audience recording.　　S: Civic Center, Providence, RI July 7 '76.　　C: Japanese CD.

STING

CD - A DAY IN THE LIFE
LAST BOOTLEG RECORDS LBR 006
Faith (5:33)/ Heavy Cloud, No Rain (4:29)/ A Day In The Life (3:37)/ Fields Of Gold (3:47)/ Synchronicity (4:31)/ Magic (4:15)/ Roxanne (6:53)/ Shape Of My Heart (4:24)/ Englishman In New York (5:10)/ King Of Pain (7:31)/ Bring In The Night, Invisible World (8:57)/ She's Too Good (3:46)/ Nothing 'Bout Me (4:00)/ Every Breath You Take (6:07)/ Fragile (4:05)
R: Exs. Soundboard.　　S: Brendon Burn Arena, New Jersey Feb. 14 '94.　　C: ECD. Dcc.

CD - HAPPY BIRTHDAY!
BABY CAPONE BC 012/2
CD1: All This Time (5:12)/ Jeremaih Blues (Part 1) (7:15)/ Mad About You (5:21)/ Driven To Tears (4:20)/ Ain't No Sunshine When She's Gone (4:55)/ Why Should I Cry For You? (9:00)/ Roxanne (5:15)/ Bring On The Night (1:52)/ When The World Keeps Running Down (7:50)/ King Of Pain (7:03)
CD2: Fortress Around Your Heart (3:23)/ The Wild Wild Sea (6:04)/ The Soul Cages (6:48)/ Purple Haze (3:05)/ If You Love Somebody Set Them Free (4:33)/ We'll Be Together (2:54)/ Walking On The Moon (3:12)/ Every Breath You Take (6:06)/ Message In A Bottle (8:06)/ Fragile (5:03)/ Russians (4:12)/ I Miss You Kate (4:48)
R: Exs. Soundboard.　　S: Hollywood Bowl, Los Angeles Oct. 2 '92.　　C: ECD. Dcc. Pic CD.

STONE ROSES

CD - COMPLETE EARLY DEMO TRACKS
3D REALITY 3D-SR-001
Here Is Comes/ Self Respect/ Swallow My Airwaves #1/ How Long/ The Saviour/ You're Not

So Good/ You're No One/ Dragging Me Down/ I Wanna Be Adored/ Swallow My Airwaves #2/ Sally Cinnamon/ Hardest Thing/ Across The Sand/ Heart On The Stares/ This Is The One/ Wanna See You Fall/ Tragic Round-About
R: Vg-Ex.

CD - STONED IN WALSALL
CHELSEA CFC 023
Adored (6:00)/ Sally Cinnamon (4:20)/ Elephant Stone (3:46)/ Waterfall (4:47)/ Going Down (2:58)/ Made Of Stone (4:43)/ Standing Here (5:02)/ I Don't Want You Now (4:18)/ Shoot You Own (3:48)/ She Bangs The Drums (3:47)/ I Am The Resurrection (10:54)/ Fools Gold, A Guy Called Gerald (remix) (5:24)*/ Adored (3:46)*/ Heart On The Staves (3:26)*/ Tell Me (4:04)*
R: Vg. Audience. *Ex. Soundboard.   S: The Walsall Junction 10 Club. *Strawberry Studio Session '85.   C: ECD. Dcc.

STONE TEMPLE PILOTS

CD - INTERSTATE LOVE SONGS
KISS THE STONE 439
Vasoline/ Silvergum Superman/ Crackerman/ Meatplow/ Still Remains/ Midnight Roundup (acoustic)/ Pretty Penny (acoustic)/ Creep (acoustic)/ Andy Warhol (acoustic)/ Army Ants/ Big Empty/ Interstate Love Song/ Plush/ Unglued/ Dead And Bloated/ Sex Type Thing
R: Exs. Soundboard.   S: Live on tour '95.
C: ECD. Dcc. Pic CD. Time 66:37.

STRADLIN, IZZY

CD - TAKE A LOOK AT THE GUY
ROCKS 92110
Bucket O Trouble/ Cuttin' The Rug/ Jiving Sister Fanny/ Time Gone By/ Rocker/ Somebody Knockin'/ Pressure Drop/ Little Red Rooster/ Amazing Grace, Highway 49/ Cuttin' The Rug/ Crackin' Up/ Time Gone By/ Rocker/ Somebody Knockin'/ Little Red Rooster/ Amazing Grace, Highway 49
R: Vg.   S: Tracks 1-9 USA '92. Tracks 10-16 Amsterdam '92.

STRAY CATS

CD - JAMMIN' WITH CATS
ALL OF US AS 34
Double Talkin' Baby (3:10)/ Rumble In Brighton (3:39)/ Routegg (4:32)/ Rockabilly Rebel (5:43)/ Blue Cadillac (3:14)/ Runaway Boys (3:31)/ Lonely Summernights (3:54)/ Too Hip, Gotta Go (2:32)/ Stray Cats Strut (5:32)/ Foggy Mountain Breakdown (2:13)/ The Racieson (1:48)/ Rev It Up And Go (3:32)/ Blue Swede Shoes (6:35)
R: Ex. Audience.   S: Tracks 1-12 Loreley Open Air Festival Aug. 20 '83. Track 13 New York Bam Majestic Theatre Aug. 18 '88.   C: ECD. Dcc.

SUEDE

CD - COVER ME
KISS THE STONE KTS 434
This Hollywood Life/ We Are The Pigs/ Killing Of A Flash Boy/ Animal Nitrate/ The Wildones/ Pantomine Horse/ The Drowners/ Metal Mickey/ The Asphalt World/ So Young/ Heroine/ New Generation
R: Exs. Soundboard.   S: Toronto, Canada Feb. 17 '95.   C: ECD. Dcc. Pic CD. Time 55:02.

SUPERGRASS

CD - DOING TIME
KISS THE STONE KTS 488
Sitting Straight (2:23)/ I'd Like To Know (3:56)/ Mansized Rooster (2:54)/ Time (3:08)/ Alright (2:48)/ Caught By The Fuzz (2:21)/ Lenny (3:02)/ Sitting Straight (2:07)/ Mansized Rooster (2:43)/ I'd Like To Know (3:51)/ Time (3:11)/ Alright (2:39)/ Odd (3:32)/ She's So Loose (3:02)/ Good Times (2:13)/ Condition (2:28)/ Lose It (2:34)/ Caught By The Fuzz (2:16)/ Strange Ones (3:47)/ Lenny (2:57)/ Weird Geezer (1:08)/ Alright (2:33)/ Caught By The Fuzz (2:19)/ Mansized Rooster (2:43)
S: Tracks 1-7 Ansom Rooms, Bristol Apr. 18 '95. Tracks 8-20 Glastonbury Festival June 23 '95. Tracks 21-24 Camdon , London July 11 '95.
C: ECD. Pic CD.

CD - FEEL ALRIGHT!
OXYGEN RECORDS OXY 038
Sitting Up Straight (2:23)/ Mansize Rooster (2:54)/ I'd Like To Know (4:08)/ Time (3:29)/ Alright (2:47)/ Odd? (3:56)/ She's So Loose (3:08)/ Susan (4:47)/ Lose It (3:05)/ Condition (2:53)/ Caught By The Fuzz (2:56)/ Strange Ones (3:40)/ Lenny (3:50)/ Susan 94:10)/ Condition (2:39)/ Time (3:09)/ I'd Like To Know (3:45)/ Odd? (5:07)/ Strange Ones (3:35)/ Lenny (2:38)/ We're Not Supposed To (2:06)
R: Exs. Soundboard.   S: Tracks 1-13 Opera House, Toronto, Canada Sept. 11 '95. Tracks 14-17 BBC Aug. '95. Track 18 BBC Jan. '95. Tracks 19-20 BBC Sept. '95. Track 21 'Mercury Music Prize', London Sept. '95.   C: ECD.

SWEET

LP - GREAT BALLS OF FIRE
PSEUDONYM RECS
S1: Mockingbird/ Chop Chop/ Tom Tom Turnaround/ Mr. Businessman/ Funny Funny
S2: Rock N' Roll Medley/ Coco/ A Message From Sweet/ Baby What Do You Want Me To Do/ Great Balls Of Fire
R: Exs.   S: Sweden '71. Radio Broadcast.
C: 10 inch disc. 500 numbered copies on orange vinyl. 500 copies as Pic-disc.

LP - TEENAGE RAMPAGE
FLASH
S1: Hellraiser (3:17)/ Blockbuster (3:16)/ Be With
You Soon (3:31)/ Teenage Rampage (3:21)/
Ballroom Blitz/ Rebel Rouser (3:55)/ Done Me
Wrong... (2:46)
S2: Little Willy (4:52)/ Teenage Rampage (3:17)/
Rock And Roll Medley (8:25)/ Ballroom Blitz
(4:25)/ Blockbuster, FBI (5:11)
S: S1 Clubgigs '72-'75. Side 2 Rainbow Theatre
X-Mas '73.

T

TAKE THAT

CD - HEARTBEATS
OCTOPUS OCTO 091
Meaning Of Love (4:42)/ Whatever You Do To Me
(8:47)/ Everything Changes (4:33)/ A Million Love
Songs (3:05)/ Babe (6:19)/ Love Ain't Here
Anymore (5:15)/ Relight My Fire (6:41)/ Pray
(5:48)/ Could It Be Magic (4:43)
R: Exs. Soundboard.   C: ECD. Dcc. Pic CD.

TAYLOR, JAMES

CD - GOT SOME FRIENDS
RSM 064 SQ
Lo And Behold (3:56)/ Mexico (3:20)/ Promised
Land (3:16)/ Gotta Stop Thinkin' (5:06)/ Rainy
Day Man (4:06)/ Frozen Man (4:21)/ Your Smiling
Face (2:56)/ Copperline (4:25)/ Carolina In My
Mind (5:08)/ Wandering (3:26)/ Memphis
Tennessee (3:27)/ Note Fade Away (3:02)/ Never
Die Young (5:11)/ Up On The Roof (4:23)/ You've
Got A Friend (5:03)/ Steamroller Blues (5:15)/
How Sweet It Is (7:32)/ Sweet Baby James (3:42)
R: Exs. Soundboard.   S: Great Woods,
Mansfield, Mass. '94.   C: ECD.

CD - NOT FADE AWAY
ZA 39/40
CD1: Sweet Baby James/ Secret O'Life/ Mexico/
The Promised Land/ Copperline/ Don't Let Me Be
Lonley Tonight/ I've Got To Stop Thinkin' Bout
That/ Never Die Young/ The Frozen Man/ Handy
Man/ 5 more tracks
CD2: California On My Mind/ Not Fade Away/ Up
On The Roof/ You've Got A Friend/ How Sweet It
Is/ Fire And Rain/ Steamroller/ You Can Close
Your Eyes/ Not Fade Away/ Up On The Roof/
You've Got A Friend/ one more track
R: Ex. Audience.   S: Sun-Plaza Hall, Tokyo
Mar. 15 '95.

TAYLOR, JAMES AND CAROLE KING

CD - ROSES FOR CAROLE
MAIN STREET MST 104
For Free/ Carolina In My Mind/ Okie From
Muskogee/ Sweet Baby James/ I Love My Babe/
Greensleeves/ Blossom/ Up On The Roof/
Country Road/ Night Out/ That Restless Feeling/
Where The Golden Rainbows End/ Riding On The
Railroad/ Highway Song/ Fire And Rain/ You Can
Close Your Eyes
R: Exs. Soundboard.   S: Second show,
Berkeley Community Theater '70.   C: ECD.
Dcc. Time 63:58.

TAYLOR, MICK

CD - GIMMIE SOME BLUES
IMPROVISATION LABEL IL-366812
Tasks/ Put It Where You Want It/ Red House
Blues/ Giddy-Up/ Rock Me Baby/ Hope Water
Music
R: Exs. FM broadcast.   S: Yubin Chokin Kaikan,
Tokyo Apr. 11 '87.

THIN LIZZY

CD - THE BOYS ARE BACK AGAIN '94
CD1: Jail Break/ Waiting For An Alibi/ Don't
Believe A Word/ Cold Sweat/ Emerald/ The Sun
Goes Down/ Angel Of Death/ Are You Ready/ Bad
Reputation/ Suicide
CD2: Got To Give It Up/ Still In Love With You/
Cowboy Song/ The Boys Are Back In Town/
Rosalie/ Black Rose/ Thunder And Lightning
R: Exs. Soundboard.   S: Tribute to Phil Lynott
by members of Thin Lizzy.   C: Japanese CD.
Dcc. Group signatures on discs.

CD - GARY'S JIG
NIGHTLIFE N-023
Black Boys On The Corner/ Crawlin/ Little Darlin/
Slow Blues/ Show Down/ Every Little Thing About
You/ It's Only Money/ Gary's Jig/ Sitamoia/ The
Rocker/ Hard Driving Man/ Rock'N'Roll With You
R: Vg-Ex. Audience recording.   S: Bristol
Locarno Apr. 14 '74.

CD - RETURN OF THE LEGEND
SBN 24
Jailbreak/ Waiting For An Alibi/ Don't Believe A
Word/ Cold Sweat/ Emerald/ The Sun Goes
Down, Keyboard Solo/ Angel Death/ Are You
Ready?/ Bad Reputation/ Got To Give It Up/ Still
In Love With You/ Cowboy Song/ The Boys Are
Back In Town/ Rosalie
R: Exs. Soundboard recording.   S: Tokyo,
Japan Nov. 24 '94.

THOMPSON, RICHARD

CD - CLOWN TIME IS OVER
MOONTUNES MOON 002
Ride In Your Slipstream/ Easy There Easy Now/
The Way That It Shows/ Tear Stained Letter/ Al
Bowleys Heaven/ Mascara Tears/ Shoot Out The
Lights/ Valerie/ Wall Of Death/ I Feel So Good/
Vincent Black Lightning/ Now That I'm Dead/
Read About Love/ Don't Roll Those Bloodshot
Eyes At Me/ Turning Of The Tide/ Feel So Good

R: Ex.   S: Tracks 1-10 Circus, Stockholm Mar. 25 '94. Tracks 11-14 Borderline, London July 6 '91. Track 15 Nov. '88. Track 16 Oct. '91. C: ECD. Dcc. Time 71:26.

CD - COLUMBIA GOLD
SOUNDBOARD MUSIC SBM CD 001/002
CD1: I Misunderstood, Killing Jar (8:12)/ Mystery Wind (5:13)/ 1952 Vincent Black Lightning (5:30)/ I Misunderstood (5:18)/ Two Left Left (5:25)/ Shoot Out The Lights (5:18)/ Waltzing For Dreamers (5:33)/ Turning Of The Tide (5:38)/ Now That I'm Dead (4:07)/ Jerusalem On The Jukebox (3:53)/ God Loves A Drink (5:29)/ I Feel So Good (5:22)/ She Moves Through The Fayre (4:39)/ Wall Of Death, Needles And Pins (5:15)
CD2: Days Of Our Lives (2:18)/ You'll Never Walk Alone (2:47)/ Can't Win (6:06)/ Valrie (6:01)/ Down Where The Drunkards Roll (4:20)/ C'Est Plein Pour Moi (5:01)/ Waltzing For Dreamers (3:48)/ Don't Roll Those Bloodshot Eyes At Me (3:52)/ Mingues Eyes (acoustic version) (3:44)/ I Can't Wake Up To Save My Life (acoustic version) (2:59)/ Why Must I Plead (4:02)/ Wall Of Death, Needles And Pins (4:20)/ Shake Rattle And Roll (4:07)/ Substitute (3:36)
R: CD1-CD2 track 10 Ex. Soundboard. CD2 tracks 11-14 Ex. Audience.   S: CD1 track 1 soundcheck, Columbia Feb. 27 (cover says '27' but it may be the 17th or perhaps the 17th should be the 27th. Whatever, it's excellent) '91. CD1 tracks 2-14 and CD2 tracks 1-8 Columbia Feb. 17 '91. CD2 tracks 9 and 10, CD2 acoustic radio session, UK '94. CD2 tracks 11-14 Glastonbury Festival, UK summer of '92.

CD - NOCTURNAL EMMISSIONS
NIXED RECORDS NIX 004
Night Comes In/ I'm A Dreamer/ I Want To See The Bright Lights Tonight/ Shoot Out The Lights/ You're Gonna Need Somebody/ Dargai/ Dimming The Day/ Night Comes In/ Jet Plane In a Rocking Chair/ Honky Tonk Blues/ Its Just The Motion/ The Choice Wife/ Two Lonely Hearts/ Honky Tonk Blues/ Further Along/ Move It On Over/ Banish Misfortune/ How Many Times/ Break My Mind
R: Vg-Ex. Soundboard. Some hiss.   S: Tracks 1-8 BBC TV 'A Little Night Music' broadcast Aug. 19 '81. Tracks 9-13 Granada TV 'Music From The Flags' broadcast Aug. '80. Tracks 14-17 Sugarhill Records demos Aug. '82. Tracks 18-19 Capitol Radio session June 22 '80.   C: ECD. Dcc. Pic CD.

THOMPSON, LINDA AND RICHARD

CD - HARD LUCK STORIES
95-RTL-04-01
Backstreet Slide/ Just The Motion/ Honky Tonk Blues/ I'll Keep It With Mine/ You're Gonna Need Somebody/ Pavanne/ Withered And Died/ Man In Need/ For Shame Of Doing Wrong/ Down Where The Drunkards Roll/ Danny Boy/ Dimming Of The Day/ I'm A Dreamer/ Hard Luck Stories

R: Ex. Soundboard.   S: Bottom Line, NYC May 17 '82. Tracks 1-12 early show. Tracks 13-14 late show.   C: Japanese CD. Time 71:09.

CD - RAFFERTY'S FOLLY
NIXED RECORDS NX 001
Don't Reneg On Our Love/ Back Street Slide/ Walking On A Wire/ The Wrong Heartbeat/ Shoot Out The Lights/ For Shame Of Doing Wrong/ I'm A Dreamer/ Modern Woman/ Just The Motion/ Wall Of Death/ Lucky In Life/ How Many Times Do You Have To Fall?/ Poor Will And The Jolly Hangman/ Wall Of Death/ Sword Dance, Young Black Cow/ I Want To See The Bright Lights Tonight
R: Ex. Soundboard.   S: Tracks 1-10 the complete Gerry Rafferty produced version of the 'Shoot Out The Lights' album, Chipping Norton Studios Sept. - Oct. '80. Tracks 11-12 demos, Woodworm Studios, Oxfordshire June '80. Tracks 13-16 Granada TV Show Oct. '81 with Fairport Convention.   C: ECD. Dcc. Time 68:56.

CD - ROCKPALAST
SILVER RARITIES SIRA 177/178
CD1: For Shame Of Doing Wrong/ Strange Affair/ Hard Luck Stories/ Crying In The Rain/ You're Gonna Need Somebody/ Pavanne/ Sunnyvista/ Don't Let A Thief Steal Into Your Heart/ Lonely Hearts/ Sisters/ Civilisation, Pipeline/ Night Comes In
CD2: I'm A Dreamer/ Borrowed Time/ I Want To See The Bright Lights Tonight/ No Particular Place To Go/ Man In Need/ Withered And Died/ New Fangled Flogging Reel, Kerry Reel/ Shoot Out The Lights/ Just The Motion/ Backstreet Slide/ Night Comes In/ Lucky In Life Unlucky In Love/ Just The Motion/ Backstreet Slide/ Walking On A Wire
S: CD1-CD2 tracks 4 Hamburg Jan. 10 '80. CD2 tracks 5-11 BBC Radio I 'In Concert' May '82. CD2 tracks 12-15 'Richard Digance Show', Capitol Radio Dec. 7 '80.   C: ECD. Time CD1 73:38. 69:37.

THOROGOOD, GEORGE

CD - IF YOU DON'T START DRINKING
SAVE THE EARTH STE 030
Born In Chicago/ Who Do You Love/ Born To Be Bad/ No Particular Place To Go/ I Drink Alone/ One Bourbon, One Scotch, One Beer/ If You Don't Start Drinking/ Sky Is Cryin'/ Madison Blues/ Back To The Bone/ Move It On Over/ Hello Little Girl
R: Exs. Soundboard.   S: Live in the USA '93. C: ECD. Time 74:01.

CD - VIVA LAS VEGAS
THE SWINGIN' PIG TSP CD 178
Who Do You Love/ No Particular Place To Go/ Night Time/ I Drink Alone/ One Bourbon, One Scotch, One Beer/ I'm Ready/ Get A Haircut/ Bad To The Bone/ Move It On Over/ You Talk Too

Much/ Johnny B. Goode
R: Exs. Soundboard.   S: Las Vegas, '93.
C: ECD. Time 69:05.

THUNDERS, JOHNNY

CD - LIVE CRISIS
MOGUL NIGHTMARE RECORDS MNR 003
Waste My Time/ M.I.A./ Cool Operator/
Personality Crisis/ Countdown Love/ Little Bit Of
Whore/ In Cold Blood, Steppin' Stone, Hit The
Road Jack/ Pipeline/ Sad Vacation/ Disappointed
In You/ Just Another Girl/ Too Much Junkie
Business/ Wipe Out/ Born To Lose
R: Exs. Soundboard.   S: Europe '85 and '86.
C: ECD. Dcc. Time 55:57.

CD - STICKS & STONES
TOTONKA CD PRO 7
Help The Homeless/ Disappointed/ Children Are
People/ Glory, Glory/ Familiarity Breeds
Contempt/ Bird Watching/ Tell The Truth/ The
Night Of The Living Dead/ Intro, Ask Me No
Questions, Wizard/ Pipeline/ (I'm Not) Your
Stepping Stone/ Great Big Kiss/ The 10
Commandments Of Love/ These Boots Are Made
For Walking/ Like A Rolling Stone/ Endless Party/
Pills/ Hootchie Coochie Man/ Personality Crisis
R: Ex. Soundboard.   S: Tracks 1-7 studio
demos. Tracks 8-18 Max's Kansas City, NYC.
C: ECD. Dcc. Time 69:32.

TOWNSHEND, PETE

CD - THE LIFEHOUSE DEMOS
HOWDY CD 555-09
Pure And Easy/ Behind Blue Eyes/ Love Ain't For
Keeping/ Mary/ Getting In Tune/ Going Mobile/
Too Much Of Anything/ Time Is Passing/ Won't
Get Fooled Again/ The Song Is Over/ Baba
O'Riley
R: Exs. Soundboard.   S: studio demos.
C: Asian CD. All tracks from vinyl sources. 62:33.

CD - LIFEHOUSE DEMOS
YELLOW DOG RECORDS YD 056
Pure And Easy (8:35)/ Behind Blue Eyes (3:26)/
Love Ain't for Keeping (1:33)/ Mary (Ian
Anderson) (4:17)/ Getting In Tune (4:05)/ Goin'
Mobile (4:15)/ Too Much (Of Anything) (5:38)/
Magic Bus (5:10)/ Party And Lies (6:39)/
Motherland Feeling ('67) (6:54)/ Real ('67) (3:10)
R: Exs. Soundboard. Tracks 10 and 11 G.
S: Tracks 1-7 Lifehouse demos.   C: ECD. Dcc.
Color. Time 53:54.

CD - QUADROPHENIA DEMOS
BLACK DOG RECORDS BD 005
The Real Me (4:02)/ Dirty Jobs #1 (4:04)/ Punk
Meets The Godfather (4:44)/ I'm One (2:24)/ Dirty
Job #2 (4:14)/ Bell Boy (4:40)/ Cut My Hair (3:32)/
Drowned (4:14)/ Instrumental (1975) (2:55)/ I'm
Gonna Fight To Make You Mine '75 (3:19)/ Who
Are You (demo) (7:26)/ Baba O'Riley (instrumen-

tal demo) (9:44)/ Dogs ('68 demo) (3:25)
R: Vg-Ex. Soundboard.   C: ECD. Dcc.

TRAFFIC

CD - WOODSTOCK 1994
OCTOPUS OCTO 045
Pearly Queen (5:13)/ Medicated Goo (5:37)/ Rock
'N' Roll Stew (6:13)/ Mozambique (5:22)/ The Low
Sparks Of High Heeled Boys (11:43)/ Glad,
Freedom Rider (10:35)/ Empty Pages (4:28)/
Light Up Or Leave Alone (12:40)/ Dear Mister
Fantasy (7:28)/ Gimme Some Lovin' (6:33)
R: Exs. Soundboard.   S: Woodstock '94.
C: ECD. Dcc. Pic CD.

TRAGICALLY HIP

CD - EAT ME COMPLETELY
GOLDEN BOYS COMPACT DISCS
Blow At High Dough/ It's Just As Well/ Locked In
The Trunk Of A Car/ Cordelia/ Get Back Again/
Radio Show/ Small Town Bringdown/ Greasy
Jungle*/ 2000 Light Years/ The Changeling/ New
Orleans Is Sinking, Nautical Disaster/ Hey Maria/
Suzie Q/ Baby Please Don't Go/ Thugs/ Crack My
Spine Like A Whip/ Train Kept A Rollin
R: Ex. Soundboard. *Ex. Audience.   S: Tracks
1, 15-16 Ontario Place Forum, Toronto June 22
'90. Track 2 86th St. Music Hall. Track 3
Landsdowne Hotel, Sydney Mar. 18 '93. Track 4
Molson Park, Barrie July 1 '92. Tracks 5-6
'Swinging On A Star' CBC studios fall '92. Track 7
Molson Canadian Rocks Tent, CNE, Toronto Aug.
'89. Track 8 Orpheum Boston Nov. 10 '84. Tracks
9, 12-13 Grand Central Station, Ottawa '87.
Tracks 10-11, 14 Kumbaya Festival, Ontario
Place Forum, Toronto Sept. 5 '93.   C: Dcc. Time
70:50.

TROWER, ROBIN

CD - DAYDREAM
VINTAGE RARE MASTERS VRE-005
Lady Love/ Somebody Calling/ Falling Star/ Too
Rolling Stoned/ Smile/ Daydream/ The Fool And
Me/ Bridge Of Sighs/ Day Of Eagle/ Little Bit Of
Sympathy/ Messin' The Blues/ Further On Up The
Road
R: Exs. Soundboard.   S: USA Oct. 18 '77.

TYPE O NEGATIVE

CD - EXPRESS YOURSELF, SAY YES!
Machine Screw/ Too Late, Frozen/ Gravital
Constant/ Summer Girl/ Paranoid/ Xero
Tolerance/ Christian Woman/ Prelude To Agony/
Unsuccessfully Coping With The Natural Beauty
Of Infidelity/ Summer Girl
R: G-Vg. Audience. Track 10 Ex. Soundboard.
S: Tracks 1-9 Ludwigsburg, Rockfabrik Oct. 16
'94. Track 10 demo version.   C: ECD. Dcc.
Time 76:19.

U

U2

CD - BAND ON THE RUN
MEN AT WORK WORK 5541-2-2
CD1: All Along The Watchtower (4:42), Slow Dancing (1:47) (Ahoy Hallen, Rotterdam Jan. 10 '09)/ Helter Skelter (3:33), Help (1:49) (Justin Herman Plaza, San Francisco Nov. 13 '87)/ C'Mon Everybody (1:46) (Hippodrome De Vindennes, Paris July 4 '87)/ Love Rescue Me (5:12) (London with Keith Richard and Ziggy Marley)/ Knockin' On Heaven's Door (4:43) (Teatro Tenda, Bologna Feb. 5 85)/ People Get Ready (2:45) (Dublin Dec. 31 '81)
CD2: Running To Stand Still (4:35), Dirty Old Town (1:53), The Times They Are A-Changing (1:52) (Dublin Dec. 31 '88)/ Stand By Me (4:34) (J.F. Kennedy Stadium, Philadelphia Sept. 25 '87)/ Rain (2:00), Hard Rain's Gonna Fall (1:47) (Milton Keynes Bowl June 22 '85)/ New Gold Dream (1:48), Take Me To The River (1:50), Light My Fire (2:06) (Barrowlands, Glasgow Jan. 4 '85)/ Someone Somewhere In Summertime (6:27) (Werchter July 3 '83)
R: G-Vg. Soundboard and Audience.   C: ECD. Super deluxe packaging on this one. The outer cardboard box has sepia-tone pictures and red type. Inside there's a quad-fold cardboard full color die-cut cover. This houses the 2 CDs and a full color book of photos and text. Finally, there's a 4 panel die-cut stand-up. All of this is topped off with pic CDs.

CD - BONO IS A DINKY TRABANT
INSECT RECORDS IST 34/35
CD1: Zoo Station/ The Fly/ Even Better Than The Real Thing/ Mysterious Ways/ One/ Until The End Of The World/ Who's Gonna Ride Your Wild Horses?/ Tryin' To Throw Your Arms Around The World/ Angel Of Harlem/ Satellite Of Love/ Bad (Medley)/ Bullet In The Blue Sky
CD2: Running To Stand Still/ Where The Streets Have No Name/ Pride (In The Name Of Love)/ I Still Haven't Found What I'm Looking For/ Desire (Medley)/ Ultraviolet (Light My Way)/ With Or Without You/ Love Is Like Blindness/ Mysterious Way/ Even Better Than The Real Thing/ Zoo Station/ Angel Of Harlem/ Satellite Of Love
R: G-Vg. Audience. CD2 Tracks 9-13 G. Audience.   S: CD1 and CD2 Tracks 1-8 Frank T. Erwin Centre, Austin, TX Apr. 7 '92. CD2 Tracks 9-13 soundcheck, Reunion Arena, Dallas, TX. Apr. 5 '92.   C: ECD. Dcc. Pic CD. Time CD1 60:58. CD2 62:56.

CD - DUETS
OXYGEN OXY 019
Miss Sarajevo (Bono, Edge, Eno and Pavarotti, Modena, Parco Novi Sad Sept. 12 '95 - 6:37)/ One (Bono, Edge and Eno Modena, Parco Novi Sad Sept. 12 '95 - 5:20)/ People Get Ready (U2 with Maria Mckee, The Point Depot, Dublin Dec. 27 '89 - 3:55)/ Sun City (U2 with Little Stevan, Nona Hendrix and Lou Reed, Giants Stadium, East Rutherford June 15 '86 -3:39)/ When Love Comes To Town (U2 and Keith Richard, A Concert For Smile Jamaica, London Oct. 16 '88 - 4:09)/ Bad, The First Time (U2 and J. Shankar, Wembley Stadium, London Aug. 12 '93 - 7:24)/ Invisible Sun (The Police and Bono, Giants Stadium, East Rutherford June 15 '86 - 5:25)/ I Shall Be Released (U2, Peter Gabriel, Sting, Bryan Adams and Lou Reed, Giants Stadium, East Rutherford June 15 '86 - 7:46)/ Gloria, Shaking All Over (Van Morrison and Bono, The Point Depot, Dublin Feb. 6 '93 - 13:01)/ It's All Over Now, Baby Blue (Van Morrison, Bono, Bob Dylan, Chrissy Hynde, Elvis Costello, Kris Kristofferson and Steve Windwood, The Point Depot, Dublin Feb. 6 '93 - 10:03)/ The Cross (Prince and Bono, The Pod, Dublin Mar. 30 '95 - 5:41)
R: Ex.   C: ECD. Dcc. Pic CD.

CD - FOUR WILD IRISH ROSES
OCTOPUS OCTO 096
I Will Follow (Richard Skinner session Sept. 9 '80 - 3:49)/ Two Hearts Beat As One (take 1 '83 demo - 3:51)/ Sunday Bloody Sunday (alternative studio version Feb. '83 - 4:37)/ Like A Song... (alternative studio version Feb. '83 - 3:35)/ Surrender (alternative studio version Feb. '83 - 4:11)/ Two Hearts Beat As One (take 2 '83 - 3:39)/ Tonight ('78 demo - 1:58)/ Trevor ('78 demo - 3:10)/ Inside Out ('78 demo - 1:59)/ I Threw A Brick Through A Window (Kid Jensen sessions Oct. 14 '81 - 4:16)/ Be There ('82 outtake - 4:44)/ Two Hearts Beat As One (take 3 '83 instrumental demo - 3:38)/ The Fool ('78 demo - 4:04)/ Two Hearts Beat As One (take 4 '83 demo - 3:37)/ Wire ('84 remix - 4:40)/ Jack In The Box ('78 demo - 1:59)/ New Year's Day (different version from Japanese TV Nov. '83 - 4:38)/ Love Comes Tumbling (different lyrics '84 - 4:37)/ My Wild Irish Rose (from the documentary film 'The Roots Of Irish Rock' - 6:54)
R: Ex. Soundboard.   C: ECD. Pic CD.

CD - JESUS WAS A COOL GUY
OXYGEN OXY 015
Stay (Faraway So Close) (Roundhay Park, Leeds Aug. 8, '93 - 5:06)/ One (Thalia Theatre, Hamburg Jan. 31 '93 - 4:47)/ Happy X-Mas (War Is Over) (Rte Studios, Dublin Dec. 16 '88 - 2:55)/ Lost Highway (D.I.R. Radio Sept. 8 '87 - 1:18)/ Slow Dancing (M.M.M. Aussie Radio Oct. 22 '89 - 1:55)/ I Still Haven't Found What I'm Looking For (Feyenoord Stadium, Rotterdam May 11 '93 - 4:32)/ Who's Gonna Ride Your Wild Horses (Dodger Stadium, Los Angeles Oct. 30 '92 - 3:20)/ She's Gonna Blow Your House Down (Long Island Beach Sept. '87 - 4:34)/ Lucille (D.I.R Radio Sept. 8 '87 - 1:39)/ Dirty Old Town (Feyenoord Stadium, Rotterdam May 9 '93 -

1:57)/ Acrobat (Take 1) (Hersey Stadium (SCK), Hersey Aug. 6 '92 - 3:07)/ Redemption Song (Vancouver Place Stadium, Vancouver, BC Nov. 3 '92 - 2:00)/ Norwegian Wood (Valle Hovin Stadium, Oslo July 27 '93 - 1:01)/ I Will Follow You (R.D.S Arena, Dublin Aug. 27 '93 - 2:32)/ She's A Mystery (Take 1) (Hersey Stadium (SCK), Hersey Aug. 6 '92 - 2:42)/ The Fly (Hersey Stadium (SCK), Hersey Aug. 6 '92 - 1:27)/ Whiskey In The Jar (CNE Stadium, Toronto Sept. 6 '92 - 1:57)/ Party Girl (Festivalterrein, Werchter May 29 '93 - 2:41)/ Wild Irish Rover (Feyenoord Stadium, Rotterdam May 11 '93 - 1:30)/ When Love Comes To Town (O' Connel Street, Dublin Oct. 27 '88 - 3:34)/ Acrobat (Take 2) (Hersey Stadium (SCK), Hersey Aug. 6 '92 - 3:41)/ She's A Misery to Me (Take 2) (Wembley, London Aug. 12 '93 - 1:41)/ Stand By Me (O' Connel Street, Dublin Oct. 27 '88 - 2:25)/ Springhill Mining Disaster (Late Late Show, Irish TV Mar. 16 '87 - 3:48)/ All I Want Is You (Gaint's Stadium, East Rutherford Aug. 13, 92 - 2:59)/ Can't Help Falling In Love (CNE Stadium, Toronto Sept. 6 '92 - 2:34)/ Are You Lonesome Tonight? (Feyenoord Stadium, Rotterdam May 11 '93 - 1:01)
R: Ex.   C: ECD. Dcc. Pic CD.

CD - MELON REMIXES FOR PROPOGANDA
ISLAND
Lemon (The Perfecto Mix)/ Salome (Zooromancer Remix)/ Numb (Gimme Some More Dignity Mix)/ Mysterious Ways (The Perfecto Mix)/ Stay (Underdog Mix)/ Numb (The Soul Assassins Mix)/ Mysterious Ways/ Even Better Than The Real Thing (The Perfecto Mix)/ Lemon (Bad Yard Club Mix)
R: Exs. Soundboard.   C: ECD. Yellow cover with red type. Time 63:49.

CD - PARTY AT TIFFANY
HERMES REC. 01
Gloria/ I Threw A Brick Through A Window/ A Day Without Me/ Seconds/ New Years Day/ Sunday, Bloody Sunday/ Electric Company/ I Fall Down/ Tomorrow/ Two Hearts Beats As One/ Out Of Control/ Party Girl/ Sunday, Bloody Sunday/ Maggie's Farm/ Help/ Sun City
R: Exs. Soundboard.   S: Glasgow, Scotland Mar. 24 '83.   C: ECD. Dcc. Pic CD. Time 69:08.

CD - RAIN ON YOU
TEDDY BEAR RECORDS TB 27
C'mon Everybody (2:57)/ Pride (In The Name Of Love) (4:33)/ Sunday Bloody Sunday (5:39)/ Maggie's Farm (6:30)/ Bad, Candle In The Wind, Walk On The Wild Side (9:35)/ M.K.L., Pride (In The Name Of Love) (5:19)/ Maggie's Farm, Cold Turkey (4:57)/ Help (2:24)/ Sun City (3:32)/ Sunday Bloody Sunday (5:37)/ Bad, Ruby Tuesday, Street Fighting Man, Walk On The Wild Side (12:36)
R: Vg-Ex. Soundboard.   S:Tracks 1-5 'Self Aid' Dublin, Ireland May 17 '86. Tracks 6-9 'Conspiracy Of Hope Tour' East Rutherford, NJ

June 15 '86. Tracks 10-11 'Live Aid' London July 13 '85.   C: ECD. Dcc. Pic CD.

CD - UNPLUGGED
KMACD 010
Angel Of Harlem (Stockholm '92) (5:20)/ Dancing Queen (Stockholm '92) (4:00)/ One (Washington Jan. 20 '93) (4:31)/ Redemption Song (Munich '92) (5:01)/ Lucille (US Radio '87) (4:16)/ Lost Highway (US Radio '87) (3:26)/ Oh Jeanie (recorded on an airplane '87) (4:30)/ Country Medley: 'The Daltons' - Francine, I Walk The Line, Lost Highway (Houston '92) (3:42)/ Knockin' On Heaven's Door (Chicago '85) (4:55)/ Slow Dancing (studio session Austrian radio '89) (4:53)/ Dirty Old Town (Rotterdam '93) (3:18)/ C'Mon Everybody (Dublin '86)/ People Get Ready (Dublin '89) (2:45)/ She's A Mystery To Me (Dublin '89) (3:40)/ Help (San Francisco '89) (3:38)/ October (Glasgow Radio' 82) (3:40)/ Tomorrow (Glasgow Radio '82) (1:10)/ I Will Follow (The Riot Show, Hamburg '81) (2:20)/ Angel Of Harlem, When Love Comes To Town, I Still Haven't Found, Stand By Me (U2 busking on O'Connell Street, Dublin at the 'Rattle And Hum' film premiere) (4:24)
R: G-Vg. Some poor-G.   C: ECD. Dcc.

CD - ZOOCOUSTIC
OCTOPUS OCTO 148
Satellite Of Love (3:52)/ Angel Of Harlem (4:13)/ When Love Comes To Town (2:45)/ Stay (Farewell So Close) (5:48)/ One (4:18)/ Dancing Queen (2:49)/ My Girl (2:00)/ All I Want Is You (2:52)/ Dear Prudence (2:16)/ I Still Haven't Found What I'm Looking For (4:04)/ Stand By Me (1:52)/ Slow Dancing (2:38)/ New York, New York (2:04)/ So Cruel (2:16)/ Wild Rover (Traditional) (1:48)/ Knockin' On Heaven's Door (4:25)/ Redemption Song (2:29)/ Who's Gonna Ride Your Wild Horses (3:05)/ Rain (1:53)/ Van Diemen's Land (3:36)/ Party Girl (3:04)/ Dirty Old Town (1:59)/ Help (1:55)/ When Love Comes To Town (2:43)/ Unchained Melody (1:51)/ I Can't Help Falling In Love With You (2:20)
R: Ex.   S: Recorded live on The 'Zoo TV', The 'Zoo TV Outside Broadcast', The 'Zoomerang' tours and over tours during the last decade.
C: ECD. Dcc.

CD - ZOOROPA 1993
RDSM 001/002
CD1: Introduction (5:14)/ Zoo Station (4:44)/ The Fly (4:45)/ Zoo TV Channel Hopping (1:05)/ Even Better Than The Real Thing (3:47)/ Mysterious Ways (6:42)/ One (4:57)/ Unchained Melody (1:16)/ Until The End Of The World (5:00)/ New Years Day (5:04)/ Zoo Interference (:16)/ Numb (4:00)/ Trying To Throw Your Arms Around The World (3:58)/ Angel Of Harlem (4:16)/ When Love Comes To Town (2:47)/ Stay (Faraway, So Close) (6:20)/ Satellite Of Love (2:04)/ Bad (7:15)
CD2: Bullet The Blue Sky (5:28)/ Running To Stand Still (5:32)/ Where The Streets Have No

Name (5:40)/ Pride (In The Name Of Love) (5:09)/ Zoo Confessions (6:58)/ Desire (4:33)/ A Word From MacPhisto And A Phone Call To The United Nations (3:09)/ Help (:51)/ Ultra Violet (Light My Way) (4:56)/ With Or Without You (3:50)/ Love Is Blindness (5:11)/ Can't Help Falling In Love With You (2:49)/ Zooropa (2:57)/ Baby Face (4:17)/ I Will Follow (2:32)
R: Exs. Soundboard.   S: The RDS Stadium, Dublin, Ireland Aug. 28 '93. CD2 tracks 13-15 Wembley Stadium, London Aug. 12 '93.
C: ECD. Dcc. Pic CD. Available with two different covers.

UFO

CD - FRANKFURT SPECIAL
BANG! BANG-017/18
CD1: Natural Thing/ Mother Mary/ Let It Roll/ Out In The Street/ This Kids/ Only You Can Rock Me/ Open And Willing/ Positive Forward/ Hot'N'Ready/ Too Hot To Handle
CD2: Love To Love/ Lights Out/ Doctor Doctor/ Rock Bottom/ Shoot Shoot
R: Vg audience recording.   S: Frankfurt Dec. 16 '93.

CD - LANDED LONDON
BONDAGE MUSIC BON 035
We Belong To The Night/ Let It Rain/ Long Gone/ The Wild, The Willing And The Innocent/ Only You Can Rock Me/ No Place To Run/ Love To Love/ Doing It All For You/ Makin' Moves/ Too Hot To Handle
R: Exs. Soundboard.   S: Hammersmith Odeon, London '82.   C: Japanese CD. Dcc. Time 50:47.

CD - RE-FLYIN'
SQS013/014
CD1: Positive Forward/ Peace/ Natural Thing/ Mother Mary/ Let It Roll/ Out In The Street/ This Kids/ Only You Can Rock Me/ Love To Love
CD2 Hot'N'Ready/ Too Hot To Handle/ Lights Out/ Doctor Doctor/ Rock Bottom/ Shoot Shoot/ C'Mon Everybody
R: Exs. Soundboard.   S: Sun Plaza Stadium, Tokyo June 16 '94.

UNREST

7" - COMPLETE
S1: Teenage Suicide/ Firecracker
S2: X-Mas Cookies/ Miles Davis
R: Ex. Soundboard.   S: Peel Sessions, UK '92.
C: USA. Limited numbered edition of 1,000. 45 RPM.

URGE OVERKILL

7" - WHAT TO DO
S1: What To Do
S2: She's Not There
R: Ex.   C: USA. Blue/black sleeve. Limited numbered edition of 500 on green vinyl. 33 RPM.

URIAH HEEP

CD - KILL THE KING DAVID
RAG DOLL MUSIC RDM-94201A/B
CD1: Sunrise/ Sweet Lorraine/ Traveller In Time/ Easy Livin'/ July Morning/ Gypsy/ Tears In My Eyes
CD2: Circle Of Hands/ Look At Yourself/ Love Machine/ Rock N'Roll Medley: Roll Over Beethoven, Blue Suede Shoes, Mean Woman Blues, Hound Dog, At The Hop, Whole Lotta Shakin' Goin' On, Blue Suede Shoes
R: Good audience recording.   S: Osaka Mar. 21 '72.   C: Japanese CD.

V

VAI, STEVE

CD - INDEDIDLE STRINGS GUITAR
IMPROVISATION LABEL IL-366809/810
CD1: An Earth Dweller's Return/ Here And Now/ Greasy Kid's Stuff/ Sex And Religion/ The Animal/ Touching Tongues/ Thunder Kids/ Dirty Black Hole/ Dr. Solo, State Of Grace/ Survive/ Ashes To Ashes/ Miss A Lable/ Still My Bleeding Heart
CD2: I Would You Love To/ Vocal Solo, In My Dreams/ Call It Sleep/ Pain/ Pig/ For The Love Of Got/ Liberty/ Attitude/ Sisters/ Answers
R: Vg audience recording.   S: NHK Hall, Tokyo, Japan Apr. 3 '94.

CD - MY FATHER'S PLACE
ALL OF US AS 09
Viv Woman (4:04)/ The Attitude Song (5:27)/ The Riddle (11:02)/ Bledsoe Bluvd (5:59)/ Call It Sleep (4:48)/ Liptown (6:49)/ One Of All (8:09)/ No Parties (5:04)/ Hard Times (5:04)/ Slow Fingers (3:19)/ Zoot Allures (5:42)/ Baby To Shake Your Monster (3:00)
R: Ex. Audience.   S: My Father's Place, New York Mar. 18 '83.   C: ECD. Dcc.

VAN HALEN

CD - BLASTIN' !
OXYGEN OXY 001
The Seventh Seal (5:44)/ Ain't Talkin' 'Bout Love (3:59)/ Right Now (6:43)/ You Really Got Me (2:58)/ When It's Love (5:20)/ Jump (5:06)/ The Seventh Seal (6:26)/ Big Fat Money (3:50)/ Finish What Ya Started (5:59)/ Eruption, Why Can't This Be Love (6:22)/ Feelin' (6:13)/ Right Now (5:54)/ Dreams (4:49)
R: Exs. Soundboard.   S: Tracks 1-6 Wembley Stadium, London June 24 '95. Tracks 7-13 Civic Center, Pensacola, FL Mar. 11 '95.   C: ECD. Dcc. Pic CD.

CD - CAN'T SLEEP AT NIGHT
BANG! BANG-014/5
CD1: On Fire/ Show Me Your Love/ Running With

The Devil/ Atomic Punk/ Little Dreamer/ You're No Good/ Feel Your Love Tonight/ Ain't Talkin' Bout Love
CD2: Ice Cream Man/ Somebody Get Me A Doctor/ Eruption/ D.O.A./ You Really Got Me/ Bottoms Up/ Summertime Blues
R: Vg audience recording, hiss.   S: Koseinekin Hall, Osaka June 24 '78.

CD - DON'T EVER SET ME FREE
BANG! BANG-019/20
CD1: On Fire/ I'm The One/ Running With The Devil/ Atomic Punk/ Little Dreamer/ You're No Goodman/ Feel Your Love Tonight/ Ain't Talkin' Bout Love
CD2: Ice Cream Man/ Somebody Get Me A Doctor/ Eruption/ D.O.A./ You Really Got Me/ Bottoms Up
R: Vg audience recording.   S: Sun Plaza Hall, Tokyo June 22 '78.

CD - IMPULSE BALANCE
IT'S ITS-1010/11
CD1: Announcement, Opening/ The Seventh Seal/ Big Fat Money/ Run Around/ Don't Tell Me (What Love Can Do)/ Amsterdam/ When It's Love/ Can't Stop Lovin' You/ Bass Solo/ After Shock/ Drum Solo
CD2: Best Of Both Worlds/ Feelin'/ Eagles Fly/ Take Me Back (Dejavu)/ 316/ Why Can't This Be Love/ Finish What Ya Started/ Right Now/ Panama/ Dreams
R: Exs. Soundboard.   S: Pensacola, Florida Mar. 11 '95.   C: ECD. Dcc. Time CD1 60:03. CD2 61:07.

CD - RAKE IT AND ROCK IT - FEATURING NEIL YOUNG
RHP 567
High Hopes (5:37)/ Finding Love Again (3:57)/ Feel Like Bugs (4:05)/ Going Down (4:00)/ Red (4:21)/ One Way To Rock (3:50)/ Down By The River (17:24)/ The Love (3:49)/ Love Walks In (4:32)/ Right Now (6:26)/ Best Of Both Worlds (5:13)
R: Tracks 1-7 Ex. Soundboard. Tracks 8-11 Vg-Ex. Audience.   S: Tracks 1-7 San Francisco, Brammies Mar. 5 '94. Tracks 8-11 acoustic set, San Francisco, Bridge Benefits Nov. 6 '93.
C: ECD. Dcc.

CD - RAPES STOCKHOLM
BONDAGE MUSIC BON 051/52
CD1: Unchained/ Hot For Teacher, Drums Solo/ On Fire/ Runnin' With The Devil/ House Of Pain, Bass Solo/ I'll Wait/ Everything Wants Some!
CD2: Pretty Woman/ 1984, Jump/ Guitar Solo, Eruption/ Panama/ You Really Got Me, Happy Trail/ Hot for Teacher*
R: Ex. Soundboard.   S: Stockholm, Sweden Aug. 25 '84. *Castle Donnington, UK Aug. 18 '84.
C: Japanese CD. Dcc. CD1 46:29. CD2 41:26.

CD - ROCKS THE BEER HALL
KISS THE STONE KTS 495/96
CD1: Right Now/ Big Fat Money/ Standing On Top Of The World/ Not Enough/ Amsterdam/ Mine All Mine, Drum Solo/ Can't Stop Loving You/ Feelin'/ When The Eagle Flies/ Guitar Solo
CD2: Why Can't This Be Love/ Dreams/ Poundcake/ Don't Tell Me (What Love Can Do)/ Panama/ Seventh Seal*/ Ain't Talking About Love*/ Right Here Right Now*/ You Really Got Me*/ Where's Love*/ Jump*
R: Exs. Soundboard.   C: Molson Amphitheatre. Toronto, Canada Aug. '95. *London '95.
C: ECD. Dcc. Pic CDs. Time 64:38. CD2 58:54.

CD - SECRET GIG
KISS THE STONE KTS 405
Poundcake (5:55)/ Judgement Day (5:24)/ Don't Tell Me (5:39)/ Amsterdam (8:01)/ Panama (4:45)/ Standing On Top Of The World (4:57)/ Feelin' (6:12)/ Best Of Both Worlds (6:39)/ Ain't Talking 'Bout Love (4:20)
R: Exs. Soundboard.   S: Lixor, Arnhem, Holland Jan. 27 '95.   C: ECD. Dcc. Pic CD. Time 51:54.

CD - STAND BY YOUR SIDE
RAG DOLL MUSIC RDM-951021
On Fire/ Show Me Your Love/ Running With The Devil/ Feel Your Love Tonight/ Atomic Punk/ Little Dreamer/ Ain't Talkin' 'Bout Love/ Mean Street/ Ice Cream Man/ You Really Got Me/ Dead Or Alive/ Summertime Blues/ Bottoms Up
R: Vgs. Audience recording.   S: Matador Theatre, Paris May 10 '78.   C: Japanese CD.

VAN ZANT, JOHNNY

CD - THE LAST OF THE WILD ONES
MAGIC MUSHROOMS RECORDS MMR 9302
Who's Right Or Wrong/ Can't Live Without Your Love/ Last Of The Wild Ones/ It's You/ Good Girls Turning Bad/ Hard Luck Story/ No More Dirty Deals/ Only The Strong Survive/ Standing In The Darkness/ Free Bird (Rossington Collins Band - instrumental version)/ Call Me The Breeze, Sweet Home Alabama (Lynyrd Skynyrd - Farm Aid '92)
R: Ex. Soundboard.   S: Live early 80s in Illinois, USA.   C: ECD. Dcc. Pic CD. Time 72:43.

VARIOUS ARTISTS

CD - DUETS
OXYGEN OXY 019
C: See listing under 'U2'.

CD - FOREVER YOUNG
GAMBLE RECORDS BSGR-09
CHUCK BERRY WITH BRUCE SPRINGSTEEN AND THE E STREET BAND: Johnny B. Goode/ BRUCE SPRINGSTEEN AND THE E STREET BAND: Shake, Rattle And Roll/ Hey Bo Diddley, She's The One/ JERRY LEE LEWIS WITH BRUCE SPRINGSTEEN AND THE E STREET BAND: Great Balls Of Fire/ Whole Lotta Shakin'

Goin' On/ BRUCE SPRINGSTEEN AND THE E STREET BAND: Darkness On The Edge Of Town/ BOB DYLAN: All Along The Watchtower/ Just Like A Woman/ The Real You At Last/ Highway 61 Revisited/ BOB DYLAN WITH BRUCE SPRINGSTEEN: Forever Young/ CHUCK BERRY WITH BRUCE SPRINGSTEEN AND MELISSA ETHERIDGE: Rock And Roll Music R: Exs. Soundboard.   S: Rock And Roll Hall Of Fame concert, Cleveland Municipal Stadium Sept. 2 '95.   C: ECD. Dcc. Time 58:23.

CD - ROCK AND ROLL HALL OF FAME
MOONRAKER 014/15/16/17/18/19
CD1: INTRO CHUCK BERRY WITH BRUCE SPRINGSTEEN AND THE E STREET BAND: Johnny B. Goode/ Segue/ JOHN MELLENCAMP: R.O.C.K. In The U.S.A./ JOHN MELLENCAMP AND MARTHA REEVES: Wild Night/ BON JOVI: With A Little Help From My Friends/ ERIC BURDON WITH BON JOVI: It's My Life/ We Gotta Get Out Of This Place/ Segue/ MELISSA ETHERIDGE: Be My Baby/ Love Child/ Leader Of The Pack/ DR. JOHN: Blueberry Hill/ What'd I Say/ AL GREEN: Tired Of Being Alone/ A Change Is Gonna Come
CD2: THE PRETENDERS: My City Was Gone/ The Needle And The Damage Done/Classic Performance From Muddy Waters/ JOHNNY CASH: Ring Of Fire/ JACKSON BROWNE: Redemption Song/ Tracks Of My Tears/ JACKSON BROWNE AND MELISSA ETHERIDGE: Wake Up Little Susie/ ARETHA FRANKLIN WITH AL GREEN: Freeway Of Love/ JOHN FOGERTY: Born On The Bayou/ Fortunate Son/ Classic Performance From Otis Redding/ SOUL ASYLUM AND IGGY POP: Back Door Man/ LOU REED WITH SOUL ASYLUM: Sweet Jane/ GIN BLOSSOMS: Wait/ I'll Feel A Whole Lot Better
CD3: SHERYL CROW: Let It Bleed/ Get Off Of My Cloud/ Classic Performance From Jimi Hendrix/ Segue Backstage Interviews/ GEORGE CLINTON AND THE P FUNK ALLSTARS WITH LARRY GRAHAM: Thank You (Falettinme Be Mice Elf Agin)/ I Want To Take You Higher/ THE KINKS: All Day And All Of The Night/ Lola/ HEART: Battle Of Evermore/ Love Hurts/ Segue/ BRUCE SPRINGSTEEN AND THE E STREET BAND: Shake, Rattle And Roll/ Bo Diddley, She's The One/ JERRY LEE LEWIS WITH BRUCE SPRINGSTEEN AND THE E STREET BAND: Great Balls Of Fire/ Whole Lotta Shakin' Goin' On
CD4: BRUCE SPRINGSTEEN AND THE E STREET BAND: Darkness On The Edge Of Town/ Classic Performance From John Lennon/ NATALIE MERCHANT: I Know To Do It/ ROBBIE ROBERTSON: The Weight/ Classic Performance From Janis Joplin/ Segue Basckstage Interviews/ Classic Performance From Bob Barley/ BRUCE HORNSBY: I Know You Rider/ Scarlet Begonias/ BOB DYLAN: All Along The Watchtower/ Just Like A Woman/ The Real You At Last/ Highway 61 Revisited
CD5: BOB DYLAN WITH BRUCE SPRING-

STEEN: Forever Young/ BOOKER T. AND THE MGS: Green Onions/ SAM MOORE: When Something Is Wrong With My Baby/ Hold On, I'm Comin/ Segue/ THE ALLMAN BROTHERS BAND: Blue Sky/ THE ALLMAN BROTHERS BAND WITH SHERYL CROW: Midnight Rider/ THE ALLMAN BROTHERS BAND: One Way Out/ JON BON JOVI & RICHIE SAMBORA: Imagine/ Give Peace A Chance/ Classic Performance From Creem/ SLASH & BOZ SCAGGS: Red House/ JAMES BROWN: Cold Sweat
CD6: JAMES BROWN: It's A Man's Man's World/ I Feel Good/ Classic Performance From Page, Plant And Young/ LITTLE RICHARD: Good Golly Miss Molly/ Tutti Frutti/ JOHN FOGERTY AND SAM MOORE: In The Midnight Hour/ MARTHA AND THE VANDELLAS: Dancing In The Street/ CHUCK BERRY WITH BRUCE SPRINGSTEEN AND MELISSA ETHERIDGE: Rock & Roll Music R: Exs. Soundboard.   S: Rock And Roll Hall Of Fame concert, Cleveland Municipal Stadium Sept. 2 '95.   C: ECD. Box set. Book has song info, pictures from the broadcast and the Hall Of Fame's list of the 500 songs that shaped R&R. Time CD1 61:14. CD2 73:48. CD3 72:29. CD4 70:05. CD5 72:44. CD6 44:25.

VAUGHAN, STEVIE RAY

CD - ALONE IN THE OZONE
TEDDY BEAR TB 79
Voodoo Chile (Slight Return) (10:52)/ Lost Your Good Thing Now (8:24)/ Honey Bee (2:48)/ Mary Had A Little Lamb (3:28)/ Lovestruck Baby (3:13)/ Tin Pan Alley (11:00)/ Cold Shot (4:27)/ Couldn't Stand The Weather (4:53)/ Texas Flood (9:02)/ Lenny (9:40)/ Stan's Swang (2:44)/ Rude Mood (4:19)
R: Exs. Soundboard.   S: California '84. C: ECD. Dcc. Pic CD.

CD - THE HAWK ON FIRE
BABY CAPONE BC014
Testify (3:37)/ So Excited (4:07)/ Voodoo Chile (6:44)/ Pride And Joy (4:30)/ Tell Me (3:04)/ Mary Had A Little Lamb (3:15)/ Texas Flood (9:53)/ Love Struck Baby (2:42)/ Hug You Squeeze You (3:46)/ Third Stone From The Sun (7:07)/ Lenny (8:45)/ Wham (4:49)/ Little Wing (8:29)/ You'll Be Mine (5:08)/ Love House (3:27)
R: Exs. Soundboard.   S: El Mocambo Toronto, Canada Apr. 15 '83.   C: ECD. Pic CD.

CD - IN MEMORIAM
SWINGIN' PIG TSP CD 205-3
CD1: Testify/ So Exited/ Voodoo Chile (Slight Return)/ Pride And Joy/ Texas Flood/ Love Struck Baby/ Mary Had A Little Lamb/ Tin Pan Alley/ Little Wing, Third Stone From The Sun/ Lenny/ Rude Mood/ Tell Me/ Scuttle Buttin'
CD2: Say What!/ Testify/ Voodoo Chile (Slight Return)/ The Things (That) I Used To Do/ Honey Bee/ Mary Had A Little Lamb/ Couldn't Stand The Weather/ Cold Shot/ Tin Pan Alley

CD3: Love Struck Baby/ Tell Me/ Texas Flood/ Wham/ Stang's Swang/ Lenny/ Pride And Joy/ Rude Mood
S: CD1 Ripley's Music Hall, Philadelphia '83. CD-3 Montreal, Canada '84.   C: ECD.

CD - THE LAST LIVE SHOW
THE LAST BOOTLEG RECORDS LBR 039/2
CD1: Testify (4:26)/ The House Is Rockin' (2:58)/ Tightrope (5:34)/ Things I Used To Do (4:56)/ Let Me Love You Baby (3:23)/ Leave My Girl Alone (5:20)/ Pride And Joy (4:27)/ Wall Of Denial (6:04)/ Riviera Paradise (9:17)
CD2: Superstition (6:53)/ Couldn't Stand The Weather (4:47)/ Going Down (6:05)/ Crossfire (4:15)/ Voodoo Chile (12:05)/ Sweet Home Chicago (15:19)
R: Ex. Audience.   S: Alpine Valley, East Troy, Wisconsin Aug. 26 '90.   C: ECD. Dcc. Pic CD.

CD - TOUCH THE SKY STUDIO SESSIONS
CAPRICORN RECORDS JCR-2005
Little Wing (1:53)/ Little Wing (2:11)/ Little Wing, 3rd Stone From The Sun (14:04)/ Life Without You (7:17)/ So Excited (3:41)/ Boiler Maker (5:44)/ Shake & Bake (2:55)/ Treat Me Right (6:05)/ The Sky Is Crying (4:49)/ Slip Sliding Slim (1:55)/ Come On (3:55)/ Come On (4:43)/ Hug, Kiss And Squeeze (2:01)/ Hang Nails And Boogers (4:33)/ Right Or Wrong (5:19)
R: Exs. Soundboard.   S: Studio Sessions '84 - '85.

VEGA, SUZANNE

CD - SOME VELVET MORNING
BABY CAPONE BC 042
99.9 F. (4:23)/ Blood Sings (4:12)/ (If You Were) In My Movie (4:25)/ Marlene On The Wall (4:49)/ Small Blue Thing (4:13)/ Left Of Center (4:10)/ Blood Makes Noise (3:54)/ Luka (3:53)/ Tom's Diner (3:26)/ Bonus Extras Tracks: Straight Lines (4:05)/ Cracking (2:58)/ Undertow (3:31)/ Solitude Standing (4:56)/ Language (4:23)/ Neighborhood Girls (4:34)/ Marlene On The Wall II (4:06)
R: Exs. Soundboard.   S: Coach House, San Juan Capistrano, CA May 24 '93.   C: ECD. Dcc. Pic CD.

VELVET UNDERGROUND, THE

CD - CONCRETE DREAMS
TEDDY BEAR TB 67
I'm Waiting For The Man (5:35)/ Sister Ray (5:27)/ That's The Story Of My Life (2:15)/ Jesus (3:10)/ I'm Set Free (4:10)/ Run, Run, Run (7:10)/ What Goes On (3:50)/ Candy Says (3:50)/ Beginning To See The Light (5:21)/ White Light, White Heat (5:29)/ Pale Blue Eyes (6:00)
R: G. Audience.   S: The Boston Tea Party - Tracks 1-4 Mar. 13 '69. Tracks 5-11 Jan. 10 '69.
C: ECD. Pic CD.

CD - THE FIRST NIGHT
AULICA A 2151
CD1: It's Just Too Much (3:04)/ Waiting For The Man (5:13)/ I Can't Stand it (5:11)/ I'm Set Free (4:45)/ Beginning To See The Light (5:40)/ Ocean (6:08)/ Venus In Furs (5:00)/ What Goes On (5:32)/ Heroin (7:40)/ I'll Be Your Mirror (2:35)/ Femme Fatale (2:52)
CD2: Pale Blue Eyes (5:27)/ Candy Says (3:54)/ Jesus (3:28)/ Story Of My Life (1:58)/ I Found A Reason (2:39)/ Sunday Morning (2:48)/ Afterhours (2:19)/ The Countess Of Hong Kong (3:19)/ Ride Into The Sun (3:44)/ Real Good Time Together (2:33)/ I Found A Reason (3:15)/ End Cole Ave. Jam (16:16)
R: G. Audience.   S: End Cole Avenue, Oct. 27 '69.   C: ECD. Dbw/red. Pic CD.

CD - WITH US FROM THE PAST
THE FLYING TIGERS FTCD 0019/20
CD1: We're Gonna Have A Real Good Time Together (4:04)/ Sweet Jane (4:50)/ Femme Fatale (3:35)/ Venus In Furs (5:09)/ Some Kinda Love (8:11)/ All Tomorrow's Parties (6:19)/ I'm Sticking With You (3:34)/ Beginning To See The Light (5:05)/ The Gift (9:55)/ I Heard Her Call My Name (4:48)/ Afterhours (2:36)
CD2: Heroin (12:40)/ White Light/ White Heat (4:13)/ Rock 'N' Roll (7:13)/ Waiting For My Man (5:48)/ Pale Blue Eyes (7:26)/ What Goes On (6:30)/ Coyotes (5:39)/ Guess I'm Falling In Love (3:52)/ Hey Mr. Rain (7:21)
R: Vg-Ex. Audience.   S: Reunion tour.
C: ECD. Pic CD.

VERLAINE, TOM

CD - GLORY
BTM 93-TV-05
Rotation/ Souvenir From A Dream/ Dissolve-Reveal/ Bomb/ The Scientist Writes A Letter/ Penetration/ Swim/ Clear It Away/ Kingdom Come/ Marquee Moon/ Glory/ Psychotic Reaction/ Red Leaves
R: Vg. Audience.   S: The Quasimodo, Berlin 3-4-87.   C: Time 70:25.

VERUCA SALT

CD - LIVE AT THE CHOCOLATE FACTORY
KTS OF AUSTRALIA 024 A
I Am 14 (4:35)/ All Hail Me (3:05)/ Once Twice (3:10)/ Forsythia (5:05)/ Straight (3:00)/ My Car (4:35)/ Seether (4:00)/ Spiderman "79 (5:50)/ Victrola, Happy Birthday Nina (2:26)/ Supernova, 25 (10:40)/ Straight (2:41)/ She's A Brain (2:32)/ All Hail Me (3:27)/ Stacey Please (1:37)
R: G-Vg. Audience. Tracks 11-14 Ex. Soundboard.   S: The Chocolate Factory, The Seattle Moore Theatre Nov. 14 '94. Tracks 11 and 12 BBC Maida Vale Studios Aug. 22 '94. Tracks 13 and 14 unreleased outtakes.   C: Australian CD. Dcc.

WAITS, TOM

CD - ON A FOGGY NIGHT
CRACKER CR-8
Introduction, On A Foggy Night/ The Heart Of
Saturday Night/ Ol' 55/ Diamonds On My Wind
Shield/ I Can't Wait To Get Off Work/ Better Off
Without A Wife/ Big Joe And Phantom 309/ Ice
Cream Man/ Piano Has Been Drinking/ Interview
R: Vg. FM broadcast.   S: Passims, Cambridge,
MA Nov. 10 '74.

CD - ON BROADWAY
LUNATIC 2008
Tom Trauberts Blues/ Small Change - Big
Spender/ Romeo Is Bleeding/ Annie's Back In
Town/ Jitterbug Boy - Better Off Without A Wife/ I
Wish I Was In New Orleans/ When The Saints/
Since I Fell For You/ Red Shoes/ Xmas Card
From A Hooker In Minneapolis/ Pasties And A
G-String/ Burma Shave
R: Ex. Soundboard.   S: Live USA '84.
C: ECD. Dcc. CD looks like a record. Time 75:02.

WATERS, MUDDY

CD - CHECKERBOARD LOUNGE
ARCHIVIO ARC 002
Mannish Boy (7:59)/ Next Time I See You (5:00)/
I'm Your Hoochie Coochie Man (4:20)/ Long
Distance Call (4:47)/ Ugly Woman Blues (6:53)/
I'm Gonna Get High (4:42)
R: Vg.   S: The Checkerboard Lounge, Chicago
Nov. 22 '81.   C: ECD. Dbw. Songs fade out.

WELLER, PAUL

CD - ANOTHER WOOD
3D REALITY 3D-PW-003
Into Tomorrow/ Here's A New Thing/ That Spiritual
Feeling/ Arrival Time/ Foot Of The Mountain/ Sexy
Sadie/ Bull-Rush, Magic Bus/ Ohio/ All The
Picture On The Wall/ You Do Something/ Shadow
Of The Sun/ Sun Flower/ Wild Wood/ Sun Flower/
Kosmos
S: Rare tracks.

CD - END OF THE WORLD
INSECT RECORDS IST 37
What's Going ON/ Uh Hu Oh Yeh (Always There
To Fool Ya!)/ Bull-Rush/ Above The Clouds/ Arrival Time/ Everything Has
A Price Today/ Ends Of The Earth/ All Year
Round/ Amongst Butterflies/ Head Start For
Happiness/ Ohio/ Into Tomorrow/ I Didn't Mean To
Hurt You/ Bitterness Rising
S: City Square Club, Milan, Italy Oct. '92.

CD - 5TH SEASON
MOD 001-2 (PW 01/02)

CD1: Opening/ Has My Fire Really Gone Out/
The Weaver/ Sunflower/ Unknown/ Wild Wood/
Fly On The Wall/ Out Of The Sinking/ Unknown/
All The Pictures On The Wall/ Hung Up/ This Is
No Time/ Amongst Butterflies/ Remember How
We Started, Dominoes
CD2: Unknown/ Can You Heal Us (Holy Man)/ 5th
Season/ Foot Of The Mountain/ Into Tomorrow/
Shadow Of The Sun/ Bull-Rush, Magic Bus
R: Vg audience recording.   S: Hiroshima Kose-
Nenkin Hall Oct. 2 '94.   C: Japanese CD. Dbw.
Pic CD.

CD - GLASTONBURY FESTIVAL 1994
FESTIVAL MUSIC FMCD-003
The Weaver/ Has My Fire Really Gone Out/ Bull
Rush, Magic Bus/ No Time/ That Sinking/
Remember How We Started/ Above The Clouds/
Hung Up/ Sunflower/ Wild Wood/ Can You Heal
Us Holy Man/ 5th. Season/ You Do Something/
Into Tomorrow/ Foot Of The Mountain/ Shadow Of
The Sun
R: Vg-Ex. Soundboard.   S: Glastonbury
Festival, England June '94.   C: ECD. Dbw.
Orange type. Pic CD. Time 78:54.

CD - I'D RATHER GO BLIND
3D REALITY 3D-PW-002
CD1: Hung Up/ Has My Fire Really Gone Out?/ I
Didn't Mean To Hurt You/ Remember How We
Started/ About The Clouds/ Wild Wood/ Fly On
The Wall/ Out Of Sinking/ Whirl Pools' End/ All
Picture On The Wall
CD2: This Is No Time/ Foot Of The Mountain/
Amongst Butterflies/ I'd Rather Go Blind/ Time
Passes/ (Can You Heal Us) Holy Man/ 5th
Season/ Sunflower/ Into Tomorrow/ Shadow Of
The Sun/ The Weaver/ Ohio
R: G. Audience.   S: Various dates Oct. '94.

WETTON, JOHN

CD - BOOK OF SEPTEMBER
WYVERN JW-27S 1/2
CD1: Heat Of The Moment/ Don't Cry/ Right
Where I Wanted To Be/ Rendezvous/ Caught In
The Crossfire/ Easy Money/ Dead Of Night/ 30
Years/ Only Time Will Tell/ Did It All For Love
CD2: Hold Me Now/ Starless/ Book Of Saturday/
Crime Of Passion/ Battle Line/ Open Your Eyes/
Smile Has Left Your Eyes/ Sole Survivor
R: Ex audience recording.   S: Sept. 27 '94.
C: Japanese CD.

WHITE SNAKE

CD - IS THIS LOVE
10106-010/020
CD1: Shake My Tree (Opening)/ Bad Boys/ Slide
It In/ Love Ain't No Stranger/ Judgement Day/ Is
This Love/ Soldier Of Fortune/ Adrian's Guitar
Solo/ Don't Leave Me This Way/ Oil, Denny's
Drum Solo

CD2: Ain't No Love In The Heart Of The City/
Slow'N'Easy/ Fool For Your Loving/ Here I Go
Again/ Introduction/ Give Me All Your Love/ Still
Of The Night/ We Wish You Well (End)
R: Vg audience recording.   S: Century Hall,
Nagoya, Japan Oct. 10 '94.

CD - MISTREATED FIRST NIGHT
WYVERN WV-2319C1/2
CD1: Bad Boys/ Slide It In/ Love Ain't No
Stranger/ Judgement Day/ Is This Love/ Adrian's
Solo/ Don't Leave Me/ Oil, Denny's Solo/ Ain't No
Love In The Heart Of The City
CD2: Slow And Easy/ Fool For Your Lovin'/ Here I
Go Again/ Give Me All Your Love/ Still Of The
Night/ Slide It In/ Rock And Roll/ Here I Go Again/
Shake My Tree, Whole Lotta Love/ Still Of The
Night
R: Ex audience recording.   S: Osaka Oct. 4 '94
CD2 tracks 7-12 Coverdale-Page - Nagoya Dec.
22 '93.   C: Japanese CD.

CD - ROCK ME BABY
REEL MUSIC RMCD-95201A/B
CD1: Come On/ You And Me/ Walking In The
Shadow Of The Blues/
Ain't No Love Heart In The City/ Micky Mood
Guitar Solo/ Love Hunter/ Mistreated/ Soldier Of
Fortune/ Keyboards Solo
CD2: Belgian Tom's Hat Trick K Drums Solo/
Might Just Take Your Life/ Lie Down/ Take Me
With You/ Rock Me Baby/ Breakdown
R: G. Audience.   S: Tokyo Apr. 15 '80.

CD - SPOKANE '84
BONDAGE MUSIC BON 016
Gambler/ Guilty Of Love/ Love Ain't No Stranger/
Walking In The Shadow Of The Blues/ Crying In
The Rain/ Slow An' Easy/ Ready An' Willing
R: Ex sound.   S: Spokane Coliseum, WA July
24 '84.   C: Japanese CD.

CD - SUCK MY SHAKE
CRYSTAL SOUND CS-14
Sweet Talker/ Walking In The Shadow Of The
Blues/ Ain't Gonna Cry No More/ Love Hunter/
Mistreated/ Soldier Of Fortune/ Ain't No Love In
The Heart Of The City/ Fool For Your Loving/
Lady Luck/ Belgian Tom's Hat Trick
R: Tracks 1-8 FM broadcast.   S: Reading
Festival Aug. 24 '80. Tracks 9-10 London July 15
'78.

CD - SYKE'S WIND
CRYSTAL SOUND CS-008
Intro/ Gambler/ Guilty Of Love/ Love Ain't No
Stranger/ Ready An' Willing/ Slow An' Easy/ John
Skyes Guitar Solo/ Crying In The Rain/ Soldier Of
Fortune/ Cozy Powell Drum Solo (Mars)/ Ain't No
Love In The Heart Of The City/ Don't Break My
Heart Again/ Walking In The Shadow Of The
Blues/ We Wish You Well
R: Good audience recording.   S: Super Rock
'84, Nagoya, Japan Aug. 4 '84.

CD - THREE MUSKETEERS FEATURING JOHN SYKES
BONDAGE MUSIC BON 13
Yellow Pearl/ Old Town/ A Night In The Life Of A
Blues Singer/ Sarah/ Unknown/ Parisienne
Walkways/ Solo In Soho/ King's Call/ Cold Sweat/
Baby Drives Me Crazy/ The Boys Are Back In
Town/ Dancing In The Moonlight
R: Ex audience recording.   S: Gothemburg,
Sweden July 29 '83.

WHITE ZOMBIE

CD - ASTRO - JUNKIES: 1995
OXYGEN OXY 025
Electric Head Pt. 1 (4:59)/ Super-Charger Heaven
(3:36)/ Real Solution #9 (5:04)/ More Human
Than Human (4:20)/ Electric Head Pt. 2 (The
Ecstasy) (5:33)/ Thunder Kiss '65 (4:02)/ Super-
Charge Heaven (3:51)/ Real Solution #9 (5:36)/
Welcome To Planet Motherfucker, Psychoholic
Slag (4:47)/ Electric Head Pt. 2 (The Ecstasy)
(4:43)/ More Human Than Human (5:21)/ Thunder
Kiss '65 (4:08)/ Grindhouse (A Go-Go) (3:48)/
Cosmic Monsters Inc. (5:47)/ Spider Baby (Yeah-
Yeah-Yeah) (3:14)/ I Am Legend (4:46)
R: Exs. Soundboard.   S: Tracks 1-6 Donnington
Festival, UK Aug. 26 '95. Tracks 7-12 Bizarre
Festival, Cologne, Germany Aug. 19 '95. Tracks
13-16 Palladium, Hollywood, CA '92.   C: ECD.
Dcc. Pic CD.

CD - YOU ONLY LIVE ONCE
HAWK HAWK 027
Intro/ Grindhouse A Go Go/ Thirst!/ Black
Sunshine/ Welcome To The Planet Motherfucker,
Psychotic Slag/ Soul-Crusher/ Spiderbaby (Yeah-
Yeah-Yeah)/ Thunder Kiss
R: Exs.   S: USA, summer '93.

7" - ZOMBIE KISS
S1: God Of Thunder
S2: Thrust
R: Ex. Audience.   S: CBGBs, NYC.   C: USA.
B&w sleeve. 45 RPM.

WHO, THE

CD - BEHIND BLIND EYES
DYNAMITE STUDIO DS94A079/80
CD1: I Can't Explain/ Substitute/ My Wife/ Baba
O'Riley/ Behind Blue Eyes/ Dreaming From The
Waist/ Magic Bus
CD2: Amazing Journey, Sparks/ The Acid Queen/
Fiddle About/ Pinball Wizard/ I'm Free/ Tommy's
Holiday Camp/ We're Not Take It/ Summertime
Blues/ My Generation/ Won't Get Fooled Again
R: Vg audience recording.   S: The Garden,
Boston Apr. 1 '76.   C: Japanese CD. Dcc. CD1
actually has 8 tracks with 'Squeezebox' as track
5, 'Behind Blues Eyes' as track 6, 'Dreaming
From The Waist' as track 7 and 'Magic' as Track
8. Time:CD145:09. CD2: 55:09.

CD - DANGEROUS
ON STAGE CD 12055 AAD
Who Are You (6:42)/ Cry If You Want (7:03)/ Baba
O' Reily (5:27)/ Eminence Front (5:46)/ Drowned
(8:10)/ Sister Disco (5:16)/ Dangerous (3:25)/
Behind Blue Eyes (3:42)/ Boris The Spider (3:26)/
Dr. Jimmy (4:50)/ 5:15 (6:41)
R: Exs. Soundboard.   S: Maple Leaf Garden,
Toronto Dec. 17 '82.   C: Dcc. The Who's '82
farewell concert. Time 60:32.

CD - EXCITEMENT AT YOUR FEET
THE RECORD COMPANY
CD1: Overture/ It's A Boy/ 1921/ Amazing
Journey, Sparks/ Eyesight To The Blind/
Christmas/ Cousin Kevin/ Acid Queen/ Pinball
Wizard/ Do You Think It's Alright?/ Fiddle About/
There's A Doctor/ Go To The Mirror/ Tommy Can
You Hear Me?/ I'm Free/ Sally Simpson/
Sensation/ Welcome/ We're Not Gonna Take It
CD2: I Can't Explain/ Substitute/ Baba O' Reily/
Love Reign O'er Me/ I'm A Man/ Friend Is A
Friend/ My Wife/ Join Together/ You Better, You
Bet/ Behind Blue Eyes/ Won't Get Fooled Again
R: Vgs.   S: Radio City Music Hall, NYC June 27
'89.   C: Dcc. Marred by broadcast static. No
track separation. Titled 'Rockin'' by the Detours
on the discs. Time CD1 65:10. CD2 65:02.

CD - LIVE AT FILLMORE EAST
EXIL CD-EX-002
Summertime Blues (4:08)/ Fortune Teller (2:18)/
Tattoo (2:48)/ Little Billy (2:37)/ I Can't Explain
(2:22)/ Happy Jack (2:09)/ I'm A Boy (2:41)/ Relax
(7:22)/ A Quick One While He's Away (8:00)/ Easy
Going Guy (2:17)/ Shakin' All Over (9:42)/ Boris
The Spider (2:33)/ My Generation (4:40)
R: Gs. Soundboard. Surface noise throughout.
S: The Fillmore East. NYC Apr. 5 '68.   C: Color
drawing. Time 60:47.

CD - MAXIMUM BBC
HIWATT WHO 001
Just You And Me/ Leaving Here/ Good Lovin'/
Anyway Anyhow Anywhere/ The Goods Gone/ My
Generation/ La La La La Lies/ Man With Money/
Substitute/ Dancing In The Street/ Disguises/ I'm
A Boy/ So Sad About Us/ Run Run Run/ Boris
The Spider/ Happy Jack/ See My Way/ I Can't
Reach You/ Our Love Was/ I Can See For Miles/
Pictures Of Lily/ Summertime Blues/ I'm Free/
The Seeker/ Heaven And Hell/ Shaking All Over/
Substitute/ Pinball Wizard
R: Ex. Soundboard.   S: BBC recordings -
Tracks 1-2 May 25 '65. Tracks 3-4 June 19 '65.
Tracks 5-7 Apr. 22 '65. Tracks 8-10 Mar. 15 '66.
Tracks 11-13 Sept. 13 '66. Tracks 14-17 Jan. '67.
Tracks 18-22 Oct. 10 '67. Tracks 23-28 Apr. 13
'70.   C: Japanese CD. Dcc. Booklet has lots of
great photos. Time 77:28.

CD - PINBALL WIZARD
OIL WELL RSC 007 CD
The Real Me/ Bell Boy/ Doctor Jimmy/ I Can't

Explain/ Summertime Blues/ My Generation/
*Pinball Wizard/ *We're Not Gonna Take It/ Won't
Get Fooled Again
R: Exs. Soundboard.   S: Capitol Center,
Landover, Maryland Dec. 6 '73 . *The Spectrum,
Philadelphia Dec. 4 '73.   C: ECD. Fuzzy Dcc.
Copy of Swingin' Pig's 'American Tour 1973'
(TSP-CD-029). Time 48:30.

CD - THE PUNK MEETS THE GODFATHER
WHOOPY CAT WKP 0031
The Real Me/ The Dirty Jobs/ The Punk And The
Godfather/ I'm The One/ I've Had Enough/ Bell
Boy/ Cut My Hair/ Brrr/ Drowned (rehearsal with
band)/ I'm One (rehearsal with band)/ Pure And
Easy*/ Baba O'Reily*/ Won't Get Fooled Again*
R: Exs. Tracks 9 and 10 Vg.   S: Quadrophenia
demos '73. *Lifehouse demos '71.   C: Japanese
CD. Dbw. Copy available on the Red Robin label.
Time 74:59.

CD - PURE ROCK THEATER
HIWATT ZA59
Heaven And Hell/ I Can't Explain/ Fortune Teller/
Tattoo/ Young Man Blues/ Substitute/ Happy Jack/
I'm A Boy, A Quick One/ Overture/ Its A Boy/
1921/ Amazing Journey, Sparks, Underture/
Tommy's Holiday Camp/ We're Not Gonna Take
It/ See Me Feel Me/ Summertime Blues/ Shaking
All Over/ My Generation
R: Ex. Soundboard.   S: US tour fall '69 and in
the UK January '70.   C: Japanese CD. Dcc. 'My
Generation' listed but not on CD.Time 76:39.

CD - ROUGH ACTIONS
RAG DOLL MUSIC RDM-942001A/B
CD1: Summertime Blues/ My Wife/ My
Generation/ I'm The Sea, The Real Me/ The Punk
Meets The God Father/ I'm One/ Helpless
Dancer/ 5:15/ Sea And Sand/ Drowned
CD2: Bell Boy/ Dr. Jimmy, Love Reign O'er Me/
Won't Get Fooled Again/ Pinball Wizard/ See Me,
Feel Me/ Magic Bus/ Naked Eye
R: Poor audience recording.   S: Cobo Hall,
Detroit, MI Nov. 30 '73.   C: Japanese CD.

CD - SAN FRANCISCO 1971
BLACK DOG BD 003
Substitute (2:50)/ Summertime Blues (4:02)/ My
Wife (6:58)/ Baba O'Riley (7:24)/ Behind Blue
Eyes (4:09)/ Bargain (7:54)/ Won't Get Fooled
Again (8:56)/ Pinball Wizard (3:11)/ See Me, Feel
Me (6:32)/ My Generation (7:30)/ Naked Eye
(12:24)/ Magic Bus (3:30)
R: Gm. Soundboard.   S: Civic Centre, San
Francisco Dec. 12 '71.   C: ECD. Dcc. 75:27.

CD - SEE ME, FEEL ME
STARLITE CDS 51144 AAD
I'm Free (2:19)/ 1921 (2:22)/ Can't Explain (2:16)/
Fortune Teller (2:30)/ Tattoo (2:56)/ Young Man
Blues (5:26)/ Summertime Blues (3:35)/ See Me,
Feel Me (4:41)/ I'm A Boy (2:35)/ Pinball Wizard

(2:39)/ Substitute (2:01)/ Happy Jack (2:11)/ My Generation (13:16)
R: Exs. Soundboard.   S: Amsterdam Opera House Sept. 29 '69.   C: ECD. Dcc. Time 48:53.

CD - SHAKIN' ALL OVER
GOLD STANDARD
Summertime Blues/ Fortune Teller/ Tattoo/ Can't Explain/ Happy Jack/ Relax/ A Quick One/ My Way/ Shakin' All Over/ Boris The Spider/ My Generation Young Man Blues
R: Exs. Soundboard.   S: The Fillmore East, NYC Apr. 5 '68.   C: ECD. Dcc. Time 65:28.

CD - THE VIOLENT SIDE
COUNTDOWN FACTORY CDF-942006A/B
CD1: Heaven And Hell/ I Can't Explain/ It's A Boy/ 1921/ Amazing Journey/ Sparks/ Eyesight To The Blind (The Hawker)/ Christmas/ The Acid Queen/ Pinball Wizard/ Do You Think It's Alright?/ Fiddle About
CD2: Summertime Blues/ Shakin' All Over/ My Generation/ Getting Tune/ Barbain/ Pinball Wizard, See Me Feel Me, Baby Don't Do It
R: Vg sound. CD2 tracks 4-5 good audience recording.   S: Woodstock Festival, Aug. 16 '69. CD2 tracks 4-6 Young Vic, London Apr. '71.

CD - WHO IS TOMMY?
DYNAMITE STUDIO DS94A077/78
CD1: Sparks/ Heaven Hell/ I Can't Explain #1 Fortune Teller #1/ Tattoo/ Young Man Blues #1/ My Generation/ Fortune Teller #2/ Summertime Blues/ Shakin' All Over/ Young Man Blues #2
CD2: I Can't Explain/ Young Man Blues/ Water/ Seeker/ Substitute/ Overture/ It's Boy/ 1921/ Amazing Journey, Sparks/ Eyesight To The Blind (The Hawker)/ Christmas/ The Acid Queen
R: CD1 Vg soundboard recording. CD2 poor.
S: CD1 Leeds '70. CD2 The Convention Center, Dallas, TX June 19 '70.   C: Japanese CD.

WILSON, BRIAN

CD - COME BACK, BRIAN!
VIGOTONE VT 125
Intro/ Turning Point/ Heavenly Bodies/ Black Widow/ In The Nightime/ Love And Mercy/ Walkin' The Line/ Melt Away/ Baby Let Your Hair Grow Long/ Little Children/ One For The Boys/ Up In The Sky (There's So Many)/ Meet Me In My Dreams Tonight/ He Couldn't Get His Poor Body To Move/ Don't Let Her Know She's An Angel/ Someone To Love/ Water Builds Up/ Don't Let Her Know She's An Angel/ Let's Get Together/ Smart Girls/ We Love You/ Fantasy Is Reality - Bells Of Madness/ Outro
R: Vg-Ex. Some good.   S: Demos - 2, 3, 4, 5, 7, 10, 12, 15. Live - 6, 8. Alternates - 7, 9, 11, 13, 14, 21. From the first mix of 'Sweet Insanity' 16, 17, 18, 19. From Wasserman's 'Tries' compilation 20 - 22.   C: Dcc. Time 65:40

CD - IN MY ROOM
INVASION UNLIMITED IU 9422-1
Interview With Brian Wilson (BBC-TV '84)/ My Diane (original Brian Wilson studio version without Beach Boys overdubs)/ Stevie (unreleased studio outtake)/ Sherry, She Needs Me (In '76 Brian recorded his vocals to a '65 backing track he produced for The Beach Boys. Unreleased)/ You've Lost That Lovin' Feeling (cover version of Righteous Brothers hit From '66)/ Still I Dream Of It (piano demo for unreleased album 'Adult Child')/ It's Over Now (See Track 6)/ Let's Put Our Hearts Together (piano-demo)/ Lines (unreleased studio outtake)/ Lazy Lizzie (unreleased studio outtake)/ Little Children (piano demo)/ I'm Begging You (piano demo of unreleased song)/ That Special Feeling (see track 12)/ Da Doo Ron Ron/ I'm So Lonely/ Male Ego/ California Girls/ Sloop John B./ The Boogie's Back In Town/ Love And Mercy/ Walkin' The Line/ Melt Away/ God Only Knows
R: Ex. Soundboard. Tracks 14-23 G-Vg. Audience.   S: This CD is a collection of studio outtakes and home demos recorded by Brian 'In His Room' Between '76-'78. Tracks 14-18 are from a charity performance Brian gave in May '85 with guests The Bangles, John Stewart and Stephen Stills. Tracks 19-23 are from a Beach Boys concert in '87.   C: ECD. Dcc.

WINTER, JOHNNY

CD - WOODSTOCK REVIVAL
SWINGIN' PIG CD 213
Introduction/ Hideaway/ Messin' With The Kid/ Johnny B. Goode/ Come On In My Kitchen/ Rollin' And Tumblin'/ Help Me/ Stranger/ Jumping Jack Flash/ Bony Moronie
S: The Woodstock Ten Year Anniversary Festival '79.   C: ECD.

WISHBONE ASH

CD - REUNION LIVE '91
WBA 01
Strange Affair/ The King Will Come/ Lost Cause In Paradise/ Throw Down The Sword/ Standing In The Rain/ Blowin' Free/ Hard Times/ Jail Bait
R: Exs. Soundboard.   S: FM broadcast, Kawasaki, Japan '91.   C: Japanese CD. 55:21.

XTC

CD - DEMOS 3
EXTATIC EX-003
Mayor Of Simpleton/ Blue Beret/ Miniature Sun/ Chalkhills And Children/ Here Comes President Kill Again/ Merely A Man/ My Train's Coming/ Hold My Daddy/ Across The Antheap/ Poor Skeleton Steps Out/ The Loving/ Pink Thing/

Brainge's Daughter/ Everything/ Don't Ever Call The Chickenhead/ Ella Guru
R: Vg.   S: 'Oranges & Lemons' sessions.

Y

YES

CD - AND YOU AND I
RAG DOLL MUSIC RDM 942007A/B
CD1: Siberian Khatru/ Heart Of The Sunrise/ Sakura Sakura/ Mood For A Day/ And You And I/ Close To The Edge
CD2: The Six Wives Of Henry The VIII/ Roundabout/ Yours Is No Disgrace/ Starship Trouper
R: Ex. Audience.   S: Mar. 12 '73.
C: Japanese CD. Dcc. Time CD1 63:32. CD2 48:43.

CD - CHICAGO OF HEAVEN '79
CAT FOOD 002
CD1: Siberian Khatru/ Heart Of Sunrise/ Future Time, Rejoice/ Time And A Word, Long Distance Runaround, The Fish, Perpetual Change, Soon/ The Clap
CD2: And You And I/ Rick Wakeman Solo/ Awaken/ Circus Of Heaven/ Starship Trooper/ Tour Song (Thank You, Chicago)/ I've Seen All Good People/ Roundabout
R: Vg sound.   S: Chicago June 4 '79.

CD - GIMME MORE
INSECT IST 775/76
CD1: Perpetual Change, The Calling/ I Am Waiting/ Rhythm Of Love/ Hearts/ Real Love/ Changes/ Heart Of The Sunrise
CD2: Owner Of A Lonely Heart/ And You And I/ Where Will You Be/ I've Seen All Good People/ Walls/ Endless Dream/ Roundabout
R: Ex soundboard recording.   S: Broome County Arena, Binghamton, NY June 18 '94.

CD - 1971 IN THE BEGINNING IS A FUTURE...
ROCKET SOUND RS-1002
Yours Is No Disgrace/ Your Move, All Good People/ The Clap/ Perpetual Change/ Roundabout
R: Ex. Soundboard.   S: Tracks 1-4 New Haven, CT July 27 '71. Track 5 demo from Advision Studio, London Sept. '71.   C: Japanese CD. Time 46:19.

CD - PERPETUAL CHANGE
HIWATT YS001
Yours Is No Disgrace/ Your Move/ I've Seen All Good People/ The Clap/ Perpetual Change/ Perpetual Change/ America
R: Vg. Soundboard.   S: Yale Bowl, New Haven, CT July 24 '71. Tracks 6-7 Berlin June 5 '71.
C: Japanese CD.

YOUNG, NEIL

CD - A RUNNER IN PERU
F*!#IN' UP FUPCD 2022/023
CD1: On The Way Home/ Don't Cry No Tears/ Everybody Knows This Is Nowhere/ Cowgirl In The Sand/ If You Got Love/ Soul Of A Woman/ Are You Ready For The Country?/ Southern Man/ Old Man/ Little Thing Called Love/ The Needle And The Damage Done/ Birds
CD2: The Band Introduction/ Nils 'Tune/ Like An Inca/ Hey Hey, My My (Into The Black)/ Cinnamon Girl/ Like A Hurricane/ Sample And Hold/ Mr. Soul
R: Ex. Soundboard.   S: Sherwood Hall, Salinas, CA 8/12/82.   C: Japanese CD. Dcc. With the Trans Band. Time CD1 48:42. CD2 44:13.

CD - BROKEN ARROW
PLANET NO 0871-22
Out On The Weekend/ Old Man/ Journey Through The Past/ Heart Of Gold/ Don't Let Me Bring You Down/ A Man Needs A Maid/ Love In Mind/ See The Girl Dance/ Tonight's The Night/ Mellow In Mind/ Roll Another Number/ Tired Eyes/ Speakin' Out/ Walk On/ For The Turnstiles/ Bad Fog Of Loneliness/ New Mama/ Winterlong/ Borrowed Tune/ Traces
R: Poor. Hiss. *Surface noise.   S: Tracks 1-8 BBC sessions Feb. 23 '71.*Tracks 9-20 acetates from 'Tonight's The Night' '75.

CD - CAROLINA QUEEN
F*!#IN' UP FUPCD-2018/19
CD1: Mr. Soul/ The Old Laughing Lady/ Journey Through The Past/ Pocahontas/ Mellow My Mind/ The Needle And The Damage Done/ Roll Another Number (For The Road)/ A Man Needs A Maid/ Sugar Mountain
CD2: Country Home/ Don't Cry No Tears/ Down By The River/ Bite The River/ Lotta Love/ Like A Hurricane/ After The Goldrush/ Cortez The Killer/ Cinnamon Girl/ Helpless
R: G-Vgs audience recording.   S: Palladium Theatre, New York Nov. 20 '76.   C: Japanese CD. With Crazy Horse.

CD - THE DAYS THAT USED TO BE
EUREKA MMCX 11/12
CD1: Comes A Time/ Sugar Mountain/ Needle And The Damage Done/ After The Goldrush/ For The Turnstiles/ Silver And Gold/ The Ways Of Love/ The Days That Used To Be/ Heart Of Gold/ Powderfinger/ Lady Wingshot/ Bad Fog Of Loneliness
CD2: Cocaine Eyes/ Eldorado/ Like A Hurricane/ Mr. Soul/ Cinnamon Girl/ Down By The River/ Hey Hey, My My/ On Broadway/ Tonight's The Night
R: Exs audience recording.   S: Memorial Auditorium, Eureka, CA Feb. 18 '89.

CD - THE FINAL F*#!
F*!#IN' UP FUPCD 2029/30
CD1: Arc-Like Feedback Instrumental Jam/ My Heart/ Act Of Love/ Hey Hey My My/ I Am A Child/

Cortez The Killer/ Western Hero/ Change Your Mind (Jan. 14 '95)/ Trans Am (Video Version)*/ Sleeps With Angels/ Change Your Mind/ Train Of Love/ Piece Of Crap (promotional only edit version)*

CD2: F*!#kin' Up/ Act Of Love/ Down By The River/ Powderfinger/ Sleeps With Angels/ Hey Hey My My (Jan. 15 '95)/ Sleeps With Angles (Bridge Benefit '95)*/ Down By The River (Farm Aid VII '94)*

R: CD1 tracks 1-8 G-Vg. Audience. *Ex. Soundboard.   S: Voters Choice Benefit, Daughters Of The American Revolution Constitution Hall, Washington, DC. CD1 tracks 1-8 Jan. 14. CD2 tracks 1-6 Jan. 15 '95.
C: Japanese CD. Dbw. With Crazy Horse. Time CD1 71:17. CD2 62:09.

CD - HARD TO FIND
THE LAST BOOTLEG RECORDS LBR 037
Mr. Soul (non-Lp version) (2:31)/ If I Could Have Her Tonight (2:12), I've Been Waiting For You (2:17), Here We Are In The Years (3:21), What Did You Do In My Life (1:48) (studio session mixes)/ Everybody Knows This Is Nowhere (alternate version) (2:10)/ Cinnamon Girl (edited version with different vocal) (2:42)/ Birds (alternate non-Lp version) (1:33)/ War Song (non-Lp version) (2:31)/ The Last Trip To Tulsa (live Feb. 18 '73) (4:13)/ Pushed It Over The End (live Aug. 27 '74) (7:35)/ Campaigner (original extra verse version) (4:15)/ Home On The Range (12" single version) (2:51)/ Weight Of The World (extended remix 12" single) (5:23)/ This Note's For You (live Apr. 13 '88 - unedited full length version) (5:48)/ No More (live Sept. 30 '89) (4:40)/ Don't Spook The Horse (non-Lp version) (7:36)
R: Ex. Soundboard.   C: ECD. Dcc. Pic CD.

CD - HIPPIE DREAM
TEDDY BEAR TB 36
Hawks And Doves (3:51)/ Bound For Glory (6:42)/ Southern Pacific (7:57)/ It Might Have Been (4:18)/ Soul Of A Woman (4:55)/ Field Of Opportunity (4:05)/ Powderfinger (5:17)/ Down By The River (10:00)/ If You Got Love (3:46)/ Southern Man (6:21)/ Like An Inca (9:30)/ Hippie Dream (5:21)
R: Ex. Soundboard.   S: Live in the USA. Tracks 1-8 Sept. '84. Tracks 9-11 Aug. '82. Track 12 Sept. '86.   C: ECD. Pic CD.

CD - LAST DANCE
NY 001
Cripple Creek Ferry/ Here We Are In The Years/ L.A./ Soldier/ Out On The Weekend/ Old Man/ Heart Of Gold/ The Loner/ Everybody Knows This Is Nowhere/ Time Fades Away/ New Mama/ Alabama/ Don't Be Denied/ Cinnamon Girl/ Lookout Joe/ Southern Man/ Last Dance/ Are You Ready For The Country?
R: G-Vg. Audience.   S: Carnegie Hall, NYC Jan. 21 '73.   C: ECD. Dcc. With Stray Gators. Time 74:49.

CD - LOST TALES OF EXILE
CAPRICORN RECORDS CR 2047
Long May You Run/ For What It's Worth/ Helpless/ Southern Man/ Band Intro/ Buying Time/ Evening Coconut/ Make Love To You/ Cowgirl In The Sand/ 49 Bye Byes/ Mr. Soul/ Suite: Judy Blue Eyes
R: Exs. Soundboard.   S: Springfield, MA June 27 '76.   C: Dcc. With Stephen Stills. 73:37.

CD - NEIL YOUNG
ALL OF US AS 11/2
CD1: Mr. Soul/ The Loner/ Southern Man/ Helpless/ Like A Hurricane/ Rockin' In A Free World/ Dream Machine/ Only Love Can Break Your Heart
CD2: Harvest Moon/ The Needle And The Damage Done/ Powderfinger/ Change Your Mind/ Down By The River/ Sittin' On The Dock Of The Bay/ All Along The Watchtower/ Sugar Mountain/ I'm A Child*/ Heart Of Gold*/ Rockin' In A Free World (with Pearl Jam)*
R: G. Audience. *G-Vg. Audience.   S: San Diego Sept. 12 '93. *San Francisco '92.
C: ECD. Dcc.

CD - RAGGED BUT RIGHT
GOLD STANDARD ZA 62
Love And Only Love, Love To Burn (rehearsals '90)/ Last Dance, Yonder Stands The Sinner (Winterland Mar. 18 '73)/ Bite The Bullet (early show, Palladium, NYC Nov. 20 '76)/ Mansion On The Hill, White Line, Days That Used To Be (rehearsals '90)/ Revolution Blues (Seattle, Washington July '74)/ Windward Passage (Catalyst Club, Santa Cruz, CA Aug. 27 '77)/ Don't Spook The Horse (rehearsal '90)
R: Ex. Soundboard/Audience.   C: Japanese CD. Dcc. Time 76:43.

CD - THE RANCH REHEARSALS
CAPRICORN RECORDS 2043
Mansion On The Hill/ White Line 1/ White Line 2/ Love To Burn 1/ Love To Burn (False Start)/ Love To Burn 2/ The Days That Used To Be 1/ Love And Only Love/ Everything Broken/ Pocahontas/ Crime In The City/ After The Gold Rush/ The Needle And The Damage Done/ No More
R: Ex. Soundboard.   S: Tracks 1-8 Broken Arrow Ranch June thru July '90. Tracks 9-14 Santa Monica Civic Apr. 1 '90.   C: Dcc. With Crazy Horse. Time 69:39.

CD - RIVER OF PRIDE
FUPCD-2003/4
CD1: Campaigner/ The Old Laughing Lady/ Human Highway/ Tell Me Why/ After The Gold Rush/ Harvest/ Mr. Soul/ Here We Are In The Years/ Journey Through The Past/ Heart Of Gold/ White Line/ A Man Needs A Maid
CD2: Give Me Strength/ No One Seems To Know (Don't Say You Win, Don't Say You Lose)/ Mellow My Mind/ Too Far Gone/ Needle And The Damage Done/ Pocahontas/ Roll Another Number

(For The Road)/ six other tracks
R: G-Vg sound.   S: Solo acoustic set Nov. '76.
CD2 tracks 11-12 promotional mono versions.
Track 13 taken from a rare 7".

CD - RUBY IN THE DUST
F*!#IN' UP FUPCD-1026
Tell Me Why/ Cowgirl In The Sand/ After The Gold
Rush/ Mellow My Mind/ Too Far Gone/ A Man
Needs A Maid/ No-One Seems To Know (Don't
Say You Win, Don't Say You Lose)/ Heart Of
Gold/ Country Home/ Don't Cry No Tears/ Down
By The River/ Lotta Love/ Like A Hurricane
R: Vg. Audience.   S: Pavillion, Paris Mar. 23
'76.   C: Japanese CD. With Crazy Horse.

CD - SCROUNGIN' FOR QUANTITY
BOOTH 001/002
CD1: Hey Hey My My/ Cocaine Eyes/ Razor
Love/ Comes A Time/ Don't Let It Bring You
Down/ Someday/ Crime In The City/ Eldorado/
Too Far Gone/ This Note's For You/ The Needle
And The Damage Done/ No More/ Dreamin' Man/
Fuckin' Up/ Winterlong
CD2: Heart Of Gold/ Rockin' In The Free World/
Powderfinger/ Eldorado/ Someday/ Crime In The
City Boxcar/ Don't Cry/ Heavy Love
R: Vg. Audience. CD2 tracks 4-8 Poor.   S: Ahoy
Club Rotterdam Dec. 13 '89. CD2 tracks 4-8
Times Square Studio sessions'89.

CD - THE SOUTHERN MAN
INVASION UNLIMITED IU9307-2
CD1: Mr. Soul/ The Loner/ Southern Man/
Helpless/ Helpless/ Love To Burn/ Separate
Ways/ Like A Hurricane/ Powderfinger/ Only Love
Can Break Your Heart/ Harvest Moon/ The
Needle And The Damage Done/ Dream Machine
CD2: Down By The River/ All Along The
Watchtower/ Motor Cycle Mama/ Separate Ways/
Powderfinger/ Dream Machine/ Dock Of The Bay
R: Exs.   S: Belgium, July 3 '93. CD2 3-9
Finsbury Park July 4 '93.

CD - VERDE VALLEY MUSIC FESTIVAL
GOLD STANDARD ZA 33
Intro/ My Heart/ Prime Of Life/ Drive By/ Sleeps
With Angels/ Into The Black/ Cortez The Killer/
Train Of Love/ Change Your Mind/ Piece Of Crap/
Act Of Love/ Helpless (not listed on the cover)
R: Ex. Audience.   S: Tracks 1-10 The Verde
Valley Music Festival, Sedona, Arizona Oct. 22
'94. Track 11 The Moore Theater, Seattle,
Washington with Pearl Jam Feb. 6 '95.
C: Japanese CD. Dcc.With Crazy Horse. 76:01.

CD - WEST COAST IS FALLING
F*!#IN' UP FUPCD 2016/17
CD1: Mr. Soul (Buffalo Springfield - non-LP ver-
sion) (2:31)/ Radio Spot For 'Neil Young' (0:50)/ If
I Could Have Her Tonight (2:12), I've Been
Waiting For You (2:17), Here We Are In The Years
(3:21), What Did You Do In My Life (1:48) (origi-
nal version mixes)/ Everybody Knows This Is

Nowhere (alternate version) (2:10)/ Radio Spot
For 'Everybody Knows This Is Nowhere' (0:47)/
Cinnamon Girl (edited version with different vocal)
(2:42)/ Radio Spot For 'After The Goldrush'
(0:58)/ Birds (alternate non-LP version) (1:33)/
War Song (non-LP) (2:31)/ The Last Trip To Tulsa
(live Feb. 18 '73) (4:13)/ Pushed It Over The End
(live Aug. 27 '74. CSN&Y 12" Single) (7:35)/
Campaigner (original extra verse version) (4:15)/
Home On The Range (12" single version) (2:51)/
Weight Of The World (extended remix 12" single)
(5:23)/ This Note's For You (live Apr. 13 '88.
Unedited full length version) (5:40)/ No More (live
Sept. 30 '89) (4:40)/ Don't Spook The Horse (non-
LP) (7:36)
CD2: Don't Be Denied (edit version) (1:15)/ Love
In Mind (edit version) (1:15)/ Last Dance (edit ver-
sion) (1:30)/ Drive Back (DJ mono mix) (3:24)/
Hey Babe (DJ mono mix) (3:35)/ Southern Pacific
(DJ mono mix) (3:59)/ Opera Star (DJ mono mix)
(3:35)/ Surfer Joe And Moe Sleaze (DJ mono mix)
(4:14)/ Inca Queen (edit version) (5:27)/ Too
Lonely (edit remix version) (2:46)/ Ten Men
Workin' (edit version) (3:10)/ This Note's For You
(edit of live version) (3:15)/ Crime In The City
('Sixty To Zero' Part 1) (fade version) (5:06)/
Rockin' In The Free World (edit version) (3:40)/
Mansion On The Hill (edit version) (3:19)/ Over
And Over (edit version) (3:13)/ Arc, The Single
(promotional only CD single) (3:25)/ Harvest
Moon (edit version) (3:49)/ Long May You Run
(edit version) (4:17)/ All Along The Watchtower
(edit version) (4:07)
R: Ex. Soundboard. A few cuts have surface
noise.   C: Japanese CD.

CD - WONDERING BACK HOME
CAPRICORN RECORDS CR 2053/54
CD1: Tell Me Why/ Roll Another Number/ Journey
Through The Past/ The Needle And The Damage
Done/ Harvest/ Campaigner/ Pocahontas/ A Man
Needs A Maid/ Sugar Mountain/ Country Home/
Don't Cry No Tears/ Drive Back/ Cowgirl In The
Sand
CD2: Bite The Bullet/ Lotta Love/ Like A
Hurricane/ After The Gold Rush/ Are You Ready
For The Country?/ Cortez The Killer/ Cinnamon
Girl/ Home Grown/ Southern Man
R: G-Vgs. Audience.   S: The Boston Music Hall,
Boston Nov. 22 '76.   C: Dcc. Time CD1 54:46.
CD2 48:40.

CD - WORK SONGS
JOKER JOK-022-A
My My Hey Hey/ Rockin' In The Free World/ Old
Laughing Lady/ Don't Let It Bring You Down/
Someday/ Crime In The City/ Too Far Gone/ This
Notes For You/ Needle And The Damage Done/
After The Gold Rush/ Ohio/ El Dorado/ F-!# In'
Up/ Powderfinger
R: Ex. Soundboard.   S: Hamburg, Germany
12/8/89.   C: Australian CD. Dbw. Time 68:48

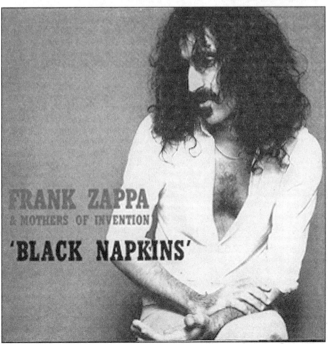

CD - YOU ARE JUST A DREAM
F*!#IN' UP FUPCD-2001/2
CD1: Tell Me Why/ Mellow My Mind/ After The Gold Rush/ Too Far Gone/ Only Love Can Break Your Heart/ A Man Needs A Maid/ No One Seems To Know (Don't Say You Win, Don't Say You Lose)/ Heart Of Gold
CD2: Country Home/ Don't Cry No Tears/ Down By The River/ Lotta Love/ Like A Hurricane/ The Losing End (When You're On)/ Drive Back/ Southern Man/ Cinnamon Girl
R: Vg. Audience.   S: Nagoya, Japan Mar. 3 '76.
C: Japanese CD. With Crazy Horse.

CD - YOUNGS HEART RUNS FREE LIVE LONDON 1993
FREE WORLD MUSIC FWM001/2
CD1: Mr. Soul (4:01)/ The Loner (4:31)/ Southern Man (6:04)/ Helpless (5:56)/ Like A Hurricane (9:26)/ Motorcycle Mama (5:14)/ Love To Burn (11:16)/ Separate Ways (6:19)/ Powderfinger (6:18)/ Only Love Can Break Your Heart (4:47)/ Harvest Moon (6:08)/ The Needle And The Damage Done (2:17)
CD2: Live To Ride (8:40)/ Down By The River (11:36)/ Sitting On The Dock Of The Bay (6:20)/ All Along The Watchtower (7:57)/ Rockin' In The Freeworld (with Pearl Jam) (7:17)/ I'm Just A Passenger (Box Car) (The Hit Factory, New York, '88) (2:14)/ Road Of Plenty (with Crazy Horse, Mansfield Sept. 21 '86 - later became 'Eldorado') (8:07)/ Forever Young (Grateful Dead, San Francisco, Nov. 3 '91) (6:59)/ Ordinary People (with The Bluenotes, Jones Beach Aug. 27 '88) (12:30)/ High Heels (with The Bluenotes at The World in New York Apr. 18 '88) (4:01)
R: CD1-2 track 17 G-Vg. Audience. CD2 tracks 6-10 Vg.   S: CD1-2 track 17 Finsbury Park, London, England July 11 '93 with Booker T And The MGs.   C: ECD. Dcc.

ZAPPA, FRANK

CD - BLACK NAPKINS
ZA 34/35
CD1: Opening Vamp (Zappa's Guitar Solo Of Inca Road Theme)/ Stink Foot, A Short Tale About The Babbled Poodle/ Dirty Love/ Filthy Habits/ Freak Out Medley: How Could I Be Such A Fool, I Ain't Got No Heart, I'm Not Satisfied/ Black Napkins/ Advance Romance
CD2: The Illusions Enema Bandit/ Wind Up Workin' In A Gas Station/ Tryin' To Grow A Chin/ Torture Never Stop/ Chunga's Revenge/ Zoot Allures/ Ship Ahoy, Miss Pinky (The Daughter Of Mrs. Pinky)/ Dinah Moe Human
R: Vgm. Audience.   S: Kyoto-Seibu Kodo, Kyoto Feb. 4 '76.   C: Japanese CD. Dbw.

CD - KREEGA BONDOLA
TRIANGLE PYCD 078-2
CD1: Heavy Duty Judy/ Carolina Hardcore Ecstasy/ Advance Romance/ I'm The Slime/ Be In My Video/ What's New In Baltimore?/ Lucille Has

Messed Up My Mind/ Ride My Face To Chicago/ Teenage Wind/ Truck Driver Divorce/ Cocaine Decision/ Nig Biz/ Sharleena
CD2: Keep It Greasy/ Honey Don't You Want A Man Like Me?/ Carol You Fool/ Chana In The Bushwop/ Kreega Bondola (Let's Move To Cleveland)/ He's So Gay/ Bobby Brown/ Crew Slut/ Camarillo Brillo/ Muffin Man/ The Illinois Enema Bandit
R: Exs. Soundboard.   S: Performing Arts Centre, Saratoga Springs Aug. 1 '84.   C: ECD. Time CD1 60:09. CD2 59:42.

CD - STREAM FLASH CONSERVATIVE
CLINTON CL 7918
Prelude To Bobby Brown/ Bobby Brown/ Conehead/ Moe's Vacation/ I Have Been In You/ The Little House I Used To Live In/ Tell Me You Love Me/ Yo Mama/ Heavy Duty Judy/ Presentation/ City Of Tiny Lights/ You Are What You Is/ Mudd Club
R: Vg soundboard recording.   S: San Francisco, New York '78.

ZEVON, WARREN

CD - THE ELECTRIC WEREWOLF STRIKES AGAIN
REAL LIVE RL CD 27
Sentimental Hygiene/ Splendid Isolation/ Detox Mansion/ Reconsider Me/ Transverse City/ Run Straight Down/ The Long Arm Of The Law/ Turbulence/ Boom Boom Mancini/ Roland The Headless Thompson Gunner/ Werewolves Of London/ Play It All Night Long/ Lawyers, Guns And Money/ Poor Poor Pitiful Me*/ Cadillac Ranch*/ Excitable Boy*
R: Exs. Soundboard.   S: 1st Avenue, Minneapolis Feb. 27 '90. *Capitol Theatre, Passaic, NJ Nov. '82.   C: ECD. Dcc. 72:39.

ZZ TOP

CD - I LOVE MY AUTOMOBILE
ZZ 1/2
CD1: World Of Swirl/ Pincushion/ Breakaway/ Waiting For The Bus/ Jesus Just Left Chicago/ I'm Bad, I'm Nationwide/ Cheap Sunglasses/ Tell It Fuzzbox Voodoo/ Just Got Back From Baby's/ A Fool For Your Stockings/ Rough Boy
CD2: Planet Of Women/ Just Got Laid/ She Loves My Automobile/ PCL/ Antenna Lead/ Legs/ Sharp Dressed Man/ Gimme All Your Lovin'/ Viva Las Vegas/ La Grange Tush
R: G-Vg. Audience.   S: Hanns-Martin Schleyer Halle, Stuttgart Dec. 14 '94.   C: ECD. Dcc.

Stay tuned...

Appendix: Bootleg Labels

For more listings of bootleg labels see

HOT WACKS BOOK XV
and
Supplements 1, 2 & 3

CD - AMERICAN FLY (AF)
AF004 Neil Young, Crazy Horse 'Afternoon Radio'
AF005/6 Phish 'Fresh From The Sea'
AF007 Amos, Tori 'I Touch Myself'
AF008 Letters To Cleo 'Babies In Paradise'
AF009 Jam, The 'Bored With The USA'
AF010/11 Clapton, Eric 'All Inspiration'
AF12/13 Nine Inch Nails 'I Feel Evil'
AF14 Green Day 'Snotheads'
AF015 Crow, Sheryl 'Missouri Watergirl'
AF016 Talking Heads 'Heads In Dallas'
AF017 Nirvana 'The First Night'
AF018 Black, Frank 'Fu Manchu In Chicago'
AF021 Grateful Dead 'Phil Lesh & Friends'
AF022/23 Etheridge, Melissa 'Concert #101'

CD - ASTEROID (AR)
AR-04 Allman Brothers 'Fillmore West'
AR-09 Ayers, Kevin 'Days In Ibza'
AR-01 Boston 'Mary Ann'
AR-12 Brand X 'London '76'
AR-06 Brand X 'San Francisco'
AR-03 Can 'Mother Sky'
AR-04 Can 'Unopened'
AR-11 Can 'Unopened #2'
AR-07-1/2 Derek & The Dominos 'The Garage'
AR-10 Wyatt, Robert 'Sea Song'

CD - BIG RECORDS (BIG)
BIG 095 Pink Floyd 'Focus'
BIG 096 Tull, Jethro 'A Slice Of Flute Cake'
BIG 097 Pink Floyd 'Re-Actor'
BIG 098 The Smiths 'The Butterfly Collector'
BIG 099 Kinks 'Kristmas Koncert'
BIG 100/01 Grateful Dead 'The Dead Don't...'
BIG 102/03 R.E.M. 'Revolution'

CD - CRACKER (CR)
CR-15 Beck 'Total Paranoia'
CR-1 Dylan, Bob 'Over The Broken Glass'
CR-7-1/2 Marley, Bob & The Wailers 'Roots Rock Reggae'
CR-10 Dinosaur Jr. 'Nothing Much To Say'
CR-17 Extreme 'Hip Today, Here Tomorrow'
CR-18 Skid Row 'This Is The Subhuman Gig!'
CR-9-1/2 Kiss 'Rock And Roll Part 1978'
CR-3 Manic Street Preachers 'Slash 'N' Burn'
CR-12 Nirvana 'Hobkan '89'
CR-11 Nirvana 'Seattle '88'
CR-14 Nirvana 'Tacoma '87'
CR-4 Pantera 'Shedding Skin'
CR-16 Pearl Jam 'Girl Find A Better Man'
CR-19 Slash's Snakepit 'Good To Be Live'
CR-5 Soundgarden 'Stingray'
CR-2 Teenage Fanclub 'On The Radio'
CR-8 Waits, Tom 'On A Foggy Night'

CD - FINGERPRINT (FP)
FP001/002 Simon & Garfunkel 'Old Friends'
FP003 Morrissey 'The More You Ignore Me, The Closer I Get'
FP004 Hole 'The Girl With The Most Cake'
FP005 Nine Inch Nails 'Sympathy For The Devil'
FP006 Elastica 'Perk Punk Noise'
FP007 Live 'Selling The Drama'
FP008 Live 'Stage'
FP009 Stone Temple Pilots 'Boggling'
FP010 The Offspring 'Live Smash'
FP011/012 Hootie And The Blowfish 'Blow Fish Blow'
FP013 Cranberries 'Unplugged And Exposed'

CD -HOME (HR)
HR5952-7 Therapy 'Absolutely Barking'
HR5953-9 Sepultura 'Brazilian Nuts'
HR5954-5 Extreme 'Caught In The Act'
HR5955-2 Pantera 'Armed & Dangerous'
HR5956/7 Steely Dan 'Steely Dan Orchestra'
HR5959-6 Pearl Jam 'The Jam Machine'
HR5960-4 Tool 'Sober'
HR5961-8 Mother Love Bone 'Sister Ass'
HR5962/63 Phish 'Jam Session'
HR5964-0 Depeche Mode 'Live In David Gahan's Pants'
HR5965-6 Eagles 'The Grand Resumption'
HR5967-3 Grateful Dead 'Cosmic Revelation'
HR5970-7 Candlebox 'Last Great Seattle Band'
HR5971/72 Metallica 'The Boys 'R' Back'
HR5973/4 Rush 'Storm In St. Petersburg'
HR5975-2 Costello, Elvis 'Youthful Elvis'
HR5976-1 Pavement 'Green Around The Gills'
HR5977-9 Nine Inch Nails 'Reznor Sharp'
HR5979-8 Allman Brothers 'Southern Silver'
HR5981-4 10,000 Maniacs 'From Natalie With Love'
HR5982-6 Pretenders 'May We Rock You?'
HR5983-0 Crow, Sheryl 'Wednesday Night State Theater'
HR5984-7 Galliano 'Antifacists On Stage'
HR5985-1 Rolling Stones 'Some Girls Are Bigger Than...'
HR5986-2 Mellencamp, John 'Strippin Down'
HR5987-9 Dylan, Bob 'Sensei'
HR5988-3 Browne, Jackson 'Alive And Kicking'
HR5991-5 Marley, Bob 'That Rasta Feeling'
HR5992-4 Counting Crow 'Adam Untouchable'
HR5993-0 Blur 'Blurred Vision'
HR5994-6 Carey, Mariah 'One Night In L.A.'
HR5995-8 Beck 'I'm A Schmoozer Baby'
HR5996-1 Phish 'Fishmen Tales'
HR5997-2 Oasis 'Crashlanding In L.A.'

HR5998-9 Big Star 'Pick Some Posies And ...'
HR5999-3 Harry, Deborah 'Debbie Does Luna'
HR6000-2 Replacements 'It Ain't Over Til The Fat Roadies Play'
HR6001-7 Clapton, Eric 'Live Rehearsals'
HR6002-5 10,000 Maniacs 'More Unplugged'
HR6003-0 Specials 'Princes At The Palace'
HR6004-8 Madness 'The Last Dementia'
HR6005-3 XTC 'Fab Oursome In Philly'
HR6006-4 Young, Neil 'Jewel Box Vol. 6'
HR6007-6 Etheridge, Melissa 'Set Yourself Free'
HR6008-1 Collective Soul 'Halloween Grove'
HR6010/11 Grateful Dead 'The Dead In Bloom'
HR6012-2 Houston, Whitney 'All My Love'
HR6013-5 Kiss 'Carnival'
HR6016-7 Sugar '100% Pure'
HR6017-0 Beastie Boys 'Lolapalooza'
HR6018 Nine Inch Nails 'Hammer Hard'
HR6019 Prince 'Juicy'
HR6020 Police 'Policemen In New York'
HR6021 Clash 'Clash Calling'
HR6022 Green Day 'Live At The Radio'
HR6023/24/25 Phish 'A Tribute To The Beatles'
HR6026/27 Black Crows 'Second Night'
HR6028 Bon Jovi 'Christmas Benefit'
HR6029 Aerosmith 'Welcome To Mama Kin'
HR6030 Wet Wet Wet 'All You Need Is Love'
HR6031/32 Cure 'Mad Bob &The Screwtones'
HR6033 Led Zeppelin 'Ultimate BBC Collection'
HR6034 Bad Religion 'Holy Smoke'
HR6035 Live 'Yorksters In Boston'
HR6036 Edmunds, Dave 'Still Rockin''
HR6037 Weezer 'Rock Candy'
HR6038 Green Day 'Kiss My Green Ass'
HR6039 Almighty 'Irish Metal Lords'
HR6040 Pearl Jam 'Vedder Me'
HR6041 Cranberries 'Lucky Charms'
HR6042 Hole 'Good Sex'
HR6043 Rem 'Ballroom Dancing'
HR6044 Shawn Colvin 'A Midwestern Night'
HR6045 Hole 'Rock's Bitch'
HR6046-3 Red Hot Chili Peppers
HR6047/48 Blues Traveler 'Sweet Talking Blues'
HR6049 Amos, Tori 'Piano Girl Up North'
HR6050-1 REM 'Toto This Isn't Athens Anymore'
HR6051 The Church 'Acoustic Sermon'
HR6052 Prince 'Open Your Fly'
HR6053 Flaming Lips 'Trippy Lip Stick'
HR6054/55 Van Halen 'Loud And Balanced'
HR6056 Veruca Salt 'Willy Wonka'
HR6057-3 Nine Inch Nails 'A Demon Possessed'
HR6058/59 Rolling Stones 'Lounging In Melbourne'

CD - IMMIGRANT (IM)

IM-002/3 Led Zeppelin 'Twinight'
IM-004/5 Led Zeppelin 'Complete 69 BBC Classics'
IM-006/7 Led Zeppelin 'Seventh Heaven'
IM-008 Led Zeppelin 'Headley Grange'
IM-009 Led Zeppelin 'Lyceum Preview'
IM-010/11 Led Zeppelin 'The Last'
IM-012/14 Led Zeppelin 'Complete Earl's Court Arena '75'

IM-015/16 Led Zeppelin 'Majestic Hollies'
IM-017/18 Led Zeppelin 'Psychedelic Raw Blues'
IM-019/21 Led Zeppelin 'One More Magic'
IM-022/23 Led Zeppelin 'Olympiahalle 1973'
IM-024/25 Led Zeppelin 'Hamburg 1970'
IM-026/28 Led Zeppelin 'Baltimore 1972'
IM-029/30 Led Zeppelin 'Blow Up'
IM-031/32 Led Zeppelin 'Missing sailor'
IM-035/36 Led Zeppelin 'Melbourne Masters'
IM-040 Led Zeppelin 'Blaze!'

CD - INVASION UNLIMITED (IU)

IU9416 Beach Boys 'Landlocked'
IU9417 Hendrix, Jimi 'Electric Lady Outtakes'
IU9418-1 Wilson, Brian 'Sweet Insanity Outtakes'
IU9419-1 Wilson, Brian 'The Wilson Project'
IU9420-1 Beatles 'The Abbey Road Companion'
IU9421 Beach Boys 'Brian's Back'
IU9422 Wilson, Brian 'In My Room'
IU9423 Pink Floyd 'The Sights And Sounds Of...'
IU9424 Hendrix, Jimi 'Get The Experience!"
IU9425 Pearl Jam 'Immortality'
IU9426-1 King Crimson 'A Weird Person's Guide To... Vol. 2'
IU9427-1 Beatles 'Live At The BBC'
IU9428 Rolling Stones 'At The Beep'
IU9429-1 Deep Purple 'BBC Radio-Tracks'
IU9430-2 Dylan, Bob 'Love Minus Zero'
IU9531 Rolling Stones 'Around And Around'
IU9532 Rolling Stones 'Songbook'
IU9533 Rolling Stones 'Have You Heard The Outtakes, Baby...'
IU9535 Rolling Stones 'Itchy Fingers'
IU9536 Rolling Stones 'It's Only Rock 'N' Roll- Outtakes'
IU9537 Rolling Stones 'Made In The Shade'
IU9538 Rolling Stones 'In The Eighties'
IU9539 Beatles 'The Alternate Versions Vol. 1'
IU9540 Beatles 'The Alternate Versions Vol. 2'
IU9541 Beatles Unplugged 'Acoustic Demos For White Album'
IU9542 Rolling Stones 'Unplugged'

CD - KISS THE STONE (KTS)

KTS 405 Van Halen 'Secret Gig'
KTS 406 Springsteen 'Loose Ends'
KTS 407 Hootie & The Blowfish 'On The Left Coast'
KTS 408 Etheridge, Melissa 'Let's Get It On'
KTS 409 Bon Jovi 'Acoustic'
KTS 410 Griffith, Nanci 'Sound Of Loneliness'
KTS 411/12 Kiss 'Rockin' In Chile'
KTS 413 Nofx 'Together On The Road'
KTS 414 Black Crows 'High Head Blues'
KTS 415 Etheridge, Melissa 'Acoustic'
KTS 416/17 Dream Theater 'Mind Control'
KTS 418/19 Pearl Jam 'Down Under'
KTS 420/21 Matthews, Dave Band 'Best Of...'
KTS 422/23 Grateful Dead 'Comes A Time...'
KTS 424 Faith No More 'Evidence'
KTS 425 Raitt, Bonnie 'Storm Warning'
KTS 426 Springsteen, Bruce 'Lost And Live'
KTS 427 Crow, Sheryl 'Acoustic'

KTS 428 Phish 'Simple'
KTS 429 Siouxsie & The Banshees 'Sister Midnight'
KTS 430/31 Grateful Dead 'Play Dead'
KTS 432 Indigo Girls 'History Of Us'
KTS 433 Lennox, Annie 'Golden Lady'
KTS 434 Suede 'Cover Me'
KTS 435/36 Dylan, Bob 'Brixton Blues'
KTS 437 Live 'Shit Town'
KTS 438 Elastica 'The Vaseline Gang'
KTS 439 Stone Temple Pilots 'Interstate Love Songs'
KTS 440 Hole 'Plugged & Unplugged'
KTS 441 Allman Brothers 'Songs From The Road'
KTS 442 Bad Religion 'Radiation Hazard'
KTS 443 Jayhawks 'Poised For Stardom'
KTS 444 Black Crowes 'Songs Of The Flesh'
KTS 445/46 Rolling Stones 'Tokyo '95'
KTS 447/48 R.E.M. 'Aneurysm'
KTS 449 Live 'Supernatural'
KTS 450/51 Page & Plant 'Simple Truth'
KTS 452 Portishead 'Nobody Loves Me'
KTS 453 Clapton, Eric 'Lost Jams'
KTS 454 Costello, Elvis 'Jesus, This Is Elvis'
KTS 455 Machine Head 'Pressure Point'
KTS 456 Hole 'Asking For It'
KTS 457/58 Clapton, Eric 'The Blues Concert'
KTS 459 Belly 'Live And Hungry'
KTS 460/61 Queensryche 'Saints And Sinners'
KTS 462 Page & Plant 'Glastonbury'
KTS 463 Oasis 'Up IN The Sky'
KTS 464/65 Bon Jovi 'Now And Forever'
KTS 466 Cure 'Dressing Up For A Day Out'
KTS 467 Soul Asylum 'Set Me Free'
KTS 468/69 Phish 'Live Bait'
KTS 470 Etheridge, Melissa 'Ten Years Of Covers'
KTS 471/72 R.E.M. 'Adhesion'
KTS 473 Matthews, Dave Band
KTS 474 Bush 'Burning'
KTS 475 The Cranberries 'Yesterday's Gone'
KTS 476 Indigo Girls 'In With The Out Crowd'
KTS 477 Bruce Springsteen 'Lost And Live 2'
KTS 478/79 Jerry Garcia 'Jerry's Home'
KTS 480/81 Dave Matthews 'With A Little Help..'
KTS 482 Sheryl Crow 'Eating Crow'
KTS 483 Blur 'Mile End'
KTS 484 Offspring 'Come Out And Play'
KTS 485 Pantera 'Noize, Booze And Tattoos'
KTS 486 P J Harvey 'Live Goes The Night'
KTS 487 Metallica 'Donnington'
KTS 488 Supergrass 'Doing Time'
KTS 489 Hole 'Vengeance Is Mine'
KTS 490 Van Morrison 'Edinburgh Castle'
KTS 491 Jethro Tull 'Velvet Flute'
KTS 492 Smashing Pumpkins 'Blackout'
KTS 493 Foo Fighters 'Reading'
KTS 495/96 Van Halen 'Rocks The Beer Hall'
KTS 498 Nine Inch Nails 'Children Of The Night'
KTS 499 Meatloaf 'It's Live For You'
KTS 500/01 Ozzy 'Let The Madness Begin'
KTS 502/03 David Bowie 'Live, Inside'
KTS 504/05 Grateful Dead 'Southern Comfort'

KTS 506/07 Grateful Dead 'Have Some Respect'
KTS 508/09 Allmand Brothers Band 'Midnight Riding'
KTS 510/11 Lenny Kravitz 'Rock & Roll Is Live'
KTS 513 Garbage 'In The Can'
KTS 514 Toadies 'Burn'
KTS 515 Alanis Morissette 'Hard To Swallow'

CD - MOONRAKER

001/2 Rolling Stones 'Olympia'
009/10/11/12 Prince 'The Park Volume One'
013 Green Day 'Attack Of Insomnia'
014/15/16/17/18/19 'Rock &Roll Hall Of Fame'
020/21 Prince 'The Park Volume Two'
022 Bjork 'Cirkusbjork'
023/24 REM 'Monster Radio'
025/26 Red Hot Chilipeppers 'One Hot Globe'
027 Foo Fighters 'Weenie Beanie'
028/29 Smashing Pumpkins 'Starlight'
030/31 Blur 'Entertainment'
032 Oasis 'Paris Is Supernova'
033/34 David Bowie 'Open The Dog'
035/36 PJ Harvey 'Pretty Polly'
037 Pulp 'Made In France'
038 Foo Fighters 'On The Air'
042/43 Simply Red 'Live Life'

CD - OCTOPUS RECORDS (OCTO)

OCTO 025 Scorpions 'Scorps Bite Back'
OCTO 026 Spin Doctors 'Hey...Spin On This'
OCTO 027 Frampton, Peter 'Frampton Comes Again (And Alive)'
OCTO 028 Pearl Jam 'Attenzione'
OCTO 029/030 Joel, Billy 'Up The Sinners'
OCTO 031/032 Yes 'Endless Dream'
OCTO 033/034 Pink Floyd 'The Glants At The Giant's'
OCTO 035 Counting Crows 'True Heart'
OCTO 036 Nirvana 'Out Of The Blue'
OCTO 037 Allman Brothers 'Southern Harmony'
OCTO O38 Red Hot Chili Peppers 'Woodstock 1994'
OCTO 039 Nine Inch Nails 'Woodstock 1994'
OCTO 040/041 'Woodstock 1994'
OCTO 042/043 Metallica 'Woodstock 1994'
OCTO 044 C. S. & N. 'Woodstock 1994'
OCTO 045 Traffic 'Woodstock 1994'
OCTO 047 James 'Sounds And Moods'
OCTO 049 Porno For Pyros 'Woodstock 1994
OCTO 050 Wet Wet Wet 'Angel Dust'
OCTO 051 Green Day 'Woodstock 1994'
OCTO 052 Prong 'Enter Nightmare'
OCTO 053/054 Rolling Stones 'The Show Must Roll On'
OCTO 055 Pink Floyd 'Just Warmin' Up (The Rehearsals In Tampa)'
OCTO 056/057 Pearl Jam 'Dedicated To The Motherf***ers'
OCTO 058 Red Hot Chili Peppers 'It's Chili Time'
OCTO 059 Marley, Bob 'Charming Haze'
OCTO 060 Metallica 'Beyond The Wall Of Sound'

OCTO 061 Amos, Tori 'Anything But Honey'
OCTO 062 Deep Purple 'The Legend Lives...'
OCTO 064/065 Rolling Stones 'Tooth And Nail'
OCTO 066/067 Kiss 'Fuego En Buenos Aires'
OCTO 068 Oasis 'Talk Tonight'
OCTO 069 Hole 'Ugly Demented World'
OCTO 071 Aerosmith 'House On Fire'
OCTO 072 Pearl Jam 'Live From The Warehouse'
OCTO 078/079 Madonna 'Physical Osmosis'
OCTO 080/81 Dream Theater 'Wake Up!'
OCTO 082 Sting 'Arigato'
OCTO 086 Oasis 'Cigarettes & Alcohol'
OCTO 087 Cranberries 'Songs Against War'
OCTO 088 (NR) Metallica 'Covering 'Em 2'
OCTO 089 (NR) Bon Jovi 'Covering 'Em'
OCTO 090 (NR) Aerosmith 'Unwired'
OCTO 091 Take That 'Heartbeats'
OCTO 092 Type O Negative 'Even Snow Dies'
OCTO 093 (NR) Stone Temple Pilots 'Unwired'
OCTO 094 (NR) Kiss ' Unwired'
OCTO 096 (NR) U2 'Four Wild Irish Roses'
OCTO 097 (NR) Collective Soul 'Atlanta Brightest Sons'
OCTO 098/099 Pearl Jam 'Aussie Dynamos'
OCTO 100 (NR) Black Crowes 'Unwired'
OCTO 101 (NR) Bon Jovi 'Unwired'
OCTO 102 (NR) Green Day 'Green Daze'
OCTO 103 (NR) Aerosmith 'Covering 'Em'
OCTO 104 (NR) Amos, Tori 'Covering 'Em'
OCTO 105/106 Rolling Stones 'Live In Japan'
OCTO 107 (NR) Etheridge, Melissa 'When I Was A Child'
OCTO 108/109 Guns N' Roses'
OCTO 110 Michael, George 'Everything You Want'
OCTO 111 U2 '1-800-U2 Live'
OCTO 112 Madonna 'Let's Do It'
OCTO 113 Van Halen 'Young & Wild'
OCTO 114/115 Metallica 'For Whom The Bell Tolls'
OCTO 116 Megadeth 'Basic Dreams'
OCTO 117 Toto 'Energy'
OCTO 118/119 Genesis 'The Lamb Lives'
OCTO 120 Tull, Jethro 'Live At The Lonestar'
OCTO 121 Sting 'Covering 'Em'
OCTO 122 U2 'Covering 'Em'
OCTO 123 Guns N' Roses 'Covering 'Em'
OCTO 124/125 Toto 'Papa Was A Sexy Dancer'
OCTO 126 Iron Maiden 'Good-Bye Bruce'
OCTO 127/128 U2 'Zootopia'
OCTO 129 Depeche Mode 'Dogma'
OCTO 130 Pearl Jam 'Covering 'Em (Selves)'
OCTO 131 Duran Duran 'Fiesta!'
OCTO 132/133 Metallica 'Blood, Sweat & Tears'
OCTO 134 R.E.M. 'Covering 'Em'
OCTO 135 Springsteen, Bruce 'Covering 'Em'
OCTO 136/137 Madonna 'Exotica'
OCTO 140/141 Aerosmith 'Skin & Bones'
OCTO 142 Clapton, Eric 'An Acoustic Tale'
OCTO 143 Pearl Jam 'The Five Musketeers'
OCTO 144 Michael, George 'I'm Your Man'
OCTO 145 Living Colour '4 Never Satisfied Friends'

OCTO 146 Guns N' Roses 'Booze'
OCTO 147 Nirvana 'Live 1994'
OCTO 148 U2 'Zoocoustic'
OCTO 149 R.E.M. 'Hitting The Note'
OCTO 150 Smashing Pumpkins 'Cutting Edge'
OCTO 151 Duran Duran 'Exposed'
OCTO 152 Metallica 'Covering 'Em'
OCTO 153 Bon Jovi 'Seattle Survivors'
OCTO 154 Sisters Of Mercy 'Welcome To The Temple Of Love'
OCTO 155 Pearl Jam 'Versus The World'
OCTO 156/157 Grateful Dead 'Unsurpassed Dead Demos'
OCTO 158 Kiss 'Flaming Years'
OCTO 159 Dream Theater 'Majestic Harmonies'
OCTO 160 Kravitz, Lenny 'On A Magic Carpet Ride'
OCTO 161 Crow, Sheryl 'Even Angels Rock'
OCTO 162 Page & Plant 'The Story So Far...'
OCTO 163 Pearl Jam 'All Night Thing'
OCTO 164 Nirvana 'Rough Tapes'
OCTO 165 Queensryche 'Unplugged & Other Stories'
OCTO 166 Beatles 'Off White Vol. 2'
OCTO 167 Beatles 'Off White Vol. 3'
OCTO 168 Pearl Jam 'In Rock We Trust'
OCTO 169 Young, Neil 'Frisco'
OCTO 170/171 Madonna 'Sexual Exposure'
OCTO 172/173 U2 'Rock's Hottest Ticket'
OCTO 174/175 Sylvian & Fripp 'A New Dream'
OCTO 176 Vaughan, Steve Ray 'Jammed Together, Texas Style'
OCTO 177 Jane's Addiction 'Live Too'
OCTO 178 Bon Jovi 'Return Of The Jersey Boy'
OCTO 179 Pearl Jam 'We're Gonna Hungry'
OCTO 180 Wood, Andy 'Communication #1'
OCTO 181 Wood, Andy 'Communication #2'
OCTO 182/183 Page & Plant 'Whole Lotta Zep'
OCTO 184 (NR) Hole 'Riot Girl'
OCTO 185/186 (NR) Matthews Band 'Riding The Rhythm'
OCTO 187 Offspring 'Revenge Of The Nerds'
OCTO 188 (NR) NOFX 'Smashing Punk Kings'
OCTO 201/202 (NR) R.E.M. 'Welcome The Freak Show'

CD - OXYGEN RECORDS (OXY)

OXY 001/2 Hootie & The Blowfish 'Blue Mirage'
OXY 003/4 Rush 'Mirrors'
OXY 005 Simple Minds 'Painting The Blue Skies Black'
OXY 006 Jeff Buckley 'Dream Brother'
OXY 007 Foo Fighters 'Tuneful Chaos'
OXY 008 Megadeth 'The Other Side'
OXY 009 Slayer 'The Sickness Within'
OXY 010 Delamitri 'Swimming With Your Boots On'
OXY 011 Van Halen 'Blastin''
OXY 012 Soul Asylum 'Misery Loves Company'
OXY 013 Lenny Kravitz 'Still Walking On Thin Ice'
OXY 014 Kiss 'Die Hard' (Unwired)
OXY 015 U2 'Jesus Was A Cool Guy'
OXY 016/17 Queensryche 'State Of Art'

OXY 018 Blur 'Blurred Vision'
OXY 019 U2 'Duets'
OXY 020 Smashing Pumpkins 'The World Is A Vampire'
OXY 021 Phil Collins 'Mr. Nice Guy'
OXY 022 Kiss 'Unplugged'
OXY 023 Red Hot Chili Peppers 'Slap Happy'
OXY 024 Silverchair 'Les Enfants Terrible'
OXY 025 White Zombie 'Astro-Junkies: 1995'
OXY 026 Rainbow 'Black Shadows'
OXY 027 Bruce Springsteen 'Railroad Tracks'
OXY 028 The Cranberries 'Strange Fruits'
OXY 029 Iron Maiden 'The Eternal Flame'
OXY 030 Melissa Etheridge 'I Wish I Was Your Lover'
OXY 031 Foo Fighters 'Fighting The 'N' Factor'
OXY 032 Garbage 'The 'G' Files'
OXY 033 Blind Melon 'Climbing The Clouds'
OXY 034 Oasis 'Undrugged'
OXY 035 Pat Metheny 'Autumn Leaves'
OXY 036 Foo Fighters 'Frenzy!'
OXY 037 Alanis Morissette 'Miss Thing'
OXY 038 Supergrass 'Feel Alright'
OXY 039 Cast 'Prime Time'
OXY 040 Simple Minds 'Don't Forget Paris'
OXY 041 Oasis '1996'
OXY 042 PJ Harvey 'My Life'
OXY 043 Pulp 'Cafe' Concerto'
OXY 044 Bush 'The Jekyll In You'

CD - RAZOR BLADE (RB)

RB501 Aerosmith 'Ruling The Planet'
RB502 Primus 'Burning Up!'
RB503 Rollins Band 'Human Pitbull'
RB504 Dinosaur Jr. 'Monsters Eat Orpheum'
RB505 Pearl Jam 'Mudfeast'
RB506 Slayer 'Rockin' Down South'
RB507 NIN 'Sex, Pain & Rock 'N' Roll'
RB508 Green Day 'Eating Burgers'
RB509 Black Crowes 'Birds Of A Feather'
RB510 Nine Inch Nails 'March Of The Devil'
RB511 Dream Theater 'Rockin' Japan'
RB513 Oasis 'British Lads In Boston'

CD - ROCK ADVENTURE (RA)

RA 1017 Metallica 'Live Before Death Vol. 1'
RA 1037 Metallica 'Live Before Death Vol. 2'
RA 1173 Nirvana 'Europe 1991'
RA 1181 Nirvana 'Smells Like Punk Spirit'
RA 1188 Metallica 'Enter Metalman'
RA 1259 Nirvana 'San Francisco 1993'
RA 1312 Nirvana 'Europe 1994'
RA 1336 Lenny Kravitz 'Acoustic 1994'
RA 1341 Nirvana 'Acoustic 1993'
RA 1149 The Doors 'San Francisco 1967'
RA 1091 U2 'Covering Them'
RA 1633 Green Day 'U.S.A. 1994'
RA 1594 The Doors 'Missing Tapes'
RA 1319 Pearl Jam 'Atlanta 1994 Vol. 1'
RA 2319 Pearl Jam 'Atlanta 1994 Vol. 2'
RA 1170 Queen 'London 1986'
RA 1203 Pearl Jam 'New Orleans 1992'
RA 1218 Guns 'N' Roses 'Covering Them'

RA 1224 Ramones 'Europe 1992'
RA 1584 Dead Can Dance 'U.S.A. 1993'
RA 1579 Bjork 'Los Angeles 1993'
RA 1343 The Cranberries 'Coming Back To My Family'
RA 1814 Metallica 'Pure Metal Vol. 1'
RA 2814 Metallica 'Pure Metal Vol. 2'
RA 1451 Rolling Stones 'Ultra Rare Trax Vol. 1'
RA 1452 Rolling Stones 'Ultra Rare Trax Vol. 2'
RA 1484 Jimi Hendrix 'Rare Masters Series 3'
RA 1804 Metallica 'Metal Masters Vol. 1'
RA 2804 Metallica 'Metal Masters Vol. 2'
RA 1307 Metallica 'Europe 1987'

CD - SILVER RARITIES (SIRA)

SIRA149 Beach Boys 'Long Lost Surf Songs 1'
SIRA150 Beach Boys 'Long Lost Surf Songs 2'
SIRA151 Beach Boys 'Long Lost Surf Songs 3'
SIRA152 Beach Boys 'Long Lost Surf Songs 4'
SIRA153 Beach Boys 'Long Lost Surf Songs 5'
SIRA154 Beach Boys 'Long Lost Surf Songs 6'
SIRA155 Beach Boys 'Surfin' Rarities Vol. 1'
SIRA156 Beach Boys 'Surfin' Rarities Vol. 2'
SIRA157 Beach Boys 'Surfin' Rarities Vol. 3'
SIRA158 Beach Boys 'Surfin' Rarities Vol. 4'
SIRA159 Beach Boys 'Surfin' Rarities Vol. 5'
SIRA160 Beach Boys 'Surfin' Rarities Vol. 6'
SIRA161/162/163 Led Zeppelin 'Listen To This Eddie' Remastered
SIRA164/165 Led Zeppelin 'No License, No Festival'
SIRA166/167 Led Zeppelin '56,800 In The Ocean'
SIRA168/169/170 Led Zeppelin 'Trampled Under Jimmy's Foot'
SIRA171/172/173 Led Zeppelin 'It'll Be Zep'
SIRA174/175 Grateful Dead 'Hardly Aged A Day'
SIRA176 Grateful Dead 'Clouds Of Dew'
SIRA177/178 Thompson, Richard & Linda 'Rockpalast'
SIRA179/180 Clapton, Eric 'Back From The Edge'
SIRA181/182 Clapton, Eric 'Cradle Music'
SIRA183/184 Plant & Page 'Paris 95'
SIRA185/186 Pink Floyd 'Not A Cloud In The Sky'
SIRA187/188 Clapton, Eric 'Milwaukee Time'
SIRA189/190/191 Grateful Dead 'We Bid You Goodnight'
SIRA192/193 Thompson, Linda & Richard 'Lonely Hearts'
SIRA194/195/196 Led Zeppelin 'Led Astray'
SIRA197/198/199 Led Zeppelin 'Destroyer II'
SIRA200/201/202 Led Zeppelin 'Rit It Up'
SIRA203/204/205 Led Zeppelin 'Sundazed'
SIRA206/207/208 Led Zeppelin 'Legendary End'
SIRA209/210/211 Young, Neil 'Journey Through The Past'

CD - STARQUAKE (SQ)

SQ-01 Deep Purple 'Never Never Before'
SQ-08 Deep Purple 'Out'
SQ-06 Kraftwerk 'Bremen'

SQ-04　New England 'See You The Next Time'
SQ-07　Uli, Jon Roth 'Hendrix Happening'
SQ-09　Hendrix, Jimi 'Live In Baltimore Civic
　　　　　Center June 13, 70'
SQ-10　Hendrix, Jimi 'Power Of Soul'

CD - SYNERGY (SY)
SY 10010　Blur 'To The End'
SY 10020　The Cranberries 'Be With You'
SY 10030　Foo Fighters 'We'll Stick Around'
SY 10040　Oasis 'Like A Ghost Train'
SY 10050　Alanis Morissette 'Perfect'
SY 10060　Therapy? 'Dead Laughing'
SY 10070　P J Harvey 'C'Mon Polly'
SY 10080　U2 '4th Of July'
SY 10091　Bon Jovi 'Wild In Germany Vol. 1'
SY 10092　Bon Jovi 'Wild In Germany Vol. 2'
SY 10100　Springsteen, Dylan & More 'Rock N'
　　　　　　Roll Hall Of Fame'
SY 10110　Massive Attack 'Protection'
SY 10120　Joe Jackson 'Ever After'
SY 10131　Pearl Jam 'Little Secrets Vol. 1'
SY 10132　Pearl Jam 'Little Secrets Vol. 2'
SY 10141　The Rolling Stones 'A Secret Gig In
　　　　　　Paris Vol. 1'
SY 10142　The Rolling Stones 'A Secret Gig In
　　　　　　Paris Vol. 2'
SY 10150　Bruce Springsteen 'Blood Brothers'
　　　　　　'The E-Street Band Reunion'
SY 10160　The Cranberries 'Acoustic'
SY 10170　Hole 'Unplugged & Reading'
SY 10180　Elastica 'Connection!'
SY 10190　Nirvana 'The Last UK Gig'

CD - TUFF BITES (TB)
TB941001　Stevie Ray Vaughan 'Montreal 89'
TB941002　Grateful Dead 'Deadly Jaws'
TB941003　Dylan, Bob 'Himself'
TB941004　Zappa, Frank 'Punk's Whips'
TB941005　Aerosmith 'Hard Nox & Dirty Sox'
TB941006　ZZ Top 'Beards Getting Rhythm'
TB941007　Winter, Johnny 'Dervish Blues'
TB941008　Captain Beefheart 'Don's Birthday
　　　　　　Party'
TB941009　Doors 'Jim's Alive'
TB941010　Grateful Dead 'Playin' Acoustic'
TB951011　Dylan, Bob 'The Real Voice Of
　　　　　　America'
TB951012　Dylan, Bob 'Songs That Made Him
　　　　　　Famous'
TB951013　Waits, Tom 'Rendevous At Midnight'
TB951014　Santana 'We Love You, Bill'
TB951015　Hendrix, Jimi 'Hovering In Winterland'
TB951016　Marley, Bob 'Death Won't Ever Kill
　　　　　　You'
TB951017　Gerry Garcia Band 'Smells Like A
　　　　　　Dead Spirit'
TB951018　Grateful Dead 'Dead Moon Rising'
TB951019　Dylan, Bob 'A Million Faces At My
　　　　　　Feet'

CD - TYPHOON RECORDS (TYN)
001/02　Rolling Stones 'Acoustic'

003　Foo Fighters 'X-Static'
008/09　Rolling Stones 'Brixton'

CD - VINTAGE RARE MASTERS (VRM)
VRM-008/9　Allman Brothers 'South Meets East'
VRM-003　Dr. John & Meters 'Groovy Days In
　　　　　　Mardi Gras'
VRM-005　Trower, Robin 'Daydream'
VRM-001/2　Clapton, Eric 'Splendor'
VRM-004　Cooder, Ry 'Stand By Me'
VRM-006/7　Beck, Jeff Group 'All Shock Up'
VRM-010/11　Clapton, Eric 'Unsteady Rollin'
　　　　　　Man'

CD - WANTED MAN (WMM)
WMM061　Bob Dylan 'Now's The Time For Your
　　　　　　Tears'
WMM062/63　Dylan, Bob 'Infinity On Trial'
WMM064/65　Dylan, Bob 'Friend Of The Devil'
WMM066/67　Dylan, Bob 'Roseland'
WMM068　Dylan, Bob 'Beacon Blues Again'
WMM069　Dylan, Bob 'Critics Choice Vol. VII'
WMM070　Dylan, Bob 'Critics Choice Vol. VIII'

CD - WEEPING GOAT (WG)
WG-014　Clash 'This Is Clash Live'
WG-016　Funkadelic 'Red Hot Mama In
　　　　　　Richmond 1976'
WG-039/40　Parsons, Gram & The Fallen Angels
　　　　　　'Legendary Live '73'
WG-011　Hound Dog Taylor & The House
　　　　　　Rockers 'Live At Florence Club '69'
WG-012　Howlin' Wolf 'Moaning For My Baby
　　　　　　Live '66'
WG-030/31　Geils, J. Band 'I Can't Do My
　　　　　　Homework Anymore!'
WG-015　Marley, Bob & The Wailers 'Live At
　　　　　　Leeds 1973'
WG-013/14　Marley, Bob 'Live At The Matrix Club'
WG-003　Marley, Bob & The Wailers 'Mystic
　　　　　　Night In Zimbabwe'
WG-002　Marley, Bob & The Wailers 'Rip This
　　　　　　Joint'
WG-017　Ramones 'Gabba Gabba Hey!'
WG-007　Rolling Stones 'Ain't Touched A Drink
　　　　　　All Night'
WG-018/19　Rolling Stones 'Bloody Night In
　　　　　　Seattle 1981'
WG-008　Rolling Stones 'Ginsoaked Barroom
　　　　　　Queen In Boston'
WG-020　Rolling Stones 'Glimmer Twins' Private
　　　　　　Tapes'
WG-005/6　Rolling Stones 'Happy Birthday Keith'
WG-025/26　Rolling Stones 'Hawaiian Top-The
　　　　　　Second Show'
WG-035/36　Rolling Stones 'Melbourne '95'
WG-037/38　Rolling Stones 'Melbourne '95'
WG-001　Sam & Dave, Otis Redding 'Triple
　　　　　　Dynamite Live'
WG-041　Tosh, Peter 'You Can't Blame The
　　　　　　Youth'
WG-042　Tosh, Peter 'Montego Bay Fest. &
　　　　　　Uptown Theater'

HOT WACKS BACK EDITIONS

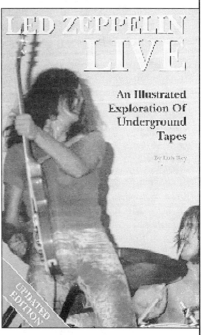

BLACK MARKET
BEATLES

BY BELMO AND BERKENSTADT - FOREWARD BY ADRIAN BELEW

Nationally-recognized Beatles recording experts Belmo (editor and publisher of BELMO'S BEATLEG NEWS) and Jim Berkenstadt (archivist and writer) have joined forces to conceive BLACK MARKET BEATLES, the most comprehensive guide ever written about the bootleg recordings of the Fab Four.

Besides containing the world's largest Beatles underground discography (which stands at a staggering 1,600 entries) the book also features interviews with several Beatle bootleggers, a photo survey of bootleg trademarks and logos, a bootleg label 'family tree' and much more, including over 225 photos and illustrations.

BLACK MARKET BEATLES also has a history of bootlegging. All in all, this is one of the most significant and unique books about The Beatles ever published.

"...intriguing and well-written..." "...excellent research..."
"...a genuine feel for Beatles music and bootleg history..."
(Allen J. Wiener - GOLDMINE)

Order your BLACK MARKET BEATLES today!

In the USA $16.95 US FUNDS (surface mail) or $18.95 US FUNDS (air mail)
In Europe / Asia $18.95 US FUNDS (surface mail) or $21.95 US FUNDS (air mail)
In Canada $19.95 Canadian Funds

Order your book today! Please send payment by cheque or money order
in US FUNDS to:

THE HOT WACKS PRESS
PO Box 544, Dept. 4
Owen Sound, ON, N4K 5R1, CANADA

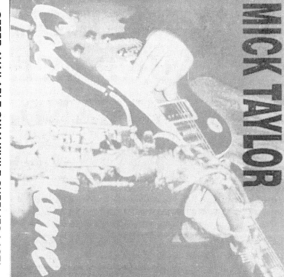

CAUFUH

HUGE COLLECTION OF GREAT RECORDINGS

RARE LIVE RECORDINGS AND AMAZING STUDIO OUTTAKES FROM

ANTRABATA, TWO SYMBOLS, IMMIGRANT, SLOW HAND, WEEPING GOAT, SPIRAL,VINTAGE RARE MASTERS, ASTEROID AND JAZZ MASTER

THE LIVE SURVIVORS

YAMETA PRODUCTIONS
MABURKA ST. ANDREA
TRIQ 1X - X
NIEN S. GWAAN
MALTA SGN04

WRITE FOR A FREE CATALOGUE

KISS THE STONE

KTS 001	THE WATERBOYS 'A GOLDEN DAY'
KTS 002	PRINCE 'PARIS AFFAIR'
KTS 003	INXS 'KICK IT IN EXCESS'
KTS 004	THE MISSION 'INTO THE BLUE'
KTS 005	REM 'IT'S THE END OF THE WORLD...'
KTS 006	VAN MORRISON 'CHURCH OF OUR LADY ST. MARY'
KTS 007	THE BLACK CROWES 'AIN'T THAT AMERICA'
KTS 008	U2 'FEEL THE NOISE'
KTS 009	THE HOTHOUSE FLOWERS 'SPIRIT'
KTS 010/11	INXS 'SOMETHING'XTRA'
KTS 012/13	BOB DYLAN 'STUCK INSIDE OF NEW YORK'
KTS 014	NEIL YOUNG 'RESTLESS'
KTS 015	NOT AVAILABLE NOW
KTS 016	ERASURE 'O L'AMOUR'
KTS 017	THE CLASH 'INTO THE 80'S'
KTS 018/19	SIMPLE MINDS 'REAL...REAL LIVE'
KTS 020	TALK TALK 'TALKING COLORS'
KTS 021	SISTERS OF MERCY 'THE NEON DREAM'
KTS 022	SIMPLY RED 'RED STARS AT NIGHT'
KTS 023	MORRISSEY 'HIGHER EDUCATION'
KTS 024	LENNY KRAVITZ 'FLOWER CHILD'
KTS 025	PIXIES 'VELOURIA'
KTS 026	THE CULT 'NEW YORK CITY BLUES'
KTS 027	U2 'THE FLAME AND THE FIRE'
KTS 028	U2 'SECOND HOMECOMING'
KTS 029	U2 'RED SUN AT MIDNIGHT'
BOX 01	U2 'BOX 579 BABY' 3 CD SET
KTS 030/31	PINK FLOYD 'A CLEAR VIEW'
KTS 032	SINEAD O'CONNOR 'BEAUTIFUL VISION'
KTS 033	PSYCHEDELIC FURS 'ROOM AT THE TOP'
KTS 034	JESUS JONES 'INFO FREAKO'
KTS 035	THE CURE 'JUST LIKE HEAVEN'
KTS 036	THE BLACK CROWES 'BLACK 'N' BLUE'
KTS 037	10,000 MANIACS 'COOL WHITE STARE'
KTS 038	ROBERT PALMER 'FEEL THE HEAT'
KTS 039	QUEEN 'A DAY AT THE STADIUM'
KTS 040	PET SHOP BOYS 'LIVE WIRES'
KTS 041	NIRVANA 'SEVENTH HEAVEN'
KTS 042/43	GENESIS 'THE INVISIBLE CAGE'
KTS 044	DEACON BLUE 'ON NEW YEARS DAY'
KTS 045	STEVIE NICKS 'CLOAKS AND DAGGERS'
KTS 046/47	STING 'THE SEAS OF SILENCE'
KTS 048	ROXETTE 'A NIGHT TO REMEMBER'
KTS 049	CARTER USM 'WHAM BAM'
KTS 050	THE WATERBOYS 'BORN TO BE TOGETHER'
KTS 051	VAN MORRISON 'SOUL LABRYNTH'
KTS 052	THE PIXIES 'ALL OVER THE WORLD'
KTS 053	LENNY KRAVITZ 'MY FLASH ON YOU'
KTS 054	IGGY POP 'METALHEAD'
KTS 055	WONDER STUFF 'INERTIA'
KTS 058	MORRISSEY 'DIGITAL EXCITATION'
KTS 059	FIELDS OF NEPHILIM 'FESTIVAL OF FIRE'
KTS 060	BILLY BRAGG 'BIG MOUTH STRIKES AGAIN'
KTS 061	PAUL YOUNG 'FOREVER YOUNG'
KTS 062	FISH 'THERE'S A GUY WORKS DOWN AT THE CHIP SHOP SWEARS HE'S FISH'
KTS 063/64	U2 'ST. STEPHENS AT THE POINT'
KTS 065	THE POGUES 'SINK THAT BOTTLE'
KTS 066	THE GODFATHER'S 'SHOOT TO KILL'
KTS 067	JANE'S ADDICTION 'DOWN IN FLAMES'
KTS 068	SISTERS OF MERCY 'TRANS-EUROPE EXCESS'
KTS 069	RIDE 'OVERDRIVE'
KTS 070	MARILLION 'GOLDEN TEARS'
KTS 071	QUEEN 'CROWNING GLORY'
KTS 072	JAMES 'LIVE AND DANGEROUS'
KTS 073	ALL ABOUT EVE 'BLESSED BY ANGELS'
KTS 074	THE MISSION 'BLOOD BROTHERS'
KTS 075	RED HOT CHILI PEPPERS 'GET THE FUNK OUT'
KTS 076	MICHAEL BOLTON 'SOUL DRIVER U.S.A.'
KTS 077/78	METALLICA 'TOTALLY DESTROY CANADA'
KTS 079	LOU REED 'MASTER CLASS'
KTS 080	PEARL JAM 'FIVE ALIVE'
KTS 081/82	THE CURE 'AND DREAMS COME TRUE'
KTS 086	SIOUXSIE & THE BANSHEES 'CASCADE'
KTS 087	THE SUGARCUBES 'HIT THE NORTH ATLANTIC'
KTS 088	JESUS & MARY CHAIN 'VENGEANCE'

KTS 089	SIMPLY RED 'RED STARS AT NIGHT VOL. 2'
KTS 090	JOHN COUGAR 'LIVE REHEARSALS'
KTS 091	L7 'MANEATER'
KTS 092	CROWDED HOUSE 'FOUR SEASONS IN ONE DAY'
KTS 093	BOB DYLAN 'SAN JOSE REVISITED'
KTS 094	RUSH 'RUN FROM THE FANS'
KTS 095	SISTERS OF MERCY 'NAPALM GODS'
KTS 096	SISTERS OF MERCY 'KISS THE BLADE'
KTS 097	SISTERS OF MERCY 'HOLOCAUST'
BOX 02	SISTERS OF MERCY 'SO DARK ALL OVER EUROPE'
KTS 098	MR. BIG 'GET BIGGER'
KTS 099	BOB DYLAN 'WANTED MAN'
KTS 100/1	U2 'ZOO TV TOUR'
KTS 102	JOHN COUGAR '4TH. OF JULY'
KTS 103	SISTERS OF MERCY 'OUT IN THE DARK'
KTS 104	RED HOT CHILI PEPPERS 'CHRISTMAS PARTY '91'
KTS 105	THE LEVELLERS 'THE FIDDLE AND THE DRUM'
KTS 106/07	GENESIS 'SUMMER NIGHTS'
KTS 108	LUSH 'KALEIDOSCOPIC HARMONIES'
KTS 109	MANIC STREET PREACHERS 'STREET PREACHING'
KTS 110/11	SOUNDGARDEN 'CROWN OF THORNS'
KTS 112	FAITH NO MORE 'LOVERS OF THEE INSANE'
KTS 113	PEARL JAM 'LOLLAPALOOZA 92'
KTS 114	LUSH/JESUS & MARY CHAIN 'LOLLAPALOOZA '92'
KTS 115	SOUNDGARDEN 'LOLLAPALOOZA '92'
BOX 003	LOLLAPALOOZA '92 VOL. 1 - 3 CD BOX + POSTER
KTS 116	MINISTRY 'LOLLAPALOOZA '92'
KTS 117	PORNO FOR PYROS/ICE CUBE 'LOLLAPALOOZA '92'
KTS 118	RED HOT CHILI PEPPERS 'LOLLAPALOOZA '92'
BOX 004	LOLLAPALOOZA '92 VOL. 2 - 3 CD BOX + TOUR PROGRAMME
KTS 110	MUDHONEY 'FUZZBUSTERS'
KTS 120	PRINCE 'DON'T CRY FOR ME ARGENTINA'
KTS 121	IRON MAIDEN 'MAIDEN EUROPE'
KTS 122	CULT 'REBIRTH OF THE PHOENIX'
KTS 123	NOT AVAILABLE NOW
KTS 124	SLAYER 'DEVIL'S DESCIPLES'
KTS 125/26	GARY MOORE 'BLUES FROM A GUN'
KTS 127/28	MICHAEL JACKSON 'LIVE AND DANGEROUS'
KTS 129/30	BOB DYLAN 'IN THE GARDEN'
KTS 133	NIRVANA 'DUMB'
KTS 134/35	ELP 'PIRATES'
KTS 136/37	MADONNA 'SOME LIKE IT HOT'
KTS 138/39	ERIC CLAPTON 'TEARS IN HEAVEN'
KTS 140	BON JOVI 'THE WILD ONES'
KTS 141	R.E.M. 'AUTOMATICALLY LIVE'
KTS 142	NEIL YOUNG 'SILVER & GOLD'
KTS 143	DON HENLEY 'AN EAGLE OUT EAST'
KTS 144	BLACK CROWES 'STARE IT COLD'
KTS 145	U2 'WATCH MORE TV'
KTS 146	BRUCE SPRINGSTEEN 'ONE WAY TICKET'
KTS 147/48	U2 'LIVE TRANSMISSION'
KTS 149	THUNDER 'SHELTER FROM THE STORM'
KTS 150	MINISTRY 'TRIP TO HELL'
KTS 151	SHAKESPEAR'S SISTER 'BACK IN YOUR OWN WORLD'
KTS 152	EMF 'ALL NIGHT RAVE'
KTS 153	UGLY KID JOE 'GET OUTTA MY FACE'
KTS 154	SONIC YOUTH 'SPLITTING THE ATOM'
KTS 155	BRYAN ADAMS 'KEEP ON RUNNING'
KTS 158	FRANK BLACK 'THE DREAM IS OVER'
KTS 158	SUEDE 'MOVIN'
KTS 159	BABES IN TOYLAND 'PLAYTIME'
KTS 160/61	BOB DYLAN 'FIFTH TIME AROUND'
KTS 162	ROXETTE 'UNCENSORED & UNCUT'
KTS 163/64	THE BLACK CROWES 'HIGH IN HOUSTON'
KTS 165	KEITH RICHARDS 'TIME IS ON MY SIDE'
KTS 166	NEIL YOUNG 'BACK TO MY ROOTS'
KTS 167	BOB MARLEY 'JAH LOVE'
KTS 168	LEMONHEADS 'SUCK ON THIS'
KTS 169	K.D. LANG 'SONGS FOR SWINGING LOVERS'
KTS 170	TOM WAITS 'COLD BEER ON A HOT NIGHT'
KTS 171	BLACK SABBATH 'BLACK BLOODY BLACK'
KTS 172	ALICE IN CHAINS 'LIVE & UNCHAINED'
KTS 173/74	SPIN DOCTORS 'ROUND AND ROUND'
KTS 175/76	U2 'THE REAL THING'
KTS 177	PANTERA 'WALK ON THE WILD SIDE'
KTS 178	RAGE AGAINST THE MACHINE 'JUSTIFY THOSE THAT DIE'
KTS 179	WORLD PARTY 'THANK YOU WORLD'

Kiss The Stone

Order

KTS *Kiss The Stone*

KTS 180	SCREAMING TREES 'TEN TONS OF FUN'
KTS 182	JOE SATRIANI 'MASTER OF THE ART'
KTS 183	LIONEL RICHIE 'ALL NIGHT LOVE'
KTS 184/85	METALLICA 'TEARING YOUR INSIDES OUT'
KTS 186	P.J. HARVEY 'BUILD ME A WOMAN'
KTS 187/88	VELVET UNDERGROUND 'TAKE A TRIP'
KTS 189	PORNO FOR PYROS 'PORNO FOR PERRY'
KTS 190/91	GRATEFUL DEAD 'HERE COMES SUNSHINE'
KTS 192	FRANK BLACK 'NO BIG DEAL'
KTS 193	SUGAR 'BLEEDING'
KTS 194	NEIL YOUNG 'WORLD ON A STRING'
KTS 195	SOUL ASYLUM 'BODY & SOUL'
KTS 196	BRIAN MAY 'OUT ON HIS OWN'
KTS 197/98	U2 'ZOO EUROPA'
KTS 199	ROBERT PLANT 'NO LOOKING BACK'
KTS 200/01	STING 'WALK IN THE FIELDS OF GOLD'
KTS 202/03	ERIC CLAPTON 'THECIRCUS HAS LEFT THE TOWN'
KTS 204/05	DEF LEPPARD 'THE CIRCUS COMES TO TOWN'
KTS 206	DEPECHE MODE 'ENJOY THE RUMOURS'
KTS 207	STONE TEMPLE PILOTS 'CLOSE YOUR EYES'
KTS 208	SMASHING PUMPKINS 'DROWN'
KTS 209	RAGE AGAINST THE MACHINE 'REVOLUTION'
KTS 210	MEGADEATH 'PUNISHMENT IS DUE'
KTS 211	THE THE 'SAVE ME'
KTS 212	LEONARD COHEN 'ABOVE THE SOUL'
KTS 213	TORI AMOS 'AFTER THE RAIN'
KTS 214	SPRINGSTEEN 'PLUGGED - THE REHEARSALS'
KTS 215	ELTON JOHN 'THE LAST SONG'
KTS 216	NEW ORDER 'ELECTRONIC ECSTASY'
KTS 217	WHITE ZOMBIE 'RESURRECTION DAY'
KTS 218	MOTORHEAD 'GONNA MAKE YOUR EARS BLEED'
KTS 219	PRIMUS 'MADHOUSE'
KTS 220	GUNS 'N ROSES 'UNPLUGGED'
KTS 221	PEARL JAM 'AGAINST'
KTS 223	THE BREEDERS 'DOUBLE TROUBLE'
KTS 224	SPRINGSTEEN 'FROM SMALL THINGS'
KTS 225/26	PRINCE 'DO U WANNA GO HOME'
KTS 227/28	GRATEFUL DEAD 'DAWN OF THE DEAD'
KTS 229	PRINCE 'THIS IS MY NIGHT'
KTS 230/31	BOB MARLEY 'GET UP AND LIVE'
KTS 233	LIVING COLOUR 'NOTHING LAST FOREVER'
KTS 234	JOHN MELLENCAMP 'WHEELS ARE TURNING'
KTS 235	BELLY 'GUT FEELING'
KTS 236	IGGY POP 'OUT ON THE STREETS AGAIN'
KTS 237	10,000 MANIACS 'HOW YOU'VE GROWN'
KTS 238	MARIEA MCKEE 'BREATHE'
KTS 239/40	U2 'ZOOROPA DOWN UNDER'
KTS 241/42	MADONNA 'LICK ME DOWN UNDER'
KTS 243	DREAM THEATRE 'DREAM OUT LOUD'
KTS 244/45	MEAT LOAF 'TO HELL AND BACK'
KTS 246	PRINCE 'FUNKY PARTY 2NITE'
KTS 247	DAVID BYRNE 'UNPLUGGED + MORE'
KTS 248	THE LEVELLERS 'BACK TO NATURE'
KTS 249	INXS 'EMPTY SUN UNDER CLEAN MINDS'
KTS 250	PAUL MCCARTNEY 'HEY, TOKYO!'
KTS 251/52	GRATEFUL DEAD 'DEAD AGAIN'
KTS 253	NIRVANA 'ALL ACOUSTICALLY'
KTS 254	BLIND MELON 'STING ME'
KTS 255/56	MADONNA 'GIRLIE SHOW EXPERIENCE'
KTS 257	MATTHEW SWEET 'SHAPE SHIFTER'
KTS 258	JACKSON BROWNE 'TOO MANY ANGELS'
KTS 259	GIN BLOSSOMS 'IN BLOOM'
KTS 260	RADIOHEAD 'CREEPSHOW'
KTS 261	SMASHING PUMPKINS 'MAYONNAISE DREAM'
KTS 262	LEMONHEADS 'SQUEEZE ME PLEASE ME'
KTS 263	TOOL 'TALES FROM THE DARKSIDE'
KTS 264	SMASHING PUMPKINS '3 FEET HIGH'
KTS 265	IZZY STRADLIN 'ROCKER'
KTS 266	CROWDED HOUSE 'IT'S ONLY NATURAL'
KTS 267	THE DOORS 'APOCALYPSE NOW'
KTS 268	BJORK 'SUGAR CANDY KISSES'
KTS 269	DURAN DURAN 'ACOUSTIC WORLD'
KTS 270/71	ELTON JOHN 'WORLD CLASS'
KTS 272	BOB MOULD 'THE CALM BEFORE THE STORM'
KTS 273/74	TOM PETTY 'SOUTHERN GENTLEMAN'
KTS 275	STING 'COMPLETE CHICAGO SESSIONS'
KTS 276	PRIMUS 'BACK IN THE MADHOUSE'
KTS 277	THERAPY? 'NO LOVE LOST'
KTS 278	SUEDE 'PERFORMANCE'

KTS 279	SEPULTURA 'WELCOME TO THE END OF...'
KTS 280	SPRINGSTEEN 'WARM AND TENDER LOVE'
KTS 281	JAMIROQUAI 'IF I LIKE IT, I DO IT'
KTS 282/83	DREAM THEATRE 'LORDS OF SOUND'
KTS 284	NIRVANA 'ROMA'
KTS 285	PRINCE 'WELCOME 2 THE BEAUTIFUL...'
KTS 286	ALLMAN BROHTERS BAND 'SWEET MELISSA'
KTS 287/88	PEARL JAM 'ATLANTA'
KTS 289	THE WONDER STUFF 'ON THE ROPES'
KTS 290	RAGE AGAINST THE MACHINE 'KILLING ZONE'
KTS 291	HEART 'UNPLUGGED'
KTS 292/93	AEROSMITH 'STRUTTIN' MY STUFF'
KTS 294/95	PINK FLOYD 'THE LIVE BELL'
KTS 296	CRACKER 'TEEN ANGST'
KTS 297	COUNTING CROWS 'CARVING OUT OUR NAMES'
KTS 298	PRIMAL SCREAM 'ROCKSUCKER BLUES'
KTS 299	CRASH TEST DUMMIES 'DUMMIES AT HOME'
KTS 300/01	BOB MARLEY 'REVOLUTION'
KTS 302	BLUR 'MODROPHENIA'
KTS 303	NINE INCH NAILS 'COMING DOWN FAST'
KTS 304/05	PHISH 'FOLLOW ME TO GAMEHENGE'
KTS 306	METALLICA 'NO LIMITS - NO LAWS'
KTS 307	SONIC YOUTH 'TAKEOUT THE TRASH'
KTS 308	BOB MARLEY 'DOWNTOWN TRENCHTOWN'
KTS 309	HUSKER DU 'SUPERNOVA'
KTS 310	KRISTIN HERSH 'SPARKLE'
KTS 311	PANTERA 'NO COMPROMISE NO SELL OUT'
KTS 312	EXTREME 'DREAMS COME TRUE'
KTS 313	SEPULTURA 'NAILBOMB'
KTS 314	PAUL WELLER 'WALK ON BY'
KTS 315	THE REPLACEMENTS 'SHIT, SHOWER & SHAVE'
KTS 316	THE WATERBOYS 'IN THE STUDIO'
KTS 317	THE CRANBERRIES 'STORIES TO BE TOLD'
KTS 318	THERAPY? 'FISTFUL OF POWER'
KTS 319	RAGE AGAINST THE MACHINE 'BULLET PROOF'
KTS 320	GRANT LEE BUFFALO 'LIKE A SHOT'
KTS 322	CROWDED HOUSE 'FLEADH'
KTS 323	BEASTIE BOYS 'SEVEN DAY WEEKEND'
KTS 324	THE PRETENDERS 'NOW AND THEN'
KTS 325	TORI AMOS 'SPIRIT IN THE SKY'
KTS 326/29	BILLY JOEL 'AFTER THE FLOOD'
KTS 329	SOUTHSIDE JOHNNY/LITTLE STEVEN 'UNPLUGGED'
KTS 330	DAVID CROSBY 'NAKED IN THE RAIN'
KTS 331	PAUL WESTERBERG 'GRAVEL PIT'
KTS 332	LENNY KRAVITZ 'ACOUSTIC'
KTS 333	AFGHAN WHIGS 'FLIP YOUR WHIG'
KTS 334	JAMES 'A STRANGE DAY'
KTS 335	MARIAH CAREY 'SOMEDAY'
KTS 336	NIRVANA 'THE ETERNAL LEGACY'
KTS 337	COUNTING CROWS 'CHILDREN IN BLOOM'
KTS 338	BLUR 'SAWDUST MEMORIES'
KTS 339/40	PINK FLOYD 'THE BELL GETS LOUDER'
KTS 341/42	GRATEFUL DEAD 'ANOTHER DAY'
KTS 343	NINE INCH NAILS 'WHEN THE WHIP COMES DOWN'
KTS 344/45	METALLICA 'ENTER MUDMAN'
KTS 346	ROLLINS BAND 'ALIEN BLUEPRINT'
KTS 347	HOLE 'KISS AWAY THE DARKEST DAY'
KTS 348	SHERYL CROW 'RUN, BABY, RUN'
KTS 349	BOB MARLEY 'REDEMPTION'
KTS 350	THE DOORS 'SHATTERED'
KTS 351	NOFX 'BACK IN THE GARAGE'
KTS 352	THE WATERBOYS 'ALIVE ON THE INSIDE'
KTS 353	TORI AMOS 'FAIRY TALES'
KTS 354	RED HOT CHILI PEPPERS 'DIRTY WEEKEND'
KTS 356/57	THE ROLLING STONES 'THE VOODOO KISS'
KTS 358	L7 'WHEN THE STINK HITS THE FAN'
KTS 359	THE OFFSPRING 'THE YEAR THAT PUNK BROKE'
KTS 356/66	METALLICA 'PILE OF SHIT'
KTS 368/69	PEARL JAM 'VORTICAL'
KTS 370	DEAD CAN DANCE 'SINFUL GARDEN'
KTS 371	PULP 'FICTON ROMANCE'
KTS 372	BIOHAZARD 'RUN FOR COVER'
KTS 373	GALLIANO 'DOWN TO EARTH'
KTS 374/75	PINK FLOYD 'OUT OF THIS WORLD'
KTS 376	THE BLACK CROWES 'TALLER'
KTS 377	THE ROLLING STONES 'SPARKS WILL FLY'
KTS 378	COLLECTIVE SOUL 'MOTOR CITY'S BURNIN'
KTS 379/80	PEARL JAM 'ATLANTA - THE DAY BEFORE'

continued on next page ->

The Ultimate In Quality!

KTS Mail

KTS 381 OASIS 'SLIDE AWAY'
KTS 382 ERIC CLAPTON 'BLUES REHEARSALS'
KTS 383 LIVE 'I ALIVE'
KTS 384/85 WHITNEY HOUSTON 'OUT OF AFRICA'
KTS 386 ELVIS COSTELLO 'UNDER THE INFLUENZA'
KTS 387 THE JAM 'SET THE SKIES ABLAZE'
KTS 388/89 THE ROLLING STONES 'MIAMI DICE'
KTS 390 CATHEDRAL ' COSMIC FUNERAL'
KTS 391/92 NINE INCH NAILS 'SLAUGHTER IN THE AIR'
KTS 393 SLAYER 'SPIRITS IN BLACK'
KTS 394 GREEN DAY 'SPITTING'
KTS 395 NIRVANA 'TRICK OR TREAT'
KTS 396 PANTERA 'LIVE BEYOND DRIVEN'
KTS 397 OASIS 'BLACK ON WHITE'
KTS 398 PEARL JAM 'SELF POLLUTION RADIO'
KTS 399 IGGY POP 'ROCK HARD'
KTS 402 THE DOOBIE BROTHERS 'REUNION'
KTS 403 JOHN MELLENCAMP 'WILD AT NIGHT'
KTS 404 LED ZEPPELIN 'ROCK 'N' ROLL HALL OF FAME'
KTS 405 VAN HALEN 'SECRET GIG'
KTS 406 SPRINGSTEEN 'LOOSE ENDS'
KTS 407 HOOTIE & THE BLOWFISH 'ON THE LEFT COAST'
KTS 408 ETHERIDGE, MELISSA 'LET'S GET IT ON'
KTS 409 BON JOVI 'ACOUSTIC'
KTS 410 GRIFFITH, NANCI 'SOUND OF LONELINESS'
KTS 411/12 KISS 'ROCKIN' IN CHILE'
KTS 413 NOFX 'TOGETHER ON THE ROAD'
KTS 414 BLACK CROWS 'HIGH HEAD BLUES'
KTS 415 ETHERIDGE, MELISSA 'ACOUSTIC'
KTS 416/17 DREAM THEATER 'MIND CONTROL'
KTS 418/19 PEARL JAM 'DOWN UNDER'
KTS 420/21 MATTHEWS, DAVE BAND 'BEST OF...'
KTS 422/23 GREATFUL DEAD 'COMES A TIME FOR ALL'
KTS 424 FAITH NO MORE 'EVIDENCE'
KTS 425 RAITT, BONNIE 'STORM WARNING'
KTS 426 SPRINGSTEEN, BRUCE 'LOST AND LIVE'
KTS 427 CROW, SHERYL 'ACOUSTIC'
KTS 428 PHISH 'SIMPLE'
KTS 429 SIOUXSIE & THE BANSHEES 'SISTER MIDNIGHT'
KTS 430/31 GREATFUL DEAD 'PLAY DEAD'
KTS 432 INDIGO GIRLS 'HISTORY OF US'
KTS 433 LENNOX, ANNIE 'GOLDEN LADY'
KTS 434 SUEDE 'COVER ME'
KTS 435/36 DYLAN, BOB 'BRIXTON BLUES'
KTS 437 LIVE 'SHIT TOWN'
KTS 438 ELASTICA 'THE VASELINE GANG'
KTS 439 STONE TEMPLE PILOTS 'INTERSTATE LOVE SONGS'
KTS 440 HOLE 'PLUGGED & UNPLUGGED'
KTS 441 ALLMAN BROTHERS BAND 'SONGS FROM THE ROAD'
KTS 442 BAD RELIGION 'RADIATION HAZARD'
KTS 443 JAYHAWKS 'POISED FOR STARDOM'
KTS 444 BLACK CROWES 'SONGS OF THE FLESH'
KTS 445/46 ROLLING STONES 'TOKYO '95'
KTS 447/48 R.E.M. 'ANEURYSM'
KTS 449 LIVE 'SUPERNATURAL'
KTS 450/51 PAGE & PLANT 'SIMPLE TRUTH'
KTS 452 PORTISHEAD 'NOBODY LOVES ME'
KTS 453 CLAPTON, ERIC 'LOST JAMS'
KTS 454 COSTELLO, ELVIS 'JESUS, THIS IS ELVIS'
KTS 455 MACHINE HEAD 'PRESSURE POINT'
KTS 456 HOLE 'ASKING FOR IT'
KTS 457/58 CLAPTON, ERIC 'THE BLUES CONCERT'
KTS 459 BELLY 'LIVE AND HUNGRY'
KTS 460/61 QUEENSRYCHE 'SAINTS AND SINNERS'
KTS 462 PAGE & PLANT 'GLASTONBURY'
KTS 463 OASIS 'UP IN THE SKY'
KTS 464/65 BON JOVI 'NOW AND FOREVER'
KTS 466 CURE 'DRESSING UP FOR A DAY OUT'
KTS 467 SOUL ASYLUM 'SET ME FREE'
KTS 468/69 PHISH 'LIVE BAIT'
KTS 470 ETHERIDGE, MELISSA 'TEN YEARS OF COVERS'
KTS 471/72 R.E.M. 'ADHESION'
KTS 473 MATTHEWS, DAVE BAND 'EAT, DRINK & BE MERRY'
KTS 474 BUSH 'BURNING'
KTS 475 THE CRANBERRIES 'YESTERDAY'S GONE'
KTS 476 INDIGO GIRLS 'IN WITH THE OUT CROWD'
KTS 477 BRUCE SPRINGSTEEN 'LOST AND LIVE - VOL.2'
KTS 478/79 JERRY GARCIA 'JERRY'S HOME'
KTS 480/81 DAVE MATTHEWS BAND 'WITH A LITTLE HELP.'

KTS 482 SHERYL CROW 'EATING CROW'
KTS 483 BLUR 'MILE END'
KTS 484 OFFSPRING 'COME OUT AND PLAY'
KTS 485 PANTERA 'NOIZE, BOOZE AND TATTOOS'
KTS 486 P J HARVEY 'LIVE GOES THE NIGHT'
KTS 487 METALLICA 'DONNINGTON'
KTS 488 SUPERGRASS 'DOING TIME'
KTS 489 HOLE 'VENGEANCE IS MINE'
KTS 490 VAN MORRISON 'EDINBURGH CASTLE'
KTS 491 JETHRO TULL 'VELVET FLUTE'
KTS 492 SMASHING PUMPKINS 'BLACKOUT'
KTS 493 FOO FIGHTERS 'READING'
KTS 495/96 VAN HALEN 'ROCKS THE BEER HALL'
KTS 498 NINE INCH NAILS 'CHILDREN OF THE NIGHT'
KTS 499 MEATLOAF 'IT'S LIVE FOR YOU'
KTS 500/01 OZZY OSBORNE 'LET THE MADNESS BEGIN'
KTS 502/03 DAVID BOWIE 'LIVE, INSIDE'
KTS 504/05 GRATEFUL DEAD 'SOUTHERN COMFORT'
KTS 506/07 GRATEFUL DEAD 'HAVE SOME RESPECT'
KTS 508/09 ALLMAND BROTHERS BAND 'MIDNIGHT RIDING'
KTS 510/11 LENNY KRAVITZ 'ROCK AND ROLL IS LIVE'
KTS 513 GARBAGE 'IN THE CAN'
KTS 514 TOADIES 'BURN'
KTS 515 ALANIS MORISSETTE 'HARD TO SWALLOW'

BIG MUSIC

BIG 001/2   JETHRO TULL 'TALES FROM THE
             CRYSTAL FLUTE'
BIG 003   UB40 'CREDIT TO THE NATION'
BIG 004   MEATLOAF 'HOT AS HELL'
BIG 005   KISS 'GODS OF THUNDER'
BIG 006   THIN LIZZY 'OUT ON BAIL'
BIG 007   ELECTRIC LIGHT ORCHESTRA
             'ROCKARIA OVERTURE'
BIG 008   THE KINKS 'ALL NIGHT STAND'
BIG 009/10   GRATEFUL DEAD 'OUT OF YOUR SKULL'
BIG 011   THE WHO 'ACCEPT NO SUBSTITUTE'
BIG 012 /13 ELVIS COSTELLO 'THIS IS TOMORROW'
BIG 014   NEIL YOUNG 'ALL NIGHT LONG'
BIG 015   THE POLICE 'CRIMEWATCH'
BIG 016   SIMPLY RED 'SIMPLY THE BEST'
BIG 017   ROD STEWART 'SKIN TIGHT'
BIG 018   THE JAM 'IT'S A MOD MOD MOD WORLD'
BIG 019   TOM WAITS 'DOWNTOWN BLUES'
BIG 020/21   VAN MORRISON 'PAGAN STREAMS'
BIG 022/23   DIRE STRAITS 'TICKET TO HEAVEN'
BIG 024   EURYTHMICS 'SWEET REVENGE'
BIG 025   STEVIE RAY VAUGAN 'COLD SHOT'
BIG 026/27   CURE 'BITE THE BIG APPLE'
BIG 028   PAUL MCCARTNEY 'A DREAM APART'
BIG 029/30   ELTON JOHN 'HEAT WAVE'
BIG 031   MADNESS 'NUTTY DREAD'
BIG 032   PINK FLOYD 'EXPLODING IN YOUR MIND'
BIG 033   ERIC CLAPTON 'BRIGHT LIGHTS IN BLUES CITY'
BIG 034/35   ROLLING STONES 'BACK IN BUSINESS'
BIG 036   LEONARD COHEN 'DIAMONDS IN THE MINES'
BIG 037   ANNIE LENNOX 'THE GIFT'
BIG 038   HANOI ROCKS 'KILL CITY BLUES'
BIG 041   BOB MARLEY 'CONQUERING LION'
BIG 042   NED'S ATOMIC DUSTBIN 'RADIO ACTIVE'
BIG 043   THE SMITHS 'LAST OF THE ENGLISH ROSES'
BIG 044/45   ROLLING STONES 'ROCKIN' AT THE FORUM'
BIG 046   THE SEX PISTOLS 'KILL THE HIPPIES'
BIG 047   VAN MORRISON 'IT AIN'T WHY, IT JUST IS'
BIG 048   S. R. VAUGHAN 'G*RAY'
BIG 049   BIG BLACK 'DEATH WISH'
BIG 050/51   ERASURE 'WELCOME TO THE GLITTER...'
BIG 052/53   PRINCE '2 LIVE 4 LOVE'
BIG 054   P.I.L. 'ROTTEN TO THE CORE'
BIG 055/56   GUNS 'N ROSES 'LIVE IN JAPAN'
BIG 057   PAUL WELLER 'GROOVE A LITTLE'
BIG 058/59   GUNS 'N ROSES 'ROCKIN' IN CHILE'
BIG 060   METALLICA 'TOWER OF STRENGTH'
BIG 061   THE SMITHS 'SAME DAY AGAIN'
BIG 062   STEVIE RAY VAUGHAN 'LET ME LOVE YOUBABY'
BIG 063   DANIEL LANOIS 'COOL WATER'
BIG 064/65   STING 'IT'S PROBABLY ME'
BIG 066   JOHN MELLENCAMP 'SOUTHERN HEMIPSHERE'

Kiss The Stone

Order

BIG 067	QUEEN 'ROCKIN' OSAKA IN 1982'
BIG 068/69	ALLMAN BROTHERS BAND 'ALL OR NOTHING'
BIG 070	LED ZEPPELIN 'ANOTHER WHITE SUMMER'
BIG 072/73	KISS 'UNCHAINED & UNMASKED'
BIG 074	ROXETTE 'BLONDE DREAMS'
BIG 075	FARM AID 6 'SOWING THE SEEDS'
BIG 076/77	METALLICA 'LIVE IN ARGENTINA'
BIG 078/079	U2 'ANYTHING IS POSSIBLE'
BIG 080	SEPULTURA 'SLAVES OF PAIN'
BIG 081	PEARL JAM 'FLASHPOINT'
BIG 083	WHITNEY HOUSTON 'LIVE IN NEW YORK'
BIG 084	MIDNIGHT OIL 'BLUE SKY RED EARTH'
BIG 085	TAKE THAT! 'KISS THIS'
BIG 086/87	GUNS N' ROSES 'LIVE IN ARGENTINA'
BIG 088/89	ROD STEWART 'IN THE SPOTLIGHT'
BIG 090	BILLY JOEL 'TEMPTATION'
BIG 091	THE SMITHS 'THANK YOUR LUCKY STARS'
BIG 092	ELTON JOHN 'FINE CHINA'
BIG 093	KISS 'ROCK AND ROLL ALL NITE'
BIG 094	ABBA 'SWEET DREAMS ARE MADE OF..'
BIG 095	PINK FLOYD 'FOCUS'
BIG 096	TULL, JETHRO 'A SLICE OF FLUTE CAKE'
BIG 097	PINK FLOYD 'RE-ACTOR'
BIG 098	THE SMITHS 'THE BUTTERFLY COLLECTOR'
BIG 099	KINKS 'KRISTMAS KONCERT'
BIG 100/01	GREATFUL DEAD 'THE DEAD DON'T HAVE...'
BIG 102/03	R.E.M. 'REVOLUTION'

COCOMELOS RECORDS

CM 001	NIRVANA 'BLIND PIG'
CM 003/4	U2 'ONE LIVE BABY'
CM 005	PIXIES 'SITUATION RED'
CM 006	SONIC YOUTH 'SONIC STARPOWER'

CM 007/08	TOM PETTY 'UNDER THE SKIES SO BLUE'
CM 009/10	'METALLICA ALL HELL BREAKS LOOSE'
CM 011	EXTREME 'TAKE IT TO THE LIMITS'
CM 012	NINE INCH NAILS 'SOLID GOLD HELL'
CM 013	DISPOSABLE HEROES OF HIPHOPRISY 'POLITICAL TECHNOCRACY'
CM 014	ALICE IN CHAINS 'DIRTY TOY TOWN'
CM 015	ICE-T & BODY COUNT 'IN YOUR FACE'
CM 016	MINISTRY 'KILL FOR KICKS'
CM 017	DEPECHE MODE 'MODE ON THE ROAD'
CM 018/19	PEARL JAM 'BRIXTON'
CM 020/21	VAN HALEN 'ROCKING MY HOMETOWN'
CM 022/23	PEARL JAM 'THE KIDS ARE ALRIGHT'
CM 024	RUSH 'NORTHERN HEROES'
CM 025/26	SOUNDGARDEN 'THE GARDEN'
CM 027/28	COVERDALE - PAGE 'LIVE IN JAPAN'
CM 029/30	PEARL JAM 'NEW SONGS'
CM 031	THE EAGLES 'THE BOYS FROM YESTERDAY'
CM 032/33	ROLLING STONES 'I CAN'T GET NEXT TO YOU'
CM 034/35	GREEN DAY 'HAVING A BLAST'
CM 036	

CD - NIKKO RECORDS

NK 001	PEARL JAM 'BLACK & WHITE'
NK 002	U2 'OUTSIDE BROADCAST'
NK 003	BLACK CROWES 'SPECIAL DELIVERY'
NK 004	SUEDE 'STRANGE FASCINATION'
NK 005 /06	PAUL McCARTNEY 'OUT IN THE CROWD'
NK 007/08	BON JOVI 'LONG WAY FROM HOME'
NK 009	10,000 MANIACS 'IN THE GARDEN OF EDEN'
NK 010/11	AEROSMITH 'OUT OF CONTROL'
NK 012	PAUL WELLER 'ANYTIME YOU WANT ME'
NK 013	THERAPY? 'ISOLATION'

CD COSTS:

	USA$	UK£	It. Lire
1 CD	22.00	12.00	25.000
2 CD	44.00	24.00	48.000
3 CD	66.00	36.00	73.000

POSTAGE COSTS:
Europe: First CD - 5.500 It. Lire / DM 6,00 / £2.30.
Each additional - 2.000 It. Lire / DM 2,50 / £1.00.
USA and Japan: First CD - $4.50.
Each additional CD - $2.00.

PAYMENT:
Send complete Credit Card information or advance payment (cash or
International Money Order) with your order.

Maximum Credit Card order eight (8) CDs. Credit Cards charged in Italian Lire.
Credit Cards accepted are: Visa, American Express, Diners Club International,
Master Card and Bank Americard.

For orders above this amount, please send an International Money Order.
Full colour catalogue: $5.00 / £2 / 5.000 It. Lire.

KTS RECORDS MAIL ORDER SERVICE

PO BOX 70, DOGANA, 47031 REP. SAN MARINO (ITALY)
PHONE 011 378 909782 - FAX 011 378 909786

The Ultimate In Quality!

On Line

HTTP://WWW.KTS.IT

HTTP://WWW.KTS.IT

Email: Mail Me@KTS.IT

Welcome to
KTS

KISS THE STONE   INTERACTIVE CATALOGUE

Artists A-Z	To order	Articles
New Releases	Search	Merchandising
Coming soon		Artist of the month

KTS Records

P.O. BOX 70 – DOGANA – 47031 REP. SAN MARINO – ITALY
TEL. 011 – 378 – 909782 – FAX. 011 – 378 – 909786

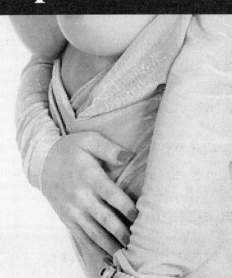

Visit

The Hot Wacks Press

on the Web at

http://log.on.ca/hotwacks

e-mail hotwacks@log.on.ca

always something new